W9-CNX-477

# AUGMENTATIVE AND ALTERNATIVE COMMUNICATION

# Augmentative and Alternative Communication

## Management of Severe Communication Disorders in Children and Adults

*by*

**David R. Beukelman, Ph.D.**
Professor
Department of Special Education and Communication Disorders
University of Nebraska-Lincoln

Director of Research and Education
Communication Disorders Division
Meyer Rehabilitation Center
Omaha, Nebraska

*and*

**Pat Mirenda, Ph.D.**
Associate Professor
Department of Special Education and Communication Disorders
University of Nebraska-Lincoln

·P·A·U·L·H·
**BROOKES**
PUBLISHING C?

Baltimore • London • Toronto • Sydney

Paul H. Brookes Publishing Co.
P.O. Box 10624
Baltimore, Maryland 21285-0624

Typeset by Brushwood Graphics, Inc., Baltimore, Maryland.
Manufactured in the United States of America by
The Maple Press Co., York, Pennsylvania.

Library of Congress Cataloging-in-Publication Data
Beukelman, David R., 1943–
    Augmentative and alternative communication : management of severe
communication disorders in children and adults / by David R. Beukelman and
Pat Mirenda.
        p.    cm.
    Includes bibliographical references and index.
    ISBN 1-55766-094-8
    1. Handicapped—Means of communication.    2. Communication devices for the
disabled.    I. Mirenda, Pat.    II. Title.
    [DNLM:    1. Communication Aids for Handicapped.    2. Communicative
Disorders—rehabilitation. WL 340 B566a]
RC429.B48    1992
616.85′503—dc20
DNLM/DLC
for Library of Congress                                        92-13583
                                                                    CIP
(British Library Cataloguing-in-Publication data are available from the British
Library.)

# Contents

# The Authors

*David R. Beukelman, Ph.D.*, is a speech-language pathologist with considerable experience in providing augmentative communication services. He is the Barkley Professor of Communication Disorders at the University of Nebraska-Lincoln and Director of Research and Education of the Communication Disorders Division, Meyer Rehabilitation Center, Omaha, Nebraska. Previously, Dr. Beukelman was Director of the Augmentative Communication Program, University of Washington Hospital, and Associate Professor in the Department of Rehabilitation Medicine of the University of Washington, Seattle.

Dr. Beukelman was Associate Editor of the journal *Augmentative and Alternative Communication,* and has published extensively in books and journals. Dr. Beukelman is the co-author of two books, *Communication Augmentation: A Casebook of Clinical Management* and *Clinical Management of Dysarthric Speakers,* and the co-editor of *Dysarthria and Apraxia of Speech: Perspectives on Management* and *Clinical Management of Communication and Swallowing Disorders in Persons with Traumatic Brain Injury.* In addition, Dr. Beukelman has co-authored two computer software programs for persons with severe communication disorders, Pacer/Tally and Cue-Write.

*Pat Mirenda, Ph.D.*, has a doctorate from the University of Wisconsin-Madison in behavioral disabilities and specializes in the education of persons with severe and profound disabilities. As Co-director, with Dr. Beukelman, of the Barkley Augmentative Communication Center, and Associate Professor in the Department of Special Education and Communication Disorders, University of Nebraska-Lincoln, Dr. Mirenda has concentrated on augmentative communication for persons with multiple disabilities. In addition, she has focused on the integration of augmented communicators into functional curricula and regular education classrooms.

Dr. Mirenda is the author of chapters and extensive research publications concerning severe disability and augmentative communication. She is Associate Editor for the journal *Augmentative and Alternative Communication* and served as chairperson for the Research Committee of the United States Society of Augmentative and Alternative Communication. In September, 1992, Dr. Mirenda begins providing a variety of training, research, and support services to individuals with severe disabilities through CBI Consultants, Ltd. in Vancouver, British Columbia.

## Contributors

*Gary Cumley, M.S., CCC-Sp*, is a speech-language pathologist with over 15 years of experience in working with young children with augmentative communication needs. Originally from California, he is a doctoral student at the University of Nebraska-Lincoln. His current interests include facilitator training, technology instruction, and developmental apraxia of speech.

*Kate Franklin, Ph.D., CCC-Sp*, is currently a Clinical Instructor in the Department of Speech Pathology and Audiology at West Virginia University in Morgantown. Previously she worked for several years at the Nebraska School for the Visually Impaired, and was a doctoral student at the University of Nebraska-Lincoln. Her current augmentative communication interests include symbol assessment and establishing a state chapter of USSAAC.

*Kathryn Garrett, M.S., CCC-Sp*, is a Clinical Supervisor in the Barkley Speech and Hearing Clinic at the University of Nebraska-Lincoln, where she is also a doctoral student. She has several years of experience working in a rehabilitation center with adults with aphasia, spinal cord injury, and traumatic brain injury. She has published extensively in the area of aphasia and augmentative communication.

*Rebecca Jones, B.S.,* is enrolled in a combined master's and doctoral program in speech-language pathology at the University of Nebraska-Lincoln. She worked as a special educator and augmentative communication consultant for Don Johnston Developmental Equipment, Inc., for several years prior to her current studies. Her current interests include educational integration, voice recognition, and dysarthria.

*Kathleen Newman, M.A.,* is an orientation and mobility specialist as well as a teacher of students with visual impairments for Lincoln Public Schools, Lincoln, Nebraska. She is enrolled in a program in educational administration at the University of Nebraska-Lincoln. Her particular interest is students with multiple disabilities who have communication needs in addition to visual impairments.

# *Preface*

*Augmentative and Alternative Communication: Management of Severe Communication Disorders in Children and Adults* is an introductory text that was written for practicing professionals, pre-professional students, and facilitators who are interested in communication options for persons who are unable to meet their daily communication needs through natural modes such as speech, gestures, or handwriting. Because severe communication disorders result from a variety of conditions, diseases, and syndromes that can affect persons of all ages, many individuals may be interested in these approaches. Several characteristics of the augmentative and alternative communication (AAC) field have shaped the format, content, and organization of this book.

First, AAC is a multidisciplinary field in which AAC users and their families, along with computer programmers, educators, engineers, linguists, occupational therapists, physical therapists, psychologists, speech-language pathologists, and many other professionals have contributed to the knowledge and practice base. We have attempted to be sensitive to these multiple perspectives and contributions by directly citing pertinent information from a wide variety of sources, and by guiding the reader to appropriate additional sources, when necessary.

Second, the AAC field has developed in many countries. For example, in 1990, individuals from 39 countries were members of the International Society of Augmentative and Alternative Communication (ISAAC). Although both authors are from the United States, we have made an effort to offer an international perspective in this book by including information about the contributions of AAC users, researchers, and clinicians from around the world. Unfortunately, within the constraints of an introductory textbook, only a limited number of these contributions can be cited specifically. Thus, we acknowledge that our primary sources of material have come from North America, and hope that our AAC colleagues in other countries will tolerate our inability to represent multinational efforts more comprehensively.

Third, AAC interventions involve both electronic and nonelectronic applications. Both are discussed in this book. In addition, much of the technology of the AAC field is highlighted in information boxes that are included in appropriate chapters. However, for several reasons, we have not included extensive descriptions of AAC technology in this book. The first reason is that AAC technology changes very rapidly, with current products being continually upgraded and new products continually introduced. Such information presented in book form would be outdated very quickly. Second, other technical information resources that are updated on a regular schedule are available. These resources provide assistive technology information in a variety of formats to meet the needs of individuals, agencies, universities, and resource centers. Three technical resources available in North America include:

1. "Features of Portable Communication Devices" (Kraat & Sitver-Kogut, 1991) is a wallchart that includes devices that are "battery-operated, can display at least 16 language items, and have a designated distributor in the United States who offers complete packages (i.e. hardware, software), warranties, and service." This chart is available from the Applied Science and Engineering Laboratories, University of Delaware/ A.I. duPont Institute, 1600 Rockland Rd., Wilmington, DE 19899 (302-651-6830).

2. *Trace ResourceBook: Assistive Technologies for Communication, Control, and Computer Access* (Berliss, Borden, & Vanderheiden, 1989) lists products designed specifically for the needs of people with disabilities. It addresses "the full range of technologies for communication, control and computer access" (p. vii). The *Trace ResourceBook* is available from the Trace Research and Development Center, S-151 Waisman Center, 1500 Highland Ave., Madison, WI 53705 (608-263-5788).

3.  Hyper-ABLEDATA is an assistive technology product database available on compact disc. The database contains over 16,000 product descriptions and pictures (in some cases), and the names and addresses of some 2,200 companies. Hyper-ABLEDATA can be ordered from the Trace Research and Development Center at the above address.

Finally, the fourth characteristic of the AAC field is that it is based on two general areas of information. The first relates to the conceptual and technical aspects of assistive technology in general and AAC in particular. The second relates to the intervention strategies and procedures that have been developed to serve the various individuals who require AAC services. In an effort to cover these two areas, the book has been divided into two sections. The first nine chapters cover conceptual and technical information about AAC, and the final ten chapters describe interventions for individuals of different ages or with different etiologies for their severe communication disorders.

Specifically, the nine chapters in Part I are organized to introduce readers to the basic concepts, terminology, and research of the AAC field. Chapter 1 introduces the reader to AAC in general and to persons with severe communication disorders in particular. Often using these individuals' own words, we attempt to convey what it means to be unable to speak and to use AAC systems to interact. Chapters 2, 3, 4, and 5 describe the basic components of AAC systems. Chapter 2 is a detailed presentation of the most common aided and unaided symbol systems used to represent messages. Chapter 3 reviews the message encoding and rate enhancement strategies used in AAC applications. Chapter 4 discusses a range of alternative access options to accommodate a variety of motor impairments. Chapter 5 outlines a variety of message input and message output options in AAC systems. In Chapter 6, we describe the service delivery systems that have been developed to deliver AAC services to persons across the range of ages and etiologies. Brief summaries of service delivery models from several countries are included in this chapter. Then, in Chapters 7 and 8, we summarize and describe the general principles of assessment and intervention that are currently used in AAC interventions. These chapters discuss in detail the participation and consensus management frameworks that the authors have utilized extensively. Finally, Part I concludes with a discussion of vocabulary selection and retention in Chapter 9.

Part II contains 10 chapters that review AAC interventions for individuals of various ages and etiologies. Six chapters discuss persons who have developmental disorders, and the remaining four chapters focus on persons with acquired communication disorders. Specifically, Chapter 10 focuses on AAC strategies to enhance communication interaction, school participation, and language learning of young children. Chapter 11 describes a framework for the educational integration of students with AAC systems. Chapter 12 outlines AAC interventions for persons who are unable to communicate through speech and/or writing because of developmental apraxia of speech, specific language impairments, learning disabilities, and primary motor impairments. AAC interventions associated with literacy issues are also described in this chapter, which was written with Gary Cumley and Rebecca Jones. Chapter 13 focuses on meeting the communication needs of individuals from school age through adulthood with severe intellectual disabilities. Chapter 14 reviews AAC issues for persons with autism; and Chapter 15, written with Kate Franklin and Kathleen Newman, provides considerable detail regarding AAC interventions for persons with visual and dual sensory impairments.

The last four chapters of the book focus on AAC users with acquired communication disorders. Chapter 16 reviews AAC interventions for persons with acquired physical disabilities, including amyotrophic lateral sclerosis, multiple sclerosis, Parkinson's disease, spinal cord injury, and brain stem stroke. Chapter 17, written with Kathryn Garrett, describes a functional classification scheme for persons with severe aphasia, and related intervention strategies and techniques. Chapter 18 addresses AAC assessments and interventions according to the cognitive levels of persons with traumatic brain injury. Finally, Chapter 19 reviews a wide range of AAC interventions for persons in intensive and acute care medical settings. Particular attention is focused on individuals who are unable to communicate due to respiratory impairments.

As we completed this book, we became keenly aware of our dependence on those who have documented their experiences in the AAC field. In order to tell the "AAC Story" we expected to cite traditional documents—professional research papers, books, and manuals. What we found is that we also made extensive use of the perspectives of AAC users, as documented in a variety of magazines, videotapes, and other popular sources. AAC facilitators have also contributed to this book, with their conclusions about the AAC experience through formal and informal case studies. Thus, we wish to thank those publishers, editors, associations, manufacturers, and institutions who supported the newsletters, bulletins, books, videotapes, and journals that now contain the historical record of the AAC field. Without these resources, we would have simply been unable to compile this document. We also want to acknowledge the role of the Barkley Trust in supporting the augmentative communication effort at the University of Nebraska-Lincoln. In addition, we have appreciated the support, encouragement, and assistance from the people at Paul H. Brookes Publishing Company, especially Melissa Behm, Carol Hollander, and Roslyn Udris.

Special appreciation is also due to a number of individuals whom we have been fortunate to work with before and during the production of this book. These include the students, families, staff, and administrators of the Lincoln Public School system, Madonna Rehabilitation Hospital, Hattie B. Munroe Augmentative Communication Center, and the Educational Center for Students with Disabilities at the University of Nebraska-Lincoln. These individuals have collaborated with us through the years and have thus greatly contributed to our AAC experiences and knowledge. Scott Cotton assisted us with photography, Cliff Hollestelle provided the illustrations, and Michelle Dombrovskis managed the reference list during the initial draft of the book. The "unsinkable" Nancy Brown was invaluably helpful as we organized, typed, proofed, checked, and rechecked the manuscript, and we are truly grateful for her support throughout the years. Finally, we thank the AAC users and their families who, through the years, have taught us about the AAC field and who have allowed us to use their stories. May their voices grow ever stronger.

## REFERENCES

Berliss, J., Borden, P., & Vanderheiden, G. (1989). *Trace resourcebook: Assistive technologies for communication, control, and computer access, 1989–90 edition.* Madison, WI: Trace Research and Development Center.

Kraat, A., & Sitver-Kogut, M. (1991). *Features of portable communication devices* [wallchart]. Wilmington, DE: Applied Science and Engineering Laboratories, University of Delaware/A.I. duPont Institute.

Trace Research and Development Center. (1991). *Hyper-ABLEDATA* (4th ed.) [compact disc]. Madison, WI: Author.

*This book is dedicated to Karoly Galyas,*
*for his leadership and pioneering contributions to the AAC field.*

# AUGMENTATIVE AND ALTERNATIVE COMMUNICATION

# PART I

# AUGMENTATIVE AND ALTERNATIVE COMMUNICATION PROCESSES

# Introduction to Augmentative and Alternative Communication

>>>>>>>>>>>>>>>>>>>>>>>>>>>>>>>>>>>>>>>>>>>>>>>>>>>

## WHAT IS AUGMENTATIVE AND ALTERNATIVE COMMUNICATION?

The definition of augmentative and alternative communication (AAC) most frequently used in North America was provided by a committee of the American Speech-Language-Hearing Association (ASHA):

> Augmentative and alternative communication is an area of clinical practice that attempts to compensate (either temporarily or permanently) for the impairment and disability patterns of individuals with severe expressive communication disorders (i.e., the severely speech-language and writing impaired). (ASHA, 1989, p. 107)

In accordance with an ASHA position paper published in 1991, it is important to emphasize that AAC interventions should always be multimodal in nature, that is, they should "utilize the individual's full communication capabilities, including any residual speech or vocalizations, gestures, signs, and aided communication" (ASHA, 1991, p. 10).

A number of other terms that are commonly used in this area also require introduction and definition. An AAC *system* is "an integrated group of components, including the symbols, aids, strategies, and techniques used by individuals to enhance communication" (ASHA, 1991, p. 10). This definition of a system also emphasizes the use of multiple components or modes for communication. As used in this definition, the term *symbol* refers to the methods used for "visual, auditory, and/or tactile representation of conventional concepts (e.g., gestures, photographs, manual sign sets/systems, picto-ideographs, printed words, objects, spoken words, Braille)" (ASHA, 1991, p. 10). It is important to note that according to this definition, the use of gestural communication (including, for example, facial expressions, eye gaze, and body postures, in addition to hand gestures) is within the overall definition of AAC. This means that interventions designed to increase the ability of persons with the most severe intellectual disabilities (e.g., profound mental retardation) to communicate through gestures and other natural modes fall within the mandate of the AAC specialist. This contrasts with other definitions that consider the use of such gestures to be AAC "prerequisites" rather than legitimate targets for AAC efforts (e.g., Shane & Bashir, 1980). This issue is discussed further in Chapter 2.

The term *aid* is used to refer to "a physical object or device used to transmit or receive messages (e.g., a communication book, board, chart, mechanical or electronic device, or computer)" (ASHA, 1991, p. 10). In this text, the terms aid and *device* are used interchangeably. A *strategy*, in the ASHA definition, is a "specific way of using [AAC] aids, symbols, and/or techniques more effectively for enhanced communication. A strategy, whether taught to an individual or self-discovered, is a plan that can facilitate one's performance" (ASHA, 1991, p. 10). Thus, role playing, graduated prompting/fading, and attending a college class to learn a word processing program are all strategies that are applicable to AAC interventions. Finally, the term *technique* refers to "a method of transmitting messages (e.g., linear scanning, row-column scanning, encoding, signing, and natural gesturing)" (ASHA, 1991, p. 10). These four components—symbol, aid, strategy, and technique—are the critical elements that comprise all AAC interventions.

## WHO USES AUGMENTATIVE COMMUNICATION?

People who use or need to have access to AAC come from all age groups, socioeconomic groups, and ethnic and racial backgrounds. The characteristic they have in common is that, for whatever reason, they require adaptive assistance for speaking and/or writing. In North America, the most commonly used definition of this population was put forth by the American Speech-Language-Hearing Association in 1991:

> Individuals with severe communication disorders are those who may benefit from [AAC]—those for whom gestural, speech, and/or written communication is temporarily or permanently inadequate to meet all of their communication needs. For these individuals, hearing impairment is not the primary cause for the communication impairment. Although some of these individuals may be able to produce a limited amount of speech, it is inadequate to meet their varied communication needs. Numerous terms that were initially used in the field, but are now rarely mentioned, include speechless, nonoral, nonvocal, nonverbal, and aphonic. (ASHA, 1991, p. 10)

The inability to speak or write without adaptive assistance can be due to a variety of congenital or acquired impairments. The most common congenital causes of such severe communication disorders include mental retardation or developmental delay, cerebral palsy, autism, specific language disorders, and developmental apraxia of speech (Mirenda & Mathy-Laikko, 1989). Acquired impairments most often resulting in the need for AAC assistance include amyotrophic lateral sclerosis (ALS or Lou Gehrig's disease), multiple sclerosis, traumatic brain injury, stroke, and spinal cord injury (Beukelman & Yorkston, 1989). Prevalence figures and demographic information related to each of these subgroups are presented in Part II of this text.

It has been estimated that approximately 2 million Americans are unable to speak adequately to meet their communication needs (ASHA, 1991). Based on a population estimate of 247.1 million people in the United States (Hoffman, 1990), this means that approximately 0.8% of the population is unable to speak, with an additional unknown incidence of individuals with severe writing and/or gestural impairments. In Canada, the number of children and adults with congenital, acquired, and progressive disabilities and severe speaking and writing impairments was estimated at 200,000 people in the early 1980s, representing 0.12% of the population (Lindsay, Cambria, McNaughton, & Warrick, 1986). In Australia, a survey conducted in the state of Victoria, which has over 4 million residents, indicated that approximately 5,000 individuals (0.12% of the population) were unable to speak adequately for communication (Bloomberg & Johnson, 1990). Thus, it appears that persons with severe communication disorders represent less than 1% of the general population. Despite this seemingly small percentage, however, these individuals number in the millions worldwide.

## WHAT DOES IT MEAN TO BE A PERSON WITH A SEVERE COMMUNICATION DISORDER?

Perhaps more relevant (certainly, more interesting) than demographic figures are the stories and experiences of people who are unable to speak and write. A number of accounts have been written by these individuals using their various communication devices, and from these we can sense what it is like to be unable to communicate. Rick Creech, a young man with cerebral palsy, wrote:

> If you want to know what it is like to be unable to speak, there is a way. Go to a party and don't talk. Play mute. Use your hands if you wish but don't use paper and pencil. Paper and pencil are not always handy for a mute person. Here is what you will find: people talking; talking behind, beside, around, over, under, through, and even for you. But never with you. You are ignored until finally you feel like a piece of furniture. (Musselwhite & St. Louis, 1988, p. 104)

Being unable to communicate also has a dramatic impact on an individual's ability to control even the most mundane aspects of life, as noted by Sara Brothers:

I know what it is like to be fed potatoes all my life. After all, potatoes are a good basic food for everyday, easy to fix in many different ways. I hate potatoes! But then, who knew that but me? I know what it is like to be dressed in red and blues when my favorite colors are mint greens, lemon yellows, and pinks. I mean really, can you imagine? (Brothers, 1991, p. 59)

Other writers with disabilities have emphasized the importance of attentive and responsive communication partners. Christopher Nolan, in his first book of poetry and short stories, wrote of his character's gratitude for teachers and others who took the time to understand his gestural communication:

Such were Joseph's teachers and such was their imagination that the mute boy became constantly amazed at the almost telepathic degree of certainty with which they read his facial expression, eye movements, and body language. Many a good laugh was had by teacher and pupil as they deciphered his code. It was at moments such as these that Joseph recognized the face of God in human form. It glimmered in their kindness to him, it glowed in their keenness, it hinted in their caring, indeed it caressed in their gaze. (Nolan, 1981, p. 11)

Creech's and Nolan's accounts are among many that have been written by persons with congenital disabilities (in particular, cerebral palsy) who use AAC (see Huer & Lloyd, 1988, 1990, for additional sources). The experiences of these individuals differ from those with acquired disabilities since, as Creech noted:

I would like to walk, run, play the piano, talk with as little effort as most people, and everything other people do. I would like to be able to, but I don't miss not doing them, because I never have. So I have not had the trauma of accepting physical limitations which were the result of an accident or illness, which left me "handicapped." (Creech, 1981, p. 550)

As noted in this passage, persons with acquired disabilities seem to experience the loss of communication skills as traumatic to a greater extent than do persons who grew up with such impairments. Easton (1989) described the thoughts of a woman with motor neuron disease (a progressive disorder) as she wrote about what it was like for her and her family in the initial stages of impairment:

Our lives were being turned upside down; frustration, anger, exasperation, and exhaustion were very evident. No one knew what to do for the best and the family felt helpless. . . . I have tried—and to some extent succeeded—to keep calm, because with the amount of communicating I have to do to cope each day, I would be in a permanent state of frustration. If, however, I do show some signs of frustration, I am told repeatedly to keep calm! . . . (Easton, 1989, pp. 16–17)

The experience of the individual whose inability to speak is sudden rather than progressive is perhaps even more devastating. Doreen Joseph, who lost her speech following an accident, and Sue Simpson, who lost the ability to speak after a stroke at age 36, wrote about their experiences:

I woke up one morning and I wasn't me.
There was somebody else in my bed.
And all I had left was my head. (Joseph, 1986, p. 8)

Speech is the most important thing we have. It makes us a person and not a thing. No one should ever have to be a "thing." (Joseph, 1986, p. 8)

So you can't talk, and it's boring and frustrating and nobody quite understands how bad it really is. If you sit around and think about all the things you used to be able to do, that you can't do now, you'll be a miserable wreck and no one will want to hang around you long. (Simpson, 1988, p. 11)

Clearly, the experience of being a person with a severe communication disorder cannot be understood by someone who has not "been there." Similarly, it is impossible to imagine what it must be like to be able talk or write with an adaptive device after months or years of silence. Christy Brown, who first communicated by writing with chalk held in his left foot, recounts the day when he printed his first letter:

I drew it—the letter "A." There it was on the floor before me. . . . I looked up. I saw my mother's face for a moment, tears on her cheeks. . . . I had done it! It had started—the thing that was to give my mind its chance of expressing itself. . . . That one letter, scrawled on the floor with a broken bit of yellow chalk gripped between my toes, was my road to a new world, my key to mental freedom. (Brown, 1954, p. 17)

Similarly, again speaking of his own experiences through the character of Joseph Meehan, Nolan writes eloquently of the power of communication:

Joseph continued to write. He recounted his experiences, his escried creeds and his crested benediction in typewritten words selected especially to describe a glorious bountiful nightmare. He saw life recoil before him, and using the third person he rescued poor sad boyhood and casting himself inside the frame of crippled Joseph Meehan he pranked himself as a storyteller, thereby casting renown on himself and casting disability before the reader. Look, he begged, look deep down; feel, he begged, sense life's limitations; cry, he begged, cry the tears of cruel frustration; but above all he begged laughter, laugh, he pleaded, for lovely laughter vanquishes raw wounded pride. (Nolan, 1987, p. 28)

Sadly, the "magic" of AAC is not readily available to all who need it. James Viggiano, a man with multiple disabilities who uses AAC, reminds us of the many individuals who cannot tell their stories, either because of language and literacy barriers or because they lack access to appropriate interventions:

With technological advances, a new day is dawning in the lives of many nonspeaking persons . . . but what about the thousands of . . . consumers who live silent, isolated existences in an archipelago of institutions where the advances you see today never reach the potential user. It is unconscionable that thousands of nonspeaking persons have not had the opportunity . . . to access state of the art technology and optimistic professionals. . . . (Viggiano, 1981, p. 552)

Anne McDonald, who spent 10 years in an institution for persons with severe/profound mental retardation before she was given access to a simple communication system, echoes Viggiano's sentiments in even more straightforward terms: "Crushing the personalities of speechless individuals is very easy: just make it impossible for them to communicate freely" (Crossley & McDonald, 1984, p. 142).

Professionals and AAC users alike remind us that along with technology come the costs, both financial and personal (Beukelman, 1991). In the following excerpt, McDonald writes about the cost of technology from a consumer's perspective:

I am not a fan of high technology. . . . The more severely disabled one is, the greater the effort involved in learning to use technology and the smaller the gains. I'm reluctant to make the effort until I'm certain the results will make the effort worthwhile. (Harrington, 1988, p. 7)

McDonald also reminds us that each person with a severe communication disorder has individual attitudes about disability itself, and these, in turn, influence personal choices about how and with whom to communicate. She continues:

Having a disability is an individual experience. Not only is every person with the same disability affected slightly differently, depending on their personalities they have different responses to their disability. Some see a disability as a challenge to be overcome. I see it as a nuisance to be endured. I see no reason to smile and pretend it's fine just to spare those who don't have a disability the knowledge of what it's like. Equally, I could protect others from having to come to grips with my disability by becoming independent or by restricting my life to those activities I can do without help, but I'm not going to. (Harrington, 1988, p. 7)

As is evident from the foregoing accounts, the experience of being a person with a severe communication disorder defies simple categorization. Similarly, the attitudes and priorities of these individuals and their communication partners are as important to the success of an intervention as are their abilities and the available options. It is only through consideration of all of these factors that interventions result in communicative competence.

## PURPOSES OF COMMUNICATION INTERACTIONS

### Perspective of the Person Using an AAC System

The work of Christopher Nolan, Anne McDonald, and others who use "low technology" (i.e., nonelectronic) systems reminds us that the ultimate goal of an AAC intervention is not to find a technological solution to the communication problem, but to enable the individual to efficiently and effectively engage in a variety of interactions. An extensive review of the AAC interaction research identified four agenda or purposes that are fulfilled in communicative interactions: 1) communication of needs/wants, 2) information transfer, 3) social closeness, and 4) social etiquette (Light, 1988). The characteristics of these four types of interactions are summarized in Table 1.1. As can be seen from this table, the goal of *expression of needs/wants* is to regulate the behavior of the listener toward an action-oriented response. Examples include a person asking for help or ordering food in a restaurant. Here, the content of the message is important, the vocabulary is relatively predictable, and the accuracy and rate of message production are critical. It is likely that the high degree of predictability and concreteness inherent in these messages explains why needs/wants vocabulary often tends to predominate in many communication systems. It is not unusual, for

**Table 1.1.** Characteristics of interactions intended to meet various social purposes

| | Social purpose of the interaction | | | |
| Characteristics | Expression of needs/wants | Information transfer | Social closeness | Social etiquette |
| --- | --- | --- | --- | --- |
| Goal of the interaction | To regulate the behavior of another as a means to fulfill needs/wants | To share information | To establish, maintain, and/or develop personal relationships | To conform to social conventions of politeness |
| Focus of the interaction | Desired object or action | Information | Interpersonal relationship | Social convention |
| Duration of the interaction | Limited. Emphasis is on initiating interaction. | May be lengthy. Emphasis is on developing interaction. | May be lengthy. Emphasis is on maintaining interaction. | Limited. Emphasis is on fulfilling designated turns. |
| Content of communication | Important | Important | Not important | Not important |
| Predictability of communication | Highly predictable | Not predictable | May be somewhat predictable | Highly predictable |
| Scope of communication | Limited scope | Wide scope | Wide scope | Very limited scope |
| Rate of communication | Important | Important | May not be important | Important |
| Tolerance for communication breakdown | Little tolerance | Little tolerance | Some tolerance | Little tolerance |
| Number of participants | Usually dyadic | Dyadic, small or large group | Usually dyadic or small group | Dyadic, small or large group |
| Independence of the communicator | Important | Important | Not important | Important |
| Partner | Familiar or unfamiliar | Familiar or unfamiliar | Usually familiar | Familiar or unfamiliar |

From Light, J. (1988). Interaction involving individuals using AAC systems: State of the art and future directions. *Augmentative and Alternative Communication, 4,* 76; reprinted by permission.

example, to see communication books or boards for individuals with mental retardation that consist almost entirely of such vocabulary, regardless of how motivating or relevant the person using the AAC system finds the messages.

The second area of interaction, *information transfer,* is a more difficult need to meet, since the goal is to share information rather than to regulate behavior. Examples include a child telling his or her teacher what he or she did over the weekend, an adolescent talking with friends about the upcoming senior prom, and an adult answering questions during a job interview. As is the case with needs/wants, the content of the message is quite important. Information transfer messages, however, are likely to be composed of novel (rather than predictable) words and sentences that allow the speaker to communicate about a wide variety of topics. Accuracy and rate of message production again remain paramount.

Communication related to *social closeness* differs from the first two types. As can be seen from Table 1.1., the goal of this type of interaction relates to establishing, maintaining, or developing personal relationships. Thus, the content of the message is less important than the interaction itself, and such messages are not usually predictable. Examples include a child telling a joke to classmates, a group of teenagers cheering their team at a basketball game, and a woman expressing her feelings of sympathy to a friend whose mother recently died. In such interactions, the rate, accuracy, and content of the message, as well as the independence of the person communicating, are secondary to the feelings achieved through the interaction, which are connectedness and, to a greater or lesser extent, intimacy.

The goal of the fourth type of interaction in Table 1.1., *social etiquette,* is "to conform to social conventions of politeness" through interactions that are often brief and contain predictable vocabulary. A child saying "please" and "thank you" to his or her grandmother, and an adult responding appropriately to a co-worker's comment about the weather are two examples of an exchange of social etiquette. As can be seen in Table 1.1., these messages closely resemble messages that express needs/wants, because rate, accuracy, and communicative independence are all important factors for success.

Most of the research and technical developments in the field of AAC have focused on strategies for enhancing communication of needs/wants and, to a lesser extent, information transfer (Light, 1988). The lack of attention to interactions of social closeness reflects both a narrow clinical perspective and the very real difficulties inherent in achieving the goals of social closeness interactions. Nevertheless, from the perspectives of many AAC users and their significant communication partners, this type of interaction may be more important than any other. It may well be that the majority of the interactions that most people typically have in the course of a week primarily fulfill social closeness agenda while masquerading as information transfer, social etiquette, or expression of needs/wants. When two friends chat over lunch about the problems in their offices, or when a group of people talk about their summer vacations at a cocktail party, the ostensible goal is one of information exchange, but is this really the primary agendum? Is the content of these communicative interactions really more important than the feeling of connectedness the messages allow the partners to experience?

The answer in many cases is that there are multiple goals involved in an interaction, and, in the context of AAC interventions, these goals must be identified for each person who uses AAC so that appropriate systems and vocabulary can be made available. One wonders how many times communication interventions have "failed" (e.g., "She has a wonderful communication system but refuses to use it") because of a discrepancy between the communication agenda of an AAC user and an AAC specialist. For example, some who use AAC prefer to use low technology systems that require ongoing interaction and turn taking with their communication partners (e.g., alphabet boards with messages spelled out letter by letter) because they enjoy the social closeness achieved through such approaches (R. Williams, personal communication, December 8, 1989). McDonald, who uses such a system, noted that, "if using the computer means I . . . have less personal contact then it's not worthwhile. I don't like using a machine if there's a person available to help me" (Harrington, 1988, p. 7). Similarly, when an individual using an AAC system wants to achieve social closeness, but the available vocabulary of the communication system is primarily related to needs/wants and social etiquette, problems are bound to occur. Careful attention to the needs and priorities of persons who use AAC and their partners is critically important in order to maximize competence.

## Perspective of the Communication Partner

Communicative competence from the perspective of the person who uses AAC involves the ability to efficiently and effectively transmit messages in all four of the interaction categories, based on individual interests, circumstances, and abilities. From the perspective of the communication partner, an additional set of skills may be needed. Light (1988) suggested that persons judged to be competent communicators using AAC systems are able to:

1.  Portray a positive self-image to their communication partners.
2.  Show interest in others and draw others into interactions.
3.  Actively participate and take turns in a symmetrical fashion.
4.  Be responsive to their communication partners and negotiate shared topics.
5.  Put their partners at ease with the AAC system, often by using humor as well as predictable, readable signals.

The extent to which these and other partner needs are met certainly affects the success of an interaction at least as much as does the type and quality of the messages. Thus, part of every AAC intervention should involve instruction regarding a set of strategies that can enable both the AAC user and his or her communication partners to achieve the highest level of communicative competence possible. These issues are discussed further in Chapter 8.

## AN AUGMENTATIVE COMMUNICATION SYSTEM MODEL

Symbols, aids, techniques, messages, vocabulary, strategies—the field of AAC is complex and multifaceted! Successful interventions require a team approach by AAC specialists from a variety of disciplines, including speech-language pathology, education, occupational and physical therapy, rehabilitation engineering, psychology, and medicine. Successful interventions also require that team members be familiar with the basic elements of an AAC system, which are presented in Figure 1.1.

An AAC system is composed of three main components: *alternative access, processes,* and *output.* Alternative access refers to how the person using the system interacts with it regarding message composition and motor skills. Message composition requires interaction with the *selection set* or *message display,* which is what the user sees when operating the system. The display consists of the *symbols* that represent messages and *message feedback,* which the AAC user receives when a symbol has been accessed. The second dimension of alternative access, *selection technique,* is the actual physical means by which the user controls the communication system. The third aspect of alternative access, *activation feedback,* is the information provided to the user following a selection.

The second main component of an AAC system is *processes,* which refer to the specialized techniques that can increase the *rate* of message composition (e.g., encoding) or *accuracy* (e.g., spell checking or grammar checking). Finally, the AAC system produces *output,* the third main

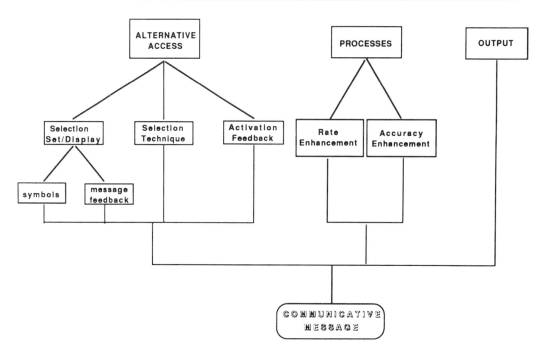

**Figure 1.1.** Basic components of an AAC system.

component, by which the message is transmitted to the communication partner. These three components—alternative access, processes, and output—interact to produce the result, the communicative message. In the chapters that follow, specific techniques related to each component are detailed.

# *Communication Symbols*

>>>>>>>>>>>>>>>>>>>>>>>>>>>>>>>>>>>>>>>>>>>>>>>>>>>>>>

Imagine what it would be like to have to rely only on speech to meet all of your communication needs. Most of us would lose our jobs for lack of the ability to communicate in writing and would probably lose friends and loved ones for lack of the ability to send nonverbal messages conveying empathy, warmth, and approval. There would be no golden arches! No mouse ears! No logos, no labels, no warning signs, or newspapers, or textbooks! Without the ability to send messages via gestures, body language, written words, and other symbols, communication as we now know it would be a vastly different—and much less rich—experience.

> "For someone who is unable to speak, to 'talk,' and for someone who is unable to write, to place words on paper. . . is improbable, it is magical" (Beukelman, 1991, p. 2).

Much of the magic of AAC lies in the vast array of symbols and signals, other than those used in speech, that can be used to send messages. Especially for individuals who cannot read and write, the ability to represent messages and concepts in alternative ways is central to communication. Acknowledgment of the importance of symbols has prompted much of the research and clinical effort devoted to studying and developing comprehensive symbol systems that are easy to use and learn. In this chapter, we review many of the most commonly used types of symbols and discuss their usefulness for various types of AAC users.

## OVERVIEW OF SYMBOLS

A number of definitions and taxonomies have been used to describe symbols and their various forms (see Lloyd & Fuller, 1986 for a review). Basically, a *symbol* is "something that stands for or represents something else" (Vanderheiden & Yoder, 1986, p. 15). The "something else" that a symbol represents is called its *referent*. The term *iconicity* refers to the continuum that describes symbols by ease of recognition. At one end of this iconicity continuum are *transparent* symbols, which visually resemble their referents and thus are high in *guessability*, and at the other end are *opaque* symbols, whose visual relationships to their referents are not obvious and may be quite arbitrary. For example, a color photograph of a shoe is transparent, while the written word "shoe" is opaque. In the middle of the iconicity continuum are *translucent* symbols, which are not readily guessable without additional information (Reichle, York, & Sigafoos, 1991). For example, the gesture commonly used in North America for "peace," in which the second and third fingers are raised to form a "V," is guessable only if one is aware of the "V for victory" slogan used during the Second World War. Translucent symbols are often described in terms of their *learnability.*

Symbols can be divided into those that are *aided*, which require some type of external assistance such as a device for production, and those that are *unaided*, which require no external device for production (Lloyd & Fuller, 1986). Examples of aided symbols include real objects and black and white line drawings, and examples of unaided symbols include facial expressions, manual signs, and natural speech and vocalizations. In addition, there are some symbol sets that incorporate the use of unaided + aided elements, and we refer to these as *combined symbol sets* (e.g., the Makaton Vocabulary).

## UNAIDED SYMBOLS: GESTURES AND VOCALIZATIONS

> "There's language in her eye, her cheek, her lip,
> Nay her foot speaks; her wanton spirits look out
> At every joint and motive of her body" (Shakespeare, *Troilus and Cressida*, Act IV, scene v).

Nonverbal behavior can repeat, contradict, substitute for, complement, accent, or regulate verbal behavior (Knapp, 1980). Nonverbal behavior includes gestures, vocalizations and other paralinguistic elements; physical characteristics (e.g., physique, body or breath odor); proxemics (e.g., seating arrangements, personal space requirements); artifacts (e.g., clothes, perfume, makeup); and environmental factors that may influence impressions and interactions (e.g., the neatness or disorder of a room may affect how one interacts with the person who lives there). While all of these are important elements of communication, gestures and vocalizations are perhaps the most extensive forms of nonverbal behavior and are therefore discussed in more detail in the following sections.

### Gestures

Gestural behavior includes fine and gross motor body movements, facial expressions, eye behaviors, and postures. A classification system was developed for describing these behaviors in terms of the communicative and adaptive purposes they generally serve (Ekman & Friesen, 1969). According to this system, *emblems* are gestural behaviors that can be "translated," or defined, by a few words or a phrase and that can be used without speech to convey messages. There is usually high agreement about the meaning of emblems among members of the same culture. For example, in North America, head shaking is generally understood as an emblem for "no," while head nodding is an emblem meaning "yes." Emblems are usually produced with the hands, although the entire body may be used (as in pantomime).

As is the case for verbal speech, emblems can be interpreted differently depending on circumstances, so, for example, a nose wrinkle may mean "I'm disgusted" or "Phew! That smells bad!" depending on the context. Some emblems, such as those used for "eating" (bringing the hand to the mouth) and "sleeping" (tilting the head to the side and closing the eyes, or placing the hands beneath the head like a pillow) have been observed in several cultures (Ekman, 1976). Other emblems are quite culture specific. For example, Figure 2.1. displays suicide emblems that reflect the methods usually used for this act (i.e., hanging, shooting, or stabbing) in three different cultures.

Some emblems are age specific, and their comprehension may depend on a person's cognitive and language abilities. For example, Hamre-Nietupski and her colleagues (1977) devised a list of 147 such emblems, which they called "generally understood gestures," which were found to have a 77% recognition rate by people serving individuals with severe disabilities (Fiocca, 1981). Doherty, Karlan, and Lloyd (1982), however, found that fewer than 40% of these gestures were understood by adults with mental retardation in sheltered workshops. Similarly, some adults with aphasia secondary to stroke have been noted to have difficulty in using and understanding even common gestural emblems (Rosenbek, LaPointe, & Wertz, 1989). For such individuals, the apparent simplicity of even common gestures may be misleading.

*Illustrators* are nonverbal behaviors that are tied to or accompany speech and illustrate what is being spoken (Knapp, 1980). Among other uses, illustrators are employed to: 1) emphasize a word or phrase (e.g., pointing emphatically to a chair while saying "sit down"), 2) depict a referent or a

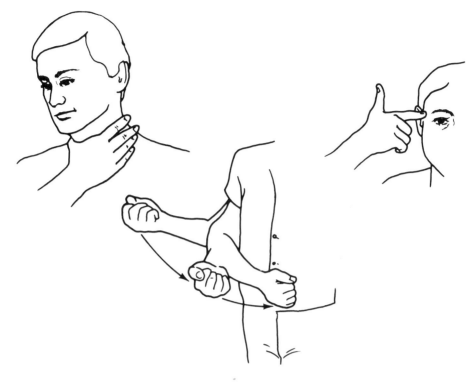

**Figure 2.1.** Emblems for suicide. Top left, Papua, New Guinea; top right, United States; bottom, Japan. (From Ekman, P. [1976]. Movements with precise meanings. *Journal of Communication, 26,* 3; reprinted by permission.)

spatial relationship (e.g., spreading the hands far apart while saying "You should have seen the size of the one that got away"), 3) depict the pacing of an event (e.g., snapping the fingers rapidly while saying "It was over with before I knew it"), or 4) illustrate a verbal statement through repetition or substitution of a word or phrase (e.g., miming the action of writing while saying "Where's my whatchamacallit?"). Knapp (1980) suggested that illustrators are used less consciously and less deliberately than emblems and that they are most likely to be used in face-to-face interactions when the speaker is excited, the receiver is not paying attention or not comprehending the message, and the interaction is generally "difficult."

*Affect displays* are facial expressions or body movements that display emotional states. Affect displays differ from emblems in that they are more subtle, less stylized, and less intentional (Knapp, 1980); in fact, in many cases, the affect display may contradict a concurrent verbal statement. These subtle gestures may be largely unconscious to the person using them, while obvious to the receiver of the message. Affect displays that convey happiness, surprise, fear, sadness, anger, and disgust or contempt may occur cross-culturally, although their contextual appropriateness is governed by specific social rules regarding age, sex, and role position (Ekman & Friesen, 1969).

> Saying "I agree completely" while shaking the head "no" and crossing the arms in front of the body is an example of an affect display that contradicts a concurrent verbal statement.

*Regulators* are nonverbal behaviors that maintain and regulate conversational speaking and listening between two or more people. Regulators may function to initiate or terminate interactions or to tell the speaker to continue, repeat, elaborate, hurry up, become more interesting, or give the other person a chance to talk, among other functions (Ekman & Friesen, 1969). Head nods and eye behaviors are the most common regulators of turn-taking interactions. For example, when one wishes to terminate an interaction, the amount of eye contact often decreases markedly, while head nodding accompanied by wide-eyed gazing can urge a speaker to continue. Like illustrators, regulators are thought to be learned from watching others interact, but, unlike illustrators, they are emitted almost involuntarily. We are usually aware of these behaviors when they are sent by those with whom we interact.

The final category of gestures, *adaptors,* are learned behaviors that are generally used more often when a person is alone, and they are not intentionally used in communication. Nevertheless, they may be triggered by verbal interactions that produce emotional responses, particularly those associated with anxiety of some sort (Knapp, 1980).

Adaptors can be divided into three types: self-directed, object-directed, and alter-directed. *Self-adaptors* refer to manipulations of one's own body and include, for example, holding, rubbing, scratching, picking, or pinching oneself. Self-adaptors are usually performed with little awareness and with no intention to communicate, and they receive little external feedback from others; in fact, other people rarely wish to be caught looking at them. Rubbing one's nose when feeling stress, or wiping around the corners of the eyes when feeling sad are a few examples of this type of self-adaptor. *Object-adaptors* involve the manipulation of objects, are often learned later in life, and have fewer social sanctions associated with them. They are often within the awareness of the person producing them and may be intended to communicate. Chewing on a pencil instead of smoking a cigarette when anxious is an example of an object-adaptor. *Alter-adaptors* are thought to be learned early in life in conjunction with interpersonal experiences, such as giving and taking or protecting oneself against impending harm. Ekman (1976) distinguished these by their ability to be adaptive. For example, a child who has been physically abused may react to any sudden advance by an adult by crouching and moving the hands toward the face in a protective motion. Later in life, this alter-adaptor may be manifested as a step backward with a slight hand movement toward the body when the person is approached by a stranger—an alteration of the initial, protective behavior.

> Beukelman (1989) noted that an AAC user's inability to communicate messages usually conveyed nonverbally—the "background" messages such as "I like you," "slow down," or "I'm worried about this," often presents as much of an intervention challenge as does the lack of verbal speech. It is critically important to attend to this issue as part of an overall intervention.

## Vocalizations and Speech

People who have difficulty with speech often exhibit vocalizations that are communicative in nature. These may range from involuntary sounds such as sneezing, coughing, hiccuping, and snoring to voluntary vocalizations such as yawning, laughing, crying, moaning, yelling, and belching that often signify physical or emotional states. Some individuals are also able to produce vocalizations that are substitutes for speech, such as "uh-huh" for "yes" or "uh-uh" for "no." Such vocalizations may be idiosyncratic and require interpretation by persons who are familiar with the individual's repertoire of vocal signals.

Vocalizations and speech may also be used by communication partners as all or part of the communication, or message, display. For example, *auditory scanning,* which may be either unaided or aided, can be particularly appropriate for AAC users with severe visual impairments who understand spoken language (Blackstone, 1988a). Beukelman, Yorkston, and Dowden (1985) described the use of auditory scanning with a young man who sustained a traumatic brain injury in an automobile accident. Among other resulting impairments, he was unable to speak and was cortically blind. He communicated by having his partner verbally recite numbers corresponding to "chunks" of the alphabet, for example 1 = *abcdef,* and 2 = *ghijkl.* When his partner gave the number of the "chunk" he desired, he indicated his choice by making a predetermined motor movement. His partner then began to recite the individual letters in the "chunk" until he signaled that the letter he desired had been announced. This laborious process continued until the message was spelled out, letter by letter. Similarly, Shane and Cohen (1981) described a commonly used process they called "20 questions," in which the communication partner asks questions and the AAC user responds with "yes" or "no" answers. Software programs are available that provide an aided form of this technique, in which the options are announced by a speech synthesizer (see Blackstone, 1988a).

> The Audscan II (Words +, Inc.) was the first commercial portable auditory scanner in North America. It can be operated via a single or dual switch and can be programmed to produce complete messages, letters, or single words. The Dynavox (Sentient Systems Technology, Inc.) and the Macaw (Zygo Industries, Inc.) are also available as auditory scanners.

## UNAIDED SYMBOLS: GESTURAL CODES

In addition to common nonverbal signals, formalized gestural codes have been developed for use by persons with communication impairments. These codes differ from sign languages because they do not have a linguistic base. Formalized gestural codes have been developed as idiosyncratic systems for individual users in nursing homes, hospitals, and residential centers (Musselwhite & St. Louis, 1988). Few gestural codes are widely used and disseminated, with the exception of Amer-Ind.

> White's Gestural System for the Lower Extremities was developed by Cathy White, who has a severe hearing loss as well as cerebral palsy with severe upper extremity involvement, with assistance from her mother, Harriet. The system consists of 125 "leg signs," which use leg, foot, toe, heel, knee, ankle, calf, and thigh touch points to convey messages in a variety of linguistic categories (e.g., people, actions, or objects) (Huer, 1987).

### Amer-Ind

Amer-Ind is based on American Indian Hand Talk, a system used by a variety of Native American tribes to communicate across intertribal language barriers. Developed by a communication specialist who was taught hand talk by her Iroquois relatives (Skelly, 1979), the current system consists of 250 concept labels that are equivalent to approximately 2,500 English words, since each signal has multiple meanings (Musselwhite & St. Louis, 1988). Additional meanings can be achieved through a process called *agglutination*, in which words can be combined to create new concepts (e.g., garage = place + drive + shelter). Skelly and her colleagues (Skelly, 1979; Skelly, Schinsky, Smith, Donaldson, & Griffin, 1975) reported that between 80%–88% of the hand signals could be recognized accurately by untrained observers. Later studies have suggested that between 50%–60% of the signals are guessable by nondisabled adults when signals are presented without reference to their conceptual categories (Daniloff, Lloyd, & Fristoe, 1983; Doherty, Daniloff, & Lloyd, 1985). Nonetheless, this is still considerably more guessable than are the 10%–30% guessability levels reported for American Sign Language (ASL) (Daniloff et al., 1983).

Amer-Ind has been used with some success with children who have severe/profound intellectual disabilities (e.g., Daniloff & Shafer, 1981) as well as with adults with aphasia, apraxia, dysarthria, dysphonia, laryngectomies, and glossectomies (Bonvillian & Friedman, 1978; Daniloff, Noll, Fristoe, & Lloyd, 1982; Rosenbek et al., 1989; Skelly, 1979; Skelly et al., 1975; Skelly, Schinsky,

Smith, & Fust, 1974). It appears that the average Amer-Ind signal can be produced at an earlier stage in motor development and requires less complex motor coordination than does the average American Sign Language sign (Daniloff & Vergara, 1984). Therefore, this system might have advantages for persons with upper extremity impairments.

A videotape of Amer-Ind gestures is available from Auditec, St. Louis, MO.

## UNAIDED SYMBOLS: MANUAL SIGN SYSTEMS

A number of *manual sign systems,* the majority of which were originally designed for and used by the deaf population, have been employed as well with persons with severe communication disorders who are able to hear. Manual signs, used alone or combined with speech, appear to be the form of augmentative communication used most often with persons in the United States labeled autistic or severely/profoundly retarded (Matas, Mathy-Laikko, Beukelman, & Legresley, 1985), the United Kingdom (Kiernan, 1983; Kiernan, Reid, & Jones, 1982), and Australia (Iacono & Parsons, 1986). This approach has also been used to some extent in the remediation of developmental apraxia (Culp, 1989).

In 1985, Bryen and Joyce published an analysis of 43 language intervention studies published in the United States or Great Britain between 1969 and 1979, of which 81% involved some type of manual sign system with persons with intellectual disabilities.

Despite the popularity of manual signing, controlled research studies with persons with intellectual disabilities have reported mixed success, with many reports indicating that self-initiated spontaneous use of learned signs or structures often does not occur (see Bryen & Joyce, 1985; Kiernan, 1983, for reviews). Failure to implement "best practice" strategies in manual sign assessment and intervention appear to be the primary reasons for such poor clinical results (Bryen & Joyce, 1985).

Regardless of concerns related to efficacy with certain populations, manual signs continue to be useful with a wide variety of persons with severe communication disorders. Lloyd and Karlan (1984) suggested six main reasons why manual sign approaches might be appropriate alternatives to speech-only approaches. First, input is simplified through the use of manual signs (i.e., verbiage is reduced and the rate of presentation is slowed). Second, expressive responding is facilitated by reduction in the physical demands and psychological pressure for speech and by the enhancement of the interventionist's ability to shape gradual approximations and provide physical guidance. Third, vocabulary that is limited, yet functional, can be taught while maintaining the individual's attention. Fourth, manual signs allow simplified language input while minimizing auditory short-term memory and processing requirements. Fifth, stimulus processing is facilitated with the use of the visual mode, which has temporal and referential advantages over the speech mode. Sixth, manual signs have the advantage over speech of symbolic representation, because signs are closer visually to their referents than are spoken words.

The term manual sign system actually refers to three main types of systems: 1) those that are alternatives to the spoken language of a particular country (e.g., American or Swedish Sign Language), 2) those that parallel the spoken language (manually coded English), and 3) those that interact with or supplement another means of transmitting a spoken language (e.g., fingerspelling). The latter two types of systems are intended to be used by nondisabled teachers or interventionists concurrently with speech and other augmentative modalities (e.g., gestures). We review the primary manual sign systems used in North America in the sections that follow, with particular reference to their applicability to AAC interventions.

## Manual Alternatives to English

   *American Sign Language*   In the United States and most of Canada, American Sign Language or Ameslan (ASL) is used within the Deaf community for face-to-face interaction. In the province of Quebec, a distinctly different system, Quebecois Sign Language (QSL), is used by people who are deaf (G. Desrosiers, personal communication, January 18, 1991).

> ASL, which is used in English Canada, is based on the French Sign Language brought to the United States in the early 1800s by Laurent Clerc. Ironically, QSL, used by French Canadians, is based on British Sign Language, which was brought to Quebec by English Catholic nuns (G. Desrosiers, personal communication, January 18, 1991).

ASL is related neither to English nor to the sign languages of other countries, so that the Deaf communities in Great Britain, Sweden, Japan, and other countries have their own distinct languages. It appears that only a few teachers of the hearing impaired in the United States use ASL with their students, and, thus, it is not a pedagogical language, although it is the predominant language of the Deaf culture (Hoffmeister, 1990). Since ASL does not follow or approximate English word order, it is not used concurrently with speech.

Pure-form ASL is rarely used with persons who have communication deficits not primarily due to a hearing impairment. Instead, an "invented" manual signing approach, in which ASL signs are combined with speech and produced in English word order, is often reported. This technique is properly termed *key word signing*, and is discussed in a subsequent section of this chapter.

> An historical note: The Paget-Gorman Sign System (Paget, Gorman, & Paget, 1976), developed in England, was the first manually coded English sign system and is composed largely of pantomimes and hand signs. Seeing Exact English (Anthony, 1971) was the first manually coded English system developed in North America, and it was originally intended for use with individuals who were both deaf and had intellectual disabilities. Duffysigns (Duffy, 1977) was developed for use by individuals with both intellectual and physical disabilities (e.g., cerebral palsy), and requires less motor control than do other MCE systems.

## Manual Sign Parallel Systems (Manually Coded English)

In North America, a number of manual sign systems that code English word order, syntax, and grammar have been developed for educational use with deaf and other individuals with communicative impairments. These systems have been referred to as "educational sign systems" (Musselwhite & St. Louis, 1988), "pedagogical signs" (Vanderheiden & Lloyd, 1986), and "manually coded English (MCE)" (Karlan, 1990; Vanderheiden & Lloyd, 1986). We use the manually coded English (MCE) term in acknowledgment of its common use in the Deaf community (Stedt & Moores, 1990).

> Outside North America, several manual sign parallel systems have been developed for use by persons with severe communication disorders. For example, in Ireland, L.A.M.H. (Language Augmentation for Mentally Handicapped) signs have been used successfully with children with intellectual disabilities (Kearns, 1990). Similarly, simplified sign lexica based on Finnish Sign Language (Pulli & Jaroma, 1990) and Swedish Sign Language (Granlund, Ström, & Olsson, 1989) have been employed.

The three most commonly used manually coded English (MCE) systems in North America are Sign English (Woodward, 1990), Signing Exact English (SEE-2) (Gustason, Pfetzing, & Zawolkow, 1980), and Signed English (Bornstein, Saulnier, & Hamilton, 1983). In addition, "key word signing," a type of MCE, has been developed primarily for use with persons with communication disorders and intellectual disabilities who can hear. These four MCE systems are discussed in the sections that follow.

> Sign English uses signs from ASL in English word order with as many ASL grammatical characteristics as possible and is usually accompanied by speech or extensive vocalizations. (Woodward, 1990).

***Sign English***   Sign English, also known as Pidgin Sign English or PSE, can perhaps best be described as "ASL-like English" when used by people who can hear and "English-like ASL" when used by members of the Deaf community (Woodward, 1990). Many versions of Sign English have evolved from interactions between skilled deaf and hearing signers. Thus, Sign English is not considered as a language separate from ASL (American Sign Language) and English; rather, it falls on the continuum between them (Woodward, 1990). Because of this intermediate status and the fact that there is considerable geographic variability in Sign English dialects, few studies have been conducted that describe the grammatical characteristics of this manual system. Sign English appears to be used extensively in the education of deaf students in a total communication context, where it is used in conjunction with speech or extensive mouthing of English words (Woodward, 1990).

> Signed English and Signing Exact English, which were developed by teachers and hearing parents of deaf children, borrow liberally from the vocabulary of ASL, but also include many non-ASL signs for word endings, verb tenses, and other elements that would ordinarily be fingerspelled or omitted (Karlan, 1990).

***Signed English***   Signed English was designed in the early 1970s as a simple and flexible alternative to existing manual English systems. Although originally designed for preschoolers with hearing impairments, it has been expanded and adapted so that it can be used by older students as well (Bornstein, 1990). Signed English consists of over 3,100 signs and uses 14 sign markers (e.g., -ed, -ing).

Signed English has been used for many years in conjunction with speech with students with intellectual disabilities, and it was the first manual sign system reported to be successfully implemented with children labeled autistic (Creedon, 1973). In their 1985 review, Bryen and Joyce reported that Signed English was identified in the majority of studies of students with intellectual disabilities that named a specific manual sign system.

> There are a wide variety of support materials for classroom and community use of Signed English, including illustrated dictionaries, texts, storybooks, flash cards, coloring books, songbooks and records, poems, and posters. These are available through Gallaudet University Press.

***Signing Exact English (SEE-2)***   SEE-2 was developed as an alternative to its predecessor, Seeing Essential English (SEE-1), after the members of a SEE-1 work group became dissatisfied with its direction (Gustason, 1990). SEE-2 consists of approximately 4,000 signs and over 70 word ending, tense, and "affix" signs (e.g., -est, -ed, -ing, -ment, un-). The system was developed around

10 basic grammatical principles that ensure internal consistency and provide guidelines for adding new signs (see Gustason, 1990).

SEE-2 is motorically and linguistically more complex than Signed English and may, therefore, be less applicable for persons with severe communication disorders not due primarily to hearing impairments (Musselwhite & St. Louis, 1988). For example, only two of the studies reviewed by Bryen and Joyce (1985) reported use of SEE-2 with students labeled as severely handicapped. It is also likely that references to the use of SEE-2 with persons with intellectual disabilities actually refer to selective use of the *signs* from this system, rather than to use of the complete system.

---

Numerous SEE-2 support materials, including articles, story books, videotapes, illustrated dictionaries, flash cards, songs, and posters are available for parents, teachers, and others through the Modern Signs Press.

---

**Key Word Signing**   In "key word signing (KWS)" (Grove & Walker, 1990; Windsor & Fristoe, 1989), spoken English is used simultaneously with manual signs for the critical words in a sentence, such as the base nouns, base verbs, prepositions, adjectives, and adverbs. Thus, the sentence "go get the cup and put it on the table" might involve the use of the signs "get," "cup," "put," "on," and "table" while the entire sentence is spoken.

The term key word signing probably most accurately describes the majority of interventions that use manual signs in English word order and that have been used with persons with disabilities other than hearing impairments. Since these interventions almost always include the use of speech in addition to manual signs, they have been referred to as *total communication* or *simultaneous communication approaches*. Bryen and Joyce (1985) reported that of 25 studies they reviewed in which some type of manual sign system was used with students with severe intellectual disabilities, 4 purported to have used ASL, 6 used Signed English, 2 used SEE-2, and 13 used other or unspecified systems. In fact, it is quite likely that KWS, using signs from the other named systems, was the approach actually used in the majority of these studies. We use the terms key word signing and total communication interchangeably in this book.

---

The distinction between ASL, Signed English, key word signing, and other manual sign systems is important in order to respect the legitimacy of ASL as the language of the Deaf culture as well as to be precise in sharing empirical and clinical results of interventions.

---

## Manual Supplements to Spoken Language

Manual systems that interact with or supplement spoken English have been used with children who have hearing impairments and, to a limited extent, with individuals with communicative disorders, to support the development of speech and literacy skills. Nevertheless, most of these techniques (including fingerspelling and gestural or eye blink codes) have not achieved widespread use in the field of augmentative communication. One exception is Cued Speech (Kipila & Williams-Scott, 1990), which has been used with people with developmental apraxia and dual sensory impairments and is discussed in Chapters 12 and 15, respectively. Readers are referred to alternative sources for overviews of other manual supplements to English (e.g., Musselwhite & St. Louis, 1988; Vanderheiden & Lloyd, 1986).

## AIDED SYMBOLS: TANGIBLE SYMBOLS

The term "tangible symbol" was coined by Rowland and Schweigert (1989) to refer to two- or three-dimensional aided symbols that are permanent, manipulable with a simple motor behavior, tactually discriminable, and highly iconic. We use the term here in a more restricted sense to refer to symbols that can be discriminated *on the basis of tangible properties* (e.g., shape, texture, and consistency); thus, most two-dimensional (i.e., pictorial) symbols are not included. Tangible symbols are typically used with individuals with visual or dual sensory impairments and severe intellectual disabilities, but they may also be appropriate for other populations (e.g., beginning communication symbols for children with visual impairments). The four types of tangible symbols discussed in this section are: real objects, miniature objects, partial objects, and artificial association symbols.

## Real Objects

Real object symbols may be identical to, similar to, or associated with their referents. For example, an *identical symbol* for "brush your teeth" might be a toothbrush that is the same color and type as the individual's actual toothbrush. A *similar symbol* might be a toothbrush of a different color and type, while an *associated symbol* might be a tube of toothpaste or container of dental floss. Other examples of associated symbols include a sponge that represents "cleaning the kitchen counter top" or a cassette tape that represents "music time" in the preschool classroom. Associated symbols may also include remnants of activities—items such as a ticket stub from the movies or the wrapper from a fast-food hamburger.

It appears that many persons with intellectual disabilities are able to match identical and nonidentical (i.e., similar) object symbols with similar accuracy (Mirenda & Locke, 1989). This suggests that both types of object symbols may be equal in enabling recognition of their referent; however, it is important to be cautious in this assumption, especially with beginning communicators. It is also important to consider the individual sensory input needs of individuals with visual impairments when selecting real objects for them to use. Rowland and Schweigert (1989, 1990) reported numerous examples of successful use of real object symbols with individuals who have visual and dual sensory impairments.

> People with visual impairments "see" with their fingers and hands, so the tangible symbols they use should be *tactilely similar* to their referents.

## Miniature Objects

Miniature objects may be more practical than real object symbols in some situations but need to be selected carefully to maximize effectiveness (Vanderheiden & Lloyd, 1986). For example, it appears that miniatures that are much smaller than their referents may be more difficult to recognize by students with intellectual disabilities than are some types of two-dimensional symbols (Mirenda & Locke, 1989). Nevertheless, miniature objects that are reasonably smaller than their referents have been used successfully with individuals with cerebral palsy (Landman & Schaeffler, 1986) and dual sensory impairments (Rowland & Schweigert, 1989, 1990).

In addition to size, tactile similarity is also critical when using miniature objects with persons who cannot see. It is unlikely that a visually impaired individual will readily recognize the relationship between a miniature plastic toilet and a real toilet, since they *feel different* with respect to size, shape, and texture. In this case, the use of a real object associated with the toilet (e.g., a small roll of toilet paper) might be more appropriate as a bathroom symbol.

## Partial Objects

In some situations, particularly those that involve referents that are large, partial objects may be useful as symbols. For example, the top of the spray bottle of the window cleaner an individual uses may be used to represent "washing the windows" at a vocational site. We also include in this category "symbols with one or two shared features" (Rowland & Schweigert, 1989, p. 229), such as thermoform symbols that are the same size and shape as their referents. The use of partial object symbols may be a good alternative when the tactile similarity requirement discussed previously cannot be met with miniature objects.

## Artificially Associated and Textured Symbols

Tangible symbols may also be constructed by selecting shapes and textures that can be artificially associated with a referent. For example, a wooden apple might be attached to a cafeteria door, and a similar apple could be used as the symbol (Rowland & Schweigert, 1989). *Textured symbols* are a subtype of this category, and these may be either logically or arbitrarily associated with their referents. A logically associated textured symbol could be a piece of spandex material to symbolize a bathing suit, since many suits are made of this material. Alternatively, a square of velvet could be arbitrarily selected to represent a favorite snack. Several case studies have documented the successful use of textured symbols with individuals with one or more sensory impairments in addition to severe intellectual disabilities (Locke & Mirenda, 1988; Mathy-Laikko et al., 1989; Murray-Branch, Udavari-Solner, & Bailey, 1991).

## Other Tangible Symbols

Case study reports have documented the usefulness of adapting line drawing symbols, such as Blissymbols, for use with persons with visual impairments (e.g., Edman, 1991; Garrett, 1986). This approach creates a tactilely discriminable "relief" symbol using a thermoform process, photo-engraving, or other method. The user then learns to associate the raised outline of the symbol with its referent.

## AIDED SYMBOLS: REPRESENTATIONAL SYMBOLS

Many types of two-dimensional symbols can be used to represent various concepts. These representational symbols include photographs, line drawings, and plastic chips that can be either made or purchased. The major representational symbol types are reviewed in this section in terms of their relative guessability (transparency) and learnability (translucency), as well as in terms of the populations of AAC users with whom they have been successfully used.

> In Canada, numerous representational symbol sets, including many of those mentioned in this chapter, are available from the Easter Seal Communication Institute.

## Photographs

Good quality color or black and white photographs may be used to represent objects, verbs, people, places, and activities. Photographs may be produced with a camera or obtained from catalogs, magazines, coupons, product labels, or advertisements (Mirenda, 1985). A research study found that persons with intellectual disabilities matched color photographs to their referents somewhat more accurately than black and white photographs (Mirenda & Locke, 1989). Another study found that persons with intellectual disabilities matched black and white photographs to their referents more accurately than line drawings (Sevcik & Romski, 1986). These findings may have implications for the use of black and white photocopies versus color originals, as well as for color versus black and white photocopies, but no data are available in this area. Dixon (1981) found that students with severe disabilities were more able to associate objects with their color photographs when the photographic objects were cut out than when they were not. Reichle et al. (1991) suggested that the context in which a photograph appears may affect an individual's ability to recognize it; for example, a photograph of a watering can may become more recognizable when it appears next to a photograph of a plant.

---

Sets of high quality color or black and white photographs are available from companies such as the Attainment Company, Imaginart Communication Products, and Communication Skill Builders.

---

## Line Drawings

*Picture Communication Symbols (PCS)*   The first column in Figure 2.2. illustrates this widely used system of 1,800 clear, simple line drawings, which is available with either written English labels or no labels (Johnson, 1981, 1985). Picture Communication Symbols (PCS) can be purchased in a variety of formats, including stamps and symbol books that can be photocopied. A Macintosh software program, Boardmaker (Mayer-Johnson Co., 1989), can generate communication boards and novel PCS symbols. A revision of the program allows symbol labels to be printed in 10 languages (T. Johnson, personal communication, July 22, 1991). In addition, a variety of PCS teaching materials are also available.

**Figure 2.2.**   Examples of Picture Communication Symbols, rebuses, Picsyms, and Blissymbols. (From Brandenburg, S., & Vanderheiden, G. [1988]. Communication board design and vocabulary selection. In L. Bernstein [Ed.], *The vocally impaired: Clinical practice and research*, p. 94. Needham Heights, MA: Allyn & Bacon. Copyright © 1988; reprinted by permission.)

Three research studies (Mirenda & Locke, 1989; Mizuko, 1987; Mizuko & Reichle, 1989) indicated that both PCS and Picsyms are more transparent than Blissymbols, for nonhandicapped preschoolers and for school-age and adult individuals with intellectual disabilities. In a comparative study of Blissymbols, PCS, PIC, Picsyms, and rebus symbols, PCS and rebus symbols were found to be the most translucent across nouns, verbs, and modifiers (Bloomberg, Karlan, & Lloyd, 1990). In general, the translucency data indicate that nonhandicapped preschoolers learned more PCS symbols over three trials than either Picsyms or Blissymbols (Mizuko, 1987) while adults with intellectual disabilities appeared to find Picture Communication Symbols (PCS) and Picsyms equally learnable (Mizuko & Reichle, 1989). PCS symbols have been used successfully in AAC interventions with persons with intellectual disabilities (Mirenda & Santogrossi, 1985), cerebral palsy (Goossens', 1989), and autism (Rotholz, Berkowitz, & Burberry, 1989), among other impairments.

A catalog of Picture Communication Symbols and related products can be obtained from the Mayer-Johnson Company.

**Rebus Symbols**   A *rebus* is a picture that visually or nominally represents a word or a syllable. For example, a rebus of a knot could be used to symbolize either "knot" or "not" (see Figure 2.2.). There are many types of rebuses (Vanderheiden & Lloyd, 1986), but the most common collection of these in North America was developed as a mechanism for teaching young nondisabled children to read (Woodcock, Clark, & Davies, 1968). This work has been adapted and expanded as a system of communication symbols for persons with communication impairments, both in the United States (Clark, Davies, & Woodcock, 1974) and in the United Kingdom (Van Oosterum & Devereux, 1985; Walker, Parsons, Cousins, Henderson, & Carpenter, 1985). The *Standard Rebus Glossary* (Clark et al., 1974) contains over 800 black and white rebuses printed with their word labels, which represent over 2,000 words.

A study of nondisabled children and young adults in four age groups found rebus symbols to be equivalent to Picsyms in transparency, and both were more transparent than Blissymbolics (Musselwhite & Ruscello, 1984). Rebus and PCS symbols were found to be more translucent than Picsyms, PIC symbols, and Blissymbols in another study (Bloomberg et al., 1990). Rebus symbols were found to be superior to Blissymbols in learning and short-term recall tasks with both nonhandicapped (Ecklund & Reichle, 1987) and language-delayed preschoolers (Burroughs, Albritton, Eaton, & Montague, 1990). Rebus symbols have been used in communication applications with a variety of individuals, including children with Down syndrome (Pecyna, 1988) and adults with autism (Reichle & Brown, 1986).

Instructional materials and a dictionary of rebuses commonly used in North America (Clark et al., 1974) can be obtained from the American Guidance Service. Information concerning British rebuses can be obtained from EARO.

**Picsyms**   Picsyms is a logical system of visual–graphic symbols that were developed according to an internally consistent set of principles. The core Picsyms system, which was developed through work with young children who were unable to speak (Carlson, 1985), consists of over 1,800 line drawings (see Figure 2.2.). Usually these are accompanied by written labels. New Picsyms can be created by following the generative rules that are included with the dictionary of symbols.

As noted previously, Picsyms appear to be similar to or slightly more difficult than both PCS and rebus symbols, and superior to Blissymbols, in both transparency and translucency (Bloomberg et al., 1990; Mirenda & Locke, 1989; Mizuko, 1987; Mizuko & Reichle, 1989; Musselwhite &

Ruscello, 1984). They have been used in AAC interventions with individuals of all ages and ability levels.

A songbook (Musselwhite, 1985), dictionary, and materials related to teaching and using Picsyms are available. The dictionary and teaching materials can be obtained from Baggeboda Press.

***Pictogram Ideogram Communication (PIC) Symbols***   Often confused with Picsyms and Picture Communication Symbols (PCS), this unique symbol set consists of 400 white-on-black symbols designed to reduce figure–ground discrimination difficulties (Maharaj, 1980). Figure 2.3. illustrates four of these symbols.

Reichle et al. (1991) and Vanderheiden and Lloyd (1986) summarized a number of studies that indicate that white-on-black pictures are not necessarily more visually salient than standard black-on-white drawings. In a study with nonhandicapped adult subjects, PIC symbols were found to be less translucent than PCS and rebus symbols but more translucent than Blissymbols (Bloomberg et al., 1990). Leonhart and Maharaj (1979) reported that adults with severe/profound intellectual disabilities learned PIC symbols faster than Blissymbols. PIC symbols have been used with persons with severe/profound disabilities (Leonhart & Maharaj, 1979; Reichle & Yoder, 1985) and with persons with autism (Reichle & Brown, 1986) with communication books or boards.

Pictogram Ideogram Communication symbols are available from The Pictogram Centre in Saskatchewan, Canada. Swedish Pictogram Symbols, which are modeled after PIC symbols, are available through the National Resource Center of Sweden. A Portuguese version of PIC symbols is also available in that country.

go          garden

wagon          sad

**Figure 2.3.**   Examples of Pictogram Ideogram Communication symbols (From Maharaj, S. [1980]. Pictogram ideogram communication. Saskatoon, Saskatchewan: The Pictogram Centre, Saskatchewan Association of Rehabilitation Centres; reprinted by permission.)

***Blissymbolics***   The history of Blissymbolics is complex and fascinating, but no attempt is made here to summarize it. The reader is referred to the original work by Charles Bliss (1965) and to historical records of Blissymbolics development in Canada in the early 1970s (Kates & Mc-Naughton, 1975). Generally, the system was developed to function as an auxiliary language for international written communication. It consists of approximately 100 basic symbols that can be used singly or in combination to encode virtually any message (Silverman, 1989). The original system consisted of 1,400 black and white symbols with written labels (Hehner, 1980), and examples are provided in Figure 2.2. New Blissymbols are added annually by an international panel affiliated with Blissymbolics Communication International (BCI). Recent additions, for example, included over 100 new symbols related to human sexuality (Wood, 1990). In addition, a collection of Blissymbols are available that have been enhanced by pink line-drawing cues (Blissymbolics Communication International, 1984). These enhanced Blissymbols are designed to remind the beginning user and the new instructor of the concepts that the symbols represent (Raghavendra & Fristoe, 1990). Figure 2.4. offers examples of enhanced Blissymbols, compared with their traditional counterparts.

> Communication aids that utilize Blissymbols have been developed and used in countries as diverse as Iceland (Magnússon, 1990), Zimbabwe (Hussey, 1991), France (Toulotte, Baudel-Cantegrit, & Trehou, 1990), Israel (Seligman-Wine, 1988), Hungary (Collier, 1991); Italy (Tronconi, 1990), India (Swartz, 1984), and South Africa (Shalit & Boonzaier, 1990). Blissymbol dictionaries, software, research reports, teaching materials, and training workshops can be obtained through Blissymbolics Communication International.

**Figure 2.4.**   Examples of enhanced Blissymbols. (From Musselwhite, C., & St. Louis, K. [1988]. *Communication programming for persons with severe handicaps* [2nd ed., p. 193]. Austin, TX: PRO-ED; reprinted by permission.)

Numerous studies have indicated that of all the representational symbols in common use, Blissymbols are the least transparent, most difficult to learn, and the hardest to retain (e.g., Bloomberg et al., 1990; Hurlbut, Iwata, & Green, 1982; Mirenda & Locke, 1989; Mizuko, 1987). Why then is this system so widely used in the AAC field? Vanderheiden and Lloyd (1986) noted some major strengths of Blissymbolics:

1. The principles and strategies for combining symbols enable expression of thoughts not on the communication board. The symbols are conceptually based and constructed using consistent, systematic rules.
2. The symbols can be introduced simply and later expanded.
3. The use of Blissymbolics is compatible with other techniques including reading and writing.
4. Extensive training and support is provided by Blissymbolics Communication International (BCI).

Originally intended for use with children with cerebral palsy, Blissymbolics has been used with various degrees of success in the remediation of virtually every known communication impairment (see Musselwhite & St. Louis, 1988; Silverman, 1989; and Vanderheiden & Lloyd, 1986, for applications).

---

Blissymbolics dictionaries, software, research reports, teaching materials, and training workshops can be obtained through Blissymbolics Communication International (Canada).

---

**Other Pictorial Systems**   Additional representational symbol systems have become available, although they have not been studied in terms of relative guessability and learnability. Some of these deserve to be mentioned, if only briefly.

---

Numerous pictorial systems have been developed to meet individual communication needs around the world. For example, the computerized COMPIC system from Australia contains over 1,700 pictographic symbols based on international symbol conventions (Bloomberg, 1990). COMPIC symbols are available through the COMPIC Development Association in Victoria, Australia. In Quebec, a line drawing symbol system, Communimage, with French labels, is available through the Association de Paralysie Cérébral du Quebec.

---

*Self Talk*   These symbols are among the few commercial symbol sets available in color as well as black and white. Originally available only on communication boards (Johnson, 1986), these simple symbols are now printed with orthographic labels and may be purchased separately (Johnson, 1988). Students with intellectual disabilities were found to match colored Self Talk and various black and white line drawing symbols with their object referents equally well, suggesting that Self Talk symbols are equivalent to these other types of symbols in guessability (Mirenda & Locke, 1989).

---

Self Talk symbols and communication boards are available from Communication Skill Builders.

---

*Pick 'N Stick*   These symbols are colored pictographs arranged categorically and available on peel-back pages. The 720 symbols currently available are not accompanied by written labels and so each symbol can be used flexibly to represent one of many related concepts (e.g., a symbol of a person sunbathing may be used to mean "sunbathe," "relax," "weekend," or "suntan"). A black and white version of these symbols, Touch 'N Talk symbols, is also available. There is no available research concerning the relative iconicity of these symbol sets.

A catalog of Pick 'N Stick, Touch 'N Talk, and other communication products is available from Imaginart Press.

*Brady-Dobson Alternative Communication (B-DAC)* These symbols comprise 1,255 black and white line drawings in 10 categories. The written label on each symbol is printed so that it faces the listener in a face-to-face interaction (i.e., it is upside down to the user). The accompanying manual (Brady-Dobson, 1982) claims that B-DAC symbols have been used with over 40 individuals 6–49 years of age who have intellectual disabilities, developmental disabilities, cerebral palsy, and aphasia.

B-DAC symbols are available from the author, Ginny Brady-Dobson.

*Talking Pictures I, II, and III* These are kits of black and white line drawings on cards, with printed labels in English, Spanish, French, German, and Italian on the reverse of each card. They depict a wide range of functional, community living, and daily living vocabulary words. They are available in a variety of formats with support materials.

Talking Pictures I, II, and III can be ordered from the Crestwood Company.

*Oakland Schools Picture Dictionary* This representational symbol system consists of over 500 black and white line drawings (Kirstein, 1981). Included are symbols for vocational concepts and adult vocabulary items not found in other similar sets of symbols. Oakland symbols compared favorably to PCS and rebus symbols on both transparency and translucency tasks with nondisabled and intellectually disabled adults in a study of symbols representing emotions (Francis, Nail, & Lloyd, 1990).

The Oakland Schools Picture Dictionary is available from the Oakland Schools Communication Enhancement Center.

## AIDED SYMBOLS: ABSTRACT SYMBOL SYSTEMS

In this category, we include symbols for which the form does not suggest its meaning. Blissymbolics is not considered abstract because at least some symbols are pictographic. The two most widely known and used abstract symbol sets are Yerkish lexigrams and Non-SLIP symbols.

### Yerkish Lexigrams

These abstract symbols resulted from a primate research project designed to develop a computer-based system for studying language acquisition in chimpanzees (Rumbaugh, 1977). The lexigrams are composed of nine geometric forms used singly or in combinations of two, three, or four to form symbols. As depicted in Figure 2.5., they may appear as white element combinations on black backgrounds (Romski, Sevcik, & Pate, 1988). They may also be reproduced on one of seven color-coded backgrounds (Silverman, 1989). Generally, the lexigrams are used on an illuminated computer-assisted AAC device (Romski et al., 1988) that produces synthetic speech when the lexigram is touched (Romski & Sevcik, 1988b).

Lexigrams were originally used in studies investigating the symbol learning abilities of institutionalized adolescents and young adults with severe intellectual disabilities (Romski, White,

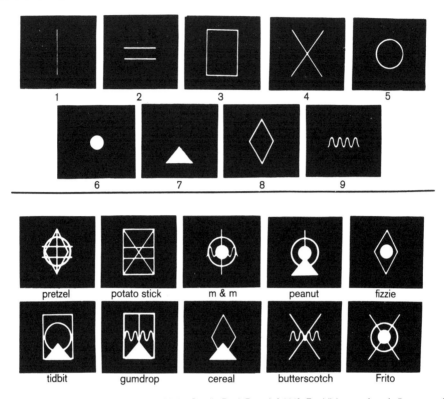

**Figure 2.5.** Examples of lexigrams. (From Romski, M. A., Sevcik, R., & Pate, J. [1988]. Establishment of symbolic communication in persons with severe retardation. *Journal of Speech and Hearing Disorders, 53*, 98; reprinted by permission.)

Millen, & Rumbaugh, 1984; Romski et al., 1988). They have been used successfully as symbols on voice output communication devices with children with moderate and severe disabilities (Project FACTT: Facilitating Augmentative Communication Through Technology, [Romski & Sevcik, 1988c; Romski & Sevcik, 1992]). So successful was this community-based project that the Clayton County (Georgia) school district where it was based has continued the use of lexigrams in the regular curriculum (R. Sevcik, personal communication, January 22, 1991). It would seem, at least intuitively, that the success reported with lexigrams might have been even greater if a more iconic symbol set had been used instead, although this is an empirical question. Lexigrams probably will not gain widespread popularity as an AAC system because they are so opaque, and they should probably not be used except with AAC systems that translate them into some type of intelligible speech.

> More information about Project FACTT and Yerkish lexigrams can be obtained from the Language Research Center, Georgia State University.

## Non-SLIP (Non-Speech Language Initiation Program)

The symbols in this set were in many ways the predecessors to Yerkish lexigrams since they originated in the early chimpanzee language work (Premack, 1971). The symbols are plastic or masonite chips that vary in color, shape, and size and are accompanied on the reverse side by printed English word meanings (Carrier & Peak, 1975). Clark (1981) reported that nonhandicapped preschoolers were able to learn both rebuses and Blissymbols more easily than either Non-SLIP symbols or written words. The Non-SLIP method has been used with individuals with global aphasia (Glass, Gazzaniga, & Premack, 1973), children with autism (McLean & McLean, 1974), and children with severe/profound intellectual disabilities (Hodges & Schwethelm, 1984).

## AIDED SYMBOLS: ORTHOGRAPHY AND ORTHOGRAPHIC SYMBOLS

*Traditional orthography* refers to the written characters used to transcribe a particular linguistic system (e.g., English alphabet or Chinese characters). Orthography has been used in AAC systems in the form of single letters, words, syllables (e.g., prefixes and suffixes), sequences of commonly combined letters (e.g., "ty," "ck," "th"), and phrases or sentences (Beukelman, Yorkston, & Dowden, 1985; Goodenough-Trepagnier, Tarry, & Prather, 1982). The interested reader is referred to Musselwhite and St. Louis (1988) for a comprehensive overview of traditional orthography and AAC applications.

The term *orthographic symbol* is used to refer to aided techniques that represent traditional orthography, such as braille, Morse code, and phonemic symbols. We differentiate these from orthographic *codes*, which use letters as message abbreviations. (These are discussed with numeric and other codes in Chapter 4.) Morse code, braille, and phonemic symbols are reviewed here briefly.

### Morse Code

Morse code is an international system that uses series of "dits" (dots) and "dahs" (dashes) to represent letters, punctuation, and numbers (see Figure 2.6.). When used in AAC applications, the dits

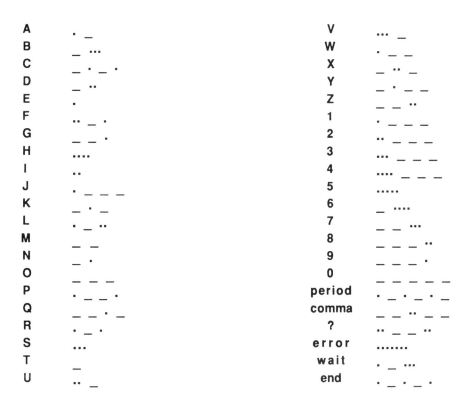

**Figure 2.6.** International Morse code.

and dahs are transmitted via microswitches through a device called an emulator that translates them into orthographic letters and numbers.

> Morse code emulators are available in many forms. These include: LightTalker (Prentke Romich Co.), RealVoice (Adaptive Communication Systems), Adaptive Firmware Card for Apple IIe and Apple IIgs computers (Don Johnston Developmental Equipment, Inc.), Ke:nx for Macintosh Computers (Don Johnston Developmental Equipment, Inc.), and WSKE Morse Code (Words +, Inc).

Studies investigating the learnability of Morse code by AAC users are limited. One exception is a case study of a man with a spinal cord injury who wrote using Morse code at a rate of 25–30 words per minute. He learned to produce basic Morse codes using a sip and puff switch within 2 weeks and became proficient in use of the system within approximately 2 months (Beukelman, Yorkston, & Dowden, 1985). The learning of Morse code by 10 individuals, ranging in age from 8 to 26 years, who activated their communication systems with bilateral head switches, was also described (Marriner, Beukelman, Wilson, & Ross, 1989). Eight learned to send Morse code with 95% accuracy within 4 weeks, while two required 5 months to reach this level. Based on this data, the authors suggested that the threshold for learning Morse code is a second or third grade reading level. (Readers are referred to McDonald, Schwejda, Marriner, Wilson, & Ross, 1982, for discussion of some of the advantages of Morse code.)

### Braille

Braille is a tactile symbol system for reading and writing that is used by persons with visual or dual sensory impairments. Braille characters are formed by combinations of six embossed dots arranged within a "cell" of two vertical columns of three dots each (see Figure 2.7.). The characters represent letters, parts of words, or entire words. Each character is formed according to a standard pattern within the six-dot cell.

Braille is organized and taught in three levels, or grades. Grade 2 is the most widely used form of braille and in 1932 was accepted for standard use in the United States (Scholl, 1986a). It allows certain contractions that enhance reading and writing speed. Grade 1 braille is uncontracted and

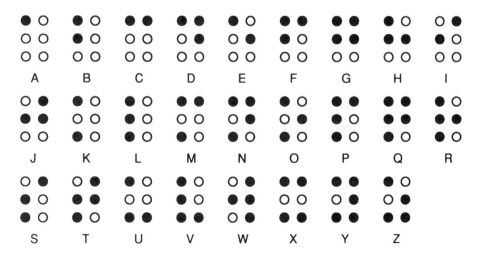

**Figure 2.7.**  English braille alphabet.

uses the alphabet symbols to spell out all words. Grade 3 braille is a rarely used shorthand form of the symbol set. Braille is used internationally, and different countries change the code to suit their language patterns and needs. Standard English braille, the official system adopted in the United States, was modified in 1959 and later revised (Olson, 1981).

In addition to being the standard literacy code for reading and writing, braille symbols are also used with different meanings for other purposes, including music code, mathematical or "Nemeth" code, and computer code. Music code assigns braille symbols to standard music notations. Nemeth code is used in performing arithmetic and mathematical computations and scientific notation. In Nemeth code, braille dots are positioned one line lower in the individual cells. The computer code is part of an effort to standardize all operational commands for different types of computer equipment (Rossi, 1986). In general, while there are hundreds of symbols in the various codes, all codes use the standard six-dot cell design but assign different meanings to the same symbol (Huebner, 1986).

## Phonemic Symbols

The most commonly used formal system of English phonemic symbols is SPEEC (Sequences of Phonemes for Efficient English Communication) (Goodenough-Trepagnier & Prather, 1981). The SPEEC-256 version, implemented on a lapboard or a 16-direction eye-gaze display, consists of 245 individual phonemes and phoneme sequences (e.g., "ile," "ch") and 11 numerals. The SPEEC-400 version, which is primarily used as a lapboard, contains 143 additional phonemes and sequences and a "space" symbol. In terms of efficiency, messages produced in SPEEC require approximately half the selections of traditional alphabet spelling (Goodenough-Trepagnier & Prather, 1981). A French phonemic system, "Par le si la b," has been developed by the same authors. Phonemes can also be used as symbols on electronic aids.

The VOIS 136 (Phonic Ear, Inc.) is a dedicated voice output communication aid that uses phonemic symbols on its display. Phoneme keys are also used on the Boswell System, a device that is used for augmented writing. Developed in Canada, the Boswell System allows a user to depress "one or more phoneme keys simultaneously to create syllables or words. . . . The [user] need not know how a word is spelled in order to input it with the keyboard, but only how it sounds. . . . The phonemes are played back through a speech synthesizer, while a software program takes the [phonemic input] and converts it into the correctly spelled word, which is displayed on a computer screen" (Boswell Industries, Inc.). The device has been used successfully for written communication by persons with learning disabilities, visual impairments, and difficulties with reading and writing. For more information, contact Boswell Industries, Inc.

## COMBINED SYMBOLS (UNAIDED + AIDED)

Formal symbol systems that incorporate the use of at least manual signs with graphic symbols became popular in North America in the 1980s and have been used with persons who do not speak. In general, use of such systems is based on the assumption that if a single augmentative communication technique works, using more than one technique should work even better. These combined systems differ from individualized communication systems that incorporate multiple modes (e.g., Hooper, Connell, & Flett, 1987) in that symbols are combined in a standard intervention package. Three combined symbol systems that have been used in augmentative communication are Visual Phonics (International Communication Learning Institute, 1986), Sigsymbols (Cregan & Lloyd, 1988), and the Makaton Vocabulary (Grove & Walker, 1990).

## Visual Phonics

Visual Phonics was developed in 1981 by the mother of three deaf children who was frustrated by her children's slow progress with reading and speech. It is a trimodal system that consists of 45 hand movements that look and "feel" like phonetic sounds, written symbols that resemble the hand in action, and pictures that are related to the hand movements (International Communication Learning Institute, 1986). Based on the reports of a small sample of attendees of Visual Phonics training seminars (Amend, 1987), this system has been used successfully to teach speech and reading skills to individuals with hearing impairments, mental disabilities, physical disabilities, learning disabilities, and other disabilities. The system has also been used with nonhandicapped preschool and elementary school children who are learning to read (Amend, 1987; International Communication Learning Institute, 1986). A videotape describing the system (International Communication Learning Institute, 1986) mentions successful use with children with autism and Down syndrome and with adults with articulation disorders secondary to stroke.

> Visual Phonics information, videotape, and training materials are available through the International Communication Learning Institute (ICLI).

## Sigsymbols

This set of approximately 350 symbols was originally designed in Great Britain for adolescents with severe disabilities who are learning or have learned manual signs. Some of the symbols (called "sigs") are simple black and white line drawings (pictographs), some are rule-based abstract symbols (ideographs), and some are drawings of manual signs (sign-linked symbols). Examples of these symbols are shown in Figure 2.8.

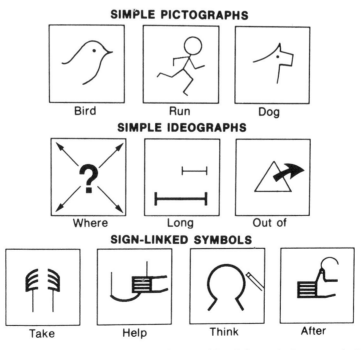

**Figure 2.8.** Examples of Sigsymbols. (From Musselwhite, C., & St. Louis, K. [1988]. *Communication programming for persons with severe handicaps* [2nd ed., p. 215]. Austin, TX: PRO-ED; reprinted by permission.)

In Great Britain, sign-linked symbols represent signs in British Sign Language (BSL) (Cregan, 1982), while in North America, the sign-linked symbols represent ASL and Signed English (Cregan & Lloyd, 1988). Sigs were developed to reinforce or elicit spoken or signed language and are used with manual signs. No information concerning the relative transparency or translucency of the Sigsymbol system and little information about its use has been published (cf. Cregan & Lloyd, 1988).

Sigsymbol information in North America is available from Don Johnston Developmental Equipment, Inc.

## Makaton Vocabulary

The Makaton Vocabulary is a program that combines speech, manual signs, and graphic symbols, and it is widely used, particularly in the United Kingdom (Grove & Walker, 1990). The core vocabulary consists of approximately 350 concepts organized in a series of nine "stages" that correspond to the order in which the words are introduced. For example, stage one consists of 39 concepts that meet immediate needs and can establish basic interactions, while stage five consists of 38 words that can be used in the general community.

No invented or modified manual signs are used in Makaton. In the United Kingdom, British Sign Language (BSL) signs are used, and the signs are largely taken from the SEE-2 lexicon in the U.S. (Gustason et. al., 1980). The graphic symbols used with the manual signs include Blissymbols (Hehner, 1980) and rebuses (Clark et al., 1974). Makaton Symbols are also available (Walker et al., 1985). These are illustrated in Figure 2.9.

The Makaton Vocabulary is "not an [AAC] system itself, but rather an organizational approach to the teaching of language and communication, which can be combined with any modality" (Grove & Walker, 1990, p. 25).

Regardless of the symbol types used, Makaton incorporates the key word signing approach, in which only the main information carrying words are signed and represented graphically. Generally, Makaton is taught through structured behavioral interventions and in natural contexts (Grove & Walker, 1990). The developers of Makaton emphasize that while the program is organized in stages and within a structure, practitioners are free to modify the system to meet individual student needs regarding the symbols used; the vocabulary introduced; and the procedures for assessment, instruction, goal setting, and data collection (Grove & Walker, 1990). The Makaton approach has been used successfully with children and adults with mental retardation, autism, specific language disorders, multiple sensory impairments, and acquired neurologic problems affecting communication (Walker, 1987).

The Makaton Vocabulary Development Project distributes a variety of Makaton resource and training materials and organizes training courses in Great Britain.

## SUMMARY

Many types of symbols are used to represent messages to AAC users in unaided and aided communication displays. Some symbol sets require that the user be able to use the visual modality to

**Figure 2.9.** Examples of Makaton symbols. (From Grove, N., & Walker, M. [1990]. The Makaton vocabulary: Using manual signs and graphic symbols to develop interpersonal communication. *Augmentative and Alternative Communication, 6*, 23; reprinted by permission.)

process and choose a message to communicate. Other symbols are displayed auditorily or tactilely, while still others require no display at all or can be presented in more than one sensory modality. These aspects are clearly important when decisions are made about communication augmentation for persons with visual, hearing, tactile, and memory impairments.

# Chapter 3

# Message Encoding and Rate Enhancement Techniques

Communication for most of us is nearly effortless. Only when speaking in formal or demanding situations, such as in front of a large audience or at a job interview, do most natural speakers think very much about the processes of communication. During ordinary interactions with family, friends, and associates, messages are prepared efficiently, timed appropriately, and spoken with the precision and completeness necessary for the situation. These spoken message-preparation skills are learned with very little effort through a combination of innate ability, exposure to a language, extensive practice, and incidental instruction from more mature language users.

The conversational speaking rates of nondisabled natural speakers vary from 150 words per minute to 250 words per minute (Goldman-Eisler, 1986). These speaking rates allow for efficient communication of extensive messages, which are formulated and spoken virtually simultaneously. One has only to view the interaction patterns among a talkative, animated group of friends to realize the importance of efficiency in communication in order for all speakers to take their conversational turns and communicate their messages before someone else "claims the floor."

In addition to communicating efficiently, natural speakers formulate spoken messages to meet the needs of the particular communicative situation. During spoken interaction, much of the meaning of a message can be derived from the context and the timing of the message. For example, we frequently mumble greetings to friends or colleagues as we pass them in the hallway at work. It is only because of the context that such poorly articulated messages can be understood. As we watch sporting events with our friends, someone may exclaim, "What an idiot!"—a message with no referent, which can be understood and appreciated only if it is produced in a timely fashion, not 3 minutes later.

Unfortunately, communication inefficiencies and message-timing limitations interfere with the communication interactions of many AAC users. For example, aided AAC rates were reported to be usually less than 15 words per minute under most circumstances (Foulds, 1980, 1987). In many cases, the rates are much less—often 2–8 words per minute. These rates are only a fraction of those achieved by natural speakers. Clearly, such drastic reductions in communication rate are likely to interfere significantly with communication interactions, especially in communicative situations with natural speakers who are accustomed to exchanging information much more rapidly. Because of this problem, the AAC field has devised a number of strategies to accelerate communication rate and improve the timing of messages. These strategies are described in this chapter.

## MESSAGE ENCODING

One factor contributing to the slowed communication rates of AAC users is that they must often compose messages by selecting component parts (e.g., pictures, words, symbols, or letters of the alphabet) one item at a time. A strategy to increase the communication rate for frequently used messages or messages that must be timed precisely is to compose complete sentences or phrases and store them in AAC systems. Rather than communicating these messages item by item, the user is able to retrieve an entire message by using the appropriate code.

A number of coding and retrieval strategies have been developed and implemented over the years. The term *encoding* is used to identify any technique in which the user gives multiple signals that together specify a desired message (Vanderheiden & Lloyd, 1986). This means that a message is encoded using a sequence of items from the selection set. How codes are represented—that is, the type of symbols used—is an individual decision that should be matched to the AAC user's capabilities. Some strategies for encoding messages include the use of numbers, letters, or icons (Table 3.1.).

## Alpha (Letter) Encoding

Letters of the alphabet are used to encode messages in a wide range of AAC systems. Generally, the selection of a code for a message is accomplished through one of the strategies discussed in the following sections.

*Salient Letter Encoding*   In *salient letter encoding*, the initial letters of salient content words in the message are used to construct the code. For example, the message "Please open the door for me" might be coded "O.D." since these are the initial letters of the primary words in the message (open door). This technique attempts to establish a logical link between the code and the message; it has, therefore, been referred to as *LOLEC* or *logical letter coding* (Adaptive Communication Systems, Inc.; Light, 1989a). Although user capability requirements for salient letter coding have not been studied in detail, it seems that some familiarity with traditional orthography and the ability to spell at least the first letter of a word are necessary. In addition, this technique would probably be most effective for users who are able to recall messages in their correct syntactic forms, as the codes are often determined by the usual word order of the most salient items.

> Multi-Talk is a Swedish communication aid that can speak several of nine available languages in four different voices. It incorporates letter encoding to recall stored message phrases, which can stand alone or be used with letter-by-letter spelling (Galyas, 1990). Multi-Talk is available through the Royal Institute for Technology.

*Letter Category Encoding*   In *letter category encoding*, the initial letter of a code is determined by an organizational scheme that categorizes messages. For example, the messages "Hello, how are you?", "It's nice to see you," "See you later," and "Goodbye for now" could be grouped in the category of "greetings." The first letter of the code for each of these messages would then be the letter "G," which represents the category. The second letter of the code would be the specifier within the category, which is based on the specific content of the message. Thus, the message "*Hello*, how are you?" might be coded as "G.H.", and the message "It's *nice* to see you today" might be coded "G.N."

**Table 3.1.**   Sample message encoding strategies

| Strategy | Code | Message |
|---|---|---|
| Salient letter encoding | H.H. | *Hello, how* are you? |
| Letter category encoding | G.H. | *(Greeting): Hello,* how are you? |
| Alpha-numeric encoding | G-1 | Hello, how are you? *(Greeting #1)* |
| Numeric encoding | 5-1 | Hello, how are you? *(Arbitrary numbers)* |
| Iconic encoding | Lei  you | Hello, how are you? *("lei" icon associated with greeting, "you" icon designates addressee)* |

Picture Communication Symbols. Copyright © 1981, 1985 by Mayer-Johnson Company; reprinted by permission. Some symbols have been adapted.

"Abbreviation expansion" is a term that has also been applied to alpha encoding techniques. Vanderheiden and Lloyd (1986) defined abbreviation expansion as "a technique that can be used in conjunction with all techniques that include an alphabet in their selection vocabulary. . . . Words, phrases, or entire sentences can be coded and recalled by the user using a short abbreviation" (p.135).

## Alpha-Numeric Encoding

Alpha-numeric coding involves the selection of codes that include both letters and numbers. Generally, the alphabetic part of the code refers to the *category* of messages, such as "G" for greetings, "T" for transportation, and "F" for food. The number is used arbitrarily to *specify* an individual message within the category. Thus, "G1" might refer to "Hello, how are you?", and "G2" might refer to "I'll see you later."

## Numeric Encoding

Occasionally, numeric codes only are used to represent messages. For example, numeric codes may be used when a communication display must be quite small in order to accommodate the user's limited motor capabilities. In this case, it is to the user's advantage if items in the selection set can be combined in many ways to code messages. Usually the relationship between the code and its corresponding message is completely arbitrary; thus, 13 might be the code for "Can we leave now?" and 24 the code for "I like this a lot." Most systems that use numeric encoding display the codes and the associated messages on a chart or menu as part of the selection display, so that neither the AAC user nor the communication partner must rely on their memories for recall or translation. Extensive learning and instruction is necessary to memorize the codes if this option is not available.

## Iconic Encoding

Baker (1982, 1986) proposed an iconic encoding technique refered to as "semantic compaction" or Minspeak (Semantic Compaction Systems). In this system, sequences of icons (i.e., pictorial symbols) are combined to store word, phrase, or sentence messages in one of the voice output devices constructed to incorporate this technique. The icons used for this encoding are deliberately selected for their rich semantic associations.

Versions of Word Strategy, a Minspeak Application Software program (Prentke Romich Co.) have been developed in German (Braun & Stuckenschneider-Braun, 1990) and Swedish (Hunnicutt, Rosengren, & Baker, 1990).

Using iconic encoding, an "apple" icon might be associated with food, fruit, snack, red, and round; a "sun" icon might be used to refer to concepts such as weather, yellow, hot, summer, and noon; or a "clock" icon might represent time, numbers, and a daily schedule. Some of the codes that might be constructed from these three icons are depicted in Figure 3.1.

As illustrated in this figure, the message "Let's have a barbecue" might be encoded with an "apple" (food) and "sun" (summer). Or, "apple" might be combined with "clock" to encode the message "It's time to have a snack." Or "sun" might be combined with "clock" to signify "It's time to catch some rays!" These sequences and their corresponding messages are stored in the electronic voice output device and are activated to produce synthetic speech for the message. Using iconic encoding, messages can be semantically organized by activities, topic, locations, or other categories to enhance retrieval.

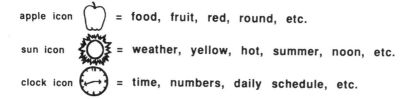

apple icon   = food, fruit, red, round, etc.

sun icon   = weather, yellow, hot, summer, noon, etc.

clock icon   = time, numbers, daily schedule, etc.


### *Codes and Rationales*

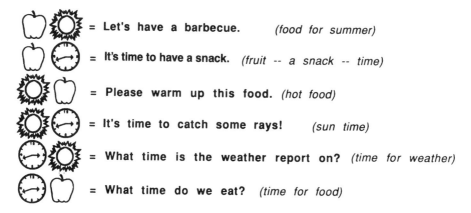

= Let's have a barbecue.     *(food for summer)*

= It's time to have a snack.   *(fruit -- a snack -- time)*

= Please warm up this food.   *(hot food)*

= It's time to catch some rays!     *(sun time)*

= What time is the weather report on?   *(time for weather)*

= What time do we eat?   *(time for food)*

**Figure 3.1.**   Examples of iconic codes. (Picture Communication Symbols. Copyright © 1981, 1985 by Mayer-Johnson Company; reprinted by permission. Some symbols have been adapted.)

---

Iconic encoding is available in a number of aided communication products. This concept has been referred to by several names that represent essentially the same technique with minor variations. These include Minspeak (IntroTalker, TouchTalker, LightTalker, and Liberator; Prentke Romich Co.), symbol sequencing (DAC, Adaptive Communication Systems, Inc.; Dynavox, Sentient Systems Technology, Inc.), keylinking (Macaw, Zygo Industries), and symbol sequencing (Talking Screen, Words+, Inc.).

---

**VoisShapes**   VoisShapes is an iconic encoding strategy based on American Sign Language (Shane & Wilbur, 1989). The VoisShapes display is depicted in Figure 3.2. Each message (i.e., each word or phrase) is encoded with three iconic symbols. One symbol in the sequence represents the hand shape, one represents the location where the sign is produced, and one represents the movement associated with the sign in American Sign Language. The assumption behind this relatively new approach to iconic encoding is that persons who know American Sign Language are able to translate this knowledge to operate VoisShapes. In addition, the developers of VoisShapes suggest that those who do not know American Sign language may be able to learn this iconic system. Research regarding the transferability or learnability of this approach has not been reported.

---

VoisShapes is used in conjunction with the VOIS160 speech output device and is available through Phonic Ear, Inc.

---

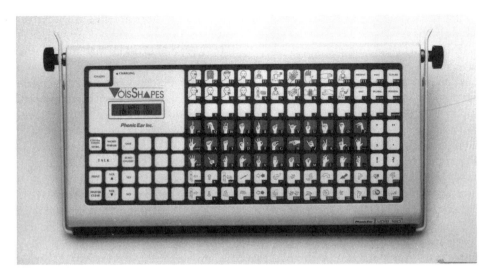

**Figure 3.2.** VoisShapes display (photo courtesy of Phonic Ear, Inc.).

## Color Encoding

Color has also been utilized to encode messages, usually in conjunction with specifiers such as numbers or symbols. Color encoding has been used to formulate messages for eye pointing communication systems (Goosens' & Crain, 1986a, 1986b, 1987). For example, the message "Turn on the music" might be coded as a red musical note and positioned, along with message symbols encoded in other colors, in the upper left corner of the eye gaze display. In order to select this message, the AAC user would first gaze at a red square on the display and then shift his or her gaze to the upper left corner; thus the code would be "red: upper left corner." The communication partner would then "read" the appropriate message and presumably follow with the requested action. Color coding can be used with other types of access techniques in addition to eye pointing.

## RETRIEVAL AND LEARNABILITY

Encoding strategies refer to the ways codes are associated with specific messages. In this section, the strategies used to retrieve messages are outlined. Generally, there are three retrieval strategies: memory-based, chart-based, and display- (or menu-) based (Vanderheiden & Lloyd, 1986).

### Memory-Based Retrieval Strategies

*Memory-based retrieval strategies* require that the AAC user memorize codes associated with specific messages. This can be accomplished either through rote memorization (e.g., for numeric encoding) or through the use of a mnemonic strategy that assists recall, such as salient letter encoding or letter category encoding. In iconic encoding strategies, the semantic associations with icons assist with retrieval.

Memory-based techniques are efficient and relatively easy to implement from a technical perspective. If users are able to retrieve codes from memory, they do not have to consult charts or menus in order to send a message. Users simply activate the appropriate codes in the selection set. Thus, static (unchanging) selection displays can be used instead of dynamic displays.

***Word Codes*** The learning curves of normal adults for five encoding strategies used to represent single words were investigated (Beukelman & Yorkston, 1984). These five strategies were:

1) arbitrary numeric codes, 2) alphabetically organized numeric codes in which consecutive numbers were assigned to words based on their alphabetic order, 3) alpha-numeric codes, 4) letter category codes, and 5) menu-prompted codes in which words were organized by their initial letters into computer menus and assigned number codes on the menus. Menu-prompted codes require the AAC user first to call up a menu by typing the first letter of a target word and then to enter the number of the target word by consulting the menu. Thus, this technique is a combined memory- and display-based encoding strategy, while the others are entirely memory-based.

Ten nondisabled, literate adults served as subjects, and two subjects served in each of the five conditions. In each condition, individuals were introduced to 200 codes and their associated words over 10 sessions. Individuals performed most accurately and retrieved the codes most quickly when using encoding approaches that group words by meaning, that is, the alpha-numeric, alphabetically organized numeric, letter category, and menu-prompted codes. They were least effective using arbitrary numeric codes. The learning curves for the random numeric codes and the alpha-numeric codes did not show as much improvement over time as did learning curves for the other three encoding strategies.

Three single-word encoding techniques were also investigated (Angelo, 1987): 1) truncation codes in which the ends of words were eliminated (e.g., hamb = hamburger), 2) contraction codes in which the most salient letters in words formed codes (e.g., comunctn = communication), and 3) arbitrary letter codes. The 66 nondisabled individuals in this study attempted to learn 20 words over a series of 10 trials. The results indicated that the individuals recalled truncation codes most accurately, followed by contraction and arbitrary letter codes, respectively.

**Message Codes**    Three studies have investigated learning and instructional issues associated with message-encoding techniques (Egof, 1988; Light, 1989a; Light, Lindsay, Siegal, & Parnes, 1990). One study used undergraduate university students as subjects (Egof, 1988), while the others (Light, 1989a; Light et al., 1990) involved individuals with disabilities. In the Light et al. (1990) study, 30 salient letter, 30 letter category, and 30 iconic codes were taught in three 15-minute sessions. In the Light (1989a) study, these same codes were taught over an extended training period with multiple sessions. Overall, the results of both studies indicated that salient letter codes were recalled most accurately, followed by letter category codes. The iconic codes were associated with the least accurate performances. (In the Light [1989a] study, this pattern applied to 8 of the 10 subjects.) The question of whether personalized codes—those selected by the AAC user rather than by a researcher or clinician—improve performance was also explored in these studies. For AAC system users, Light (1989a) did not find an overall differential effect for self-selected codes compared with nonpersonalized codes.

Clearly, the learning issues associated with memory-based encoding techniques are extensive, and little research has been done in this area. Additional investigation to clarify the relative advantages and disadvantages of various encoding strategies for both literate and nonliterate AAC users is urgently needed.

### Chart-Based Retrieval Strategies

*Chart-based retrieval strategies* may be used in a variety of encoding applications. With this strategy, codes and their corresponding messages are listed on a chart, usually in alphabetic, numeric, or categorical order. Figure 3.3. illustrates a chart-based display that might be used for eye pointing. The primary advantage of a chart-based display is that neither the AAC user nor his or her communication partner are required to memorize the codes, since the chart can be used to identify the appropriate codes and to retrieve messages. Obviously, the rate of communication depends on how efficiently the user and the partner can visually locate the desired code or message on the chart.

**Figure 3.3.** Chart-based display used for eye pointing.

**Static Chart Retrieval Strategies** *Static charts* are fixed and do not change to accommodate ongoing communication requirements. For low tech AAC techniques, such as eye gaze displays, static charts may be used by both the communication partner and the AAC user. The AAC user indicates a code, and the partner then "reads" the code and consults the chart to determine the associated message. The encoding chart may be separate from the communication display, or the chart may be located on the display itself.

**Dynamic Chart Retrieval Strategies** Several AAC systems use dynamic menus to assist with the retrieval of messages. For example, in Figure 3.4., the dynamic menu system associated with the EZKeys system (Words +, Inc.) is illustrated. Words are displayed in a word menu (or "word window") at the upper right of the screen. Each word is associated with a number code. The AAC user types a number, and the word associated with it is retrieved and inserted in the text being formulated on the screen.

This is a *dynamic chart retrieval strategy* because the specific words presented in the word menu are determined by the letters that the AAC user selects. For example, if the user types the letter "b," six common words that begin with "b" will be presented on the menu. If the word of choice is not included in the listing, the user then types the next letter, for example, "r," and six words that begin with "br" will be presented in the menu. Thus, the menu changes according to the input the user provides.

Predictive Adaptive Lexicon (PAL) software, developed at the University of Dundee (Scotland), provides a dynamic menu display similar to that described for EZKeys. The words displayed in the menus are selected by the program algorithm on the basis of frequency of occurrence and recency of use (Swiffin, Arnott, Pickering, & Newell, 1987). PAL has been used with children with physical, language/learning, and intellectual disabilities (Beattie, Booth, Newell, & Arnott, 1990), and is available through Scotlander Ltd. in the United Kingdom.

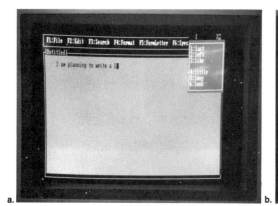

**Figure 3.4.** Dynamic menu display from EZKeys (Words +, Inc.): **a.** Screen displays the six most likely words that begin with "l" when letter is typed; **b.** Screen changes to the six most likely words that begin with "le" when a second letter is added; **c.** Screen changes to six words beginning with "let" when user hits "t."

The symbols or messages included in dynamic menus can be selected in several ways. Some devices contain preselected messages determined by the manufacturer. Other products allow users to enter specific words in the menus. Other products monitor the communication performance of the AAC user and update menu content based on frequency of word use. More than one of these options may be available in the same product.

## MESSAGE PREDICTION

Message encoding strategies for enhancing communication rate have been discussed in this chapter. In this section, a different approach to rate enhancement is discussed, that of message prediction. *Message prediction* is a dynamic retrieval process in which options offered to the AAC user change based on the portion of the message that has already been formulated. Communication prediction algorithms generally occur at one of three levels: single letter, word, or phrase/sentence.

### Single Letter Prediction

In virtually all languages that can be represented orthographically (i.e., with letter symbols), individual letters of the alphabet do not occur with equal probability. Some letters occur more frequently than others; for example, in English, the letters "e," "t," "a," "o," "i," "n," "s," "r," and "h" occur most frequently, and "z," "q," "u," "x," "k," and "v" occur least frequently (see Table 3.2.).

Orthographic languages are also organized so that the probability of the occurrence of a letter in a word is influenced by the previous letter. In English, the most obvious example of this is that the letter "q" is always followed by the letter "u." Some combinations occur with more frequency than others. For example, "ch-," "-ed," "tr-," "str-," and "-tion" are frequent letter combinations in English, while combinations such as "-sz," "-zs," "jq-" and "wv-" occur rarely if at all.

Electronic letter prediction systems rely on the probability of these letters and letter combination relationships so that when a letter is activated, a menu of the letters that are most likely to follow will be offered on a dynamic display. When this technology was first introduced, often the entire display of the scanning system was electronically reorganized each time a new letter was selected. Users complained, however, that this required extensive scanning to find the letter they wanted to enter. In response to this problem, letter prediction systems were redesigned to keep the overall letter display intact and to include an additional, dynamic line of letter prediction at the top or the bottom of the device.

## Word Level Prediction

*Word Pattern Prediction*   AAC devices provide word level prediction using a variety of strategies. Some systems predict words based on patterns of word combinations likely to occur in conversational interactions. For example, the probability is high that an article such as "a," "an," or "the" follows a preposition in a prepositional phrase (e.g., on the bed, under a tree). Designers of AAC systems have translated this word pattern information into prediction algorithms. In these

**Table 3.2.**   Letters of the English alphabet by frequency of occurrence

| Frequency of initial letters of words (text)[a] | Frequency of all letters in words (text)[a] | Frequency of letters (AAC samples)[b] |
|---|---|---|
| T | E | I |
| A | T | O |
| O | A | T |
| S | O | E |
| W | I | A |
| I | N | N |
| H | S | H |
| C | R | S |
| B | H | M |
| F | L | D |
| P | D | Y |
| M | J | R |
| R | C | U |
| E | F | L |
| L | G | W |
| N | M | F |
| D | W | G |
| U | Y | B |
| G | F | C |
| Y | B | K |
| J | V | P |
| V | K | V |
| Q | X | J |
| K | U | X |
| X | Q | Z |
| Z | Z | Q |

[a]Pratt (1939).
[b]Beukelman and Yorkston (1985).

systems, the user is offered a menu of high probability words that are likely to follow each word that is selected.

   **Linguistic Prediction**   In an effort to refine prediction strategies, some system designers have included algorithms that contain extensive information about the syntactic organization of the language. The predictions offered to the user in these systems are based on grammatical rules of the language. For example, if a first person singular noun has been selected as the subject of a sentence (e.g., Chris, mom), only verbs that agree in subject and number will be presented as options (e.g., is, likes, is going). If an article (e.g., "a," "an," or "the") is selected, the system will predict nouns rather than verbs as the next word, since it is unlikely that a verb follows an article. Obviously, the algorithms that support linguistic-based prediction are complex. This type of message enhancement is becoming increasingly available, however, with the decreasing cost of computer processing. Not only does this type of prediction enhance communication rate, it may also enhance the grammatical performance of some persons who have language and learning disabilities.

## Phrase/Sentence Level Prediction

A team of researchers in Scotland is developing several communication software programs that incorporate sophisticated algorithms for predicting language units longer than single words. For example, CHAT incorporates conversational segments, and TALK BACK employs sentence level prediction (Newell, Arnott, & Alm, 1990). Information about these prototype projects, which seek to apply artificial intelligence techniques to communication rate enhancement, is available from the Microcomputer Centre at the University of Dundee.

## RESEARCH ON COMMUNICATION RATE ENHANCEMENT

Encoding and message prediction strategies are generally employed for three purposes: to enhance message timing, to assist grammatical formulation of messages, and to enhance overall communication rate. A wide variety of encoding and prediction strategies are continually being developed and implemented for AAC systems. Nevertheless, relatively little research has examined systematically the impact of these strategies on the three functions of encoding and message prediction. For example, although anecdotal reports abound regarding the use of encoding strategies in meeting the timing requirements of interaction, no written research has documented the relative effectiveness of various encoding approaches. Similarly, while initial clinical reports support the use of prediction programs to enhance grammatical accuracy, no empirical research reports confirm these observations. Nevertheless, there have been a few studies concerning the enhancement of communication rate, and these can be grouped into those that examine enhancement of rate from a *theoretical* perspective and those that involve *actual* measurement of communication rates under various circumstances.

The study of rate enhancement in the AAC field can be illustrated by the fable about the elephant and the four wise men who could not see. The men were trying to describe an elephant and were forced, by the nature of their shared impairment, to use the sense of touch to do so. The first man ran his hands up, down, and around the beast's round, rough leg and declared, "An elephant is like a tree!" The second man felt the elephant's long, wavy trunk and announced, "No, no, an elephant is like a snake!" The third man laughed at his friends as he felt the animal's bristly tail and challenged, "You two are both wrong! An elephant is like a broom!" And the fourth man, feeling the elephant's high, broad side, exclaimed, "What are you talking about? An elephant is like a wall." In fact, all four were right—and all four were wrong, for it is only through examination of the *interaction* among the separate factors that the true picture can be understood.

## Actual Rate Enhancement

Because a number of human factors are associated with various encoding and prediction strategies, the extent to which these strategies actually enhance communication rate may not be as great as is implied by studies that have examined one factor. For example, simply measuring the average number of *motor acts*—also referred to as *keystrokes*—saved through use of an encoding technique does not take into account the visual, timing, linguistic, and cognitive factors that also influence rate. Human factors associated with dynamic displays of encoded or predicted information (e.g., EZKeys and Predict It) also vary depending on the interaction between the visual monitoring and motor control that are involved. Encoding or prediction strategies that require extensive learning and memorization (such as Word Strategy) are less efficient early in the learning phase when compared to a later stage, when the AAC user has mastered the strategy and has achieved fluency.

In acknowledgment of the complexity of this issue, Rosen and Goodenough-Trepagnier (1981) proposed that three factors be measured to predict an AAC user's rate of communication: 1) linguistic cost (i.e., the average number of selections needed to communicate a word), 2) length (i.e., the average number of motor acts required for each selection), and 3) time (i.e., the average time per motor act). In addition, Light (1989a) suggested that, "A critical fourth variable in determining rate, not included in this list, is the cognitive processing time and load involved in deciding which selections or acts are necessary" (p. 6). The original three factors were used to predict the communication efficiency of various communication systems and configurations based on a theoretical model of communication efficiency, but they have not been used extensively by other researchers to assess actual communication rates.

Very little information about human factors associated with AAC techniques has been generated by longitudinal studies of actual AAC users in actual communication exchanges. Unfortunately, research efforts in the AAC field aimed at delineating human factors related to rate enhancement are still in their infancy.

---

A cooperative project involving the Institute for Rehabilitation Research and the Institute for Phonetics in the Netherlands, and the A. I. duPont Institute in the US is addressing rate enhancement in both English and Dutch through several techniques. The KATDAS system employs a complex decoding algorithm and an adaptive lexicon, while the COMBIBOARD allows users to enter frequently occurring letter sequences with a single key (Foulds, Soede, & van Balkom, 1987; Kamphuis, 1990). Information is available through the Institute for Rehabilitation Research.

---

## Theoretical Studies of Communication Rate

Theoretical studies of communication rate typically have investigated the number of keystrokes required to communicate messages in various encoding strategies. In these theoretical studies, other human factors such as motor control, visual scanning, cognitive load, learning, and fatigue have not been considered.

The keystroke savings that might be achieved by retrieving frequently occurring words either through encoding or linguistic prediction strategies were investigated (Vanderheiden & Kelso, 1987). The authors reported that a relatively small number of words account for the majority of word usage and suggested that:

> Providing quick access to the first 100 words will have a much greater impact on the person's speed of communication than quick access to the next 1,000 words. As a result, most of the acceleration techniques tend to focus on the most-frequently-used words to optimize their effectiveness. (p. 197)

Obviously, this approach assumes that there is considerable commonality of word usage across individuals. A summary of research in this area noted that "The most-frequently used words do differ between studies. However, there is a fair degree of commonality, and a set of 50–200 'frequently used words' can be constructed which will apply across most word samples" (Vanderheiden & Kelso, 1987, p. 198).

Another factor that was considered by this report is word length. Obviously, a longer word requires more letters to spell than does a short word. Thus, encoding or prediction strategies that apply to longer words will yield greater keystroke savings than those used with shorter words. A relative keystroke analysis examined this proposition and concluded that:

> The implications of this are two-fold. First, looking only at the frequency of word use without looking at word length can result in a false positive indication for the value of the words or word sets. To get an accurate picture, the length-times-frequency analysis should be used. Further, for an optimum word set, the words should be reordered after they have been given a length-times-frequency value. However, reordering the word set has very little impact on the overall efficiency . . . [in that] efficiency would only be increased by 1 or 2 percent. (Vanderheiden & Kelso, 1987, p. 198)

A theoretical analysis of the percent of keystrokes that would be saved through the use of various encoding techniques is shown in Figure 3.5. This analysis suggested that, depending on the type of encoding, keystroke savings might range from 20% to 50% over typing letter by letter. Furthermore, this research suggested that the keystroke savings for message prediction systems would not be likely to exceed those achieved through encoding.

In a subsequent study, keystroke efficiency was compared for a number of encoding and prediction strategies, including EZKeys (Words +, Inc.), Word Strategy (Prentke Romich Co.), and the Predictive Linguistic Program (PLP) (Don Johnston Developmental Equipment, Inc.) (Higginbotham, 1990). A subset of this data is displayed in Figure 3.6. For all words in the target sample, 45% fewer keystrokes were required when EZKeys was used instead of letter-by-letter spelling, compared with 41% for the Predictive Linguistic Program (PLP), and 36% for Word Strategy. All of the words in the target sample were not included in all of the vocabularies of these AAC systems, and some words had to be spelled individually. Therefore, in a second study, keystroke savings were analyzed for only those words that were included in the vocabularies of the systems (Higginbotham, 1990). In this analysis, EZKeys saved 46% of the keystrokes required for letter by letter

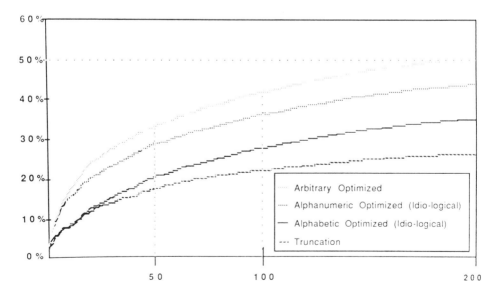

**Figure 3.5.** Theoretical keystroke savings as a function of vocabulary size for four abbreviation expansion approaches. Vertical axis = % of keystrokes eliminated, horizontal axis = abbreviated words. (From Vanderheiden, G., & Kelso, D. [1987]. Comparative analysis of fixed-vocabulary communication acceleration techniques. *Augmentative and Alternative Communication, 3,* 203; reprinted by permission.)

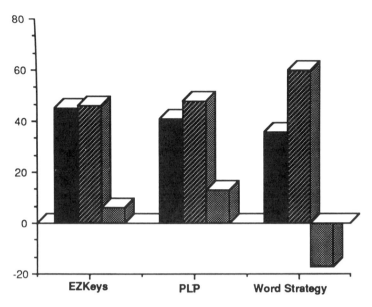

**Figure 3.6.** Theoretical keystroke savings of three rate enhancement techniques. (EZKeys = EZKeys software, PLP = Predictive Linguistic Program software, Word Strategy = Word Strategy software. Vertical axis = keystroke savings in %, horizontal axis = AAC technique. Solid bar = all words in sample, cross-hatched bar = encoded words only, dotted bar = spelled words only.) (Data based on Higginbotham [1990].)

spelling, compared with 48% for the Predictive Linguistic Program, and 60% for Word Strategy. When words *not included* in the menus of the various strategies were examined, only 6% fewer keystrokes were required when EZKeys was used instead of letter-by-letter spelling, compared with 13% for the Predictive Linguistic Program program, and 17% more keystrokes were required for Word Strategy.

## SUMMARY

The previous discussion has made clear that human and theoretical issues related to AAC rate enhancement are complex and have only recently received research attention. Communication rate and timing gains made possible by encoding and prediction strategies are potentially very important and can result in substantive interaction gains. Nevertheless, each strategy is also associated with human factors that involve learning, memory, cognitive load, and visual scanning. AAC users and their facilitators must weigh the relative benefits and costs of available strategies without much assistance from a research base. Research in message encoding and prediction should continue to clarify the interactions among various human factors, while development efforts focus on innovative strategies that minimize costs to AAC users.

# Chapter 4

# Alternative Access

It was in a junior high school in Edmonds, Washington, that I received my first extensive lesson in alternative access. Kris, a junior high student with severe athetoid cerebral palsy, was "talking" with her mother at the end of a school day. As I observed from across the room, they faced each other. Her mother stared intently at Kris's face and talked quietly throughout the interaction. Kris did not speak at all; however, after watching for a while, it was clear to me that she was communicating a great deal. At the time, I was impressed with the magic of the interaction. Her mother was "reading" Kris's face, and they were discussing the schoolwork to be completed at home over the weekend. I was listening to a sincere interaction in which both individuals were contributing, adding their opinions, and arguing a bit.

My curiosity led me to move behind Kris's mother. What I saw were a series of very rapid eye movements that were somehow being translated into letters, words, and eventually messages. As I came to know Kris and her mother better, they let me know the nature of their code. When Kris directed her eyes at her mother's *feet*, she was communicating the letter "f." When she directed her eyes toward her mother's *el*bow, she signaled an "l." When she looked at her mother's *nose*, she signaled the letter "n." After they explained these codes to me, they seemed rather logical. Then, they told me that when Kris raised her eyes and looked slightly to the left, she was signaling the letter "y,"—referring to the "*yellow* curtains in the living room," the location where this eye code had been developed!

At one point, I attempted to communicate with Kris using her system, and quickly found that, although the system was technically inexpensive, it required extensive learning and ability on the part of a listener. I didn't have the training and practice to be an effective communication partner for Kris, so her mother and her speech-language pathologist patiently interpreted for me. Eventually, Kris developed other forms of alternative access in order to control an electronic communication system, as well as computer equipment, so that she could talk with people like me, complete high school and university, and eventually enroll in a doctoral program. (D. Beukelman, personal communication, February, 1991)

Those of us who speak naturally learned our verbal communication skills at an early age. These skills and processes are now so automatic that we have little awareness or understanding of them. Only when we begin to translate our spoken language into written form do we begin to realize that messages are coded by combining and recombining a relatively small set of elements. In the English language, those who are literate are able to write nearly anything they wish by combining and recombining a set of 26 letters. The child's task in learning to write is to select the appropriate letters from the set of 26 and to formulate them so that they meet certain standards of accuracy, intelligibility, and aesthetics. Similarly, people are able to say every word in spoken English by combining approximately 45 sounds. Only those who have difficulty learning to speak need to know that words are made up of sounds, and that certain sounds require special attention in order to be spoken correctly.

Communication is based on the selection of one or more types of symbols, used alone or in combination, to communicate messages. In natural speech, a speaker is able to produce messages by combining specific sounds. In writing, orthographic symbols (i.e., letters) are formed or produced and placed in a systematic order. For persons who are unable to speak or write through traditional means, alternative strategies are necessary in order to communicate. The task of learning alternative access methods is easier to understand when the organization of natural language is first considered. For a person with a severe communication disorder, the task of learning alternative access methods involves the selection of messages or codes from a relatively small set of possibilities. These elements are then used alone or combined in ways that allow for the communication of a variety of messages. Obviously, the message must be presented to the listener in a way that the listener can understand.

In the past, many persons with disabilities were required to operate standard communication equipment such as typewriters by using headsticks and key guards in order to communicate. If individuals were unable to use these devices, they were considered to be inappropriate candidates for electronic communication options. During the 1970s and 1980s, however, alternative access options for persons with severe disabilities expanded dramatically. Every year, dozens of new communication products and devices enter the commercial market, and older products and devices are discontinued. We had to make some decisions about how to cover the influx of new technology in a way that would not make this book outdated before it went to press. In this chapter, we decided to offer limited examples of communication devices that represent specific access techniques or features. This is in no way meant to imply that the products mentioned in this chapter are the *only* examples, or even the "best" examples, of the concepts they illustrate. It was not our intention to attempt to offer a comprehensive overview of the latest technology. The Resources at the conclusion of this book contain the names and addresses of many of the major communication device manufacturers and distributors. In addition, the *Trace ResourceBook* (Berliss, Borden, & Vanderheiden, 1989) and a wallchart, "Features of Portable Communication Devices" (Kraat & Sitver-Kogut, 1991), are among the many available resources related to specific AAC devices.

## THE SELECTION SET

Typewriters and computers are perhaps the most familiar alternative communication options that are used by people who have difficulty writing by hand. It is apparent that a keyboard contains a finite set of symbols, which comprise the selection set (see Figure 4.1.). Some of these symbols include individual letters of the alphabet; punctuation symbols; numbers; and control commands for the device, such as "enter," "control," "tab," and "return." Although all AAC systems do not involve computer technology, this example of a computer keyboard is useful because many AAC systems use similar components, even if they are not electronically based.

Many AAC techniques utilize visual displays of items in the selection set. When visual displays are inappropriate due to an individual's visual impairments, however, the selection set may be displayed auditorily or tactilely. Auditory displays usually involve presentation of the selection set through spoken words or messages. Tactile displays are composed of tactile representations of items in the selection set using real or partial objects, textures, shapes, or raised dots (e.g., braille).

### Components of the Selection Set

The selection set of an AAC system includes the visual, auditory, and tactile presentation of all available symbols (Lee & Thomas, 1990). The symbols in a selection set are determined in a number of ways. In the case of standard computers, the symbols (numbers, letters, punctuation symbols, and commands) are assigned by the manufacturer. It is the task of the user to learn what the various symbols mean and how to use them. For individuals who use AAC systems, however, symbols are typically selected on an individual basis so that relevant messages can be represented

**Figure 4.1.**   A standard computer keyboard.

in a way that the user can understand and use efficiently. The components of the selection set can generally be divided into three groups: messages, symbols and codes, and operational commands.

**Messages**   Figure 4.2. illustrates a communication board with a variety of selection items. This particular board was developed to facilitate communication for a Boston Celtics fan as he watched professional basketball with his friends and family. Because this individual is able to read and spell, items of the selection set were displayed orthographically rather than pictorially or some other way. Complete messages, as well as individual alphabet items, were included for two reasons. First, some messages must be communicated immediately if they are to have meaning. For example, the message "What a great play!" is only meaningful if it can be produced at exactly the right moment during a fast moving basketball game. If the message had to be spelled letter by letter, this timing requirement would not be met, and the message—completed long after the play that elicited the comment—would lose its meaning. Other phrases are included because they are communicated frequently, and the ability to retrieve them intact saves time and reduces fatigue. "Hi, how are you?" and "See you later," are examples of such messages. Obviously, choosing messages to be included in a selection set requires cooperative effort by the user and his or her facilitators. The symbolization and coding of the messages depends on the individual's linguistic and learning abilities, as well as on personal preference.

**Symbols and Codes**   Not all items included in the selection set in Figure 4.2. are complete messages. A number of the items are symbols, and these include individual letters of the alphabet, numbers, and punctuation marks. These symbols must be combined in certain ways in order to communicate messages. One way to accomplish this is to combine the symbols, one at a time, to spell out words for a communication partner to read. Alternatively, the symbols could be used to form codes—in this case, letter or number abbreviations—that represent longer messages. For example, the AAC user might tell someone to "LMA," which means "Leave me alone now." When codes are used, the communication partner must understand the code, or the AAC device must interpret it via an output mechanism.

**Operational or Interactional Commands**   On many communication displays, a small number of items are assigned as operational or interactional commands. In electronic communica-

| How are you? | Coaches | Players | Former Players |
|---|---|---|---|
| See you later. | Red Auerbach | Bird | Cousy |
| Just a minute. | KC Jones | McHale | KC Jones |
| Thanks for coming. | J. Rodgers | Parish | Jones |
| Next time. | C. Ford | Lewis | Russell |

| This team | What a great play! | Paxson | Havlichek |
|---|---|---|---|
| | Greatest! | Shaw | Walton |
| Past teams | Fantastic! | Pinckney | Johnson |
| The Garden | Incredible! | Smith | Ainge |
| Draft pick | Awful! | Brown | |
| Championship team | Idiot! | Kleine | |

| Celtics | Never! | Points | Assists |
|---|---|---|---|
| | What's the score? | Foul | Turnovers |
| Opponents: | Legal | Personal | Free Throw |
| Bulls | Illegal | Technical | Rebounds |

| Lakers | A B C D E F G H I J K L M | Yes |
|---|---|---|
| Knicks | N O P Q R S T U V W X Y Z | No |
| Pistons | 1 2 3 4 5 6 7 8 9 0 | I don't know |
| Trailblazers | End of word | Maybe |
| Sonics | Wait, I'm not done yet | Forget it |
| | Start    over | Sorry |

**Figure 4.2.** A communication board designed to facilitate communication for a Boston Celtics fan.

tion systems, as well as in computers, some of these commands direct the operations of the technical equipment (e.g., "enter," "backspace," "delete," "print," "speak"). In other cases, commands may be used to direct communication partners. In Figure 4.2., several of these interactional commands are included on the communication board, including "End of word," "Start over," "Forget it," and "Wait, I'm not done yet." Some of these commands allow the communication partner to interpret messages formulated by the user, while others allow the user to exert some control over turn taking in the conversation.

## Physical Characteristics of Selection Set Displays

When vocabulary items to be included in a selection set have been chosen (Chapter 9) and the symbolization or encoding strategies for the various items have been identified (Chapters 2 and 3), several physical characteristics of the selection set display must be considered. Intervention decisions are based on a match between the cognitive, language, sensory, and motor capabilities of the user and the characteristics of the AAC technique.

*Number of Items*   Whether a display is visually, auditorily, or tactilely based, the actual number of items in a selection set is a compromise of many factors. The most important factor is the number of messages, symbols, codes, and commands that are required by the user. When symbols other than those representing letters (e.g., traditional orthography, braille, or Morse code) are used exclusively, the size of the selection set increases with the number of messages, since there is a one-to-one correspondence between messages and symbols. Thus, 500 symbols are required for 500 messages. When encoding strategies are used, the number of items in the selection set may be greatly reduced, depending on the number of codes used. Thus, if a large number of codes are used, the display may contain *fewer* items than if a small number of codes are used. This is because each item can be used in multiple ways to make up numerous codes; for example, literally thousands of two-letter codes can be constructed by combining each of the 26 letters in the alphabet with each of the other 25. Once symbol and encoding decisions have been made and the potential items the AAC user needs in the display have been established, the actual number of items on a visual display will be determined by size and spacing considerations.

**Size**   Two issues related to size should be considered when making selection set decisions: individual item size and overall display size. For visual displays, the actual size of the symbols or messages on the display is determined by the user's visual capabilities, the motor access technique employed, the type of symbol, and the number of items to be displayed. For many individuals, visual capability determines individual item size, and this issue is discussed in Chapter 15. For other AAC users, motor control is the critical variable, because items need to be sufficiently large to allow accurate and efficient selection.

The overall size of the visual display also involves compromises between the number of items that must be displayed, the size of individual items, the spacing of items, mounting and portability factors, and the AAC user's physical capability. For example, if the system is to be carried around by the AAC user, the shape and weight of the display must be manageable and nonfatiguing, and its exact dimensions will depend on the user's physical capabilities. If the AAC user drives a wheelchair, the display must not be so large that it obscures vision. If the AAC user selects items using finger pointing or a head stick, the overall size of the display must accommodate the user's range of movement or some items will be inaccessible.

For auditory displays, the size of the display is determined by the user's memory and ability to retain the organizational scheme of the display. When large auditory displays are employed, users need to remember that a particular item will eventually be displayed (i.e., announced) if they wait long enough. When multi-level displays are available in electronic auditory scanners, the user must be able to remember the categorical scheme used for organization. For example, if messages are organized by main topic (e.g., food, drinks, places, people), the user must remember that "Coke" is a message under "drink", while "shopping mall" is stored under "places." If more than two levels are used, this categorical scheme becomes even more complex, and "Coke" might be a message under "soda pop," which is a subcategory of "drinks."

For tactile displays, the size of the selection set depends on the tactile recognition capabilities of the AAC user. Some users, such as those who use braille, require very little information to recognize options presented tactilely, while others with less cognitive or tactile ability may require larger tactile symbols or actual objects.

**Spacing and Arrangement of Items**   Spacing and arrangement of items on a visual or tactile selection display is determined largely by the visual and motor control capabilities of the individual user. For example, the ability of some users to discriminate among items on the display is enhanced if the items are widely separated and surrounded by a large empty area. For others, performance may be improved if the space surrounding the items is colored to contrast with the rest of the communication board. Still other AAC users may have field cuts or blind spots that require irregular spacing arrangements to match their visual capabilities. Determinations such as these are made on an individual basis.

The motor control profile of each user also influences the spacing arrangement. Many persons with physical disabilities who use AAC systems have better control of one hand than the other. The items on the display should be positioned accordingly to enhance access. For example, Figure 4.3.

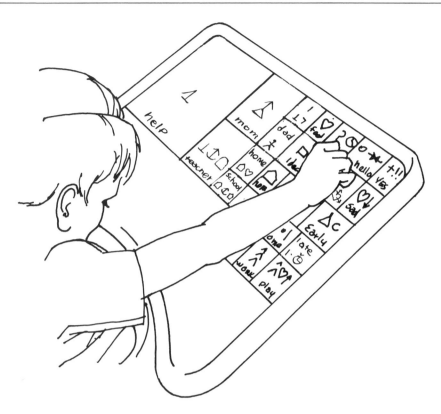

**Figure 4.3.**  A communication board for an individual with better motor control on the right side.

illustrates a communication board in which frequently used items are displayed to be most accessible to the user's right hand, which has better motor control. In addition, the size of the items in the area where the user has his or her best motor control (i.e., the right side of the board) is smaller than in areas of reduced motor control (i.e., the left side of the board).

Another example of a communication board display, a curved array, is provided in Figure 4.4. This arrangement is designed to accommodate the motor control capabilities of a person using a headstick. By positioning the items in an arch, the forward and backward movements of the head and neck are minimized, compared with movements needed to reach items in a square or rectangular display.

***Orientation of Display***   Orientation refers to the position of the display relative to the floor. The orientation of a visual or tactile display is dependent on the postural, visual, and motor control capabilities of the AAC user. Visual and motor capabilities are the most critical in a direct selection display, where the user points in some way to items on the display. If a scanning approach is used, visual and postural factors will probably determine the orientation decisions, since these are critical skills for the switch activation required by this technique. These issues are detailed later in this chapter.

A visual/tactile display mounted on a table or wheelchair tray that is horizontal to the floor (Figure 4.5.) provides considerable arm and hand support, as well as stabilization, if weakness, tremor, or extraneous movements are present. This display orientation requires that the user maintain upright posture (either independently or with adaptive equipment) while viewing and using the display.

Alternatively, a display positioned at a 30° or 45° angle to the floor (Figure 4.6.) provides a

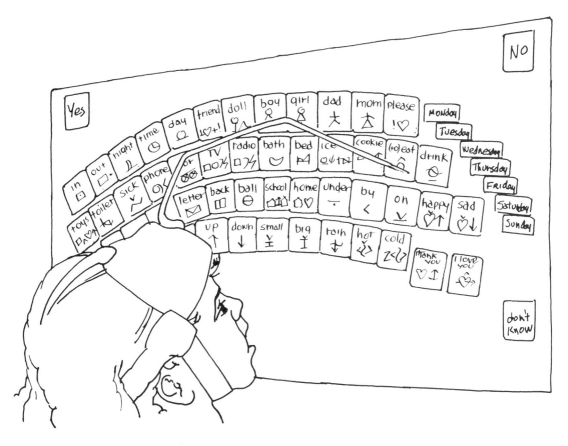

**Figure 4.4.**  A communication board with a curved array for an individual using a headstick.

compromise position for many persons with physical disabilities. This orientation allows the user to see the display clearly but avoids the neck flexion required by the horizontal display, while still providing some degree of hand and arm support and stability. Many persons with very limited motor control due to weakness or extraneous movements may experience difficulty using a display that is oriented this way. For these individuals, mobile arm supports may be used to elevate their arms and hands so that they can access a slanted display. Finally, displays that are used in combination with light or optical pointers are usually oriented at a 45°–90° angle to the floor, again depending upon the vision, motor control, and posture of the user. When a display is positioned at a 45°–90° angle, care must be taken not to obstruct the user's vision for other activities, especially driving a wheelchair or viewing instructional materials.

## Types of Displays

The display of a selection set depends on the technique and device employed in the AAC application. Displays are generally of two main types: fixed and dynamic.

***Fixed Displays***   The communication board illustrated in Figure 4.2. is a *fixed display*, because the symbols and items on the board are fixed in a particular location. Most displays used in the AAC field are of this type. The number of symbols that can be included on a fixed display is limited, depending on the AAC user's visual, tactile, cognitive, and motor capabilities. This means that AAC users typically must use a number of fixed displays in order to accommodate all needed vocabulary items. For example, if the user wishes to change the topic of discussion from profes-

**Figure 4.5.** A communication board mounted on a wheelchair, horizontal to the floor.

sional basketball to plans for an upcoming holiday, he or she might need to change the display with sports symbols to one with travel and family vocabulary items.

Because of the obvious limitations in the use of multiple fixed displays (e.g., lack of portability, inefficiency), extensive efforts have been made to compensate for the limited symbols that can be contained on a fixed display. One compensatory technique is to organize a number of displays into "levels." For example, a communication book in which symbols are arranged topically on pages is an example of a fixed display with several levels (in this case, each page is a different level). Many electronic communication aids that use visual or auditory selection sets also incorporate levels in their design and operation. Another compensatory technique involves using various encoding strategies by which multiple messages can be constructed by combining one, two, three, or more items on a fixed display. Obviously, by coding messages this way, a greater number of messages can be communicated than there are items on the display.

**Dynamic Displays**   Two types of dynamic displays are now commercially available in the AAC field. The first utilizes a computer screen with electronically produced visual symbols representing messages. Certain areas of the screen when activated automatically change the selection set on the screen to a new set of programmed symbols. For example, if the individual using the communication board in Figure 4.2. had access to a dynamic display, he might first see a screen displaying symbols related to a number of different conversational topics, such as professional basketball, plans for the day, personal care, work, or family members. By touching the "basketball" symbol, he would activate the screen so that the items contained in Figure 4.2. were displayed. When the basketball game ended, he would return to the initial screen by touching the appropriate symbol.

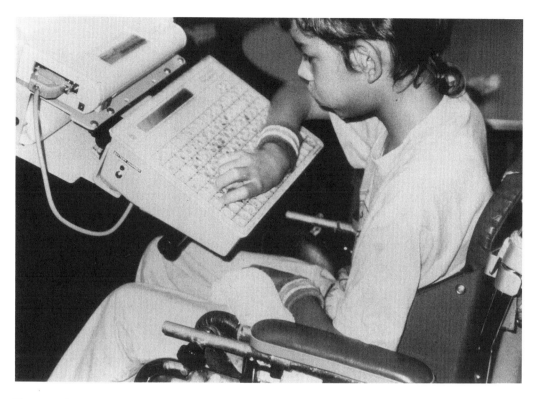

**Figure 4.6.** A communication device positioned at a 30°–45° angle.

Then he could select a new topic symbol (e.g., a calendar, representing "plans for the day") that would cause the screen to change to a new set of related vocabulary items.

This type of dynamic display is available for several commercial AAC products in North America. One dynamic display option, the Talking Symbols program for Macintosh computers, can be accessed via a mouse or mouse emulator. The second option, the Talking Screen program for IBM and compatible computers, can be used with a touch screen or scanning technique. Similarly, the Dynavox is a dedicated AAC device with a dynamic screen controlled either through a touch screen or scanning.

Talking Symbols is distributed by the Mayer-Johnson Company. Talking Screen is published by Words +, Inc. Dynavox is a product of Sentient Systems Technology, Inc.

The second type of dynamic display uses an indicator to inform the user which items in the selection set are available for activation. In this display, the symbols are static, but the indicator changes with each selection. This technique is used in the Liberator (Prentke Romich Co.), an AAC device that uses sequences of iconic codes to represent messages (see chap. 3, this volume). When a user activates the first icon in a sequence, indicators on the display screen light up next to each icon that might come next. After the user makes a selection from one of these options, the lights change to indicate the icons that might come next in the sequence. This technique was designed as a memory aid, particularly for individuals who use numerous icon sequences to communicate. Because dynamic screen technology is new to the AAC field, little information has been accumulated regarding user capabilities required for operation.

## SELECTION TECHNIQUES

The term *selection technique* refers to the way the user of an AAC system selects or identifies items from the selection set. For persons who use AAC systems, there are two general approaches to item selection: direct selection and scanning.

### Direct Selection

The AAC user directly indicates the desired item from the selection set with *direct selection* techniques. Most of us have experienced several types of direct selection. When typing, we are able to directly choose or activate any item on the typewriter or computer keyboard by depressing a key. Even those of us who are single-finger typists have the option to select any key that we wish. In addition, most of us have used natural speech and gestures, and many have either observed or used manual signing. These modes are also considered direct selection techniques, because an individual can directly select gestures or signs to communicate specific messages from a large set of options.

Direct selection via finger pointing or touching is a common selection technique for many AAC system users. Other AAC users employ headlight pointers or headsticks to select items, or point their gaze in order to indicate choices. At this time, readers may wish to review the story of Kris presented at the beginning of this chapter. Kris used eye gazing (or eye pointing), a direct selection technique in which her eyes were directed toward the body parts or environmental stimuli that symbolized the letters of the alphabet. Options for direct selection are reviewed briefly in the following sections.

#### Selection Options

*Physical Pressure or Depression*   Many AAC devices are activated by depressing a key or touch-sensitive pad. A standard keyboard uses this activation mode, as does the touch pad (i.e., membrane switch) on many microwave ovens or AAC devices. If pressure is required for activation, it is usually generated by a body part, such as a finger or a toe, or by some device that is attached to the body, such as a headstick or splint mounted on the hand or arm. The movement of the body part or body-part extension (e.g., the headstick) must be sufficiently controllable so that only a single item is activated with each depression. Pressure sensitive keys and touch pads usually can be set to a variety of adjustable pressure thresholds that enhance accurate activation.

---

A number of direct selection devices are available primarily in Europe. These include the Temac system, a keyboard emulator for Macintosh and Apple IIgs computers; Minimanus and Maximanus, miniature and expanded keyboards for IBM-compatible computers; and Handicom, a computer and environmental control system operated through a headpiece controlled by eye gaze. Information about these and other devices can be obtained from the Swedish Institute for the Handicapped.

---

*Physical Contact*   With many nonelectronic AAC options, items are selected using physical contact rather than pressure or depression. For example, the man using the communication board in Figure 4.2. identified the items from the selection set by *touching* them with his finger. Because electronic activation is not involved, pressure is not required. Manual signs and gestures fall into this category, since they are formed by hand and body movements rather than by pressure or pointing.

*Pointing (No Contact)*   Actual physical contact is not always necessary when selecting an AAC option. For example, when *eye pointing* (eye gaze) is the selection technique, the AAC user looks at an item from the selection set long enough for the communication partner to identify the direction of the gaze and confirm the selected item. Eye pointing is a selection technique often used by individuals who are unable to speak due to physical impairments, since they often retain relatively accurate eye movements. In addition, eye pointing is often employed by young AAC users who have not yet learned other communication techniques, as well as by those with poor positioning, chronic fatigue, or ongoing medical conditions that prevent them from utilizing more physically demanding options. Some nonelectronic eye gaze communication techniques are quite advanced and incorporate complex encoding strategies (Goossens' & Crain, 1987). An ETRAN eye pointing display and an eye gaze communication vest are presented in Figures 4.7. and 4.8., respectively.

Pointing without contact can also be accomplished through use of an *optical* or *light generating device* that is mounted on the head in some way (e.g., on a headband or attached to glasses), or held in the hand (Figure 4.9.). This technique can be used with both high and low tech AAC options. For example, the individual who used the communication board in Figure 4.2. could indicate his choice by directing a light beam toward a desired item. Electronic AAC systems also can be activated using optical or light pointing. Systems using this selection technique are designed to electronically monitor the position of the light beam or optical sensor and select an item if the beam or sensor remains in a specific location for a period of time. The two primary motor requirements for use of this technique are the ability to direct the light beam to a desired item and the ability to maintain the direction for a prescribed period of time. Because light pointers and optical sensors are usually mounted on the head, head control without excessive tremor or extraneous movements is required for accurate and efficient use of these options.

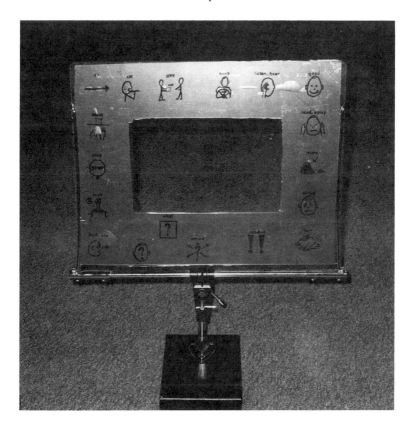

**Figure 4.7.** An Etran board for eye pointing.

**Figure 4.8.** An eye gaze vest (based on a design by Goossens' & Crain, 1986b).

Selection can also be made using *sonar* or *infrared technology* instead of direct physical contact. Sound or infrared signals that are imperceptible to human senses are generated electronically and interpreted by a receiving unit positioned near a computer screen display. By moving his or her head, the AAC user controls the cursor on the computer screen to indicate items from the selection set. The motor control requirements of sonar or infrared systems are similar to those for the light pointing and optical systems.

> The Headmaster employs sonar technology so users can control the mouse function on a Macintosh computer with their head movements. It is distributed by Prentke Romich Co. The Freewheel offers an infrared sensor for electronic head pointing on IBM-compatible computers. It is distributed by Pointer Systems, Inc.

*Voice Recognition*   Progress has been made in the area of *voice recognition* as an alternative access selection mode for persons who are able to produce consistent speech patterns. Voice recognition in the past was used primarily by individuals who could speak but were unable to write or control a computer keyboard. Depending on the technology, the selection set for voice recognition can be developed in a variety of ways. In some cases, the system is "trained" to recognize certain words, phrases, codes, or commands, as well as the voice of a specific individual. Thus, the selection set is limited to those items the system has been trained to recognize; usually these are limited to letters, numbers, and basic computer commands. In the newer commercial voice recognition systems, an extensive vocabulary of frequently occurring words is included with the system. The user selects these words by speaking the word or by speaking the alphabetic or numeric codes displayed

**Figure 4.9.** Headlight pointing with letters and numbers.

on the screen. This increases the rate of message composition considerably. In addition, as the user works with the system, recognition accuracy improves as the system continually learns and re-learns the user's voice patterns.

> DragonDictate is a general purpose voice "typewriter" that can serve as an emulator for operating commercial software programs (word processors, spreadsheets, or databases). It is published by Dragon Systems, Inc. and distributed by Adaptive Communication Systems, Inc.

*Activation Strategies* Methods to locate and identify a specific item from a selection set have been discussed. When an item is selected on an electronic display, it must then be activated so that the AAC system recognizes and translates it into usable output. Because of the limited motor control capabilities of many AAC users, alternative activation strategies must be employed. For example, some individuals may be unable to isolate a pressure key on a selection display without occasionally dragging their fingers across the display or inadvertently activating other items. Several electronic options can compensate for these difficulties.

*Timed Activation* Most electronic AAC devices that allow for direct selection have the option of *timed activation*. This strategy requires the AAC user to identify an item on the display in some way (e.g., through physical contact or by shining a light beam) and then sustain the contact for a determined period of time in order for the selection to be recognized by the device. Timed activation allows AAC users to move their fingers, headsticks, or light beams across the display surface without activating each item that is encountered. The clear advantage of this strategy is that it reduces both inadvertent activations and the motor control demands placed on the user.

*Release Activation*    Release activation is another activation strategy available in electronic AAC devices. Release activation can be used only with displays that use direct physical contact, either with a body part or with an extension of some type. The strategy requires the AAC user to contact the display, for example, with a finger and keep contact until the desired item is located. The individual can move wherever he or she wishes on the display without making a selection as long as direct contact is maintained. When the AAC user releases contact from the display, an item is selected. The advantage of this strategy is that it allows an individual to use the display itself for stability and minimizes errors for users who move too slowly or inefficiently to benefit from timed activation.

*Filtered or Averaged Activation*    Some AAC users are able to select a general area on the display but have difficulty maintaining sufficiently steady contact with a specific item for selection. In other words, their selection ability is so limited that it is impossible to set a sufficiently low activation time to accommodate them. This is particularly the case for people who are able to use head-mounted light or optical pointers but who do not have the precise and controlled head movements needed for accurate selection. Devices with *filtered* or *averaged activation* "forgive" brief movements off a specific item and sense the amount of time the pointer spends on each item in the general area. The device averages this accumulated information over a short period of time and activates the item on which the light or optical device was pointed the longest. The amount of time that elapses prior to activation can be set to personalize the system for an individual.

**Summary**    A variety of direct selection options are available to individuals who can locate specific items directly from a selection display. The best way to understand these options and their clinical applications is to operate and use a number of AAC devices that incorporate them.

## Scanning

Some individuals who require AAC systems are unable to directly choose items from the selection set. Although there may be a variety of reasons for this inability, the most common is lack of motor control. In such situations, the items in the selection set are displayed either by a facilitator (i.e., a trained communication partner) or by an electronic device in a predetermined configuration. The AAC user must wait while the facilitator or electronic device scans through undesired items before reaching the item of choice. At this point, the user indicates in some way that the desired item has been presented. This type of item selection has been called *scanning*. Various aspects of scanning selection are discussed in the following sections.

*Scanning Patterns*    The configuration in which items in the selection set are presented to the AAC user is one component of scanning. It is important that items in the selection set be identified systematically and predictably so that the intention of the AAC user and the actions of the facilitator or device are coordinated. Three primary selection set patterns are circular, linear, and group-item scanning techniques.

*Circular Scanning Techniques*    *Circular scanning* is the least complicated pattern used to present items in the selection set (Figure 4.10.). Individual items are displayed in a circle and are electronically scanned, one at a time, until the AAC user stops the scanner and selects an item. The scanner is usually a sweep hand like the "big hand" on a clock or is in the form of individual lights near each item in the selection set. Though circular scanning is visually demanding, it is cognitively relatively easy to master and, for this reason, is often introduced first to new AAC users.

*Linear Scanning Techniques*    In *visual linear scanning*, a cursor light or an arrow moves across each item in the first row, each item in the second row, and each item in the third row, until the AAC user selects an item. Figure 4.11. illustrates a visual display in which items in the selection set are arranged in three lines or rows. In *auditory linear scanning*, items are announced one at a time by a synthetic voice or a human facilitator until the AAC user makes a selection. For example, the facilitator might ask, "Which shirt do you want to wear today? The red one? The blue one? The

**Figure 4.10.** A circular scanning display for an individual in an intensive care unit. (Picture Communication Symbols. © 1981, 1985 by Mayer-Johnson Co.; reprinted by permission.)

striped one? The purple and green one?" until the user answers "Yes." Linear scanning, although more demanding than circular scanning, is straightforward and easy to learn. Nevertheless, because items are presented one at a time in a particular order, it may be inefficient if there are many items in the selection set.

*Group–Item Scanning*    *Group–item scanning* approaches have been developed in an effort to enhance scanning efficiency. Group–item scanning involves identifying a group of items and then eliminating options gradually until a final selection is made. For example, in *auditory group–item scanning*, the device or facilitator might ask, "Do you want food items?" Drink items? Personal care items?" and continue until the "group" or topic is identified by the AAC user. Then, a

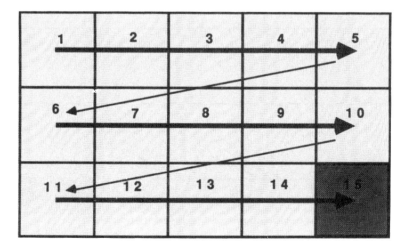

**Figure 4.11.** A linear scanning display with three rows of symbols.

predetermined list of options within that group is recited. For example, if the "drink" group is selected, the facilitator might question, "Water? Pop? Tea? Beer?" until selection is made. Clearly, this would be more efficient than first going through a list of food items and then drink items before a selection could be made.

One of the most common visual group–item strategies is *row–column scanning* (Figure 4.12.). Each row on the visual display is a group. The rows are each electronically highlighted in presentation until the user selects the row containing the target item. Then, individual items in that row are highlighted one at a time until the user stops scanning at the specific item desired.

There are also a number of row–column scanning variations. *Group row–column scanning* is a common variation of row–column scanning often used to increase efficiency in sophisticated AAC systems that contain many items in the selection set. Group row–column scanning requires the user to make three selections. First, the entire display is highlighted in two or three groups. When the AAC user identifies a group, for example, the group at the top of the screen, each row in that group is scanned. When the user selects a specific row, the scanning pattern changes to highlight each item in that row. Finally, the user identifies the desired item within a row.

Another variation is *horizontal group–item scanning.* Figure 4.13. illustrates a horizontal group–item scanning array of the type employed in the Adaptive Firmware Card and in Ke:nx, which allow Apple II or Macintosh computers to be controlled through alternative access options. The horizontal display requires minimal space on the computer screen, thus allowing the AAC user to see nearly all of the application display for word processing, games, or educational programs. Horizontal group–item scanning operation is identical to row–column scanning except that the rows are replaced by groups of symbols (in most cases, letters) that are highlighted one at a time before individual within-group items are presented.

---

The Adaptive Firmware Card (for Apple IIe and Apple IIgs computers) and Ke:nx (for Macintosh computers) are both distributed by Don Johnston Developmental Equipment, Inc.

---

**Scanning Timing and Speed**    In addition to the scanning pattern, the speed and timing of scanning must also be personalized according to the AAC user's physical, visual, and cognitive capabilities. When nonelectronic scanning is used, the facilitator can scan the items audibly or on a communication display (e.g., an alphabet or communication board) as quickly or as slowly as the user requires. The facilitator is usually able to observe the user's response patterns and adjust the

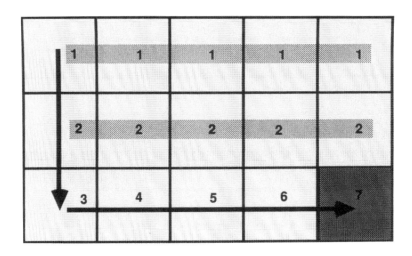

**Figure 4.12.**   A row–column scanning display.

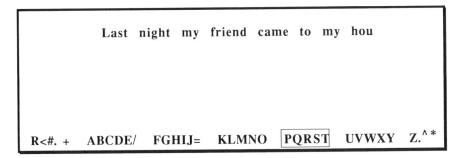

**Figure 4.13.** A horizontal group–item scanning display at the bottom of a computer screen.

speed of scanning accordingly. When electronic equipment is used, however, scanning speed must be individualized for or by the AAC user, because a facilitator is not involved in the scanning presentation. Most electronic AAC devices have sufficient scanning speed options to meet the needs of individual users.

*Selection Control Techniques* The user must be able to select an item while the items in a display are being systematically scanned. Generally, three selection control techniques are used: directed, automatic, and step scanning.

*Directed (Inverse) Scanning* In *directed scanning,* the indicator or cursor begins to move when the AAC user activates a microswitch of some type. As long as the switch is activated, the indicator moves through the preset scanning pattern (e.g., circular, linear, or row–column). The selection is made when the user releases the switch. Directed scanning is particularly useful for persons who have difficulty activating switches but who can sustain activation once it occurs and can release the switch accurately.

*Automatic (Regular or Interrupted) Scanning* The movement of the indicator or cursor in this type of scanning is *automatic* and continuous according to a preset pattern (e.g., circular or linear). The user activates the switch to *interrupt* the indicator at the group or item of choice in order to make a selection. This type of scanning is particularly useful for persons who are able to activate a switch accurately but who have difficulty sustaining activation or releasing the switch. This is also the type of scanning that is employed when the display presentation is auditory. The facilitator might recite names of movies, for example, until the AAC user stops (or interrupts) the recitation at the one he or she wishes to see.

*Step Scanning* In *step scanning,* the indicator or cursor moves through a preset selection pattern, one step (i.e., group or item) at a time for each activation of the switch. In other words, there is a one-to-one correspondence between cursor movement and switch activation. In order to select a specific item, the AAC user simply stops activating the switch for an extended period of time or activates a second switch that indicates selection of the item displayed. Step scanning is often used by individuals who have severe motor control or cognitive restrictions, or who are just beginning to learn to operate electronic scanners. Because step scanning requires repeated, frequent switch activations, it is often fatiguing for complex AAC applications.

## FEEDBACK

The two primary purposes of feedback from a communication system are: 1) to let AAC users know that an item has been selected from the selection display (*activation feedback*), and 2) to provide AAC users with information about the message they have formulated or selected (*message feedback*). Some communication systems provide neither type of feedback, some provide one but not the other, and some provide both. Feedback can be visual, auditory, tactile, or proprioceptive.

## Activation Feedback

Activation feedback has been defined as "the information sent back to the user upon activation of the input device. . ." (Lee & Thomas 1990, p. 255). Activation feedback differs from message feedback in that it informs the user that activation has occurred, but does *not* provide information about what symbol or message has been selected. It differs from output in that it provides information that is useful to the AAC user but not, generally, to the communication partner.

Activation feedback must occur in a sensory modality that is within the user's capabilities. *Auditory activation feedback* may be a beep, click, or other generic sound produced by an electronic communication device. Auditory activation feedback is not available in nonelectronic displays. *Visual activation feedback* on an electronic communication device may be provided via a light flash after a switch has been activated, or via an area or symbol flash on a backlit display. Visual activation feedback on a nonelectronic display may simply be seeing one's body part contact the device (Lee & Thomas, 1990). Contact with the textured surface of symbols on either electronic or nonelectronic devices provides *tactile activation feedback*. Finally, *proprioceptive activation feedback* is obtained when the user applies pressure against a resistant surface (a switch or key) that "gives" when the pressure threshold is exceeded. AAC users who produce manual signs and gestures also get proprioceptive and kinesthetic feedback from the position and movement of their hands in space.

## Message Feedback

Message feedback provides the AAC user with information about the symbol or message that has been formulated. Unlike activation feedback, message feedback may be useful to the communication partner as well, although this is of secondary importance. For example, when an AAC user interacts with a keyboard that echoes each letter as it is typed via synthetic speech, the echo provides the user with message feedback. The echo may also serve as output for the communication partner, if he or she can hear the echo and chooses to listen, but this is not its primary purpose. Similarly, a device may provide the AAC user with message feedback in the form of a screen display of symbols as they are activated in a sequence (e.g., the Dynavox), and such feedback may not even be visible to the communication partner.

Message feedback, like activation feedback, is available through auditory, visual, tactile, or proprioceptive modalities. *Auditory message feedback* may be provided on an electronic device as either a key echo (e.g., a speech synthesizer announces each alphabet letter as it is activated by an AAC user using orthographic symbols) or a word/phrase echo (e.g., individual words or phrases in a message are spoken by a speech synthesizer as they are produced). With nonelectronic displays (both aided and unaided), the communication partner often provides auditory message feedback by echoing each letter, word, or phrase as it is produced or selected by the user. *Visual message feedback* may be provided on electronic devices as computer screen displays of letters, words, or phrases as they are selected. Several communication devices (e.g., Dynavox) and software products (e.g., Symbol Writer) are available that provide message feedback in screen displays of symbol sequences as each symbol is selected.

Visual message feedback from aided and unaided nonelectronic devices is generally identical to activation feedback—the AAC user simply sees the symbol he or she produces. Tactile and proprioceptive message feedback is unavailable in AAC applications, except in writing aids used by persons with visual impairments (see chap. 15, this volume).

## RESEARCH AND CLINICAL NOTES

### Research on Alternative Access

The usefulness of a variety of alternative access options has been demonstrated and is illustrated more comprehensively in Chapters 10–19. There has been considerable speculation, but little systematic research, regarding the effectiveness of various alternative access options. The situation has been summarized as follows:

> It has been speculated that scanning is more difficult than direct selection for several reasons. First, scanning is a slower selection technique than direct selection. . . . Using direct selection, the rate of production ranges from 6 to 25 words per minute (Yoder & Kraat, 1983); using scanning, it ranges from 5 to 10 words per minute (Foulds, 1985). . . . The slow rate of scanning may place extra demands on . . . memory and attention. Others have speculated that scanning is cognitively more difficult than direct selection and have hypothesized that different forms of direct selection and scanning vary in their cognitive complexity. . . . However, there is limited empirical evidence to support any of these speculations about the cognitive differences between direct selection and scanning. (Mizuko & Esser, 1991, p. 44)

Research studies have addressed only some of these issues. Direct selection and row–column scanning performance was compared among normally developing children (Ratcliff, 1987). The results reported that the children "made significantly more errors, and took longer to respond" (p. xi) using scanning than using direct selection. It was suggested that scanning requires more user attention and short-term memory than direct selection. Nevertheless, the results of another study regarding the cognitive demands of direct selection and row–column scanning techniques appear to contradict those of Ratcliff (Mizuko & Esser, 1991). These authors found no significant differences among normally developing 4-year-old children on a visual sequential recall task performed with direct selection and performed with circular scanning. The task in the latter study, however, was considerably less demanding than that used in the former. In a related report evidence was presented suggesting that electronic auditory scanning places higher information processing demands on adults who are not disabled than does electronic visual scanning (Fried-Oken, 1989). These results have not been confirmed either with children or adults who have disabilities. As is apparent from this brief discussion, research examining the requirements (sensory, motor, cognitive, and language) and the effects (rate, accuracy, and fatigue) of various access options is still limited.

## Actual Use of Alternative Access

Alternative access has been used with AAC users of all ages and abilities by matching the capabilities and needs of individuals with the characteristics and capabilities of techniques. Although one might think that there is a "best" or "ideal" alternative access method for each user, in reality most individuals utilize several different access options depending upon the communication task, the time of day, and their fatigue level. The story of Kris presented at the beginning of this chapter illustrates this. Although Kris initially communicated using eye pointing, she eventually learned to control a Morse code-based AAC device with bilateral head switches in order to participate in school classes. Ten years later, she communicates with eye pointing as well as with her Morse code device, depending on the situation. She uses eye pointing when she "talks" with her family, when she is tired or ill, and when she is not in her wheelchair. She sends Morse code when she is at the university to operate her computer, write papers, and talk with persons who cannot comprehend her eye pointing system. In addition to her electronic communication device, Kris also controls other assistive devices such as a powered wheelchair and a page turner.

# *Message Input and Message Output*

It is Saturday afternoon and you have just completed your weekly grocery shopping at the local Super Duper Market, one of those big warehouse-type stores that are, to say the least, rather busy and stimulating. After standing in line at the checkout counter for 35 minutes, you finally reach the conveyer belt and unload your purchases from the cart. As the clerk moves each item across the optical scanner, a somewhat robotic female voice intones, "$.69. . .$1.49. . . $2.36. . . $210.00. . . " Whoops! $210.00?? Seems like a lot for a jar of pickles! Quickly, you glance at the cash register screen display to check the price and see $210.00 clearly written there. The clerk continues to scan items, oblivious to the mistake that has been made, so you interrupt him and request that he check the printed register tape for an error. When he checks, sure enough, the tape reads $210.00, which he agrees is a lot to pay for cucumber dills that retail for $2.10. The manager is called, the situation is resolved, and you leave the store, happily trying to figure out how to spend the $207.90 you just "saved!" You probably don't leave thinking, "Wow! I sure am grateful for the advancements made in message output over the past decade!" although you probably should! Were it not for the combined effects of synthetic speech, computer screen display, and printed tape output, you might have just bought the most expensive jar of pickles in the world!

AAC users, like all of us, are both the senders and the receivers of messages during communicative interactions. In this chapter, the term *message output* is used to refer to the information that is *sent* by the AAC user to the communication partner via the selected or composed message. Examples of message output modes include gestures, vocalizations, synthetic speech, and computer screen readouts. Conversely, the term *message input* refers to the information that the AAC user *receives* from others. Message input is usually in the form of natural speech, gestures, and vocalizations (assuming that most partners are nondisabled), although input may also be in the form of written or printed materials (e.g., letters, notes) or manual signs. It is important to distinguish input and output from *feedback*, which is primarily provided during, rather than at the end of, message construction (see chap. 4, this volume).

For some AAC users, the input mode through which they receive messages may be as much of an intervention concern as the output mode by which they send messages. For example, "The incidence of auditory reception problems among the adult population with aphasia is large" (Beukelman & Garrett, 1988, p. 119), and these individuals may need input in the form of gestures, pictures, or writing in addition to natural speech. Persons with impairments that affect cognitive, sensory, and linguistic processing (e.g., intellectual disabilities or traumatic brain injury) may also require and benefit from augmentative input techniques. In the following sections, the major types of message input and output used in AAC applications are reviewed in terms of general characteristics and the learning and performance abilities that they require of AAC users and their communication partners.

## INTRINSIC VERSUS EXTRINSIC MESSAGE PRODUCTION

In Chapter 4, we noted that the selection set of an AAC system includes the visual, auditory, and/or tactile presentation of all available symbols from which the user can choose (Lee & Thomas, 1990). For example, the selection set on a typewriter consists of the alphabet, number, punctuation, and other keys. When a user makes a selection from a set, the message that is produced can be either *intrinsic* or *extrinsic* in nature.

An *intrinsic* message is identical to the selection set symbol that is used to produce it. For example, when an individual produces a manual sign or a spoken word, the message is "sent" in the form of the sign itself or the sound of the word. When an AAC user points to a symbol on a communication board, the message is inherent in the symbol that the communication partner sees. In other words, intrinsic messages are inseparable from the symbols used to produce them—what you get is what you see/hear.

The second type of message production is termed *extrinsic*, to signify its externalized and autonomous nature. The form of an extrinsic message is separate from the symbol used to produce it. In order to understand the difference between extrinsic and intrinsic messages, consider the following examples involving orthographic symbols. If I touch several such symbols on a non-electronic communication display while you look over my shoulder, I produce a message that is intrinsic in nature—the sight of the symbols touched is all that you get. If I use a pencil to write several letters on a piece of paper, however, I produce a message that is extrinsic, since the resulting message is distinct from the symbols themselves. I can now mail the message, hand it to you, or carry it across the room. Similarly, if I were to use a computer to type, an extrinsic message would appear on the computer monitor or could be produced on a printer.

Two additional and very popular types of extrinsic messages are synthetic and digitized speech. With synthetic or digitized speech, the symbols used to produce the message are totally separate from the mode through which the message is sent. For example, an AAC user may use an electronic device on which Picsyms represent messages that are produced through digitized speech. Or, Morse code symbols may be sent to a computer that translates the symbols into computer screen, printed, and synthetic speech messages. Because symbols and extrinsic messages take different forms, many different combinations of the two are possible. This flexibility is not possible with intrinsic output systems, where, as noted previously, what you get is what you see/hear.

The distinction between intrinsic and extrinsic messages is important to the interventionist for two primary reasons. First, the interventionist must be aware of the relative advantages and disadvantages of each type of message in order to select an AAC system that will meet the *message output* needs of the partners of a prospective user. Intrinsic messages, for example, require that the partner understand the symbols used to produce them, while extrinsic messages do not have this requirement. Second, the AAC interventionist must ensure that messages can be received by the user as accurately and efficiently as messages can be sent. Thus, consideration of the *message input* needs of AAC users requires an appreciation of the relative advantages and disadvantages of the two types of messages from this perspective. For example, AAC users who have difficulty understanding natural speech may not benefit from this form of intrinsic input from their partners, and they may require an augmentative input technique or device. In the remainder of this chapter, we discuss intrinsic and extrinsic message production from both the perspectives of AAC users and their partners.

## INTRINSIC MESSAGE PRODUCTION

Intrinsic messages, those that are inherent in the symbols used to produce them, can be sent by AAC users as *output* to their partners, and can be received by AAC users as *input* from others. In the first part of this section, we provide some general guidelines regarding the advantages and disadvantages of intrinsic output. Later, we discuss the same issues as they relate to intrinsic input.

## Intrinsic Output

*Advantages* Messages produced with intrinsic output have advantages for AAC users and their communication partners. Unaided techniques (e.g., gestures, manual signs) that yield intrinsic output are easy to use, because they require no additional paraphernalia—books, boards, or computers. Unaided intrinsic output techniques are always available for use because they do not have to be switched on as do electronic devices. Similarly, aided devices that yield intrinsic output, such as communication books, boards, and wallets, require little pre-message preparation. The rate of intrinsic output can be adjusted to the situational needs and the communication abilities of the communication partner. The use of aided devices that produce intrinsic output (e.g., simple alphabet communication boards) may allow AAC users to "hold the floor" and regulate speaking turns more effectively than do aided devices that produce extrinsic output (Buzolich & Wiemann, 1988).

*Disadvantages*

*Symbol Intelligibility* The extent to which intrinsic output limits the communication partners with whom an AAC user can interact is an important consideration. For instance, readers of Chapter 2 may recall that only 10%–30% of American Sign Language (ASL) signs and 50%–60% of Amer-Ind gestures were found to be guessable by nondisabled adults (Daniloff, Lloyd, & Fristoe, 1983; Doherty, Daniloff, & Lloyd, 1985). Thus, relatively few nondisabled people are likely to understand the intrinsic messages produced in these modes.

The issue of intelligibility is not limited to unaided techniques. Whenever unfamiliar (i.e., translucent or opaque) symbols are used to form messages in communication systems that provide only intrinsic output, constraints may be placed on the range of communication partners. Aided symbols that have the potential for problems in this regard include textured symbols with arbitrarily assigned meanings, selected symbols from all the pictorial line drawing sets discussed in Chapter 2, many Sigsymbols and Blissymbols, orthographic symbols (letters, words, and phonemic symbols) for people who do not spell or read, lexigrams, Non-SLIP plastic symbols, and other symbols such as braille and Morse code.

A common strategy for maximizing intrinsic output intelligibility is to provide simultaneous written "translations" of aided messages for literate communication partners. To facilitate interactions with nonliterate partners, the solution may be to use a multimodal AAC system with at least one component that provides extrinsic output intelligible to the communication partner(s).

*Perceptual and Memory Concerns* AAC users who send intrinsic output must first get their partners' attention. Then, their partners must be able to turn toward them or move toward the AAC users in order to see the hands, boards, books, or devices that display their message symbols. Finally, communication partners must possess sufficient sensory acuity to see or hear the intrinsic output. There are many situations in which one or more of these requirements would be difficult or impossible to fulfill. Such situations include communicative interactions in which a communication partner has a visual or hearing impairment, and communication interactions in busy, crowded, dimly lit, or limited mobility environments (e.g., classrooms, factories, movie theaters, or football games). The best solution in these situations may be to introduce one or more forms of extrinsic output as part of a multimodal, individualized communication system, as discussed later in the chapter.

Unaided systems that produce intrinsic output impose memory requirements on both of the participants in the communicative exchange. Since there is no permanent display available, all of the gestures or manual signs must be recalled and produced from memory by the sender and held and processed in memory by the receiver. These may be very difficult tasks for persons who have poor memories (e.g., persons with traumatic brain injury) or who have difficulty processing transitory information (e.g., persons with autism). The use of aided systems with permanent displays has been urged as a solution when memory deficits are a problem (Mirenda & Schuler, 1989; Reichle & Karlan, 1985).

## Intrinsic Input

In order to select appropriate AAC systems, interventionists must determine the extent to which AAC users, particularly those who experience sensory, cognitive, and/or linguistic impairments, are able to process and understand various intrinsic input. The most obvious of these are the natural modes of communication—speech, gestures, and vocalizations—that are used by most nondisabled communication partners. In addition, intrinsic input may be provided via an augmentative mode to AAC users. For example, an approach termed "aided language stimulation" has been used to provide intrinsic input via pictorial symbols to young AAC users (Goossens', 1989). Similarly, the use of "graphic organization aids" that provide intrinsic input via pictorial and graphic symbols have been used (Reichle et al., 1991). More widespread is manually signed input by teachers and family members of AAC users with autism and severe intellectual disabilities (see chaps. 2 and 14, this volume). In AAC applications such as these, the pictures, words, or signs are almost always presented in a *total communication paradigm*, in which the communication partner accompanies each picture or sign with the corresponding spoken word (Carr, 1982).

*Intrinsic Input from the Perspective of the AAC User*    Simultaneous presentation of speech plus some other type of symbol that yields intrinsic input is often presumed to automatically improve the AAC user's ability to understand the message, because pictures or manual signs are somehow less cognitively demanding than is speech. This belief is not based on unequivocal evidence for either manual signs (Bryen & Joyce, 1986) or pictorial symbols (Franklin, Phillips, & Mirenda, 1991). Furthermore, numerous studies have demonstrated that AAC users with autism or severe intellectual disabilities, in particular, are unlikely to understand (or use) pictorial or signed information if it is merely *presented* along with speech (Reichle et al., 1991). Rather, the receptive meanings of AAC symbols must be taught, preferably in natural contexts, as carefully as their expressive meanings (Karlan, 1990). Thus, facilitators who provide pictorial or signed input to persons with autism or intellectual disabilities should not assume that they are automatically providing them with useful additional information. The usefulness of various forms of intrinsic input must be made on an individual basis. A similar caution has been raised regarding the aided or unaided intrinsic visual, auditory, and tactile input provided to persons with dual sensory impairments (Rowland, 1990), traumatic brain injury, and aphasia (Beukelman & Garrett, 1988). "The role and potential impact of communicative [input] . . . has been underutilized in intervention approaches to date. . . . Research focus should be directed to the influence of the partner's communication [input] in [AAC] system exchanges" (Romski & Sevcik, 1988a, p. 89).

*Intrinsic Input from the Perspective of the Communication Partner*    There is some evidence that communication partners who use key word signing (i.e., total communication) slow their rates of both speaking and signing and insert more pauses than when they use speech alone (Windsor & Fristoe, 1989, 1991). This may account, at least in part, for the expressive and receptive language gains that have resulted from the use of this approach with some autistic and other developmentally delayed persons (Kiernan, 1983). The type and amount of intrinsic input that should be provided to the AAC user are, however, major considerations. Should all or most spoken words be accompanied by pictorial or manually signed input, or should a telegraphic or key word approach be used instead? Should a total communication approach be used throughout the day or only during designated instructional periods? Unfortunately, the answers to these important questions are not available from existing research.

Regardless of how or when intrinsic output systems are used, facilitators must have the necessary symbols available for transmission and organize the environment in order to use the symbols appropriately. Data have demonstrated that, at least in classrooms for students with severe/profound intellectual disabilities, neither of the above requirements is likely to be met when manual signing is used (Bryen, Goldman, & Quinlisk-Gill, 1988). These requirements may not be any easier to achieve when pictorial symbols are used in aided language stimulation, since activity boards with the necessary symbols must be prepared in advance and be available when needed (Goossens', 1989). In short, facilitators must be committed to learning the symbols (e.g., in the case of manual signs) or preparing the displays (e.g., of pictorial symbols) in order to provide substantive intrinsic input to AAC users.

## EXTRINSIC MESSAGE PRODUCTION

As noted previously, the form of an extrinsic message is separate from the symbol that is used to produce it. Thus, extrinsic messages always involve some type of device, such as a pencil, electronic AAC aid, or computer, that is used to "translate" the symbol into another form. Because of this, devices that produce extrinsic messages (with the exception of pens and pencils) are generally more expensive than are those that produce intrinsic messages. Most devices for extrinsic message production also require regular maintenance and careful handling, and they must be protected against environmental hazards such as moisture, static electricity, and food or liquid spillage. Despite these considerations, however, many AAC users can benefit from devices that produce extrinsic messages.

### Extrinsic Output

Two primary types of extrinsic output sent by AAC users to their communication partners are auditory output, in the form of synthetic or digitized speech, and visual output, in the form of printed materials and various computer screen displays. (The clicks, beeps, light flashes, and key echoes produced by many electronic devices are not forms of extrinsic output, but rather are feedback mechanisms as discussed in Chapter 4.) Auditory and visual extrinsic output are detailed in the sections that follow.

**Auditory Output: Synthetic or Digitized Speech**  The most common method to generate synthetic speech in communication devices is *text-to-speech* synthesis. This method involves a flexible mathematical algorithm representing rules for pronunciation, pronunciation exceptions, voice inflections, and accents. In standard text-to-speech synthesis, messages must be entered orthographically into a computer, either by the AAC user or by a facilitator. Messages are retrieved when the AAC user selects the related symbols on the communication device, and the symbols are simultaneously converted into speech output through the algorithm. A second type of text-to-speech synthesis employs a *phoneme-to-speech* method, in which synthetic speech output is produced from words entered into the algorithm on a phoneme-by-phoneme basis. The resulting speech of either of these text-to-speech methods sounds less natural than that produced by other methods of speech synthesis (e.g., digitization), but the method is flexible and requires relatively little computer memory.

> Some of the most common English-speaking synthesizers in the AAC field include Street Electronic's Echo and Cricket text-to-speech synthesizers and the Votrax SC02 chip, a phoneme-to-speech synthesizer.

A third type of text-to-speech synthesis uses *concatenated diphones* to produce speech. This method employs approximately 1,300 diphones, which are sound units that begin at the steady-state frequency midpoint of one phoneme, include the natural transition to the next phoneme, and end at the steady-state midpoint of the succeeding phoneme (Boubekker, Foulds, & Norman, 1986). Since the diphones are extracted from carrier words recorded by natural speakers, the resulting speech is intended to be more natural sounding than conventional text-to-speech synthesis. Diphone-based synthesizers, however, require considerably more memory and faster micro-processing speeds in order to operate than do text-to-speech synthesizers, and they are usually housed in computer-based communication systems that are more powerful and, therefore, more expensive.

A number of English-speaking synthesizers utilizing concatenated diphone technology are available in communication devices, including First Byte's Smoothtalker 3.0 and Adaptive Communication System's RealVoice, both of which are available in male and female versions.

Another type of electronic speech used in AAC systems is *digitized speech*. This method differs from those already discussed in that it consists primarily of natural speech that has been recorded, stored, and reproduced. In digitized speech, natural speech is recorded with a microphone and passed through a series of filters and a digital-to-analog converter (Cohen & Palin, 1986). When reproduced, the speech is a close replica of the original speech entry. The primary disadvantage of this process is that it requires a great deal of computer memory and, therefore, is quite expensive. In addition, because messages can only be entered through a microphone and cannot be typed as in text-to-speech methods, it can be inconvenient to enter messages. Despite these drawbacks, a number of AAC devices with digitized speech are available, in response to consumer demand for high quality speech output.

Some AAC devices that use digitized speech include Adaptive Communication System's DAC device, Prentke Romich's IntroTalker, and Zygo Industry's Macaw and Parrot devices.

The last type of electronic speech that is considered here incorporates a *combination of text-to-speech and digitized speech techniques*. Text entered via a keyboard is converted to a pronunciation code using a dictionary and a set of rules in an algorithm. This code is further converted to produce intonation, duration, and proper stress. Finally, the code is used to create speech via a digital-to-analog converter (Cohen & Palin, 1986). The process requires a moderate amount of computer memory, involves no more time for the user than that required by the standard text-to-speech method, and results in very natural sounding speech.

Digital Equipment Corporation's DECtalk system employs combined text-to-speech plus digitization to produce a variety of voices, including: (male) "Huge Harry," "Perfect Paul," "Doctor Dennis," and "Frail Frank"; (female) "Beautiful Betty," "Rough Rita," "Uppity Ursula," and "Variable Val"; and (child) "Whispering Wendy," and "Kit the Kid." The DECtalk is also available in a portable, battery-operated unit, the MultiVoice, that weighs 3.9 pounds and can produce 2–3 hours of *continuous* speech with an overnight battery charge (Words +, Inc. 1991). It is available through the Institute of Applied Technology.

*Intelligibility*   Beukelman and Yorkston (1979) found that the ability of unfamiliar listeners to comprehend messages read by dysarthric speakers deteriorated markedly once the speakers' intelligibility fell below 81%. If this figure is used as the benchmark or cutoff point for acceptable intelligibility, very few speech synthesizers produce output that is adequately intelligible for children or adults without disabilities. Exceptions include three of the DECtalk voices ("Perfect Paul,"

"Beautiful Betty," and "Kit the Kid"), which have been found to be 81%–97% intelligible in sentence identification tasks and 60%–84% intelligible in single-word identification tasks (Mirenda & Beukelman, 1987). (The lower figures represent scores of 6–8 year old children and the higher scores are those of older children or adults.) Another exception is the Smoothtalker 3.0 male voice, which was found to be between 67%–92% intelligible in sentence identification tasks, even though it was considerably poorer (45%–64%) in word identification tasks (Mirenda & Beukelman, 1990). Votrax and Echo, which have been commonly used in AAC devices, consistently have been found to be among the least intelligible synthetic voices (Hoover, Reichle, van Tassell, & Cole, 1987; Logan, Pisoni, & Greene, 1985; Mirenda & Beukelman, 1987). Other less intelligible voices include Lightwriter, Artic R65B, and early versions of Smoothtalker male and female voices (Mirenda & Beukelman, 1990). A summary of intelligibility scores is presented in Table 5.1.

No studies have been conducted regarding the intelligibility of digitized speech, probably because it is presumed to be close to or identical to that of natural speech. There may be differences, however, in the quality of the digital-to-analog converters, playback mechanisms, or other components that produce better speech in some systems than in others. This evaluation awaits future comparative research.

---

Speech synthesizers have been developed to speak many languages. Computer chips that produce synthetic Swedish, Norwegian, German, French, Spanish, Italian, American English, and British English were developed at the Royal Institute of Technology in Stockholm, Sweden. These voices are available commercially in the Mini Voxbox, which can be used with any serial output communication aid and in a dedicated AAC device, the Polycom (Zygo Industries, Inc.).

---

*Acceptability*   If the intelligibility of synthesized speech is poor, listeners are likely to rate it poorly along other dimensions as well, such as gender/age appropriateness and overall social acceptability. Indeed, two studies that examined this issue found that for hypothetical contexts involving people, low intelligibility voices such as Echo, Votrax, and Lightwriter were consistently

**Table 5.1.**   Summary of intelligibility scores for common speech synthesizers

| Speech synthesizer | Single-word intelligibility (in %) | Sentence intelligibility (in %) |
| --- | --- | --- |
| DECtalk (male: "Perfect Paul") | 72–78 | 81–97 |
| DECtalk (female: "Beautiful Betty") | 72–84 | 90–96 |
| DECtalk (child: "Kit the Kid") | 60–68 | 81–91 |
| Smoothtalker 3.0 (male) | 45–64 | 67–92 |
| Smoothtalker 2.0 (female) | 35–49 | 41–54 |
| RealVoice (male) | 49–59 | 51–78 |
| Lightwriter | 33–44 | 42–73 |
| Artic R65B | 37–45 | 42–70 |
| Votrax SC02 (with spelling modified to maximize intelligibility) | 35–57 | 46–84 |
| Echo II + (with spelling modified to maximize intelligibility) | 34–40 | 50–68 |

Based on Mirenda and Beukelman (1987, 1990).

Scores have been rounded upward to the nearest unit. In all cases, the low scores in a range were obtained for nondisabled children (6–8 years of age), and the high scores were obtained for nondisabled adults. Scores for 10- to 12-year-olds fell within the range. Intelligibility scores obtained from the same subjects for natural speech (female) ranged from 94% to 99% for both single-word and sentence tasks.

rated no higher than 2.0 on a 5-point scale on which 1 = "I wouldn't like the voice at all," and 5 = "I would like the voice a lot" (Crabtree, Mirenda, & Beukelman, 1990; Mirenda, Eicher, & Beukelman, 1989).

But what of synthesizers whose intelligibility seems reasonably good? How do communication partners rate these voices for overall acceptability? No research data are available in this area for digitized speech, although, presumably, it would be highly rated because it is essentially natural speech that has been stored and played back. For synthetic speech, Crabtree et al. (1990) and Mirenda et al. (1989) found that listener attitudes varied considerably depending on the age and gender of the potential user, even for voices that are rated relatively high in intelligibility. For example, of the Smoothtalker 3.0 male voice and the three DECtalk voices cited, none were considered comparable in acceptability to age- and gender-appropriate natural speech. On a 5-point scale, the highest score received for hypothetical contexts involving people was 3.15 (neutral), for DECtalk's "Kit the Kid" voice when used by a female child. In these two studies, the less intelligible voices did not receive scores higher than 1.9 under any conditions. These scores can be compared to averages ranging from 4.0–4.6 for natural speech produced by speakers the same ages and genders as the listeners. In a related study, 9-year-old nondisabled children also rated a natural female child's voice as preferable to three synthetic alternatives; again, DECtalk's "Kit the Kid" voice was next, and the Smoothtalker 3.0 and RealVoice female voices tied for third (Bridges Freeman, 1990). Interestingly, when asked about their attitudes toward the hypothetical children using the four options, the children scored no significant differences across the voices on a standard attitude scale. Thus, while they appeared to prefer the natural voice, this did not seem to affect the children's attitudes toward potential synthetic speech users.

Of course, what we don't know from either the intelligibility or the acceptability studies is exactly how much any of this matters in the context of real, longitudinal communication interactions. Since intelligibility is known to improve with listener exposure and practice (Hoover et al., 1987; Huntress, Lee, Creaghead, Wheeler, & Braverman, 1990; Schwab, Nusbaum, & Pisoni, 1985), it is likely that acceptability might also improve. Furthermore, these acceptability ratings were made for hypothetical AAC users, not actual ones. It is quite conceivable that if actually faced with a friend or relative who produced synthetic speech through an AAC device, the respondents would have been much more flexible and accepting, since "any speech is better than no speech" in many circumstances. Nonetheless, given the available empirical information, the increased availability of high quality, gender- and age-appropriate synthetic speech is good news for both AAC users and their communication partners. Table 5.2. summarizes the types of speech output available in the most common AAC devices in North America.

*Advantages and Disadvantages*   Major advantages of reasonably intelligible extrinsic speech output for a communication partner are that it: 1) may significantly reduce the partner's burden in the interaction, since interpretation of the output requires only the ability to understand spoken language; 2) provides information in a mode that is relatively familiar and nonthreatening; 3) allows communication with partners who are nonliterate but understand spoken language, and with those who are visually impaired; 4) allows messages to be sent without first obtaining the partner's attention through some other mode; and 5) allows communication to occur at a distance. A few illustrations of these advantages might help to clarify them.

Consider a child with severe disabilities who is mainstreamed into a regular kindergarten classroom of 25 children and who has limited receptive language skills and no speech. If he or she uses a formal AAC system with intrinsic output, his or her teacher and classmates must also learn to use and understand the symbols in that system. If this is an aided system, they must be in close proximity to the student when he or she communicates so that they can see the symbols in the communication book or wallet. Alternatively, he or she may use an AAC device that produces high quality synthetic speech output when a symbol is touched on the display. Now, there are few learn-

**Table 5.2.** Type of speech output in selected electronic communication devices

| Device | Speech output | Device manufacturer |
|---|---|---|
| Touch/LightTalker | DECtalk (10 male, female, or child voices), Smoothtalker (male and female) | Prentke Romich Co. |
| Liberator | DECtalk (10 male, female, or child voices), Smoothtalker (male and female) | Prentke Romich Co. |
| IntroTalker | digitized | Prentke Romich Co. |
| DAC (Digitized Augmentative Communicator) | digitized | Adaptive Communication Systems, Inc. |
| RealVoice | RealVoice (male and female) | Adaptive Communication Systems, Inc. |
| Dynavox | DECtalk (10 male, female, or child voices) | Sentient Systems Technology, Inc. |
| Macaw | digitized | Zygo Industries |
| Parrot | digitized | Zygo Industries |
| Lightwriter | Lightwriter | Zygo Industries |
| Zygo Notebook | Artic R65B | Zygo Industries |
| Polycom | Polytalk, available in Swedish, Norwegian, German, French, Spanish, Italian, American English, and British English | Zygo Industries |
| Talking Screen | Smoothtalker; external Votrax, RealVoice, DECtalk, or MultiVoice | Words+, Inc. |
| EZKeys | Smoothtalker; external Votrax, RealVoice, DECtalk, or MultiVoice | Words+, Inc. |
| WSKE Scanning and Morse code | Smoothtalker; external Votrax, RealVoice, DECtalk, or MultiVoice | Words+, Inc. |
| Equalizer | Smoothtalker; external Votrax, RealVoice, DECtalk, or MultiVoice | Words+, Inc. |

ing demands made of the teacher and the student's friends regarding the output, and he or she can communicate from anywhere in the classroom, assuming that the volume on the device is sufficiently adjustable. Older persons who want to communicate with their young (nonliterate) grandchildren, adults who work in vocational environments who need to communicate with co-workers at a distance, and other potential AAC users may also find substantive advantages in the use of extrinsic speech output.

The PC-VOICE and the BLISS-VOICE were developed in Belgium and provide synthetic speech in the Dutch language (Van Coile & Martens, 1990). Through the Artificial Language Laboratory (ALL) at Michigan State University, a Hebrew-speaking voice has been developed and is used primarily in Israel (Eulenberg, 1987). The ALL is also involved in the India Voice Project, which seeks to develop a synthesizer that can speak many of the languages in India, such as Bengali and Hindi (Kaul, 1990).

Extrinsic speech output has disadvantages for communication partners as well. Even when synthetic or digitized speech is fairly intelligible, it may be difficult to hear and understand in noisy environments by persons with hearing impairments or by those with reduced receptive language ability (e.g., aphasia or congenital intellectual/learning disabilities). Such limitations must be individually considered before making a decision about whether extrinsic speech output is appropriate for a particular user.

The second type of extrinsic output is visual and includes computer screen and written or printed output. These are discussed in the sections that follow.

**Visual Output: Computer Screen or Printed**    When we were searching for material to include in this book, it became apparent that few guidelines are available to guide AAC users and their facilitators in selecting visual output monitors and displays. In fact, the type of visual output that AAC devices provide has often been an issue secondary to selection of the symbol set, access mode, and encoding technique. Nevertheless, as an increasing number of options have become available, and as stationary AAC computer displays have become increasingly common in schools and vocational settings, information concerning visual output options has become more relevant. Therefore, this information is detailed in the sections that follow.

*Computer Screen Output: CRT Monitors*    One type of screen output is that provided by the standard cathode ray tube (CRT) monitor used with all nonportable IBM-compatible, Apple II, and Macintosh computers used in AAC interventions (G. Vanderheiden, personal communication, May 17, 1991). Figure 5.1. shows a typical CRT monitor.

CRT monitors can be selected on the basis of features that appear to make them easier to read, at least by office workers who regularly view such screens for long periods. The following information was drawn primarily from Tijerina (1984) and from a report issued by the Panel on Impact of Video Viewing on Vision of Workers (1983).

Luminance    Luminance refers to the brightness of the computer screen. In general, higher luminance improves optical quality, allows viewers to see finer details on the screen, and improves overall visual performance. High-luminance screens may be particularly important when sending output to communication partners with visual impairments.

Contrast    Negative contrast screens, those with dark characters on a light background, may offer visual acuity advantages over positive contrast screens (light characters on a dark background). Ideally, the contrast ratio (C1:C2) between the characters and the background should be

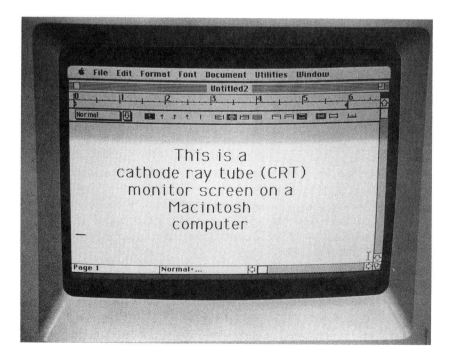

**Figure 5.1.**    Cathode ray tube (CRT) monitor.

adjustable to accommodate the individual viewer. This ratio, in which C1 refers to the brighter of two contrasting areas and C2 refers to the darker, should be adjustable from 2:1 to 15:1.

Character Generation   Characters produced by a single-line process are generally preferable visually to those with a visible dot or element structure. The latter category includes dot matrix and raster-written characters, both of which appear as a collection of dots with visible spacing in the vertical and horizontal direction. Since the characters on most CRT screens used in AAC applications are produced through a dot or raster structure, it is important to consider the features of each that appear to contribute to optimum visibility.

*Dot matrix screens* are usually described in terms of the number of dots per row by the number of dots per column in a rectangular array. A 7 × 9 or larger matrix size is preferable to smaller sizes. In addition, square characters appear to be visually better than round ones. Smaller characters are appropriate for visual screens that are used mainly for output (assuming communication partners have normal visual acuity), while larger characters are preferable for AAC applications in which the output screen is also the AAC user's display (e.g., in visual scanning). Tijerina (1984) also listed a number of more detailed guidelines drawn from the research literature regarding character height and width, inter-element and inter-linear spacing, and other factors.

*Raster-written characters* produced by CRT screens are described in terms of the number of horizontal scan lines used to produce a character. Higher numbers indicate that the raster lines are less visible, which is desirable perceptually. Generally, 729-line–1,029-line raster screens are considered optimal, because they produce characters that appear to be continuous rather than broken. Reasonable legibility for most communication partners requires a minimum of 7–9 raster lines per character, and these are equivalent to 5 × 7 and 7 × 9 dot matrix sizes, respectively.

Flicker   Flicker refers to the visual effect that can be seen on the screen as the character generating beam of the cathode ray is renewed or, in computer lingo, refreshed. Flicker is highly unlikely to induce seizures, which is a major concern for many AAC users and communication partners. This is because the "refresh rate" (the rate at which a point on the screen is renewed) in most cases greatly exceeds the typical alpha frequency region (8–14 Hz) in which seizures can be produced. Screens with refresh rates of 50 Hz–60 Hz or higher are recommended to avoid perceptible flicker and to minimize the unlikely induction of seizures (Tijerina, 1984).

Phosphor Persistence and Color   Raster-written characters are produced when an electron beam activated by voltage moves across a screen surface coated with phosphor particles, making them glow. These phosphors differ in the rates at which they fade when the beam is removed or turned off, and this property is known as *phosphor persistence*. Long-persistence phosphors include the P38 (orange) and P39 (green) phosphors in common use. When static screens (those that do not change rapidly or frequently) are used for output, long-persistence phosphors are preferable because they provide better control of flicker. Such phosphors produce "smearing" when images are moved across the screen, however, and they may have deleterious effects on legibility when scrolling screen options are used. In contrast, characters produced with short-persistence phosphors, such as P4 (white) or P1 (green), are preferable when moving screens provide output, because they disappear quickly when the screen is moved.

The color of the phosphor also determines the color of the monochrome screen characters. Color does not appear to affect readability for communication partners, provided that pure red and blue colors are not used, since the eyes may have trouble focusing on these colors. Aside from this consideration, character color is a matter of personal preference.

Reflection (Glare)   Two types of reflection concern partners reading CRT screens. The first is *specular reflection*, which occurs when light reflects off the front surface of the screen. The second, *diffuse reflection*, occurs at the phosphor surface and scatters incidental light in all directions. Specular reflection is generally of greater concern because it produces glare that may interfere most with legibility. Glare control can be achieved by tilting or reorienting the screen to avoid environmental light, selecting a screen with an etched or roughened screen surface that is less likely to act as a mirror, and using micromesh or colored filters over the screen.

> At the Artificial Language Laboratory, researchers have developed systems for languages that use a variety of non-Roman scripts, such as Arabic, Chinese, Hebrew, and Hindi. This allows for multilingual graphic capability in a single AAC system (Eulenberg, 1990).

*Computer Screen Output: LCD Monitors*    Low power consumption, low-voltage operation, compactness, and good readability of liquid crystal display (LCD) screens have contributed to their widespread use in portable computer screens (Bahadur, 1984). All IBM, IBM-compatible, and Macintosh laptop computers incorporate LCD screens, as do virtually all of the dedicated electronic devices currently used in AAC applications (G. Vanderheiden, personal communication, May 17, 1991). Figure 5.2. illustrates a typical LCD monitor.

Very simply, LCD screens consist of two plates of glass with liquid crystal material between them. When voltage is applied to areas of the liquid crystal, these areas become visibly different from the rest of the background, giving rise to alpha, numeric, or other types of characters. LCDs are passive electro-optical screens that do not generate light but simply modulate it (Bahadur, 1984).

Two types of LCD screens are commonly used in AAC applications (G. Vanderheiden, personal communication, May 17, 1991). The first type of LCD screen is the *reflective screen*, which has good visibility in bright light environments such as outdoors. Reflective screens may also be used in normally lighted rooms, but are not appropriate for low light conditions. The second type of LCD screen, the *transmissive or backlit screen*, requires more battery power to operate and was designed for good visibility in normal or low light conditions. Ideally, an AAC device should have both reflective and transmissive capabilities so that all lighting conditions are accommodated. Typically, this means that the backlight can be turned off when not in use and reactivated quickly when lighting conditions change.

The guidelines provided in the previous section on CRT screens are applicable to features such as character generation, reflection, and other elements of LCD screens. Of course, some variables

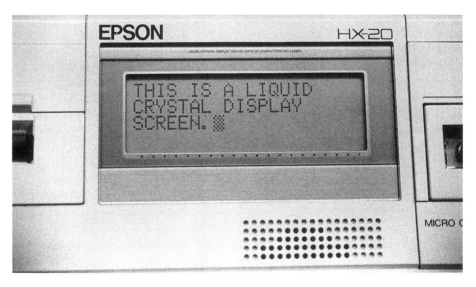

**Figure 5.2.**   Liquid crystal display (LCD) monitor.

such as flicker and phosphor persistence do not apply to LCDs, which may be advantageous. In addition, a report issued by the Bureau of National Affairs (1987) noted that unlike CRT screens, LCD screens generate no x-rays or electrostatic fields, and LCDs have lower emissions of low frequency magnetic fields. This suggests that LCD screens may be preferable, especially for long-term, frequent users and their partners, from a health and safety standpoint.

*Printed Output* Permanent, "hard copy " output is produced on paper by a printer that may be part of or an adjunct to the communication device, as illustrated in Figure 5.3.

In addition, many communication devices can be connected to standard peripheral printers or interfaced with small, portable printers. The printer may produce full-page, wide-column, or strip output in many paper and font sizes (Fishman, 1987). With some software/hardware combinations, it is also possible to print messages with other than orthographic symbols. For example, PCS symbols can be displayed and printed on a Macintosh computer using software programs such as Boardmaker and Talking Symbols (Mayer-Johnson, 1989, 1990), and Blissymbols can be printed using programs such as AccessBliss and StoryBliss (McNaughton, 1990a, 1990b).

**Advantages and Disadvantages of Visual Output** A major advantage of visual output is that it can be used for message clarification if the synthetic or natural speech is not understood. The need for message reformulation in response to a partner's request for clarification may be reduced when computer screen output is provided (Higginbotham, 1989). This may be particularly important for communication partners who are hearing impaired or unfamiliar with the AAC user and his or her system. For example, an adult with aphasia who has limited speech but good literacy skills may learn to type messages that appear on a screen so that his visiting sister, who is hearing impaired, can understand him. In addition, the permanence of printed visual output allows communication partners to save it, read it again, and correct or edit it for the AAC user. Printed output is obviously useless to partners who are nonliterate or unable to read the print.

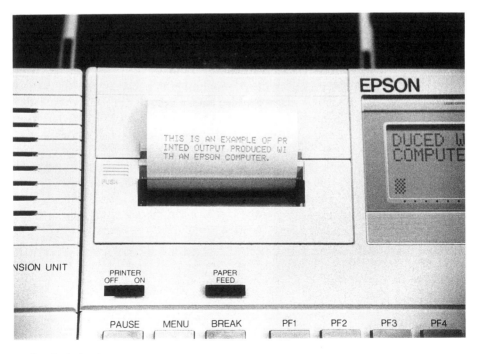

**Figure 5.3.** Sample of printed output.

## Extrinsic Input

AAC users may find themselves in the position of receiving synthetic speech, computer screen, or written or printed input from their partners. Some issues related to these input applications are reviewed in the following sections.

**Synthetic Speech**    Most studies that have examined the intelligibility of synthetic speech have been conducted with nondisabled individuals. In order to assess the generalizability of these studies, however, it is important to know whether persons with disabilities (preferably, potential users of AAC systems) experience synthetic speech in the same way as their nondisabled peers. Two studies attempted to provide this information as it relates to persons with aphasia. The studies examined synthetic speech intelligibility for individuals with aphasia using the Votrax SC-01 chip (Huntress et al., 1990) and the Smoothtalker 3.0 male, RealVoice male, and Echo II+ voices (Frecks, Beukelman, & Mirenda, 1989). The results of the first study, conducted with adults with mild auditory comprehension problems, indicated that the subjects initially comprehended natural speech better than Votrax. This difference almost disappeared, however, after four practice sessions (totaling approximately 2 hours) over a 2-week period. The second study, which involved adults with varying degrees of aphasia, indicated no significant differences in their Revised Token Test scores (McNeil & Prescott, 1978) for natural speech, Smoothtalker 3.0 male, and RealVoice male voices after a single experimental session. However, 10 of the 12 subjects in this study rejected the experimental task when the Echo II+ voice was employed, presumably because they could not understand it. These results suggest that high quality synthetic speech and sufficient exposure and practice over time appear to positively affect the intelligibility of this type of extrinsic input for adults with aphasia.

One of the few studies in which children with disabilities were subjects (Massey, 1988) examined use of the DECtalk male synthesizer with elementary school–age students with language impairments using the Token Test for Children (DiSimoni, 1978). The results indicated after one experimental session that not only did the children with language impairments have significantly more difficulty with synthetic speech than did nondisabled children, but they also scored significantly lower on a test presented by synthetic speech than on the same test using natural speech. The inter-speech differences among the children with language impairment, while statistically significant, were small in magnitude (e.g., a range in scaled scores of 486–498 with synthetic speech versus 486–504 with natural speech). Another study in this area compared DECtalk, Votrax, and natural speech intelligibility for nondisabled elementary school–age children and those with learning disabilities or mild mental retardation (Dahle & Goldman, 1990). The results indicated that: 1) for all three subject groups, significant differences existed across the intelligibility scores for the three voices, with natural speech (95%) better than synthetic speech, and DECtalk (83%) better than Votrax (32%); 2) the response times to the experimental stimuli for all children followed an identical pattern: fastest to natural speech, slower to DECtalk, and slowest to Votrax; and 3) in comparison to the other subjects, those with mild mental retardation exhibited significantly slower response times for both types of synthetic speech and made more invalid responses when listening to Votrax. These results suggest that even when the intelligibility of a voice is high (i.e., DECtalk), individuals with cognitive impairments may require more time to process information presented via synthetic speech.

**Computer Screen or Printed Output**    Certainly, when AAC users are capable of comprehending computer screen or printed input, these forms offer them many of the advantages noted previously for communication partners. For example, Beukelman and Garrett (1988) described the use of written input via notepads, typewriters, and dual monitor screens to communicate to AAC users with aphasia who retained intact literacy skills. In addition, a number of authors have described the successful use of devices that produce extrinsic input (visual and auditory) to communicate to persons with autism (Biklen, 1990; Crossley, 1990), Down syndrome (Meyers, 1990), and moderate/severe intellectual disabilities (Romski & Sevcik, 1992). Goossens' (1989) also used extrinsic speech input with young AAC users with widely varied disabilities in applications of the aided language stimulation strategy discussed previously. Other clinicians have suggested that the communication partners of AAC users with extrinsic output devices should use these devices themselves during interactions to provide natural pragmatic, linguistic, and operational models (e.g., Bruno, 1986; Goossens', 1989; Musselwhite, 1986b; see Musselwhite & St. Louis, 1988, for a review).

The availability of extrinsic input appears to facilitate receptive language comprehension in some cases. Persons with autism, for instance, have been found to process concrete visual–spatial information more readily than temporal or visual–temporal information such as speech or manual signs (Biklen, 1990; Mirenda & Schuler, 1989). Hypothetically, it could also be argued that providing visual input models to AAC users might enhance their communication and language abilities or literacy skills, although little empirical evidence exists in this regard (cf. Romski & Sevcik, 1991).

# Chapter 6

# Service Delivery

## FROM PIONEERING TO PUBLIC POLICY

As is apparent from the previous chapters, knowledge about AAC has increased dramatically since the 1970s. Specifically, AAC technology has evolved at a remarkable pace, and intervention strategies have been developed for persons with a wide array of severe communication disorders. Concurrently, models for delivering AAC services have also undergone changes in order to accommodate the growth in the knowledge and resource base of the field. Such changes in the patterns of service delivery can perhaps best be characterized as a "transition from the pioneering to the public policy phase" of the AAC field (Beukelman, 1990).

### The Pioneering Phase

During the pioneering phase of development, successful AAC interventions were viewed as the exception rather than the rule. When children or adults with severe communication disorders were successfully provided with AAC systems, and when they learned to use the systems to communicate effectively, their achievements were often celebrated through the local media, presented at professional meetings, and perhaps written up as a case study in a professional journal. The successful intervention demonstrated what was possible at that point in the AAC field, and it was viewed as a pioneering effort.

As is common during the pioneering phase, successes were celebrated, and failures were often minimized or ignored. For example, it was the responsibility of potential AAC users, their families, or professionals to make the unusual efforts necessary to obtain services. When there was no one to make such efforts for a severely communicatively impaired child or adult, minimal or no services were provided. Thus, there was a far greater incidence of service delivery inequity than success, although the inequities were not publicized or acknowledged.

### The Public Policy Phase

The impetus to move the AAC field beyond the pioneering phase to a public policy phase has differed from country to country. In the following sections, we have invited two AAC "pioneers" to describe this transition in their respective countries. Penny Parnes, director of augmentative communication services at the Hugh MacMillan Medical Centre in Toronto, explains Ontario, Canada's, transition to the public policy phase.

> I would say that, prior to 1982, the AAC effort in Ontario was in the pioneering phase, in that services were provided but there was not a systematic service delivery framework or funding base. However, in 1982, the International Year of the Disabled, the province moved into the public policy phase, as the Health Ministry of the Ontario Government introduced a program known as the "Assistive Devices Program." Initially, the devices funded through this program included the more "traditional" rehabilitation technology such as wheelchairs, artificial limbs, and orthotic devices. The program focused on the needs of children, and funding covered devices for persons up to 19 years of age. The program funded 75% of the cost of these devices, and the family was responsible for the other 25%.
>
> After intense lobbying by consumers, parents, and professionals, AAC devices were included in the mandate in 1984. The AAC program differed in some important ways from the service delivery programs for other devices. Some of the key features of the Ontario AAC delivery system are:

1.  The range of AAC devices that are approved is extensive, and covers simple signalling devices, to custom communication boards, to state-of-the-art voice output and writing aids.
2.  Devices are added to the approved list through a systematic device evaluation procedure, which includes technical and clinical evaluation.
3.  "High-technology" devices are only approved for funding if prescribed through an authorized communication clinic.
4.  "High-technology" devices are usually leased to the user, instead of through the shared purchase arrangement employed for most other device categories.
5.  Technology used in the province is pooled to optimize cost efficiency and to allow for easy recycling of devices.
6.  Currently, the program is being expanded systematically to include other age groups, recognizing that device provision will not be successful without appropriate clinical services.
7.  There are four levels of authorization for communication devices, depending on the complexity of the AAC system required. This authorization mechanism encourages appropriate evaluation and prescription of AAC technology and services.
8.  The program is now beginning to fund research and development activities. (P. Parnes, personal communication, July 22, 1991)

A description of the transition to public policy in Sweden is provided in the next section, which was written by Gunnar Fagerberg, who currently directs the INROADS Project through the University of Western Ontario and the Thames Valley Children's Centre in Canada.

In his Viking epic, *The Long Ships*, the Swedish novelist Frans G. Bengtsson relates a story about a very early AAC device. One crew member returns to Scandinavia from the Eastern campaign unable to speak and see. He had witnessed the secret burial of a great treasure by the Dnieper River and was captured by Russians, who removed his eyes and tongue to prevent him from disclosing the site. Back in Sweden, however, his brother carves out the 16 runic characters in relief on a wooden board, thus providing him with a means of alternative communication. He is able to convey his secret; and the Vikings go back east to bring home the fortune.

Today, a thousand years later, Sweden has 8.5 million inhabitants, an area the size of California, and has stopped raiding other countries! It also has a long history of providing services for persons with disabilities. One of those services is the nationwide program established in 1968 for the free provision of assistive devices through hospital-based centres across the country. The delivery of AAC services, technical and non-technical, has been closely tied to this program and its expansion over the years. In the early 1970s, AAC services were largely limited to persons with laryngectomies and weak voices. Artificial larynxes and voice amplifiers were the only devices available. They were provided by speech pathologists working in phoniatrics clinics in hospitals. For other groups, communication boards, made by local technicians and therapists, were the only available fruits of technology. Sign language was only used by deaf persons among themselves and was not officially accepted in the schools. But, under the vaults of the Royal Institute of Technology, in the Department of Speech Communication, researchers were busy working on "artificial speech." Maybe one of their machines could be used one day.

On its victory tour from Ontario around the world, Blissymbolics was introduced in Sweden in 1976. Two schools for disabled children led the introduction: Bräcke Östergård and Ekhaga. The use of Blissymbols spread rapidly and spawned the creation of other symbol systems, as well as research and development of devices for converting Blissymbols into written Swedish and vice versa. About this time, The Swedish Handicap Institute, the government agency responsible for assistive devices and their provision, realized that very little was being done for persons with speech and language impairments. They started to look around the world for activities in the field. Some of the most interesting programs and persons were invited to present lectures and workshops, and the idea of creating an international project was launched. Canada, Great Britain, and, later, the United States joined Sweden in the IPCAS (International Project on Communication Aids for the Speech-impaired) project, devoted to the development of devices and services in AAC (a not-yet-invented term).

By the end of the seventies, there were several AAC devices around: Auto-Com from the U.S., the Talking Brooche and Splink from the U.K., Blisstalk and Multitalk from Sweden, and the Japanese Canon Communicator, based on a Dutch concept. The Swedish devices had been created at the Royal Institute of Technology, based on their work on speech synthesis, but also on a genuine dedication by the researchers to use their achievements for the benefit of persons with disabilities. Still, there were no well-organized nationwide services to make assessments, fit, and prescribe the devices. It was largely left up to individual speech pathologists and to the technical aids centres, whose main responsibility was the provision of devices for persons with mobility impairments, to take on the new devices and do the best they could. In Great Britain, the IPCAS project was the direct inspiration to start six new communication aids centres with multidisciplinary staffs, a development which we regarded with equal amounts of surprise and envy.

The formation of ISAAC (the International Society for Augmentative and Alternative Communication) in 1983 acquainted us for the first time not only with new terminology, but also with a number of people in other countries who, like us, were struggling to organize their service delivery programs. It became increasingly evident that something new had to be created for the provision of AAC services and the new high technology devices. The technical aids centres, staffed mainly by occupational therapists and focused on mobility devices, were not suitable for this function. Thus, the Swedish Handicap Institute initiated and coordinated the establishment of seven new centres across the country for the provision of computer-based communication devices and systems. The multidisciplinary staff at each centre also has responsibilities in information dissemination, education, evaluations, and research.

The formation of a Swedish chapter of ISAAC in 1989 was another boost to the field. Membership soared, and now a newsletter and annual conferences provide a vehicle for interaction and information dissemination. The 1990 ISAAC Conference in Stockholm generated a lot of interest and activity in AAC, both inside and outside the field itself. So, with the help of international inspiration and interaction, we have established a nationwide system for the provision of AAC services to all age groups. Still, many problems remain to be solved: integration with educational, vocational and other programs; the role and participation of facilitators; involvement of local community resources; services for persons with multiple disabilities; and the quantity and quality of services. No doubt, we will continue to look for models and ideas in other countries when approaching these and other issues for the future. (G. Fagerberg, personal communication, July 25, 1991)

In the United States, several factors continue to encourage the transition from a pioneering to a public policy phase. First, the Education for All Handicapped Children Act of 1975 (P.L. 94-142) and the Individuals with Disabilities Education Act Amendments of 1991 (P.L. 102-119) mandate that all children receive a publicly funded education in the least restrictive environment. Among other things, this legislation means that public school districts can no longer disqualify students from educational services because of their severe disabilities. In addition, courts and some school districts have interpreted the "least restrictive environment" to mean a regular classroom attended primarily by nondisabled children. Thus, all children with severe communication disorders are eligible for public education, and some find themselves in traditional classrooms with nondisabled peers. The need for AAC and other services has increased in direct proportion to the available educational opportunities so that students can be competitive, or at least active, in classroom settings.

Second, the Technology-Related Assistance for Individuals with Disabilities Act of 1989 (P.L. 100-407) provides financial incentives in the form of grants to enable states to make assistive technology services equitably available. This law stipulates that efforts should be made to provide assistive technology services to all citizens in a state, regardless of age, disability, or location. Thus, as these state grants are implemented, individuals in rural areas should have access to services similar to those available in urban areas. In addition, adults and children of all abilities should become eligible for services. Clearly, the implications of this law and the assistive technology practices that this legislation fosters are having a tremendous impact on the AAC field. Because the delivery of educational, medical, and technical services in the United States is organized on a local or state level, there are many patterns of AAC service delivery. Some of these patterns are reviewed later in this chapter.

Finally, AAC users recently formed a non-profit organization, Hear Our Voices, which is supported through membership dues, grants, government funding, and private donations. The goals of the organization are: 1) to provide a vehicle through which consumers can "speak for themselves, advocate for themselves, and thereby empower themselves to change their own lives" (Broehl, 1990, p. 13); and 2) to "help users of AAC systems . . . effect change in . . . public policy arenas" (Broehl, 1990, p. 12). As the AAC field moves into the public policy stage of development, organizations such as Hear Our Voices are likely to assume increasingly important leadership roles.

Information about Hear Our Voices can be obtained from David Broehl, 105 W. Pine Street, Wooster, OH 44691 (216) 262-4681

The AAC field is maturing and changing, and is becoming increasingly institutionalized in many countries. Personnel are being trained at an increasingly rapid rate to provide AAC services through efforts of the International Society for Augmentative and Alternative Communication (ISAAC) and its national chapters, regional AAC societies, university programs, and commercial organizations. In addition, professional journals, periodicals, and newsletters document and communicate international developments in the AAC field.

Journal: *Augmentative and Alternative Communication (AAC).* Periodicals and Newsletters: *Communicating Together, Communication Outlook, The ISAAC Bulletin,* and *USSAAC Newsletter.*

## COMPONENTS OF SERVICE DELIVERY

Three components can be used to assess an AAC service delivery system: structures, processes, and outcomes (S. Blackstone, personal communication, July 22, 1991). Although these components are considered throughout this book, each is introduced briefly below.

### Structures

The structure of an AAC service delivery program includes elements such as administration, team management, staff assignment, staff development, space, equipment, and materials. During the pioneering phase of the AAC field, structural issues at a local level were often ignored entirely or handled as they occurred. Organized and systematic efforts were rarely instituted to ensure proper administration, appropriate staff training, and equipment availability. In the public policy phase, proper support structures became required, so that services could be provided efficiently and equitably. Often, professionals who first began to provide AAC services during the pioneering phase must now pay special attention to these components in their agency or center, since these structural components may not be in place. Table 6.1. suggests some of the symptoms that may indicate that a service delivery program has structural deficiencies.

### Processes

This component of service delivery refers to the specific AAC assessment and intervention procedures that are used by the agency providing services. Clearly, this is the central component of any AAC delivery model, since process weaknesses mean that potential AAC users will not be well served. Because most of this book is concerned with the processes of AAC service delivery, detailed discussion of this component is not included here.

### Outcomes

The quality of a service delivery program must be assessed in terms of its outcomes. The purpose of the service delivery program is to provide communication opportunities and access techniques to persons with severe communication disorders so that they can communicate and participate appropriately. Thus, a review of service delivery outcomes should include measurements of AAC users' performance in terms of: 1) their ability to participate in a wide range of communicative events; 2) the number of their communication needs that are met; and 3) their operational, social, linguis-

**Table 6.1.** Symptoms of structural difficulties in AAC service delivery programs

1. Because the AAC program includes people from many professional disciplines, there is no administrator who assumes overall responsibility for the program.

2. The agency has no policies regarding use of AAC equipment or materials.

3. There is no staff development plan for the AAC team members.

4. An AAC user is placed in a classroom at the beginning of the school year in which the "new" teacher has had no preparation regarding AAC.

5. The AAC efforts of the agency are inefficient or haphazard because there is no designated team leader.

6. AAC interventions are often "stalled" because it is not clear who is responsible for obtaining funds to purchase AAC systems for potential users.

7. Funds for purchasing the AAC equipment and materials that are needed for assessment must be "squeezed out" of the budgets of the speech-language pathology and occupational therapy departments because the AAC program has no independent budget.

8. Clients with AAC systems receive as much (or less) intervention time from the speech-language pathologist as clients with mild communication impairments (e.g., mild articulation disorders).

9. Although one or two schools in a school district have well-developed AAC programs, there is no systematic plan for establishing such programs in other schools that serve students who are potential AAC users.

10. Although a potential AAC user and family desire AAC services, they cannot figure out how to obtain them or who is responsible for delivering services.

tic, and strategic competence with the AAC system. These issues are discussed in much more depth in Chapter 8.

## MODELS OF SERVICE DELIVERY

Shewan and Blake (1991) reported the results of a survey of all facilities in the United States that offer speech-language pathology services. The survey indicated that 49.9% of these facilities provide AAC services. Table 6.2. presents the proportion of facilities that provide these services. The authors reported that one third of the AAC clients served by speech-language pathologists and audiologists are young children, one half are adults, and the remainder are school-age children.

Regardless of the type of facility, a number of service delivery models have been developed to meet the AAC needs of persons with severe communication disorders. Coston (1988) edited a volume that described many of these models in detail, and readers are referred to this excellent source for comprehensive information. Several models that are used in a variety of countries are reviewed briefly in the sections that follow.

**Table 6.2.** Facilities that provide AAC services

| Type of facility | Percent providing AAC services |
| --- | --- |
| School | 44.7 |
| College/university | 3.4 |
| Hospital | 24.2 |
| Residential health care facility | 12.8 |
| Nonresidential health care facility | 13.3 |
| Other | 1.6 |

Based on Shewan and Blake (1991).

## Regional Specialty Center

Regional specialty centers were the primary sources of AAC services during the early years of the profession. Typically, these specialty centers were located within regional medical centers, regional rehabilitation centers, or state or provincial educational agencies and served AAC users from a wide geographic area. At a time when few professionals were trained in the AAC field, the regional center model appeared to be an efficient way to utilize a limited number of personnel to meet the needs of a large number of persons with severe communication disorders.

Today, regional center programs are run by individuals from a variety of disciplines who have had extensive experience in the AAC area. The centers are equipped with typical AAC equipment and materials, and services are usually obtained through self-referrals by potential AAC users or their families, or by referrals from educational, social service, vocational, or medical personnel or agencies. The roles of regional centers generally include: 1) evaluating individuals with severe communication disorders, 2) describing their capabilities and deficits, and 3) recommending intervention programs that may or may not include AAC technology. Personnel from the regional specialty center often do not deliver direct intervention services, but provide technical assistance and prescriptive advice regarding intervention. In addition, these centers may provide training to staff in local agencies or to families who will actually implement an AAC program with a specific user.

The strengths of the regional specialty center are that staff are experienced with meeting the AAC needs of a variety of individuals and have extensive technical resources. The major weakness of the regional specialty center is that follow-up is difficult, and the actual AAC intervention is often implemented by persons outside the center. This means that the intervention may be implemented by individuals who may not consider themselves to be responsible for providing it, who may not have received adequate training in AAC processes, and who may not have received appropriate technical instruction.

## Educational/Regional Network

As a result of efforts to provide equitable AAC services to students in public schools, state or provincial agencies have formed educational or regional AAC networks. These networks assume responsibility for training personnel in a designated geographic region, provide assessment equipment, and provide technical, intervention, and follow-up assistance. Some regional networks also manage AAC equipment loan banks. Colleen Haney, an augmentative communication specialist and Associate Director of the Pennsylvania Assistive Device Center, describes the regional network established in her state:

> In 1985, the Pennsylvania Assistive Device Center was created through federal funding (PL 94-142, PL 89-313, and PL 99-457) that was dispersed through the Department of Education in Pennsylvania. Over the past 6 years, approximately 7 million dollars of funding have been provided for specific pieces of assistive technology and the necessary support services. During these years, 726 students (aged 3 to 21 years) have received computers, software, vocal output devices, writing aids, vision equipment, amplification systems, and environmental control units—that is, "high technology" that is otherwise too expensive or not provided through other means. Mobility aids such as wheelchairs or eyeglasses, "light technology," or "high technology" devices under $500 are not provided through this program.
>
> Three equipment loan programs are available; these include:
>
> 1. Short-Term Loan Program: Assistive devices are available to professionals through the short-term loan program. Professionals may borrow devices for a period of 4 weeks to evaluate and experiment with the technology. Professionals who wish to provide students with a particular piece or pieces of assistive technology may do so by applying for a long-term equipment loan.
> 2. Long-Term Loan Program: This equipment will stay with the student for the entire length of time that the student is enrolled in an educational program in Pennsylvania. When the student graduates or leaves the state, the equipment is returned to the center to be upgraded and recycled. Equipment may be used by a student at home or school (24 hours a day, if necessary).
> 3. Equipment Exchange Program: When equipment no longer meets the needs of a student, it may be upgraded or changed through the exchange program.

In addition, in 1986, the Pennsylvania Assistive Device Center developed a multidisciplinary network of local assistive technology specialists. These specialists provide community-based assistive technology expertise to the students in schools located in the 29 educational regions of the state. Therefore, services are provided in the students' natural environments. The specialists receive ongoing training from the center through workshops, a newsletter, technology sheets, a reference library, and an equipment demonstration laboratory. As the specialists provide AAC assessment and intervention services, they are also supported by a toll-free telephone "hotline" that allows for technical and consultative services from the center. In addition, technical assistance and consultation is provided by center staff at the local school sites. (C. Haney, personal communication, July 23, 1991)

AAC networks are organized in several ways. Some are housed in a regional specialty center with outreach capabilities. Others provide intervention assistance and consultation through a specialty center, but complete all AAC assessments and interventions locally. Other regional networks are totally decentralized and promote a great deal of peer instruction and assistance among people in local agencies. For example, AAC specialists employed by a specific local educational agency may travel throughout the network region to serve as AAC consultants to other school districts in areas such as assessment, education, and intervention. Consultative services may then be reciprocated by other AAC specialists in the network so that resources are shared equitably. Betsy Minor Reid, senior consultant for the Colorado Department of Education, describes such an AAC network in Colorado:

In the spring of 1986, the Department of Education in Colorado began to address the assistive technology needs of persons with severe communication disorders, by bringing together groups of special education administrators and direct service personnel. As a result of those meetings, the extensive need to provide additional communication services to students with severe communication disorders and the willingness of some school districts to form an AAC network was clarified. During August 1986, the first AAC training workshop was held. Personnel from 18 of the 50 educational administrative units in the state of Colorado attended. That was the beginning. Today, all 50 administrative units in the state of Colorado participate in a statewide AAC network, and over 300 professionals have been trained to serve on the AAC teams that are supported by the network.

Throughout the schools of Colorado, 35 multidisciplinary AAC teams have been formed. Each of these teams is composed of professionals from either a single or a number of different school districts. When a local school district refers a student for AAC services, the local AAC team cooperates with personnel from the student's home school team to assess, plan the intervention, and monitor the referred students. The home school team contains those persons from the local district (or administrative unit) who are responsible for providing day-to-day AAC and educational services. Once students have been referred for AAC services, they remain part of the program until they leave the Colorado public schools through graduation or transfer. The AAC team assigned to that child has a "follow along" responsibility to ensure that appropriate services are provided.

Individual school districts (or administrative units) decide whether or not to participate in the network. In order to participate, an individual school district must provide personnel to work within the network. The amount of service that each district can expect from the network is dependent on the personnel time that it contributes toward the effort. The AAC teams are supported through several different programs. Initially, the Department of Education in Colorado supplies each AAC team with a package of equipment including a membrane keyboard, Adaptive Firmware Card, computer software, switches, and materials to develop communication boards. Through the years, each team can request additional equipment and materials to support its ongoing efforts. The Department also has purchased some dedicated AAC equipment that can be loaned to an AAC team or team member, so they may learn to operate a device, assess a student, or provide the student with a short-term loan (from 2 weeks to 2 months in duration). Each summer, an intensive 3-day training workshop is provided for the members of all of the teams. Through a "trainer of trainers" model, additional support and instruction is provided to school personnel who request it. The Department of Education supports the "trainer of trainers" program by paying the trainers' expenses, including the costs of hiring substitutes to cover the trainers' ongoing responsibilities. (B. Minor Reid, personal communication, July 25, 1991)

The strength of an educational/regional network is that it requires a commitment to equitable AAC services across the region through establishment of an "umbrella" agency that has the responsibility for implementing these services. Networks are generally committed to providing local personnel with at least some training and ongoing intervention support. In addition, there may be a commitment to provide on-site technical assistance. A potential weakness of the educational/regional network model is that the expertise with AAC processes may not be adequate to provide a full range of AAC interventions. Also, the technical expertise needed to personalize complex AAC systems may not be available if a regional facility is not accessible.

## Local Agency

Some local educational agencies or individual schools provide their own AAC intervention programs. Usually, these programs are led by a single individual who makes it his or her primary professional responsibility to become proficient in the AAC area. Although the local educational agency model was prevalent in the beginning of the AAC era, it is less common today, and local agencies are usually part of larger networks or consultative arrangements. The major problem with a local agency model is maintaining high quality services over time, especially if the individual providing expertise and leadership leaves. It is also difficult for most local agencies to provide adequate technical and equipment support for conducting assessments, which can help to identify a variety of communication options that can be explored. If adequate staff training and expertise can be maintained within the district, this model clearly has advantages related to ongoing AAC implementation in relevant natural settings.

## Private Practice or Consultant Model

AAC services are also delivered through a private practice or consultant model. Consultants generally provide direct AAC assessment and intervention services in the homes, schools, or workplaces of potential AAC users in one of two ways. First, for adults who have severe communication disorders but who have no AAC support network, a person in private practice may be hired by the family, insurance company, social agency, or nursing center. In this case, the AAC specialist provides assessment, prescriptive and technical assistance, intervention services, and contracts for the assistance of other professionals, as needed. Second, there is an increasing trend for persons in private practice to serve as consultants to agencies such as public school districts, hospitals, or nursing homes. In this case, consultants may provide AAC services to individual clients while helping the agency develop the capacity to deliver AAC services. These consultants often utilize professionals from a variety of disciplines within the agency to deliver ongoing services and conduct staff training in the area of individual client assessments and interventions. Thus, as part of the consultation, these individuals also develop the abilities of individuals to work as a team, assist the agency's AAC team to prepare technical prescriptions and intervention plans, and oversee the overall AAC program. In addition, consultants frequently assist the agency to improve administrative management of the AAC program. Sarah Blackstone, an AAC specialist in private practice, describes her role as an AAC consultant to a school district:

> For 2 years, I have served as a consultant to the Berkeley School District in Berkeley, California. My role is, and has been, primarily a facilitative one—that is, working with the personnel from the various agencies that are involved in the lives of children with severe communication disorders enrolled in the district, so that appropriate services are made available to these children in a coordinated fashion. The number of different agencies differs from student to student. Obviously, administrators and direct service personnel from the school district are involved, in addition to consultants within the school system (e.g., vision, hearing, and educational psychology staff), and professionals, like myself, in private practice (e.g., occupational therapists, rehabilitation engineers, physical therapists, and audiologists). The family is also involved, as are any agencies they choose to access, including day care workers, personal care attendants, regional centers (e.g., for consultation regarding behavior problems), local rehabilitation centers, vocational rehabilitation staff, university programs, physicians (e.g., ophthalmologist, orthopedic specialists), the Disabled Children's Computer Group, and state deaf–blind programs.
>
> Through the years, my role has changed somewhat. Initially, I was more directly involved in evaluations and day-to-day programming for each student. The concept, from the school district's perspective,

was that I would assist their staff to provide AAC services to children, and coincidentally provide inservice instruction to staff. Initially, Sue Procter (an occupational therapist with AAC expertise), and, more recently, Peggy Barker (a rehabilitation engineer with AAC expertise) and I have worked closely as the team's primary AAC consultants. The performance and progress of students are reviewed at a monthly meeting with each student's Augmentative Communication Team (ACT) involved. The purposes of the meetings are to monitor and plan the program of each student and to develop the capability of the ACTs. Meetings are almost always attended by the families and by some of the older students. I facilitate these meetings, as well as prepare and distribute the action plans we develop. These plans supplement IEPs [Individualized Education Programs] and are written into IEPs as a primary mechanism for measuring student progress. They document the activities of the ACT and the personnel responsible for completing goals and objectives, often on a monthly basis.

As the experience of the ACTs has increased and the expertise has grown within the Berkeley area, Mary Berg, a speech-language pathologist consultant, has taken on more and more of the ongoing responsibility for supporting the individual ACTs. Several teachers, occupational and physical therapists, instructional assistants, families, and administrators are rapidly becoming AAC specialists. I consult with Mary and others on a regular basis over the telephone; and for now, I continue to run the monthly meetings.

The functional and educational outcomes of the children served by the Berkeley ACTs over the past few years are demonstrably good. Perhaps, my greatest frustration has been related to the education of the adults on the ACTs. It has become apparent that all adults do not learn the same way. Some learn very well during the monthly meetings; some quickly take advantage of printed, videotaped materials and phone consultations; some attend special workshops and conferences. Not surprisingly, many require direct instruction and coaching in the context of their own programs. Unfortunately, some never really become interested. To truly have a quality and cost-effective program, we need to find ways to identify adults early in the process who will develop AAC expertise and then support their growth and development. In addition to planning and monitoring the progress of each student, we have begun to plan and monitor the development of each AAC team member, as well. The need to actively involve district supervisory personnel in this process, both for support and accountability, is becoming increasingly apparent.

I expected my role with the Berkeley District Augmentative Communication Team to decrease over time, and it has. It may be discontinued at the end of the third year, or it may continue on with additional modifications. Due to changes in personnel within the school district, I may be asked to assist in the development of new generations of leadership from time to time. I have learned a great deal from working with the Berkeley ACTs. (S. Blackstone, personal communication, July 22, 1991)

## Combination Models

Combinations of various service delivery models are being utilized as the AAC field matures. These combinations are often developed so that the strengths of a regional center, a consultant, and a local educational agency are merged to provide improved AAC services. Some examples of combined models are provided below.

***Regional Specialty Center—Mobile Team—Local Agency***  Howard Shane, director of the Communication Enhancement Center at Children's Hospital in Boston, described this agency's mobile outreach program:

At Boston Children's Hospital, we began the Communication Enhancement Center (CEC) several years ago as a regional AAC center. In time, the limitations of the regional center approach became increasingly evident, so we initiated the Institute on Applied Technology, designed to develop and market AAC-related technology. Then, a few years ago, we started the Mobile Outreach Program (MOP) in an effort to extend the services of the CEC into our region. This program utilizes a large van with two complete workstations and a power lift. It travels throughout the region with two staff members who have broad AAC and technology expertise. These personnel also have an office at the CEC, and receive support in terms of staff development, equipment availability and repair, and mobile telephone contact.

The MOP allows us to provide follow-up services to individuals whom we have seen in the regional center. These services take several forms. First, we can complete assessments begun in the regional center with observations in clients' usual environments. Second, we can provide inservice training to the various facilitators who will be responsible for implementing the AAC program. Third, we can monitor AAC intervention programs and provide assistance to the local agency personnel.

The MOP also allows us to provide AAC services to individuals who cannot come to the regional center. Many persons who are medically fragile are seen for assessment, intervention, and follow-up in their own residences. At times, we provide the complete intervention program; however, often we work in conjunction with agency personnel who are able to deliver some communication disorders services but who do not have AAC expertise. In these cases, we serve as consultants to local personnel as they complete those aspects of the assessment and intervention with which they feel comfortable. MOP also allows us to provide AAC services to individuals for whom financial constraints prevent access to the regional center because of release time or travel restrictions.

After a few years of operation, we have found that approximately 60% of MOP clients are adults, and 40% are children. Through the years, there has been a gradual but consistent shift toward serving more and more adults. Over the years, we have also learned some things about running a mobile outreach program. Generally, two individuals travel with the van on each trip. We try to select people who have complementary skills, yet it is still difficult for two people to meet the wide range of technology needs. It would be nice to send the entire team, but of course that would be too expensive. Unfortunately, the staff assigned to the program tend to "wear out" rather quickly, as they spend a good deal of time driving the van, and are away from home a fair amount. In addition, it seems that our original plan to use the van itself as a site for AAC assessments has become less important as communication devices have become increasingly portable. Thus, we have plans to replace our large van with a minivan. Assessments and interventions will then be completed in the person's home or local agency, and the van will be used primarily to transport equipment and personnel. (H. Shane, personal communication, August 10, 1991).

### Regional Specialty Center–Consultant–Local Agency    Pamela Mathy-Laikko, director
of the Hattie B. Munroe Augmentative Communication Program, describes that facility:

The Meyer Rehabilitation Institute [Nebraska] provides a variety of different AAC services. The Hattie B. Munroe Augmentative Communication Center, along with the Hattie B. Munroe Habilitation Technology Center, provides assessment and technology assistance services for persons from a wide geographic area. Persons who come from a considerable distance receive follow-up services through periodic visits to the center. In the metropolitan (Omaha) area, some school districts have also contracted for consultative AAC services. The regional center employs the consultants and provides them with technical support, a limited AAC equipment bank, and staff development activities. The regional center also collaborates with the consultants to provide staff development opportunities for the AAC teams within the cooperating school districts. (P. Mathy-Laikko, personal communication, July 21, 1991)

### Regional Specialty Center–Private Practice–Local Agency    Kathryn Yorkston, head of
the Division of Speech Pathology, Department of Rehabilitation Medicine, University of Washington, describes the Neuromuscular Speech and Swallowing Clinic:

The University of Washington Hospitals have developed a program for serving persons with amyotrophic lateral sclerosis (ALS) that contains a number of different service delivery components. Actually, persons with a variety of different neurological diseases and syndromes are referred to our clinic, called the Neuromuscular Speech and Swallowing Clinic. These referrals are made by the patient's physician, the Muscular Dystrophy Association, neurologists, physiatrists (i.e., rehabilitation physicians), or visiting nurses. The clinic meets weekly and is staffed by a dietician, neurological nurse, otolaryngologist, and speech-language pathologist. Referrals are made at different times, depending upon the patients. Some are referred when they begin to experience speech and/or swallowing problems; however, increasingly, referrals are being made shortly after diagnosis. The clinic provides medical, swallowing, and communication services including evaluation, treatment, referral, and monitoring.

When deterioration of speech performance is first detected by the person with ALS and the monitoring clinical staff, a referral is made to the speech-language pathologist who serves in the Assistive Technology Clinic, for an educational session regarding the AAC options that are available to persons with ALS. The two clinics are in the same facility and visits to both are coordinated on the same day. When it is clear to the staff of the Speech and Swallowing Clinic that an individual will need an AAC system, the Assistive Technology Clinic provides an interdisciplinary evaluation to select the communication option appropriate for the individual. Because the Assistive Technology Clinic manages a bank of AAC devices dedicated to the use of persons with ALS, the patient usually is provided with a device from the bank. As the capabilities or communication needs of the individual change, the AAC system can be exchanged, if necessary. The equipment bank was initiated with a gift from a foundation. It is sustained by gifts and memorials from families and friends of persons with ALS.

When persons with ALS live in the Seattle area, they usually continue to attend the Speech and Swallowing Clinic for follow-up services. If their symptoms are progressing slowly, they return on a monthly or bi-monthly basis. If their symptoms are progressing rapidly, they return as often as needed. When ALS patients live a distance from the Seattle area, staff from the Assistive Technology Clinic consult with speech-language pathologists in private practice or working within a service agency such as a nursing center, visiting nurse agency, or the Muscular Dystrophy Association, to provide follow-up services. Some of these professionals have attended instructional workshops provided by the Assistive Technology Clinic, and others are provided with video tapes of the instructional workshops. Telephone consultation is frequent between the clinic and the professionals in distant locations. (K. Yorkston, personal communication, July 18, 1991)

## AAC TEAMS

Regardless of the AAC service delivery model utilized, nearly without exception a team of individuals is required to complete the multiple activities of AAC assessment, intervention, and follow-up. In order for these to be accomplished efficiently, the members of the team need to utilize a variety of consensus-building strategies throughout these processes. Without such consensus building, the team runs the risk of realizing that all of its members are not in agreement with an assessment or an intervention plan, even after considerable time and effort have already been devoted to these processes. In Chapters 7 and 8, we discuss specific strategies for building consensus during assessment and intervention planning. In this section, the rationale, structures and membership of AAC teams is described.

### Rationale for an AAC Team

AAC intervention decisions are based on a broad range of information. For example, information regarding the cognitive, language, sensory, and motor capabilities of the individual is required. In addition, information is needed regarding the operational, linguistic, social, and strategic competence of the individual's current communication. Information about current and future communicative contexts is important, as is information about the support system available to the potential AAC user. Also, the preferences of the AAC users, their families or guardians, and their personal advisors must be identified and respected. Few AAC specialists are capable of assessing and intervening in all these areas, and, therefore, it is nearly always necessary to involve a team of individuals to provide appropriate AAC services.

Yorkston and Karlan (1986) suggested areas of expertise appropriate for AAC teams and their roles, which are summarized in Table 6.3. The age and needs of an individual AAC user determine the specific areas of expertise likely to be needed in the AAC assessment and intervention. In addition, it is essential to involve AAC users and individuals close to them (i.e., parents, guardians, family members, and communication partners) on assessment and intervention teams. Finally, individuals who are involved in particular aspects of the AAC user's life are also critical team members. Thus, teachers, employers, residential supervisors, and other managers who will be affected by an AAC intervention should be included in the process of service delivery from the outset. This important issue is discussed in more detail in Chapter 7.

### Team Structures

Three team models are commonly used to provide AAC services: multidisciplinary, transdisciplinary, and interdisciplinary. Although these terms are often used interchangeably, they refer to models that are, in fact, quite distinct, which has important implications for service delivery.

***Multidisciplinary Team*** The concept of the multidisciplinary team concept was developed from the medical model and involves direct service delivery by several different specialists. Each specialist independently assesses the individual with a communication disorder, records the assess-

**Table 6.3.** Areas of expertise for an AAC team

| | |
|---|---|
| Speech-Language Pathology<br>  Communication sciences<br>  Normal and disordered communication<br>  Receptive and expressive language<br>  Development and disorders<br>  Alternative and augmentative aids, symbols, techniques,<br>    and strategies<br>  Management of communication interventions | Education<br>  Planning for appropriate social and academic<br>    experiences<br>  Development of cognitive/conceptual objectives<br>  Assessment of socio-communicative components<br>    in the classroom<br>  Integration of augmentative components in the<br>    classroom<br>  Development of an appropriate vocational curriculum |
| Medicine<br>  Management of therapeutic program<br>  Natural course of the disorder<br>  Medical intervention<br>  Management of medication regimes | Psychology<br>  Documentation of level of cognitive functions<br>  Selection of appropriate learning styles<br>  Estimation of learning potential |
| Physical Therapy<br>  Mobility aids<br>  Motor control and motor learning<br>  Positioning to maximize functional communication in<br>    all environments<br>  Maintenance of strength and range of motion<br>  Physical conditioning to increase flexibility, balance,<br>    and coordination | Social Services<br>  Evaluation of total living situations<br>  Identification of family and community resources<br>  Provision of information about funding options |
| Occupational Therapy<br>  Activities of daily living<br>  Positioning to maximize functional communication in<br>    all contexts<br>  Adaptive equipment<br>  Mobility aids<br>  Access to aids, computers, splints | Vocational Counseling<br>  Assessment of vocational potential<br>  Identification of vocational goals<br>  Education of co-workers<br>  Identification of augmentative components in<br>    vocational settings |
| Engineering<br>  Application and modification of existing electronic or<br>    mechanical aids and devices | Computer Technology<br>  Evaluation of software programs for potential use<br>    by clients<br>  Modification of existing software programs<br>  Developing programs to meet existing<br>    communication needs |

Adapted from Yorkston and Karlan (1986).

ment results, and makes intervention decisions appropriate to his or her specific discipline. The team members then share the assessment results and intervention plans at a team meeting, after which each team member provides direct services to the client. Thus, depending on how well-coordinated the individual service efforts are, specialists in a multidisciplinary model function to a greater or lesser extent as a true team of collaborative professionals.

**Interdisciplinary Team**    In an interdisciplinary team, professionals assess students individually as in the multidisciplinary approach; however, there is an attempt to control information fragmentation through formal communication channels (Hart, 1977). Thus, following individually conducted assessments, team members meet to discuss their individual findings and make collaborative recommendations regarding an intervention plan. However, once intervention decisions are made, the team members may not meet again until problems arise or re-evaluation is necessary, because intervention implementation may be the responsibility of one team member (e.g., a classroom teacher). Alternatively, the interdisciplinary team members may meet regularly to discuss progress and make revisions in the intervention. Yorkston and Karlan (1986) suggested that this is the most commonly used approach in the AAC field.

**Transdisciplinary Team**    The transdisciplinary model involves the transfer of information, knowledge, or skills across discipline boundaries (Hutchison, 1978). In this model, information is shared among professionals so that direct service providers become proficient in areas other than their primary specialties (Locke & Mirenda, in press). Assessment is often completed through the collaborative efforts of all team members and is followed by a team meeting to establish the goals and objectives for intervention. According to Hart (1977), once decisions are made, each team member is responsible for the care of the whole individual, rather than only one facet of his or her life.

Several levels of transdisciplinary involvement may be included within this model. *Role extension* refers to an increase in a professional's knowledge of his or her own field as he or she learns from other fields and incorporates that knowledge. *Role exchange* occurs when team members are supervised and taught skills by professionals from fields other than their own. *Role release* occurs when professionals release their traditional roles, so that all members of the team can work in a more holistic fashion. For example, teachers may be taught to conduct specific physical therapy interventions, or physical therapists may be taught to carry out communication interventions.

## Roles and Responsibilities of the AAC Team

Roles and responsibilities of individual AAC team members may vary, depending upon a number of factors. First, the team model adopted influences the nature and flexibility of members' responsibilities. For example, on a multidisciplinary team, professional roles across interventions may be quite consistent, while on inter- or transdisciplinary teams roles may shift considerably to accommodate the needs of an AAC user.

Second, the age of the individual AAC user may influence the size of the team and the roles of team members. If an AAC user receives services within a school setting, the roles of team members must be defined in terms of the education and communication program. If an AAC user is a young adult who no longer receives school-based services, the roles of team members may need to shift to support vocational or adult educational services.

Third, the disability of a specific AAC user may affect the responsibilities of individual team members. For example, if an individual's inability to speak results from a cognitive or language disorder, the composition of the team and roles of team members will be quite different than if the communication disorder results from a physical disability. Fourth, roles of team members are often influenced by the AAC user and his or her family. In some cases, the AAC user and family want to be responsible for aspects of the AAC process such as funding or ongoing instruction. In other cases, these team members may wish to take a less active role or to assume different responsibilities. As is clear in the chapters on assessment (Chapter 7) and intervention (Chapter 8), it is critically important to include AAC users and their families as active team members.

Fifth, the roles of team members are influenced by their knowledge and skills in the AAC field. Unfortunately, many professionals receive only limited instruction regarding AAC issues in pre-professional programs. Therefore, during the early years of practice, these individuals may need to rely on other team members to teach them skills in this area. As team members develop their own capabilities, their roles often change to accommodate their increased knowledge and skills.

# Chapter 7

# Principles of Assessment

In the broadest sense, the goal of AAC interventions is to assist individuals with severe communication disorders to become communicatively competent *today* in order to meet their current communication needs and to prepare them to be communicatively competent *tomorrow* in order to meet their future communication needs. AAC assessment involves the processes by which information is gathered and analyzed so that users of AAC systems and those who assist them can make informed decisions throughout the course of intervention. In this chapter, the *general principles and procedures of AAC assessment* are presented.

## AAC ASSESSMENT MODELS

### Candidacy Models

A primary goal of an AAC assessment is to determine whether an individual requires, or continues to require, AAC assistance. Initially, this might seem a trivial task, as it would seem apparent that persons who are unable to meet their daily communication needs through natural speech require AAC interventions. Nevertheless, since the 1970s, considerable controversy has been generated about candidacy for AAC services.

A review of the history of the field reveals that a variety of candidacy requirements have been in effect. Formerly, AAC assistance was provided primarily to those persons who demonstrated chronic expressive communication disorders along with relatively strong cognitive and linguistic capabilities. For example, AAC services were often provided to persons with degenerative diseases such as amyotrophic lateral sclerosis, in which the ability to speak is lost, but cognitive and linguistic functions are not impaired. Similarly, persons with spinal cord injuries were considered to be good candidates for AAC services directed toward improving their writing abilities, because their primary deficit was motoric rather than cognitive or linguistic in nature. Persons with severe speech disorders due to cerebral palsy were also considered to be appropriate candidates for AAC services at that time, *if* they demonstrated relatively intact cognitive and language skills.

Along with this, there was a tendency *not* to provide AAC systems to persons who might eventually develop natural speech. Thus, children with developmental apraxia of speech were often excluded from services, because the hope was that their phonologic abilities might improve. There was also the assumption (or fear) that if they were given AAC systems, they might not exert the effort required to become natural speakers. Similarly, adults with aphasia and individuals with traumatic brain injury were often considered to be inappropriate candidates for AAC interventions until it became clear—sometimes months or even years after their injuries—that speech recovery had failed to occur. Consequently, these individuals were deprived of the ability to communicate their wants, needs, preferences, and feelings, often during the very period of time when they were attempting to restructure their lives in order to live with their severe communication and other disabilities.

In these early years, a strong bias also existed against providing AAC services to persons with developmental cognitive limitations. Many of these individuals had severe expressive communication problems secondary to mental retardation, autism, congenital dual sensory impairments, or multiple handicaps, and their cognitive and linguistic limitations were taken as evidence that they were not appropriate candidates for AAC services. This thinking was so predominant that the service delivery guidelines of local educational agencies often imposed specific requirements of cognitive or linguistic performance before an individual could be considered an appropriate AAC candidate. This effectively excluded most individuals with moderate, severe, and profound intellectual disabilities from receiving AAC services.

## Communication Needs Models

The "candidacy" guidelines for AAC intervention have been gradually replaced by guidelines based on communication needs. These changes were due to several influences. First, the definition of AAC services was expanded to include communication strategies and technologies that could be used by individuals who were not literate—that is, those who could not type messages letter by letter. Initially, this expanded view of AAC provided communication options to persons who were preliterate, such as preschoolers (see chap. 10, this volume). In time, these options were also extended to persons who were nonliterate, such as persons with intellectual disabilities, autism, and aphasia (see chaps. 13, 14, and 17, this volume).

---

Marvin and his teacher sat facing each other on low chairs. The teacher would say, "Look at me," and Marvin would occasionally comply. The teacher would then give him a raisin to eat. After a while, the teacher began to touch some of her body parts—head, nose, and eyes—and would prompt Marvin to imitate her actions. When he did, he received a sip of juice. I asked, "Why are you doing these activities?" and the teacher replied, "To teach him the prerequisites for communication." (P. Mirenda, personal communication, June 26, 1991)

---

Second, it became increasingly clear that when people were excluded from AAC services because of "inadequate" capabilities, they were also usually excluded from the experiences, instruction, and practice necessary to improve their capabilities (Kangas & Lloyd, 1988; Reichle & Karlan, 1985). Persons so excluded worked on "perpetual readiness" activities that were hypothetically designed to teach them the "prerequisite" skills that they lacked. Most of these activities, such as learning about object permanence by finding toys hidden under towels, or learning about visual tracking by following stuffed animals moved across the line of visual regard, were nonfunctional and often age-inappropriate.

In time, the concept of prerequisite skills was abandoned, and interventions were organized to match the individual's needs and capabilities for today while building future capabilities for tomorrow (see chap. 8, this volume, for more complete discussion). As a result of these changes, candidacy for AAC is now determined based on an *individual's unmet communication needs* rather than on some profile of his or her capabilities. Beukelman, Yorkston, and Dowden (1985) described the Communication Needs Model and its goals to: 1) document the communication needs of an individual, 2) determine how many of these needs are met through current communication techniques, and 3) reduce the number of unmet communication needs through systematic AAC interventions (see also Dowden, Beukelman, & Lossing, 1986).

The Communication Needs Model works well for assessment and intervention when the communication needs of an individual are easy to define. For example, some adults with severe communication disorders have well-established life-styles with consistent support systems. They are often successful in reaching consensus, with their families and attendants, about their communicacation needs, and the resulting intervention plans can be quite straightforward as a result. Determining the communication needs of individuals with less clearly defined or with changing lifestyles is, however, more difficult. For them, the Communication Needs Model has limitations.

## Communication Participation Model

In an effort to broaden the Communication Needs Model, Beukelman and Mirenda (1988) expanded on concepts that were initially described by Rosenberg and Beukelman (1988) to guide AAC decision making and intervention. The Participation Model, shown in Figure 7.1., provides a systematic process for conducting AAC assessments and designing interventions based on functional participation requirements of nondisabled peers of the same chronological age as the potential AAC user.

In this chapter, and throughout the following chapters, the Participation Model is used to discuss assessment and intervention strategies in AAC. First, however, basic principles that underlie the Participation Model are defined and examined. These include the need for multiphase assessment and the importance of consensus building.

> Principle 1: Assessment is not a one-time process. Assess to meet today's needs, then tomorrow's, and tomorrow's, and tomorrow's. . . .

## PHASES OF AAC ASSESSMENT

AAC interventions are usually ongoing, long-term processes, because the individuals who require them usually are unable to speak or write due to chronic, rather than temporary, disabilities. The communication problems of these individuals are persistent because of severe physical, cognitive, language, and sensory impairments. Nevertheless, as AAC users mature and age, their communication needs and capabilities often change. Some people experience an expanding world with increased opportunities, while others become less able to participate as they age or as their impairments become more severe. Thus, AAC assessment and intervention is a dynamic process and usually consists of three general phases.

### Phase I: Initial Assessment for Today

The individual's current communication interaction needs and physical, cognitive, language, and sensory capabilities are assessed during this phase so that efforts to support immediate communication interaction and communication can begin. Thus, the goal of initial assessment is to gather information to design an initial intervention to match today's needs and capabilities. These initial AAC interventions usually undergo continual, subtle refinements as users learn about the operational requirements of their AAC techniques. Gradually, a basic conversational communication system is developed to facilitate interactions with family members, friends, and other persons familiar with the AAC user. Detailed discussions of useful assessment processes in the initial phase were reported by Beukelman, Yorkston, and Dowden (1985); Blackstone, Cassatt-James, and Bruskin (1988); Culp and Carlisle (1988); Goossens' and Crain (1986a); and Musselwhite and St. Louis (1988).

### Phase II: Detailed Assessment for Tomorrow

The goal of assessment for this phase is to develop a communication system for tomorrow, which is one that will support the AAC user in a variety of specialized settings, beyond the familiar ones. These settings reflect the individual's life-style, and may include school, employment, independent

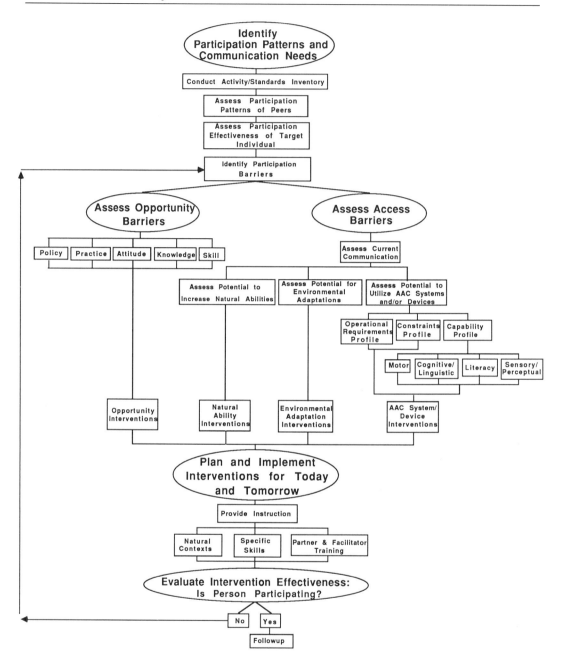

**Figure 7.1.** The Participation Model.

living, and recreation and leisure environments. Such settings require basic conversational communication and also specialized communication that matches the participation requirements of each setting. For example, a child in a classroom must have access to a system that allows academic and educational participation as well as social participation. Similarly, an adult at work might need to write and talk on the telephone as well as to converse with co-workers during break times. Thus, this phase requires careful assessment of the individual's expected participation patterns, as well as assessments to refine the basic communication system to accommodate future participation.

## Phase III: Follow-Up Assessment

Follow-up, in general, involves maintaining a comprehensive AAC system that meets the changing capabilities and life-style of the individual. Assessment in this phase may involve periodically examining communication equipment to detect replacement and repair needs, assessing the needs and abilities of communication partners and facilitators, and re-assessing the capabilities of the AAC user if his or her capabilities change. For individuals whose life-styles and capabilities are relatively stable, follow-up assessment may occur irregularly and infrequently, while for others, such as those with degenerative illnesses, follow-up assessments may be a major part of intervention planning.

> Principle 2: Early efforts to build inclusionary, cooperative teams during the assessment process may prevent problems and discord later on, or: Consensus today keeps dissension away.

## CONSENSUS BUILDING DURING ASSESSMENT

In Chapter 6, we described the team and service delivery models most commonly used in the AAC field, as well as some of the advantages and disadvantages of each. We also noted that regardless of the specific model in place, it is essential to involve the AAC user as well as family members and other significant individuals as members of the team. In fact, the commitment of the AAC user and his or her family to the overall intervention is often gained or lost during either the initial or subsequent phases of assessment. Negative consequences may result if these individuals are excluded from or ignored during assessment. First, information that is important to subsequent intervention efforts is likely to be lacking. Second, AAC users and their families may not assume "ownership" of interventions that are formulated, without their input and agreement, by others on the team. Third, distrust of the agency delivering AAC services may develop if the family is not permitted to participate in the assessment process, regardless of the quality of the evaluation or interventions. Fourth, AAC users and family members may not learn to participate as team members if they have been excluded from the assessment phase when team dynamics and interaction styles are established.

These consequences are also likely to result if team members, especially those who manage the environments in which the AAC user participates, are excluded or ignored during any assessment phase. For example, regular and special education teachers usually manage a child's educational environment, speech-language pathologists often manage the communication–conversational environment, employers manage the work environment, and residential staff may manage the living environment. One or more of these individuals is likely to be affected by any decisions made during the assessment process. Therefore, their involvement during assessment is absolutely critical in order to avoid later problems that are related to a lack of ownership or a failure to follow through with team decisions. When conflicts occur regarding an AAC intervention or the integration of a person using an AAC system in a school or work setting, the roots frequently can be traced to early failure to develop productive consensus patterns among team members. Unfortunately, it may be nearly impossible to achieve consensus once a long-standing disagreement exists regarding the needs, participation patterns, and capabilities of an AAC user.

### Strategies for Building Consensus

As is apparent from the previous discussion, effective AAC interventions involve the cooperative participation of many individuals. One major goal of initial assessment should be the development of a process for long-term consensus building and management. Consensus building and management form the basis for cooperation and compromise for subsequent intervention decisions. Implementing the process of consensus-building requires participation by all of the decision makers involved in an AAC intervention. Unfortunately, strategies for building consensus in the assessment process have received scant attention in the literature, despite the numerous studies that have documented their importance (see Locke & Mirenda, in press, for a review). Nevertheless, several aspects of consensus building are becoming more common, including:

1. *Invite the participation* of the AAC user, his or her family, other significant individuals, and the various environmental managers (i.e., teachers, employers, residential staff) early in the assessment process. These individuals should be included in addition to other professional team members.

2. *Develop strategies to encourage participation* by each team member throughout the assessment and decision-making process. For example, each member of the team might be asked to write down his or her communication priorities on a separate sheet and then to individually present these to the group. This allows less assertive members of the team to be heard before more dominant or powerful team members are able to shape or control opinions and decisions. It also discourages team members from sitting back quietly with hidden agendas.

3. *Use arena assessment strategies* that require the simultaneous presence of many team members for at least some phases of assessment. In this way, key aspects of the assessment can be completed with most of the members of the team participating. This allows simultaneous evaluation of the individual's motor, sensory, linguistic, and cognitive abilities and acknowledges the interaction of these. An obvious illustration is the need for appropriate positioning to facilitate accurate responses during the assessment of an individual's ability to use various types of symbols. Or, a vision specialist may contribute information valuable to an assessment of motor control for alternative access. In addition, intervention options can be explored and discussed by the team much more effectively in an arena setting than they can at a team meeting where the members do not have a shared frame of reference and must rely on verbal or written descriptions of assessment results.

Table 7.1. lists 10 symptoms commonly seen in AAC teams that do not practice consensus-building strategies during assessment and decision making.

## IDENTIFY PARTICIPATION PATTERNS AND COMMUNICATION NEEDS

We now return to the Participation Model depicted in Figure 7.1. The top part of the model depicts the process for describing the participation patterns and communication needs of the individual, referenced against the participation requirements made of same-age, nondisabled peers. This process is described in the sections that follow.

> Principle 3: The purpose of an AAC intervention is to facilitate meaningful participation in daily life activities.

### Conduct an Activity/Standards Inventory

The assessment of a potential AAC user's participation patterns begins with an Activity/Standards Inventory (Table 7.2.). As can be seen from this form, all specific daily activities in which the individual is required to participate, at home, school, work, or other settings, are outlined by the AAC team. Obviously, specific activities for an individual will depend on social, vocational, and educational considerations. In any case, it is important at this stage of assessment that the team members reach consensus regarding the activities included on the Activity/Standards Inventory,

**Table 7.1.**   Ten symptoms of AAC teams that do not practice consensus building

1. Parents or guardians who have not been included in the assessment or decision-making processes are asked to sign Individualized Education Programs (IEPs) or Individualized Habilitation Plans (IHPs) that delineate AAC interventions.
2. AAC users are not asked for input during assessment or intervention planning.
3. A person's new AAC system is a surprise to his or her classroom teacher, parents, or employer.
4. Although many team members attend a meeting, only a few give reports. These few team members also control the discussion so that other members are neither required nor expected to contribute their opinions or preferences.
5. A parent or guardian refers to an AAC intervention as something "they" said to do.
6. Paraprofessionals, educational aides, or direct care staff are not invited to attend team meetings.
7. A school administrator rejects an intervention plan without having attended the team meeting at which it was formulated.
8. Parents or guardians are not provided with opportunities early in the assessment process to express their opinions and preferences.
9. When parents speak at a team meeting, team members do not take notes as they do when other team members speak.
10. The members of the AAC team have never met the staff who manage the AAC user's residence or employment site.

since this list will influence the subsequent assessment process and intervention program. Furthermore, if consensus about the activities important in a person's life cannot be achieved, it will be very difficult to determine later on if the AAC intervention has been effective. (The term "standards" is used throughout this work to refer to standards of performance and does *not* imply that participation standards are based on arbitrary or norm-referenced criteria.)

## Assess the Participation Patterns of Peers

The next step of the assessment is to determine the participation patterns of peer individuals. The importance of this step varies depending on the individual of concern. For example, if the potential AAC user is a young child or an elderly adult who is involved in few regular activities outside of the home, documentation of peer participation may be inappropriate. In most cases, such as with a potential AAC user who is involved in educational, vocational training, employment, or residential settings, this step of the assessment is quite important.

Again, a form similar to that in Table 7.2. can be used to gather and record information. A peer of the same gender and approximately the same age as the individual, whose participation is representative of the desired performance in a given situation, should be selected as the model. This may necessitate several peers, depending on the environments involved in the analysis. As the participation patterns of the peer are observed and documented in each delineated activity, performance standards are based on the following criteria:

1. Independent: The peer is able to participate in the activity without human assistance.
2. Independent with Set-Up: The peer is able to participate independently once human assistance has been provided to set up the activity (e.g., art materials are laid out for an individual student, or the raw data for an engineering report are compiled for an employee).
3. Verbal Assistance: The peer is able to complete an activity if provided with verbal prompts or instruction (e.g., in an educational setting, it is very common for a teacher or educational aide to prompt students verbally as they work through a new assignment or process).
4. Physical Assistance: The peer is able to participate in an activity if provided with physical assistance (e.g., a parent or a teacher provides hand-over-hand guidance, or holds certain materials while the peer completes the activity).
5. Unable to Participate: The peer cannot or does not participate in the activity.

Accurately determining participation patterns of peer individuals is an important step in the AAC assessment process. AAC users, their teachers, co-workers, or family members may at times set unrealistic standards for an activity. For example, we know of a junior high school social studies

**Table 7.2.** Activity/standards inventory

Directions:
1. List the *primary and secondary activities* in which nondisabled peers are expected to participate.
2. Select one or more nondisabled peers who are typical in terms of their ability to achieve the expected standards. After observing one of the peers in each activity listed, indicate the *level of peer participation* achieved, by entering a "P" in the appropriate category for each activity.
3. After observing the target individual in each activity, indicate the *level of participation* achieved by entering a "T" in the appropriate category for each activity.
4. In the Discrepancy column, indicate *yes* if a participation gap exists for the target individual compared to peers, and *no* if a participation gap does not exist.
5. Based on your observations and impressions, indicate if the barrier to participation appears to be related to *opportunity barriers, access barriers, or both.*

| Activity | Level of peer participation | | | | | Discrepancy? | | Type(s) of barrier(s) | |
|---|---|---|---|---|---|---|---|---|---|
| | Independent | Independent with setup | Verbal assistance | Physical assistance | Unable to participate | Yes | No | Opportunity | Access |
| 1. | | | | | | | | | |
| 2. | | | | | | | | | |
| 3. | | | | | | | | | |
| 4. | | | | | | | | | |
| 5. | | | | | | | | | |
| 6. | | | | | | | | | |

teacher who indicated that a student in her class who had severe cerebral palsy should be prepared to attend class and to discuss the assigned readings during every class. An assessment of the peer participation patterns in the classrooms revealed that few, if any, of the peer students were prepared to discuss the readings daily, and, in fact, some of them were almost never prepared to do so. If the AAC assessment team had accepted the teacher's standard as its goal, excessively high expectations would have been placed on the student with the AAC system. Instead, the teacher, who was a member of the team, agreed to alter her expectations of the target student once the results of the peer participation analysis were presented to her.

## Assess the Participation Effectiveness of the Target Individual

When the participation standards for peer individuals have been identified, the actual participation patterns of the target individual can be assessed and documented by the team using the same criteria for performance standards. The individual may be able to participate in some activities at a level similar to the peer, and there is no participation gap in such situations. For other activities, however, discrepancies will be evident between the participation level of the peer and that of the individual. There is a space to designate whether such a discrepancy is present on the form in Table 7.2. In addition, the form encourages a preliminary assessment of the types of barriers to participation in each activity.

## Identify Participation Barriers

According to the Participation Model, failure to participate can be explained by two types of barriers—those related to opportunity and those related to access. *Opportunity barriers* refer to barriers that are imposed by persons other than the individual with the severe communication disorder and that cannot be eliminated simply by providing an AAC system or intervention. For example, an individual may be unable to participate at the desired level because of the attitudes of those around him or her, even though an appropriate AAC system has been provided. *Access barriers* are present primarily because of the current capabilities of the individual of concern or his or her immediate support system. Thus, an access barrier would be present if the individual does not participate because there is no AAC system in place, or because the vocabulary in the AAC system is outdated. Assessments aimed at identifying the source of barriers to participation are needed in order to formulate effective assessment and intervention strategies for each barrier.

> Principle 4: The mere provision of an AAC system is often not enough. Thus, identification of actual or potential opportunity barriers is a critical component of the assessment process.

## ASSESS OPPORTUNITY BARRIERS

An Opportunity Assessment can be completed using the form in Table 7.3. First, a summary of the activity inventory is listed in the left column. After observations in various environments, the assessment team meets to discuss and identify opportunity barriers that might apply to each activity. Five types of opportunity barriers (see Table 7.3.) should be considered during this assessment process.

> "Severe-profound students in our school district don't qualify for AAC services until they've reached sensorimotor stage 5. It's the school district policy" (a speech-language pathologist, 1989).

**Table 7.3.** Opportunity assessment

Directions:
1. List the activities for which potential opportunity barriers have been identified for the target individual.
2. Indicate the nature of the opportunity barrier (e.g., policy, practice, attitude, knowledge, skill).
3. Briefly describe the intervention plan and persons responsible for implementation.

| Activity | Opportunity barrier | | | | | Intervention plan and person(s) responsible |
| | Policy | Practice | Attitude | Knowledge | Skill | |
| --- | --- | --- | --- | --- | --- | --- |
| 1. | | | | | | |
| 2. | | | | | | |
| 3. | | | | | | |
| 4. | | | | | | |
| 5. | | | | | | |
| 6. | | | | | | |

## Policy Barriers

Policy barriers are the result of legislative or regulatory decisions that govern the situations in which AAC users find themselves. In schools, vocational environments, residential centers, hospitals, rehabilitation centers, and nursing homes, policies are usually outlined in the written documents that govern the agency. In less formal situations, such as the AAC user's family's home, policies may not be written but are nonetheless set by the decision makers (e.g., parents or guardians) in the environment. A wide variety of policies can be barriers to participation, and two of the most prevalent are described below.

***Segregation Policies***   Many educational agencies and school districts in North America still have policies that segregate students with disabilities into classrooms or facilities that are not shared by their nondisabled peers. In such situations, by policy, students with disabilities cannot be integrated into regular classrooms, participate in the school district's regular curriculum, or communicate regularly with friends who are nondisabled. Furthermore, since many school districts with segregation policies offer such educational programs only in "cluster sites" or special schools, students may be bussed to facilities far away from their neighborhoods. These students not only have no or limited access to nondisabled peers during the school day, but they also have no opportunities to make friends in their neighborhoods. The combination of these restrictions severely limits the communication opportunities afforded to students with disabilities. Similar situations can be found in sheltered workshops, segregated group homes or institutions, and in other "disabled-only" settings.

***Limited Use Policies***   It is still fairly common for educational agencies to limit the use of AAC systems that are purchased with school district funds. Usually, limited use policies mean that students who use AAC devices in school are not permitted to take them home after school or, in some cases, are not permitted to take them out of the school building for community-based instruction (e.g., vocational training). Thus, by policy, some students cannot use their communication systems during evenings, weekends, holidays, and summer vacations, unless the systems are purchased with nonschool funds. The opportunity barriers to participation imposed by such policies are obvious.

Similarly, limited use policies may exist in intensive care units that contain complicated and expensive equipment. In order to prevent interference with this equipment, some hospitals have stringent policies regarding other types of equipment that can be brought into intensive care units. Persons with electronic AAC devices may face opportunity barriers in some medical settings due to such policies. This situation may also exist in agencies or nursing homes that serve adult AAC users.

> "If parents ask that their handicapped child be placed in a regular classroom, we see what we can do. We cross that bridge when we come to it. It's certainly not something that we encourage, but I guess we don't really have a policy against it" (school administrator, 1990).

## Practice Barriers

While policy barriers are legislated or regulated procedures, practice barriers refer to procedures or conventions that have become common in a family, school, or workplace, but are not actual policies. The staff of an agency may think that long-standing practices are legislated policies, but a review of actual agency policies usually reveals that this is not the case. For example, it is a matter of practice in many school districts to restrict the use of district-funded AAC equipment outside the school, although this is not part of official district policy. We know of several cases in which school district representatives have told families and staff that such practices are state education department policies, although no such policies existed. The same may be true of the segregation practices of many schools or businesses. In fact, it is illegal in many countries, including the United States, to institute policies that prevent students with disabilities from attending regular classes or that prevent workers with disabilities from obtaining competitive employment. Nevertheless, there are often very strong practices in place that do not encourage or permit such participation.

Professional practices may also limit participation opportunities for persons with AAC needs. Early in the AAC field, for example, some speech-language pathologists made it their practice not to work with persons who were unable to speak, believing that this would be inappropriate, since they were trained to assist people with speech problems. Subsequently, this practice has been largely eliminated, although it may still exist as an attitude barrier posed by some individuals.

---

I had just described the summer school program of a young girl who is unable to speak and has cerebral palsy. She has an AAC system, and for 8 weeks during the previous summer she had worked for 3 hours each morning on an intensive literacy program. I explained that the program was designed to assist the student to compete at the third-grade level during the following school year. An experienced special education teacher in the audience raised her hand and indicated that she would never recommend such a summer school program for her students. "Summer is a time for socialization and fun," she said. Then she added, "We don't expect these children to be competitive students, anyway." (D. Beukelman, personal communication, April 1991)

---

## Attitude Barriers

An attitude barrier occurs when an individual, rather than an agency or establishment, presents a barrier to participation. The authors of this work were involved in a situation in which a university professor did not want to permit a student with a disability to enroll in his class. The policy of the university was clear: Persons with disabilities who had been admitted to the university were entitled to attend all classes. It was also the practice of the university to comply with this policy, even if this meant moving classes to more accessible locations. Nevertheless, an individual professor, because of his attitude toward students with disabilities, attempted to set up a barrier. Of course, he was not permitted to maintain this barrier in the face of the actual policies and practices of the institution.

The negative or restrictive attitudes that can form barriers to participation are extensive. Negative or restrictive attitudes may be held by parents, relatives, co-workers, supervisors, professionals, peers, and the general public. At times, attitude barriers are quite blatant, but, more often, they are subtle and insidious, since most people realize the social unacceptability of such views. The result of most attitudinal barriers is that family members, professional personnel, and employers have reduced expectations of persons with disabilities, resulting in limited participation opportunities. It is impossible to discuss the wide range of attitude barriers that may be present. However, the assessment process should be sensitive to attitudes that may prevent an individual with a severe communication disorder from participating in daily life activities.

---

While we were writing this book, a junior high teacher called the authors and said that her school district would be enrolling a student with a severe vision impairment at the beginning of the next school year. During a team meeting in preparation for the student's arrival, it became clear that no one in the school knew very much about the technology available for visually impaired individuals. The teacher was calling because she had volunteered to learn about this technology and identify services that might be of assistance to the team.

## Knowledge Barriers

A knowledge barrier refers to a lack of information by someone other than the AAC user that results in limited opportunities for participation. Lack of knowledge about AAC intervention options, technology, and instructional strategies often presents tremendous barriers to effective participation by individuals with disabilities. Knowledge barriers on the part of some members of the intervention team are likely to exist at some point during nearly every AAC intervention. One purpose of assessment is to identify these barriers in advance, so that information can be provided in order to eliminate or minimize them.

> "Where is Steven's communication device?" I asked. "In the closet," his group home supervisor replied sheepishly. "No one knows how to turn it on since Marge left last year. I guess we should have called sooner, but we were so embarrassed. . . ."

## Skill Barriers

Skill barriers may exist for individuals who assist AAC users. Numerous technical and interaction skills are often necessary to assist someone to become a competent communicator. It is important to assess the skill level of individuals who will be responsible for various aspects of the AAC user's intervention plan, in order to identify skill deficits and to design interventions to reduce these barriers to communicative competence.

## ASSESS ACCESS BARRIERS

In the Participation Model (Figure 7.1.), barriers to access pertain to the capabilities, attitudes, and resource limitations of potential AAC users themselves, rather than to limitations of their societies or support systems. Many types of access barriers could interfere with an individual's participation. Although access barriers related to communication are of primary importance in this book, it is important to remember that access barriers might also be related to mobility (i.e., the inability to move around), manipulation (i.e., the inability to hold and manage objects), cognition (i.e., problems with cognitive functions and decision making), and sensory perceptual factors (i.e., vision, hearing, or touch impairments). The purpose of an AAC access assessment is to identify the nature and extent of the potential AAC user's capabilities as they relate to communication.

> Principle 5: Everyone *can* communicate. Everyone *does* communicate.

## Assess Current Communication

It is important to remember that everyone communicates in some fashion. Thus, the initial step in assessing communication access is to determine the effectiveness and the nature of the individual's current communication system.

Profiles for assessing and documenting the individual's communication abilities and techniques are provided in Table 7.4. and Figure 7.2. Table 7.4. helps the AAC team gather information about different communication techniques, since most individuals use a variety of techniques as part of an overall communication package. The assessment of current communication focuses on two aspects of communicative competence: *operational* and *social*. Some individuals have a very difficult time using a particular communication technique. For example, a child may be unable to use eye gaze consistently, or an adult with aphasia may be unable to write legibly with a standard pen or pencil. Some individuals, however, may be operationally competent and yet not be socially

**Table 7.4.** Current communication techniques

Directions:

1. List all of the various *techniques* the target individual currently uses to communicate. *Examples:* natural speech, vocalizations, gestures, body language, manual signs, pointing to a communication board with pictures, eye gaze to photographs, scanning with _____ device, typing on a typewriter, headlight pointing to _____ device.
2. Describe the *body part* used for each technique listed (e.g., both eyes, right hand, left thumb, right side of head).
3. Describe any unique *adaptations* needed for each technique (e.g., must sit on Mom's lap, uses keyguard, needs to have eye gaze chart held 6 inches from face).
4. After observing use of the technique, *rate* the person's *operational competence* (1 = poor, 5 = excellent). (Operational competence is the person's ability to use the technique *accurately and efficiently* over time without becoming fatigued.)
5. After observing and interacting with the person, *rate* his or her *social competence* (1 = poor, 5 = excellent). (Social competence is the person's ability to use the technique in an interactive, socially appropriate manner.)

| Technique | Body part | Adaptations | Operational competence<br>Poor 1  2  3  4  Excellent 5 | Social competence<br>Poor 1  2  3  4  Excellent 5 |
|---|---|---|---|---|
| 1. | | | | |
| 2. | | | | |
| 3. | | | | |
| 4. | | | | |
| 5. | | | | |
| 6. | | | | |

| | | Not at all | | | | Very much | | Context-specific comments |
|---|---|---|---|---|---|---|---|---|
| **Expression of needs and wants** | | | | | | | | |
| | Overall | 1 | 2 | 3 | 4 | 5 | NA | |
| | Home | 1 | 2 | 3 | 4 | 5 | NA | |
| | School | 1 | 2 | 3 | 4 | 5 | NA | |
| | Work | 1 | 2 | 3 | 4 | 5 | NA | |
| Other _____ | | 1 | 2 | 3 | 4 | 5 | NA | |
| Other _____ | | 1 | 2 | 3 | 4 | 5 | NA | |
| **Sharing information** | | | | | | | | |
| | Overall | 1 | 2 | 3 | 4 | 5 | NA | |
| | Home | 1 | 2 | 3 | 4 | 5 | NA | |
| | School | 1 | 2 | 3 | 4 | 5 | NA | |
| | Work | 1 | 2 | 3 | 4 | 5 | NA | |
| Other _____ | | 1 | 2 | 3 | 4 | 5 | NA | |
| Other _____ | | 1 | 2 | 3 | 4 | 5 | NA | |
| **Social closeness** | | | | | | | | |
| | Overall | 1 | 2 | 3 | 4 | 5 | NA | |
| | Home | 1 | 2 | 3 | 4 | 5 | NA | |
| | School | 1 | 2 | 3 | 4 | 5 | NA | |
| | Work | 1 | 2 | 3 | 4 | 5 | NA | |
| Other _____ | | 1 | 2 | 3 | 4 | 5 | NA | |
| Other _____ | | 1 | 2 | 3 | 4 | 5 | NA | |
| **Social etiquette routines** | | | | | | | | |
| | Overall | 1 | 2 | 3 | 4 | 5 | NA | |
| | Home | 1 | 2 | 3 | 4 | 5 | NA | |
| | School | 1 | 2 | 3 | 4 | 5 | NA | |
| | Work | 1 | 2 | 3 | 4 | 5 | NA | |
| Other _____ | | 1 | 2 | 3 | 4 | 5 | NA | |
| Other _____ | | 1 | 2 | 3 | 4 | 5 | NA | |

**Figure 7.2.** Communication interaction effectiveness.

competent with a specific technique. For example, an individual might be able to operate an electronic communication device but never uses it to initiate interactions. Therefore, when assessing the current communication system, it is necessary to rate both the individual's operational and social competence for each technique currently used.

Figure 7.2. helps the team gather information about *what* the individual currently communicates. This form is deliberately open ended, so that the team can supply the communicative functions of interest to the individual. Nevertheless, efforts should be made to compile information in all four of the areas outlined, through observation, interview, or both.

The potential of various solutions to the existing communication barriers can be assessed, when the current communication system and how it is used have been described. One solution might be to increase the person's natural communication abilities, as discussed briefly in the following section.

## Assess Potential To Increase Natural Abilities

Many individuals with severe communication disorders demonstrate some ability to communicate using natural speech. Functionally, the effectiveness of natural speech for communicative interaction can be divided into five levels:

1. The individual can convey messages through vocalizations (to signal attention, discomfort, pain, or pleasure).
2. The individual can say a few intelligible words or phrases.
3. The individual can convey brief messages, if listeners are aware of the topic or the context of the messages.

4.  The individual can communicate extensive messages, but requires assistance to resolve communication breakdowns.
5.  The individual can communicate extensive messages with few communication breakdowns.

During the assessment process, it is important to consider the role of natural speech in an individual's communication system and to predict the role of natural speech in the future. Unfortunately, it is beyond the scope of this chapter to provide detailed information regarding the assessment of natural speech potential, since such assessment varies considerably depending on the specific speech impairment. In Part II of this book, a number of these specific situations are addressed (e.g., developmental apraxia of speech, speech impairments secondary to traumatic brain injury). Because all AAC teams should include a speech-language pathologist, these professionals are responsible for completing a natural speech assessment and for clarifying for the AAC team the role that natural speech may play in the overall communication system.

## Assess Potential for Environmental Adaptations

> The authors observed a young girl who used an electric wheelchair and a communication board that did not have voice output. An attempt was being made to integrate this child into a busy preschool classroom in which most of the children were not disabled. The teacher was experiencing difficulty during "circle time" as the children gathered around her to discuss the calendar, weather, and the schedule for the day. Because the nondisabled children could move quickly, they would cluster around the teacher, who was seated with her back to a wall. By the time the disabled student approached the group with her wheelchair, there was no way for her to make her way through the crowd. Thus, she was always positioned at the back of the class and off to the side, with relatively poor access to instructional materials and few opportunities to communicate. After assessing the communication barrier in this situation, the staff decided to institute a number of environmental adaptations. The teacher began to position herself in the center of the room and had the children sit on a rug in front of her. In this configuration, the disabled student was able to drive her wheelchair around the cluster of students and position herself alongside the teacher, close to her peers. This allowed her to use her communication board successfully and to be near the instructional center of the class.

Environmental adaptations may be successful and relatively simple solutions to communication access barriers. As illustrated in the above example, such adaptations may include altering physical spaces or locations, or altering physical structures themselves. Assessment of the need for such adaptations is a commonsense process and can almost always be determined by observation in problematic situations.

## Assess Potential To Utilize AAC Systems or Devices

In the Participation Model (Figure 7.1.), three assessments determine an individual's ability to use AAC systems or devices in order to reduce access barriers. These include: an operational requirements profile, a constraints profile, and a capability profile.

*Operational Requirements Profile* Often, either low tech (nonelectronic) or high tech (electronic) techniques will need to be instituted to reduce the existing access barriers to communication. Thus, it is necessary to identify which of the many AAC device options may be appropriate. The first step is to become familiar with the operational requirements of the various AAC techniques. For example, there may be display requirements regarding the size, array, and number of items in the selection set. There are always alternative access system requirements regarding the motor and sensory interface between the individual and the device, so that the device can be operated accurately and efficiently. In addition, the output provided by the device may require the individual to have certain skills or abilities. Readers are referred to Chapters 2, 3, 4, and 5 for descriptions of the operational and learning requirements of many AAC options.

> Principle 6: Technology alone does not make a competent communicator any more than a piano makes a musician or a basketball and a hoop make an athlete.

**Constraints Profile**   Practical issues, aside from those directly related to potential AAC users and techniques, may influence the selection of an AAC system and the strategies for instruction. Such constraints should be identified early in the assessment process so that subsequent decisions do not conflict with the constraints and so that efforts can be made to reduce them whenever possible. The most common constraints are those related to: 1) user and family preferences, 2) the attitudes of other communication partners, 3) the abilities of partners and facilitators, and 4) funding.

*User and Family Preferences*   Undoubtedly, the most important constraints that must be assessed are those related to user and family preferences (Blackstone, 1989b; Norris & Belair, 1988). These may include concerns about: 1) system portability, durability, and appearance (i.e., cosmesis); 2) time and skills required to learn the system (this may be particularly relevant for manual sign and high tech approaches); 3) quality and intelligibility of synthetic speech output; and 4) the "naturalness" of the communication exchange achieved through the system. For example, some users and families may prefer to use low tech AAC approaches (e.g., gestures, alphabet boards) because they feel that these techniques allow greater social closeness and are less cumbersome than are electronic devices (Harris, 1982). Some users and their families have strong negative reactions to technological solutions for other reasons, such as the amount of learning time or physical effort that may be required (see chap. 1, this volume). Family members may express hesitation at assuming the extra maintenance of a high tech system, or may be averse to the robotic speech of some devices, though this problem has been greatly reduced with increased availability of high quality speech output. While some AAC users may be unable to express their preferences as straightforwardly as others, careful observation of affective, motor, and other behaviors are usually good indicators in this regard (Campbell, 1989).

It is not at all uncommon to find that family members and potential users do not share the same concerns or preferences. For example, one parent of a child with a communication disorder may be very interested in an electronic AAC option, while the other parent may strongly prefer a low tech approach. The basis for such disagreements may come from a variety of sources. One individual may be more experienced with technology than the other, or one of the parties involved may be lured by the magic of technology, regardless of its appropriateness to a given situation.

Potential users and their families may be completely negative about using AAC techniques of any kind. This most often occurs in one of three situations. First, the parents of young children may be biased against AAC because they are worried that natural speech will not develop if an alternative option is available. (In Chapter 8, we detail suggestions for consensus building in this situation.) Second, resistance to AAC options may occur among the families of elderly persons. For example, it is often very difficult for the spouse and children of an elderly individual to accept the sudden onset of communication impairments secondary to stroke. In this situation, family members may reject AAC options because of a strong desire that their spouse or parent regain the use of natural speech. At other times, concerned individuals reject certain electronic options because they just can't imagine their elderly relative operating a system that produces artificial speech. (Readers are referred to Chapter 17 for more extensive discussion of this issue.) Third, individuals may reject AAC options when they are overwhelmed with a medical situation. For example, some individuals do not wish to attempt alternative forms of communication in an intensive care unit, even if they cannot communicate important information because of a temporary absence of speech. It often seems that such individuals simply do not have the cognitive or emotional resources that are needed to acquire simple operational skills in the midst of high levels of existing stress. (This situation is discussed in more detail in Chapter 19.)

In an assessment of constraints, it is important to help potential users and their families identify their preferences and attitudes concerning various AAC options so that these can be considered during the subsequent decision making. Sensitivity and attention through consensus building are critical in an assessment of constraints, even if this means that the final assistive device decision is less than perfect from the perspective of the AAC professionals on the team. After all, it is the AAC user and his or her family, usually, who will have to live with whatever decision is made. Failure to consider user and family preferences will almost certainly result in the widespread lament: He or she has this great system/device but hardly ever uses it! (Creech, Kissick, Koski, & Musselwhite, 1988).

*Preferences and Attitudes of Other Communication Partners*    Less important than user and family preferences, but still of concern, are the preferences and attitudes of other individuals with whom an AAC user either regularly or occasionally interacts. Little research exists in this area, although a few studies have sought to empirically measure the influence of various communication techniques on the perceptions of unfamiliar communication partners. Nonhandicapped subjects in these studies typically have watched videotapes of interactions between an AAC user and a natural speaker and have rated their perceptions or attitudes along a number of dimensions. For example, a study indicated that college-age young adults had less favorable attitudes about an AAC user of a low tech (i.e., alphabet board) system than one who used a high tech (i.e., voice output) device, regardless of whether they were provided with written information about the AAC users (Gorenflo & Gorenflo, 1991). Persons with previous personal exposure to AAC users have displayed the opposite preference pattern, however, preferring low tech devices because they allowed more active involvement in the communication process (Mathy-Laikko & Coxson, 1984).

Other studies examined observer attitudes about AAC users themselves. Blockberger, Armstrong, O'Connor, and Freeman (1990) reported the results of the only available study of children's attitudes in this regard. In this study, children rated videotaped scenes of a peer using aided electronic, aided nonelectronic, and unaided (i.e., manual sign) systems. The results indicated that regardless of the type of system used by the target peer, fourth-grade children gave similar estimates of her chronological age and school grade and responded similarly to an attitude measure of social acceptability. This is in contrast to a report suggesting that adult unaided AAC users are often perceived by nondisabled adults as less competent than are aided high tech users (Gorenflo & Gorenflo, 1991). Clearly, much educational work and advocacy remains to be done to change perceptions such as those reflected in the latter report. In addition, information about attitudes of communication partners from various cultural, ethnic, and socioeconomic backgrounds is needed in order to consider these preferences realistically and sensitively. At present, assessment of communication partner attitudes is generally completed on an informal basis from interviews and observations.

*Abilities of Communication Partners and Facilitators*    Assessment of the general abilities of potential communication partners is also essential since it is imperative that they be able to understand the messages conveyed through a communication system. For example, if the system output cannot be readily understood by unfamiliar listeners, as may be the case with manual signs or low quality synthetic speech, frequent communication breakdowns will occur (see chap. 5, this volume). Other constraints that may guide the selection of one system over another are the ages and literacy skills of potential partners and other display-related issues (see chap. 2, this volume). At present, commonsense considerations such as these guide the assessment of partner abilities, because the field has accumulated little empirical research investigating the impact of such issues on communicative competence.

Partners affect communication in other ways as well. Literature in the AAC field abounds with empirical studies of interactions between users and partners. These studies clearly indicate that the skills of partners are at least as critical as those of users in creating successful communicative exchanges (e.g., Higginbotham, Mathy-Laikko, & Yoder, 1988; Kraat, 1985). Facilitators, those who provide extensive support to AAC users by virtue of either their family or professional roles, play a unique role during initial and long-term intervention. The knowledge and skills of these individuals frequently must exceed those needed to interact with natural speakers. For example, it is not uncommon to find that facilitators are operationally competent in the programming, use, and maintenance of the user's electronic AAC device. Facilitators must also demonstrate social and strategic competence with AAC techniques in order to provide good models and instruction to the users they support. For these reasons, lack of adequate facilitator skills may place constraints on the intervention selected, simply because the necessary, ongoing expertise is unavailable. Failure to specifically consider adequate facilitator skills in the assessment process will almost always result in implementation failure later on, and this is especially true for more demanding high tech devices.

Unfortunately, few assessment tools for evaluating the capabilities of potential facilitators are in widespread use. One exception is a simple rating scale designed by Culp and Carlisle (1988) that can be used to evaluate facilitator attitudes and knowledge concerning AAC techniques. Selected items from the Partner Rating Scale are provided in Figure 7.3. In lieu of such instruments, the AAC team must evaluate facilitator expertise more informally.

In addition, several later chapters in this book extensively discuss the role of communication partners and facilitators in AAC applications. For example, Chapter 8 discusses some general principles for facilitator training, and Chapter 10 discusses these issues specifically for young children. Chapter 13 relates to persons with severe intellectual disabilities, Chapter 14 addresses persons with autism, and Chapter 17 discusses the assessment and training of partners and facilitators for adults who have severe aphasia.

*Funding*    The funding of AAC technology and intervention services is a complex process within and across countries. As the AAC field has moved into the public policy phase of development, the funding base to cover AAC services and equipment has shifted and expanded. In some countries with nationalized (i.e., centralized) health and social service systems, the shift to a public policy phase has meant the inclusion of new groups of people eligible to receive support for AAC services and the development of service delivery capacities to meet the needs of these individuals. In such instances, increased funding support has generally accompanied the authorization of new service delivery programs.

---

Directions:
The partner is asked to use the following scale to respond to all questions:
Strongly disagree, disagree, neutral, agree, strongly agree

1. I like _____ (AAC user's name) to use his/her _____ (augmentative technique).

2. Other people like _____ (AAC user's name) to use his/her _____ (augmentative technique).

3. I feel good about the way _____ (AAC user's name) uses his/her _____ (augmentative technique).

4. I think it is important for _____ (AAC user's name) to use his/her _____ (augmentative technique).

5. I understand how to use _____ (AAC user's name)'s _____ (augmentative technique).

6. When using _____ (augmentative technique), _____ (AAC user's name) can say most things he/she wants to say.

7. When _____ (AAC user's name) uses the _____ (augmentative technique), he/she can make most people understand.

8. Using the _____ (augmentative technique) may improve _____ (AAC user's name)'s speech.

9. The rewards for using _____ (augmentative technique) justify my efforts to do so.

10. _____ (AAC user's name)'s present augmentative technique(s) suits his or her current needs and abilities.

---

**Figure 7.3.**   Selected items from the Partner Rating Scale (based on Culp & Carlisle, 1988).

In contrast, in countries with decentralized or individualized health and social programs, funding patterns are more difficult to summarize because they are so diverse. Thus, it is simply impossible to cover this adequately in a book such as this. An excellent resource is *The Many Faces of Funding* (Hofmann, 1988), which describes procedures and strategies for AAC funding in the United States, an example of a country with decentralized funding.

It may be helpful to develop a funding profile for an individual AAC user by using the forms contained in Figure 7.4. and Table 7.5. when attempting to locate AAC funding in a decentralized system. The Funding Sources Checklist (Figure 7.4.) can be used to identify potential funding sources available to an individual AAC user. The Personal Funding Worksheet (Table 7.5.) contains intervention activities and potential funding sources for each activity. These two tools can be used together to develop funding strategies that vary, depending on the individual AAC user's age and available support services.

First, we will consider a kindergarten-age child in a school district with an AAC program. In this case, the AAC referral will probably be managed by the school district. The assessment and evaluation will also be funded by the district, and these, most likely, will be completed by school district personnel, perhaps with the assistance of a consultant. In difficult cases, a child might be referred by the school district to a regional specialty center, with the school district assuming the costs. Any resulting AAC prescription and report will probably be funded as part of the evaluation process. The actual procurement of necessary equipment, however, may or may not be supported by the school district. If it is not, health insurance, social service, or other agencies will need to be approached for funding support in this area. Finally, intervention training for the student will probably be delivered directly by school district personnel, although it would not be uncommon for the school district to enlist the services of a consultant to prepare school staff to provide this training.

Now, let's consider a 45-year-old individual with amyotrophic lateral sclerosis. The referral for services in this case will probably be made by the individual, a family member, or the primary physician. Assessment, evaluation, and prescription of an AAC program will probably be completed by a regional specialty center or by a professional in private practice. These services will probably be paid for, at least in part, by the individual's health insurance company or by a social agency. Individuals who do not have such support may need to use personal finances or obtain community support. The purchase of needed technical equipment may be difficult for this adult, because there may be no social agency responsible for this individual's equipment. The person's health insurance company may or may not support the purchase of equipment, depending on a variety of factors. If a funding request is rejected by an insurance agency, it may be necessary to prepare an appeal or to enlist the assistance of a social agency. As a last resort, the family may need to seek community funding of some type for the AAC equipment. Similarly, funding for intervention training may or may not be covered by insurance or social agencies. Thus, such support may simply be lacking, or it may have to be paid for with private funds.

As is obvious from this discussion, patterns of funding vary tremendously from individual to individual. The following general steps are recommended as an approach to developing a funding strategy for an individual client:

1.  Survey the funding resources that are potentially available to the individual (Figure 7.4.).
2.  Identify potential funding sources for the various activities in an AAC intervention (Table 7.5.).
3.  Prepare a funding plan with the AAC user and family members.
4.  Assign responsibility to specific individual(s) for pursuing funding for each aspect of the AAC intervention.
5.  Prepare necessary documentation for the funding request. Be sure to make all requests in writing so a written record is available if an appeal is necessary.

**Patient Name** _____

Address _____

City _____ State ____ Zip _____

Telephone _____

Patient status:      ____ Mother

                      ____ Father

                      ____ Son

                      ____ Daughter

_____ Other (specify)

Sex:  M  F  Year of birth _____

Disability/medical diagnosis:

_____

Time of onset: Birth _____

If later: Year _____

**Family status:**

| | Employed? | Where? (name of employer) | Group insurance | Name of insurance co. |
|---|---|---|---|---|
| Mother | Y  N | _____ | Y  N | _____ |
| Father | Y  N | _____ | Y  N | _____ |
| Other _____ | Y  N | _____ | Y  N | _____ |

Any family insurance?  Y  N

If yes: (name of carrier) _____

Anyone member of a labor union?  Y  N

If yes: Who? _____

What union? _____

**Patient education:**

Attending school?  Y  N  If yes: Elementary ____  HS ____  College ____  Other _____

**Patient employment:**

| | Where? (name of employer) | Dates employed From | To | Group insurance |
|---|---|---|---|---|
| Employed?  Y  N | _____ | ____ | ____ | Y  N |
| Ever Employed?  Y  N | _____ | ____ | ____ | Y  N |

**Public services provided to date:**

____ Medicare

____ Medicaid

____ Veterans Administration

____ Education for Handicapped PL 94-142/Section 504

____ Vocational rehabilitation

____ Crippled children's services (CCS)

____ Other (specify) _____

**Steps toward seeking funding:**

File applications with:

  1.  Public services provided

  2.  Group insurance or private insurance

  3.  Labor union membership

If the foregoing do not provide funding, investigate nonpublic programs:

  Corporate foundations—investigate local offices of large corporations

  Local businesses with benevolent funds for community programs

  Private foundations

  Volunteer agencies: Kiwanis, Rotary, Lion's International, United Cerebral Palsy, Sertoma, Bell Telephone Pioneers of America, Elks, Knights of Columbus, Soropt i mists, Optimists, ALS, Churches—especially patient's affiliation, Advocacy groups for help/direction—Write for name of local representative: Closer Look, Box 1492, Washington, DC 20013; Pilot Parents, 3212 Dodge Street, Omaha, NE 68131

  © Phonic Ear Handvoice/Vois

**Figure 7.4.**  Funding Sources Checklist. (From Hofmann, A. [1988]. The many faces of funding. In *Phonic Ear, Inc.,* 3380 Cypress Dr., Petaluma, CA 94954; reprinted by permission.)

**Table 7.5.**  Personal Funding Worksheet

| Funding source | AAC intervention activities | | | |
|---|---|---|---|---|
| | Assessment/ prescription | Equipment purchase | System personalization | Instruction and follow-up |
| Adult service agency | | | | |
| Adoption/foster care agency | | | | |
| Community organizations | | | | |
| Disability organizations | | | | |
| Employer | | | | |
| Legal settlement | | | | |
| Long-term disability insurance | | | | |
| Medicaid | | | | |
| Medicare | | | | |
| Parent/family/self | | | | |
| Private health insurance | | | | |
| School | | | | |
| State agency | | | | |
| Vocational rehabilitation | | | | |
| Other: | | | | |

6.  If the initial request is denied, appeal (with the AAC user's permission) for reconsideration or identify new funding sources.
7.  Proceed to a hearing (with the AAC user's permission) if appeals are denied or identify new funding sources.

Despite careful planning, families and potential users may have to wait to receive services while funding is sought (Beukelman, Yorkston, & Smith, 1985). Similarly, after the assessment process is completed and assistive device decisions have been made, an AAC user may face a lengthy wait while additional third-party payment for the device is secured. Unless private funds are readily accessible, the "least dangerous assumption" (Donnellan, 1984) with regard to funding is that such time lags will occur. Therefore, the AAC team must plan during assessment to: 1) institute an interim system or device; 2) seek minor funding for equipment rental, which itself may take considerable time to obtain; 3) use an equipment loan service if one is available; and 4) arrive at some creative solution to this constraint. Federal funds available in response to the Americans with Disabilities Act of 1990 and the Technology-Related Assistance for Individuals with Disabilities Act of 1988 should allow states to develop cohesive and coordinated interagency plans for funding AAC devices and systems.

> Principle 7: A primary purpose of AAC assessment is to identify strengths and abilities, not weaknesses and deficits.

**Capability Profile**   Capability profiling (i.e., assessment) is the process of gathering information about the capabilities of an individual in a variety of areas in order to determine the appropriate AAC options. Capability assessment is considered in two ways in this book. In this chapter, some general principles for constructing a capability profile will be presented. In Chapters 10–19, specific capability assessment considerations for persons with various disabilities are reviewed.

According to Yorkston and Karlan (1986), capability assessment involves identification of an individual's level of performance in critical areas that pertain to AAC intervention, such as cognition, language, literacy, and fine motor control. The result of such an assessment should be a profile of the individual's capabilities that can be matched to operational requirements of particular AAC options. One of the characteristics of a capability profile is that it emphasizes an individual's strengths and unique skills, rather than his or her deficits. A "strengths" approach is critical to the endeavor, because it is these strengths that will be matched to one or more AAC techniques. Basically, there are two or three approaches to capability profiling that might be considered by the AAC team.

*Maximal Assessment*   Most AAC specialists have been trained in a maximal, or comprehensive, assessment approach. The goal of this approach is to construct a comprehensive profile of, for example, an individual's receptive language level, reading level, and motoric capabilities. Examples of broad-based comprehensive assessment tools include the Comprehensive Screening Tool for Determining Optimal Communication Mode (House & Rogerson, 1984) and The Nonspeech Test (Huer, 1983).

Maximal assessment is a time consuming task for the target individual and the professional staff involved. Maximal assessment often results in a great deal of information about the person's capabilities, only a small portion of which is actually used to make AAC intervention decisions. For these reasons, maximal assessment strategies are often unnecessary and impractical for AAC applications and have been replaced by criteria-based assessment.

---

Principle 8: Less is more.

---

*Criteria-Based Assessment*   Criteria-based assessment is used if a client meets the performance thresholds necessary for successful operation of specific communication techniques or devices. The Non-Oral Communication Assessment (Fell, Linn, & Morrison, 1984) and the Assessment for Non-Oral Communication (Mills & Higgins, 1983) are representative of such assessment packages. Yorkston and Karlan (1986) described this approach in detail:

> The team frequently has at its disposal some basic information regarding the client. This information is usually obtained through a screening procedure that may involve a survey of the broad areas of cognitive and language function, hearing, and speech as well as environmental factors. Based on this screening, a decision is generally made not to conduct a comprehensive assessment. For example, when the goal of assessment is to select a portable writing/text editing system for an individual who has successfully attended a community college, in-depth assessment to identify the specific grade level in spelling or grammatical composition may not be necessary.
>
> The criteria-based assessment approach is used to expedite assessment because it is based on a series of branching decisions that allow the team to exclude a large number of possible questions and proceed to critical decisions. For example, when selecting the most appropriate interface by which an individual can access an augmentative communication device, one of the first questions asked is, "Can this individual access the aid in a direct selection mode?" If the answer is no, then a number of scanning options are explored in more detail. However, if the answer is yes, then a large number of scanning options are eliminated from consideration, and attention is focused on selecting the most appropriate direct selection option. (pp. 175–176)

From this description, it should be clear that criteria-based assessment requires the professionals involved in the process to work together when gathering information and making decisions. Thus, criteria-based assessments are often best conducted with a model that uses arena assessment strategies, as discussed previously in this chapter.

*Predictive Assessment*   Yorkston and Karlan (1986) suggested predictive profiling as an extension of the criteria-based approach. Capabilities of the individual are first assessed using a number of carefully selected tasks in predictive assessment. Based on this information, the AAC team *predicts* the efficiency with which the individual might utilize one or more devices or techniques. Predictive profiling requires that AAC team members be knowledgeable and experienced about the operational and learning requirements of a wide variety of AAC options. Nevertheless, the advantage of this approach is that, based on the predictions, the team can often arrange for short-term acquisition of the most promising equipment for a trial period. If the AAC team does not use predictive profiling, it is often necessary to have many AAC options available at the assessment or later, so that successive trials can be completed with each device. In many settings, such equipment availability is simply impossible.

When the team has decided which capability assessment approach will be used, the specific assessment strategies will depend on the individual's age, disability, and other factors. Some of the assessment strategies used most frequently are described briefly in the sections that follow.

## ASSESS SPECIFIC CAPABILITIES

### Limitations of Norm-Referenced Standardized Tests

Many professionals in fields such as psychology, education, and speech-language pathology have been trained to use norm-referenced tests designed to compare an individual's abilities to those of same-age peers. These professionals may be frustrated when they attempt to evaluate persons who require AAC systems, because they cannot administer the norm-referenced tests in a standardized manner. For example, tests that require verbal responses cannot be used if the individual is unable to speak. Tests that require object manipulation may be useless with persons who have upper extremity impairments. Even instruments that incorporate multiple choice formats, which often can be used to assess persons with limited speech and motor abilities, may not be able to be completed within standard time limitations.

Fortunately, AAC assessment rarely requires that norm-referenced tests be administered in a standardized manner, because the purpose of the assessment is *not* to compare the individual to peers of the same age. Thus, many professionals use norm-referenced tests for AAC assessments when they contain appropriate content and simply modify them to obtain capability or predictive profiling information. For example, some individuals may require response options to be presented in a yes/no format instead of in an open-ended or multiple choice array. Many formal language assessment instruments can be adapted for use with persons who have poor upper extremity use and need to use eye gaze or other alternative techniques to respond (for adaptations see Bigge, 1991; Goossens' & Crain, 1986a; Johnson-Martin, Wolters, & Sowers, 1987; and Wasson, Tynan, & Gardiner, 1982).

Although standardized tests usually are not necessary for AAC assessment, there are certainly situations in which educational or similar agencies require standardized test administrations in order to verify client eligibility for services. This is one of the most frustrating aspects of agency policy and practice for those who serve persons with severe communication disorders. Frequently, these "verification" tests simply cannot be administered in a standardized fashion to AAC users, and, at times, persons with AAC systems do not receive services because of this. This is an excellent example of a policy and practice barrier to communication opportunity that the AAC team may need to address. Professionals, AAC users, their families, and involved individuals may need to advocate to change such policies or practices so that service availability is not limited by this barrier.

> Principle 9: The goal of motor assessment in AAC is to discover motor capabilities, not to describe motor deficits.

## Assess Motor Capabilities

The purpose of the motor assessment is to determine the mobility, manipulation (i.e., fine motor), and other capabilities that can be used in alternative access. (At this point, readers might wish to review the alternative access options presented in Chapter 4.) Generally, there are two approaches to indicate items from the selection display: direct selection and scanning. The initial task of a motor assessment is to gather relevant information to determine which general approach is most appropriate. The philosophy of the AAC team influences the depth and detail of this portion of the assessment. Some teams prefer a maximal assessment strategy, in which they assess the voluntary control of all sites of the body that might be utilized for alternative access (e.g., Lee & Thomas, 1990). More often, the team will use a criteria-based assessment to determine if an individual can access an AAC system through a direct selection technique. Regardless of the approach, several assessment activities are usually undertaken.

*Posture/Positioning*     It is possible to grossly underestimate an individual's motor capabilities if the individual is not properly positioned and supported. First, therefore, the individual's positioning should be optimized so that motor control capability can be assessed. This does *not* mean that all AAC assessments should be delayed until the optimum wheelchair or seating insert has been developed to assist an individual's posture. Rather, it means that the team members who are experts in physical posturing and control should be prepared to at least temporarily position the individual so that an appropriate motor assessment can be completed. Perhaps in no other area is the interdisciplinary team more necessary than during this initial phase of the motor assessment.

*Direct Selection*     "Direct selection techniques can be more efficient for individuals with sufficient motor control, and are generally preferred to scanning selection techniques" (Lee & Thomas, 1990, p. 98). Therefore, motor assessment usually focuses first on direct selection, and scanning assessment is initiated only if the AAC user's control of direct selection options is inaccurate, very slow, or fatiguing. Although the philosophy stated above is quite prevalent in the AAC field, a word of caution is in order. As more and more AAC devices are manufactured with both scanning and direct selection options, many AAC users can incorporate both into their systems. For example, some AAC users communicate using direct selection in the morning but change to scanning in the afternoon or evening when they are tired. Other AAC users are able to use a direct selection technique when they are properly positioned in wheelchairs, and they control their communication systems or computers through scanning when they are in bed or in other types of chairs.

An assessment of direct selection capabilities generally occurs in the following order (Lee & Thomas, 1990): 1) assessment of hand and arm control, 2) assessment of head and orofacial control, and 3) assessment of foot and leg control. Upper limbs are assessed first because the hand potentially provides the most discrete control and has the greatest social acceptance as an alternative access site. Second, head, neck, and orofacial movements (e.g., eye pointing and head pointing) may be used but often interfere with natural movements and actions. Third, foot and leg control is usually assessed last, because few individuals with physical impairments have the necessary fine motor control of their lower extremities needed for direct selection techniques.

The form in Table 7.6. has been developed to collect and summarize the information from a direct selection survey. Some of the techniques that may be used to gather this information are summarized in the sections that follow.

*Observation and Interview*     First, an assessment of direct selection capabilities is usually begun by observing the individual for a period of time to determine the types of movements he or she makes during communication or other routine activities. Interviews with the individual, family members, caregivers, and others will also provide information about current movement patterns and activities. For example, some individuals may already point with their hands or their eyes to indicate items of choice. Such information is useful in guiding the assessment.

**Table 7.6.** Direct selection survey

| Movement pattern | Direct selection device | Adaptations used (e.g., splint, textured surface, keyguard) | Target (size, number, distance/orientation to body) | Times hit/missed target | Negative impact (e.g., muscle tone, reflexes, postures, fatigue) | Comments |
|---|---|---|---|---|---|---|
| Right upper limb | | | | | | |
| Left upper limb | | | | | | |
| Head/neck | Headlight pointer | | | | | |
| Head/neck | Headstick/mouthstick | | | | | |
| Eyes | | | | | | |
| Other (e.g., lower limbs, voice recognition) | | | | | | |

*Assess Range and Accuracy of Movement*   Next, the assessment generally involves testing the range and accuracy of movements without using adaptations. Hand or headstick control is usually assessed using a horizontal surface, and eye pointing or headlight pointing is assessed using a vertical surface. Obviously, the individual must understand the task requirements in order for the results to be valid. Thus, the team should endeavor to minimize the cognitive, linguistic, and technical aspects of the assessment so that motor control can be isolated and studied. For this reason, we usually do *not* use AAC symbols or technology during this initial screening process. Rather, we begin by placing various types of targets on the display surface and indicating that the individual is to touch/look at/shine the light on each target. We have found that coins make excellent targets for children, especially when the children realize they can keep each coin that they touch with their hands or feet, "hit" with a headstick or light pointer, or look at using eye gaze. We have found that even children with severe cognitive impairments often understand this task almost immediately.

Targets may need to be enlarged to assess headlight (optical) pointing, at least initially, so that the individual experiences success. With adults who understand the task, colored circles of construction paper positioned on a large display surface, such as a light colored wall, may be sufficient. For children, the assessment may include asking them to shine the headlight on large animal pictures or some other motivating targets. Some children are also willing to try to play "tag" with the light pointer in an assessment. By "chasing" people, the assessor's hand, toy animals, or large pictures as they move slowly across a solid background, children may be able to demonstrate the range and accuracy of their head control. Many of these same techniques can be used to screen for eye pointing capabilities as well.

*Optimizing Control*   For motor techniques with which the individual was somewhat successful during screening, additional assessment can help to further define capabilities in areas such as: 1) the degree of accuracy with which the technique can be used to access targets of various sizes, 2) the maximum range and number of targets that can be accessed, and 3) the extent to which adaptations such as keyguards, various display surface angles, various textured surfaces (e.g., slick versus rough), head supports, and trunk supports can be used to optimize the accuracy, efficiency, and range. Because persons with severe disabilities may have had little experience with the access options used in the assessment, the AAC team should be quite conservative in their judgments about motor control. During an initial evaluation, an individual may demonstrate little of the ability that instruction and practice might produce. This is particularly true for techniques such as headlight pointing, since few individuals are likely to have had any experience with this method of alternative access prior to an evaluation. Thus, options that appear even marginally viable should be reassessed, if possible, after the individual has practiced for a few weeks.

*Assess Negative Impact*   Throughout the motor control assessment, the AAC team should also focus on the *overall impact* each access technique has on the individual. For example, some direct selection control techniques can elicit unwanted consequences such as persistent abnormal reflexes, excessive muscle tone, abnormal postures, or excessive fatigue. In the assessment, the AAC team must determine the extent to which the negative impact of various alternative access options can be minimized while preserving the potential benefits. Often, a compromise may be reached; however, the negative consequences associated with a particular alternative access option occasionally can be so detrimental that the option must be abandoned for the moment. Such techniques often can be considered later with additional instruction, practice, or adaptations.

**Manual Signing**   Assessment of the fine motor skills to use manual signs or formalized gestures, such as Amer-Ind, may be undertaken if this mode is being considered for an individual. Papers by Dennis, Reichle, Williams, and Vogelsberg (1982) and Doherty (1985) reviewed a number of studies that examined the motoric dimensions that appear to be related to manual sign acquisition and retention. In addition, formal protocols for fine motor assessment related to the use of signs were developed by Dunn (1982) and described by Dennis et al. (1982). Although available assessment protocols in this area lack formal reliability measures, some are based on the research literature and thus appear to be reasonably valid. They are summarized in Table 7.7.

**Switch Assessment for Scanning**   A switch assessment for scanning will need to be completed if an individual is unable to directly select items from a display. This involves identification of body sites that can be used to activate one or more switches, as well as assessment of the individual's ability to use various scanning strategies and arrangements (see chap. 4, this volume).

Screening for a switch activation site on the body is the first step of a scanning assessment. A note of caution: There is a tendency to utilize tasks that are too complex when identifying switch activation sites. Instead, attempts should be made to *reduce* the cognitive, visual, and communicative demands in a switch control assessment, and, for this reason, we rarely use AAC equipment to gather this information. We have found that having an individual activate a tape recorder and play music (or turn on a battery-operated toy) is an effective way to provide a consequence during the scanning assessment. Thus, a switch is attached to the remote control port of a tape recorder, and a cassette tape appropriate for the age and interests of the potential AAC user is inserted. As the team assesses various motor control sites, such as fingers, hands, head, and feet, different switches can be tried.

Generally, we use a criteria-based assessment approach to identify a switch activation site. Thus, we begin a switch assessment with the most socially appropriate body site for switch control: the hands. If hand or finger control of a switch sufficiently allows accurate, efficient, and nonfatiguing alternative access, we do not continue the assessment with other body parts. If hand control seems insufficient, the head is usually assessed next, followed by the feet, legs, and knees.

*Components of Switch Control*   There are essentially *six components* of switch control. In order to operate an electronic scanner, the individual must first be able to *wait* for the right moment, in order to avoid activating the switch inadvertently. Some individuals have difficulty waiting, because of cognitive or motor control problems. The second step in controlling a switch is *activation*, or closing the switch. Assessment should determine if the individual can activate a variety of switches, the approximate length of time it takes for such activation to occur, and the efficiency with which activation movements are made. The third step is to *hold* the switch in an activated position for the required time. Some individuals who are able to activate the switch accurately and promptly are not able to hold or maintain switch closure. The fourth step in switch control is to *release* the switch accurately and efficiently, which may be problematic for some individuals. Finally, the fifth and sixth steps involve *waiting* and then *reactivating* the switch at the appropriate times.

Each of these components can be assessed using the tape recorder or toy strategy described previously. The individual is instructed to turn the tape recorder on and off according to directions

**Table 7.7.**   Selected instruments for assessment of manual signing capabilities

| Instrument | Source |
|---|---|
| Pre-Sign Language Motor Skills (Klein, 1988) | Communication Skill Builders, P.O. Box 42050-E91, Tucson, AZ 85733 |
| Purdue Perceptual Motor Survey (Roach & Kephardt, 1966) | Charles E. Merrill, Publishers, Columbus, OH 43216-0508 |
| Illinois Test of Psycholinguistic Abilities, Manual Expression Subtest (Kirk, McCarthy, & Kirk, 1968) | University of Illinois Press, Urbana, IL 61801 |
| Early Manual Communication Skills Assessment (Sweeney & Finkley, 1989) | D. Blackstone, E. Cassatt-James, & D. Bruskin (Eds.), *Augmentative communication: Intervention resource* (pp. 3-159–3-168). Rockville, MD: American Speech-Language-Hearing-Association |

designed to assess each component, such as "Wait, don't play it yet," "Okay, play it now," "Stop," and "Play it again." Individuals who are unable to follow verbal directions because of cognitive or other limitations may need to be observed as they use switches to control appliances in natural environments for their assessments. Regardless of the environment, this assessment should give the team an overall indication of the individual's ability to activate switches at various motor control sites. A form to record the results of this assessment is provided in Table 7.8. Again, readers are reminded that although many body parts are listed on this form, it is often unnecessary to evaluate all of them.

*Cursor Control Techniques and Switch Control Capabilities*    The choice of cursor control technique for scanning (e.g., automatic, directed, step scanning) is influenced by an individual's motor control capabilities. This match between techniques and capabilities is illustrated in Tables 7.9. and 7.10. The types of scanning are included across the top of Table 7.9., and the six components of switch control described previously are listed along the side. The motor component skill accuracy requirements for each type of scanning are listed in the table. Thus, for automatic scanning, in which the cursor moves automatically across the selection set and the AAC user is required to stop it at a desired item, there is a high skill accuracy requirement for the user to wait until the cursor is in the correct location. There is also a high skill accuracy requirement for the the user to activate the switch to stop the cursor. Because the item is selected at the moment of switch activation, it does not matter how long the user holds the switch closed, and the accuracy requirements for holding are low. The release phase also has a low skill accuracy requirement, because nothing is required during this phase of automatic scanning. High skill accuracy is required for waiting and reactivating the switch. Automatic scanning relies on timing rather than repeated movements or endurance, so it produces a low level of fatigue.

In directed scanning, the cursor only moves to the desired item when the switch is activated, and the user must release the switch to make a selection. A review of Table 7.9. for this type of scanning indicates that waiting prior to activation has a medium skill accuracy requirement. Although waiting does not affect accurate item selection directly, inadvertent activation at this point will initiate cursor movement before the individual is ready to begin. Switch activation has a low skill accuracy requirement in directed scanning, because activation does not involve precise timing. Holding in directed scanning has a high skill accuracy requirement because the individual must hold the switch closed until the cursor is positioned at the desired item. Thus, inability to adequately hold the switch closed will result in a selection error. During directed scanning, switch release has a high skill accuracy requirement in directed scanning, because selection is actually made during this phase. Waiting and reactivation have medium skill accuracy requirements in directed scanning. The fatigue value in directed scanning is medium, because the switch must be held closed for a period of time, which requires some motor endurance.

In step scanning, the cursor moves one step with each activation of the switch. Thus, the ability to wait has a low skill accuracy requirement because it is not involved in item selection. Activation has a medium skill requirement because it does not have to be rapid, accurate, or well timed, but the activation aspect may be quite fatiguing. Because the cursor moves one step with each activation and holding is not part of the selection process, holding is a low skill accuracy requirement in step scanning. Releasing is also a low skill accuracy requirement for the same reason. Waiting and reactivation require medium motor control abilities, since inadvertent switch activation at these phases will result in erroneous selections. Fatigue is high in step scanning due to the multiple, repeated switch activations.

The preceding discussion is based on clinical experience, not research, and, in fact, we are unaware of any research that exists to support this model. Nonetheless, professionals with whom we have worked have told us that these guidelines generally applied help them achieve effective

**Table 7.8.** Assessment of motor (switch) control for scanning

| | Voluntary motor control (single switch) | | | | | | | | | | | | |
| | Is able to wait | | Is able to activate | | Is able to hold | | Is able to release | | Is able to wait | | Is able to reactivate | | Accuracy[a] |
| | Yes | No | Yes | No | Yes | No | Yes | No | Yes | No | Yes | No | |
|---|---|---|---|---|---|---|---|---|---|---|---|---|---|
| Fingers on left hand | | | | | | | | | | | | | |
| Fingers on right hand | | | | | | | | | | | | | |
| Left hand (palm? back?) | | | | | | | | | | | | | |
| Right hand (palm? back?) | | | | | | | | | | | | | |
| Left shoulder | | | | | | | | | | | | | |
| Right shoulder | | | | | | | | | | | | | |
| Head rotation (r? l?) | | | | | | | | | | | | | |
| Head flexion | | | | | | | | | | | | | |
| Head–side flexion (r? l?) | | | | | | | | | | | | | |
| Head extension | | | | | | | | | | | | | |
| Vertical eye motions | | | | | | | | | | | | | |
| Horizontal eye motions | | | | | | | | | | | | | |
| Tongue or chin | | | | | | | | | | | | | |
| Left outer leg/knee | | | | | | | | | | | | | |
| Right outer leg/knee | | | | | | | | | | | | | |
| Left inner leg/knee | | | | | | | | | | | | | |
| Right inner leg/knee | | | | | | | | | | | | | |
| Left foot (up? down?) | | | | | | | | | | | | | |
| Right foot (up? down?) | | | | | | | | | | | | | |

[a]Accuracy = rate of overall accuracy on a 0–4 scale on which 0 = never and 4 = always.

**Table 7.9.** Skill accuracy requirements of cursor control techniques for scanning

| Motor component | Cursor control technique | | |
|---|---|---|---|
| | Automatic scanning | Directed scanning | Step scanning |
| Wait | High | Medium | Low |
| Activate | High | Low | Medium |
| Hold | Low | High | Low |
| Release | Low | High | Low |
| Wait | High | Medium | Medium |
| Reactivate | High | Medium | Medium |
| Fatigue value | Low | Medium | High |

matching between an individual's motor control capabilities and a cursor control pattern for scanning. We illustrate clinical applications of these guidelines in the following sections by discussing three AAC users who use scanning for alternative access.

*Clinical Illustration: Francesca (athetosis)*   The results of a switch assessment for Francesca, a child with athetoid cerebral palsy, are illustrated in Table 7.10. In Table 7.10., the ease with which Francesca was able to accomplish the various components of switch activation are described as either difficult, medium, or easy. As is the case for many individuals with athetosis, accurate waiting was difficult for her. Because of involuntary motor movements ("overflow") associated with her athetosis, Francesca inadvertently activated the switch during the waiting phase. Similarly, accurate and efficient switch activation was also difficult, because Francesca's overflow movements are accentuated in times of stress or anticipation. Thus, she was unable to activate the switch quickly on command. We see that the holding phase was of medium ease for Francesca, because she was able to maintain contact with the switch once she managed to activate it. In contrast, the release phase was easy for this child, and she was able to release the switch efficiently and accurately. Finally, waiting and reactivation were again difficult because of her extraneous motor movements.

A comparison of Francesca's switch control profile with the requirements of cursor control in Table 7.9. suggests that directed scanning might be an alternative access mode for her. Directed scanning has high skill accuracy requirements for holding and releasing, which match her capabilities. Conversely, automatic scanning has high skill requirements for waiting and activating, the two phases of switch activation that Francesca found most difficult. Step scanning would probably exacerbate her involuntary motor movements, because it requires the greatest amount of actual motor activity and is quite fatiguing.

*Clinical Illustration: Isaac (spasticity)*   The switch activation profile for Isaac, a young man with severe spasticity following a traumatic brain injury, is also summarized in Table 7.10. Isaac

**Table 7.10.** Clinical illustrations of ease of motor control and capabilities for scanning

| Motor component | Ease of motor control | | |
|---|---|---|---|
| | Francesca (athetosis) | Isaac (spasticity) | Jin (weakness) |
| Wait | Difficult | Medium | Easy |
| Activate | Difficult | Medium | Medium |
| Hold | Medium | Easy | Difficult |
| Release | Easy | Difficult | Easy |
| Wait | Difficult | Medium | Easy |
| Reactivate | Difficult | Medium | Medium |
| Fatigue value | Medium | Medium | Difficult |

had medium ease with waiting and switch activation. His activations were rather deliberate and slow. He found it easy to hold the switch closed briefly, but difficult to release it in a timely and accurate manner. Release was difficult because the spasticity prevented him from relaxing his contact with the switch when he wanted. He experienced medium ease with waiting and reactivation.

A review of the requirements of cursor control patterns suggests that Isaac's difficulty with switch release will probably make it difficult for him to use directed scanning successfully. Rather, automatic scanning might be a more appropriate choice for him, since it has high waiting and activation requirements, which Isaac found moderately easy. Automatic scanning also has low skill requirements for switch releasing, the phase with which this young man has the most difficulty.

*Clinical Illustration: Jin (weakness)*   Jin, a woman with amyotrophic lateral sclerosis that caused severe weakness in all body parts, could operate a very sensitive switch affixed just above her eyebrow by raising her forehead slightly. Jin found waiting quite easy and was able to activate the switch with moderate ease when asked. She experienced difficulty holding the switch closed because of her weakness, but she could release it with ease. She then had no difficulty waiting and reactivated the switch with medium ease. As can be seen by consulting Table 7.9., the optimal cursor control pattern for Jin appeared to be automatic scanning, since this option requires the greatest amount of waiting and presents the least fatigue, a major concern for someone with little motor stamina.

The reader is cautioned that the clinical interpretations made in these examples are illustrations only. In no sense do we mean to suggest that all individuals who experience athetosis, spasticity, or weakness will demonstrate switch activation profiles similar to those in this section. We present these examples to illustrate the process of matching an individual's capabilities with the motor control requirements for scanning. It should also be noted that the goal of the type of motor assessment described here is to screen an individual's motor capabilities so that intervention can begin. In addition, motor control should be continually assessed when an intervention is in place to further refine the alternative access technique and ensure that the AAC user's performance becomes increasingly more accurate and efficient and less fatiguing.

> Principle 10: Assessment of cognitive and linguistic capabilities should enhance the process of matching an AAC user to an appropriate AAC technique or device. Thus, the goals of such assessment are *inclusionary*, not *exclusionary*.

## Assess Cognitive/Linguistic Capabilities

*Cognitive Assessment*   The purpose of cognitive assessment in AAC is to determine how the individual of concern understands the world and how communication can best be facilitated within this understanding. Ultimately, this information should be used to achieve a good match between the person and one or more AAC techniques. Unfortunately, however, the cognitive requirements of most AAC options have been described only minimally in the clinical and research literature. Yet, it is quite obvious that the operation of AAC techniques requires various types of cognitive abilities, ranging from basic to quite sophisticated. For example, in order to use even a basic communication board with pictorial symbols, the AAC user must understand that when he or she indicates an item on the board, the communication partner will respond accordingly. This basic concept of communicative cause and effect may be poorly understood by some beginning AAC users.

No formal tests are currently available that predict the ability to meet the cognitive requirements of various AAC techniques. Rather, the AAC team is required to analyze the cognitive requirements of a particular approach and then estimate the extent to which the individual will be able to meet these requirements. Intervention trials with one or more AAC techniques or devices may be required in order to determine an individual's capabilities for AAC techniques. Thousands of successful AAC interventions have been instituted without formal documentation of users' cognitive abilities required by various techniques.

Aside from the goal of achieving a good match, there are often other situations in which assessment of an individual's cognitive abilities may be necessary or useful. The assessment measures listed in Table 7.11. may yield useful information concerning the sensorimotor skills of beginning communicators. Some basic sensorimotor skills include:

1. Alertness
2. Attention span
3. Vigilance (i.e., ability to visually or auditorily process information over time)
4. Understanding of cause and effect
5. Ability to express preferences
6. Ability to make choices
7. Understanding of object or pictorial permanence
8. Symbolic representation skills

Informal modifications of Piagetian assessment tasks have also been developed by clinicians working with individuals with physical and sensory impairments (e.g., Goossens', Heine, Crain, & Burke, 1987).

There are also reasonably reliable and valid standardized tests, which can be used with children as young as 2½ years of age who are unable to speak, such as the Columbia Mental Maturity Scale (Burgemeister, Blum, & Lorge, 1972), Bracken Basic Concept Scale (Bracken, 1984), Pictorial Test of Intelligence (French, 1964), and Leiter International Performance Scale (Arthur, 1950). Johnson-Martin et al. (1987) presented an excellent review of these and other nonverbal cognitive measures along with suggestions for empirically validated adaptations, and they also discussed the pros and cons of such tests for AAC assessment.

***Symbol Assessment*** A majority of the messages included in AAC systems are represented by symbols or codes. Persons who are unable to read or write may use one or more of the symbol options described in Chapter 2. It is not uncommon to see AAC users successfully utilize a variety of types of symbols. Thus, the goal of a symbol assessment is not to identify a single symbol set to represent all messages. Rather, the goal of a symbol assessment is to select the types of symbols that will meet the individual's current communication needs and match his or her current abilities, as well as to identify symbol options that might be used in the future.

An assessment of an individual's ability to use symbols usually involves several steps. First, the items or concepts that the individual understands are identified. Then, the types of symbols the individual recognizes as representative of these items or concepts are determined. Figure 7.5.– Figure 7.8. provide forms that might help organize the processes of symbol assessment.

**Table 7.11.** Selected instruments for sensorimotor assessment related to curriculum

| Instrument | Source |
| --- | --- |
| Callier-Azusa Scales for the Assessment of Communicative Abilities (Stillman & Battle, 1985) | University of Texas at Dallas, Callier Center on Communication Disorders, Dallas, TX 75235 |
| Nonverbal Prelinguistic Communication (Otos, 1983) | Oregon Dept. of Education, 700 Pringle Parkway SE, Salem, OR 97310 |
| Sequenced Inventory of Communication Development (Hedrick, Prather, & Tobin, 1984) | University of Washington Press, Seattle, WA 98195 |
| Sensorimotor Assessment Form (Robinson, Bataillon, Fieber, Jackson, & Rasmussen, 1985) | Meyer Rehabilitation Institute, 44th & Dewey, Omaha, NE 68198-5450 |

An assessment format for initial symbol screening is illustrated in Figure 7.5. Prior to the assessment, 10 or so items with which the individual is familiar should be identified by the team members responsible for the symbol assessment, based on the recommendations of family members, teachers, or frequent communication partners. These can be listed in the appropriate column in Figure 7.5. Next, the assessment team members should reach consensus about the familiarity of the selected items. One of the most common errors is to attempt a symbol assessment using items that the individual does not understand or know. When consensus has been reached, this can be indicated in the column of the form, and items may be replaced if they are found to be unfamiliar. Then, symbols that represent the selected items should be compiled from a variety of sources. These symbols might include color and black and white photographs, miniature objects, various types of line drawing symbols (see chap. 2, this volume), and written words.

*Receptive Language and Yes/No Formats*　　Receptive language labeling is often attempted first in the symbol assessment, since this is the most straightforward way to establish if an individual can recognize a symbol as representing its referent. The person conducting the assessment simply presents two or more symbols of a particular type to the individual and asks him or her to "Point to/look at/give me/show me the [presented item]." Of course, the requested motor response depends on the person's motor abilities. Alternatively, a yes/no format can be used, in which the assessor holds up one symbol at a time and asks, "Is this a ___?" Trials should be ar-

---

Format used ____ Receptive language ____ Yes/no
Number of items in the array _____
Instructions used _____
Response accepted as correct _____

List items used                                              Confirmation of item knowledge by team?

_____ | _____
_____ | _____
_____ | _____
_____ | _____
_____ | _____
_____ | _____
_____ | _____
_____ | _____

Indicate if trial is correct (+) or incorrect (−) in appropriate column

| Trial no. | Target item | Real objects | Color photographs | Line drawings | Other: | Other: |
|---|---|---|---|---|---|---|
| 1 | | | | | | |
| 2 | | | | | | |
| 3 | | | | | | |
| 4 | | | | | | |
| 5 | | | | | | |
| 6 | | | | | | |
| 7 | | | | | | |
| 8 | | | | | | |
| 9 | | | | | | |
| 10 | | | | | | |
| 11 | | | | | | |
| 12 | | | | | | |

**Figure 7.5.** Symbol assessment: receptive language and yes/no formats.

ranged so that yes/no questions are presented randomly across all target items. Obviously, this is only appropriate if the individual understands the concept of yes/no and has a clear and accurate way of answering yes/no questions. Several types of symbols can be assessed, one type at a time, using one of these formats. The assessor records if the individual can identify target items from the various symbol sets on the form in Figure 7.5. Some individuals cannot be assessed in either format, because they do not understand the task expectations, the verbal labels presented, or because of a lack of motivation. A visual matching format, indicated in Figure 7.6., may serve as a useful alternative.

*Visual Matching Format*   In a visual matching assessment, familiar objects selected by the team prior to screening are placed one by one in front of the individual being assessed. In a standard matching assessment, two or more symbols of a particular type, one of which matches the target object, are presented by the assessor, and the individual is asked to match the correct one to the target. This may be done via eye gaze, pointing, or other modes. Alternatively, a sorting format may be used in which several different types of symbols representing two or more items are presented simultaneously. The individual is given verbal instruction and/or a model to indicate that the task is to sort the symbols into two boxes by item (e.g., all symbols representing a ball in one box and all of the symbols representing a key in another). Various symbol sets may be assessed individually in this manner, as with the receptive language protocols.

Format used  _____ Standard matching  _____ Sorting
Number of items in the array _____
Instructions used _____
Response accepted as correct _____

| List items used | Confirmation of item knowledge by team? |
|---|---|
|  |  |
|  |  |
|  |  |
|  |  |
|  |  |
|  |  |
|  |  |
|  |  |

Indicate if trial is correct (+) or incorrect (−) in appropriate column

| Trial no. | Target item | Real objects | Color photographs | Line drawings | Other: | Other: |
|---|---|---|---|---|---|---|
| 1 |  |  |  |  |  |  |
| 2 |  |  |  |  |  |  |
| 3 |  |  |  |  |  |  |
| 4 |  |  |  |  |  |  |
| 5 |  |  |  |  |  |  |
| 6 |  |  |  |  |  |  |
| 7 |  |  |  |  |  |  |
| 8 |  |  |  |  |  |  |
| 9 |  |  |  |  |  |  |
| 10 |  |  |  |  |  |  |
| 11 |  |  |  |  |  |  |
| 12 |  |  |  |  |  |  |

**Figure 7.6.**   Symbol assessment: visual matching format.

This is not a standardized testing protocol, but it is a flexible format that can be altered to suit the individual's abilities and interests. For example, many persons with limited cognitive abilities may need to be taught how to match items and symbols before actual assessment. This can usually be accomplished in a short time using a "teach–test" approach. During the "teach" phase, physical or other prompts can be introduced and gradually faded, in order to teach the person to match identical real objects. Once he or she can do this independently and fairly accurately, various object–symbol matching tasks can be presented as described previously (see Mirenda & Locke, 1989, for a more complete description of this approach).

A variety of other strategies can also be used to facilitate an accurate matching assessment. One variation involves changing the manner in which the items are displayed. As noted previously, two or more symbols are usually presented by the assessor, and the individual's task is to match the correct one to a target object. It is also possible to reverse the format, so that the assessor presents two or more objects, which the individual must then match to a target symbol. The configuration, number of items in the array, and spacing of items can also be adjusted to meet the needs of specific individuals. The point is to make systematic adjustments that facilitate the acquisition of accurate and useful information about the person's symbolic abilities.

*Question and Answer Format* Because real communication rarely involves either receptive language labeling or symbol matching, we have found it useful to extend the assessment beyond these tasks to determine if an individual can use symbols in a more functional manner. Figure 7.7. presents a form to be used in assessing if symbols can be used to answer verbal questions. Again, items or concepts that the individual knows should be identified before the assessment by familiar communication partners and listed in this form. The assessor then selects two or more symbols of a specific type, such as objects, photographs, or line drawings, and presents them to the individual. The assessor then asks a question that can be answered correctly by indicating one of the symbols. Questions such as "Can you show me the car?" or "Where is the picture of your dog?" should not be used in this situation, since these are examples of receptive labeling questions. Rather, simple knowledge-based questions such as "What did you eat for breakfast?" with choices such as the person's favorite breakfast food, a car, and a dog could be used, or "Who likes to ride in the car?" with choices such as a boy and a horse.

In order to successfully complete this task, the individual must understand the task expectations, the questions, and the symbol options presented, and must be motivated and cooperative during the evaluation. If poor performance occurs, it is important to try to determine which of these is responsible. Alternative formats, such as question and answer assessments in natural contexts, may be useful to counteract some factors contributing to poor performance, especially with persons who experience severe cognitive impairments. For example, many individuals may be able to answer the "breakfast" question if they are seated in the kitchen where they usually eat, rather than in a classroom where breakfast never takes place. Figure 7.7. allows the assessor to provide relevant information related to context.

*Requesting Format* Individuals with severe communication and cognitive limitations may be able to match symbols to objects and even answer simple questions using symbols, but be unable to use symbols for requesting. In Figure 7.8., a form is provided to guide the assessment of symbol use in this requesting format. This assessment is usually conducted in an appropriate natural context, such as snack time, play activity, domestic task (e.g., washing the dishes), or other context of interest to the person being assessed. As before, items that the person knows and that are available in the context are listed and confirmed. Then symbols representing two or more of the available options are provided, one type at a time. The interaction is structured to provide opportunities for the person to request objects or actions by selecting one of the available symbols without being instructed to do so by the assessor. Indirect cues, such as "I don't know what you want. Can you help me out?" may be used to elicit requests, but direct instructions such as "Touch the picture to

Number of items in the array _____
Instructions used _____
Context _____ Out of context _____ In context (specify): _____
Response accepted as correct _____

| List items used | Confirmation of item knowledge by informant? |
| --- | --- |
| | |
| | |
| | |
| | |
| | |
| | |
| | |

Indicate if trial is correct (+) or incorrect (−) in appropriate column

| Trial no. | Question asked | Real objects | Color photographs | Line drawings | Other: | Other: |
| --- | --- | --- | --- | --- | --- | --- |
| 1 | | | | | | |
| 2 | | | | | | |
| 3 | | | | | | |
| 4 | | | | | | |
| 5 | | | | | | |
| 6 | | | | | | |
| 7 | | | | | | |
| 8 | | | | | | |
| 9 | | | | | | |
| 10 | | | | | | |
| 11 | | | | | | |
| 12 | | | | | | |

**Figure 7.7.** Symbol assessment: question and answer format.

tell me what you want" should be avoided, since the purpose of this assessment is to determine if the individual can make spontaneous, unprompted requests.

*Pulling It All Together*    Virtually no research has been conducted about how different assessment tasks—receptive language labeling, visual matching, question and answer, and requesting—relate to various levels of symbol use. In clinical practice, we often encounter individuals who can use symbols for one function but not for another. This is particularly prevalent among those who have been taught to identify or label symbols with highly structured approaches, such as traditional, massed trial teaching (e.g., "Show me the ___"). If extensive symbol instruction has been administered in this manner, it is not surprising that the individual can only use symbols when asked, but not to answer questions or make requests.

Given the effect of instruction and knowledge on a person's ability to understand and use symbols, how does one utilize the assessment information to make decisions about the types of symbols to use? Generally, we introduce one or more of the types of symbols with which the individual demonstrated success during assessment. In other words, the *initial symbol sets* should enable accurate, efficient, and nonfatiguing communication with very little instruction required. More sophisticated types of symbols can be taught over time and used *tomorrow*. Symbols such as

Number of items in the array _____

Instructions used _____

Were options  _____ Visible?   _____ Out of sight?

Context  _____ Out of context  _____ In context (specify:) _____

Response accepted as correct _____

| List items used | Confirmation of item knowledge by informant? |
|---|---|
| | |
| | |
| | |
| | |
| | |
| | |
| | |

Indicate if trial is correct (+) or incorrect (−) in appropriate column

| Trial no. | Items available | Real objects | Color photographs | Line drawings | Other: | Other: |
|---|---|---|---|---|---|---|
| 1 | | | | | | |
| 2 | | | | | | |
| 3 | | | | | | |
| 4 | | | | | | |
| 5 | | | | | | |
| 6 | | | | | | |
| 7 | | | | | | |
| 8 | | | | | | |
| 9 | | | | | | |
| 10 | | | | | | |
| 11 | | | | | | |
| 12 | | | | | | |

Figure 7.8.   Symbol assessment: requesting format.

manual signs, Blissymbols, and others that require extensive learning and practice may be excellent choices for the future, but may not be appropriate for initial use.

When several options exist to meet today's needs, compromises between an individual's capabilities, the requirements of a particular AAC technique, and the logistics of specific situations may need to be made. For example, line drawing symbols are more easily used from a practical perspective than objects or photographs. Line drawing symbols can be photocopied, generated by computer, expanded, and reduced in ways that accommodate a variety of communication techniques. Real object symbols are cumbersome, less flexible, and may be difficult to incorporate on electronic communication displays. Photographs must be shot and developed, or located and cut out. If an individual demonstrates the ability to use all three types of symbols, line drawings will probably be selected, because they offer logistical advantages over the others.

### Language Assessment

*Single-Word Vocabulary*   Two types of language assessment typically are completed for AAC purposes. In the first assessment, an attempt is made to measure vocabulary (i.e., single-word receptive language) comprehension in relation to the individual's overall level of functioning. Assessment instruments such as the Peabody Picture Vocabulary Test (Dunn & Dunn, 1981) may be used to assess *nonrelational words,* which have been defined as "words that have referents in the real world such as chair, dog, shirt, etc." (Roth & Cassatt-James, 1989, p. 169). This test is often preferred for AAC evaluations because it can be modified easily, without sacrificing validity, to meet the needs of individuals with motor limitations. For example, Bristow and Fristoe (1987) compared Peabody Picture Vocabulary Test (PPVT) scores obtained using the standard protocol with those obtained using six alternative response modes, including eye gaze, scanning, and head-light pointing. The subjects were nondisabled children in four age groups. The results indicated that with few exceptions, scores obtained under the modified conditions were highly correlated with those obtained using standard test protocols. In addition, it is important to assess comprehension of *relational* words (i.e., those that do not have real-world referents), such as in/out or hot/cold (Roth & Cassatt-James, 1989). The Boehm Test of Basic Concepts (Boehm, 1986) is one example of an instrument that might be used in this regard. For individuals who are unable to complete formal tests, an estimate of vocabulary comprehension is often obtained by having family members, caregivers, and school personnel develop a diary of the words and concepts that individuals appear to understand.

*Language Abilities*   An attempt to determine the individual's syntactic or grammatical knowledge may be made, depending upon the nature and extent of the severe communication disorder. For persons who can participate in formal testing, the Test of Auditory Comprehension of Language (Carrow, 1973) is often used because it screens a variety of syntactic functions in an adaptable, multiple-choice format. Speech-language pathologists are generally well acquainted with a variety of assessment instruments that may be used to gather information related to semantic, morphological, syntactic, and other language areas. Once again, it must be emphasized that the purpose of using such formal tests is not to assign a score or developmental age to the individual, but rather to take advantage of existing methods for gathering needed information. Readers are referred to Roth and Cassatt-James (1989) for additional information about language assessment.

Traditional language sampling usually cannot be completed because most individuals participating in AAC assessments have no formal communication systems. This technique, however, often yields useful information and should be attempted when appropriate. Alternatively, family members, caregivers, and school personnel may be asked to keep a diary of the word combinations that the individual is able to understand and produce through either natural speech or augmented modes.

## Assess Literacy Capabilities

*Reading Assessment*   Persons who are even partially literate may be able to use their reading skills in AAC applications. Assessment of reading skills for AAC usually involves both word recognition and reading comprehension. A variety of assessment instruments incorporate these components, including the Metropolitan Reading Readiness Test, Level II (Nurss & McGauvran, 1986); Gates-MacGinitie Reading Test (MacGinitie, 1978); reading subtests of the Peabody Individual Achievement Test (Dunn & Marquardt, 1970); and the Woodcock Reading Mastery Tests—Revised (Woodcock, 1987). All of these require a simple pointing response or can be adapted for use with alternative response modes.

It is often advisable to conduct an informal, interactive word recognition reading assessment as well, especially with individuals who demonstrate limited skills on standardized tests. For example, some people may be able to recognize "sight words" in natural contexts, although they cannot identify them in more isolated assessment situations. In such cases, natural environment testing can be conducted using words that are likely to be required in the individual's AAC system (e.g., "hello," "goodbye," "help me," "buzz off"). Alternative approaches will not be required for words that are recognized in such functional situations.

*Spelling Assessment*   Spelling abilities are also important targets for AAC assessment. Because various AAC techniques require different types of spelling skills, a nontraditional language or spelling evaluation may be necessary.

Overall, there are three components of spelling ability that need to be assessed: recognition spelling, spontaneous spelling, and first-letter-of-word spelling. In *recognition spelling* tests, an individual is asked to recognize either the correct or the incorrect spelling from a series of options. For example, the words "eresir," "eraser," and "esarer" might be presented with a picture of an eraser, and the task is to identify the correctly spelled word. A test that measures recognition spelling ability is the Peabody Individual Achievement Test (Dunn & Marquardt, 1970). In *spontaneous spelling*, the individual is required to actually spell words letter by letter. The spelling subtest from the Wide Range Achievement Test (Jastak, Bijou, & Jastak, 1978) provides good estimates of spontaneous spelling abilities. Several AAC techniques require *first-letter-of-word spelling* so that the individual can retrieve menus of words that begin with each of the letters of the alphabet. Thus, it is also important to evaluate the extent to which people can spontaneously indicate the first letters of words, even if their other spelling skills are minimal or nonexistent. Tests such as the Brigance Diagnostic Inventory of Basic Skills (1977) allow assessment of this skill.

In our experience, individuals with minimal performance on spontaneous spelling tests can perform quite well on first-letter-of-word tasks. Furthermore, many individuals who acquired literacy skills without appropriate writing systems may have learned to spell on a recognition basis. Therefore, their recognition spelling performance may be significantly greater than their spontaneous spelling abilities. The spelling skills of individuals with such uneven profiles should not be overestimated, since the AAC implications for each type of spelling skill differ considerably. For example, in order to learn Morse code, it appears that people need spontaneous spelling skills to at least the second-grade level (Marriner et al., 1989). Nevertheless, individuals who are not this proficient but who have first-letter-of-word spelling abilities and adequate reading abilities may be able to use EZKeys or another word menuing technique. As with other types of assessments, it is important that the AAC team be aware of the available AAC options and their operational requirements to ensure a good client–system match.

## Assess Sensory/Perceptual Capabilities

Assessments of an individual's sensory/perceptual capabilities should be made using the materials, items, and devices that are being considered for the individual's AAC system. For example, the symbols and configuration considered for a visual display might be used in a vision assessment so that the assessor can evaluate their appropriateness. Or, the synthetic speech output device being considered might be used during an audiometric exam to assess its functionality. Criteria-based sensory assessments are often completed by the AAC team members rather than by specialists, especially if there appear to be no uncorrected deficits in these areas.

**Visual Assessment**   The sensory demands on individuals who use AAC techniques relate primarily to selection set displays and feedback options provided by their systems (see chap. 4, this volume). Typically in AAC applications, selection sets are displayed graphically, either as symbols or codes. Assessment of the visual capabilities of AAC users is necessary in order to determine the size, spacing, and layout of the items in the selection set. Obviously, the individual's motor control skills also contribute to this determination. The operational and message feedback of many electronic AAC devices is also provided visually. For example, when a selection is made in some devices, a flash of light indicates the activation. In other devices, the message or a portion thereof is presented on a display as feedback. Thus, visual assessment may determine possible feedback options.

Chapter 15 focuses specifically on AAC options for persons with visual impairments and provides descriptions of components of the visual system and how they affect selection set decisions. Some of the most relevant formal vision assessment tests for visual components of AAC systems are presented in Table 7.12. (Cress, 1987; Cress et al., 1981). In addition, informal vision assessment procedures such as Langley's (1980) Functional Vision Inventory may provide AAC team

**Table 7.12.**  Selected instruments for vision assessment

| Instrument | Source |
|---|---|
| Lippman HOTV (Lippman, 1971) | Good-Lite Company, 7426 W. Madison St., Forest Park, IL 60130 |
| Lighthouse Flashcard Test | New York Association for the Blind, 111 E. 59th St., New York, NY 10022 |
| Parsons Visual Acuity Test (Spellman, DeBriere, & Cress, 1979) | Bernell Corporation, 422 E. Monroe St., South Bend, IN 46601 |
| Teller Acuity Cards (Teller, McDonald, Preston, Sebris, & Dobson, 1986) | Vistech Corporation, 4162 Little York Road, Dayton, OH 45414 |
| Vision Assessment and Program Manual for Severely Handicapped and/or Deaf-Blind Students (Sailor, Utley, Goetz, Gee, & Baldwin, 1982) | San Francisco State University, Bay Area Severely Handicapped Deaf Blind Project, San Francisco, CA 94132 |

members with useful classroom-based strategies for gathering information relevant to visual competency.

**Hearing Assessment**  Assessment of hearing capabilities is important, especially if the selection set is displayed auditorily, as with auditory scanning. Auditory display systems are usually selected for persons with severe visual impairments, and these require that users be able to hear and understand the items in the selection set as they are announced. If auditory scanning via synthetic or digitized speech is being considered as an option, the hearing assessment also needs to determine the individual's ability to comprehend the particular type of synthesized speech. In many electronic devices, feedback is auditory also. This feedback may be in the form of a beep to indicate that an item has been selected, or be a spoken echo produced via synthetic or digitized speech. Finally, many AAC devices utilize speech synthesis or digitization for output. Although such output is provided primarily for the benefit of the communication partner, not the AAC user (see chap. 5, this volume), auditory comprehension of the output signal by the user is generally desirable.

Assessment of hearing capabilities is usually straightforward and can be conducted by a qualified audiologist who does not necessarily have experience with AAC. Evaluation of a potential user's ability to understand synthetic or digitized speech may need to be requested as an additional service, however. Of course for some individuals, alternative response modes may need to be utilized during testing. For example, Bristow and Fristoe (1988) reported data supporting the use of a speech audiometry procedure incorporating eye gaze as the response mode for persons with physical disabilities. In addition, persons with severe cognitive limitations may require considerable instruction prior to formal testing in order to establish a reliable operant response to sound. The empirically validated procedures developed by Goetz, Gee, and Sailor (1983) may be useful in this regard.

**Tactile Assessment**  Some AAC applications utilize tangible (i.e., tactile) symbols in the selection set. These applications are used most with individuals who have severe visual impairments or combined visual and hearing impairments. Tactile feedback is also used in a variety of electronic AAC devices where depression of a key or membrane surface is associated with tactile feedback to indicate that an item has been selected.

Systematic procedures for assessing tactile capabilities are noticeably lacking in the literature. Interested readers are referred to an article by Hart and Spellman (1989) that summarized the few existing studies in the area and also referred to a number of experimental procedures that might be useful in conducting assessments of tactile capabilities.

> "Assessment is a process during which information is gathered in order to make clinical, educational, or vocational management decisions" (Yorkston & Karlan, 1986, p. 164).

## CONCLUSION

The goal of assessment is to gather a sufficient amount of information for the AAC team—the user, family members, professionals, and other facilitators—to make intervention decisions that meet both current and future communication needs. Because of the many complex issues that must be considered in such assessments, there is a widespread tendency to *over*assess capabilities. Too much testing of an individual's motor, cognitive, linguistic, and sensory performance can actually interfere with an AAC intervention, because it takes so much time and places so many demands on the family and the potential user. In this chapter, we have attempted to provide a framework for completing assessments that are broad-based in scope but not necessarily exhaustive. Additional details regarding the assessment of persons with specific types of severe communication impairments are presented in Chapter 10–Chapter 19.

# *Principles of Decision Making and Intervention*

>>>>>>>>>>>>>>>>>>>>>>>>>>>>>>>>>>>>>>>>>>>>>>>>>>>>>

When the assessment process has been completed, the AAC team can begin to make decisions about intervention. Some guidelines for decision making were presented in Chapter 7, particularly those related to consideration of motor control. In this chapter, we discuss additional principles that can be used in the intervention process. Then, in Chapters 10–19, we provide specific intervention guidelines and techniques for AAC users with various types of disabilities. Thus, the issues discussed in this chapter are general.

> Principle 1: Build on the consensus already achieved during the assessment process.

## CONSENSUS BUILDING DURING INTERVENTION

In Chapter 7, we discussed the importance of building consensus among members of the team during the assessment process. During decision making and intervention, the AAC user, his or her family, and the professionals involved must continue to share information about preferences and strategies. Two strategies in particular are important during this phase of the process:

1. Continue to make decisions as a team after the assessment has been completed, rather than asking team members to "sign off" on an idea or decision in which they have not been involved. If even one member of the team disagrees with a decision, negotiation and compromise should be clearly established as the appropriate team responses.
2. Create an atmosphere in which team members feel free to raise issues or problems. Team members may not be comfortable expressing concerns for fear of "hurting someone's feelings" or "making someone angry." It is far preferable to make team decisions regarding the effectiveness of an intervention and the need to make adjustments.

A consensus approach to team management may be ineffective if the basic principles of consensus building are violated. In *ineffective* consensus building, an agreement to compromise typically means that one or more of the team members (almost always those in the minority) have been manipulated, intimidated, coerced, or otherwise persuaded to agree with the rest of the team. This may resolve the immediate conflict, but will come back later to haunt the overall team efforts through subtle (or not so subtle) sabotage of the plan. Instead, the goal should be a compromise that emerges when all team members engage in an open dialogue about the issue and arrive at truly "reciprocal concessions" (Chadsey & Wentworth, 1974, p. 121).

To accomplish this compromise, all members of the team must be willing to state their opinions openly, engage in dialogue to share rationales and information, and state their revised opinions. Team members must be willing to repeat the dialogue as many times as necessary to resolve the conflict. In order to negotiate, the consensus facilitator (i.e, team leader) must be prepared to confront the behavior of individual team members who refuse to engage in discussions or reveal their biases and opinions, or who otherwise remain uninvolved in the decision-making process. The team must work to achieve consensus without anyone "losing face" or agreeing to tasks that are clearly "above and beyond the call of duty." Finally, all team members, including administrators and support personnel, should be prepared to state their understanding of the compromise and their willingness to participate. Again, we emphasize that the long-term detrimental effects of a failure to build consensus far outweigh the efforts that may be needed to achieve consensus.

In this chapter, we continue discussion of the steps in the Participation Model and focus on steps that take place after the assessment of participation needs, opportunity barriers, current capabilities, and constraints. Following the Participation Model, assessment information is compiled and compared with the requirements of various communication options. Two sets of communication options are generally available: 1) those designed to increase natural abilities, and 2) those designed to utilize environmental or communication adaptations. It cannot be sufficiently emphasized that these are *not* mutually exclusive. Indeed, many individuals may be best served by a combination of natural ability and adaptive approaches.

## NATURAL ABILITY INTERVENTIONS

The first decision that the team must make often involves the relative emphasis to be placed on natural ability interventions and adaptive approaches. Of course, this consideration depends on the origin, stage, and course of the AAC user's communication disability. For example, an individual with end-stage amyotrophic lateral sclerosis (ALS) will not benefit from interventions designed to increase natural speech, while a preschool child with cerebral palsy is likely to require extensive attention in this area. (Readers are directed to the chapters discussing specific disabilities in Part II of this book.) Regardless, the team may need to resolve misconceptions and disagreements concerning this decision.

### Resolving Misconceptions

Discussions about the relative emphasis of AAC versus natural ability interventions can be perceived as leading to dichotomous, either/or outcomes. Perhaps the most common scenario is one in which family members are resistant to AAC interventions because they are afraid that these will inhibit natural speech development. For example, the family of a young adult with traumatic brain injury, who has some speech but who cannot be understood by unfamiliar people, may perceive a recommendation to provide an AAC system as an indicator that no further therapeutic work will be done for speech, even if this is not the intent. Or, the motor specialists working with a young child with severe cerebral palsy may recommend a single-switch scanning device with a head switch, since this best matches his or her current capabilities. The other members of the team and the family may view this decision negatively if they interpret it to mean that current therapeutic interventions to improve the child's upper extremity motor function will be discontinued.

Such misconceptions must be identified and articulated early in the decision-making process so that they can be discussed and corrected. If these misconceptions are not dealt with, the issue is almost certain to surface again, either during intervention planning or implementation. Sometimes, providing those concerned with information from research regarding the effects of AAC on natural speech development is sufficient to alleviate their concerns. We have summarized such information in Table 8.1.

Simple assurances that AAC interventions are unlikely to be detrimental to natural speech development are usually insufficient to dispel such misconceptions. A plan describing: 1) the amount of speech therapy services that will be provided, 2) the intervention goals, and 3) information about the approaches to be used should be included in the individual's educational or rehabili-

**Table 8.1.** Impact of augmentative communication intervention on attempts at speech communication by diagnosis

| Reference | Number of clients | Children or adults | Impact of speech attempts[a] | | |
|---|---|---|---|---|---|
| | | | Increased | Decreased | None |
| **Diagnosis: aphasia** | | | | | |
| Eagleson, Vaughn, and Knudson (1970) | 31 | Adults | "Success with this nonspeech mode of communication increased the apparent motivation of patients to persevere in learning verbal modes of communication." | | |
| Goodwin and Goodwin (1969) | 2 | Children | 2 | | |
| Schlanger (1976) | 5 | Adults | 3 | | 2 |
| **Diagnosis: apraxia** | | | | | |
| Ellsworth and Kotkin (1975) | 1 | Child | 1 | | |
| Skelly, Schinsky, Smith, and Fust (1974) | 6 | Adults | 5 | | 1 |
| **Diagnosis: autism** | | | | | |
| Creedon (1975) | 30 | Children | "Some" | | |
| Fulwiler and Fouts (1976) | 1 | Child | 1 | | |
| Konstantareas, Oxman, Webster, Fischer, and Miller (1975) | 5 | Children | 2 | | 3 |
| Miller and Miller (1973) | 19 | Children | 2 | | 17 |
| Offir (1976) | 30 | Children | 20 | | 10 |
| Schaeffer, McDowell, Musil, and Kollinzas (1976) | 3 | Children | 3 | | |
| **Diagnosis: dysarthria** | | | | | |
| Gitlis (1975) | 1 | Child | 1 | | |
| Kates and McNaughton (1975) | 19 | Children | "Symbol use appeared to encourage vocalization and speech." | | |
| Kladde (1974) | 3 | Children | 1 | | 2 |
| Levett (1971) | 12 | Children | 1 | | 11 |
| Ontario Crippled Children's Centre Symbol Communication Programme (1973) | 141 | Children | 45 | 2 | 94 |
| **Diagnosis: mental retardation** | | | | | |
| Balick, Spiegel, and Greene (1976) | 5 | Children | 5 | | |
| Brookner and Murphy (1975) | 1 | Children | | | 1 |
| Duncan and Silverman (1977) | 32 | Children | 15 | | 17 |
| Kimble (1975) | 4 | Children | 2 | | 2 |
| Lebeis and Lebeis (1975) | 27 | Children | 6 | | 21 |
| Linville (1977) | 4 | Children | 2 | | 2 |
| Prinz and Shaw (1981) | 17 | Children | Most showed "increase in the use of speech." | | |
| Schmidt, Carrier, and Parsons (1971) | 10 | Children | 10 | | |
| Wills (1981) | — | Children | 38% | | |
| Wilson (1974) | 26 | Children | 5 | | 21 |

(From Silverman, F.H. [1989]. *Communication for the speechless: An introduction to augmentative communication for the severely communicatively impaired* [2nd ed., pp. 47–48]. Englewood Cliffs, NJ: Prentice Hall; reprinted by permission.)

[a]Given in numbers of individuals, except where noted.

tation plan, if applicable. In addition, it is important to share information about any progress in natural abilities with the entire team on a regular basis to avoid the perception that agreement to work on these skills was a token rather than a serious commitment.

## Resolving Disagreements

More than simple misconceptions about the intended emphasis of natural ability interventions in the overall communication plan may be present. The intent of some team members may be, in fact, to suggest that work on natural abilities either not be initiated, be terminated after a trial period, or be increased or decreased markedly. Typically, disagreements about recommendations to *terminate or decrease* instruction arise from perceptions or evidence that efforts to increase natural ability have not proved effective for the individual of concern. For example, an older person with aphasia secondary to stroke who has had years of speech therapy may indicate that he or she no longer wishes to receive such services, against the wishes of his or her spouse. Disagreements about whether to *initiate* natural ability interventions almost always stem from differing opinions about the prognosis of such efforts. For example, the family of a youngster with autism and little speech may be unwilling to place the child in a nonacademic curriculum, because they believe that he or she may be able to communicate through reading and writing if given the necessary instruction. Finally, disagreements about whether to *increase or maintain* the current emphasis on natural ability often arise when team members are more familiar with natural ability options than with AAC options. Consider the example of a child with severe motor and speech apraxia who has been using both AAC and natural speech approaches for several years. Her family moved to a new town where she attends a school in which there has never been a child who uses an AAC approach. None of the professionals involved in her educational program are familiar with either the AAC field or her particular system. Hence, a recommendation is made at the initial team meeting to place major emphasis on developing her natural speech and to minimize or discontinue the use of the AAC system at school. Her parents protest that intensive speech therapy was tried for several years with minimal results and insist that her AAC system be fully incorporated into the overall plan.

Whatever the source of the disagreement, certain outcomes can be predicted if a consensus is not achieved prior to intervention planning. First, members of the team representing the minority position are at risk for being labeled by the others as uncooperative, unrealistic, or "in denial" about the abilities in dispute. The parents of the child with apraxia in the previous example were labeled overly pessimistic because they did not wish to expend undue time and energy on natural speech, and they were considered to be "parents who think technology will solve everything" because of their support of the child's AAC system. Second, the intervention plan as a whole is at risk for failure, since it is almost certain that the team members who disagree will pursue implementation of the plan with less than full commitment and enthusiasm. Third, and most important, the AAC user is at risk for continued and future communication problems as a result of the interpersonal conflicts and intervention failures that are likely to occur as a result of the lack of consensus.

Clearly, none of these outcomes is acceptable. Concerted and ongoing efforts to resolve the disagreement through consensus building are critical if an impasse occurs. The first step in resolution is to identify the source of the disagreement through a discussion with all team members—including parents, the AAC user when appropriate, and professional, support, and administrative staff. In many cases, the real source of the disagreement may stem from policies or practices of the agency. Failure to involve agency administrators can result in ineffective and inefficient consensus building. For example, consider a disagreement between the family of a 17-year-old with learning disabilities and the student's speech-language pathologist and teachers. The family wants their son to be allowed to use a portable computer in the classroom with a spell checker, grammar checker, and linguistic predictor to produce written work such as tests and reports. The professionals on the team refuse, ostensibly because they believe that he should work to remediate his natural reading and writing skills exclusively. In fact, however, they are acutely aware that none of them possess sufficient computer skills to provide the student necessary support, and they are worried about the implications for their workloads if this adaptation is instituted. Of course, none of the team members admits these real issues to the family, and it is only when one of the teachers makes a reference to being wary of computers and other gadgets at the consensus meeting that the real problem begins to be identified. The disagreement was eventually resolved, with the help of the principal, who had the authority to initiate district-wide interventions to increase computer skills among the staff. Although this particular situation may be unique, similar situations in which the apparent source of the disagreement is different from the real source are not. Regardless of the issue, resolution of a disagreement is impossible until its source and dynamics are clear to all team members.

In situations where neither clear evidence nor history supports one position over another, outcomes that reflect compromise are preferable to those in which some team members win while others lose. Compromise is a likely solution in most cases, considering the advances in both natural and augmented communication approaches. For example, who is to say that the family of the aforementioned youngster with autism is wrong in their assessment of his potential academic abilities? Indeed, splinter skills in literacy are fairly well documented in this population, and some believe that they may be more common than previously thought (Biklen, 1990). In reality, for decisions about natural ability interventions, the evidence for one position and the accuracy of predictions concerning outcomes are often weak at best. Therefore, in order to reach consensus, professionals, family members, support personnel, and AAC users all must be willing to grant the possibility that a novel approach or combination of approaches merits consideration (see Vanderheiden & Smith, 1989, for a case study).

> Principle 2: Communication is multimodal in nature. AAC interventions should also be multimodal in nature.

One of the most important principles in AAC intervention is that communication is multimodal in nature. Most likely, some professional time and effort devoted to developing a natural ability such as speech will result in at least some positive outcomes. Often, we approach compromise with the analogy of an investment portfolio, in which negotiable percentages of professional time are allocated to natural speech and AAC investments, respectively. Thus, a decision might be made to invest 50% of available intervention time in therapies to increase natural speech and motor skills, and 50% in AAC system development and use; or 10% in natural ability areas and 90% in the AAC area; or whatever reasonable compromise can be reached by the team. When a compromise is reached, it is critical that the team follow through with the negotiated plan and meet regularly to share progress or lack thereof so that adjustments can be made in the "investment portfolio" accordingly.

## ENVIRONMENTAL ADAPTATION INTERVENTIONS

The second intervention option in the access strand of the Participation Model (Figure 7.1.) involves resolving communication difficulties through environmental adaptations. The need for environmental adaptations may have been identified in the assessment of participation patterns or in the capability assessment, or both. Environmental adaptations, when indicated, are as critical to the overall success of the communication intervention as are other options. These adaptations can be divided into two main categories: space or location adaptations and physical structure adaptations.

### Space/Location Adaptations

It is important to distinguish space/location adaptations from those identified as opportunity barriers. Major life-style concerns regarding physical segregation and isolation from people because of lack of opportunity require policy- and practice-level interventions such as legislation, regulation, or education, and are not solved by simple space/location adaptations. Space/location issues are specific and should be solvable by the AAC team without major policy-level changes—assuming that consensus building has been effective, as discussed previously.

Space adaptations may be necessary to remove physical barriers to the AAC system itself. For example, a woman with a brain stem stroke who lives in a residential care home may be unable to bring her communication device into the cafeteria because the tables and chairs are too close together for the device to pass when mounted on her power wheelchair. Or, a college student with cerebral palsy may not be able to install his adapted word processing equipment in his dormitory room because there is not enough space. In the first case, the necessary adaptations are simple: move the chairs and tables further apart, but in the second case, more complex accommodations will be necessary.

Location adaptations are more related to the location of the AAC user him- or herself than to the equipment. For example, a young girl with an AAC system in a classroom may be seated in the back of the room, making it difficult for her to regularly interact with the teacher. In addition, if she has an AAC device with synthetic speech output, her teacher may have difficulty hearing this without being near the student for every interaction. We are aware of one case where the teacher's initial solution was to turn off the speech output, since, "No one could hear it anyway!" More appropriate was a location adaptation to move the child's seat near the front of the room, which eventually was done.

### Physical Structure Adaptations

Physical structure adaptations go beyond space and location adjustments and are those necessary to accommodate the communication system or to facilitate its use. Obvious examples include tables or classroom desks that need to be lowered, raised, or otherwise adjusted to accommodate a student and his or her AAC system. Other examples include beds adapted with adjustable swing arms in order to mount AAC systems for users who are partially bedridden, and doorways that are widened to allow passage of wheelchair-mounted equipment. Physical structure adaptations related to making public places accessible are required by the Americans with Disabilities Act of 1990.

## AAC SYSTEM/DEVICE INTERVENTIONS

AAC system or device interventions include both unaided and aided techniques, and both high tech and low tech applications. In Chapter 7, we discussed strategies for constructing a technology requirement profile and a capability profile to achieve an appropriate match between the AAC user's current abilities and the requirements of the available options. We also discussed what information is needed to compile a profile of constraints that might affect the AAC system or device plan. The process of achieving an effective match between a user and an AAC intervention involves a number of important considerations related to both long- and short-term communication goals. These considerations are explored in the sections that follow.

---

Principle 3: Plan for today and tomorrow.

---

## PLAN AND IMPLEMENT INTERVENTIONS FOR TODAY AND TOMORROW

With initial assessments completed, the team should be prepared to make a decision about AAC devices or systems for the individual. Actually, two sets of decisions should be made from the outset: those aimed at "today" and those aimed at "tomorrow" (Beukelman, Yorkston, & Dowden, 1985). Figure 8.1. depicts the relationship between decisions for today and decisions for tomorrow. The today decisions should meet the user's immediate communication needs and match the current capabilities and constraints identified during the assessment process. The tomorrow decisions are based on projections of future opportunities, needs, and constraints, as well as capabilities that result from instruction. Both decisions are critical to the long-term success of an intervention plan.

## Interventions for Today

The major consideration in planning for today's needs is that the AAC technique(s) selected to meet the user's immediate needs, within the available opportunities, be accurate, efficient, and non-fatiguing. An *accurate system* is one that the AAC user can use to produce intended messages with a minimum number of communication breakdowns and errors. A system for today should enable the AAC user to achieve an acceptable degree of accuracy without extensive training. This means that the system for today should match the user's current linguistic, cognitive, sensory, and motor abilities as closely as possible. An *efficient system* is one that enables the AAC user to produce messages in an acceptable amount of time, again without extensive practice or training. This requirement can be accomplished by achieving a good match between the user's motor and sensory abilities, in particular, and those motor and sensory abilities required by the system. A *nonfatiguing system* is one that enables the AAC user to communicate for as long as necessary without becoming excessively tired or experiencing significantly reduced accuracy or efficiency. This requirement, like accuracy, is met only through consideration of linguistic, cognitive, motor, and sensory factors. In short, today's system should require a minimum of training and practice in order for the individual to use it effectively to communicate messages about his or her most important and immediate needs. Of course, a today system is selected with consideration of the existing constraints and unresolved opportunity barriers.

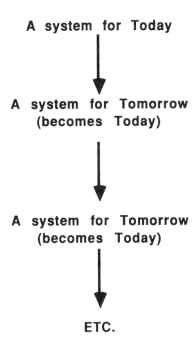

**Figure 8.1.**  The longitudinal nature of AAC interventions.

When we first got the light talker [sic], Ana had very poor head control. Getting the light to hit the right squares became a daily battle. But she carried on with a determination I found extraordinary. She must have known that this device was eventually going to liberate her, at least from the confines of speechlessness. I have never been so proud of my daughter as I was during those times. (Cy Berlowitz, 1991)

Why is the ability to almost immediately use a system such an important issue? The reason is to avoid situations in which an AAC user must wait for months or years before he or she can communicate effectively. For example, a recent study of 118 school-age students labeled severely/profoundly mentally retarded who were provided with manual sign instruction indicated that the average student was able to imitate nine signs and spontaneously produce four signs after 2.9 years of instruction (Bryen, Goldman, & Quinlisk-Gill, 1988). Obviously, this is an unacceptable outcome but, unfortunately, not altogether uncommon. From the information in the study, it appears that this unsatisfactory result can be accounted for by two primary failures: a failure to gather sufficient assessment information for decision making, and a failure to consider the need for instituting a today system that matched students' current abilities (Bryen et al., 1988). Although the problems in this case were two-fold, it is just as likely that this result could have occurred even if the assessment had been complete. For example, most readers can probably think of at least one AAC user who has struggled for months or even years to learn to operate a manual AAC system despite severe upper extremity athetosis, or a headlight pointer despite insufficient head control, while, in the meantime, having no way to achieve accurate, efficient, and nonfatiguing communication. What a disappointment it must be for people who have never been able to communicate to discover that communication involves a great deal of hard work with very little payoff! Of course, some initial instruction or training must occur in most situations. The point is that this should be minimized and should not require long periods of time to achieve.

## Interventions for Tomorrow

Decision making for tomorrow should be concurrent with decision making for today under most circumstances. That is, as plans are developed to institute an AAC system that matches current abilities and immediate needs, plans should also be developed for broadening the user's skill base in preparation for a tomorrow system. These plans might involve providing instruction to improve specific motor, symbol recognition, pragmatic, or literacy skills. The plans might involve remediating identified barriers that limit the quantity or quality of communication opportunities. Whatever the focus of the planning for tomorrow, the goal should be to institute an intervention that will enable more of the user's communication needs to be met and/or to increase the accuracy, efficiency, and ease of use of the today system.

The tomorrow system may be an expansion or extension of the today system, or it may involve a different device or technique. For example, a component of the today system for a young man with traumatic brain injury early in recovery may be a series of eye gaze communication boards with color photographs, which represent the major choices available in his day. An expansion of this system for tomorrow might introduce PCS symbols for the same messages by placing them next to the photographs and then fading the photos as he is able to accurately eye point to the PCS symbols. As another example, perhaps the photographic eye gaze system for today was intended as a temporary measure to allow the motor therapists to develop the adaptations and skills needed for more effective hand and arm use. If this is the case, the eye gaze system might be discontinued when motor control is sufficient and replaced with a laptray communication board containing the same photographs. In either case, once the tomorrow system has been instituted, it becomes the new today system, and planning can begin immediately for yet another tomorrow.

Thus, a longitudinal AAC plan should always be two-pronged: planning for today and tomorrow, although the time between successive tomorrows is likely to lengthen as the AAC system comes closer and closer to meeting all of the user's communication needs.

Another example illustrating the ongoing nature of today and tomorrow interventions might prove useful. Mirenda, Iacono, and Williams (1990) described one possible series of such interventions appropriate for a student with profound intellectual and physical disabilities who has some volitional movement of the head. A today system for such a student might consist of a head-activated microswitch that turns on single, prerecorded cassette tapes for eliciting attention and requesting foods, objects, or activities (Wacker, Wiggins, Fowler, & Berg, 1988). Other components might include the use of nonsymbolic gestures, vocalizations, and other natural modes in the context of predictable routines to signal rejection, emotions, and preferences (Siegel-Causey & Guess, 1989). At the same time, a tomorrow intervention consisting of a "calendar box" with real object symbols for daily activities (Rowland & Schweigert, 1989) could be introduced, although this is beyond the student's current level of ability. The purpose of introducing the calendar box at this point would be to begin teaching symbol–activity associations in natural contexts. Once the student begins to show ability to make such associations, the object symbols could be used for making simple choices with eye gaze (if the student has sufficient vision), or with direct selection of the object symbols through a tactile mode (if the student's vision is limited). As the student's eye gaze or tactile symbol skills develop, one of these options could become the new today system and replace the initial, limited microswitch and tape device. At this point, planning and instruction would begin for the next tomorrow system that will continue to meet communication needs and to build skills in natural contexts. Additional examples of the today and tomorrow principle can be found in a number of case studies (e.g., Beukelman, Yorkston, & Dowden, 1985; DeRuyter & Donoghue, 1989; Goossens', 1989; Light, Beesly, & Collier, 1988; Yorkston, 1989).

In some cases, it might be fairly obvious what the today system should be, but not at all clear how to logically plan for tomorrow. This is often the case if the individual's motor impairments are very severe and not easily remediable. In such cases, it is often advisable to institute multiple and simultaneous training programs for tomorrow, each designed to improve the AAC user's ability to control and use a different motor site. For example, consider the example of a young man with severe athetoid cerebral palsy and good literacy skills. It was apparent from assessment that a simple orthographic eye gaze system (Goossens' & Crain, 1987) combined with dependent auditory scanning (a 20-questions approach) was the best match for his current abilities. It was also apparent that in order for him to access a more efficient and comprehensive system, he would need to achieve increased control of at least one motor movement sequence. It was not at all clear, however, which motor movement sequence would be most amenable to intervention. Therefore, training programs designed to increase his ability to operate a single switch using his head, right hand, and left foot, respectively, were instituted at the same time. It became apparent that his head control was improving at a faster rate, and the result was that after 6 months of work, he was able to use a head switch to control a single switch scanner accurately, efficiently, and without unreasonable fatigue. When the logical direction for tomorrow is not clear, such a multiple target approach is vastly preferable (and certainly less frustrating!) to one in which single training targets are selected in succession until one finally is successful.

## PROVIDE INSTRUCTION

After a comprehensive plan for natural skill development, environmental adaptations, and assistive device adaptations is established, the vocabulary items that will be represented on the system need to be selected (see chap. 9, this volume). Instruction of the AAC user, communication partners, and the facilitators who manage the ongoing intervention must be initiated. While many of the instructional techniques are specific to the AAC user and his or her impairment (see chaps. 10–19, this volume), there are general principles that guide instruction. These are discussed briefly in this section.

---

Principle 4: Provide both contextual and specific skill instruction, as needed.

---

## Natural Contexts

Instruction in AAC techniques has come a long way from the days when the majority of such work was done in isolated therapy rooms by one or two professionals (Musselwhite & St. Louis, 1988). It is now well established in the AAC literature that much, if not most, of the focus of intervention should take place in natural contexts such as classrooms, homes, community settings, and workplaces (Calculator, 1988b; Montgomery, 1987). Instructional plans that emphasize natural context intervention appear to result in better response generalization (i.e., to novel targets within the same response class) and better stimulus generalization (i.e., to novel people, environments, materials, and situations) than do instructional plans that emphasize isolated skill training (Musselwhite & St. Louis, 1988; Reichle, York, & Sigafoos, 1991). Natural context instructional strategies specific to AAC users with various backgrounds and abilities are discussed in Part II of this book.

## Specific Skills

The importance of natural context instruction notwithstanding, it is also important to provide specific skill instruction, which may occur in separate training sessions, into the intervention plan when necessary. Specific skill training, unfortunately, may be labeled "nonfunctional" and discounted or ignored by proponents of natural context instruction, even if it is the most functional response to a skill deficit (e.g., Arwood, 1983). Specific skill training is particularly useful if there is a need for instruction in new skill areas and to compensate quickly for past instructional deficiencies.

*Initiating New Skill Learning*   Basic instruction of most new skills is best conducted from the very beginning in natural contexts. However, if the skill is sensory or motor, at least some specific skill instruction in separate training settings may be necessary as well as desirable. It is important to remember that the motor skills necessary for natural speech or to use an AAC device usually involve fine discrete movements, and most AAC users have motor impairments, sometimes quite severe. In addition, many AAC users are easily startled and distracted by noise, movement, activity, or other extraneous environmental stimuli. For all of these reasons, concentration is often difficult to maintain, and control of the target motor site is not easily achieved. An individual with such multiple obstacles in busy, distracting, ever-changing natural contexts may not make steady improvement in the skill being taught, and to expect so is simply unrealistic. Rather, a judicious blend of natural and specific skill training is often necessary to achieve the desired result in a reasonable period of time.

---

Principle 5: Minimize the cognitive, linguistic, sensory, and motor demands of specific skill training.

---

Specific skill training is appropriate only when the target skill is particularly challenging for the AAC user, so it stands to reason that the other skills required during training sessions should be minimally demanding. For example, if an adult with spinal cord injury is learning to use a sip and puff switch so that he or she can send Morse code, it does not make sense to teach him or her to control the switch at the same time that the individual is learning and memorizing Morse codes.

Rather, nonlinguistic practice tasks (e.g., pattern imitations) designed to teach him or her to sip and puff accurately and efficiently should be introduced. Then, using a visual display chart, he or she could be taught to produce Morse code sequences for single letters or numbers in some practice sessions, while learning and memorizing the codes without using the switch during others. Finally, the motor and the symbol skills could gradually be integrated toward the goal of mastery (Matas & Beukelman, 1989). Similarly, the cognitive, linguistic, and sensory requirements for training the motor skills for tasks such as headlight pointing (Blackstone, 1988b), manual signing (Carr & Kologinsky, 1983), and visual scanning (Blackstone, 1989f) should be reduced as much as possible during initial instruction.

This principle also applies to cognitive/linguistic and sensory skills. For example, Keogh and Reichle (1985) recommended providing difficult-to-teach students with intellectual disabilities opportunities for specific "match-to-sample" training when introducing new pictorial symbols. Similarly, specific skill instruction for the linguistic and pragmatic components of a low tech communication system for an elderly AAC user with Broca's aphasia has been described (Garrett, Beukelman, & Low-Morrow, 1989). Other examples of this principle can also be found in Beukelman, Yorkston, and Dowden (1985).

***Compensating for Past Instructional Deficiencies*** In some cases, the institution of an optimal tomorrow system is entirely dependent on the AAC user acquiring complex, rather specific skills. Perhaps the clearest examples of this situation are young adult AAC users, many of whom have severe cerebral palsy, who have the ability and the motivation to learn to read and write, but who have not been provided with sufficient instruction (Berninger & Gans, 1986b; Smith, Thurston, Light, Parnes, & O'Keefe, 1989). These individuals need to acquire literacy skills in order to use AAC systems with flexible, orthographic displays. In addition, many who use and are satisfied with nonorthographic AAC systems may want to be able to read and write for personal or educational reasons. Intensive specific skill instruction in literacy skills will be necessary to compensate for past instructional deficiencies in this area.

> Principle 6: Provide information, training, and support to AAC users, their communication partners, and their facilitators to build communicative competence.

## Partner and Facilitator Training

Light (1989b) identified four types of competencies that are necessary for successful augmented communication: 1) operational competence, 2) linguistic competence, 3) social competence, and 4) strategic competence. AAC users need the ongoing support of facilitators and communication partners in order to acquire all the skills needed for each competency (see Light et al., 1988, for an excellent example). Basic principles of facilitator training are discussed in this section.

***Operational Competence*** The most immediate need for the user and those who support him or her is to acquire operational competence as quickly as possible when an AAC system is introduced. This requires instruction in all operational and maintenance aspects of the device or system (see Lee & Thomas, 1990, for details). Often, the AAC user is not the primary recipient of much of this instruction, and trained support personnel, whom we refer to as "facilitators," may take on much of the responsibility for operational competence. These facilitators may be parents, spouses, or other family members; educational or residential staff; friends; and other people who are involved in and committed to the AAC user's communicative well-being. In school settings, new facilitators may have to be trained in AAC operation each school year to keep pace with staff turnover and teacher and staff rotations. For example, one fourth-grade student we know of, who has had the same speech-language pathologist and paraprofessional working with her since kindergarten, has nonetheless had 16 people trained in operational aspects of her system over a 5-year period (Beukelman, 1991). The AAC user, the facilitators, or both need to: 1) keep the vocabulary in the device up-to-date; 2) construct overlays or other displays as needed; 3) protect the device against breakage, damage, or other problems; 4) secure necessary repairs; 5) modify the system for tomorrow's needs; and 6) generally ensure day-to-day availability and operation. Generally, operational competence is less demanding for unaided or low tech devices, and this is one reason why they may be preferable when facilitator availability is identified as a constraint (see chap. 7, this volume).

**Linguistic Competence**    Linguistic competence involves a functional mastery of the symbol system or linguistic code used for the display. Equally important, the AAC user must learn the native language spoken by communication partners in order to receive messages. For the bilingual user, this may mean learning the family language as well as that of the community at large (Light, 1989b). For AAC users with acquired disabilities, much of this learning may be in place at the time of intervention, leaving only the AAC-specific tasks to be mastered. For persons with congenital disabilities, however, all of these skills must be learned within the physical, sensory, or cognitive constraints that the AAC user experiences.

Parents, communication specialists, friends, and other facilitators can play a major role in assisting AAC users to master this formidable set of tasks. First, facilitators can offer ongoing opportunities for practicing expressive language (both native and augmentative) in natural contexts (Berry, 1987; MacDonald & Gillette, 1986a). In some cases, this may be simply helping the AAC user learn the augmentative symbol system or code through drill and practice sessions. In other cases, especially if the user has a history of poor generalization, facilitators may themselves have to learn the symbol system in order to provide sufficient opportunities for practice (e.g., manual signing [Loeding, Zangari, & Lloyd, 1990; Spragale & Micucci, 1990]). Specific strategies for assisting linguistic competence in relation to the AAC system are discussed in greater detail in the chapters in Part II of this work.

It is also important for facilitators to provide receptive language models in the spoken language of the community and family and in the symbols or codes used in the AAC display. Receptive language input strategies may include aided language stimulation vests or boards (Goossens', 1989), symbol song strips used with music (Musselwhite & St. Louis, 1988), joint use of the AAC user's display by the facilitator (Bruno, 1986), or providing key word input through manual signing (see Blackstone, Cassatt-James, & Bruskin, 1988, for additional strategies). These strategies are discussed in more detail in Part II of this volume.

> Principle 7: Meaningful communication is a shared responsibility.

**Social Competence**    Of the four areas identified by Light (1989b), social competence has been the focus of most of the research in the AAC field (e.g., Kraat, 1985; Light, 1988). Social competence requires the AAC user to have knowledge, judgment, and skills in both the sociolinguistic and sociorelational aspects of communication, or "competence as to when to speak, when not, and as to what to talk about, with whom, when, where, in what manner" (Hymes, 1972, p. 277). For example, sociolinguistic skills include abilities to: 1) initiate, maintain, and terminate conversations; 2) give and take turns; 3) communicate a variety of functions (e.g., requesting, rejecting); and 4) engage in a variety of coherent and cohesive interactions. Light (1988) suggested that some sociorelational skills that are important for AAC users include: 1) a positive self-image, 2) an interest in others and a desire to communicate, 3) active participation in conversation, 4) responsiveness to partners, and 5) the ability to put partners at ease.

Opportunities to practice social competence skills in natural contexts may be critical for the

AAC user and his or her primary facilitators. A number of "facilitator training" manuals or programs have been developed for AAC users who have a variety of backgrounds and AAC system needs (e.g., Blackstone et al., 1988; Culp & Carlisle, 1988; Light, McNaughton, & Parnes, 1986; MacDonald & Gillette, 1986b; Manolson, 1985; McNaughton & Light, 1989; Reichle et al., 1991; Siegel-Causey & Guess, 1989). Both the number and the quality in recent years of such efforts are indicative of the importance of providing extensive training in social competence skills to both AAC users and their facilitators.

Information, training, and support efforts related to social competence must often go beyond specific training for the AAC user and facilitators. Direct work with communication partners who encounter the AAC user only socially is also important in many cases. For example, the AAC user's friends and peers may need information about how to adjust their interactions to accommodate the requirements of the AAC system (e.g., allowing sufficient pauses for message composition). Or, explanations of how to interact with the user of a low tech display (e.g., the need to echo messages as they are indicated in order to provide feedback) may be necessary. Brief inservice training to an AAC user's entire school class to demystify the AAC system may be useful, and, in many cases, users can participate in or conduct these sessions. Whatever the content and however brief, communication partner interventions such as these are often just as critical as more extensive facilitator training endeavors.

**Strategic Competence** Because even the most flexible AAC systems impose some interactive limitations on their users, knowledge, judgment, and skills are needed that allow the users to "communicate effectively within restrictions" (Light, 1989b, p. 141). Instruction in strategic competence involves teaching various adaptive or coping strategies to use when communication breakdowns occur. For example, an AAC user may learn to transmit the message "Please slow down and wait for me to finish," or use a gesture that means "No, you misunderstood." This is another area of training from which partners, as well as facilitators and AAC users, can benefit. For example, many AAC users appreciate the increased efficiency that results if the communication partner helps to co-construct messages by guessing. In order for this to occur, however, a facilitator or the AAC user him or herself must teach the partner how to guess accurately. Unfortunately, few guidelines for facilitator or partner training exist in this domain.

**Assigning Responsibilities** In addition to providing instruction in operational, linguistic, social, and strategic competence, facilitators also assume other responsibilities. For example, someone must be responsible for planning and executing the AAC user's educational and vocational programs, securing funding for AAC interventions, providing ongoing technical supports, and ensuring that efforts are coordinated and properly sequenced. Usually, the facilitators for these tasks are members of the AAC user's assessment and intervention team. One team member/facilitator is usually responsible for each area, and others are assigned to assist. For example, the speech-language pathologist is usually responsible for managing interventions to increase the AAC user's linguistic competence, and teachers, parents, and paraprofessionals may serve as assistants. An adult AAC user and his spouse may agree to manage funding for the intervention with assistance from a social worker or vocational rehabilitation specialist. As part of decision making and planning, the team (including the family and AAC user) must determine how various facilitator instructional and support responsibilities will be delegated. Specifically, the team decides who will serve as the manager and who will assist in each major area. One of the greatest mistakes a team can make is to fail to make these roles and responsibilities explicit, assuming that everyone understands what needs to be done and who will do it. The result is that efforts are poorly coordinated and that important tasks do not get done. In addition, unless facilitator roles are explicitly assigned to specific team members, accountability is difficult to achieve. Table 8.2. provides a planning form (Cumley, 1991) that can be used by the team to decide who will perform which facilitator roles and responsibilities.

**Table 8.2.** Team member/facilitator responsibilities and roles

Directions: In the appropriate box, indicate who is responsible for each role:
Manager (M): Assumes primary responsibility (usually one person for each area of responsibility)
Assistant (A): Provides instructional assistance or other supports (one or more persons per area of responsibility)

| Area of responsibility | AAC user | Parent/ guardian/spouse | Speech-language pathologist | Regular/ special educator | Personal assistant/ paraprofessional | Motor therapist (OT, PT) | Other: | Other: |
|---|---|---|---|---|---|---|---|---|
| AAC operational competence | | | | | | | | |
| AAC linguistic competence | | | | | | | | |
| AAC social competence | | | | | | | | |
| AAC strategic competence | | | | | | | | |
| Educational program | | | | | | | | |
| Vocational program | | | | | | | | |
| Home program | | | | | | | | |
| Overall coordination | | | | | | | | |
| Funding | | | | | | | | |
| Technical support | | | | | | | | |
| Other: | | | | | | | | |
| Other: | | | | | | | | |

Team member/facilitator responsible

Based on Cumley (1991).

***Social Network Interventions*** In addition to facilitators who assume instructional and managerial roles, other members of an AAC user's social network may also need specific support and guidance. The availability and skills of communication partners affect the overall quality of AAC users' social environments and are thus critically important. Initiation of an AAC system may require more social adjustment than anything else, particularly for adults with acquired and degenerative impairments. Friends and relatives may need be to be encouraged to visit as the individual becomes less able to use natural speech and as communication becomes more difficult. An elderly individual may require glasses or hearing aids in order to hear or see the AAC system of his or her companion. Grandchildren may need to be reassured that even though grandpa's speech sounds different after his stroke, his is still able to "read" stories to them by pointing to pictures or by using another technique. AAC users with acquired disorders may find themselves "all dressed up with no one to talk to" as their social lives become limited to immediate family members and caregivers, if concerted efforts are not made to maintain a broad social network.

Social network interventions may also be necessary for persons with congenital impairments, particularly during times of transition. The first years spent in a preschool, elementary school, junior high, senior high, college or university, new job, or new neighborhood—these are all periods when social network interventions may be particularly necessary to help the AAC user adjust interaction habits and priorities. To assume that an AAC user will be able to initiate and establish social networks without assistance during transitional periods is often unrealistic and is likely to result in disappointment. Clearly, the overall AAC intervention plan must anticipate such transitions and attempt to minimize their impact through social network interventions.

## EVALUATE INTERVENTION EFFECTIVENESS: IS THE PERSON PARTICIPATING?

The final steps of the Participation Model (Figure 7.1.) refer to generic strategies for evaluating the effectiveness of communication interventions. Blackstone (1989c) identified five main problems in evaluating effectiveness: 1) lack of time and money for evaluation, 2) poor validity of available assessment instruments, 3) difficulty obtaining reliable measurements, 4) lack of functional assessment tools, and 5) evaluation constraints imposed by the service delivery model. Effectiveness evaluation can be conceptualized as occurring at three levels: evaluation related to impairment, evaluation related to disability, and evaluation related to handicap (Beukelman, 1986).

*Impairment* refers to "any loss or abnormality of psychological, physiological, or anatomical structure or function" (Wood, 1980, p. 377). Evaluation of the degree to which communication interventions compensate for impairments involves measuring specific cognitive, language, motor, and sensory skills that may change as a result of intervention. Culp (1987) referred to two types of measures in this area: operation parameters and representation parameters. *Operation parameters* reflect the AAC user's ability to interact with the system itself. For example, evaluation at this level of an effort to teach headlight pointing might entail trial-by-trial assessment of correct and incorrect responses to various targets. *Representation parameters* evaluate the AAC user's symbol and grammatical abilities. For example, measurement of the effectiveness of a pictorial symbol intervention might entail daily or weekly data collection of an individual's ability to identify and match the symbols with their referents.

Data collection in educational and rehabilitation settings has traditionally focused on evaluating the impact of an intervention on the impairment. While this assessment may be useful for measuring operational and representational skill acquisition, it may not be sensitive to larger issues related to functional social or strategic competence (Calculator, 1988b). Many measurements for operational and representational skill acquisition evaluation are norm-referenced, such as the Nonspeech Test (Huer, 1983), or are standard measures of spoken language. Readers are referred to published accounts in which AAC effectiveness has been measured in terms of impairment (e.g., Goossens', 1989; Osguthorpe & Chang, 1988; Sutton, 1989).

*Disability* is the aspect of a disorder that is related to the reduced ability of an individual to meet the needs of daily living (Beukelman, 1986). Effectiveness evaluations related to disability seek to judge various communication techniques as they relate to communication in actual school, community, vocational, recreational, and domestic environments. The Participation Model emphasizes this level of evaluation by determining the AAC user's participation in the activities identified during the initial needs assessment. Intervention effectiveness can be quantified based on the observed or reported level of participation. If the desired level of participation is not achieved, the Participation Model requires reexamination of opportunity and access factors that may be barriers.

Culp (1987) referred to effectiveness evaluation related to disability in terms of a number of "interaction parameters" (p. 174), including measurements such as: 1) how many and what modes of communication the user produces, 2) how many times the user initiates or responds to a partner's message, and 3) how the user repairs message breakdowns. A number of specific evaluation tools, both criterion- and norm-referenced, have been used to measure the impact of intervention on the AAC user's disability (e.g., Bolton & Dashiell, 1984). Examples of protocols in this area can be found in Culp (1987, 1989), Culp and Carlisle (1988), Garrett et al. (1989), and Romski and Sevcik (1988b).

Finally, *handicap* refers to the societal disadvantage that results from either impairment or disability (Beukelman, 1986). Related evaluations seek to measure the degree to which a communication intervention affects the attitudes of and acceptance by communication partners and others. Culp (1987) referred to evaluation measures in this area as "psychosocial parameters" (p. 174), such as the attitudes of AAC users and their partners about the communication system or the adjustment patterns of users and significant others. Protocols adapted from empirical studies may be useful to gather some of this information. For example, Mathy-Laikko and Coxson (1984) used a 7-point scale for communication partners to rate their reactions to various types of AAC output devices in terms of pairs of opposites (e.g., intelligible/unintelligible, fast/slow, clear/unclear). Unfortunately, few validated reliable instruments currently exist in this area. Exceptions include the assessment tools in *PACT: Partners in Augmentative Communication Training* (Culp & Carlisle, 1988) and more generic instruments such as the Parenting Stress Index (Abidin, 1983).

> "[My daughter] says she wants to be a veterinarian. Can someone with severe cerebral palsy come close to that goal? In 10 or 15 years, will medicine and technology have caught up with Ana's aspirations?" (Cy Berlowitz, 1991)

## FOLLOW-UP

According to the principle of interventions for today and tomorrow discussed previously, most AAC interventions never end! That is, once an AAC user has mastered a device or system for today, parallel training and practice can begin to prepare for one that is even more accurate, efficient, and nonfatiguing for tomorrow. Once these new skills are acquired, today becomes yesterday, tomorrow becomes today, and planning can begin for a new "tomorrow!"

If the AAC user is a child, this cycle is likely to require repetition at each transition from preschool to kindergarten, from elementary school to junior high, from junior high to senior high, and from senior high to either employment or post-secondary school. Adults with either congenital impairments (e.g., cerebral palsy) or acquired, nondegenerative impairments (e.g., spinal cord injury) are likely to experience less frequent need for system alterations, unless their employment, residence, or family status changes markedly. Adults with degenerative illnesses (e.g., ALS, multiple sclerosis), however, may require frequent system changes as their abilities deteriorate and living situations change. Finally, long-term AAC users will require additional modifications to their systems as they approach retirement age, begin to shift priorities, and experience changes in ability (see Light, 1988).

# Chapter 9

# *Vocabulary Selection and Retention*

> "Vocabulary selection [in AAC] can be viewed as the process of choosing a small list of appropriate words or items from a pool of all possibilities" (Yorkston, Dowden, Honsinger, Marriner, & Smith, 1988, p. 189).

The process of selecting the messages to be included in a communication system is unique to the AAC field. Because word selection and message formulation are such efficient processes for most nondisabled speakers, these speakers enter communication situations without giving much consideration beforehand to the words and phrases they will use. Indeed, vocabulary selection during natural speech and written communication interactions is so automatic that most AAC specialists themselves have little experience selecting vocabulary items in advance of the act of speaking or writing. Even professionals who have regular contact with persons who experience communication disorders such as stuttering, voice problems, articulation problems, and cleft palate rarely need to pre-select messages to support conversational or written communication. Because the vocabulary selection process in AAC *is* unique, this chapter provides an overview to supplement information that is included in Chapters 10–19, which cover specific interventions.

## VOCABULARY NEEDS FOR DIFFERENT COMMUNICATION MODES AND CONTEXTS

The words that we use to communicate with are greatly influenced by the communication context and modality. For example, we speak more colloquially and casually when conversing with friends than we do when orally presenting a formal report to a class, business meeting, or professional group. When adults speak to young children, they use different words and grammatical structures than when they speak to other adults. Furthermore, written communication is somewhat different from spoken communication. General knowledge of these different vocabulary use patterns is important when vocabulary items are selected for inclusion in AAC systems.

### Spoken and Written Communication

Although speaking and writing may seem to be different, but equivalent, ways of communicating, there are actually inherent differences between these two modes of communication that may not be immediately apparent (Barritt & Kroll, 1978). In general, spoken communication involves the use of more personal references and more first and second person pronouns (e.g., I, we, you) than does written communication. Less lexical (vocabulary) diversity is present in speech than in writing, because words tend to be repeated more often. Speech also tends to contain shorter thought units, more monosyllabic and familiar words, and more subordinate ideas than writing.

In a study that compared these two types of language in the classroom, McGinnis (1991) collected 1,000-word spoken and written samples from 34 third-grade students in a regular education setting. She found that the students' written vocabulary was considerably more diverse than their spoken vocabulary. For example, the type-to-token ratio (i.e., number of different words divided by the total number of words in a sample) was lower for spoken (TTR = .30) than for written language samples (TTR = .46). This indicates that spoken words were produced more repeatedly than written words, because fewer spoken words represented a greater proportion of the total language sample than did a similar sample of written words.

### School Talk and Home Talk

Vocabulary use also varies for spoken communication depending on the communication context. For example, "school talk" can be quite different from "home talk." In school, language is not used for the same purposes, such as to meet immediate needs and achieve social closeness with familiar partners, as it may be at home. Instead, children talk primarily with relatively unfamiliar adults in school in order to build a theory of reality, share their understanding of actions and situations, and acquire knowledge (Westby, 1985). They are required to "shift away from the expectation of shared assumptions (implicit meaning) to interpreting overtly lexicalized intentions (explicit meaning)" (Westby, 1985, p. 157).

Few investigations have documented in detail the vocabulary use patterns of children or adults at home and in school. One exception is the work of Marvin, Beukelman, and Vanderhoof (1991), which recorded the vocabulary spoken by five preschool-age, nondisabled children in home and school. Approximately one third of the words produced by these children were spoken only at school, one third were spoken only at home, and one third were spoken both at home and school. (In Chapter 10, we provide additional details related to this study.)

Differences across specific school environments might also be expected to have dramatic effects on the words communicated in classrooms. For example, the content of elementary and secondary school curricula in various subjects requires access to vocabulary items that may change daily or weekly. As the topics in a student's science unit shift from plants, to planets, to prehistoric animals, and to rocks, the extent to which he or she can communicate successfully in the classroom will depend largely on the availability of the appropriate vocabulary. The vocabulary set designed to support a student's conversational interactions, which are relatively stable and predictable, is unlikely to be useful in meeting frequently changing curricular communication needs.

---

Greg's friends came to me one day and said, "You need to put some cool stuff in Greg's machine [an electronic communication device]. He sounds weird now." "What do you mean?" I asked, "What's wrong with what's in there?" "Well, you know how he says 'Hello, how are you?' when he comes into the class in the morning?" his friends replied. "No one talks like that. We say 'How you doin', dudes?' or 'Hey, guys, what's happening?' or something." (P. Daharsh [Greg's teacher], personal communication, March, 1991)

---

### Age and Gender Variables

*Age*   Research reports suggest that age, gender, and cultural (e.g., ethnic) differences may affect the topics and vocabulary words used during interactions. For example, the communication patterns of elderly persons have been investigated from at least two different perspectives. One perspective has been to study and document the language differences between elderly and younger persons in order to describe the language deficits that people experience as they grow older. Studies from this perspective have suggested that people produce fewer proper nouns, more general nouns, and more ambiguous references as they age. In addition, the lexical variety of their nominal and syntactic structures decreases (Kemper, 1988; Kynette & Kemper, 1986; Ulatowska, Cannito, Hayashi, & Fleming, 1985). Goodglass (1980) reported that the size of individuals' active expressive vocabularies decreases quite markedly during the individuals' seventh decade.

A second perspective has been to view aging in terms of a model of human cognitive development, in which the performance of elderly persons is seen as a legitimate, adaptive stage of development (Mergler & Goldstein, 1983). Viewed from this perspective, elderly people appear to tailor their communicative interactions to the unique task of "telling," that is, information sharing. In their role as "tellers," elderly individuals relate to the past as a resource for assigning meaning to the present (Boden & Bielby, 1983). For example, the topical references made by five elderly women, ranging in age from 63 to 79 years, during conversational exchanges were examined (Stuart, Vanderhoof, & Beukelman, 1990). The younger women made more "present oriented" comments and referred much more frequently to topics related to family life than did the older women. In contrast, the older women referred to their social networks outside the family much more often than did their younger counterparts.

**Gender**  A number of researchers have written about the influence of gender on language and word use. For example, men and women appear to use parts of speech differently. Men use fewer pronouns, and more adjectives, unusual adverbs, and prepositions than do women. Women use more auxiliary words and negations than do men (Gleser, Gottschalk, & John, 1959; Poole, 1979). Men also appear to speak about different topics than women. Gleser et al. (1959) found that women make reference to motivations, feelings, emotions, and themselves more often than men, while men refer to time, space, quantity, and destructive actions more often than women.

Stuart (1991) summarized the work of a number of different researchers who examined the differences between "male talk" and "female talk" as follows:

> The studies were conducted in a Spanish village; a traditional working-class family in England; among Kung Bushmen in Africa; sidewalk conversations in New York City, Columbus, Ohio, and London, England; women working in a telephone company in Somerville, Massachusetts; blue collar couples in New York; and participants in the draft resistance movement in the United States. The results were impressively similar and can be reported collectively. Female topics were found to be: people (themselves, other women, men), personal lives/interpersonal matters (age, lifestyles, life's troubles), household needs, books, food, clothes, and decorations. Male topics were found to be: work (land, crops, weather, animals, prices, business, money, wages, machinery, and carpentry), legal matters, taxes, army experience, and sports or amusements (baseball, motorcycles, sailing, hunting, mountain climbing, and cockfighting). (p. 43–44)

Although information about vocabulary use patterns of various groups of nondisabled persons is gradually increasing, information about the vocabulary use of AAC users of different genders, ages, or cultural backgrounds is very limited. Until such information is available, AAC specialists must be sensitive to how these factors and others (e.g., cultural differences) may affect the vocabulary selection process. Peer informants are perhaps the best source of specific vocabulary needs and should be used as a resource to guard against the selection of inappropriate vocabulary.

## VOCABULARY NEEDS OF PERSONS WITH DIFFERENT COMMUNICATION CAPABILITIES

The overall communication capability of the individual who will use an AAC system is another important factor that should be considered as vocabulary is selected. In this section, three types of individuals will be considered: 1) those who are preliterate, such as young children who have not yet learned to write and read; 2) those who are nonliterate, such as individuals who have not been able to learn to read or write and people who have lost these abilities because of their impairments; and 3) those who are literate.

> "They are unable to create spontaneously their own lexicon and must operate with a vocabulary selected by someone else or preselected, not spontaneously chosen by themselves" (Carlson, 1981, p. 240).

## Preliterate Individuals

Individuals who are preliterate have not developed reading and writing skills but are likely to do so. These individuals are often young children, but they may also be older children or even adults who were never given the instruction needed to become literate. Thus, the vocabulary items in their AAC systems are represented by one or more of the symbols or codes discussed in Chapters 2 and 3. Generally, the vocabulary requirements of preliterate individuals can be divided into two categories: vocabulary that is needed to communicate essential messages and vocabulary that is needed to develop their language systems.

**Coverage Vocabulary**    Vocabulary that is needed to communicate essential messages is referred to as *coverage vocabulary* (Vanderheiden & Kelso, 1987), because it contains messages that are necessary to "cover" an individual's basic communication needs. Because preliterate individuals are unable to spell out unique messages letter by letter, care must be taken to include as many such messages as will be required, regardless of how frequently they are used. For example, a person may use a message such as "I am having trouble breathing" very rarely, but if this is even an occasional occurrence, it should be included in the coverage vocabulary.

> "The objective of this type of word set [coverage vocabulary] is to try to provide the individual with the ability to communicate most effectively and about the widest range of topics, given the limited word set" (Vanderheiden & Kelso, 1987, p. 196).

Coverage vocabulary is highly dependent on the communication needs of the AAC user. As noted previously, these needs are likely to change, depending on the user's age and the communicative context. For example, the coverage vocabulary needed at a birthday party would be very different from that required during a physical therapy session. Coverage vocabularies for preliterate individuals are selected through careful analysis of their environmental and communication needs. The details of this process are discussed later in this chapter.

Coverage vocabularies for preliterate individuals are commonly organized by context so that they are available when needed. Thus, separate communication "miniboards" may be designed to contain the vocabulary items needed while eating, dressing, bathing, playing a specific game, or participating in specific school activities. These miniboards are often located strategically in the environment where each particular activity takes place, such as the kitchen, bathroom, or specific classroom area, so that they are readily available when needed. At other times, these miniboards may be stored in a carrying case or notebook so that the appropriate board is available for a specific communication context. Additional miniboard strategies are discussed in detail in Chapter 10 and Chapter 13. Alternatively, vocabulary items may be programmed into an electronic communication device with speech output, using "themes" or "levels" that are contextually relevant to the individual. An excellent example of this type of application with iconic encoding (i.e., Minspeak) was proved by Bruno (1989).

**Developmental Vocabulary**    The vocabulary set for an AAC system may also include words that the individual does not yet know and that are selected to encourage vocabulary growth. For example, if a preliterate child is about to encounter a new experience for the first time, such as a circus, vocabulary items associated with the new context may be included on the communication display, although the child has never before used them. During the circus, the child's parent or friend may point to various vocabulary items on the display that are associated with the circus events such as "clown," "lion," "funny," and "scary." It is hoped that the child will begin to learn to use these new vocabulary items to communicate about the new experience. For young children, vocabulary items that are selected to enhance vocabulary learning are usually based on developmental information in much the same way that words are selected to enhance the semantic systems of nondisabled children. This is discussed in more detail in Chapter 10.

Vocabulary selected for preliterate individuals should also include words or messages that encourage them to use various language structures and combinations. For example, words should be available such as "more" to indicate continuation, "no" to indicate negation, and "there" to indicate location. A variety of nouns, verbs, and adjectives might be included to support the individual's use of word combinations (e.g., "more car," "no eat"). As the person's language abilities expand, vocabulary should be selected to encourage the use of two-, three-, four-, and longer word combinations. Generally, these words are chosen from a developmental perspective; for example, the language patterns of speaking children of the same age may be examined to identify the words most commonly combined in early language.

## Nonliterate Individuals

The term "nonliterate" refers primarily to those individuals who are unable to spell well enough to formulate their messages on a letter-by-letter basis and who are not expected to develop or regain these spontaneous spelling skills. Most of these individuals are also unable to read, except perhaps for a few functional sight words that they have memorized. The vocabulary selection process for nonliterate individuals primarily aims to meet their communication needs. Nevertheless, the coverage vocabularies for these individuals differ in a number of ways from those discussed for preliterate individuals.

First, vocabulary items selected for nonliterate AAC users are nearly always chosen from a functional rather than a developmental perspective. Single words or, more often, whole messages are selected to meet individual daily communication needs. These vocabulary items are represented by one or more types of symbols, as discussed in Chapter 2. Second, it is even more important that the vocabularies selected for nonliterate individuals be age and gender appropriate. Many of these individuals, especially those with intellectual disabilities, may be adolescents or adults, and special care must be taken not to select words and messages for them that are only appropriate for infants or young children. For example, a symbol of a happy face may be used for a young child to represent the word "happy," while for an adolescent, this same symbol might be translated to mean "awesome." Even better, a "thumbs up" symbol might be used to represent "awesome" or "way to go" on an adolescent's display.

It is also appropriate to include at least some developmental vocabulary in the AAC systems of nonliterate individuals. For example, new vocabulary items should be added whenever new environments or participation opportunities are included in the individual's life. However, the goal is to expand the words and concepts about which the individual can communicate, not necessarily to increase his or her use of complex syntactical forms. Again, efficient, functional communication in a variety of age-appropriate contexts is of paramount importance for these individuals. Additional guidelines for selecting vocabulary to be used in the AAC systems of nonliterate persons are provided in Chapters 13, 14, and 17.

> To a 17-year-old, mother is "Mom," not "Mommy"; father is "Dad" or "Pop," not "Daddy"; and food tastes "gross" or "bad," not "yucky."

## Literate Individuals

AAC users who are able to read and spell have access to a greater variety of message preparation options. Literate individuals are able to formulate messages on a letter-by-letter and word-by-word basis and to retrieve complete messages, with appropriate AAC equipment, once they have been stored. Depending on the communication needs of an individual, three different types of messages may be prepared for quick retrieval: those related to timing enhancement, those related to message acceleration, and those related to fatigue reduction.

*Timing Enhancement*   Some messages require careful timing in order to be appropriate. Although a literate AAC user may have the ability to spell timely messages letter by letter, their meanings are lost if they are not communicated quickly. For example, consider the message "Please pick up my feet before you roll my wheelchair forward." If this message is not delivered in a timely manner, it loses its relevance, as the wheelchair may have been moved while the person was formulating the message. Thus, messages that have important timing requirements are usually stored and retrieved in their entirety. Additional examples of such messages include: "Wait just a minute, I'm not finished yet," "Before you go, would you help me with this?" and "When will we meet again?" AAC users and their facilitators are the best sources for unique messages related to timing enhancement.

*Message Acceleration*   In addition to timing enhancement, vocabulary items are often selected to accelerate a user's overall communication rate. Vanderheiden and Kelso (1987) introduced the term *acceleration vocabulary* to refer to words or messages that occur so frequently and are so lengthy that the use of an encoding strategy to retrieve them results in substantial keystroke savings for the AAC user. (Readers are referred to Chapter 3 for a more complete discussion of message encoding and communication rate.) Thus, the words chosen for a message acceleration vocabulary set are not chosen to allow an AAC user to communicate particular ideas, but rather to speed up the rate at which they can communicate them.

---

"Typically, the first 50 [most frequently occurring] words will account for 40%–50% of the total words communicated, even though they account for only 1/2% of a 10,000-word vocabulary. One hundred words would account for approximately 60%, 200 words 70%, and 400 words 80%" (Vanderheiden & Kelso, 1987, p.196).

---

*Fatigue Reduction*   The third type of vocabulary set typically selected for persons who are literate is one that results in reduced fatigue. In many cases, words and phrases that comprise the acceleration vocabulary set are the same as those that are encoded to reduce fatigue. In certain situations, however, fatigue reduction requires a slightly different approach to vocabulary selection. For example, fatigue is a cumulative problem for some AAC users. Early in the morning, they may be able to use their AAC systems with more physical efficiency than later in the day or the evening. In such cases, fatigue reduction vocabulary items should be selected to cover their communication needs during the portion of the day when their fatigue levels are highest. In this way, they can avoid having to spell out words letter by letter when they are tired. Analyses of communication patterns during periods of high fatigue can guide the selection of words and messages that will be most helpful to reduce fatigue.

## VOCABULARY SOURCES

Rarely does one individual have enough knowledge and experience to select all the vocabulary items needed by an AAC user in a specific environment. Rather, it is necessary to obtain this vocabulary information from a variety of sources. The sources that are commonly used to help in vocabulary selection are summarized in this section, along with indications of the situations in which a particular source is most useful.

## Core and Fringe Vocabularies

Generally, the vocabulary needed in a given communication situation is composed of two types of words: core and fringe vocabulary. *Core vocabulary* refers to words and messages that are commonly used in a particular situation. Core vocabulary items are generally identified through empirical research or clinical reports that assess vocabulary use patterns of a number of individuals. *Fringe vocabulary* refers to vocabulary words and messages that are specific to the individual. For example, these might include names of specific people, locations, and activities of interest. Identification of items for a fringe vocabulary set occurs after analysis, by a variety of informants, of the specific communication needs of an individual. The relationship between the concepts of core and fringe vocabularies, as discussed here, and the concepts of coverage and acceleration vocabularies, discussed previously, are depicted in Figure 9.1. A variety of vocabulary selection resources and analysis procedures have been developed to compile core and fringe vocabularies. These are highlighted in the following sections.

**Core Vocabulary**   Three sources have been used to identify core vocabularies for specific individuals: 1) word lists based on the vocabulary use patterns of other successful AAC system users, 2) word lists based on the use patterns of the specific individual, and 3) word lists based on the performance of natural speakers or writers in similar contexts.

*Vocabulary Use Patterns of AAC Users*   Of particular interest in developing core vocabulary lists is the performance of persons who are operationally and socially competent with their AAC systems. Communication samples have been collected from these individuals, over extended periods of time, and their word use patterns have then been analyzed. The first of these studies collected the entire communication corpuses produced on a letter-by-letter basis over 14 days by five disabled young adults who used Canon Communicators (Beukelman, Yorkston, Poblete, & Naranjo, 1984). From a composite list that consisted of all words produced by all five subjects, the 500 most frequently occurring words were identified, and these are presented in Table 9.1. Approximately 80% of the words communicated by the five subjects were represented by these 500 most frequently occurring words, as displayed in Figure 9.2.

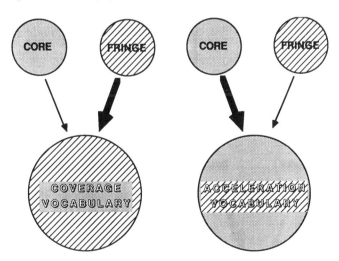

**Figure 9.1.**   Relationship between core/fringe and coverage/acceleration vocabularies. A coverage vocabulary is composed mainly of fringe words, in addition to some core words. An acceleration vocabulary is made up primarily of core words, with fringe words added to meet individual needs.

**Table 9.1.**  Five hundred most frequently occurring words produced by five adult AAC users (listed from most to least frequently occuring)

| | | | | | | | |
|---|---|---|---|---|---|---|---|
| I | very | new | since | miss | such | hot | two |
| to | use | nice | boy | pay | seeing | water | live |
| you | can't | pants | damn | cars | kept | always | yesterday |
| the | work | never | words | able | he's | board | pick |
| a | now | fix | knee | these | stereo | which | anyway |
| it | more | lunch | gets | clothes | walked | hospital | number |
| my | didn't | tape | talking | called | laundry | love | box |
| and | help | call | hurts | stop | going | money | their |
| in | him | used | problem | show | put | getting | minutes |
| is | who | been | mouth | hand | take | pee | she's |
| me | right | light | what's | haven't | we | hate | fine |
| on | that's | hope | nurse | save | did | leave | hair |
| have | day | thought | while | broke | please | arm | leaving |
| do | tomorrow | under | came | sun | time | pack | stay |
| of | foot | pretty | write | easy | know | old | year |
| that | long | mean | cookies | second | one | garage | place |
| get | were | kind | weight | thanks | see | hard | sit |
| for | an | way | into | pass | just | pop | plus |
| what | today | crib | bath | moved | am | doctor | important |
| but | by | might | wrong | tapes | off | guess | mind |
| if | over | great | being | makes | as | week | months |
| can | them | push | you'd | gone | think | let | handle |
| don't | I've | even | years | full | there | working | juice |
| be | really | head | big | gift | make | once | track |
| I'm | walk | both | radio | feels | had | shoes | food |
| with | two | wouldn't | looking | everything | dad | plug | afraid |
| are | any | far | happened | apple | need | glad | dumb |
| like | let's | set | told | nothing | where | many | word |
| was | chair | things | rather | speed | room | whole | between |
| mom | tonight | game | oh | must | here | man | run |
| how | again | hurt | bring | dead | he | yet | carry |
| this | only | stuff | care | piece | back | took | supper |
| so | feel | music | breakfast | already | some | red | lay |
| will | bag | wait | he'll | late | still | because | doctors |
| go | eat | next | life | part | I'll | ago | ice |
| not | has | done | six | normal | look | blue | cost |
| or | find | also | hit | wrap | bed | walker | instead |
| want | then | anyone | face | type | play | block | job |
| would | four | our | suppose | sleep | wish | line | door |
| when | maybe | sorry | huh | notes | may | name | wondering |
| up | left | until | most | insure | sure | hold | low |
| all | last | wear | understand | real | something | ever | hello |
| out | those | making | twenty | asked | buy | fell | toilet |
| it's | dinner | book | girl | horn | night | towel | lap |
| your | doing | cave | close | guy | say | isn't | surgery |
| at | first | eyes | lot | might | talk | floor | sound |
| she | stand | skin | shirt | days | his | doesn't | probably |
| they | pleased | paper | myself | tired | should | table | clear |
| about | battery | away | tube | slow | ask | looks | purse |
| no | said | TV | started | sitting | try | forgot | Friday |
| could | people | enough | least | nose | little | bit | cream |
| down | won't | walking | there's | lift | than | half | brain |
| tell | a lot | school | best | comes | better | saw | fall |
| home | give | move | almost | card | does | mine | tight |
| her | I'd | heard | thank | coming | before | made | diamond |
| good | clean | hour | through | thinking | thing | beautiful | awful |
| too | turn | bad | minute | month | same | three | shop |
| why | watch | using | later | sounds | keep | therapy | free |
| ok | well | noise | cut | study | eye | program | |
| because | remember | side | yourself | pins | went | own | |
| from | other | check | morning | read | cold | building | |
| much | yes | pot | listen | feet | | open | |
| car | anything | believe | wonder | trying | | every | |

From Beukelman, D., Yorkston, K., Poblete, M., and Naranjo, C. (1984). Frequency of word occurrence in communication samples produced by adult communication aid users. *Journal of Speech and Hearing Disorders, 49*, 367; reprinted by permission.

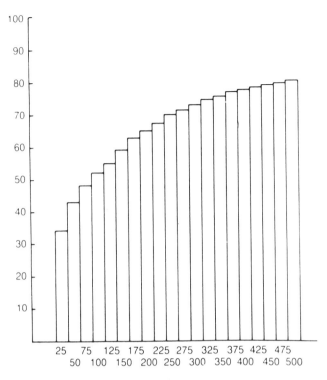

**Figure 9.2.** Mean percentage of total communication samples (averaged across five subjects) represented by vocabulary lists of various sizes. (Vertical axis = mean percentage of total sample, horizontal axis = core list size in number of words.) (From Beukelman, D., Yorkston, K., Poblete, M., & Naranjo, C. [1984]. Frequency of word occurrence in communication samples produced by adult communication aid users. *Journal of Speech and Hearing Disorders, 49,* 364; reprinted by permission.)

The Canon Communicator is a small, portable AAC device. It allows messages to be formulated on a letter-by-letter basis and displayed on strips of paper tape. The device does not provide either speech output or computer access. It is manufactured by the Canon Corporation.

In subsequent research, the vocabulary lists produced by 10 AAC users during communicative interactions were compared with six different composite word lists selected from published vocabulary sources (Yorkston, Smith, & Beukelman, 1990). The 10 subjects all used letter-by-letter spelling to express their messages. The results indicated that the subjects actually used between 27%–60% of the words included in the various published lists.

In a companion article, Yorkston, Beukelman, Smith, and Tice (1990) analyzed multiple word sequences from the communication samples investigated in Yorkston, Smith, and Beukelman (1990). They reported that a number of two-word sequences produced by the AAC users occurred frequently both within and across the samples. Word sequences that were longer than two words, however, occurred much less frequently. Both the two- and three-word sequences are listed in Table 9.2. The authors suggested that such two-word sequences be included in message acceleration vocabularies for similar AAC users and that three-word sequences be selected for timing enhancement on an individual basis.

*Vocabulary Use Patterns of a Specific AAC User* Individualized word lists, which are word lists compiled from the past performance of the specific individual for whom an AAC system is being developed, are even more efficient vocabulary sources than are composite lists (Yorkston,

**Table 9.2.**    Frequently occurring two- and three-word sequences in communication samples from AAC users

Frequent three-word sequences

| | | |
|---|---|---|
| I have to (4) | I want to (4) | are you going (3) |
| I don't know (3) | to go to | did you know (2) |
| have to go (2) | I am going (2) | I do not (2) |
| talk to you (2) | to talk to (2) | what are you (2) |
| what is for (2) | you going to (2) | |

Frequent two-word phrases

| | | |
|---|---|---|
| I have (10) | I was (10) | to be (10) |
| do you (9) | going to (9) | have to (9) |
| I don't (9) | want to (9) | in the (8) |
| are you (7) | I can't (7) | I want (7) |
| to go (7) | but I (7) | go to (6) |
| have a (6) | I can (6) | I get (6) |
| in my (6) | me to (6) | out of (6) |
| you have (6) | I didn't (5) | I do (5) |
| I had (5) | I think (5) | if I (5) |
| so I (5) | to do (5) | to the (5) |
| you get (5) | you know (5) | and I (4) |
| don't know (4) | get a (4) | I am (4) |
| I feel (4) | I know (4) | let me (4) |
| like to (4) | of the (4) | on the (4) |
| to get (4) | when I (4) | will be (4) |
| a lot (3) | can I (3) | do it (3) |
| how I (3) | I just (3) | I need (3) |
| I really (3) | I will (3) | I would (3) |
| me a (3) | on my (3) | thank you (3) |
| that I (3) | to you (3) | would you (3) |
| you going (3) | you want (3) | a little (2) |
| and my (2) | at the (2) | came in (2) |
| did not (2) | do I (2) | do not (2) |
| for a (2) | get me (2) | give me (2) |
| he is (2) | how are (2) | how much (2) |
| how to (2) | I did (2) | I go (2) |
| I got (2) | I hate (2) | I like (2) |
| I through (2) | I'll be (2) | I'll have (2) |
| I'm not (2) | if you (2) | in a (2) |
| if for (2) | is my (2) | is that (2) |
| it in (2) | it is (2) | it was (2) |
| last night (2) | my room (2) | not know (2) |
| see you (2) | take a (2) | talk to (2) |
| tell you (2) | that is (2) | the computer (2) |
| the phone (2) | the time (2) | to play (2) |
| to see (2) | what are (2) | what I (2) |
| what is (2) | what time (2) | where is (2) |
| why don't (2) | you can (2) | you do (2) |
| you later (2) | | |

From Yorkston, K., Beukelman, D., Smith, K., and Tice, R. (1990). Extended communication samples of augmented communicators II: Analysis of multiword utterances. *Journal of Speech and Hearing Disorders, 55,* 230; reprinted by permission.

These word sequences occurred at or above a frequency of 1:1,000 in two or more of the subjects' samples. The number in parentheses following the phrase indicates the number of subjects who used the phrase frequently.

Smith, & Beukelman, 1990). This is not unexpected, as it could be assumed that the past performance of an individual AAC user would be the best predictor of his or her future performance. Unfortunately, in many cases, it is difficult to obtain and analyze communication samples from an individual AAC user in order to develop an individualized word list. Nonetheless, efforts to obtain this information appear to be important.

   *Vocabulary Use Patterns of Nondisabled Speakers or Writers*    A considerable number of studies have examined vocabulary use patterns of nondisabled natural speakers and writers. These composite lists provide a rich source of core vocabulary information and can be useful when developing vocabulary lists for specific AAC users. A detailed summary of these word lists is beyond the scope of this chapter. Therefore, Table 9.3. provides a chart that identifies the various studies, the contexts in which the vocabularies were sampled, and the types of subjects involved.

As noted previously, Yorkston, Smith, and Beukelman (1990) indicated that vocabulary selection for individual AAC users is quite complex, since a composite vocabulary list contains only a fraction of the total words that will be needed. These authors summarized their views about the role of core vocabularies in AAC applications in the following statement:

> This is not to suggest that standard [i.e., composite] words lists should be abandoned. On the contrary, our data . . . suggest that they are an excellent source of potential words to be included in an AAC application. The inclusion of standard word lists in the memory of an AAC device is a great time savings for augmented communicators and their facilitators. However, these standard lists must not be taught without careful consideration. Systematic strategies are required to eliminate unnecessary or "costly" words from the standard vocabulary lists as an AAC device is individualized for a given client. In some cases, unnecessary words need not actually be eliminated from the system. In other cases, codes for useful words can simply be taught first. Thus, the sequence of teaching codes is individualized rather than curricular. (p. 223)

***Fringe Vocabulary***   Fringe vocabulary refers to those messages that are unique to the individual AAC user. Such words are used to personalize the vocabulary included in an AAC system and to allow expression of ideas and messages that do not appear in core vocabulary lists. By their very nature, fringe vocabulary items must be recommended by AAC users themselves, or by informants who know them or their communicative situations quite well. The most important potential informant is the individual who will be using the AAC system. AAC users' abilities to act as informants about their own vocabulary and message needs depends on factors that include age, cognitive ability, and language ability, as well as facilitator support provided.

In clinical work, there is a tendency for one or two team AAC team members, often professionals, to select fringe vocabulary items without consulting a sufficient number of informants. The most obvious informants are spouses, parents, siblings, teachers, and other caregivers. Informants such as employers, co-workers, peers, and friends often offer valuable vocabulary suggestions as well. Whenever possible, the AAC user should identify potential informants as well as suggest words and messages to be included or retained in the vocabulary.

Although there has been very little research regarding the development of fringe vocabularies, important suggestions to guide this process have been made. Musselwhite and St. Louis (1988) suggested that initial vocabulary items should: 1) be of high interest to the individual, 2) have potential for frequent use, 3) denote a range of semantic notions and pragmatic functions, 4) reflect the "here and now" for ease of learning, 5) have potential for later multiword use, and 6) provide ease of production or interpretation. Two similar processes have been widely used in the AAC field to facilitate achievement of these criteria. These two processes are described in the sections that follow.

*Environmental Inventory*   In an effort to personalize the vocabulary of AAC users, Carlson (1981) presented an environmental inventory process that can be used to document how the individual participates in and observes various activities. Carlson stated, "By discriminating between observation and participation events, it is possible to gain a better picture of the child's actual experiences within the area rather than the adult's perception of the experience" (p. 42). The environmental inventory process first requires that special equipment, physical positioning, other persons, and materials present in the environment be documented. Then, vocabulary words that might enhance communication interaction are listed after observing the individual during specific activities. Finally, this pool of vocabulary items can be reduced to a smaller list of the most critical words that can be managed on the communication system by the individual who uses it.

*Ecological Inventory*   Mirenda (1985) and Reichle, York, and Sigafoos (1991) described an eco-

**Table 9.3.**   Selected composite vocabulary source lists from nondisabled subjects

| Subject group providing sample | Context/environment in which sample was obtained | Reference |
|---|---|---|
| Nondisabled persons, general | Samples of English writing analyzed statistically to identify the 5,000 most frequently occurring words | Carrol, Davis, and Richman, 1971. *Word frequency book.* |
| Nondisabled persons, general | Unknown. Contains vocabulary lists for academic subject areas such as math and science, words that express feelings, words that sound alike, common abbreviations | Fry, Polk, and Fountoukidis, 1984. *The reading teacher's book of lists.* |
| Nondisabled persons, general | Spoken English words | Howes, 1966. *A word count of spoken English.* |
| Nondisabled persons, general | Spoken words used as an introductory vocabulary for learners of English as a second language | Ogden, 1968. *Basic English: International second language.* |
| Nondisabled preschoolers | Integrated preschool classrooms (i.e., both disabled and nondisabled children attended) | Beukelman, Jones, and Rowan, 1989. *Frequency of word usage by nondisabled peers in integrated preschool classrooms.* |
| Nondisabled preschoolers | Home and preschool contexts | Marvin, Beukelman, and Vanderhoof ,1991. *Vocabulary use patterns by preschool children in home and school contexts.* |
| Nondisabled and disabled preschoolers | Language samples and environmental inventories compiled by educators/speech-language pathologists and parents | Fried-Oken and More, 1992. *A suggested core vocabulary for the augmentative communication of 3- to 6-year-old preliterate children: Data from developmental and environmental samples.* |
| Nondisabled first grade children | Spoken interviews during which children were asked to tell the interviewer a story and to talk about their favorite game, their favorite television show, and the best/most exciting things that ever happened to them | Moe, Hopkins, and Rush, 1982. *The vocabulary of first-grade children.* |
| Nondisabled first grade children | Spoken words, gathered in a variety of contexts | Stemach and Williams, 1988. *Word express: The first 2,500 words of spoken English.* |
| Nondisabled third grade children | Spoken and written academic vocabulary | McGinnis, 1991 . *Development of two source lists for vocabulary selection in augmentative communication: Documentation of the spoken and written vocabulary of third grade students.* |
| Nondisabled adults living in and. near Kent, OH: primarily businessmen, white collar workers, and skilled laborers | Unguarded conversations in public places; samples obtained by eavesdropping over a 2-year period on unknowing subjects | Berger, 1967 . *The most common words used in conversation.* |
| Elderly women, ages 63–79 | Spoken conversations in home and community contexts | Stuart, Vanderhoof, and Beukelman , in press . *Topic and vocabulary use patterns of elderly women.* |
| Elderly men and women in two age groups | Spoken conversations in home and community contexts | Stuart , 1991 . *Topic and vocabulary use patterns of elderly men and women in two age cohorts.* |

logical inventory strategy that can be used to select fringe vocabulary for persons who are not literate. This process has six phases: 1) identify the current and future environments in which a severely disabled individual is required to function, 2) conduct detailed on-site analyses of communication requirements of nondisabled persons during actual activities in these environments, 3) conduct detailed on-site analyses of the communication requirements of disabled individuals during the same activities in these environments, 4) conduct discrepancy analyses to determine the communication needs of disabled individuals, 5) interview significant others regarding communication needs, and 6) create instructional adaptations, such as AAC systems, to address these needs (Mirenda, 1985). This vocabulary selection strategy ensures that individuals have the relevant vocabulary available to communicate in a variety of natural, age-appropriate environments.

## INFORMANTS

Very little research has examined the performance or role of informants in vocabulary selection. One exception is a study of three types of informants—parents, speech-language pathologists, and teachers—often used to select vocabulary for AAC users (Morrow, Beukelman, Mirenda, & Yorkston, in press). Results indicated that each of the informants contributed an important number of unique words to composite vocabularies for an individual child and that none of the informants could be eliminated from the vocabulary selection process. Specifically, for three of the six subjects involved in the study, the parents (all mothers) contributed the most unique words. For the other three subjects, the speech-language pathologist offered the most unique words. Words contributed by teachers, although fewer in number, were, however, critically important to classroom participation, in particular.

In another aspect of this same study, Morrow et al. (in press) studied the informants' reactions to three different vocabulary selection techniques: a blank sheet of paper, an environmental inventory (after Carlson, 1981), and a vocabulary checklist (Bristow & Fristoe, 1984). The results indicated that the informants' overall satisfaction level was relatively consistent and that none of the three informants was more satisfied than the others. Across informants, the blank sheet and environmental inventory methods were similarly rated as being moderately easy to use, and the checklist was rated as slightly more satisfactory.

In addition, a series of studies using parents and educators/speech-language pathologists as informants to select vocabulary for preschool children has been conducted (Fried-Oken & More, 1992). One study reported that for the 100 most frequently occurring words, subjects in the two informant groups agreed 50%–56% of the time (Yorkston, Fried-Oken, & Beukelman, 1988). More information about the core vocabulary items recommended in this series of studies is provided in Chapter 10.

> Parental vocabulary diaries . . . are invaluable supplements to professional observations. I find it is not possible to rely on such diaries for information about pronunciation or grammar, but most parents have little trouble learning how to keep a list of words used by the child during the day. (Crystal, 1987, p. 41)

## VOCABULARY RETENTION

Various aspects of the initial vocabulary selection process have been discussed in this chapter. An equally important process involves decisions regarding the vocabulary words to retain over time. Some words and phrases are used so commonly that it is easy for AAC users and their facilitators to decide to retain them in the system. Other words and phrases may be used much less often, either because they were poorly chosen in the first place or because they have outlived their usefulness. The latter applies particularly to vocabulary items that were selected for specific contexts, such as a particular unit of study in the classroom, or for special events, such as Thanksgiving or other holidays. Items with limited use should be eliminated from the available lexicon, to make space for other, more important words and to reduce the cognitive load for users, who must scan many items prior to selection. No research information is available about systematic vocabulary retention processes or decision making involved in these processes. Obviously, this is an important research need.

# PART II

# AUGMENTATIVE AND ALTERNATIVE COMMUNICATION INTERVENTIONS

# *Serving Young Children with AAC Needs*

≫≫≫≫≫≫≫≫≫≫≫≫≫≫≫≫≫≫≫≫≫≫≫≫≫≫≫≫≫≫≫≫≫≫≫≫≫≫≫≫≫≫≫≫

> We purchased [our son] Dustin's computer system in February of 1984. He was 3½ years old. . . . We did not pay attention to psychologists' reports. They said that Dustin functions at an 8-month level. Considering that the evaluations have been based on motoric indicators, an 8-month level might be generous. It tells us nothing, however, about Dustin's strengths: his personality, his ability to learn, his appreciation of music, his ability to make friends. (Webb, 1984, p. 4)

## INTERVENTION PHILOSOPHY

In this quotation, Webb highlights a number of important points that are appropriate to guide AAC interventions for young children. First, she alludes to the dearth of assessment tools to accurately and meaningfully measure the abilities of children with complex sensory, motor, and speech problems. Second, she cautions against putting much credence in the results of such assessments, especially if observation provides information and impressions that are contradictory to the test results. Third, she emphasizes the importance of building upon the child's strengths rather than focusing on the child's deficits. Finally, she reminds us that AAC interventions with young children should operate under the assumption that all children have the potential to make significant skill gains.

In addition to these basic principles, communication interventions should be conducted with the view that outcome predictions are almost always inappropriate when addressing the needs of young children. Thus, without exception, strategies for supporting the development of natural speech should *always* be included in communication interventions for this age group. Similarly, strategies for supporting the development of literacy skills (e.g., reading and writing) should be included in all intervention plans, even for those children who may seem unlikely to acquire such skills. Finally, intervention strategies should be based on the assumption that regular kindergarten placement is the goal for *all* young children. This aggressive approach can result only in positive outcomes for the child and will guard against the all too frequent later realization that a child with many skill deficits might also possess a corresponding number of skills, if not for a lack of communication access and opportunity in earlier years. Interventions designed to increase communication opportunities, as well as those designed to teach specific communication and social interaction skills, are usually both necessary for positive outcomes.

> "Participation in mainstreamed [preschool] programs is an essential component for improving the peer social competence of young handicapped children" (Guralnick, 1990, p. 11).

## EARLY INTERVENTION AND PRESCHOOL SERVICES

Early intervention services are usually delivered to the child in the home through his or her primary caregivers for the first few years of life. These services are generally provided by visiting teachers and therapists who regularly come to the home to teach caregivers to provide appropriate input and supports, including those related to communication. At approximately 2–3 years of age, the child usually begins to attend a preschool program for at least part of the day, where direct services are provided by professional staff. The type of preschool program may vary greatly, from one that accommodates only children with disabilities to one that serves primarily nondisabled children.

There is no doubt that preschool settings that include at least some nondisabled children are vastly preferable to segregated classrooms for social interaction and communication (Hanson & Hanline, 1989; Peck & Cooke, 1983). As Guralnick (1990) noted, "A mainstreamed preschool appears to provide a challenging and developmentally appropriate social/communicative environment for the handicapped child, one that cannot be replicated in specialized programs due to the linguistic and other limitations of the handicapped children themselves" (p. 10). In this chapter, we assume that some amount of regular, systematic integration with nondisabled peers exists in the preschool setting, and, if it does not, this should be recognized as an opportunity barrier and targeted for remediation. We will also use the generic term "children" to refer to the persons targeted for early intervention, and this may include infants, toddlers, and preschoolers, depending on the intervention discussed.

## PARTICIPATION INTERVENTIONS

Planning and implementation within the context of the Participation Model (Figure 7.1.) require assessment of the child's participation needs, including communication needs, in natural contexts such as home and preschool settings. As was discussed in Chapter 7, the Participation Model requires that the participation patterns of nondisabled peers in relevant environments be assessed for comparison. The participation patterns of the target child are assessed in the same contexts and compared to those of the peer. Interventions are then designed to increase the participation levels of the target child so that they more closely match peer levels. For infants and toddlers, this requires analyzing the interaction patterns of peers in home and community settings, while for preschoolers, this examination is also needed in the classroom. Table 10.1. displays an example of a participation analysis and intervention plan for a preschool-age child in activities of her school day.

In the example in Table 10.1., discrepancies were identified between the participation patterns and expectations of the target student and other children. In some cases, such as during music and pretend-play time, assistive device and environmental adaptations were designed to reduce discrepancies. In other cases, such as during snack time, the need for both adaptations and instructional modifications (e.g., working on standing at the sink) were identified. In all cases, the basic principle of the Participation Model is reflected: The first step to increasing communication is to increase meaningful participation in natural contexts.

### Creating Predictable Routines

Daily living routines can provide many opportunities for communication, if they are structured with this purpose in mind. In most homes and classrooms, routines such as dressing, bathing, toileting, eating, and changing the motorically involved child's position occur at regular times and intervals throughout the day. If this is not the case, these routines should be regularized as much as possible so that the child can begin to anticipate their occurrence. In addition, routines should be conducted in the same sequence each time, again so that the child can begin to anticipate what

**Table 10.1.** Sample participation analysis and intervention plan for a preschool-age child

| Activity | How do peers participate? (What is expected?) | How does child currently participate? | Intervention plan |
|---|---|---|---|
| Music (group) | Choose songs, sing repetitive parts of songs, put record on player, do hand or body movements to songs | Does not choose or sing, does not put on record, does hand or body movements with aide's assistance, mostly sits and watches/listens | Provide taped songs that she can turn on with a switch to "sing along," provide picture symbols representing songs so she can choose, continue to imitate hand/body movements with aide |
| Snack time (group) | Wash hands with help, sit down, ask for snack item, ask for drink, ask for help as needed, eat/drink appropriately, take dirty plate/cup to sink and rinse, wash hands/face with help | Washes hands and sits with help; does not ask for snack, drink, or help; needs help to eat and drink; does not take or rinse plate/cup at sink; hands and face washed by aide | Provide real object choices of two snack and drink options, look for eye gaze or reach to indicate choice; talk to physical therapist about facilitating standing at sink so she can participate in cleanup routine |
| Pretend-play time (solo or small group) | Doll play in kitchen or grooming area, block and car play, dressup play: children expected to play appropriately with peers while teacher encourages verbal language according to IEP goals | Tues. & Thurs.: sits in wheelchair and watches peers play in an area. Mon., Wed., & Fri.: practices switch use with battery toys (solo) | Encourage peers to use her laptray as a play surface, adapt toys with Velcro so she can pick up with adapted Velcro glove, use Fisher-Price stove and sink on laptray instead of large play kitchen furniture, adapt battery-operated blender and mixer for switch activation, use activity frame to display small items within reach |

happens next. Finally, whenever possible, sufficient time should be included in the routine so that contextual communication instruction can be conducted concurrently with the activity. Specific strategies for using regular, predictable routines to teach communication skills are discussed later in this chapter.

> Participation is the only prerequisite to communication. Without participation, there is no one to talk to, nothing to talk about, and no reason to communicate. For young children, the primary participation context is *play*.

## Adaptive Play

Much of an intervention plan for a young child is specifically designed to promote communication in natural self-care contexts such as mealtimes, bathtimes, and dressing and grooming times. Since the primary business of young children is play, however, their primary communicative opportunities occur in play contexts. By increasing participation in play activities, we automatically increase the quality and quantity of communication opportunities (Brodin, 1991).

*What Is Play?* In *Adaptive Play for Special Needs Children* (Musselwhite, 1986a), it is noted that play is an intrinsic activity that is "done for its own sake, rather than as a means to achieving any specific end. . . . [It is also] spontaneous and voluntary, undertaken by choice rather than by compulsion. . . . Play includes an element of enjoyment, something that is done for fun" (Musselwhite, 1986a, p p. 3–4).Unfortunately, when play skills are taught in classrooms, these character-izations of play are often ignored, and play becomes, quite literally, the child's "work." This is not to imply that play cannot be used as a vehicle to promote specific skill development in gross motor, fine motor, social, cognitive, self-help, and (of course) communication domains. In fact, whenever possible, it is desirable to "telescope" goals and activities by working on one primary and one or more secondary goals simultaneously in a play context (Musselwhite, 1986b). For example, a pre-school child in a "dress the doll" activity might be working primarily on fine motor skills related to dressing, and secondarily on social and communication skills. Nevertheless, it is important to pre-serve the integrity of the activity as playful, not simply one in which toys are used as vehicles for work. This requires careful selection of play materials and the ways they are activated and used, as discussed in the sections that follow.

*Selecting and Adapting Toys*   For play activities to foster the development of communica-tion skills, toys and play materials must be selected with interaction goals in mind. For example, some types of toys (e.g., blocks, balls, toy vehicles, and puppets) have been found to be more facilitative of peer interactions than other, more solitary play materials (e.g., books, paper and crayons, play dough, and puzzles) (Beckman & Kohl, 1984). Other important considerations in selecting a toy include safety, durability, motivational value for children with various types of disabilities, and attractiveness (Musselwhite, 1986a). Another consideration is reactivity: Does the toy do something (e.g., produce sound, sustain movement, create a visual display)? Some research has demonstrated that young children with severe disabilities engage in longer periods of manip-ulative play with reactive toys than with nonreactive toys (Bambara, Spiegel-McGill, Shores, & Fox, 1984). Finally, toys should be selected to cover the range from realistic to imaginative, so that children have opportunities to engage in both concrete and pretend (i.e., symbolic) play.

Another way to increase the probability that toys will be played with is to make them easy to hold, carry, and manipulate. This is particularly important for individuals with motor impair-ments, since the quality of early communication and the motor ability to manipulate objects ap-pear to be related (Granlund & Olsson, 1987). Goossens' and Crain (1986b) and Musselwhite (1986b) have described numerous low tech assistive device adaptations that can be made at home or at school. These include activity frames, adjustable easels, learning boxes, playboxes, and other means of stabilizing and presenting manipulable toys so that they are accessible to children with limited hand and arm control. Toys can be attached to laptrays with Velcro or elastic cords so they are within reach. Books can be adapted with small foam or carpet tape squares pasted to the corners to separate pages for easier turning. Small magnets or squares of Velcro can be attached to toys so that the child can then pick them up with a headstick or mitten affixed with the same material. Toys with movable parts (e.g., levers, knobs) can be adapted with plastic or Velcro extenders for children with sensory or motor impairments (Wright & Nomura, 1987). Numerous other strategies for adapting toys can be found in an excellent chapter by Williams, Briggs, and Williams (1979). Fig-ure 10.1. illustrates some of the many possible toy adaptations.

*Using Microswitches*   Strategies for adapting battery-operated toys and appliances (e.g., blenders, slide projectors) to run with simple microswitch technology have been described by a number of authors (Burkhart, 1988; Goossens' & Crain, 1986a, 1986b; Levin & Scherfenberg, 1988; Wright & Nomura, 1987). The switches can either be purchased through commercial dis-tributors or manufacturers (see Berliss, Borden, & Vanderheiden, 1989, for a complete listing) or constructed inexpensively at home or at school using readily available components (Burkhart, 1980, 1982, 1988; Goossens' & Crain, 1986a, 1986b; Wright & Nomura, 1987). Such endeavors should be used as the means to an end (i.e., participation), not as ends in themselves. All too often, children with motor or other impairments can be found sitting in the corner of a classroom with a paraprofessional, a battery-operated toy, and a microswitch while the other preschoolers are having fun playing house, garage, or dress-up! Unfortunately, this is often worsened by the practice of

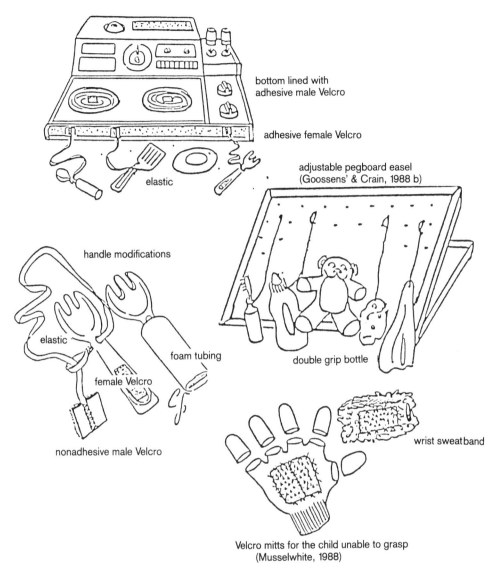

bottom lined with
adhesive male Velcro

adhesive female Velcro

adjustable pegboard easel
(Goossens' & Crain, 1988 b)

elastic

handle modifications

elastic

foam tubing

female Velcro

double grip bottle

nonadhesive male Velcro

wrist sweatband

Velcro mitts for the child unable to grasp
(Musselwhite, 1988)

**Figure 10.1.** Examples of play adaptations that can be made at home. (From Goossens', C. [1989]. Aided communication intervention before assessment: A case study of a child with cerebral palsy. *Augmentative and Alternative Communication, 5*, 17; reprinted by permission.)

providing only one or two battery-operated toys for switch activation, apparently under the assumption that watching a monkey (or a bear, or a dog) hit a drum (or crash a pair of cymbals, or ride a car) is so fascinating that it will sustain a child's attention for an extended period of time, day after day! Neither of these practices reflect an understanding of the principles of the Participation Model nor the appropriate use of microswitch technology in general, and they are almost certain to result in the widespread lament: "We spent all that money to buy a switch/a toy and he (or she) gets bored with it after 2 minutes!" York, Nietupski, and Hamre-Nietupski (1985) described a step-by-step process for determining the appropriateness of microswitch usage that provides a useful alternative. Table 10.2. summarizes some suggestions for using microswitches to enhance participation in home and preschool activities for children.

**Table 10.2.**    Suggestions for using microswitch technology to enhance participation of preschoolers

| Environment | Activity | Participation via microswitch technology |
| --- | --- | --- |
| School | Transition from one activity to another | Child activates switch attached to a cassette tape recorder with a recorded tape of the teacher singing the cleanup song or saying, "Time to get ready for *x*," or whatever the verbal transition routine usually is. |
| Same as above | Snack time | Child uses a switch to operate a toy car or truck that "delivers" the snack of the day to each of his or her friends at the table. |
| Same as above | Free-play time | Child uses a switch to operate a simple computer game with a peer (e.g., Interaction Games, Don Johnston Developmental Equipment, Inc.). Child controls a battery-operated toy in play interaction with a peer. |
| Home/school | Play time | Child in a crib accidentally activates a switch placed near a mobile body part to turn on a toy that provides stimulating and enjoyable feedback (e.g., a light display, music tape, mobile). |
| Same as above | Music time | Child activates a switch to turn on a sing-along tape, or a prerecorded tape of a same-gender child singing his or her part in a song. |
| Same as above | Pretend-play time | Child uses a switch to activate a battery-operated car, truck, robot, toy blender, or toy mixer, depending on the theme of the pretend play. |
| Same as above | Art time | Child uses switch to operate a broken record player (no arm or needle) with paper affixed to the turntable and a blob of paint placed on the paper to make a swirly design pattern. Child provides power for electric scissors used by a peer or adult to cut paper. |
| Same as above | Story time | Child uses a switch to operate a recorded tape of an adult reading the "story of the day," as he or she looks at the book to read along. |
| Same as above | Cooking | Child operates a blender with a switch to make a milkshake, or a mixer to make cake batter, or a food processor to make salad. |

***Adapting Arts Activities***    Communication opportunities can arise or be created in the context of music, movement, puppetry, acting, and other fine arts activities for young children. Like other play activities, these may require adaptation in order to be accessible to children with disabilities. Musselwhite (1985, 1986b) described strategies and resources for combining adaptive play and music and for using music to create opportunities for interaction and communication. For example, she described strategies for writing simple songs that can be easily represented through manual signs or pictorial symbols and for adapting songs to enhance their usefulness as contexts for encouraging speech and manual sign skills.

Movement activities (e.g., finger play songs such as "Where Is Thumbkin?" and gross motor games such as "Red light, green light") are excellent vehicles for teaching basic cognitive/communication skills such as following directions, imitation, sequencing, and concept development. However, many standard movement activities and songs require one or more of the following modifications to be used for communication purposes (Musselwhite, 1985): 1) simplifying target movements so that the child can participate meaningfully (this is also a good place to incorporate movement goals identified by therapists); 2) slowing the speed of the song/activity; 3) making directions shorter, simpler, and more repetitive; 4) simplifying the vocabulary; 5) pairing words with manual signs; 6) accompanying movements with sounds or words to encourage speech; and 7) including visual aids or concrete materials for children who do not yet engage in pretend play (Musselwhite,

1985). Alternatively, children with motor impairments can be provided with single-message cassette tapes and tape recorders operated with a microswitch. In this way, children can assume the role of the activity leader by playing a tape that announces movements to be performed by the other children, such as "Put your right foot in, put your right foot out. . ." or "Simon says . . ." or "Duck, duck, goose. . . ."

Arts activities such as acting and puppetry can also be used to create communication opportunities. Stuart (1988) provided guidelines for acting with young children, and Musselwhite (1985) discussed using puppets as communication partners and models. These authors offered suggestions for adapting and modifying activities to enhance participation, such as attaching a puppet to the child's foot or wrist rather than insisting that it be manipulated with the hand, or decorating the child's wheelchair so that it can be used as a prop or stage in a play or puppet show.

## COMMUNICATION INTERVENTIONS

Communication interventions to teach relevant skills can be designed when communicative opportunities in the context of self-care, play, and other routines have been identified. What communication skills are appropriate to teach to young children? Obviously, the specific answer depends on the age of the child, but, generally, communication skills can be grouped into three categories: those related to social interaction, those related to receptive language (understanding), and those related to expressive language (production). It is possible for deficits to occur in each or all of these areas. For example, some children may understand age-appropriate language input and may have age-appropriate social skills, but they experience an expressive language (production or output) problem. Some children may understand and produce spoken language, but do so in ways that reflect social interaction deficits. Still other children may show evidence of significant delays in all three areas. The targets and approaches for communication intervention should address the child's specific areas of difficulty while building on the areas of relative strength.

### Beginning Communication Strategies

*Expressing Preferences*   Three essential building blocks of communication are signals for attention-seeking, acceptance, and rejection. Children can often communicate these basic messages with even a limited repertoire of gestural or vocal behaviors. Attention-seeking signals are those the child uses primarily to initiate social interactions with others, such as laughing, crying, or making eye contact. Acceptance signals are those used by the child to communicate that whatever is currently happening is tolerable, okay, or enjoyable. Caregivers are usually able to describe these behaviors if asked questions such as "How do you know when your child doesn't mind or likes something?" or "How do you know when your child is happy?" Rejection signals are used to communicate that the child finds his or her current status unacceptable, not enjoyable, or intolerable for some reason. Caregivers will often describe these behaviors when asked questions such as "How do you know when your child doesn't like something?" or "How do you know when your child is unhappy or in pain?" Thus, the ability to signal "acceptance" and "rejection" is *not* the same as the ability to respond to yes/no questions—the latter involves a much more sophisticated set of skills. Accept and reject signals may be overt and obvious, such as smiling, laughing, frowning, or crying, or may be very subtle, such as averted eye gaze, increased body tension, increased rate of respiration, or sudden passivity. Most children are able to signal acceptance and rejection in some way, although this may be quite idiosyncratic. If clear attention-seeking, acceptance, and rejection signals are not part of a child's communication repertoire, initial interventions will need to include strategies for developing these behaviors.

*Sensitizing Facilitators*   The term "facilitator" refers to any individual who assumes or is assigned responsibility for supporting the child's communicative attempts. A study has highlighted the importance of teaching facilitators (in this case, teachers and paraprofessionals) to identify and respond to children's emerging signals (Houghton, Bronicki, & Guess, 1987). The authors observed 37 students with severe multiple disabilities across 12 classrooms. They coded the frequency of student initiations related to expression of preferences, as well as facilitator responses to these initiations. The results indicated that body movements and facial expressions were the most frequently observed communicative behaviors produced by the students. The students initiated such behaviors approximately once per minute in both structured and unstructured situations, but facilitators responded to these communications only 7%–15% of the time! Unfortunately, similarly dismal data were reported recently in a study of preschoolers with dual sensory impairments (Rowland, 1990). In general, these data suggest that: 1) the facilitators were largely unaware of or insensitive to student attempts to communicate, and/or 2) the constraints imposed by the demands of the classrooms precluded the level of facilitator attentiveness that is desirable. Regardless, the critical need for training and environmental adjustments in this area is obvious.

---

"Be related, somehow, to every one you know" (E. Deloria, 1943).

---

In their excellent text on nonsymbolic communication interactions, Siegel-Causey & Guess (1989) suggested that the first step in teaching facilitators to "tune in" to a child's early preference behaviors is to foster an atmosphere of security and warmth through nurturing relationships. This includes encouraging facilitators to provide comfort, support, and affection; create positive settings for interactions; and focus on the child's interests at the moment. For example, facilitators working with young beginning communicators should be encouraged to use animated facial expressions such as smiles and wide eyes to display enjoyment and simple verbalizations with rhythmic intonation patterns to convey affection and emotional warmth.

*Responding to Spontaneous Signals*    Children who communicate primarily through gestures and vocalizations initially do so when the need arises, rather than in response to queries or directives from their communication partners. A child's initial spontaneous signaling behavior is not intended to be communicative but simply occurs at random. When facilitators consistently interpret and respond to such behaviors as if they were intentional, children gradually learn to initiate them intentionally. Interpretation and responsiveness continue to be important facilitator techniques to expand communication repertoires, even after children begin to attach meaning to their gestures and vocalizations. Although most adults are attuned to gestures and vocalizations of typical children, they may often either ignore or misinterpret many of the more subtle and idiosyncratic behaviors exhibited by children with disabilities (Houghton et al., 1987; Rowland, 1990).

---

Parents rely heavily on their own intuition and ability to interpret their child . . . . [This] involves a great degree of guesswork . . . . Parents are often regarded with suspicion about the validity of their interpretations. They often hear from other people that they overinterpret the child and that their comprehension is only an expression of wishful thinking . . . . Parents have a unique competence in knowing their children and understanding their children's communication. (Brodin, 1991, p. 237)

---

It is particularly important that facilitators be attuned to attention-seeking behaviors initiated by the child. Initially, facilitators should respond to *any* such behavior that is socially and culturally acceptable so that the young child can repeatedly experience the communicative results of his or her efforts (Smebye, 1990). For example, a facilitator might respond to a child's behavior such as pounding on a laptray or vocalizing loudly as an indicator of a desire for attention (Baumgart, Johnson, & Helmstetter, 1990). Nevertheless, behavior such as grabbing, hitting, or throwing items is socially unacceptable and would not be a proper target for response. After a repertoire of acceptable attention-seeking behaviors has been established and is used intentionally by the child, facilitator responsiveness can be limited to the most desirable and frequent behaviors only.

The basic principles of contingent interpretation and responsiveness are the cornerstones for building other communicative behaviors, including those signaling acceptance or rejection. These signals may be subtle; for example, a child might not evidence behavior changes when he or she is content but might whimper slightly when distressed or uncomfortable. In other cases, a child might give more overt indicators such as limb movements, smiling, or crying. In still other cases, children may use unconventional behaviors to signal acceptance or rejection. For example, some children engage in self-stimulatory behaviors (e.g., spinning objects, light gazing) and aggressive behaviors (e.g., tantrums, self-injury), both of which can be interpreted as "reject" messages, when they are in situations that are boring or unpleasant (Siegel-Causey & Downing, 1987). Other children may flap their hands, squeal repetitively, or become aggressive when they are happy or excited, which are two clear "accept" messages.

Initial facilitator responsiveness to and compliance with any communicative behaviors that can be socially and culturally tolerated is necessary in order to strengthen the behaviors over time and teach the child the power of communication. Occasionally, facilitators express concern about the implications of this strategy, worrying that children will become "spoiled" if they always "give them what they want." This need not be a concern if facilitators are attuned to the amount and level of responsiveness the child needs so that they can decide when to begin to respond intermittently to these signals.

*Teaching in Routine Contexts*　In addition to responding to spontaneous attention-getting, acceptance, and rejection signals, facilitators can provide structured opportunities for children to practice these behaviors in the context of naturally occurring routines (e.g., Baumgart et al., 1990; Carlson, Hough, Lippert, & Young, 1988; Oregon Research Institute, 1989a). The need for predictable routines was discussed earlier in this chapter in reference to activities such as dressing, eating, changing positions, and toileting. Routines can be established informally or formally through the use of planned "dialogues" (Siegel-Causey & Guess, 1989) or "scripted routines." Table 10.3. displays part of a scripted routine created for Adam, a toddler with multiple disabilities, while preparing for swimming. As can be seen from this example, scripted routines may consist of four elements, depending on the type of routine and the child's disability. These four elements, a touch cue, verbal cue, pause, and action, are described with reference to Table 10.3.

1. Touch cue. Touch cues are information provided in addition to the spoken words and should be given to the child before each step in the routine. The touch cue for a step should be the same each time, and the same cues should be used by all facilitators. Touch cues are critical for children with one or more sensory impairments (e.g., vision, hearing, or both) and are often useful with other children. For example, in step 2 of Table 10.3., the touch cue associated with putting on Adam's swimsuit is the feel of the suit against his wrist.

2. Verbal cue. The verbal cue is a general description of what the facilitator should say to the child while providing the touch cue. For example, while rubbing Adam's swimsuit against his wrist before putting it on, the facilitator might say, "It's time to put your swimsuit on" (step 2, Table 10.3.). Facilitators should not be rigid about the precise structure of verbal cues but should provide necessary information as naturally as possible. Verbal cues should always be used, even with children who have hearing impairments, since most of these children have at least some residual hearing.

3. Pause. After each touch cue + verbal cue pair, the facilitator should *pause* for at least 10 seconds and *observe* the child for a response. "Response" means any motor movement or vocalization that appears to be deliberate or can be interpreted as deliberate. If the child responds with a signal that can be interpreted as an accept signal after the pause, the facilitator should con-

**Table 10.3.**   Part of a scripted routine for undressing/dressing prior to swimming

| Touch cue (how you give nonverbal information) | Verbal cue (what you say) | Pause (wait for at least 10 sec. and look for a response) | Action (what you do after the child accepts or the second pause is over) |
|---|---|---|---|
| 1. Rub seat belt under Adam's elbow. Release buckle so that a sound is made. | "Time to get ready for a swim." | Pause, observe. | Go to step 2. |
| 2. Rub the waistband of swimsuit against his wrist. | "It's time to put your swimsuit on." | Pause, observe. | Go to step 3. |
| 3. Unzip coat/sweater | "It's time to take your coat/sweater off." | Pause, observe. | Go to step 4. |
| 4. Rub Adam's back. | "Let's lean forward now." | Pause, observe. | Lean him forward. |
| 5. Tug coat collar behind Adam's head and rub your hand on the back of his head. | "Going to pull this over your head now, Adam." | Pause, observe. | Pull up back of coat over Adam's head. |
| 6. Pat one arm where the sleeve ends. | "Time to take your sleeve off." | Pause, observe. | Remove hand from sleeve. |
| 7. Pat the other arm where the sleeve ends. | "Let's take the other sleeve off now." | Pause, observe. | Remove hand from sleeve. |
| 8. Tap one shoe, hard. | "Time to take your shoes off." | Pause, observe. | Untie shoe and remove. |
| 9. Tap the other shoe, hard. | "Time to take your other shoe off." | Pause, observe. | Untie shoe and remove. |

tinue the routine. If the child gives a reject signal, the facilitator may stop the routine briefly and then try again, explore an alternative way of proceeding, or terminate the routine altogether. If neither type of signal is produced, the facilitator should repeat the touch + verbal cue pair and wait 10 seconds for a signal. If there is still no signal, the facilitator simply continues the routine. The length of the pause depends largely on the child's level of responsiveness and the extent of motor involvement. Children with severe disabilities require much longer pauses in order to have time to formulate and produce signals.

4.   Actions. Actions are the actual steps in the routine that are identified through a task analysis. As the facilitator performs each step after the child's accept signal, verbal feedback in the form of a comment about what the child did and what action the facilitator will do in response should be provided. For example, at the end of step 2 in Table 10.3., the facilitator might say, "Oh, you moved your foot, okay, I'll unzip your coat first," or "I see you moved your arm, here, I'll help you take your coat off."

A simplified format similar to that used for the dressing/undressing routine, but without the touch and verbal cues, can be used to create scripted routines for play. For example, an interaction routine for "Row, row, row your boat" can be created by having the facilitator sit on the floor facing the child while holding his or her hands. As the facilitator sings the song, he or she rocks to and fro in a boatlike motion with the child. Once the routine has been established and the child is seen to enjoy it, the facilitator pauses after every two lines in the song and watches for any indication that the child wants to continue the game. This basic format—action, pause, action—can be used with other interactive games and songs. Such joint action routines (or "resonance" activities: see chap. 13, this volume) form excellent contexts for assessment as well as intervention. Readers are referred to McLean, McLean, Brady, and Etter (1991); and Snyder-McLean, Solomonson, McLean, and Sack (1984) for informative suggestions in this regard.

**Making Choices**  The ability to make choices is another critical building block of communication (Guess, Benson, & Siegel-Causey, 1985; Shevin & Klein, 1984). In school, children can be offered choices of foods for snack time, toys to play with, music to listen to, and friends to sit next to, and there are probably dozens more choices that can be offered just in the few hours spent in a preschool classroom each day. At home or in the community, even more choices exist, for example, what clothes to wear in the morning, which cereal to eat for breakfast, or what TV shows to watch after school.

*Choice-Making Formats*  The choices offered must be motivating, provided in natural contexts, and presented in a manner that is understandable to the child in order for choice-making interventions to be successful. Making the choices simple enough so that the child can successfully choose involves careful consideration of the child's symbolic, yes/no, and receptive object labeling abilities, because one or more of these skills are needed for many choice-making formats typically used in natural settings. Table 10.4. displays clinically derived formats that can be used to present choice-making opportunities, arranged from simple to complex. Choices should be presented to the child using the format corresponding to his or her abilities. The skills needed for more sophisticated levels can be taught concurrently.

*Choice-Making Arrays*  In addition to the choice-making format, the types of items in the choice-making array must also be selected. The types of items are determined by the decision to use: 1) two preferred options (Writer, 1987), 2) one preferred and one nonpreferred option (Burkhart, 1988), or 3) one preferred option and a "blank" or "distractor" option (Reichle, York, & Sigafoos, 1991; Rowland & Schweigert, 1990) for teaching initial choice making. (Note that a fourth option promoted by some in the past, which involves one preferred and one aversive or disliked item, is not included in our list of acceptable strategies.) There simply are no empirical data to guide decisions in this area, and reasonable arguments can be made in support of each option. Our preference is to start out with two preferred options (i.e., items known to be acceptable to the child) since this is the most natural choice format. If there are indications that the child is having difficulty making choices, for example, if he or she frequently chooses an option and then rejects it, or if he or she always chooses the item on one side of the array, one of the other array formats might be helpful to clarify the task. Other strategies to consider for children who seem to find choice-making difficult include spacing options closer together or farther apart, aligning them vertically rather than horizontally, and holding them out of reach from children who are impulsive (Burkhart, 1988).

*Natural Consequences*  We cannot overemphasize the importance of providing opportunities for choice making in a nonevaluative atmosphere, which is an atmosphere in which "right" and "wrong" choices have not been predetermined by the facilitator. Professionals may designate choice options as right or wrong in order to record data on the basis of "correct/incorrect," or because they forget that people learn to make effective choices by experiencing both the pleasant and the unpleasant consequences of their actions. How many of us, for example, have not at some time bought a shirt or a pair of shoes that we disliked after a single wearing or, even worse, have not experienced the pain of making a relationship choice that later proved to be problematic? Perhaps we even made such choices against the advice of friends or family, and we hope we were able to learn from our mistakes!

Children, too, need to experience natural consequences in order to learn, even if this means that sometimes they do not get what they want because they were not paying sufficient attention or failed to weigh the options adequately. A common mistake in this regard is to offer the child two options, and then to correct the child if the one that is known to be less preferred is selected.

**Table 10.4.** Choice-making formats in approximate order of difficulty (levels 1–4)

| Level | Strategy | Examples |
|---|---|---|
| Level 1: Simple active/passive choice system with two options. | Child gets choice A when passive (i.e., for doing nothing) and choice B when active (i.e., for doing something) (Wacker, Wiggins, Fowler, & Berg, 1988). | The child is in the preschool classroom. Choice A is a toy doll, choice B is a music box. The child gets A by default unless he or she does something, in this case, emits a vocalization of any type. Whenever he or she vocalizes, he or she gets choice B for 3 minutes. He or she then is given choice A again, and the cycle repeats. |
| Level 2: Two-item active choices using real objects or object symbols in natural contexts. Does not require yes/no or object labeling concepts. | Show two objects or symbols and ask "What do you want?" Look for an indicator (e.g., eye gaze, reaching) that one is preferred over the other and comply. | Music time is about to begin. The teacher holds up two albums and asks the child "Which should we listen to?" The child reaches for one of the albums, and the teacher complies. |
|  | Show one object or symbol and ask, "Do you want the *x*? Show second item as well and finish; "Or the *y*?" Provide the item indicated (Baumgart, Johnson, & Helmstetter, 1990). | Dad is helping the child with self-care activities in the morning. These consist of toothbrushing, hair combing, and face washing. Dad holds up a toothbrush and says, "Should we brush your teeth first?" He holds up the comb and finishes, "Or comb your hair?" The child looks at the toothbrush and Dad complies. After this activity is done, Dad repeats the routine with the washcloth and the comb. |
| Level 3: Two-item choices using real objects or object symbols in natural contexts. Requires yes/no concept but not object labeling. | Show one option and ask "Do you want the *x*?" Pause and look for an accept response, comply if given. If the child gives a reject or no response, hold up a second option and ask, "Do you want the *y*?" Continue until the child accepts an option (Musselwhite, 1986a). | The child is in the bathtub at home with his sister. She holds up a rubber ducky, asks "Do you want the ducky?" and pauses. He does not respond, so she holds up a plastic boat, asks, "How about the boat?" and pauses again. He grins and reaches for the boat, and they play. |
|  |  | At a fast food restaurant, Aunt Mary shows the child an empty french fry container and an empty apple pie container and says, "You can have french fries or apple pie today." She then holds out only the french fry container and asks, "Do you want french fries?" The child stiffens her body, an indication of acceptance, so Aunt Mary complies. |
| Three-item choices using real objects in natural contexts. | Same as Level 2, except three items are offered simultaneously (Burkhart, 1988). | The teacher arranges a car, a horn, and a doll on the table and asks the child, "Which one do you want to play with?" The child reaches toward the horn and the teacher complies. |
| Level 4: Multiple option choices with invisible objects. Requires yes/no and object labelling concepts. | Ask, "Do you want the *x*?" or "Do you want to go to the *x*?" without the item or an object symbol of the item present. | The art teacher asks, "Do you want some paint now?" without showing the child a jar of paint or a symbol representing paint. The child shakes her head "No." |

*(continued)*

**Table 4.** (*continued*)

| Level | Strategy | Examples |
|---|---|---|
| Level 4: Multiple option choices with invisible objects. Requires yes/no and object labeling concepts. | | The paraprofessional asks the child, "Do you need to go to the bathroom?" without showing her an object symbol that represents "bathroom" (e.g., an almost-finished roll of toilet paper, a plastic toilet seat insert). The child jumps up and down, signalling "Yes." |
| Two item choices using pictorial symbols | Provide photos or simple pictorial symbols of the options. Use the language appropriate to the child's level. (Burkhart, 1988). | Grandma shows the child photos of the child on a swing and in a sandbox and asks, "Should we go play on the swings or in the sandbox outside?" The child looks at the photo of the swing and Grandma complies. |

*Example: A scene in a fast-food restaurant. T = teacher, C = child. (The child is known to prefer juice to milk most of the time.)*

T:  Do you want milk [shows empty carton] or juice [shows container]?
C:  [Looks at/points to milk.]
T:  [With rising inflection]: Do you want milk?
C:  [Looks at/points to juice.]
T:  Yes, okay, you want the juice.

Providing corrective feedback this way almost certainly ensures that problems will occur later in instruction. The child is learning that it is not necessary to pay attention or think about his or her response, since the teacher will always "make it better" in the end. Instead, it would be preferable to let the natural consequence of a "mis-choice" occur and then offer an opportunity for the child to try again:

*Example: A scene in a fast-food restaurant. T = teacher, C = child. (The child has just made a "mis-choice.")*

T:  [Gives the child the item that was selected.]
C:  [Pushes the item away or begins to whine/cry/scream.]
T:  Oh, you don't want [the item]? Okay, we'll try again in a minute. [Removes the item, pauses at least 30–60 seconds and presents a new opportunity to choose.]

Another common feedback error is to check a child's response for correctness by providing a second or even a third opportunity to make the same choice:

*Example: A scene in a video arcade. M = mother, C = child.*

M:  Do you want to play Pac-Man [points] or Space Invaders [points]?
C:  [Gestures towards Pac-Man.]
M:  Okay, let's try it again. Do you want to play Pac-Man [points] or Space Invaders [points]?
C:  [Assumes she must have misunderstood the first time and gestures toward Space Invaders.]
M:  You need to start paying attention. Do you want to play Pac-Man [points] or Space Invaders [points]?
C:  [Does not respond, since there seems to be no way to win this game!]

Such a "massed trial" approach to choice making, as seen in this example, is inappropriate and almost certain to be confusing, because it means that the consequence of choice making is unclear to the child. Instead, each choice-making opportunity should be followed by a natural consequence so that the child can gradually learn the effects of his or her actions.

**Gestural Dictionaries**    By the time interventions have been successfully instituted to teach the child to signal for attention, acceptance, rejection, and to make choices, the child has probably developed a fairly large repertoire of vocalizations and gestures for communication. Many of these signals may be idiosyncratic, so that a few close facilitators (e.g., parents, teachers) are able to understand and respond to them consistently, while people less familiar with the child have difficulty understanding and interpreting the messages. This may result in unnecessary, and sometimes problematic, communication breakdowns. For example, the babysitter may not know that the child's way of asking someone to change the channel on the television is to walk over to the TV and bang on it repeatedly with moderate force. If the sitter tries to dissuade the child from engaging in this seemingly destructive act, the child's efforts simply intensify until both parties are frustrated and dissatisfied. Such communication breakdowns may be avoidable through a "gesture dictionary" in which descriptions of the child's gestures, along with their meanings and suggestions for appropriate responses, are compiled. The dictionary may be in the form of a wall poster in the classroom or home, or may be an alphabetized notebook with cross-referenced entries. For example, in the above situation, the babysitter might look in the child's gesture dictionary under "B" for "banging" or "T" for television. Under either (or both), he or she might find a description of the behavior, its meaning, and how to respond (e.g., "This means he wants you to change the channel on the TV. Get him to try to say 'Help me,' and then change the channel for him"). Table 10.5. displays a portion of a gesture dictionary created for Shawn, a young child with visual and cognitive impairments.

## Limited Context Communication

Strategies exist that allow young children to communicate a limited number of messages in specific contexts. These strategies are particularly applicable to children who have developed the basic skills of attention getting, accepting, rejecting, and choice making. It is important to expand the repertoire of these children to include functional skills such as initiating requests, sharing information, and engaging in social routines (e.g., greeting and departure routines as well as basic etiquette routines). Readers are encouraged to refer to the many excellent clinical resources already cited for limited-context communication strategies for children across the ability range. In this section, a few of the most prevalent or innovative techniques are summarized briefly.

**Topic-Setting Strategies**    Topic-setting strategies allow beginning communicators to introduce and establish topics of conversation. Three topic-setting approaches are discussed in this section: collections, topic-setter or remnant books, and topic-setter cards (Musselwhite, 1990).

*Collections*    Children of all ages enjoy collecting various objects. Even preschoolers may begin to accumulate collections of items such as play necklaces, bracelets, message buttons, toy cars, squirt guns, or small stuffed animals. Such collections, if systematically encouraged and appropriately displayed, can stimulate adult and peer interactions with children across the ability range. For example, a child could wear a different message button from her collection to school every day, or have his "transformers" collection displayed on a bulletin board at school. Both adults and children could be reminded to notice and comment on the newest addition to the collection, and peers could be encouraged to look at the collection items and talk with the child about them. Items in some collections may also be shared by children as play materials (e.g., toy cars).

*Remnant Books*    A remnant book provides a way for beginning symbol users with limited verbal skills to tell people about past events, such as those that occurred during the day at school, or over the weekend. "Remnants" or scraps from activities are simply saved (rather than discarded) and inserted into a photo album or other book. The remnant book allows the child to answer questions such as "What did you do at school today?" or "What did you do over the weekend?" and to

**Table 10.5.**   Example of a gesture dictionary

| What Shawn does | What it means | What you should do |
|---|---|---|
| Manual sign for "T" to chin | Wants to go to the bathroom. | Give him permission and help him to door. |
| "Sshh" sound | "Yes" | Respond according to situation. |
| Shakes head back and forth | "No" | Respond according to situation. |
| Reaches out his hand to other person | "I want to shake your hand." [Greeting] | Shake his hand. |
| Clapping other's hand when offered | "I'm feeling sociable/affectionate." | Respond according to situation. |
| Puts both arms around his stomach | Wants a hug. | Encourage him to shake your hand by prompting or give him a hug, if appropriate. |
| Hands crossed at chest and tapping both shoulders | | |
| Pulls your hand to bring you close to him | | |
| Tapping his opposite shoulder with one hand | | |
| Hand flat across mouth | Wants food. | If mealtime or near mealtime, help him to table or ask him to wait a few minutes. |
| Hand sideways to mouth | Wants a drink. | |
| Hand to mouth with grinding teeth | "I'm *really* hungry!" | If in between meals, provide small amount of milk or bland food (ulcer). |
| Jumping up and down | In a good mood. | Respond in kind. |
| | Needs to go to the bathroom. | Give permission and take to the door |

initiate a topic of conversation about an interesting past event. Initiating a topic of conversation may be particularly useful for children who are able to talk somewhat but who have poor articulation. Once such a child has narrowed down the topic of conversation by referring to a remnant in the book, his or her communication partner may find it easier to guess the spoken words that are difficult to understand. Figure 10.2. displays a strategy sheet that can be used at home or school to establish a remnant book.

In addition to the general strategies discussed in Figure 10.2., Musselwhite (1990) included suggestions for teaching children to use remnant books, including a "sequenced partner training approach," which consists of three steps. She suggests that after the child and the facilitator select a remnant and place it in the book, they rehearse using the remnant to introduce a topic through role playing or puppets. Next, a third person is introduced, and the facilitator coaches the child to use the remnant with this person. Finally, the third person is asked to facilitate an interaction with another person. Musselwhite also suggests that written cues be provided with the remnants to assist literate communication partners to engage in multi-exchange conversations with the child. For example, a cue card might read "Ask me what I did this weekend," "Who did I go with?" or "Ask me what funny thing happened there."

*Topic-Setter Cards*   Topic-setter cards are simple drawings or symbols on self-adhesive notes or index cards that present topics of interest to the child (Musselwhite & St. Louis, 1988). Topic-setter cards may be used in conjunction with collections, remnant books, or other techniques. For example, a card might have a symbol of a television on it that faces the child and a written message that faces the communication partner (i.e., upside down to the child) stating "My favorite TV show is Bart Simpson. Do you have a favorite show? Do you like Sesame Street?" The cards can be placed

---

**Putting Things in the Remnant Book**

1. When you go somewhere in the community with the child, save a remnant of the place you went. "Remnant" is a fancy word for "garbage," something that the child used or encountered during the activity. The remnant should be something that is meaningful to the child and that he or she is able to associate with the place it came from. Let the child help select the remnant. Examples: If you go to a movie, you might save a ticket stub, the popcorn container, or the candy box, whichever the child prefers and finds most meaningful. If you go out to eat, you might save a napkin, the hamburger wrapper, the chicken box, or the empty paper cup, whichever the child prefers and finds most meaningful. If you do something interesting or special at home, save a remnant from that occasion, such as birthday parties, watching a video, or a friend visiting.

2. With the child, put the remnant in the communication book on the page under the correct day of the week (e.g., Monday, Tuesday). You may have to flatten the remnant to put it on the page or under the plastic page cover. It will be bulky, but there's not much to do about that.

**General Strategies for Using the Book**

Don't:
   Ask the child "accuracy questions" with the book, such as "Show me where you went first on Monday," or "Show me what you did next," that have a "right" and "wrong" answer. This is not much fun for the child and will make him or her hate the book very quickly!

Do:
   Make the interactions fun and casual.

   Use the book when the child indicates that he or she is interested.

   Encourage the child to say the words for the place or activity the remnant represents.

   Make the book readily available to the child at all times so that he or she can initiate interactions by simply opening the book and pointing to remnants. Have a conversation about the place or activity the remnant represents when the child does initiate an interaction with the book.

   Ask the child what happened today/last night/over the weekend and encourage him or her to get out the book. Talk about the places and activities the remnants represent ("Oh, I see you went to the zoo. Did you have a good time?").

   Just get out the book with the child and go through it together to talk about what he or she has been up to lately. It is sort of like reading a story together, but it's the child's story that's being read!

---

**Figure 10.2.**   Starting and using a remnant book.

on a laptray, in a communication book, or on an electronic device that can be programmed to speak the message (Musselwhite, 1990).

**Loop or Cassette Tape Strategies**   Simple cassette tapes or loop tapes, such as those used to record answering machine greetings, can be used to facilitate effective limited-context communication (Fried-Oken, Howard, & Prillwitz, 1988; Musselwhite, 1986a). The advantage of using a loop tape is that rewinding is never necessary, since the tape cycles continuously, but loop tapes are considerably more expensive than standard cassette tapes. Loop or cassette tape strategies might be particularly appropriate for beginning communicators who use wheelchairs for mobility and who are learning to use microswitches to participate in communication. (This strategy is more fully discussed in Chapter 13.)

*Activating the Tape*   The tape strategies basically involve teaching the child to activate a battery-operated tape recorder to play a recorded spoken message. Activation may be direct (i.e., the child with sufficient fine motor skills simply turns on the tape recorder) or, more likely, indirect (i.e., the child uses a microswitch attached to the recorder to turn it on). The indirect method may require an adapter to connect the switch to the recorder and a switch-latching device for children who cannot hold the switch down when it has been activated (see Berliss, Borden, & Vanderheiden, 1989; Fried-Oken et al., 1988). Burkhart (1988) has described methods of constructing similar low-cost devices that children can activate by using headlight pointers or scanning techniques.

*Single Message Tapes*   Loop tape strategies are easiest to initiate by using multiple tapes, each with a single message. The same message, interspersed with pauses, is recorded one or more times. Ideally, the person recording the message should be the same age and gender as the child, although this is less important for young children than for older children. The tape is inserted into the recorder, and the child simply activates the tape to play the message in the relevant context.

The most obvious context for using a single message tape is one in which the child can request a predetermined, preferred activity. Single message tapes might also be used at preschool during: 1) opening "circle time" (e.g., the child uses a tape to "sing" his or her part in the greeting song), 2) transition times (e.g., the child activates a tape of someone singing the cleanup song, or of a voice saying "Time to clean up!"), 3) when a request for continuation is appropriate (e.g., the child plays a tape that says "More, please" or "Let's do it again"), and 4) any time the schedule dictates that a specific activity take place (e.g., in the morning, the child plays a tape that says "Take my coat off please"). At home, single message tapes can be used for similar purposes, and they can allow the child to participate in family rituals such as saying the blessing before a meal, or singing "Happy Birthday" at a party. Children can also "talk" on the phone by activating a single message tape, which is a nice way for a preschooler to keep in touch with grandparents and other relatives. Use of the single message loop tape strategy is limited only by the budget available for the equipment and by the facilitator's imagination.

*Multiple Message Tapes*  Two loop tapes, each in a separate recorder with its own switch, can also allow the child to make choices. Each switch can be labeled with a symbol representing the associated message, using object, tactile, or pictorial symbols that are appropriate for the child (Fried-Oken et al., 1988; Mathy-Laikko et al., 1989). More than two options can be made available by using additional recorders or a device such as the Loquitur 250 (Don Johnston Developmental Equipment, Inc.), which allows multiple switch activation of up to four prerecorded messages through a single system.

Another way to provide a child with multiple message options is to record two or more choices sequentially on the same tape as an independent auditory scanning system (Fried-Oken et al., 1988; Musselwhite, 1986a). For example, a tape might say "play with dolls," "play with trucks," and "play with blocks" in a repeated sequence with pauses interspersed. The child activates the recorder to start the tape and then stops the tape when the desired message has been heard. Multiple message options require better receptive language ability and better motor control of the switch than do the single message or multiple tape options, but may be a low tech method of introducing auditory scanning to children who have these skills.

*Miniboards*  Many young children begin using pictorial or other graphic symbol displays through topic-specific miniboards or minidisplays. These can be used as overlays on electronic devices or as stand-alone low tech communication aids (see Musselwhite & St. Louis, 1988, for examples). These communication boards serve two primary purposes: They allow the child to participate in special events and regular activities by ensuring that needed vocabulary items are available, and they provide vehicles for promoting language development and more complex expressive output by the child.

*Participation Through Miniboards*  Participation is enhanced when multiple limited context communication displays are available, perhaps in addition to a generic communication board or overlay that is used routinely. For example, Cook (1988) described a "What I did on the 4th of July" laptray miniboard that contained symbols such as "fireworks," "loud," "outside," "see," and "Statue of Liberty." Several authors have discussed the construction of minidisplays for children who use eye gaze, rotary scanners, communication books, and other display formats (Goossens', 1989; Goossens' & Crain, 1986b; & Musselwhite & St. Louis, 1988). Minidisplays can also be mounted in specific locations, such as on the wall (e.g., in each room of the home at the child's height), on aquatic flotation devices (e.g., kickboards or inner tubes) so the child can communicate while in the water, or on the dashboard of the car. The advantage of using miniboards is that individual boards can be put together quickly using only the vocabulary items appropriate to the activity or event. Miniboards for special events can be constructed and stored until the next occasion for their use (e.g., next Christmas, or the next time Grandma visits). This strategy enhances the probability that specialized vocabulary items needed in limited contexts are available to the young child.

*Language Development Through Miniboards*    In addition to enhancing participation, mini-boards can be used to promote the child's use of multiword linguistic structures and to build a strong receptive language base. Unfortunately, many children do not have access to vocabulary items that can be flexibly combined; instead, they have "noun boards" or "wants and needs" boards that contain only symbols representing basic objects, people, places, and food items, plus a few verbs such as "eat," "drink," and the inevitable "go bathroom." Thus, it is not surprising that their language development and use patterns often lag behind those of their peers. Relevant vocabulary items from a variety of semantic categories can be provided for specific activities with mini-boards. Some guidelines for vocabulary selection were discussed in Chapter 9 and are expanded later in this chapter. Figure 10.3. displays an example of a miniboard for the specific activity of "playing space explorer."

---

Power in Play (Van Tatenhove, 1989) is a voice output communication program designed for children up to 4 years of age that can be used with a Touch Talker or Light Talker. It contains rhymes, songs, story books, bedtime prayers, special messages, and other interactive routines that can be used with miniboards. It can also be customized with individual vocabulary items. For information, contact the Prentke Romich Co.

---

## Receptive Language Augmentation

Three strategies, using some type of symbols in addition to speech, are often used to provide receptive language input to children. The strategies include total communication, aided language stim-

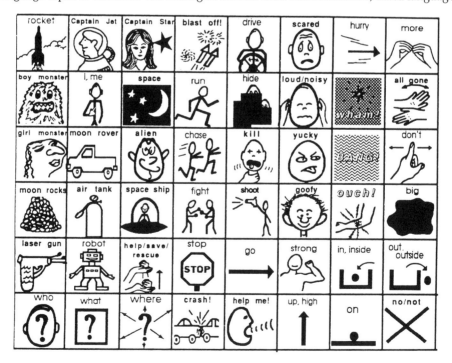

**Figure 10.3.**   A miniboard designed for a preschool-age child to encourage language development (Picture Communication Symbols © 1981, 1985 by Mayer-Johnson Co.; reprinted by permission. Some symbols have been adapted.)

ulation, and calendar/schedule boxes. These may involve the use of manual signs, pictorial symbols of some type, or real object symbols.

**Total Communication**   Total communication, also known as "simultaneous communication" or key word signing, provides the child with manual sign input of the key (i.e., critical) words in each spoken communication interaction. Thus, during play, a teacher might tell the child, "The doll is so tired, she wants to go to sleep now," while at the same time manually signing the words "doll," "tired," "want," and "sleep." This approach has been used extensively with children with autism, intellectual disabilities, and other impairments. Because it is so widely known in the educational and speech-language communities, this approach will not be discussed in detail here. Readers are referred to Chapter 14 of this book and to Goossens' & Crain (1986a, 1986b), Karlan (1990), Musselwhite and St. Louis (1988), and Reichle et al. (1991) for more information.

**Aided Language Stimulation**   Aided language stimulation is a "total immersion" approach to teaching children to understand and to use pictorial symbols. Aided language stimulation is similar in concept to total communication (Goossens', 1989; Goossens' & Crain, 1986b). The purpose of this technique is to provide children with models for combining symbols in a flexible manner and opportunities to do so. Thus, this strategy is closely related to the use of miniboards to promote language development, as discussed previously.

In the context of an ongoing activity, the facilitator simply points to key pictorial symbols from the selection set while speaking. For example, the facilitator might say, "It's time to put the cookie mix in the bowl," while pointing to the symbols "put," "cookie," "in," and "bowl" on an eye gaze vest or board, electronic device, miniboard, or other type of display. Obviously, in order for this to occur, displays that contain necessary key vocabulary items for each activity in the child's day must be prepared in advance and be accessible to the facilitator. Numerous opportunities for interaction must also be available in the context of natural routines and play activities, as discussed previously in this chapter. Table 10.6. details the steps of selecting vocabulary for aided language stimulation displays and basic strategies for generic use of the technique. Readers are referred to the primary sources cited previously for additional information, and to Figure 4.8. as an example of an eye gaze vest used to provide aided language stimulation to children with severe motor impairments.

**Calendar/Schedule Boxes**   This strategy came from the work of Stillman and Battle (1984) and other practitioners working with children with dual sensory impairments. It has been disseminated and described by Rowland and Schweigert (1989, 1990) for use with children with visual

**Table 10.6.**   Aided language stimulation example application

Example: Doll play

1. *Choose* an augmentative modality that incorporates pictorial symbols: This could be eye gaze, a communication board, or a voice output device, for example.

2. *Delineate* a variety of doll play activity themes (e.g., cooking, doctor, kitchen, baby care).

3. *Delineate* subthemes associated with the activities (e.g., baby care—changing diapers, mealtime, dressing/undressing, grooming, bedtime).

4. *Select* vocabulary to reflect the interactions that can occur within each subtheme (e.g., baby care, changing diapers: stinky, wet, dry, change, pin, cry, no way, yucky, put on, take off, baby, mommy, wipe, bottom, powder, diaper, finished).

5. *Include* vocabulary commonly used across subthemes (e.g., more, yes, no, help).

6. *Develop* pictorial symbol displays for each subtheme and post in the relevant activity area for easy access (e.g., in the doll play area of the classroom).

7. *Use* the pictorial symbols during interactions with the child, much as key word manual signing would be used. Encourage and support the child in attempts to use the symbols as one component of a multimodal communication system that might include speech/vocalizations or gestures, for example.

Adapted from Goossens' (1989); Goossens' and Crain (1986a, 1986b).

impairments only, as well as with children with cognitive or multiple handicaps. The calendar or schedule box uses symbols to represent each activity in the child's day. The calendar or schedule box may serve several purposes: 1) to provide an overview of the sequence of activities; 2) to provide information about what will happen next; 3) to introduce the child to the concept of symbolization, which is the idea that one thing can stand for another; and 4) to make transitions from one activity to the next easier for the child. Figure 10.4. displays a summary of suggestions for organizing and using a schedule box.

---

**Organizing the Calendar/Schedule Box**

1. The first step in putting together a schedule box is to identify the child's daily schedule at home, in the classroom, or both. This means all of the activities he or she does in the setting every day—from grooming to dressing to eating to swimming. Make a list of the activities in order as they occur each day that can be posted near the schedule box.

2. Second, symbols to represent each of these activities should be identified and gathered. For most young children who are beginning communicators, these will probably be real object or partial object symbols, although they may be photographs, line drawings, or any type of symbol the child might understand. If real objects are used, a cassette tape might be used for "listening to music," a spoon for "eating," and a toothbrush for "grooming," for example. Collect the symbols in one place (e.g., in a cardboard box) so they are readily available. The same objects should be used to represent the activities every time.

3. Third, a schedule box should be constructed. The "box" is really a series of shallow containers arranged from left to right. The box may consist of a series of empty shoe boxes or cardboard magazine holders taped together, or a series of transparent plastic bags hung on cup hooks, or maybe just a long cardboard box with cardboard dividers taped at intervals. The symbols for each activity in the child's morning should be laid out, one in each container from left to right. For example, if the schedule box is used at school, it might look something like this for the first several activities of the day:

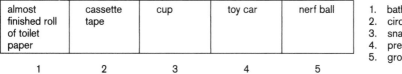

| almost finished roll of toilet paper | cassette tape | cup | toy car | nerf ball |
|---|---|---|---|---|
| 1 | 2 | 3 | 4 | 5 |

1. bathroom time
2. circle time (music)
3. snack time
4. pretend-play time
5. gross motor activity

4. Fourth, a "discard box" should be placed near the schedule box, into which the child places the activity symbol after he or she has completed the activity.

**Using the Calendar/Schedule Box**

1. Before each activity, the child should be prompted or taken to the schedule box. Starting with the far left container, he or she should be prompted to feel inside each container in order, until he or she comes to one that has a symbol in it. He or she is then prompted to take out the symbol and proceed to the activity.

2. The child should use the symbol at the beginning (or close to the beginning) of the activity. For example, the symbol for "circle time" (a cassette tape) might have been selected because the first part of this activity is that all the children sing the "Good Morning Song" that is on the tape. Perhaps the child could put the tape in the player at the start of circle time and turn it on as his or her way of participating in this activity. This will help the child make the connection between the symbol and the activity.

3. When the activity is completed, the child should put the symbol in the discard box. The discard box should be readily accessible to the child at all times so that he or she has the option of going to the box and taking out a symbol for something that has been completed, if he or she wants to ask to repeat that activity. If this happens, facilitators should make every attempt to respond to the child's request and let him or her do the activity the symbol represents, if at all possible!

4. Positive signs that indicate that the child is making the connection between a symbol and the activity it represents:
   a. Taking a symbol and then proceeding to the room or area where the activity typically occurs (e.g., in the bathroom for grooming or to the table for eating)
   b. Smiling or laughing when he or she picks up a symbol for something he or she likes to do
   c. Resisting taking a symbol, throwing it off his or her tray, or making a negative facial expression when he or she sees a symbol of something he or she doesn't like to do.

---

**Figure 10.4.**   Organizing and using a calendar/schedule box.

## Vocabulary Selection

Basic principles for selecting vocabulary items for miniboards, total communication, aided language stimulation, and other AAC applications were discussed in Chapter 9. Several issues in vocabulary selection for young children deserve emphasis here.

First, it is critical to remember that multimodal communication is the ultimate goal of an AAC intervention. In practical terms, this means that if the child can already communicate a particular message through eye gaze, gestures, or vocalizations in an acceptable and intelligible manner, it is generally not necessary to include that item in the AAC display. In fact, it is likely that if such items are included, they will not be used. For example, when preschoolers with physical disabilities had the necessary symbols available on their communication boards, they primarily used eye gaze, gestures, and vocalizations to initiate, confirm/deny, and request objects or actions (Light, Collier, & Parnes, 1985). They used their communication boards to provide information or clarification and to answer questions (other than yes/no). Eliminating redundant messages from the initial lexicon also allows more space for needed vocabulary items.

Second, it is important to provide young children with vocabulary items that are both developmentally and chronologically age appropriate and that include words in many semantic classes so that they have opportunities to learn and use language. Lahey and Bloom (1977) suggested that initial vocabulary should include at least the following words:

1.  Substantive words (people, places, things)
2.  Relational words (e.g., big, little)
3.  Generic verbs (e.g., give, get, make)
4.  Specific verbs (e.g., eat, drink, sleep)
5.  Emotional state words (e.g., happy, scared)
6.  Affirmation/negation words (e.g., yes, no, not)
7.  Recurrence/nonrecurrence words (e.g., more, all gone)
8.  Proper names for people first and personal pronouns later. Initially, proper names can be used instead of pronouns for possessives ("Mommy car") as well as object/agent relations ("Pat want" instead of "I want").
9.  Single adjectives first (e.g., hot, dirty) and their polar opposites later (e.g., cold, clean). Initially, "not" + adjective can be used for a polar opposite (e.g., "not" + hot = cold).
10. Relevant colors
11. Relevant prepositions

Recent studies have added substantially to the information base concerning the core vocabulary words for preschooler communication displays. These studies have examined various aspects of the spoken vocabulary of 3- to 5-year-old children. For example, Beukelman, Jones, and Rowan (1989) reported that 100 words accounted for 60% of those produced at school by six nondisabled children, 3 to 4 years of age, when 3,000-word samples from each child were analyzed. Marvin, Beukelman, and Vanderhoof (1991) reported that a similar percentage was represented by the most frequently occurring 100 of 2,000 words collected from 3- to 5-year-old children in home and in school settings. In a related study, Fried-Oken and More (1992) reported a vocabulary core list derived from comparing actual language samples from nondisabled 3- to 6-year-old children with the top 100 words chosen by parents and speech-language pathologists for 3- to 6-year-old children who were unable to speak. The top 100 words, or composite core vocabularies, derived from these databases are listed in the appendix by source.

## Literacy Activities

Because it is generally inappropriate to make assumptions about young children's future reading, writing, and spelling potentials, it is important to include literacy activities from a young age.

While it is beyond the scope of this chapter to provide detailed strategies in this area, a summary of early childhood literacy approaches is presented in the following sections.

**Reading and Storytelling**   Adult AAC users with congenital disabilities who learned to read as children have consistently identified the high expectations and encouragement of family members as having a major role in their success (Koppenhaver, Evans, & Yoder, 1991). Blackstone (1989e) noted that children with severe communication disorders often have less access to literacy experiences when young than do their nondisabled peers. This may account for the poor outcomes of literacy instruction for this population as a whole.

Blackstone (1989e) identified dozens of strategies that can be used by family members, teachers, and others to encourage skill development of literary skills. For example, age-appropriate stories should be read out loud frequently and repeatedly, since young children enjoy hearing the same stories over and over. Children should be positioned on or next to the person reading so that they can see the pictures and words on a page. As children become familiar with a story, they can be encouraged to indicate key pictures, use their vocalizations to "fill in the blanks" of a refrain, or participate in other ways to help tell the story. Similarly, loop tapes with single repetitive phrases (e.g., "I'll huff and I'll puff and I'll blow your house down") can allow children who use microswitches to participate in story telling. Once children become interested in this aspect of reading, it is important to indicate key words to them by pointing to the words or using other cuing techniques. Many children also enjoy learning the meaning of logos for places or activities in the environment, and many children learn to read the names of fast food restaurants and favorite breakfast cereals long before they begin kindergarten! Another way to encourage the child's literacy development is through involvement in story times such as those sponsored by many libraries, as well as by visiting the library with the child to borrow books from an early age (Koppenhaver et al., 1991). Relatives and friends may need to be reminded to purchase books and other printed materials for young children with disabilities, forgetting that without such early stimulation, later interest in literacy may be difficult to develop. Seventy-one percent of the adult AAC users surveyed by Koppenhaver et al. (1991) reported that they were read to as children at least 2–3 times per week, and an even greater number reported receiving books as gifts for their personal libraries.

**Writing and Drawing**   Children also need opportunities to learn writing, drawing, and other composition skills that involve the use of output tools. Many children, even those with severe physical disabilities, are motivated to manipulate crayons, paint brushes, and the other drawing and writing aids they see their peers using, and they should be given opportunities to do so whenever possible. Occupational therapists or other motor specialists may recommend adaptations to standard drawing or writing tools. Children should also be encouraged to compose and produce, if possible, drawn and written materials such as art projects (to be posted on the refrigerator at home, of course!) and letters to Santa Claus so that they learn to enjoy artistic and written expression. Of course, emphasis on composition and spelling accuracy is generally not appropriate for young children.

**Microcomputer Interventions**   Software programs are available to teach language and preliteracy skills to young children. Perhaps the best known of these applications in language has been reported by Meyers (1983, 1984, 1990), who used computers with speech output capabilities with toddlers with Down syndrome and other impairments. For example, Programs for Early Acquisition of Language (PEAL) software was developed specifically for this purpose and incorporates synthetic voice output, alternative keyboard access, and graphic displays in an interactive environment (see Table 10.7.). Research by O'Connor and Schery (1986) compared this approach with traditional language therapy for eight toddlers with handicaps over twelve 20-minute sessions. The marked improvements found between the pre-test and post-test assessments were similar under both conditions for all children. This is consistent with reports by Meyers (1983, 1984) that documented dramatic communication gains in some instances; however, this study also suggests that similar gains might be possible with more traditional approaches. Computerized language interventions may provide extra motivation and opportunities for practice to enhance language learning.

Simple software programs are also available to encourage early drawing skills and to teach letter and number recognition, preliteracy concepts (e.g., matching), basic keyboarding skills, and other skills related to literacy development. Table 10.7. summarizes some programs used with young children to develop literacy skills. These programs can be readily used with expanded keyboards, touch windows, single switches, and other alternative access modes with the addition of necessary computer hardware. Delineation of these hardware and software options is beyond the scope of this chapter, and readers are referred to Blackstone, Cassatt-James, and Bruskin (1988) for articles related to implementation and to the manufacturers in Table 10.7. for information about specific products.

> The *Trace ResourceBook* (Berliss et al., 1989), the *Apple Software Reference Guides* (Apple Computer, Inc.), and the resource catalog produced annually by Closing the Gap are excellent directories of literacy-related hardware and software materials.

## Transition to Elementary School

The ultimate goal of communication and other interventions for young children is to facilitate their entry into the educational mainstream (Brown et al., 1989; Salisbury & Vincent, 1990; Vincent

**Table 10.7.**  Examples of early literacy software for young children

| Literacy area | Software | Available from |
|---|---|---|
| Preliteracy/language development skills | First Words I and II, First Verbs, First Categories, Talking Nouns I and II, Talking Verbs, others | Laureate Learning Systems, Inc., 110 East Spring St., Winooski, VT 05404 |
| | Music Play, Action Play, Exploratory Play, Representational Play | Peal Software, 5000 N. Parkway Calabasas, #105, Calabasas, CA 91302 |
| | Touch 'N See, Touch 'N Match | Don Johnston Developmental Equipment, Inc., P. O. Box 639, Wauconda, IL 60084 |
| Reading, storytelling | Explore-A-Story | D.C. Heath & Co., 125 Spring St., Lexington, MA 02173. |
| | Gateway Stories | Don Johnston Developmental Equipment, Inc. (see above) |
| | Stickybears ABC and Stickybear Reading | Weekly Reader Software, Xerox Educational Publishers, Middletown, CT 06456. |
| | Reader Rabbit | Learning Co., 6493 Kaiser Dr., Fremont, CA 94555 |
| Drawing | Delta Drawing | Spinnaker, 1 Kendall Square, Cambridge, MA 02139 |
| | Create with Garfield | DLM, One DLM Park, Allen, TX 75002 |
| | Picture Perfect | Mind Play, 100 Conifer Hill Park, Building 3 #301, Danvers, MA 01923 |
| Keyboarding | Keytalk | Peal Software (see above) |
| | Stickybear Typing | Weekly Reader Software (see above) |

et al., 1980). Increased attention has focused on developing support mechanisms so that children who are not academically competitive by kindergarten age can enter and benefit from regular classes with other children of their own ages (e.g., Ford et al., 1989; Sailor et al., 1989; Stainback & Stainback, 1990). Several federally funded projects (e.g., Project TEEM in Vermont) have successfully demonstrated that this can be accomplished at the kindergarten level, to the benefit of children and to the satisfaction of their parents (Conn-Powers, Ross-Allen, & Holburn, 1990; Hamblin-Wilson & Thurman, 1990).

Early intervention specialists have described some components necessary to facilitate transitions into mainstreamed kindergarten settings (e.g., Conn-Powers et al., 1990; Salisbury & Vincent, 1990). From a communication perspective, one of the most important elements in such mainstreaming efforts is to ensure that the child has been receiving comprehensive services from a young age, so that the foundation has been laid for communication before beginning elementary school. It is also important to ensure that by the time the child reaches first grade, he or she has the tools necessary for academic participation and instruction. These tools may include an augmented writing system (either electronic or nonelectronic) in addition to whatever spoken communication system is in place. The tools may also include computer or software technology necessary for formal augmented reading instruction (see Blackstone, 1989e). Alternatively, tools may be necessary to ensure partial participation in the educational activities of a regular classroom. Whatever the case, it is important to start planning for the child's kindergarten placement approximately 2 years before the end of preschool so that necessary adaptations and arrangements can be instituted. If regular class placement is not an option, preparation time is equally important for the next environment, whatever it is.

An important technique for facilitating a smooth transition to kindergarten is to visit the target classroom, well before the beginning of the school year, in order to gather information about the participation patterns of the typical children in that setting. Some kindergarten settings are quite structured and academically oriented, while others emphasize building concepts through play, exploration, and cooperative learning. The nature and expectations of the kindergarten setting greatly influence the interactive requirements made of the child, which will, in turn, influence the direction of planning in the preschool years. "Kindergarten survival skills" curricula have been developed in response to what will be expected of the child (e.g., Rule, Fiechtl, & Innocenti, 1990; Vincent al., 1980).

Pre-transition visits also facilitate dialogue with the kindergarten teacher and professional staff concerning the child's needs and abilities, as well as the supports necessary for accommodation. For example, architectural modifications may be needed to facilitate physical accessibility, or a part-time paraprofessional may need to be hired to assist the teacher in facilitating optimum classroom participation. The speech-language pathologist and motor specialists in the new school may want to establish a plan for learning to use whatever communication equipment is in place, or for sharing the day-to-day management of the communication program. Family involvement in the transition and planning process is also critical, since family members are likely to be the only stable people in the child's life until the transition is complete (Hamblin-Wilson & Thurman, 1990). Thus, family members often play a critical role in the transfer of information about technology, interaction, and other components of the child's communication program (Berry, 1987). While the specific transition planning process depends on the school district and the individuals, it is clear that careful attention and anticipation of the child's needs are critical in order to avoid "reinventing the wheel" for the first several months in the new location.

# *Composite Initial Vocabulary List for Preschoolers*

>>>>>>>>>>>>>>>>>>>>>>>>>>>>>>>>>>>>>>>>>>

| Word | School (Beukelman, Jones, & Rowan, 1989) | Parent/SLP language samples (Fried-Oken & More, 1992) | School (Marvin, Beukelman, & Vanderhoof, 1991) | Home (Marvin, Beukelman, & Vanderhoof, 1991) |
|---|---|---|---|---|
| A | x | x | x | x |
| Again | | | | x |
| All | x | x | x | x |
| Am | x | | | |
| And | x | x | x | x |
| Are | x | x | x | x |
| At | x | | x | x |
| Back | | x | x | |
| Be | x | x | x | x |
| Because | x | x | x | x |
| Bed | | x | | |
| Big | x | | | |
| Boo | x | | | |
| Boy | | x | | |
| But | x | | x | x |
| By | | | x | |
| Can | x | x | x | x |
| Car | | x | | |
| Chair | x | x | | |
| Come | x | x | | x |
| Could | | | | x |
| Dad | | x | | x |
| Did | x | x | x | x |
| Do | x | x | x | x |
| Does | x | | | |
| Dog | x | x | | |
| Done | x | | | |
| Door | | x | | |
| Down | x | x | x | x |
| Duck | | | x | |
| Eat | x | x | | |
| For | x | x | x | x |
| Get | x | x | x | x |
| Girl | | x | | |
| Go | x | x | x | x |

| Word | School (Beukelman, Jones, & Rowan, 1989) | Parent/SLP language samples (Fried-Oken & More, 1992) | School (Marvin, Beukelman, & Vanderhoof, 1991) | Home (Marvin, Beukelman, & Vanderhoof, 1991) |
|---|---|---|---|---|
| Going | x | x | x | x |
| Gonna | | x | x | x |
| Good | x | | | |
| Got | x | x | x | x |
| Grandma | | x | | |
| Had | | | x | |
| Has | x | | | |
| Have | x | x | x | x |
| He | x | x | x | x |
| Her | | x | | |
| Here | x | x | x | x |
| Hey | x | | x | x |
| Him | | x | | |
| His | | x | | |
| Home | x | x | | |
| House | x | x | | |
| How | x | x | x | x |
| Huh | | | x | x |
| I | x | x | x | x |
| If | | | x | x |
| I'll | | x | x | x |
| I'm | | x | x | x |
| In | x | x | x | x |
| Is | x | x | x | x |
| It | x | x | x | x |
| Just | x | x | x | x |
| Kind | | | | x |
| Know | x | x | x | x |
| Let | x | x | | x |
| Like | x | x | x | x |
| Little | x | x | x | x |
| Look | x | x | x | |
| Long | | | x | |
| Make | x | | x | x |
| Man | | | x | |
| Me | x | x | x | x |
| Mine | x | | x | x |
| Mom | | x | | x |
| Mommy | | | | x |
| More | x | x | x | |
| My | x | x | x | x |
| Muffin | | | x | |
| Name | x | | | |
| Named | | | | x |
| Need | x | x | x | x |
| No | x | x | x | x |
| Not | x | x | x | x |

| Word | School (Beukelman, Jones, & Rowan, 1989) | Parent/SLP language samples (Fried-Oken & More, 1992) | School (Marvin, Beukelman, & Vanderhoof, 1991) | Home (Marvin, Beukelman, & Vanderhoof, 1991) |
|---|---|---|---|---|
| Now | x | x | x | x |
| -n't | | x | x | x |
| Of | x | x | x | x |
| Off | x | | x | |
| Oh | x | | x | x |
| Okay | x | x | x | x |
| On | x | x | x | x |
| One | x | x | x | x |
| Out | x | x | x | x |
| Over | x | x | | |
| Paint | x | | | |
| Person #1 | x | | x | x |
| Person #2 | | | x | x |
| Person #3 | | | | x |
| Person #4 | | | | x |
| Person #5 | | | | x |
| Play | x | x | | x |
| Please | x | | | |
| Pop | | | | x |
| Put | x | x | x | x |
| -'re | | x | x | |
| Red | | | x | |
| Right | x | x | x | x |
| -s, 's | | x | x | x |
| Said | | | x | |
| Say | | | x | |
| See | x | x | x | x |
| She | x | x | | |
| Show | x | | | |
| Sleep | | x | | |
| Sit | x | x | | |
| Snake | | | x | |
| So | x | x | x | x |
| Some | x | x | x | x |
| Something | | | | x |
| Take | x | x | x | x |
| That | x | x | x | x |
| The | x | x | x | x |
| Them | x | x | x | x |
| Then | | x | x | x |
| There | x | x | x | x |
| These | x | x | x | x |
| They | x | x | x | x |
| Thing | | | x | |
| This | x | x | x | x |
| Those | x | | | |
| Three | x | | | |

| Word | School (Beukelman, Jones, & Rowan, 1989) | Parent/SLP language samples (Fried-Oken & More, 1992) | School (Marvin, Beukelman, & Vanderhoof, 1991) | Home (Marvin, Beukelman, & Vanderhoof, 1991) |
|---|---|---|---|---|
| Through | | | x | |
| Time | | x | | |
| To | x | x | x | x |
| Too | x | x | x | |
| Try | | | | x |
| Two | x | x | x | x |
| Uh | | | x | x |
| Um | | | x | x |
| Up | x | x | x | x |
| Us | x | | | |
| Watch | | x | | |
| Wanna | | x | | |
| Want | x | x | x | x |
| Was | | x | x | x |
| We | x | x | x | x |
| What | x | x | x | x |
| When | | | x | x |
| Where | x | x | | x |
| Who | x | | | |
| Why | | | | x |
| Will | x | x | x | x |
| With | x | x | x | x |
| Yeah | | | x | x |
| Yes | x | x | | |
| You | x | x | x | x |
| Your | x | | x | x |

This composite list is composed of the 100 most frequently occurring words from each list.

# *Educational Integration of AAC Users*

>>>>>>>>>>>>>>>>>>>>>>>>>>>>>>>>>>>>>>>>>>>>>>>>>>>>>>

> Education is a specialized form of communication. Human beings have developed particular times and places in which the scripts of their cultures are to be communicated from one generation to the next. We have come to call the set of practices by which this communication of cultural scripts is accomplished "education." The communication that occurs in educational contexts happens in oral, written, verbal, and nonverbal modes. . . . [Our] role is to facilitate the communication, thus the education, that occurs in the classroom. (Hoskins, 1990, p. 29)

In response to legal and societal pressure, what are considered as appropriate educational environments for children with severe communication disorders have changed dramatically in the 1980s and 1990s. The "least restrictive environment" for these students increasingly has come to mean the regular classroom, for at least a substantial part of each school day. Since participation in the regular classroom requires many kinds of extensive communication, effective AAC systems that are age- and context-appropriate are critical tools for school success. This applies to students across the ability range, regardless of their communication disorders.

Unfortunately, it is not uncommon for children with severe communication disorders to attend kindergarten and then to enter first grade without access to writing and drawing tools, the reading tools, or the conversational tools available to their fellow students. Although these students cannot hold pencils or crayons, they may not have access to augmented writing systems. Although they cannot hold books, turn pages, or use their voices to practice phonics, they may not have been given adapted reading equipment or computers. Although they may have difficulty answering questions in class and participating in social conversations, they may not have been provided with AAC systems for interaction. Thus, it is not at all surprising that many of these students fail to participate successfully in regular education classrooms, since they are at a distinct disadvantage for both academic and social learning. When participation failure occurs, these students are often labeled as "nonacademically oriented" and are then assigned to either segregated classrooms or to adapted curricula delivered in resource rooms or other separate settings. In time, they find themselves increasingly isolated from the mainstream, and integrated only during nonacademic classes such as music, art, or physical education. Until recently, it was only under exceptional circumstances that any of these students were retained in regular classrooms and provided with the adaptive devices and supports that enable them to be successful.

As placement of students with severe communication disorders in regular classrooms becomes routine, there is a critical need for policies, practices, and strategies to replace the prevailing "management by exception" approach. This chapter presents a framework for delivering integrated communication and educational services to children who require AAC systems across the ability range.

> Principle 1. Begin early, so the AAC user is prepared for the regular classroom experience.

## PREPARING AAC USERS FOR THE CLASSROOM

Students with severe communication disorders often enter early elementary grades without communication systems that permit them to participate in the regular curriculum. Needless to say, the educational experiences of these students are quite different from those of their peers. For example, these students are unable to write or speak in class when other students are expected to do so. Instead, they must either passively observe other students or communicate through an aide or paraprofessional. Students with severe communication disorders often spend months and even the first years of school in assessment and instructional activities related to AAC system use. These activities may conflict with regular classroom activities, causing them to fall further behind the regular students as they must forfeit "academic time" in favor of "communication time."

A clear solution to this dilemma is to begin providing AAC services to children with severe communication disorders during their preschool years. As discussed in Chapter 10, early attention allows children to develop linguistic, operational, and social competencies necessary to support participation in elementary school. In the United States, P.L. 99-457, which mandates publicly funded preschool education for children over the age of 3 with disabilities, provides the base for early AAC interventions. Such AAC interventions must be designed to meet the conversational and interaction needs of young children—communication for today—as well as the academic and social needs of the regular classroom—communication for tomorrow. Thus, AAC team members involved with preschool students must have a solid understanding of the participation requirements of elementary school programs, in order to adequately prepare children for these settings. (This issue was discussed in Chapter 10 regarding preschool–kindergarten transitions.)

Transitions between kindergarten and elementary school must be managed with care. First, the AAC team should not modify the AAC system unnecessarily during the first year of school. If a child has been well prepared for school, drastic changes in the system should not be necessary. If substantive changes are made, the child is at risk for falling behind the other students academically while learning to use the revised system. If AAC preparation has been inadequate, the elementary school AAC team faces a difficult problem and may need to intervene, although the timing is not optimal.

Second, the AAC team in the elementary school should have the knowledge and skills to facilitate communication efforts of young AAC users. If team members must learn about an unfamiliar AAC system over the course of the school year, the student's ability to participate in the classroom will probably be affected adversely. We have found that one way to avoid this problem is for a paraprofessional to follow an AAC student from preschool to kindergarten to elementary school, especially if the technical requirements of his or her system are sophisticated. When this is not possible, providing facilitator training for the elementary school staff *prior to the beginning of the academic year* should be a primary goal of transition planning.

> Principle 2. Whenever possible, hold the student in the regular curriculum.

## INVOLVING STUDENTS IN THE REGULAR CURRICULUM

The primary reason for integrating students with severe communication disabilities is to make available to them the educational and social benefits of the regular classroom. Several negative consequences are likely if integration does not occur.

First, when students "fall out" of the curriculum, teachers (often special educators) are required to develop personalized educational plans to meet their needs. This instruction is delivered either in a segregated setting (e.g., a resource room or special education classroom) or in the regular classroom during activities that are parallel to, but not the same as, those for other students. Early curricular failure often results in a student receiving a personalized curriculum for the duration of his or her public school experience. While this may not be problematic in theory, the reality is that a personalized curriculum often lacks continuity, since its content depends on the preferences and philosophies of individual educational staff. Therefore, the curriculum may change dramatically with the arrival of each new teacher or speech-language pathologist. Furthermore, inadequate longitudinal management of a personalized curriculum over the years usually results in a splintered educational program that is replete with gaps, redundancies, and oversights. In contrast, the regular curriculum provides an overall program structure for educational staff that, at a minimum, encourages a cohesive scope and sequence of instruction.

Second, failure to be involved in the regular curriculum appears to reduce available peer pressure and support. For example, in the early elementary years, there is considerable peer pressure related to learning to read and write. Children with disabilities in regular classroom environments are subject to this pressure as much as their nondisabled classmates, so that they often respond with the desire to learn what their peers are learning. Children with disabilities are also encouraged to learn at a similar rate to that of other students, so that they don't stand out from their peers. Such opportunities for peer pressure and support are eliminated in a personalized curriculum in which no other students participate.

Third, failure to be involved in a regular curriculum diminishes opportunities for peer interaction and instruction. Even if a student with disabilities is physically present in a regular classroom, opportunities for social and academic involvement with other students are reduced if he or she has a personalized curriculum. In addition, opportunities for peer instruction in either direction (i.e., tutor with disabilities–nondisabled peer or nondisabled tutor–peer with disabilities) are virtually eliminated.

Fourth, lack of participation in the regular curriculum may shape students' perceptions of themselves negatively, as well as those of their classmates, teachers, and family members. If, however, students are involved successfully in regular-classroom curricular experiences, they learn to see themselves as able and active in the same arena as their nondisabled peers.

---

In order to foster change in regular education, special educators need to reduce their current emphasis on classifying, labeling, and offering "special" programs for students who do not fit within the present regular education structure. Instead, they should put more emphasis on joining with regular educators to work for a reorganization of or modifications in the structure of regular education itself so that the needs of a wider range of students can be met within the mainstream of regular education. (Stainback, Stainback, Courtnage, & Jaben, 1985, p. 148)

---

## THE PARTICIPATION MODEL

We use the Participation Model (Figure 7.1.) as a framework for making decisions associated with integrating AAC users into educational programs. In the following sections, applications of the model to meet the needs of AAC users in regular classrooms are discussed and illustrated.

### Identify Participation Patterns

In the past, students who were not academically competitive were usually excluded from regular classroom settings. More recently, mainstreaming has become more widespread, although there may still be several participation patterns available within this model for regular classroom integration. We propose four variables that can be manipulated to achieve a participation pattern that is appropriate to the needs and capabilities of an individual student. These include three levels of integration, four levels of academic participation, four levels of social participation, and three levels of independence, which are depicted in Figure 11.1.

**Integration**   The term *integration* refers to the physical presence of a student with disabilities in a regular classroom attended by same-age peers. There are three basic levels of integration: full, selective, and none. These levels are defined in Table 11.1.

An increasing number of students with AAC needs are *fully integrated* into regular classroom settings, which means that they are physically present in the same classrooms attended by their same-age peers during a significant part of the school day. Thus, they, their classmates, and the regular class teacher all consider them as part of the class. Physical integration may be all that is needed for social and academic advantages to accrue, but the mere physical presence of students with AAC needs in regular classrooms usually is not enough to ensure participation. Thus, integration as we have defined it is *necessary but not sufficient* to ensure regular classroom participation.

*Selective integration* into regular classrooms is an option that may be appropriate in some situations, depending on a student's individual academic or social needs. For example, we know of high school students with severe disabilities who choose to spend one or two periods of their school day receiving remedial literacy instruction in a resource room setting rather than attending study hall, music, art, or other regular elective classes. Parents may prefer the option of selective integration so that their child can receive specialized remediation services. We know at least one adolescent girl with physical disabilities whose parents prefer that she receive physical therapy in a separate room, because they are uncomfortable having therapy administered in physical education class while her nondisabled friends play basketball or do aerobics. Some students may spend considerable amounts of school time in community settings receiving vocational, recreational or other instruction appropriate to their long-term needs. These selectively integrated students participate at various levels in the regular school curriculum for the remainder of the school day.

Students may be selectively integrated as part of the process of moving from "no integration"

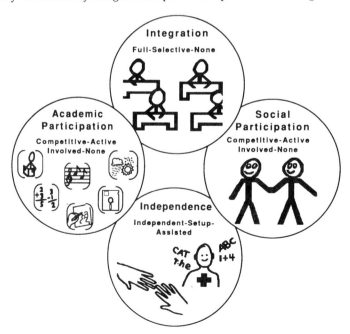

**Figure 11.1.**   Four variables that can be manipulated to achieve a participation pattern for an individual student.

**Table 11.1.** Levels of regular classroom integration

| Level | Definition |
|---|---|
| Full | Physically present in age-appropriate regular education settings for the entire school day. At times, activity patterns may vary from those of peers. |
| Selective | Physically present in age-appropriate regular education settings during some, but not all, of the school day. Receives educational services in separate classroom, resource room, community, or other settings during the remainder of the school day. |
| None (excluded) | Physically excluded from age-appropriate regular education settings during all of the school day. There may be access to hallways or other settings used by regular peers but at times separate from regular peers. |

to full integration. For example, it is not uncommon for students with intellectual disabilities to spend most of their school day in a school or classroom separate from their peers, with the exception of one or two classes. These classes are often the nonacademic areas mentioned previously, such as art, music, library time, lunchtime in the cafeteria, or recess. Although this type of selective integration may be a laudable first step toward full integration, it is rarely sufficient to offset the negative consequences of falling out of the curriculum that were mentioned previously.

Some students with AAC systems may attend *no* regular classes during one or more years of their school programs. As noted previously, a variety of social, legal, and educational mandates are rapidly reducing this segregation in many parts of the world. Special circumstances, however, may exist in which AAC and educational services provided in separate settings benefit the children involved. For example, we know of separate classrooms in the United States in which children with severe multiple handicaps receive intensive *short-term* instruction from AAC specialists with extensive technical and educational expertise. The explicit goals of these specialized classrooms are to: 1) provide the children with suitable alternative access methods, 2) teach them to use their AAC systems efficiently, 3) provide extensive literacy instruction, and 4) eventually integrate the students into regular classrooms. When professional expertise and the commitment to long-term academic and AAC gains are not available in integrated settings, separate educational programming for these students may be a *short-term* option.

An educational cooperative in upstate New York operates a specialized Option 4 classroom for children with multiple (i.e., severe/profound) handicaps. Two years ago, eight children between 5–12 years of age were assigned to this classroom to receive "intensive technology assistance" aimed at facilitating their eventual placement into other segregated classrooms in the system. All of the students were nonreaders and non-AAC users at that time. The classroom was staffed with a full-time speech-language pathologist, extensive occupational and physical therapy supports, a full-time teacher, and three paraprofessionals. Two years later, seven of the eight children read within 1–2 years of their age levels and are proficient AAC users. Two entered regular classrooms as competitive students, [and] the academic placements for the other children are being negotiated, with the hopes of having them all placed in integrated situations. (K. Erickson, personal communication, July 25, 1991)

**Academic Participation** The four levels of academic participation are described in Table 11.2. These are discussed from the highest to lowest level of participation.

*Competitive* *Competitive academic participation* requires that a student with AAC needs meet the academic standards expected of regular peers. Nevertheless, this does not necessarily mean that all of the activities completed by peers will be completed by the student with disabilities to the same degree. For example, students with AAC systems often cannot write as rapidly as their peers, and, therefore, the seat work they are expected to complete may be reduced, as long as the

**Table 11.2.**   Levels of academic participation

| Level | Definition |
|---|---|
| Competitive | Academic expectations are the same as for peers, although the workload may be adjusted. Academic progress is evaluated in the same way as peer performance. |
| Active | Academic expectations are less than for peers, although similar content is taught. The workload may be adjusted. Academic progress is evaluated according to individualized standards. |
| Involved | Academic expectations are minimal. Student is included in classroom activities to the extent possible, with alternative activities available when needed. Progress is evaluated according to individualized standards. |
| None | No academic participation expectations at all. Student is passive during most learning activities in the regular classroom. Progress may not be evaluated at all. |

same academic standards are met. Some students may choose to reduce their total academic workloads in order to fulfill the requirements of classes in which they are competitive. For example, it is not uncommon for students with severe disabilities at the post-secondary level to enroll in only one or two classes each semester so that they can be academically successful and still have time to participate in the social opportunities available on a college campus. It is also important to note that students may be competitive in one, several, or all areas of the curriculum. Thus, an elementary-school student may be competitive in math, reading, music, and art, while meeting somewhat lower expectations in other areas. The level of academic participation should be determined on an individual basis.

Competitive academic participation requires that families, teachers, and specialists coordinate efforts so that the student can be maximally efficient. The expectations of competitive academic participation do not allow for an adapted or remedial curriculum, taught by specialists, which is different from that of the regular classroom. If competitive participation is expected, educational specialists must act as consultants to regular classroom teachers so that all school activities contribute to the overall educational goal. In short, the goal of competitive participation is to expect that competitive standards will be met while modifying activities and workloads as appropriate, *not* to modify standards while expecting the same quantity of work as produced by peers.

*Active*   Not all students with AAC systems can be academically competitive in all areas. Nevertheless, many students can be *academically active* and participate in the regular curriculum, although they cannot meet the same academic standards as their peers. Maintaining these students as active participants in regular classrooms allows them to experience many of the benefits of integration, such as exposure to a structured educational sequence, peer social contact, and peer instruction. Meanwhile, agreements among educational staff and parents regarding the students' active status can reduce the pressures of competitive expectations and the negative experiences that might result.

Many students with AAC systems will be competitive in some academic areas and active in others. Alternatively, some students may be active in all areas and competitive in none; yet they are expected to participate in the curriculum at some level, to be involved with and learn at least part of the same academic content as other students, and to be evaluated according to their individual goals. An active student may receive supplementary instruction to develop particular skills in certain areas such as math or reading. Depending on the academic expectations, the focus of the curriculum may shift from an academic to a functional orientation as they progress through school.

*Involved*   Some students, together with their educational teams and parents, may decide that participation in certain academic areas will be limited to *academic involvement*, rather than competitive or active participation. In this case, the student attends the regular class activities along with peer students but is less active as a participant. For example, some students who are unable to speak or sing may enjoy being involved in the school choir. Because of their disabilities, they are not expected to be competitive or active on a routine basis, but they like music, the music teacher is fun to be around, the social atmosphere of the choir is very positive, and the students thus benefit in a number of ways from the experience.

Involvement should not be limited to elective areas such as music and art. Involvement may be desirable, although academic participation is expected to be minimal, perhaps because of the social atmosphere of a classroom or a student's interest in a subject area. For example, we know of one selectively integrated junior high school student with severe disabilities who was involved in regular social studies, English, shop (e.g., woodworking), and health classes in one school year and who also received instruction in a variety of community settings. Some of the regular classes were of special interest to him (e.g., woodworking and health), while others were offered because the teachers were known to be accepting of students with AAC needs, regardless of their level of participation. It is important that in none of these classes was the student merely a passive observer with no involvement whatsoever. Again, students may be involved in some areas, active in others, and competitive in still others.

*None* The level of *no academic participation* is never acceptable or defensible, although it occurs far too often. In the level of no participation, the student is physically present in a regular classroom for a particular lesson or activity, but is passive and uninvolved for the majority of time. This may occur for a number of reasons, not the least of which is that the student does not have the AAC tools needed for participation. Even fully integrated students may be nonparticipants in one or more classroom activities, and this undesirable option requires prompt remediation.

> It is wise to choose a school that your neighborhood friends attend. I was no surprise to the majority of my classmates; they had known me and how I did things for many years before I became a fellow classmate. They also were able to explain about me to any new students who had never met me or had any exposure to a person with disabilities. (Victor Valentic, a fully integrated, competitive AAC user, 1991, p. 9)

**Social Participation** School involves more than just academic learning, since all curricular and extracurricular activities occur within social contexts. Parents of regular students show their awareness of this aspect of school when they request that their child be assigned to the same classroom as a friend, or to a specific teacher who encourages social development. The participation patterns of students with disabilities also involve social considerations along four levels similar to those in academic participation. These are defined in Table 11.3.

*Competitive* *Socially competitive* students are active participants in a social group of peers. They are involved in the activities of the group, at the least by making choices about whether to engage in activities, and they exert influence over group decisions. For example, a socially competitive student might initiate activities such as birthday or slumber parties on occasion and, in turn, is invited to similar activities by other group members. The student who is socially competitive typically plays, visits, "hangs out," or otherwise interacts with his or her classmates after school hours (e.g., on weekends or evenings).

*Active* Not all regular or disabled students are socially competitive, but many are *socially active*, and they make choices about and are involved in social activities, although they may not exert much influence over the social climate of a group and its interaction patterns. Some readers will be able to apply this designation to themselves when they were children because they were "shy" or "studious" individuals who were not socially isolated but who did not have a wide circle of friends. Socially active students with AAC needs may spend more time alone after school than do socially competitive students, although they may have some opportunities for interaction with nondisabled peers. As with levels of academic participation, students may be socially active in some areas and competitive or involved in others.

**Table 11.3.**   Levels of social participation

| Level | Definition |
|---|---|
| Competitive | Chooses whether to be involved in social contexts with regular peers. Actively participates in social interactions. Actively influences the activities of the social group. |
| Active | Chooses whether to be involved in social contexts with regular peers. Actively participates in social interactions. Usually, does not directly influence the activities of the group. |
| Involved | Chooses whether to be involved in social contexts with regular peers. Participation may be passive. Does not directly influence the activities of the group. |
| None | Is not involved in social interactions with regular peers. |

*Involved*   *Socially involved* students attend class with their regular peers and may be involved in some extracurricular activities. Socially involved students, however, do not influence social situations and often are passive observers in social activities. Students who are socially involved in school rarely maintain contact with their peers after school hours. Thus, they may spend their evenings and weekends engaged in activities primarily with family members rather than friends.

*None*   Students who have *no social participation* have limited access to their peers during school hours and thus have no opportunities to form friendships or make acquaintances. They are not members of a social group during school or nonschool hours. As is the case with academic participation, no involvement is generally undesirable and requires remediation.

Social participation patterns co-exist with the patterns of integration and academic participation described previously. For example, when students with disabilities are at least selectively integrated in regular classrooms, they have opportunities for social inclusion at some level, regardless of whether they are academically competitive, active, or involved. The extent of integration and social involvement for students with AAC needs depends on many factors. Students may be integrated, that is, physically present in regular classrooms, as a result of school policy. Nevertheless, the educational staff and the family may still need to encourage the active social involvement of these students. An active or competitive level of social participation requires that mutual friendships be formed with some peer students. (Approaches for encouraging and facilitating such friendships, such as the "Circle of Friends" process, are described in Chapter 13.) Because the peer group plays such an important role in determining the level of social participation, educational personnel and family members can directly influence this component only to a limited extent.

*Independence*   School personnel must also plan for the level of independence expected in each academic area. Three levels of independence are useful to consider for students who are integrated into regular classrooms, and these are defined in Table 11.4.

As can be seen from this table, some students may be *completely independent* in at least some activities. Many AAC students, however, require appropriate environmental and technical assistance at the outset of an activity to *set up* their work environments or change position in the classroom. When these set-up activities are completed, the students can be independent. Some other students need to be *assisted* in order to participate in regular classrooms. The teacher is not the only available source of ongoing human assistance, and perhaps the primary (and most underutilized) source of assistance is the regular classroom peer group.

Ideally, all students who use AAC systems should have opportunities to be independent (either with or without initial set-up assistance) during some, but not necessarily all, parts of each school day. Language arts is often a subject in early grades in which the AAC team can easily facilitate such independence, because students tend to work in small reading groups with other students at a similar academic level. At least some independent participation is important because it communicates to the students themselves and to their classmates that they are legitimate members of the class in both learning and social areas. Independence also requires well-coordinated efforts in support of a student by the AAC team. For example, if a student is unable to independently partici-

**Table 11.4.** Levels of independence

| Level | Definition |
| --- | --- |
| Complete | Able to participate in an activity without human assistance. |
| Independent with set-up | Independent in an activity with human assistance to set up educational materials, AAC or other equipment, or physical position, for example. |
| Assisted | Able to participate in an activity with physical or verbal assistance from a teacher, paraprofessional, or peer student. |

pate in a subject area for several days, it is often a sign that the AAC team is not meeting its responsibilities in keeping the vocabulary in the AAC system current or in maintaining the device. Selective independent participation frees the educational staff from expecting that the child must be independent throughout the entire school day in order to be included in a regular classroom. We cannot emphasize enough that neither independence nor academic competitiveness are appropriate prerequisites to regular classroom integration.

> We can, whenever and wherever we choose, successfully teach all children whose schooling is of interest to us. We already know more than we need in order to do this. Whether we do it must finally depend on how we feel about the fact that we haven't done it so far. (Edmonds, 1979, p. 29)

## Individual Participation Patterns

The discussion of patterns of participation in regular classrooms is meant to be both a conceptual and a practical tool. We intend that the various levels of integration, academic and social participation, and independence be used by the AAC team, which includes the family and the AAC student, to make decisions about the desired participation profile prior to the beginning of each school year. This approach is in contrast to a less systematic approach to integration that basically involves placing the student in a regular classroom and then "seeing what happens." We have found that for many students with AAC needs, such an approach almost guarantees confusion, frustration, and often failure. In order to facilitate systematic planning, we have provided a simple matrix in Table 11.5. that the AAC team can use to discuss and make decisions about integration, academic and social participation, and independence.

The first decision concerns the integration pattern: Will the student be placed in a regular classroom full time, selectively, or not at all? If integration is to be selective, in which specific curricular or extracurricular activities will it occur? Numerous factors influence these decisions, not the least of which may be the policies or practices of the school district, and these may need to be resolved before further planning can occur. While our bias is toward full integration or nearly full integration with very selective specialized classes, some families may choose a less integrated participation pattern for their children for a variety of reasons. The family, AAC user, and the AAC team will need to arrive at consensus concerning this issue for the individual.

Assuming that some level of integration is desirable and feasible, the next set of decisions relates to academic and social participation. For each area targeted for integration, what is the desired level of academic participation for the student? That is, is the student expected to be competitive, active, or involved? In Table 11.5., this information can be entered for each academic ("A") subject. Then, similar decisions can be made for the desired level of social participation in each area of integration, using the corresponding line ("S") to record decisions. Decisions regarding the desired level of independence in each area can be coded according to the scheme in Table 11.5. Use of this matrix is designed to facilitate team decision making in these areas, rather than to approach

**Table 11.5.** Integration/academic and social participation/independence matrix

| Integration | | Participation | | | |
|---|---|---|---|---|---|
| | | Competitive | Active | Involved | None |
| Full | A | | | | |
| | S | | | | |
| Selective | A | | | | |
| | S | | | | |
| None | A | | | | |
| | S | | | | |

A = academic areas, S = social areas; I = independent, Is = independent with set-up, As = assisted.

integration haphazardly or, in the worst case, not at all. Two brief examples of the application of this multidimensional matrix follow.

*Chad*   Table 11.6. illustrates the participation profile that was targeted for Chad, a 13-year-old student. The AAC team in Chad's school began plans to integrate him into regular classes when he entered junior high. Prior to this, he received all of his education in a separate special education classroom for students with severe physical and intellectual disabilities. He operated an electronic scanning device with a head switch to communicate in social situations, and he was able to access a standard computer by connecting the device to the computer via a special cable. The first decision made by Chad, his parents, and the rest of the education team was to aim for selective integration for the next school year. The team identified the following learning priorities for Chad: 1) literacy skills, 2) music (an activity that he enjoyed), 3) functional math, 4) computer skills, 5) physical therapy, and 6) community-based vocational instruction. In addition, social studies was included because the teacher was a supportive facilitator of social interactions between regular and disabled students. Thus, it was decided that Chad would be selectively integrated into regular social studies, music, and beginning computer classes, and he would receive his literacy (e.g., reading), functional math, vocational instruction, and physical therapy in specialized classes. An involved level of aca-

**Table 11.6.** Integration/academic and social participation/independence matrix for Chad

| Integration | | Participation | | | |
|---|---|---|---|---|---|
| | | Competitive | Active | Involved | None |
| Full | A | | | | |
| | S | | | | |
| Selective | A | | As: **computer class,** reading, math, physical therapy, vocational | As: **social studies** Is: **music** | |
| | S | | active/involved in all integrated classes | | |
| None | A | | | | |
| | S | | | | |

A = academic areas, S = social areas; I = independent, Is = independent with set-up, As = assisted. Bold type = regular classes.

demic participation was planned for social studies and music, while an active level was chosen for the remaining subject areas. Chad, his family, and the rest of the team wanted him to be socially active or involved as much as possible. Finally, it was agreed that Chad would need assistance in order to participate at the desired levels in all areas except music.

**Heather**    Table 11.7. depicts the desired participation profile for Heather, a young student with severe athetoid cerebral palsy. Planning for integration into first grade began for Heather at the end of kindergarten. During her kindergarten year, she received an electronic direct selection AAC device with a small, portable printer that were mounted on her powered wheelchair. The AAC team determined that Heather should be fully integrated into first grade, and, after negotiation, the school district agreed to this goal. Further, the team felt that Heather should be expected to be competitive in all academic areas, active in elective areas such as art and music, and involved in physical education. In addition, the AAC team and her family recommended that Heather should receive specialized instruction in the use of her AAC device three times per week, when her classmates engaged in free reading time. Everyone agreed that she could be socially competitive or active in all areas. A combination of total independence and independence with set-up, as well as assisted independence in some areas, was identified to facilitate this high level of participation.

These two examples of Chad and Heather illustrate that although independent, competitive participation in all aspects of regular school life may not be possible for many students with severe communication disorders, some variation of this level is usually possible. Careful, thoughtful planning and decision making in both academic and social areas allows for flexibility in an educational program, which permits a mix of competitive, active, and involved participation. Careful planning also allows parents and school staff to tailor the academic and social expectations to the needs and abilities of a specific child, so that the responsibilities of each team member can be clarified and evaluated.

---

Once the decision about my education was made by myself and my parents, plans for how to manage that education were soon underway, and still are today as I complete high school and head for college. We have a formula; as problems present themselves, solutions are sought, and, at times, we have learned that you never give up, just keep on trying. (Valentic, 1991, p. 9)

---

## Activity/Standards Inventory and Barrier Assessment

When the team has established the desired level of regular class participation, actual implementation can be accomplished through following the preliminary steps of the Participation Model (Figure 7.1.). The first step is completing an Activity/Standards Inventory in the actual classroom at the beginning of the school year using the form in Table 7.2. This inventory involves a detailed list of all activities in which regular students are expected to participate during the school day, along with expected levels of academic participation. (Readers will note that the levels of independence listed in Table 7.2. are more specific than those in Table 11.5. This is because actual implementation requires a more precise breakdown of the levels of assistance according to the types of assistance [e.g., verbal or physical] that need to be provided.)

Next, a similar analysis of the actual participation of the AAC student in the regular classroom for activities identified as integration targets is completed. Again, it is important to conduct this analysis as early in the school year as possible so that discrepancies among the expectations for peers, the target student's current level of participation, and the desired level of participation can be identified and remediated. Next, observations about the types of barriers preventing participation are included on the inventory. For example, Table 11.8. displays part of the Activity/Standards Inventory completed for Heather.

**Table 11.7.**   Integration/academic and social participation/independence matrix for Heather

| Integration | | Participation | | | |
|---|---|---|---|---|---|
| | | Competitive | Active | Involved | None |
| Full (except no silent reading time 3 x/week; replace with AAC instruction) | A | I or Is: **reading, writing, spelling, math, science, health, social studies** | Is or As: **music, art** | As: **Physical education** | |
| | S | competitive or active in all areas | | | |
| Selective | A | | | | |
| | S | | | | |
| None | A | | | | |
| | S | | | | |

A = academic areas, S = social areas; I = independent, Is = Independent with set-up, As = Assisted. Bold type = regular classes.

It became clear as the Activity/Standards Inventory was being completed in the first month of school that most of Heather's peers were independent learners after they had been set up. The team had agreed that this was a reasonable goal for Heather as well. The Activity/Standards Inventory revealed that she was unable to participate at this level of support and was falling rapidly behind her classmates as a result. This was felt to be the result of an opportunity barrier rather than a problem with access, since she had the necessary AAC equipment at school to participate in math. The math curriculum used in her classroom, however, required her to work with manipulable items in various configurations, which she could not do because of her physical impairments. She was also unable to complete work on the chalkboard because of her physical impairments. She also could not complete her homework because she was not allowed to take her school-owned AAC device home after school. In order to overcome the first two barriers, a paraprofessional was assigned to provide Heather with assistance during math. Her parents agreed to assist her with homework and have her solve problems for which they wrote down the answers. Because these obstacles were identified early in the year, Heather quickly regained much of the ground she had lost.

As can be seen from this example, the Activity/Standards Inventory process is critical in order to translate integration planning and desired levels of academic participation into realities. In situations where several educational staff are involved in an instructional activity, completing this inventory can be useful for bringing the educational team to a consensus.

> "It should be emphasized that saying it can be done is not the same as saying it will be easy" (Stainback & Stainback, 1990, p. 7).

## Assess Opportunity Barriers

As noted in the previous discussion about Heather, both opportunity and access barriers can account for discrepancies between the participation patterns of AAC users and those of their peers. Both types of barriers can limit academic or social participation. Since the AAC team's ability to

**Table 11.8.** Activity/standards inventory for Heather

Directions:
1. List the *primary and secondary activities* in which nondisabled peers are expected to participate across the school day.
2. Select one or more nondisabled peers who are typical, in terms of their ability to achieve the expected standards. After observing one of the peers in each of the activities listed, indicate the *level of peer participation* achieved, by entering a "P" in the appropriate standards category for each activity.
3. After observing the target individual in each activity, indicate the *level of participation* achieved by entering a "T" in the appropriate standards category.
4. In the Discrepancy column, indicate *yes* if a participation gap exists for the target individual as compared to the peers, and *no* if a participation gap does not exist.
5. Based on your observations and impressions, indicate whether the barrier to participation appears to be related to opportunity barriers, access barriers, or both.

| Activity | Level of peer participation | | | | | Discrepancy | | Type(s) of barrier(s) | |
|---|---|---|---|---|---|---|---|---|---|
| Math | Independent | Independent with set-up | Verbal assistance | Physical assistance | Unable to participate | Yes | No | Opp'ty | Access |
| 1. Complete worksheets from book. | | P, T | | | | | X | | |
| 2. Answer questions in class. | | | P, T | | | | X | | |
| 3. Do work on board. | | P | | | T | X | | X | |
| 4. Work with manipulable items: count, sort. | | P | | | T | X | | X | |
| 5. Complete homework. | | P | P | P | T | X | | X | |

215

overcome these barriers often makes the difference between successful and failed integration efforts, we will discuss them in this and the following sections. First, we consider a variety of *opportunity barriers* that may interfere with integration efforts.

It is often helpful to identify opportunity barriers during a team meeting among representatives of the family, educational staff, and educational administrators. A thorough assessment of opportunity issues using a format similar to that in Table 7.3. (Opportunity Assessment) is likely to reveal that each party is responsible for one or more barriers. Acknowledging this shared responsibility tends to diminish unnecessary blaming or finger-pointing among team members. For example, Table 11.9. contains a portion of the Assessment of Opportunity Barriers that was completed for Heather.

A review of Table 11.9. reveals that the school district policy prohibiting children from taking school-owned AAC devices home with them was limiting Heather's ability to participate in homework and social interaction. Unfortunately, the team's inability to resolve this policy barrier meant that Heather's family had to obtain funding to purchase equipment for Heather to use at home.

In addition, a long-standing practice in Heather's school was that young elementary students received motor specialty services such as physical and occupational therapy in the morning, while the older elementary students received these services in the afternoon. This practice interfered with Heather's ability to participate in both math and language arts activities, which occurred every morning in her first grade class. Furthermore, the speech-language pathologist did not employ a curriculum-based approach to service delivery. Pull-out speech therapy began to compete for academic time with curricular activities. These issues were resolved through an agreement with Heather's parents that she would receive motor specialty services during the regularly scheduled physical education class each morning instead of during math and language arts. In addition, the speech-language pathologist agreed to discontinue pull-out speech therapy, and , instead, she worked with Heather during her regularly scheduled language arts class to help her develop and use her speech in her reading group.

Another identified barrier pertained to the attitude of the special education teacher. She was experienced in planning individualized educational programs for students with disabilities, but had no experience acting as a consultant to a regular classroom teacher in the context of an established curriculum. Moreover, she was not interested in taking the time to familiarize herself with the curriculum used in the first grade. Clearly, in order to integrate students while offering appropriate supports to regular education staff, cooperative, not antagonistic or competitive, attitudes must prevail. Unfortunately, Heather's first grade teacher did not receive appropriate educational supports, although the paraprofessional, Heather's parents, and the speech-language pathologist all helped to fill in the major gaps.

Knowledge and skill barriers existed everywhere. Although the speech-language pathologist and the paraprofessional were both able to operate and program Heather's AAC device, the other school personnel—the regular education teacher, special education teacher, and students—were largely unfamiliar with the equipment. In addition, as with the special education teacher, the paraprofessional and other staff were unfamiliar with the first-grade curriculum, although they were willing to familiarize themselves with its content. Because Heather was the first AAC user to be fully integrated in the district, the administrator had no experience or knowledge base concerning the role of the paraprofessional assigned to the first grade classroom. As can be seen from Table 11.9., much of the planning related to these knowledge and skill barriers required careful, ongoing attention at many levels. This is not unusual and should be expected, especially during the pioneering phase of integration efforts within a school or district. What is important is that opportunity barriers are seen as just that—*barriers that can be overcome*—not as reasons to abandon the integration plan for either an individual student or the district as a whole.

**Table 11.9.** Assessment of opportunity barriers for Heather

Directions:
1. List the activities for which potential opportunity barriers have been been identified for the target student.
2. Indicate the nature of the opportunity barrier (e.g., policy, practice, attitude, knowledge, skill).
3. Briefly describe the intervention plan and those responsible for its implementation.

| Activity | Opportunity barrier | | | | | Intervention plan and person(s) responsible |
|---|---|---|---|---|---|---|
| | Policy | Practice | Attitude | Knowledge | Skill | |
| 1. Math, work on board and work with manipulables | | X | | | | Hire a paraprofessional to provide assistance. |
| 2. All homework, social interactions after school hours | X | | | | | Family will need to purchase AAC equipment with private funds. |
| 3. Math, language arts conflicts with PT, OT, SLP schedule | | X | | | | Schedule PT during PE activities, SLP to offer direct services in the first grade during language arts |
| 4. All curricular areas: lack of familiarity with first grade curriculum; SpEd teacher not interested in learning content | | | X, SpEd | X, SLP, para., OT, PT | | Education and familiarization of all specialty staff regarding first-grade curriculum; education regarding consultant role of special educator. |
| 5. Operating and programming the AAC device | | | | X, all but SLP, para. | X | Orientation to first graders and teacher by SLP; para. to assume primary role for programming and maintenance until others are adept |
| 6. Paraprofessional assignment and role | | X | | X | | Assign para. to Heather and other AAC student in another 1st grade, meet biweekly to see if this works, adjust as needed, write district job description for para. by end of year. |

The removal of opportunity barriers is sometimes sufficient to allow a student to achieve the desired pattern of participation. Nevertheless, there may be access barriers to consider as well with students who require AAC assistance.

"When education happens, it happens in the mind of the student" (Anonymous).

## Assess Access Barriers

Assessment procedures to identify access barriers and strategies for instituting access-related interventions were discussed in detail in Chapters 7 and 8. Generic interventions such as those related to natural abilities, environmental adaptations, and AAC systems or devices were identified in the Participation Model (Figure 7.1.) because they are applicable to individuals of all ages and disabilities. In addition, there are a number of intervention issues that require special attention for students in classroom settings, and these are discussed in the sections that follow.

***Adapting the Educational Environment*** Adjustments in the physical environment may be necessary to enhance access in a classroom. For example, it is not uncommon for students in wheelchairs to be positioned off to the side or at the back of a room, because their chairs make it difficult for others to get around them. Creating wider aisles between student desks and classroom furnishings is a preferable solution to this problem, since this allows the AAC user to stay with the group instead of being physically marginalized. Wider doors adapted with special open buttons or electric eyes allow easy entrance into the classroom and through other areas of the building, such as the music room, gymnasium, and cafeteria. Student working surfaces should be positioned at appropriate heights for comfort and efficiency through the use of adjustable desks and tables. Cut-out desktops may be necessary so that there is a suitable distance between students and their working surfaces. Chalkboards at lower than usual levels and extended slightly out from walls allow students in wheelchairs to position themselves appropriately for writing activities. Other stems such as door knobs, pencil sharpeners, coat racks, and light switches can also be lowered to heights accessible to all. Finally, classroom assignments should be made after considerations of the accessibility needs of students, since some classrooms are usually more accessible than others.

Hyper-ABLEDATA is an extensive database of assistive devices and is available on compact disc, floppy disk, or tape. This database contains information about the sources, descriptions, and prices of a wide variety of equipment that might be useful when adapting an educational environment for an AAC user. Hyper-ABLEDATA is available through the Trace Center.

***Managing the Academic Workload*** Educational specialists can increase the academic workload of a disabled student unnecessarily without realizing it. For example, Jason was an AAC student in a combined fifth- and sixth-grade regular class who received resource room assistance to increase his literacy skills. Using an Apple IIe computer with an Adaptive Firmware Card, he operated a software program, Predict It (Don Johnston Developmental Equipment, Inc.), which is a writing program with rate enhancement features. Early in his augmented writing program, Jason was given writing assignments by the special education teacher in the resource room, without regard for the writing assignments required by his regular education teacher. It soon became apparent that this student, who wrote very slowly anyway, was being asked to manage a workload that was far beyond his capabilities. Through collaborative efforts, the regular and special education teacher began to coordinate their writing assignments so that Jason had sufficient writing practice and was still able to complete his regular classroom assignments. For example, the regular teacher agreed to accept the letters and stories that Jason wrote as his resource room assignments as fulfilling his fifth-grade language arts requirements. In addition, the resource room teacher agreed to make assignments related to subject matter covered in the regular class.

**Assisting Students To Be Active Learners**   Because the communication content in regular classrooms changes so rapidly, it may be difficult to keep the vocabulary in the AAC system current. This leads to a tendency to provide AAC students with communication systems that are solely designed to address wants/needs and social interaction functions rather than the information-sharing functions that are integral to classroom participation. If this happens, AAC users are often forced to be passive learners: They cannot ask or answer questions in class, deliver topical reports, or otherwise participate in subject-oriented discussions because they do not have the vocabularies to do so. It is critical that the AAC support team aggressively attempt to translate the curriculum into communication units that will allow the AAC user to participate in these classroom interactions. This is particularly critical during the early elementary years before students are able to spell well enough to compose their own messages. In this case, the demands on the AAC support team are reduced if the AAC student has adequate rate enhancement techniques available. Support staff, however, will still need to institute strategies that help students manage the time constraints of the regular classroom.

**Assisting Students To Manage Time Constraints**   Students with severe communication and motor impairments often find it difficult to keep pace in a regular education classroom, because they have difficulty manipulating educational materials such as books and worksheets. Without accommodations to these difficulties, students may experience academic failure because they cannot complete their work, although they have mastered the content. Several approaches are routinely used to accommodate the time constraints of disabled students.

*Advance Preparation*   It may be necessary to work with regular education staff to preview upcoming assignments, topic areas, and class projects, so that ample time is available to create related adaptations. For example, if the AAC support team knows that upcoming science units will include the planets, rocks, and dinosaurs over the next 2 months, they can begin to construct related communication miniboards, or plan how to program the needed vocabulary words into an electronic AAC device.

In addition, students can be encouraged to use strategies such as preparing questions in advance or composing their answers to assigned questions at home in order to compensate for their reduced communication rates. For example, in her teen living class, Ginger was involved in a unit on sex education. Although she was not able to grasp all of the class material, she clearly understood at least some of the discussion related to dating etiquette. She managed to convey to her special education teacher that she had some questions in this regard. Prior to class, the teacher recorded Ginger's questions on a cassette tape, which Ginger activated in class using a single switch. This technique was also used when Ginger was assigned class reports in a cooperative learning group. She worked with her classmates after school to prepare the report, and they recorded it on tape. Ginger was then responsible for playing the taped report the next day in class. Such advance-preparation strategies allow students with AAC systems to be active participants in regular classes without requiring teachers and peers to wait while they compose messages or questions.

*Use of Educational Paraprofessionals*   Educational paraprofessionals have been employed for years to assist persons with severe communication disorders in regular classroom experiences. The paraprofessional may be assigned directly to a student with disabilities and assume the role of a personal educational assistant or tutor. Alternatively, he or she may be assigned to a specific classroom and teacher as a general assistant to all the students in the class, including the disabled student. Our recent experiences with the second approach have been quite positive. The general assistant approach allows the paraprofessional to provide services that benefit the AAC user as well as the teacher and other students. This approach also makes better use of the paraprofessional's time, allows the AAC user more opportunities for independence, and provides the regular teacher with additional assistance. The role of the paraprofessional is discussed more completely later in this chapter.

*Use of Peer Students*   Cooperative or peer instruction is increasing in regular education (Gartner & Lipsky, 1990; Sapon-Shevin, 1990). Applying cooperative or peer instruction approaches to students who use AAC systems can be very effective in helping them meet classroom time demands. In addition, when students with disabilities are included in small cooperative learning or informal peer instructional groups, they are often able to participate more effectively than they can in large classroom situations.

In junior high, senior high, and college or university classes, peer students can also be enlisted to take notes in class for students with disabilities. Their notes are photocopied or carbon paper is inserted between pages of their notebooks so that a copy is made automatically. At the University of Nebraska, we initially paid peers a small wage to take notes for students with disabilities, but we found that they were more cooperative and reliable when they were enlisted as volunteers than as paid employees. We have also found that regardless of the grade level, students with AAC systems should be encouraged to at least outline their class notes whenever possible, in order to stay mentally involved in the subject matter of the class. Alternatively, many students prefer to tape classroom lectures and use the tapes to clarify information from the peer notes. Some tape recorders have a feature that allows the student to press a button to mark specific sections while recording them. Then, as they review the tapes with the notes, they can "fast forward" to the marked sections rather quickly. This reduces their listening time and encourages students to stay involved in the class so that they can mark important segments on the tape.

*Adapting Academic Testing*   Competitive students with disabilities usually have difficulty completing academic tests in the same amount of time as their nondisabled peers. If adjustments in time limits are not made, these students are either penalized for their disabilities or must rely on the assistance of a paraprofessional to complete tests in the time allotted. To be penalized is clearly unacceptable, and relying on a paraprofessional often leaves the teacher wondering who is really taking the test, the student or the paraprofessional.

One solution is to provide an adapted environment in which students can take tests under close supervision. For example, the University of Nebraska has a policy that students with disabilities may take their academic tests at the Center for Students with Disabilities. All test taking at the center is monitored to confirm that students have completed their own work. Time limits are removed, however, and all tests thus become instruments for evaluating competence rather than speed. The faculty members at the university have no choice but to cooperate if students choose to use the center. Many junior high and senior high schools provide similar options to students with disabilities through the assistance of resource teachers.

*Reduced Workloads*   Students who are expected to participate at a competitive level (i.e., held to the same standards as their nondisabled peers) do not necessarily have to complete the same *amount* of work as their peers. If a teacher is willing to allow a student to discontinue an assignment once he or she has demonstrated mastery of a concept or a process, precious time can be saved. In many cases, *not* to allow this to occur can be frustrating for all involved. For example, it is not uncommon to hear parents report how upsetting it is to watch their child work long hours to complete several pages of math problems when it is clear that he or she understands the concepts by the end of the first page.

Another selective participation strategy favored by some students and families is simply not to enroll in classes that are not required, or for which the requirements can be met in a different way. For example, some students who are unable to participate as involved students in a physical education program may choose to meet this requirement through physical therapy after school hours. This way, they can use the regular physical education period to complete other academic work. As another example, a competitive student may wish to be exempted from elective classes in order to complete required coursework. Obviously, such decisions must be made by the student, family, and educational staff, with consideration of the social as well as the educational consequences that might result.

*Selective Retention*     In the United States, children with disabilities are eligible to remain as public school students past the age of 18 when most of their peers graduate. This extra time for students who use AAC systems means that rather than rushing through an educational program at the same pace as their nondisabled peers, they and their families may opt for retention at a grade level in order to meet specific academic goals. Such retentions tend to occur at four different times. First, some students may not have the AAC equipment that is needed to enter first grade. Their parents may choose to retain them in kindergarten for an additional year so that the AAC team has time to develop the appropriate communication supports. Second, we know of a number of parents who have elected to retain their children in the third or fourth grade. This option has been chosen particularly for children whose literacy skills were not sufficiently developed to support their need to read in order to learn. The additional work in reading and writing that these students received was often sufficient to narrow the gap in this area. Third, some students may participate in junior high school for an additional year. In schools in the United States, much of the junior high curriculum is an enhanced version and review of the concepts and processes taught in earlier years to ensure that students are fluent in this material before they enter high school. Students who do not master this material in elementary school may benefit from an extra year in junior high for academic reasons. Finally, students may choose to extend the length of their high school programs in order to complete academic requirements.

The decision to retain a student should be made only with the agreement of the student and his or her parents. If parents are aware of this option, they will often encourage their child to make friends with students who are younger so that the social consequences of a possible retention are less drastic. Of course, in many cases the detrimental social impact of retention may outweigh any potentially positive academic benefits. In fact, it is primarily the social implications of selective voluntary retention that makes this such a controversial topic. In addition, many regular educators and administrators seem to believe that retaining regular students serves no constructive purpose, which may or may not be true. Regardless, applying the same logic to students with disabilities, or rejecting the notion of selective retention for philosophic reasons only, appears equally non-constructive. To our knowledge, there is simply no reason not to consider this option for competitive or active students who experience academic difficulties simply because of their reduced communication efficiency.

---

Principle 3. When students with disabilities are not successful in high school and college, it is usually because of their limited literacy skills and limited world knowledge base.

---

**Developing the Student's Knowledge Base**     The development of adequate literacy skills, coupled with a cultural and world knowledge base, is increasingly viewed as an important factor for educational success. Those who assist students with disabilities at the post-secondary level suggest repeatedly that the primary source of most of these students' academic difficulties lies in deficiencies in these two related areas.

The knowledge base is developed in many different ways. The family contributes to it, as does television, other media, and printed materials. The contributions of the family, community, and media are supplemented when students with disabilities are provided with extensive access to printed materials at school and are associated with the regular school curriculum. Even if they cannot read and write, elementary-age students are able to learn a great deal about the world around them through experience and exposure. Nevertheless, as they progress through school, students increasingly are required to read in order to learn. Students who experience reading problems are at risk for missing out on much of the information and knowledge imparted in schools. This problem becomes even worse in high school and college. The result is that students who are unable to read often lag far behind their peers in world knowledge, not necessarily because they are unable to learn the information, but because they have limited access to it.

---

Initially, [eighth-grade] science was selected because the teacher was an enthusiastic individual who was very interested in involving all learners in the class. The team struggled with how science related to a functional, life space domain curriculum but went ahead with the plans to include the learner [with a severe disability] in the class anyway. After several weeks in the class, it became apparent that the student enjoyed the science subject area. His spoken vocabulary increased dramatically to include science jargon including e.g., "rocks," "rivers," [and] "stars." (York & Vandercook, 1989, p. 16)

---

Another factor contributing to an insufficient world knowledge base for many students with disabilities is the amount of time they spend outside the regular classroom. At the time this book is written, it is not uncommon for students with AAC systems to be selectively integrated into regular educational activities. This usually means that they participate in elective, resource room, or segregated classes for much of their school day, especially when their regular peers are engaged in academic subjects. An obvious consequence of this arrangement is that students who are AAC users miss the classes in which world knowledge is taught.

Decisions to exclude students from academic classes may be made because the students cannot be competitive with their nondisabled classmates. Nevertheless, as previously noted, there are often other valid levels of participation that should be considered for the sake of building a student's world knowledge base. For example, we know of a high school student with a severe learning disability who used an augmented software writing program to compensate for his spelling deficits. He was enrolled primarily in vocational education courses, yet he was interested in history, government, and earth science. So, he participated in these courses as an active student. He attempted to read the assignments, and he participated in class discussions. Because the continued development of his literacy skills was an important goal of his educational program, he wrote short essays to meet the class requirements rather than taking the tests required of the competitive students.

Some students may be involved, but not active, in academic classes in order to have access to world knowledge. For example, Felipe attended a junior high biology class that was considerably beyond his academic ability level. Nevertheless, he was involved in various plant experiments with his peer group, enjoyed learning to use a microscope to examine cells, participated in a presentation about ecology by collecting examples of recyclable materials, and listened to recorded portions of the textbook using a tape recorder and a single switch. Thus, he benefited both academically and socially from this opportunity for involvement.

It is important to emphasize that we are not advocating placing students in academic classes in which they are neither able to participate nor benefit. For example, placing Felipe in a junior high math class would have been quite pointless since he was not interested in or able to learn the material at all. If the student sits passively in the classroom, day after day, it is unlikely that much world knowledge is being absorbed or that much social benefit will accrue.

*Role of Parents and Caregivers* Parents, siblings, relatives, and caregivers can play an important role in assisting students with disabilities develop their knowledge bases. They are often willing to take this role seriously once they are aware of the importance of this information to the student's ongoing educational development. For example, they can involve the student in their own hobbies, vocations, and daily chores and impart a wide range of information through direct experience and incidental teaching. As they watch television or videos, they can also interact with the student to provide background information and discuss the implications of the material presented. A parent or relative might wish to assume primary responsibility for teaching the student a specific content area. In one instance, a student's father taught her much of the school's science curriculum at home for several years. The school district supported their efforts by providing textbooks, workbooks, and videotapes. School personnel evaluated the student's performance and documented her progress. During her usual science period, the student attended the resource center to develop her writing skills. This unique arrangement allowed the student to master the content of the science curriculum, while receiving much needed remedial instruction in the literacy area.

---

Principle 4. Specialists must complement, not compete with, the academic program.

---

## COLLABORATIVE TEAMING AND CONSENSUS BUILDING

In Chapter 6, we described a variety of team models that can be used to provide AAC services, and we noted that depending on the specific situation, various team members may play different roles in this process. In an integrated educational program, the primary role of educational specialists such as speech-language pathologists, motor therapists, and special education teachers is to assist the AAC student to participate successfully in the regular classroom. This may include the provision of some direct AAC services, or it may involve some direct skill instruction. The overriding responsibility of the specialist, however, is to serve as a consultant to the regular teacher, and to assist in adapting the educational environment and the curriculum. This may constitute a major shift in the specialist's role from direct to indirect instructional provider.

---

[Collaborative teaming is] an interactive process that enables teams of people with diverse expertise to generate creative solutions to mutually defined problems. The outcome is enhanced, altered, and produces solutions that are different from those that the individual team members would produce independently. (Idol, Paolucci-Whitcomb, & Nevin, 1986, p. 1)

---

### Consensus Building

As we discussed in Chapters 7 and 8, collaborative efforts between regular education and specialist staff require the use of a variety of consensus-building strategies that allow team members to articulate their priorities, identify potential conflicts, and design proactive solutions to resolve these conflicts before they become problematic. In addition, successful collaborations often require creative solutions aimed at accomplishing multiple objectives within a single activity. Collaborative efforts also require careful deployment of personnel and adequate delineation of their roles and responsibilities (see Pugach & Johnson, 1990). The range of strategies that may be used to accomplish these goals are illustrated through several examples.

   **Heather**   As we discussed previously, when Heather was in first grade, her math curriculum involved extensive use of manipulable objects (e. g., stones, beads, bottle caps). These were used to teach the children about basic mathematical concepts such as counting, grouping, and combining. Because of her cerebral palsy, Heather was unable to manipulate these items independently, necessitating the involvement of a paraprofessional to provide assistance. When the paraprofessional was hired, the question then became: What is her role? Should she become Heather's "hands," and simply manipulate objects for her? Or, should her role be that of a tutor for Heather, providing separate remedial math activities under the first grade teacher's direction? Or, should she be involved as part of the team to devise strategies so that Heather can participate in the standard math program as independently as possible? After much discussion, the regular teacher, special educator, speech-language pathologist, and paraprofessional decided that, in fact, their combined role should be to help Heather participate in the math program as independently as possible. Thus, they proceeded to work collaboratively to develop a math communication board that allowed Heather to interact with her classmates and participate in peer instructional activities. In addition, they developed an adapted "touch math" system that enabled Heather to use a modified number line to learn about numerous mathematical principles. The paraprofessional assumed a major role in this collaborative effort, by modifying and updating the system, as well as by assisting Heather during regular math activities.

*Ginger*   During high school, Ginger was integrated into several nonacademic classes such as teen living (a health and personal responsibility class), home economics, computers, and art. She was also involved in a functional curriculum, where she received vocational and community-referenced instruction. Ginger was unable to participate in the basic sewing unit of her home economics class because of her severe physical impairments. The motor specialists on the AAC team collaborated with the regular education teacher to devise a relay system that Ginger controlled with a single switch. With this, she could turn the sewing machine, electric scissors, and other sewing appliances on and off. She also used a simple sewing communication board devised by the speech-language pathologist to participate in making decisions about the fabrics, thread, buttons, and patterns to use for class projects. Ginger was paired with a regular peer, who was responsible for actually manipulating the appliances and fabrics, for the duration of the sewing unit. Thus, the collaborative efforts between the AAC specialists and the home economics teacher resulted in a solution that enhanced Ginger's participation, both academically and socially.

*Lakota*   Lakota was just beginning to learn to operate an electronic AAC device in kindergarten, and her speech-language pathologist and a paraprofessional were her primary instructors. Early in the spring, Lakota's kindergarten teacher was planning to present a unit about plants, and the class was to visit the Sunken Garden, a city park with an extensive floral display. The children would be accompanied on the field trip by a class of landscape architecture students from the local university, who were there to observe the interests and interaction patterns of young children in a public garden. In an effort to combine AAC device instruction with support for Lakota's participation in kindergarten activities, the specialist staff devised an AAC overlay that contained messages pertaining to the plant unit and subsequent field trip. During the field trip, the AAC device was mounted on Lakota's wheelchair so that she could "talk" with the student observers and interact with her classmates.

## Roles and Responsibilities of Team Members

*Student and Family Members*   Federal law in the United States requires that students with disabilities and their families be actively involved, to the extent of their interests and abilities, in the educational process. When parents and students are active in establishing individualized patterns for academic and social integration and in setting expectations in these areas, their satisfaction with the efforts of the professionals involved is usually enhanced. Indeed, much of the conflict that occurs between school personnel and families results from the failure to involve families in decisions regarding educational opportunities and expectations. For example, parents are often asked to approve an Individualized Education Program (IEP) for their child although they have had a minimal role in its development. As a result, it is hardly surprising that they take minimal "ownership" of the educational program. Students and families are integral members of both integration and AAC efforts and should always be included as full team members.

*Speech-Language Pathologist*   The speech-language pathologist is usually the overall manager in school situations of AAC interventions for children with severe communication disorders. In this role, he or she is responsible for leading the AAC team during both the assessment and intervention. If assistance is needed from a regional AAC center, the speech-language pathologist arranges for services. In addition, the speech-language pathologist is responsible for developing an intervention program designed to instruct the AAC user in required interaction and conversational skills. Finally, he or she often provides input to the educational paraprofessional regarding communication issues.

---

Firstly, you must have teachers who are willing to teach students who are disabled. A good teacher will be able to cope with varying the style of his or her teaching subjects. There must also be back-up resource and support people who can give tips on teaching areas that seem to be presenting difficulties to the student and the teacher. (Valentic, 1991, p. 9)

---

***Regular Education Teacher*** The regular teacher is responsible for establishing the educational agenda for students in his or her classroom, including those who use AAC systems. As the educational manager, the teacher sets academic standards for the classroom and evaluates the extent to which the standards are met by all students. In addition to planning educational activities, the regular teacher is responsible for communicating this information to other members of the AAC team so that they can support the student's classroom communication efforts appropriately. The regular teacher is also responsible for the social environment and standards in the classroom. This includes instituting strategies as needed to encourage acceptance and to facilitate friendships between nondisabled and disabled students. If students with disabilities are excluded or teased, the teacher is responsible for intervening. Finally, the regular teacher is responsible for supervising paraprofessionals assigned to the classroom with regard to educational issues.

***Special Education Teacher*** The special education teacher is usually responsible for evaluating the academic and social strengths and weaknesses of the student during the initial AAC assessment, as well as helping to determine the student's AAC needs and how best to meet them. Following this, the role of the special educator in an integrated classroom largely depends on the participation pattern of the student. If the student is fully and competitively integrated, the special education teacher is likely to serve primarily as a consultant to the regular teacher and the paraprofessional. Students who are selectively integrated, or who participate at active or involved levels, may receive some direct instruction from the special education teacher during designated periods. Alternatively, the special educator may consult with the regular education teacher to design personalized curricula for these students, which is delivered by a paraprofessional in the regular classroom. As the student moves into a middle school, junior high, and high school, the special education teacher may assume a major role in coordinating the efforts of subject-area teachers and support personnel. During summer sessions, special education teachers may be active in planning and delivering remedial and supplementary education to students with AAC systems.

***Occupational and Physical Therapists*** The occupational therapist is a very active member of the AAC team in the initial AAC assessment and intervention processes and assumes the primary responsibility for recommending alternative access AAC and computer control options. Together with the physical therapist, the occupational therapist is responsible for planning a program of intervention that will enhance the accuracy and efficiency of alternative access techniques. In the regular classroom, occupational and physical therapists are likely to be consultants to the regular teacher regarding motor control, positioning, and mobility issues. For example, the occupational therapist can be an invaluable resource for adapting the environment or materials used in the classroom. Therapy staff generally remain involved over the years as the physical demands of the educational and AAC program change.

***Computer Specialist***    Because of the increasing role of computer technology in elementary and secondary education, the involvement of a computer specialist on a school-based AAC team is becoming increasingly necessary. The computer specialist possesses technical knowledge that is useful to the team, especially in attempts to coordinate a student's AAC system with the computers utilized in the school curriculum. Computer specialists are also valuable consultants concerning computer programs that might be used to supplement the educational programs of students with disabilities.

***Paraprofessional***    The educational paraprofessional, in our experience, is critical to the successful integration of students with AAC systems. This individual is generally responsible for ensuring that the AAC system contains the vocabulary items and symbols that are needed for participation in regular classroom activities. He or she is usually assigned the task of programming a student's electronic AAC device, assembling communication miniboards or other materials as needed, and coaching the student to use the system appropriately in the classroom. In addition, the paraprofessional assists the disabled student with self-care and positioning activities when necessary. In many cases, the paraprofessional also provides assistance to the peer students in the classroom, as we discussed previously. Although the paraprofessional may be assigned classroom duties other than those directly related to the AAC student, he or she often moves with the student through the grade levels. When this occurs, the paraprofessional, along with other members of the AAC team, is able to provide continuity between the educational and communication programs, although the regular classroom teacher changes from year to year.

In elementary school, the paraprofessional usually functions under the direction of the regular classroom teacher to whom he or she is assigned, with input from the special education teacher and speech-language pathologist. In a departmentalized junior high or high school, the paraprofessional may be assigned to a special education teacher or speech-language pathologist for supervision. This supervisor is responsible for guiding the paraprofessional, assigning tasks, and ensuring that there is adequate coordination between the efforts of regular education staff and the AAC team. Paraprofessionals are often expected to provide, with little or no preparation, critically important services to students with AAC systems. The AAC field must begin to develop strategies and materials to prepare paraprofessionals for this role.

***Educational Administrators***    Successful integration of students with AAC devices into regular classrooms requires extensive planning and cooperation over many years. Inevitably, a student with disabilities in the classroom requires longitudinal administrative attention. Initial administrative support for integration and participation can substantially reduce the practice and attitude barriers that may otherwise limit educational opportunities. Active administrative involvement also facilitates the review of policies and practices that may discourage effective integration. Administrative involvement can enhance the transition planning as the student moves from grade to grade. Without clear administrative guidance for the educational personnel who each year are involved with the student, the family, and the AAC system, smooth transitions are often difficult to achieve.

## CLOSING COMMENTS

The occasional integration of persons with severe communication disorders into regular educational settings has occurred for many years, as documented in autobiographies such as those by Nolan (1987) and Rush (1986). Nevertheless, these unique personal accounts also serve to emphasize that integration for many individuals with disabilities has been the exception to the rule rather than the routine educational practice. In response to multiple societal and legal pressures, the educational environments considered to be appropriate for children with severe disabilities are rapidly changing. As is apparent in this chapter, parents, as well as a variety of school personnel, must learn to work collaboratively in order for these efforts to be cohesive and successful. Although it is beyond the scope of this book to describe in detail the wide range of integration strategies now in place in many parts of North America to achieve this objective, numerous texts are available in this regard. In particular, readers are referred to Biklen (1985), Fullwood (1990), Secord (1990), and Stainback and Stainback (1990) for additional information in this area.

# Persons with Primary Speech, Language, and Motor Impairments

## with Gary Cumley and Rebecca Jones

>>>>>>>>>>>>>>>>>>>>>>>>>>>>>>>>>>>>>>>>>>>>>>>>>>>>>>>

A number of individuals experience spoken or written communication difficulties as a result of primary speech, language, or motor impairments. These include developmental apraxia of speech (DAS), specific language impairments (SLI), learning disabilities (LD), and primary motor impairments (PMI). Little has been written about AAC interventions for some of these individuals, probably because of the difficulties inherent in meeting their diverse needs. In this chapter, we review some current trends and communication approaches used to treat these impairments.

> Katie is an 8-year-old girl with developmental apraxia of speech who was adopted at age 2 after spending her infancy in a number of different foster homes. Her mom recalled that at first, "Katie was easily distracted, particularly in groups or where there was a lot going on in the environment. She . . . was constantly on the move [and] . . . did not stick with any task for more than a few minutes (or less). . . . She had very poor fine motor skills—i.e., *difficulty* stringing beads, buttoning, doing puzzles, etc. She screamed frequently, not in rage or anger, but I interpreted this as the only way she could 'communicate'." (Katie's mother, personal communication, July 17, 1991)
>
> Katie continues to be a very active child who shows evidence of upper limb apraxia, in addition to an extremely limited vocal repertoire. In January, 1991, her speech consisted primarily of single sounds, with imitative attempts at two-word syllables or sound patterns. Her primary communicative behaviors included pointing, nodding "yes," waving, various facial expressions, and pantomimes. She achieved age-equivalent scores of 4 years, 11 months on both the PPVT and the TACL. Her hearing and vision are within normal limits.

## DEVELOPMENTAL APRAXIA OF SPEECH (DAS)

### Overview and Characteristics

The term developmental apraxia of speech (DAS) has been used in the United States since the 1970s to refer to children with congenital articulation problems that are moderate to severe in nature and that are resistant to traditional methods of treatment (Haynes, 1985; Yoss & Darley, l974a). These children may exhibit mixed hand laterality and often come from families with a history of speech and/or language problems. Males are three times more likely than females to be diagnosed with DAS (Marquardt, Dunn, & Davis, 1985), which is also known as developmental articulatory apraxia, childhood verbal apraxia, and childhood dyspraxia, among other terms.

Blakeley (1983) described DAS as a "syndrome-like" disorder, due to the frequent presence of other symptoms in conjunction with the oral motor difficulty. Marquardt et al. (1985) noted that positive "soft" neurologic signs are frequently present, including difficulty with gait and coordination, electroencephalogram (EEG) abnormalities, and delayed development or clumsiness in dressing, feeding, writing, and walking. In addition, DAS is often associated with other impairments, including language delays and disorders, mental retardation, and neuromuscular disorders (Marquardt et al., 1985). Even in children who do not demonstrate delayed intellectual functioning, severe delays in speech development are often related to later difficulties in speech, language, school placement, reading, writing, and behavioral/social adjustment (Aram & Nation, 1982).

Apraxia in children is relatively difficult to identify, but a diagnosis later in life as a result of identified and documented neurologic damage is more straightforward (Haynes, 1985). Regardless, apraxia of speech can be defined generally as a "nondysarthric, nonaphasic sensorimotor disorder of articulation and prosody" (Rosenbek, 1985). Typically, children with DAS have difficulty with volitional or imitative production of speech sounds and sequences (Bernthal & Bankson, 1988; Eisenson, 1968; Rosenbek & Wertz, 1972). There is considerable disagreement concerning specific symptomatology, although a number of authors appear to agree at least about the following characteristics:

1. Difficulty in imitating both nonspeech movements and speech sounds in the absence of abnormalities of the tongue, lips, or palate
2. Difficulty in initiating speech movements
3. Unawareness of articulator positions, resulting in prominent phonemic errors
4. Impairment in production of sound sequences
5. Occasional telegraphic speech
6. Disturbances in repetition of speech and in conversation, with frequent prosodic disturbances (e.g., slowed rate, uneven stress)
7. Inconsistency of articulatory output and errors (Haynes, 1985; Rosenbek & Wertz, 1972)

In addition, oral apraxia, delayed or deviant speech development, and markedly better receptive language abilities are usually present (Rosenbek & Wertz, 1972). Research related to the physiology of speech production has indicated that DAS is the result of faulty timing, coordination, and transitioning between dynamic motor subgroups (Blackstone, 1989c). The assumption is made that these problems are due to a neurologic impairment that affects motor programming, the nature of which has not been documented empirically (Guyette & Diedrich, 1981).

It is also important to note what DAS is not. It is not a delay or disorder of language per se (i.e., aphasia), although it may occur concurrently with language deficits (Haynes, 1985; Rosenbek, Hansen, Baughman, & Lemme, 1974). As noted previously, there is none of the muscle weakness, slowness, or uncoordination that is characteristic of dysarthria. Finally, Rosenbek and Wertz (1972) suggested that at least four symptoms can be used to differentiate DAS from a functional articulation disorder. They include: 1) the presence of vowel errors, 2) an increasing number of errors on longer responses, 3) oral nonverbal apraxia (e.g., difficulty puffing the cheeks, sticking out the tongue), and 4) groping trial and error behavior during speech production.

> At one point, Katie's family contacted two speech-language pathologists to inquire about possible speech therapy for her. They were told, "We cannot work on speech until we *have* speech" (Katie's mother, personal communication, July 26, 1991).

## Communication Interventions

*Natural Speech*   Intensive work to improve natural speech production should be part of every intervention for children with DAS. As Blackstone (1989c) noted, "Every intelligible word/

phrase is worth it!" (p. 4). Since an extensive discussion of natural speech interventions is beyond the scope of this book, readers are referred to Table 12.1. for a summary of recommendations for natural speech interventions for children with developmental apraxia.

> At age 3, Katie received early childhood home-based services for 1 year before entering a preschool classroom for hearing impaired children. The preschool placement was chosen because it was felt that she should be taught to use manual signs to communicate. Signing Exact English (SEE-2) was used in the classroom, and her parents used it at home as well. Her mom recalls that due to Katie's fine motor problems and hyperactivity, it was very difficult for her to focus when someone signed to her. One day, out of frustration, she said to Katie, "Don't you want to learn sign language so we can talk?" and Katie shook her head "No." Finally, the family's continued frustration with Katie's lack of progress in signing prompted them to withdraw her from school in order to provide her with home schooling.

***Augmentative Communication Interventions***     In addition to interventions to improve natural speech, children whose speech is largely unintelligible may benefit from an intervention package that includes AAC techniques. It is critical to support the child's attempts to communicate successfully while concurrently engaging in vigorous, systematic speech therapy until speech is adequate to meet ongoing communication needs. If speech does not develop sufficiently over time, the AAC system can be revised to function on a long-term, multipurpose basis for the individual.

Another equally important goal is to provide AAC interventions that can support language learning. Children with DAS may show evidence of significant language delays that can be traced (at least hypothetically) to their inability to "practice" language in their early years. Many older children with DAS cannot formulate even two-word combinations, show limited ability to use all but the most basic language structures, and have not developed conversational competence because they have had no means to converse. In order to address these concerns, many such children have been introduced to manual signing, but if they show evidence of upper extremity apraxia, this modality can be almost as frustrating for them as natural speech.

Simply put, delayed language and conversational development are high prices to pay while either waiting for speech to develop naturally or while devoting 99% of the available therapy time to speech intervention. Rather, it is critically important to provide children with DAS with one or more appropriate augmentative modalities from an early age so that they have ample opportunities to use and "play" with language. From the outset, such AAC systems should be multimodal in nature and should almost always include at least gestures and visual–spatial (i.e., pictorial) symbols in addition to manual signs, if these are appropriate.

> Katie was home schooled (a legal educational option in her state) for approximately 2 years, along with several other children. In January 1991, when Katie was 8 years old, her family contacted a speech and hearing clinic at the state university to inquire about possible services. After assessment was completed, a multimodal intervention was introduced with the goals of improving Katie's natural speech and augmenting her communication while building her language skills through the use of communication miniboards. A modified phonological processing approach (Hodson & Paden, 1991), with hand gestures used to cue specific sounds, was initiated. Functional, motivating games and activities—not drill and practice sessions—formed the context for systematic speech intervention.

*Gestures and Manual Signs*     Several natural-speech treatment approaches for DAS have incorporated movement techniques such as arm swinging (Yoss & Darley, 1974b) and conventional

**Table 12.1.**    Summary of recommendations for natural speech interventions for children with developmental apraxia

| Natural speech intervention recommendations | Selected references |
| --- | --- |
| Imitate sustained vowels, establish vowels before consonants. | Blakeley (1983), Haynes (1985), Marquardt, Dunn, and Davis (1985), Yoss and Darley (1974b). |
| Imitate visible consonants and visible sounds. | Blakeley (1983), Haynes (1985), Marquardt et al. (1985), Thompson (1988), and Yoss and Darley (1974b) |
| Present early developing consonants first. Later, introduce voiceless sounds, which are more difficult. | Blakeley (1983) and Haynes (1985). |
| Use contrast therapy to teach consonants. | Marquardt et al. (1985). |
| Teach frequently occurring consonants early in treatment that will improve functional intelligibility. | Blakeley (1983) and Haynes (1985). |
| Use single whole words or syllables first and then move to phrases and sentences. Do not teach nonsense syllables. | Blakeley (1983), Haynes (1985), Marquardt et al. (1985), and Thompson (1988). |
| Use tasks continually generated according to phonetic principles and phonetic features. | Blakeley (1983), and Rosenbek, Hansen, Baughman, and Lemme (1974). |
| Extend sequencing efforts by using carrier phrases. | Blakeley (1983), Haynes (1985), and Yoss and Darley (1974b) |
| Teach use of longer pause times preceding difficult sounds or words. Slow rate as needed, especially at the phrase and sentence level. | Blakeley (1983), Haynes (1985), and Marquardt et al. (1985). |
| Do not use auditory discrimination drills. They are generally not productive. | Haynes (1985) and Yoss and Darley (1974b). |
| Use the visual modality to teach sounds and blends. | Blakeley (1983), Rosenbek et al. (1974), and Thompson (1988). |
| Associate tactile and visual symbols with sounds; associate auditory stimuli. | Blakeley (1983), Haynes (1985), Marquardt et al. (1985), and Thompson (1988). |
| Work in front of a mirror so the child can get visual feedback (imitation). | Marquardt et al. (1985) and Yoss and Darley (1974a). |
| Facilitate response adequacy with systematic use of rhythm, intonation, stress and motor movements (gestures). | Haynes (1985), Marquardt et al. (1985), Rosenbek et al. (1974), Thompson (1988), and Yoss and Darley (1974a, 1974b). |
| Use intensive, frequent, systematic drills for short periods of time. | Haynes (1985), Marquardt et al. (1985), Rosenbek et al. (1974), and Thompson (1988). |
| Introduce self-monitoring systems. | Haynes (1985), Thompson (1988), and Yoss and Darley (1974). |
| Ensure a high level of success. | Haynes (1985) and Thompson (1988). |

gestures (Klick, 1985) in conjunction with speech. Klick (1985) described the successful use of what she termed an "adapted cuing technique" (ACT), in which manual cues that reflect the shape of the oral cavity, the articulatory placement and movement pattern, and the manner in which a sound is produced are presented with the speech sounds. Similarly, a "touch cue method" (Bashir, Graham-jones, & Bostwick, 1984) and the PROMPT (Prompts for Restructuring Oral Muscular Phonetic Targets) system (Chumpelik, 1984) incorporate systematic manual–tactile cues to the face concurrent with speech to elicit specific sounds in therapy sessions.

   In a related study, the efficacy of "melodic intonation therapy" was reported for two children with DAS (Helfrich-Miller, 1984). This multiphasic technique involves the use of manual signs (in this case, Signed English) with intoned phonemic sequences, and the technique was reported to result in a gradual decrease in articulation and sequencing errors over the course of training. Similarly positive results were reported as a result of "signed target phoneme" therapy, in which fingerspelled letters from American Sign Language are paired with difficult sounds during therapy (Shelton & Garves, 1985).

In addition to their potential as adjuncts to natural speech therapy, gestural and manual sign interventions are also useful for their own sake to augment the child's communication output. Children whose fine motor abilities are not compromised (i.e., children without accompanying limb apraxia) may benefit from a total communication approach all day (not merely as a component of therapy only), or an approach that incorporates the use of highly iconic gestures such as Amerind (Crary, 1987). The primary advantages of unaided techniques for children with DAS are their portability, which is a critical consideration because, almost without exception, these individuals are fully mobile, and flexibility, in that an infinite number of semantic elements can be represented with manual signs. Nevertheless, considerable learning time is needed in order for the child as well as family members, school personnel, and friends to become sufficiently fluent at signing for the advantage of flexibility to be realized.

---

Concurrent with intensive work on natural speech, miniboards with black and white line drawing symbols were introduced to Katie in the context of motivating activities. The boards were designed to encourage multiword combinations, teach Katie to use specific language structures (e.g., prepositions, descriptors), and enhance her overall communication. Katie also began to use the miniboards at home during activities with her family (e.g., making cookies or popcorn, playing with dolls). A remnant book was also introduced at home and in the clinic to help Katie to introduce and establish topics.

---

*Aided Communication*   In conjunction with unaided techniques, nonelectronic communication/conversation books, miniboards, wallets, and other formats are often useful, as are aids that supply voice output (Blackstone, 1989c). The advantage of these methods, particularly if they incorporate line drawings or orthographic symbol output, is that they are often more intelligible to unfamiliar communication partners than are manual signs. The main disadvantages are the vocabulary and portability constraints that they can impose on the AAC user. Kravitz and Littman (1990) emphasized the importance of providing an adequate number of vocabulary items, noting that for many DAS clients with whom they have worked, communication books are often nonfunctional unless they have 400–500 items. In terms of motor ability, individuals with DAS can almost always manage multiple overlays and pages, so extensive vocabulary displays can be carried, worn, or strategically placed in the environment.

Careful, flexible combinations of aided and unaided approaches can be effective in enhancing the advantages and minimizing the disadvantages of each approach. For example, Blockberger and Kamp (1990) reported the use of multimodal systems consisting of natural speech, gestures, manual signs, and voice output communication aids with school-age children with DAS. The children and their families generally preferred to use unaided approaches and only resorted to aided techniques when communication breakdowns occurred (S. Blockberger, personal communication, February 19, 1991). Another example was provided by Kravitz and Littman (1990) in their discussion of an adult client who had DAS, among other impairments. This woman uses sign language to exchange basic information rapidly, while she uses her communication book primarily to achieve social closeness and to engage in more elaborate conversational interactions. She also uses a simple AAC device with voice output for specific situations such as introductions, asking for assistance at the bank, or ordering at fast-food restaurants.

In the only known published account describing an AAC intervention with a DAS child, Culp (1989) described the use of a multimodal system consisting of the four components mentioned previously: natural speech, gestures, manual signs, and voice output communication aids. This case study emphasized the importance of teaching AAC users and their communication partners to use appropriate interaction skills, rather than assuming that the mere provision of an AAC system will result in improved communication. The child in this case study, as those cited previously, relied primarily on speech, gestures, and manual signs largely because of the lack of portability of her communication book. Some alternative techniques that may help to circumvent the lack of portability include communication miniboards mounted on walls, mealtime placemats, car dashboards, refrigerators, bathtub tiles—in short, in any and all of the places the child may go, so that opportunities and vocabulary for communication are abundantly available (Blackstone, 1989c). Many of the currently available direct selection electronic devices are also appropriate for literate and preliterate children and can be transported with shoulder straps, carrying cases, or briefcases.

*Pragmatic Considerations*   Three important sets of skills that individuals with DAS need to learn are: strategies for topic setting, strategies for clarification and repair, and strategies for decision making about when to use which communication modality. Strategies for topic setting are usually related to the use of natural speech, which is almost always the child's mode of choice even when intelligibility is poor. The difficulty is that when the child attempts to introduce a new topic of conversation with one or more poorly articulated words, the communication partner is required to guess what the word is from a virtual universe of possibilities. If the child can narrow the range of possibilities by referring to a remnant book or topic-setter card (see chap. 10 and chap. 13, this volume), his or her communication partner may find it easier to guess the spoken words that are difficult to understand.

Clarification and repair strategies include repetition, rephrasing, adding or changing communication modes, using a cuing display (e.g., first sounds or rhyming words), gesturing, using body language/pantomime, and pointing to environmental cues (Blackstone, 1989c). Instructions for communication partners concerning useful ways to resolve breakdowns are often necessary and beneficial as well (e.g., "Try asking me the question another way"). The child may need to learn a decision-making strategy regarding when to use manual signs, a communication book, or an electronic aid. For example, Reichle and Ward (1985) taught an adolescent with intellectual disabilities (not DAS) to point to the orthographic message "Do you use sign language?" when asked a question by an unfamiliar person and then to use either manual signs or his electronic aid depending on the partner's response.

After 7 months of multimodal communication work, Katie's mom reported that, "Within a few days (maybe 2 weeks), I saw some changes as we continued working intensely at home. . . . After a few weeks—a month or so . . . I began to hear others, outside the family, remark at the improvement in Katie's speech. I have seen gradual but fairly steady improvement—the changes may seem quite slight to anyone else. . . . Katie is making a greater effort to take time to get more information across. Often, with a simple reminder, she will attempt a word again with greater clarity. She is beginning to attempt combinations of words (occasionally). . . . She has enjoyed making use of her book to communicate information to others. We as her family have learned a lot that will help her, too. [For] example, I will no longer hesitate to use the book, signs, pictures, or whatever else seems appropriate to help Katie get started with some dialogue or provide a beginning point for others." (Katie's mother, personal communication, July 17, 1991)

The family has decided to have Katie reenter the public school system, where she will receive educational and related services in both regular classroom and specialized settings. The use of a multimodal approach for communication will continue.

## SPECIFIC LANGUAGE IMPAIRMENT (SLI)

### Overview and Characteristics

Considerable attention has focused on describing a heterogeneous group of children who have considerable difficulty with spoken receptive and expressive language (e.g., Lahey, 1990; Leonard, 1991; McCauley & Demetras, 1990). The terms specific language impairment (SLI), childhood aphasia, developmental aphasia, dysphasia, and language disability (among others) have been used interchangeably to refer to these problems (Leonard, 1982). SLI is considered to be a primary, rather than a secondary, disorder. It is not the result of mental retardation, autism, or other etiologies. Prevalence estimates for SLI range from just above 3% (Leske, 1981) to 5.7% of the preschool population (Stevenson & Richman, 1976). This figure abruptly declines to close to 1% in the school-age population (Leske, 1981), probably because children with SLI who enter elementary school are often assigned different labels, such as learning or language-learning disabled (Snyder, 1984). Leonard (1982) cited an overall prevalence figure of 1 in every 1,000 children overall. SLI is far more common in males than in females (Swisher, 1985) and appears to run in families; that is, the family members of SLI children are more likely than those of normal children to have had language impairments (Tomblin, 1991).

SLI is considered to be a deficit in language expression, comprehension, or both, in the absence of apparent neurologic damage or hearing impairment. Children with SLI often demonstrate age-level performance on nonverbal tests or subtests of intelligence, even when verbal scores are significantly below the norm (Leonard, 1991; Stark & Tallal, 1981). This does not mean, however, that the children's cognitive abilities are unaffected, and, in fact, areas such as symbolic functioning and cognitive processing are frequently impaired as well (Johnston, 1991b). Language development is not simply delayed, but, rather, the language limitations are long standing, at least in the absence of remediation. Development of language is uneven, typically affecting the use of grammatical morphemes and function words more than other language subskills (Johnston, 1991a; Leonard, 1991). Some authors have described individuals with SLI as "hearing but not understanding" (Bloom & Lahey, 1978, p. 510), referring to their relatively poor auditory processing skills, including short auditory memory, difficulty with temporal sequencing, and difficulty with repetition of auditory patterns (Eisenson & Ingram, 1972). In his review of the SLI research literature, Leonard (1982) noted that the symptoms experienced by this heterogeneous population can range from mild to severe and may encompass a wide range of communication difficulties that affect listening, speaking, reading, and writing. Thus, persons with SLI may also qualify for services under the category of learning disabilities, depending on the specific criteria used for identification in their locales.

### Communication Interventions

Little has been written about AAC interventions for SLI individuals, because natural speech and language interventions are emphasized almost exclusively. One exception described the use of a total communication approach (speech + manual signs) with an 8-year-old girl who had severe receptive and expressive language impairments (Roth & Cassatt-James, 1989). In this case, total communication appeared to have positive influences on both language domains. In the expressive realm, the girl's use of total communication for several years appeared to reduce frustration and facilitate the use of speech, which eventually became her primary mode of expression. The authors noted that when her communication partners decreased their use of manual signs in response to her improved expressive language, her ability to comprehend directions and stories decreased. When speech was again paired with manual signs, her comprehension improved. These authors echoed the advice of other researchers (e.g., McCauley & Demetras, 1990) who emphasized the importance of conducting broad-based language assessments with SLI individuals in order to arrive at accurate diagnoses and provide appropriate intervention recommendations.

**Computer Interventions**    Virtually every catalog of materials for speech-language pathologists or special educators contains software products designed to teach basic to advanced language skills. The effectiveness of computer language interventions has been documented through research (e.g., O'Connor & Schery, 1986), but most available software programs have not been tested empirically. Nonetheless, there are a number of case study reports that indicate that at least for some children with SLI, these approaches may offer important advantages over more traditional language therapy (e.g., Larson & Steiner, 1985; Steiner & Larson, 1991). Factors such as increased motivation, improved attention span, reduced frustration, and opportunities for repeated practice are frequently cited as among the reasons for improvement when computer software programs are used.

Software should be selected to meet clients' individual language needs and not used simply to include technology as part of the intervention. Programs such as Representational Play and Exploratory Play (Peal Software), and Micro-LADS and Speak Up (Laureate Learning Systems) were designed specifically for children with language disorders. Other generic software programs, such as First Words and First Verbs (Laureate Learning Systems), the Stickybear series (Communication Skill Builders), and The Factory (Sunburst Communications) can be useful in combination with more specific programs to meet a wide range of student needs. Catalogs from the software manufacturers are excellent sources of ideas for individual interventions.

Larson and Steiner (1985) offered clinical guidelines to assist facilitators in the use of computer software with individuals with SLI and other individuals. These include:

1. Integrate microcomputer interventions with other, state-of-the-art intervention approaches.
2. Do not substitute a computer for a clinician. Spontaneity, flexibility, and sensitivity are important intervention elements that cannot be provided by technology.
3. Affiliate with microcomputer and user groups for current information about professional issues and recent developments (e.g., Closing the Gap, ASHA).
4. Emphasize functional communication and ensure generalization by practicing skills learned on the computer in natural settings.
5. Ensure that software programs adhere to what is known about communication development and learning principles.
6. Do not purchase or implement software that has not been field tested with individuals similar to the anticipated client population.

## LEARNING DISABILITIES (LD)

---

The first time I remember shame was when I used the wrong word or got words in the wrong order. Everyone always laughed at me. Perhaps I could have laughed too if I had been able to see the mistakes I had made. But I couldn't. (Loftus-Brigham, 1983)

"Yesterday, our seven-year-old daughter was reading a book and asked her father to help her with a word. He grew red in the face, ran out of the room, and I found him crying. He admitted the truth. He can't read. He told me that he just can't recognize letters and words," (letter to a reading problems clinic, in Lerner, 1988, p. 350).

---

### Overview and Characteristics

Learning disabilities, as other impairments discussed in this chapter, are known by a variety of names, including language-learning disabilities, dyslexia, minimal brain dysfunction, and specific reading disabilities, among others (Wallach & Liebergott, 1984). The definition accepted by the National Joint Committee on Learning Disabilities (NJCLD) is as follows:

> Learning disabilities is a general term that refers to a heterogeneous group of disorders manifested by significant difficulties in the acquisition and use of listening, speaking, reading, writing, reasoning, or mathematical abilities. These disorders are intrinsic to the individual, presumed to be due to a central nervous system dysfunction, and may occur across the life span. Problems in self-regulatory behaviors, social perception, and social interaction may exist with learning disabilities but do not by themselves constitute a learning disability. Although learning disabilities may occur concomitantly with other handicapping conditions . . . or with extrinsic influences . . . they are not the results of those conditions or influences. (National Joint Committee on Learning Disabilities, 1991, p. 19)

Based on this definition, it appears that the term learning disabilities may, in fact, describe the larger disorder of which SLI is a subcategory; that is, children with SLI may be LD individuals whose specific impairment is in listening and speaking, as listed in the above definition. There is a research base to suggest that some LD individuals are also language impaired in one or more areas, regardless of the labels they are assigned (McKinney & Feagans, 1984; Moran, 1988). Overall, approximately 5% of the total school population in the United States was identified as LD during the 1986–1987 school year, comprising 44% of all students with handicaps receiving special education services (U. S. Department of Education, 1988). Approximately 72% of LD students were males and 28% were females (Lerner, 1988). In 1985–1986, about 62% of these children were served in regular classrooms and resource rooms, 21% in separate classrooms, and 15% in regular classrooms only (U. S. Department of Education, 1988). As adults, people with LD are most often identified because they are unable to read and write, and this widespread illiteracy has received considerable attention in the 1980s and 1990s.

## Augmented Literacy Instruction

*Reading*    Although persons with LD may have difficulties in many areas, poor reading is the major academic problem reported for 80% of them (Lerner, 1988). There are almost as many approaches to teaching literacy skills as there are terms that have been used to describe LD. These teaching methods include various phonics approaches, direct instruction (DISTAR), language experience or "whole language" approaches, the Orton-Gillingham method, and many, many others. It is far beyond the scope of this chapter to review the many remedial literacy strategies currently in use, and readers are referred to other texts for this information (e.g., Engelmann & Bruner, 1984; Gillingham & Stillman, 1970; Kamhi & Catts, 1989; Stauffer, 1980). We will, however, review briefly some of the most prevalent techniques used in augmented, or computer-assisted, literacy instruction with LD individuals. These techniques may be useful with a broader range of communicatively impaired individuals as well, since the literacy problems associated with LD may occur with other types of disabilities (i.e., primary motor impairments such as cerebral palsy).

Computers cannot (and should not) take the place of books for teaching reading, but computer technology can expand the instructional possibilities. A number of pre-reading programs for young children were summarized in Table 10.7. In addition, computer programs are available to teach specific reading skills, which include basic skills, such as phonics and word recognition, comprehension, word meaning or vocabulary instruction, and language experience. Table 12.2. summarizes some of the many software programs available in each of these areas. Since these programs can be used with both standard keyboards or alternative access modes, they are applicable to students with physical disabilities and reading difficulties as well as to "typical" LD students.

*Writing*    The process of writing is closely related to that of reading, and, in fact, when adults write, over one half of their time is actually devoted to reading activities (Stephens, 1987). Current research emphasizes the importance of teaching the writing *process* instead of simply concentrating on the written *product* (Lerner, 1988). This means placing less initial emphasis on technical

**Table 12.2.**   Examples of reading instruction software

| Reading skill | Software | Available from: |
|---|---|---|
| Basic skills (e.g., blending, phonics, sight-word recognition) | Sentence Master | Laureate Learning Systems, 10 East Spring St., Winooski, VT 05404 |
| | Hint and Hunt I, Construct-a-Word I | DLM/Teaching Resources, One DLM Park, Allen, TX 75002 |
| Comprehension | Comprehension Connection | Milliken Publishing Co., 1100 Research Blvd., P.O. Box 21579, St. Louis, MO 63132 |
| | Dragon's Keep | Sierra On-Line, Sierra On-Line Building, Coarsegold, CA 93614 |
| | Readable Stories | Laureate Learning Systems (see above) |
| | Ace Reporter | Mindscape, Inc., 3444 Dundee Rd., Northbrook, IL 60062 |
| Word meaning or vocabulary instruction | Word Attack Plus | Davidson & Associates, 3135 Kashiwa St., Torrance, CA 90505 |
| | Semantic Mapper | Teacher Support Software, PO Box 7130, Gainesville, FL 32605 |
| Language experience | Language Experience Primary Series | Teacher Support Software (see above) |
| | Writing to Read System | IBM, PO Box 1329, Boca Raton, FL 33422 |
| | Talking Textwriter | Scholastic Software, 2931 E. McCarty St., Jefferson City, MO 65102 |

variables such as correct spelling, grammar, organization, and word choice in favor of teaching students to translate ideas, thoughts, and feelings into written form for a particular audience. In this regard, computerized writing programs have gained popularity in the 1980s and 1990s, since they allow LD students to write without worrying about handwriting (which is often difficult for them) and to revise without crossing out words or otherwise ruining their drafts. Table 12.3. displays some examples of writing instruction programs. Many writing programs also provide assistance with spelling, which is discussed in the next section.

The most significant advantage of computerized approaches to writing may be in the area of student attitudes. At all age levels, persons with LD seem to be more willing to attempt writing tasks and to experiment with word choice and sentence structure when they are less frustrated by the technical aspects of the process (e.g., Bowles-Bridwell, 1987; Collins & Price, 1987; Morocco & Neuman, 1986; Rosegrant, 1985).

**Spelling**   Spelling is considered to be much more difficult than reading, and LD students who are able to read may have great difficulty with spelling, which, in turn, is likely to affect their ability and motivation to write (Lerner, 1988). As with other literacy-related areas, there are numerous approaches to spelling instruction. One approach is "invented spelling," in which children with a basic understanding of phonics are encouraged to write by listening to the sound units of words and associating letters with them, even if this does not result in correct spelling. Thus, children might spell "telafon" for "telephone," or "peetza" for "pizza." A substantial body of research shows that children who write in this manner at an early age either become better spellers or at least as good as those who are limited to correct spelling (Ehri & Wilce, 1985). Another approach often used with LD children involves teaching cognitive learning strategies that give students a way to think systematically about spelling challenges. Finally, more traditional phonics and sight word reading approaches are also used widely with students with literacy problems (Lerner, 1988).

In recent years, a number of computer-assisted spelling programs have become available,

**Table 12.3.**    Examples of writing instruction software

| Writing skill | Software | Available from: |
|---|---|---|
| Basic keyboarding and word processing | Keytalk | Peal Software, 5000 N. Parkway Calabasas #105, Calabasas, CA 91302 |
| | Magic Slate | Sunburst Communications, 39 Washington St., Pleasantville, NY 10570 |
| | Appleworks | Claris Corp., 440 Clyde Ave., Mountain View, CA 94043 |
| Graphics and text combination to create "books" | Storymaker | Bolt, Beranek & Newman, Inc., 10 Moulton St., Cambridge, MA 02238 |
| | Kidwriter | Gessler Education Software, 900 Broadway, New York, NY 10003 |
| Interactive, creative writing | Story Tree | Scholastic Software, 2931 E. McCarty St., Jefferson City, MO 65102 |
| | The Writing Adventure | DLM/Teaching Resources, One DLM Park, Allen, TX 75002 |

ranging from standard spell checkers, which identify misspelled words and suggest alternatives, to programs that provide considerably more adaptive support. For example, Cue-Write (Communication Skill Builders) provides word processing along with spelling assistance and practice via customized word lists that are arranged and activated on an initial letter basis. EZKeys (Words + , Inc.) and Write Away (Institute of Applied Technology) provide similar spelling and other types of writing assistance for IBM-compatible computers. Predict-It for the Apple IIe series and Co:writer for Macintosh computers (both from Don Johnston Developmental Equipment, Inc.) actually predict the next word in a sentence based on numerous grammatical and linguistic variables. If the student indicates that the prediction is accurate, the program automatically inserts the word (correctly spelled, of course) into the text. Thus, some software programs emphasize spelling instruction while others allow writers to circumvent the spelling process through adaptive techniques.

An example of the potential effects of computer-assisted writing and spelling for persons with LD is provided in the manual that accompanies the Cue-Write software program (Beukelman, Garrett, Lange, & Ticé, 1988). The authors illustrated use of the program through a case study of a high school senior with such severe learning disabilities that he spent approximately one half of his day receiving tutorial assistance in a resource room. Although he was able to read at approximately a ninth-grade level, his writing and spelling were virtually unintelligible to unfamiliar readers. For example, he produced the following writing sample, which is approximately 63% intelligible, without computer assistance:

> Shoup is my 2the perepe class We are now workeing on a pknake taBal You have to cutet the wood to santk lanks and angles. sanbing is prably the loung parte of maki it weve gout the top of it on no and are yousing wood skrous to hoould it ot grather and poniting wood plouts over the wood skrous sow it wale show up on the prajate now all I have to dow is stain it an varnshi it. (Beukelman et al., 1988, p. 29)

The story translates as follows:

> Shop is my second period class. We are now working on a picnic table. You have to cut the wood to certain lengths and angles. Sanding is probably the long part of making it. We've got the top of it on now and are using wood screws to hold it together, and putting wood plugs over the wood screws so it will show up on the project. Now all I have to do is stain it and varnish it. (Beukelman et al., 1988, p. 29)

The student was instructed in the use of Cue-Write for 1 month, until he could generate text, print documents, edit vocabulary files, and operate the hardware independently. He was given functional practice assignments during this time, such as describing a photograph he brought in, writing short paragraphs of personal interest, or writing letters to friends. He used the program in the "assist mode," which allowed him to activate word tables on the bottom of the computer screen by typing in the beginning letter of the desired word, which he could do quite accurately, as can be seen from the example. He would then simply copy the word from the table into his text on the top of the screen. His primary difficulty was in copying the words accurately, but after 1 month of daily 1-hour sessions with the software, he produced the following story about archery. This is as it appeared prior to editing, with the most unintelligible words translated in brackets:

> You csan use qcamoflage it will help you alout [a lot] it makes you you bland in with the back ground. And it allows you to move a[nd] not be seen. Last yer I shot my deer. It toke me three trise to get one. I was on the west side of the rever the ddere wor moceing [was moving] up the side of the rever and comeing tward me I was in my tree stand it was a 15 yard short [shot] I hit him the sholder it dikn't no what him [hit] him. It is a lot of fun and it takes a lot of patience. (Beukelman et al., 1988, p. 31)

This sample represents a 20% improvement in writing intelligibility, with approximately 83% of the words spelled correctly. A final edited version was then produced using standard spell checker and grammar checker programs to correct the remaining errors. Such computer support may act as a long-term writing prosthesis for individuals such as this young man.

*Handwriting*   The final component of literacy instruction that is difficult for many LD individuals is handwriting, or the mechanics of actually producing words on paper. This difficulty with handwriting, often referred to as dysgraphia, may be related to underlying fine motor skill or eye–hand coordination problems, visual–spatial impairments, or attention deficits (Lerner, 1988). Individuals whose progress with handwriting instruction has not matched their writing needs, or who write very slowly may benefit tremendously from word processing programs operated through standard keyboards or alternative input devices. It simply does not make sense to deprive children or adults of the enjoyment of writing simply because of their poor handwriting. Unfortunately, however, many professionals are reluctant to allow access to a keyboard for young children in particular, possibly because they fear that the computer will become a permanent crutch and that handwriting will not develop as a result. As with all such decisions, this one need not be made on an either/or basis (see chap. 8, this volume, for a related discussion).

Software programs to teach keyboarding and beginning typing skills are available for persons across the age range. Typing Tutor III (Scholastic Software) and Master Type (Mindscape) are two examples of these programs. In addition, rather expensive voice recognition programs for IBM-compatible computers, such as Dragon Dictate (Dragon Systems, Inc.) are available. These allow writers to speak their text into a small microphone, and the computer then translates the speech into written form (see chap. 4, this volume, for more information about voice recognition software). Such approaches are probably most applicable to adolescents and adults with LD who have severe handwriting and spelling problems (especially the former), as well as to persons in the same age range with physical disabilities, such as spinal cord injury, that prevent them from writing altogether.

## PRIMARY MOTOR IMPAIRMENTS (PMI)

A large number of individuals experience severe communication disorders as a result of primary motor impairments (PMIs) that limit their ability to speak and write. These include persons with congenital impairments such as cerebral palsy and arthrogryposis, as well as those with physical impairments (e.g., spinal cord injury). In general, individuals with PMI do not experience significant sensory, intellectual, or learning problems that contribute to their communication difficulties. Thus, the main characteristics common across persons in this group are that their motor impairments are primarily responsible for their difficulties with spoken and written communication, and, if provided with appropriate alternative access techniques, their communication difficulties are likely to be largely resolved. In the sections that follow, we describe briefly some primary motor impairments that may require AAC intervention.

## Cerebral Palsy

The term *cerebral palsy* typically refers to a developmental neuromotor disorder that is the result of a nonprogressive abnormality of the developing brain (Hardy, 1983). There are a number of etiologies that are known to result in early lesions or malformations of developing brain tissue, which are summarized in Table 12.4. The cause is unknown in approximately 40% of all cases of cerebral palsy. The incidence of cerebral palsy is between 2–2.5:1000, with a prevalence of about 400,000 school-age children. Figures for adult incidence of cerebral palsy are difficult to obtain (Erenberg, 1984; Lord, 1984).

Several types of motor problems may be present in persons with cerebral palsy, depending on the location of the brain lesion. The most common type, spastic cerebral palsy, results in hypertonic muscle tone and occurs in about 50% of all cases (McDonald, 1987). According to McDonald, the other types of cerebral palsy include:

1. Athetosis, causing uncontrollable involuntary movement (10%)
2. Rigidity, causing resistance to flexion and extension movements (7%)
3. Ataxia, resulting in difficulty in maintaining balance (5%)
4. Tremor, resulting in repetitive involuntary contractions of the flexor and extensor muscles (less than 1%)
5. Atonia, in which muscle tone is lacking or deficient (1%)
6. Mixed type, in which there are combinations of two or more of the above problems (12%)

Primarily because of these motor impairments, persons with cerebral palsy often experience severe speech and writing difficulties that present significant challenges to the AAC team.

In addition, associated disorders are also common in persons with cerebral palsy. These include cognitive impairments (60%–70%); vision problems (40%), hearing impairments (20%), and seizure activity (35%–45%) (Mirenda & Mathy-Laikko, 1989). Discussion in this chapter is limited to individuals with cerebral palsy whose communication disorders are primarily a result of their motor impairments.

## Arthrogryposis Multiplex

*Arthrogryposis multiplex* is a chronic nonprogressive disorder, which appears to be hereditary and occurs because of an absence of fetal movement. As a result, multiple joints remain immobile because of weak or absent limb muscles, and spinal curvature may also appear. The disorder is quite rare, occurring in approximately .03% of all newborns (Bigge, 1991). Early surgical intervention may facilitate standing, but functional use of the upper extremities is often minimal. Individuals

**Table 12.4.**   Primary known causes of cerebral palsy

| Cause | Percent of cases |
|---|---|
| First trimester events such as exposure to radiation, intrauterine infection, ingestion of teratogenic drugs, and chromosomal abnormalities | 7 |
| Later pregnancy events such as abruptio placentae and fetal–placental exchange abnormalities | 32 |
| Complications of labor and delivery | 17 |
| Neonatal complication such as sepsis, asphyxia, and prematurity | 39 |
| Meningitis, head trauma, lead intoxication, and other early childhood disorders | 5 |

Adapted from Batshaw and Perret (1986).

with arthrogryposis usually have normal or near-normal speech and language capabilities. Therefore, communication needs usually involve reading (i.e., managing printed material), writing, and computer control. Because arthrogryposis is a congenital condition, alternatives to written communication must be developed to support these individuals while they are in school.

## Osteogenesis Imperfecta

*Osteogenesis imperfecta* refers to a group of connective tissue disorders that are hereditary and involve fragile and brittle bones that break easily (thus, the lay term *brittle bone disease*). In addition, 26%–60% of these individuals experience mild to moderate hearing loss during the second or third decade of life. There are no concomitant intellectual or language impairments. The incidence of osteogenesis imperfecta has been estimated at 2–5 per 100,000 births (Jung, 1989). The frequent fractures experienced by these individuals may make written communication difficult, and they may require alternative access techniques for this reason.

## Muscular Dystrophy

*Muscular dystrophy* is a hereditary disease that is characterized by progressive muscle weakness. The most common form, Duchenne dystrophy, follows a hereditary sex-linked pattern and affects 1 in every 3,500 males (Bigge, 1991). It is generally manifested between the ages of 2–6 years when the child begins to have difficulty climbing stairs and running. Weakness usually begins in the muscles of the pelvic girdle, necessitating the use of a wheelchair by age 10–14 years in most cases. Spinal curvature, upper extremity involvement, and decreased respiratory function gradually follow, with death occuring in adolescence or young adulthood primarily from heart or respiratory failure. The primary AAC needs of individuals with muscular dystrophy are in the areas of augmented writing, when the upper extremities have been severely affected, and, in the terminal stages, in augmentative or alternative conversational communication, when the oral muscles can no longer support natural speech.

## Other Impairments and Disorders

Juvenile rheumatoid arthritis, congenital limb deficiencies of the upper extremities, and fibrocystis are but a few of the many other PMIs that can necessitate the use of AAC techniques for spoken or written communication. In addition, acquired disorders such as spinal cord injuries often necessitate the use of adaptive written communication and other literacy supports.

In Chapter 16, we discuss AAC interventions for acquired disorders that usually occur in adults. In the sections that follow in this chapter, we summarize briefly the AAC techniques that are most commonly applied to school-age children and youth with PMIs for conversation and classroom participation and for augmented literacy (i.e., writing, reading, spelling, and drawing).

## AAC FOR CONVERSATION

Many individuals with PMI are able to function as competitive or active students in regular classrooms if given appropriate assistive technology and instructional supports. Most of these individuals will be able to meet their conversational needs through natural speech, although they may require technological assistance to read and write independently. Some individuals with cerebral palsy, however, need AAC systems for conversational interactions, as well as for reading and writing, because of their severe motor speech disorders. Some of the most salient issues in providing AAC systems for individuals with severe speech and physical impairments are discussed briefly in this section.

### Intensive Emphasis on Developing Language Skills

If individuals with augmented conversational systems are to be successful in school, their language knowledge and skill base must be well-developed by the time they enter the elementary grades. As we discussed in Chapter 10 concerning young children, language learning (both incidental and formal) must be accomplished by these individuals using AAC approaches. Thus, parents and preschool professionals must adapt AAC approaches to support the language-learning process. Although this is true for all preschool children who are unable to speak, it is even more essential for children who are likely to be competitive students. These students must master considerable language knowledge before entering elementary grades so that they can participate at a level similar to their peers. Students who are not academically competitive have some additional time to develop and expand their language skills.

## Supporting Preliterate Students

Conversational AAC users who will be competitive or active students spend their early elementary-school years engaged in intensive schooling. The extent to which their facilitators support their conversational needs as these students learn to read and write often determines their long-term success. Persons working with young preliterate conversational AAC users face some difficult decisions in this regard. Young children with PMI who cannot speak are also unable to read and spell in order to prepare their messages. Obviously, these young AAC users must have some means to interact conversationally, and they cannot wait until they are able to spell in order to achieve this. Therefore, some type of AAC symbol approach must be taught to them, which may itself have significant learning requirements. For example, systematic instruction and experience are necessary in order for a child to learn the Blissymbolics system or iconic encoding (e.g., Minspeak or VoisShapes). At the same time, many of these children are attempting to learn the orthographic form of their native language. Since young AAC users may need to accomplish both of these learning tasks while they are enrolled in regular elementary-school classrooms, the competition for learning time can be considerable. There is no simple solution to this dilemma. An important task for the AAC field is to learn more about how to assist young AAC users with PMI to be communicatively competent, while allowing them to participate successfully as competitive students.

## Differences Between Social and Classroom Communication

***Content Variability***    AAC systems that are designed to support social interactions may not be designed to support classroom participation. It would seem that social conversation is very dynamic, but it appears that classroom communication is even more so, as students change vocabularies from math to language arts to science to music to art. Furthermore, the content in each subject area changes regularly. For example, in language arts, the topics for class discussion change from story to story. In science and social studies, the vocabuary needed to participate in written and spoken classroom communication changes from unit to unit. In addition, an AAC system designed to meet conversational needs probably will not contain the specialized vocabulary words used in the classroom. Thus, in order for AAC users to communicate successfully in their classrooms, the content of their AAC systems must be changed to accommodate ongoing activities.

During their early years, when students cannot spontaneously spell their messages, classroom communication needs place a considerable burden on the AAC team. Even when students are able to spontaneously spell their messages, they may still need considerable assistance to communicate the vocabulary of the classroom. We are reminded of one young AAC user we know who struggled to talk with her teacher and classmates about the various types of dinosaurs included in a science unit. None of the students in the class could spell the difficult dinosaur names, but the nondisabled students were able to talk about them and answer the teacher's questions without difficulty. In order to participate in the discussions, the AAC student needed the symbols representing these messages available, a task that was time consuming but nonetheless essential to her competitive-student status (see Figure 12.1. for an example).

***Grade-Level Variability***    Spoken communication in the classroom also appears to vary as a function of grade level. Although little information has been published in this area, there are some

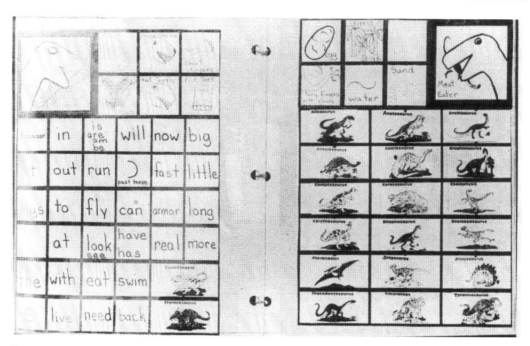

**Figure 12.1.** A communication board with dinosaur vocabulary items needed in a regular science class. (Reprinted with the permission of Merrill, an imprint of Macmillan Publishing Company from *Teaching individuals with physical and multiple disabilities* [3rd ed.], p. 168, by June L. Bigge. Copyright © 1991 by Macmillan Publishing Co. Copyright © 1982, 1976 by Merrill Publishing Co. Figure reprinted courtesy of Janie Kelly.)

fragments that should encourage facilitators who help AAC users to analyze their classroom communication requirements. For example, Trevor and Nelson (1989) reported that choral speaking was common in the first-grade classrooms, rarely occurred in the third-grade classrooms, and never occurred in the fifth-grade classrooms that they observed. They also reported that third-grade students spoke a slightly greater number of total words and more different words in the classroom than first graders, and they spoke nearly twice as many words as did fifth graders. Thus, it would seem that classroom verbal expression by elementary students decreases as they reach higher elementary grades.

*Teacher Variability*    Variability among patterns of verbal classroom expression also appears to depend on the individual teacher. For example, the spoken communication of students in four third-grade classrooms in the same school building was recorded (McGinnis, 1991). Children in some classrooms spoke four times the number of total words than did students in other classrooms.

To summarize, classroom instructional staff must communicate effectively with other members of the AAC team to ensure that a student's AAC system is personalized to meet both conversational and academic needs. Because the vocabulary of successful academic participation is so variable, the AAC approach used to symbolize messages (especially prior to the acquisition of spontaneous spelling abilities) should be selected carefully, as there is little time to teach symbol or symbol sequence relationships. The student's communication program should be managed to provide some rehearsal time for the student before he or she is expected to be competitive or active in the classroom.

## AUGMENTED LITERACY

Most individuals with PMI are likely to have problems with written communication at some point, because their motor impairments make handwriting or even regular typing difficult. Individuals with PMI who are able to speak, however, typically have no more difficulty acquiring basic literacy skills than do their nondisabled peers. In contrast, individuals with cerebral palsy and who have insufficient speech for functional communication often experience serious difficulties learning to read and write for a variety of reasons. In the sections that follow, we discuss augmented writing and augmented reading for persons with PMI.

## Reading and Writing Problems

The literacy learning difficulties experienced by many persons with severe speech and physical impairments, primarily cerebral palsy, have been documented by a number of authors. Approximately 50% of children in this group with measured intelligence scores in the average range appear to demonstrate reading skills significantly below grade-level expectations (Berninger & Gans, 1986b; Koppenhaver & Yoder, 1992). Even when they can read, these individuals often experience difficulties with written communication into adolescence and throughout adulthood. Analyses of writing samples of these young people consistently indicate incorrect usage of grammatical forms and errors in spelling performance (e.g., Kelford Smith, Thurston, Light, Parnes, & O'Keefe, 1989).

Why are literacy deficits so common in persons with severe speech and physical impairments? Unfortunately, no one really knows the answer. The motor impairments that prevent these individuals from being able to write no doubt account for some of the problem. Some authors have suggested that "reading is parasitic upon the surface codes of spoken language" (Berninger & Gans, 1986a, p. 57), implying that the reading difficulties these individuals experience are somehow related to their speech impairments. It also appears that from the time they enter school, many individuals with severe speech and physical impairments receive very little actual literacy instruction. For example, Koppenhaver and Yoder (1990) reported that in the classrooms of three adolescent boys with cerebral palsy, 30%–42% of the instructional time allotted to literacy each day was devoted instead to nonliteracy activities such as toileting, waiting, or booting up a computer. Most of the instructional time was spent working one-to-one on workbook pages, an activity that has been found to be unrelated to gains in reading in nondisabled children (Rosenshine & Stevens, 1984). The students seldom read for more than 2 minutes per hour of instruction, and they wrote text, other than single words, on only 9 occasions out of 45 observed days. Thus, the areas that seem to be most related to literacy learning in nondisabled students—silent reading and text composition (Anderson, Wilson, & Fielding, 1988)—are areas in which these students had virtually no opportunities during a typical school day. Sadly, these data are similar to those reported by a number of other authors as well (see Koppenhaver & Yoder, 1992, for a summary).

## Promoting Development of Reading and Writing Skills

In an effort to identify factors that may contribute to the development of literacy skills, researchers analyzed the results of survey information obtained from literate adults with severe communication and physical impairments. In a retrospective survey, Koppenhaver, Evans, and Yoder (1991) examined some early reading and writing experiences of 22 literate individuals with cerebral palsy, ranging in age from 16–55 years. These individuals reported that when they were in school, they participated regularly in a variety of reading experiences that included: 1) reading and listening to taped stories, 2) reading the same texts repeatedly, 3) reading texts to answer questions proposed by their teachers or in textbooks, 4) visiting classroom and school libraries, and 5) participating in independent and silent reading sessions. Many of them indicated that they were taught new vocabulary words before reading stories. Some individuals also noted that their teachers spent time reading aloud to them.

Many individuals in this study emphasized the critical role of family members in facilitating their literacy learning. Two particularly important factors included family members reading aloud to them while they viewed the text, and family members providing them with opportunities for social interaction and attention through discussions of the stories read. These individuals recalled that a variety of different types of printed materials were accessible to them as children through visits to libraries and bookstores. Regular opportunities to choose their own reading materials and to observe others reading were also evident. The respondents suggested that the most significant factors contributing to their successful acquisition of literacy skills were the support and high expectations of their parents, in addition to their own talents and persistence.

While the results of this study indicate that the early experiences of people with PMI who learned to read are generally positive, a related study suggests that are substantial differences between nondisabled and disabled children in learning to read. A survey found that while non-disabled preschoolers' parents reported reading to them daily, children with severe speech and motor impairments were read to approximately 2–3 times per week (Light & Kelford Smith, in press). Nondisabled children were typically asked to respond verbally to many questions during reading activities, while their counterparts with speech and motor impairments remained quite passive, typically looking at or pointing to pictures. Writing and drawing materials seemed to be much less available to preschoolers with disabilities than to nondisabled preschoolers (Light & Kelford Smith, in press). All of the above activities have been found to be important in promoting the development of literacy.

Persons with severe speech and physical impairments also experience serious writing difficulties in many cases. Kelford Smith et al. (1989) analyzed the written output completed in home environments by six adolescents and young adults with severe communication and congenital physical impairments. Although these individuals exhibited deficits in their speech production, utilized telegraphic output in their spoken communication, and had limited access to technology and literacy instruction until the later years of their educational programs, they all demonstrated basic levels of proficiency in producing and reading written text. The individuals and their caregivers suggested that several factors contributed to this acquisition of literacy skills, including: 1) involvement in an integrated educational program at some point in their school careers, 2) access to computers for word processing, 3) the support of a specific teacher, and 4) their previous use of Blissymbolics for face-to-face communication.

### Augmented Reading and Referencing

*Alternative Access*   A primary need of many persons with PMI is to be able to hold printed material, turn the pages, and generally have access to printed matter in order to support the development of reading skills and to learn academic content. It is important, however, to put this need in perspective and determine if independent access should be the primary goal for all individuals. While student independence is certainly a worthwhile goal, it is also clear that this goal must be balanced with considerations of how to best use valuable instructional time. It might be more efficient, for example, to have a regular-class peer or paraprofessional provide assistance with some printed materials, or to use one of the many available low tech options. Figure 12.2. displays home-made devices for holding books or pages, and Table 12.5. contains a summary of some of the commercial options.

In addition, computer-based options that involve word processing software to host reading materials have also been outlined (Wolverton, Beukelman, Haynes, & Sesow, 1992). Such computer applications, along with alternative access and screen reader (i.e., speech synthesis) options, allow students to choose and load text from a diskette, display it on a computer monitor, and advance through the text independently, using commands such as "page up," "page down," and "go to." Students can have words, lines, or entire screens of text read aloud to them by the computer as they visually follow the text when a speech synthesizer is used in conjunction with the software. (Examples of reading software that can be used in this manner were provided in Table 12.2. and Table 12.3. Readers are referred to Table 10.9. for examples of early literacy software for beginning or pre-readers.)

**Figure 12.2.** Homemade devices for holding books and pages. (Reprinted with the permission of Merrill, an imprint of Macmillan Publishing Company from *Teaching individuals with physical and multiple disabilities* [3rd ed.], p. 168, by June L. Bigge. Copyright © 1991 by Macmillan Publishing Co. Copyright © 1982, 1976 by Merrill Publishing Co.)

Technology-assisted reading generally requires the creation of computer diskettes containing the text to be read. This can be accomplished by simply entering text into a standard word processing program and saving it on a diskette, or by using an optical scanner to accomplish this function. The optical scanner reads standard printed materials and translates the written characters into computer text that can be saved on a diskette. This option, which is much less time consuming than entering text by hand, has become more widely used due to improved optical scanning technology. Table 12.6. is a summary of some of the most common optical scanners.

Augmented referencing systems that incorporate compact discs, a computer network, and alternative access options may facilitate literate students' abilities to access and read library re-

**Table 12.5.** Assistive devices for print access

| Print access tool | Product | Available from |
|---|---|---|
| Reading stands/book holders/easels | Wire Frame Bookholder, Book Butler, Miller Deluxe Bookholder, Overhead Book Holder/Easel, Tilt Desk, Easi-Reader, Reading Desk with Storage, Book Maid, Bed Reader, Uni-Reader | Fred Sammons, Inc., 145 Tower Dr., Burr Ridge, IL 60521 |
| | Miller Deluxe Book Holder, Overhead Book Holder/Easel | J.A. Preston Corporation, 60 Page Rd., Clifton, NJ 07012 |
| Page turners | | |
| Mouth-held | Wand Mouthstick, Vacuum Wand | Fred Sammons, Inc. (see above) |
| | Mouth Held Page Turner | Maddak, Inc., 6 Industrial Ave., Pequannock, NJ 07440 |
| Hand-held | Page Turner and Cuff Wand | Fred Sammons, Inc. (see above) |
| Mechanical/electronic | Automaddak Page Turner | Maddak, Inc. (see above) |
| | Automatic Page Turner | Lakeland Products, 21 Birnamwood Dr., Burnsville, MN 55337 |
| | Gewa Page Turner | Zygo Industries, Inc., P.O. Box 1008, Portland, OR 97207 |
| | Saltus Reader | Dickey Engineering, 3 Angel Rd., North Reading, MA 01864 |
| | Touch Turner | Touch Turner, 443 View Ridge Dr., Everett, WA 98203 |

**Table 12.6.** Optical scanners for augmented reading

| Optical character recognition scanners | Product | Available from: |
| --- | --- | --- |
| IBM-compatible scanners | Adhoc Reader | Adhoc Reading Systems, Inc., 28 Brunswick Woods Dr., East Brunswick, NJ 08816 |
| | DeskScan 2000 | Chinnon America Inc., 660 Maple Ave., Torrance, CA 90503 |
| | Discover 7320 Models 10, 20, 30 | Kurzweil Computer Products, Inc., 185 Albany St., Cambridge, MA 02139 |
| | Jet Reader | Datacopy Corporation, 1215 Terra Bella Ave., Mountain View, CA 94043 |
| | Omni-Reader | G.A.S. International, Inc., P.O. Box 1281, Euless, TX 76040 |
| | PC Scan | DEST Corporation, 1201 Cadillac Ct., Milpitas, CA 95035 |
| | Personal Computer Scanner | CompuScan, Inc., 300 Broad Acres Dr., Bloomfield, NJ 07003 |
| | Personal Reader | Kurzweil Computer Products, Inc., (see above) |
| | PS-2000 | Electronic Information Technology, Inc., 25 Just Rd., Fairfield, NJ 07006 |
| Macintosh-compatible scanners | DeskScan 2000 | Chinon America Inc., 660 Maple Ave., Torrance, CA 90503 |
| | Jet Reader | Datacopy Corporation (see above) |
| | Omni-Reader | G.A.S. International, Inc. (see above) |
| | Read-It Personal | Olduvai Corporation, 7520 Red Rd., Suite A., South Miami, FL 33143 |

sources. Basically, augmented referencing systems allow students to read encyclopedias, dictionaries, atlases, and other multivolume reference materials through a computer. Shell, Horn, and Bruning (1989) have implemented such a system for university students who have "print impairments" due to a visual, language, and/or physical inability to manage books. Although augmented referencing is still new, research and development in this area are clearly important.

***Instructional Techniques*** Technology for reading is a means to an end, but it is not an end in itself. Unfortunately, we know very little, from either a clinical or a research perspective, about instructional techniques that are likely to be successful in teaching persons who cannot talk how to read (Koppenhaver & Yoder, 1992). As noted previously, it appears that positive, varied, and interactive reading experiences from an early age and the support of family members in this area are influential in preparing for reading. So, too, is the determination of the individual, as noted by Brown in *My Left Foot*:

> When mother was busy I worked on by myself, trying to make out new words whenever I came across them. I used to try to spell out the names of objects around me at home, like fire, picture, dog, door, chair, and so on. I was very proud of myself when I had mastered a new word and could write it down for mother to show her what a great scholar I was. (1954, p. 27)

Students with PMI and speech impairments also need alternative strategies for acquiring word decoding and encoding skills, which are learned by their nondisabled peers through speech. Berninger (1989) suggested that one way to "learn the correspondence between the whole spoken word and the whole written word" (p. 125) is to have the student look at a word on a flashcard or computer monitor, hear the teacher or speech synthesizer pronounce the word, and then write the word using an appropriate alternative access technique. Or, in order to "learn the relationship between the phoneme and letter" (Berninger, 1989, p. 125), the student might look at phoneme sequences presented one-by-one on flashcards or a monitor, hear the teacher or synthesizer pronounce the phonemes separately and then blend them together into a word, and write the word or answer questions about it. Whatever strategy is used, the ability to encode and decode words is both important and difficult, as noted by Creech (1988):

> I honestly can't imagine reading without phonetics. I couldn't say the words I read; therefore, my parents taught me to sound them out in my head; and this takes a mastery of phonetics. . . . Reading presents us with abnormal difficulties. Normally children learn to read by reading out loud. They learn the physical shape of sounds and words, which reinforces their reading. I have no idea what "can" feels like, its shape, its texture. To me, "can" is completely abstract. It is a combination of three phonemes that, combined, form a morpheme. However, speakers know what "can" feels like. (p. 12)

In addition to phonics approaches, Bigge (1991) and Koppenhaver and Yoder (1992) summarized some basic interactive instructional practices that appear to hold promise for teaching basic literacy skills. These include strategies included in the "whole language" approach, which centers on the idea that "teaching literacy should focus on meaning and the experience of the child, rather than on the teaching of [isolated] skills. . ."(Chaney, 1990, p. 244).Whole language strategies for teaching include:

1. Reading or listening to taped or slide-taped stories
2. Multiple readings of a text, paired with interactive activities related to the text (e.g., art, music, cooking, and writing activities)
3. Regular visits to in-class, community, and school libraries
4. Teacher previewing that establishes the purpose of reading a particular text
5. Vocabulary instruction prior to reading
6. Regular in-class silent reading periods
7. Frequently being read to while observing the text

Adaptive techniques that allow students to participate in the usual classroom reading activities are also essential. This can be accomplished through alternative access modes (e.g., using symbol displays to answer questions in class) that are identical to those used for augmentative communication.

---

Art is an affable, determined university student with arthrogryposis. No AAC assistance was available to him when he was growing up, and, thus, he developed his own method of writing. He lies on his stomach on the floor, in front of a computer keyboard, and types with his tongue. No mouthstick, no headstick—just his tongue! He types in this manner, error-free, at a rate of *200 keystrokes per minute!* Now that he is required to produce frequent written work as a university student, Art often experiences neck and shoulder pain because of the muscle strain caused by his method of computer access. He is currently learning Morse code so that he can type in a comfortable upright position with a sip and puff switch. With practice and rate enhancement techniques such as linguistic prediction and abbreviation expansion, he hopes to be able to match his current tongue-typing rate within the next 6 months.

---

## Augmented Writing

***Alternative Access*** Nondisabled students enter elementary school with the ability to hold and manipulate pencils and other writing implements. The educational program then takes responsibility for developing the motor and language skills needed for writing. When students with PMI enter school without a way to write, much of the written literacy instruction is inaccessible to them. Thus, they need to enter school with a way to write so that they can benefit from regular classroom instruction and avoid the need for personalized literacy curricula. These students also need a way to produce printed output so that their work can be reviewed by their peers and corrected by the teacher in a manner similar to that of their classmates.

Rosenthal and Rosenthal (1989) suggested that school personnel utilize a "backwards elimination" approach to determine the writing adaptations needed by an individual student. Using this approach, the teacher simply works backward from the standard materials and procedures that are used by nondisabled students. Thus, initial adaptations might involve simple modifications of regular worksheets or textbooks. For example, assignments such as workbook pages might be simplified by changing fill in the blank questions to those that require multiple choice or matching responses. Then, the answer options can be coded with a letter or number so that the student can respond by writing, typing, or pointing to a single character. In some cases, simply enlarging a worksheet by photocopying may be sufficient to allow a student with a motor disability to use a pencil to fill in answers. Alternatively, shortening the length of assignments or modifying the overall workload may be appropriate strategies that allow the teacher to evaluate the quality of a student's work without lowering the academic standards.

If simple solutions to participation are ineffective, the backwards elimination approach requires that low tech adaptive equipment or materials then be tried as solutions. For example, simple headsticks; splints with pencil attachments; modified pencil holders; or large pencils, crayons, and markers may be useful. Examples of these adaptations are displayed in Figure 12.3.

If simple writing adaptations prove ineffective, or if the student experiences undue fatigue when writing with such equipment, electronic alternate access methods should be investigated (see chap. 4, this volume). The process of writing for students with PMI is often time consuming and slow, even if electronic alternate access methods are used. For example, Kelford Smith et al. (1989) analyzed the writing samples of six individuals with PMI and reported mean typing rates of 1.5

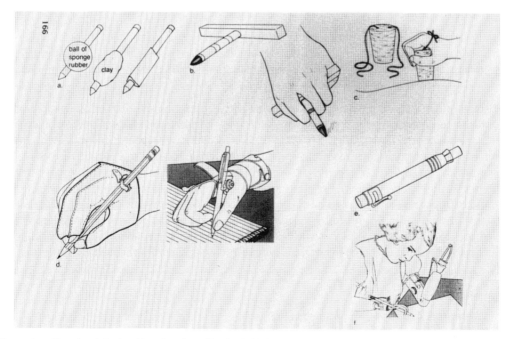

**Figure 12.3.**  Examples of simple writing adaptations. (Reprinted with the permission of Merrill, an imprint of Macmillan Publishing Company from *Teaching individuals with physical and multiple disabilities* [3rd ed.], p. 166, by June L. Bigge. Copyright © 1991 by Macmillan Publishing Co. Copyright © 1982, 1976 by Merrill Publishing Co.)

words per minute. To enhance the speed of alternative access, rate enhancement techniques such as encoding or linguistic prediction are often essential (see chap. 3, this volume, for discussion of this issue). Software programs that provide augmented writing and spelling assistance were presented in a previous section of this chapter that concerned students with learning disabilities.

> Because of her severe athetosis, Lydia is unable to use her hands to type. She had no alternative keyboard access until she was 12 and was provided with a single head switch. This allowed her to use an Adaptive Firmware Card scanning routine to type with software in an Apple computer. Initially, she used a spelling and writing assistance program (Cue-Write, Communication Skill Builders) to write simple, familiar stories such as "The Three Pigs" or "Goldilocks." Then she watched movies on videotape, and she recounted the stories in text form. For example, she watched the film "The Manikin" and then rewrote it with herself as the heroine. She also wrote poems, short stories, letters to friends, and even a short class play. Lydia and her family decided to have her retained in elementary school for 1 year so that she could engage in intensive literacy instruction. Lydia composed text on the computer an average of 1 hour each day during the school year, and 2–3 hours per day during summer school. She is now a sophomore in high school and is academically and socially involved in selected regular education classes. Lydia now uses a headlight pointer and RealVoice to produce written work, with assistance from rate enhancement software programs such as Predict It (Don Johnston Developmental Equipment, Inc.). Because instruction in reading and writing started so late, Lydia's literacy skills still lag far behind those of her peers.

**Instructional Techniques**    Just as students appear to learn to read by reading, they appear to learn to write by writing. For many, this is a slow and laborious process, even with adaptive equipment, but it appears essential that students with PMI have ample opportunities to compose written text, not just to write single words in isolation as part of workbook exercises (Koppenhaver & Yoder, 1990). Simply allowing students to get their thoughts down on paper is much more important than emphasizing correct grammar, spelling, and punctuation, at least initially. Consistent with a whole language approach, students should have frequent opportunities to "creat[e] literacy events by dictating stories, labeling, creating charts or bulletin boards, writing journals, stories, poems, and by producing their own books" (Chaney, 1990, p. 245). In addition, it appears that auditory feedback (i.e. synthetic speech) that echoes each letter, word, or phrase as it is written may result in spelling, word recognition, and comprehension improvement (Koppenhaver & Yoder, 1992). Other instructional strategies for writing that appear promising include teaching organizational skills for planning, generating, and revising written output and expanding the language base for writing through multimodal communication (Bigge, 1991).

# Persons with Severe Intellectual Disabilities

≫≫≫≫≫≫≫≫≫≫≫≫≫≫≫≫≫≫≫≫≫≫≫≫≫≫≫≫≫≫≫≫≫≫≫≫≫≫≫≫≫≫≫≫≫≫≫

> The day and hour had finally arrived. This was to be the day when the consulting speech pathologist was going to let us know when Vi was finally going to get her augmentative communication system. Anticipation loomed like the hot sticky July air, which pervaded her unit cubicle [in the institution where she lived], where we all had gathered to hear the news. Five minutes into his polite but rambling recitation, though, it became apparent that the only news he had for us that day was no news at all: a glitch had developed here or there, a microswitch had failed, a proverbial monkey wrench had been thrown into the works again. . . . I asked how much longer it'd take to get back on track this time. "Why," he quizzically replied, "Is there any special reason for all the rush???" "No, no special reason," I said. . . . "No, no special reason at all . . . except that she has had 50 years of no special reasons." (Williams, 1989, pp. 16–17)

People like Vi who are labeled "severely/profoundly mentally retarded" have only recently been recognized as appropriate candidates for AAC interventions. Indeed, many school districts, adult service agencies, and residential facilities still maintain candidacy criteria to ascertain whether such individuals are likely to qualify for AAC services. Nonetheless, the 1980s and 1990s have seen important positive changes in societal and professional attitudes toward these individuals. People with severe intellectual disabilities are being increasingly provided with the opportunities and technology needed to assist them to communicate in inclusive, dynamic environments. In this chapter, we discuss some of the AAC approaches that have been demonstrated or appear to show promise in this regard (see also Mirenda, Iacono, & Williams, 1990).

## WHO ARE THESE INDIVIDUALS?

Their names are Peter, Elias, Eduardo, Min, Jason, Beverly, and Quinta. They are not a "population," but they are individuals from every age, race, and ethnic background whose intellectual abilities lag far behind those of same-age peers. Historically, individuals with severe intellectual disabilities have been among the most devalued and disenfranchised citizens living in any country in the world. As a group, they have been segregated in large institutions, sterilized, denied immigration visas, jailed for marrying, and put to death because of their intellectual disabilities (Wolfensberger, 1975). They comprise approximately 2% of the school-age population (Evans, 1991) and have traditionally been labeled "deaf/blind," "severely/profoundly mentally retarded," and "multihandicapped," among other things. We will refer to these individuals as "people with severe disabilities," for want of a better term. According to the definition accepted by The Association for Persons with Severe Handicaps (TASH), people with severe disabilities include:

> Individuals of all ages who require extensive ongoing support in more than one major life activity in order to participate in integrated community settings and to enjoy a quality of life that is available to citizens with no or fewer disabilities. Support may be required for life activities such as mobility, communication, self-care, and learning as necessary for independent living, employment, and self-sufficiency. (Meyer, Peck, & Brown, 1991, p. 19)

People with severe disabilities can live, work, play, communicate, and form relationships with a wide variety of people in their communities, schools, and workplaces, and they deserve to be provided with opportunities to do so.

> Suddenly the scene changed. A new group of young waterfowl came up to the [Ugly] Duckling and invited him to dive in and swim with them. But he held back. Then came the parents, and . . . the mother said, "You belong with us! You're a swan!" . . . And . . . the little guy said, "Belong? A swan? You mean I'll grow up to be . . . like you?" and the adult said he would. . . . (Perske & Perske, 1988, p. 27)

## OPPORTUNITY INTERVENTIONS

Belonging—living in a home with people who choose to live with you, going to school with your friends and neighbors, working at a real job, getting invited to birthday parties, funerals, and employee picnics—these are a few of the opportunities that people with severe disabilities should have. Most don't have access to such events on a regular basis because of societal or institutional policy or practice, or because of attitudinal, knowledge, and skill barriers that may take years to change. It is beyond the scope of this book to address strategies for eliminating policy and practice barriers to integration and community participation (see Appendix A for related resources). Nevertheless, since one of the underlying principles of the Participation Model is that opportunities are critical to communication success, a chapter about communication for individuals with severe disabilities would be incomplete if it did not include some of the strategies that have been demonstrated to be effective in breaking down attitude, knowledge, and skill barriers in this regard.

### Communication Environments

Since the mid-1970s, a number of authors have argued that citizens with severe disabilities, like other citizens, should spend a substantial portion of their adult lives engaged in community activities such as going to work, shopping for groceries, or riding public transportation when it is available (e.g., Brown, Nietupski, & Hamre-Nietupski, 1976). In order to accomplish this, instruction in functional skills needed to participate in such activities must be taught during their school careers. More recently, the move toward regular classroom integration has emphasized inclusion in the community of the school—participating in recess, science, home economics, music, art, and other activities in which other students participate. According to this community-referenced curriculum and instructional approach, skills targeted for instruction should be: 1) age-appropriate; 2) functional—that is, directly useful in daily activities; 3) taught in the actual environments where they are needed, either in school, in the community, or both; and 4) taught with reference to the cues and corrections that are naturally available (Falvey, 1989; Ford & Mirenda, 1984). Such skills may occur in domestic, recreational and leisure, general community, vocational, or school environments.

Adoption of a community-referenced approach to instruction has a direct impact on the quantity and quality of the participation and communication opportunities that are available. Suddenly, the individual needs to order food in a restaurant, cheer for the basketball team, ask for help at the library, greet the school secretary when bringing the attendance list, chat with co-workers at break time—the list of natural opportunities for things to say and people to say them to becomes endless.

Careful analysis of the settings in which the individual participates helps to identify the opportunities available for communication and to ensure that necessary adaptive and AAC techniques are included in an intervention. The "ecological inventory" process has been used successfully for this purpose for many years and has been recently described as it applies to communication interventions (Reichle et al., 1991). Briefly, the ecological inventory process involves:

1. Observing a nondisabled person of the same age engaged in the activity of interest
2. Writing a step-by-step list of the skills required
3. Assessing the target individual against the skill inventory to identify discrepancies
4. Designing communication adaptations and instructional programs to teach compensatory skills

Table 13.1. provides excerpts from an ecological inventory completed for a young adult in a community setting, along with suggested participation and communication adaptations in discrepancy areas. This basic format can be easily applied to activities at school, at home, or in the community. If the individual is not allowed to participate in functional, age-appropriate activities in a wide variety of settings, this clearly should be considered an opportunity barrier and targeted for remediation. Appendix A lists some resources for planning community-referenced instruction.

## Communication Partners

Who is there to talk to? For most people with severe disabilities, the answer is family members, adults who are paid to be communication partners, and, perhaps, other people with severe disabilities. These are all perfectly acceptable communication partners—they are simply not sufficient communication partners. Imagine what it would be like, day after day, to communicate only with your parents, teachers, and other people who have at least as much difficulty as you do in getting messages across. Models for increasing the number and types of communication partners—also known as acquaintances and friends—are described in the following sections.

---

*In te grate* (in te grayt) *v.* 1. to combine or form (a part or parts) into a whole. 2. to bring or come into equal membership of a community.
*In clude* (in klood) *v.* to have or regard or treat as part of a whole  (O'Brien, Forest, Snow, & Hasbury, 1989).

---

*Circle of Friends and the MAPS Process*    Circle of Friends and MAPS are two related processes that have been used primarily to facilitate the inclusion of school-age individuals with severe disabilities into regular classroom settings, although they certainly can be used to create inclusive neighborhoods, workplaces, and other settings as well. When applied to school integration, these dynamic processes involve family members, school principals, both regular and special education teachers, paraprofessionals, support personnel, and, *most of all*, regular class peers. The processes in this context involve strategies for building school communities in which an individual with severe handicaps can be supported and develop friendships (O'Brien et al., 1989; Vandercook, York, & Forest, 1989).

One strategy involves building a Circle of Friends around the target individual and supporting these friends as they begin to include the person with severe disabilities in integrated activities. Another strategy, the McGill Action Planning System (MAPS) process, is used to develop IEP goals by involving family members, professionals, and regular education friends in planning and implementation. Some examples of successful results of these processes can be found in *Circles of*

**Table 13.1.**   Example of an ecological inventory with suggestions for participation and communication adaptations

Environment: Prendle's Drug Store
Target Individual: Sarah, age 20
Activity: Purchasing personal care items
Set-up: In the store with a friend who also needs to do some shopping, friend is wheeling Sarah in wheelchair

| Skill (as performed by nondisabled peer) | Participation (person with disability) | | | Possible participation or communication adaptations |
|---|---|---|---|---|
| 1. Enter store. | − | | | Pause before entering, wait for signal indicating anticipation/acceptance. |
| 2. Greet salesperson at jewelry counter, if present. | + (vocalized) | | | In addition, consider single message loop tape with greeting that can be activated with microswitch by left hand. |

| | **Items to Purchase** | | | |
| | #1 | #2 | #3 | |
| **Repeat for each item:** | | | | |
| 3a. Walk/wheel along front of store, looking down each aisle until desired aisle is identified. | − | − | − | Encourage Sarah to look down aisle, pause and look for accept signal, proceed down aisle after signal. |
| 3b. Walk/wheel down aisle. | − | − | − | Friend can wheel her slowly down aisle. |
| 3c. Locate correct section. | − | − | − | As she wheels past the sections, look for an accept signal and stop. |
| 3d. Examine options. | P | P | P | Friend can hold up two options at a time to make this easier. |
| 3e. Choose desired item. | P | P | P | Look for eye gaze or arm movement toward one of the two options presented. If none, try another two options. |
| 3f. Converse with friend as desired/needed. | P | − | P | Consider a multiple message loop tape with topic-setter statements that can be activated with microswitch by left hand: "Have you seen any good movies lately?" |
| 3g. Check to see if next item is in the aisle. If yes, go to step 3a. If no, go to step 2. | − | − | − | Friend can push her down aisle again slowly, looking for signal to stop. |

| | Participation | | | |
|---|---|---|---|---|
| 4. Locate checkout stand. | − | | | Wheel to front of store and pause within view of stand, pause and wait for a signal to proceed. |
| 5. Greet cashier. | P (smiled slightly) | | | Consider single message loop tape as in step 2. |
| 6. Put items on counter. | − | | | Friend can do this. |
| 7. Get out money. | − | | | Friend can do this. |
| 8. Give cashier money when requested to do so. | − | | | Place a Velcro strap around her left hand and tuck bills under it. Have her extend her left hand toward the cashier, who can then remove the money. |
| 9. Receive change. | − | | | Friend can do this. |
| 10. Put change away. | − | | | Friend can do this. |

*(continued)*

**Table 13.1.** *(continued)*

| Skill (as performed by nondisabled peer) | Participation (person with disability) | Possible participation or communication adaptations |
|---|---|---|
| 11. Take bag with purchases. | − | Take bag from counter and hold in front of Sarah, and pause. Look for an accept signal and place bag on lap. |
| 12. Exit store. | − | Pause before door, look for an accept signal and leave store. |

+ = performed independently by target individual, − = not attempted by target individual, P = attempted by target individual and then performed with assistance.

*Friends* (Perske & Perske, 1988) and in a videotaped case study, "With a Little Help from My Friends" (Forest, 1988). This model has been used successfully across Canada and in many places throughout the United States.

**Lifestyle Planning and Personal Futures Planning**   The Lifestyle Planning (O'Brien & Lyle, 1987) and Personal Futures Planning (Mount & Zwernik, 1988) models are ongoing problem-solving processes that help groups of people "focus on opportunities for people with severe handicaps to develop personal relationships, have positive roles in community life, increase their control of their own lives, and develop the skills and abilities to achieve these goals" (Mount & Zwernik, 1988, p. 1). The processes can be used to facilitate community integration of individuals of all ages, but they have been particularly successful in assisting adults with severe disabilities to make successful transitions from institutional to community settings and from segregated community settings to more integrated ones.

Lifestyle Planning and Personal Futures Planning consist of three basic steps. First, a "personal profile" is developed from a group interview of the "focus person" and all of the people involved in his or her life to gather information about past events, relationships, places, preferences, choices, ideas about the future, obstacles, and opportunities. The goal of this first step is to develop a personal profile that emphasizes the person's capacities and gifts, rather than his or her deficits and problems. Second, both short- and long-term plans are developed by the group, based on the personal profile. Third, individuals in the group make commitments of various types and levels to help the individual carry out the plan over time. A booklet, "It's Never Too Early, It's Never Too Late" (Mount & Zwernik, 1988), and a videotape, "A New Way of Thinking" (Minnesota Governor's Planning Council on Developmental Disabilities, 1987), are among the resources that describe these processes and their outcomes. Lifestyle Planning and Personal Futures Planning have been used widely across North America (Mount, 1987).

**Local Models**   Many school districts, adult service agencies, and other organizations have developed their own models for integration and inclusion by individualizing and modifying the processes described to particular community circumstances. Some organizations have documented their efforts, and two of the best known examples are described briefly.

*Comprehensive Local School Model*   The Comprehensive Local School (CLS) model was developed through a federal project in conjunction with the San Francisco, California Unified School District (Sailor et al., 1989). The CLS model combines best practice strategies for community-referenced instruction with integration and inclusion strategies. The model assists regular and special education professionals to develop individualized integration plans for students with the most severe disabilities and to set up support structures that will facilitate integration into regular education classrooms. Considerable emphasis is placed on helping teachers to adapt curricula so that all students can be included at an appropriate level.

The California Research Institute (CRI) continues to disseminate the results of research and development efforts based on the CLS model, which has been incorporated into restructuring efforts by school districts in Arizona, Delaware, Iowa, Nebraska, and Texas, among other states (California Research Institute [CRI], 1990a). Some of the available resources include a quarterly newsletter, "Strategies" (CRI, 1990a), and videotapes describing various aspects of the model (e.g., "The Way to Go," CRI, 1990b).

*Syracuse Model*   Another local integration model was developed in the Syracuse, New York School District through collaboration with Syracuse University (Ford et al., 1989; Schnorr, Ford, Davern, Park-Lee, & Meyer, 1989). As with the CLS model, processes in the Syracuse model combine strategies drawn from the research base on community-referenced instruction with those related to inclusion. Emphasis is placed on individualized planning that combines elements of regular classroom instruction in academic areas and community-referenced instruction in functional areas. An award-winning videotape, "Regular Lives" (Biklen, 1988), as well as the written resources already mentioned, describe this model, which has been used by school districts in Arizona, Iowa, Maine, Nebraska, New Hampshire, Virginia, and Wisconsin, among others (Schnorr et al., 1989).

## The Bottom Line

Over and over again in schools, work settings, and homes, friends, parents, professionals, and community members have documented the incredible impact of integrated communication opportunities—or the lack thereof—on the communication abilities of people with severe disabilities (e.g., Perske & Perske, 1988). There is simply no doubt about it: The availability of genuine and motivating communication opportunities in integrated and inclusive settings is *at least* as important to the success of a communication intervention as is the availability of an appropriate access system. This is perhaps more true for people with severe disabilities than for anyone else, because these individuals are among those with the fewest personal resources and the most need for interdependence with others. If those others do not include a substantial number of people who are not paid to be there, who are not likely to leave for a new job next year, and who do not believe that their primary task is to make the individual more like everyone else, the impact of communication interventions are almost certainly going to be limited.

## COMMUNICATION INTERVENTIONS

When communication opportunities have been identified and provided, a variety of strategies can be used to teach and encourage communication. Strategies must be selected to match actual opportunities and actual communication needs identified through the ecological inventory or other assessments. Communication opportunities that go beyond simple requesting, rejecting, and identifying wants and needs should be recognized, although these are clearly important as well. For example, if an adolescent is sitting in the cafeteria with his high school friends, and one of them is helping him eat lunch, he probably does not have to communicate many wants and needs messages, since his needs are already being met. Rather, he may be asked by his friends to share information about what he did last weekend, or be expected to contribute to the conversation by sharing the latest teenage joke. Communication in areas such as information sharing, social closeness, and social etiquette (Light, 1988) are often overlooked in needs assessment for people with severe disabilities, perhaps because of the erroneous assumption that these are not important agenda for these individuals.

## Loosely Structured Naturalistic Interventions

Loosely structured naturalistic interventions encompass a variety of intervention strategies that are characterized by the following: they are conducted only in natural (as opposed to artificial) contexts, and, although they require that facilitators develop appropriate communicative contexts and opportunities, they do not require that such opportunities be artificially set up or fabricated. Some strategies, although in widespread clinical use, have not been empirically validated in published research, and such strategies were included in this chapter only if there appeared to be substantial anecdotal evidence of their effectiveness with persons with severe disabilities. Some strategies were introduced in Chapter 10 as they applied to young children. Readers are encouraged to familiarize themselves with the contents of that chapter before proceeding, since the basic principles discussed in Chapter 10 are not repeated here. Instead, we reintroduce loosely structured beginning communication strategies in terms of their applicability to persons with severe disabilities across the age range, as well as additional techniques to enhance communication.

> Everyone can communicate. Everyone does communicate.

***Movement-Based Approach***     Dr. Jan Van Dijk (1966) and colleagues at the Institute for the Deaf in Sint Michielsgestel, the Netherlands, first described this approach for enhancing the social and communicative abilities of young children with dual sensory impairments (i.e., deafness and blindness). The Van Dijk technique and its adaptations are based on the principle that "learning through doing" enables people to acquire concepts, form social relationships, and influence the environment as communicators. Thus, these approaches emphasize movement as a way for the individual to be actively involved in the ongoing activities of daily life.

It is perhaps not surprising that movement-based techniques were first developed for use with individuals who can neither see nor hear, and for whom movement in its many forms, such as touch, motion, or object manipulation, for example, represents the most viable way of learning about the environment. This approach has been successfully adapted and used since the 1960s with individuals with severe/profound intellectual disabilities, multiple disabilities, autism, and other disabilities in addition to sensory impairments (e.g., Rowland & Schweigert, 1989, 1990; Siegel-Causey & Guess, 1989; Sternberg, 1982; Stillman & Battle, 1984; Writer, 1987). The six levels of the approach described by Van Dijk are summarized in the sections that follow, with particular emphasis on adaptations described by Writer (1987).

*Nurturance*     The aim of this component is to develop a warm, positive relationship between the individual with disabilities and the facilitator. Siegel-Causey and Guess (1989) described this as a relationship "that promotes interest in communicative interactions and enhances a willingness to participate in social exchanges" (p. 23). According to Writer (1987), Van Dijk's suggestions for establishing this social bond include: 1) limiting the number of people working with the individual so the facilitator and the person can get to know each other through continual contact, 2) building a routine of daily activities for the individual, and 3) distributing external stimuli to avoid over- or understimulation. Siegel-Causey and Guess (1989) suggest that nurturance is provided when the facilitator: 1) gives support, comfort, and affection; 2) creates a positive setting for interaction; 3) expands on behaviors initiated by the individual; and 4) focuses on the individual's interests. They offered the following example:

> When it is time to go out to recess, the paraprofessionals need to make sure everyone is dressed properly in coats, gloves, and hats. Sarah, one paraprofessional, using an affectionate tone of voice, directs Ken, a student, toward the coat rack. She holds his hand and as they walk, they swing their arms back and forth slightly. While smiling at Ken, Sarah's voice is warm as she says to him, "It's almost time for recess now, what do you need to do?" Ken returns the smile and looks delighted as he reaches for his coat. He obviously enjoys the attention Sarah pays him and uses his nonsymbolic behaviors (e.g., reaching, smiling) to communicate with her. (Siegel-Causey & Guess, 1989, p. 28)

*Resonance*     Activities related to resonance are designed to shift the individual's attention from the self to the external world of people and objects. Resonance activities consist of rhythmic movements that the individual and the facilitator perform while in direct physical contact. For example, the facilitator might use a full hand-on-hand prompt to assist the individual to wipe a tabletop with a sponge. After several back and forth wiping movements, the facilitator pauses and waits for a signal that the movement should start again. Or, the facilitator may sit on the floor with a young child between the legs and rock back and forth to music, pausing regularly to provide opportunities for the child to signal a desire to continue. Many of the techniques associated with resonance were discussed in Chapter 10 and are also included in this chapter, including: 1) establishing natural and scripted routines, 2) utilizing patterns in games, 3) providing turn-taking opportunities, 4) encouraging participation, and 5) using calendar boxes or "anticipation shelves" (Writer, 1987). Tactile and object cues associated with specific activities, people, or items may also be used by the facilitator to communicate with the individual (Oregon Research Institute, 1989b).

*Coactive Movement*   Coactive movement is an extension of resonance with the basic difference being the amount of physical distance between the facilitator and the individual with disabilities. (Siegel-Causey & Guess, 1988). The goal of coactive movement is to develop sequence and anticipation by gradually building activities that the individual and the facilitator do together (Sternberg, 1982). The establishment of such predictable sequences facilitates communicative development by allowing the individual to anticipate and become actively involved in daily routines.

Coactive movements are executed by the individual parallel to, or side by side with, a peer or adult model (Writer, 1987). The facilitator may use full body movements, limb or hand gestures (e.g., kicking a ball, waving goodbye, making the manual sign for "eat"), and tactile cues to help the individual initiate the coactive movement, with the goal of fading these cues. Coactive movement activities, like resonance activities, follow a "start-stop" format, in which the facilitator is sensitive and responsive to signals from the individual.

*Nonrepresentational Reference*   Nonrepresentational reference involves teaching the individual to identify body parts on models that are initially three-dimensional (e.g., a doll or other person) and later, two-dimensional (e.g., a stick figure or line drawing) (Writer, 1987). These activities develop body image, teach pointing, and encourage the individual to be somewhat independent of the facilitator (Sternberg, 1982). These activities should be conducted as much as possible during routine activities (e.g., during a dressing routine or pretend-play time in a preschool classroom).

*Deferred Imitation*   Deferred imitation teaches the individual to imitate movements after the facilitator has completed them, starting with full body movements (e.g., standing up, sitting down) and eventually proceeding to functional limb and hand movements (e.g., putting on a hat, kicking a ball). Van Dijk (1966) recommended that such imitative movements be taught with familiar objects and through natural daily routines, using the types of cues described in the section on coactive movement. In fact, deferred imitation is the direct result of further fading of the cues used during coactive movement.

*Natural Gestures*   This final component of the movement-based approach involves encouraging the individual to produce communicative gestures that are "self-developed" (Sternberg, 1982, p. 214) and that motorically represent how the target individual typically uses an object or participates in an event. Writer (1987) noted that many manual signs that are highly iconic (e.g., the sign for "car," which involves the bilateral holding and moving of an invisible steering wheel) represent how an adult facilitator typically experiences a car. Thus, this particular gesture would not be appropriate to introduce at this point, according to the principles set forth by Van Dijk. Other iconic gestures or manual signs typical of the individual may be encouraged during this stage, such as waving goodbye, patting the mouth to ask for food or drink, or pointing at a desired item to request it.

*More About AAC for Persons with Dual Sensory Impairments (DSI)*   In addition to the movement-based approach, communication techniques for persons with severe intellectual disabilities in general are also used with individuals with dual sensory impairments. Readers are referred to Chapter 2 for a discussion of tangible symbol techniques and to Chapter 10, as well as other sections of this chapter, for discussions of scripted routines, gestural dictionaries, microswitch technology, loop-tape strategies, and communication miniboard techniques that are directly applicable to persons with dual sensory impairments. To supplement this information, additional references relating to communication interventions for persons with DSI are provided in Appendix B. Readers are also referred to Chapter 15 for information regarding AAC techniques for persons with DSI who do not have intellectual disabilities.

**Scripted Routines and Gestural Dictionaries**   Many individuals benefit from interventions to teach them to produce consistent gestural and other signals for attention getting, acceptance, and rejection (see Siegel-Causey & Guess, 1989). In Chapter 10, we discussed facilitator training, responsiveness to spontaneous signals, and using scripted routines to provide opportunities for developing these signals in natural contexts. A gestural dictionary strategy was also presented, which can document the idiosyncratic behaviors of beginning communicators.

All of these techniques may be necessary and all are appropriate for use with older individuals as well, with some adjustments needed to make them age appropriate. For example, a scripted routine can be used in self-care contexts such as eating, drinking, dressing/undressing, and toileting (see Table 10.3. for a script appropriate for both children and adults). Individuals older than 5 years of age are unlikely to engage in play routines such as "Row, row, row your boat" with their friends, and they may swim, play video or pinball games, run relay races, go to dances, listen to music, or engage in a wide variety of other recreational activities instead. Table 13.2. illustrates how some of these activities can be adapted for scripted routines. Additional applications of the "pause-wait-act" sequence from the scripted routine that are appropriate for older individuals can be found in McLean, McLean, Brady, and Etter (1991) as well as in the ecological inventory displayed in Table 13.1. Finally, the example of the gesture dictionary in Table 10.5. can be used without modification for individuals well beyond preschool age. In fact, we have seen this technique used effectively in group homes or other residential settings with high staff turnover as a method of orienting new staff to the communication patterns of a resident with severe disabilities.

The types of cues used during scripted routines require adaptations for individuals with visual or dual sensory impairments in particular. Persons who cannot see and who may not be able to hear must rely on olfactory, tactile, movement, and object cues in order to understand their environments. At a minimum, such cues should be standardized and used by all facilitators across all environments in order to: 1) greet the individual (e.g., a pat on the arm), 2) provide information to identify the facilitator (e.g., an object cue such as the partner's glasses or olfactory cue such as perfume), 3) identify the next activity (e.g., tangible symbols in a calendar box), 4) identify available choices (e.g., tangible symbols), 5) signal the completion of an activity (e.g., use of a hand-on-hand manual sign), and 6) communicate that the facilitator is leaving (e.g., a touch cue). Excellent examples of these principles are offered in the videotape "Getting in Touch" (Oregon Research Institute, 1989b).

**Choice Making**   The choice-making formats summarized in Table 10.4. can also be used successfully with persons with severe disabilities by relying on natural consequences to teach the effects of choice making. The contexts and examples in Table 10.4. were specifically intended for use with young children and should not be applied per se to older children or adults. Some alternative contexts are obvious: choices of food to eat or drink, music to listen to, TV shows to watch, and clothes to wear. Other alternative contexts may be less obvious, such as choices of whom to sit next to (or avoid!) during an activity, when to terminate an activity, how to complete an activity, and the order in which to complete a multicomponent task (e.g., a personal care routine in the morning). Still other choice-making opportunities depend on the extent to which the individual is included in integrated school and community life. These include, for example, choices about what brand of beer to order in the pub, which team to cheer for, which store to shop in, who to call on the phone tonight, or who to invite to a slumber party. Without exception, the number of choices available to

**Table 13.2.**    Examples of scripted routine segments for older individuals

| Touch cue (how you give nonverbal information) | Verbal cue (what you say) | Pause (wait for at least 10 sec. and look for a response) | Action (what you do after the person accepts) |
|---|---|---|---|
| **Swimming** | | | |
| 1. Move an inner tube up and down when the person is safely seated in it. | "Get ready to float. 1, 2, 3. . . ." | Pause, observe | Verbally acknowledge and push the inner tube gently across to a partner, 2–3 feet. Repeat. |
| 2. Float the person in a life jacket under the spray fountain in the middle of the pool. Let the water spray on his or her body. | "Getting wet, going under the water. . . ." | Pause, observe | Verbally acknowledge and keep the person in the spray for 2–3 minutes. Repeat. |
| **Video or pinball game** | | | |
| 1. Place hand on video joystick or pinball lever. | "Okay, it's time to fire/ shoot. Here we go." | Pause, observe | Verbally acknowledge and use hand-on-hand assistance to fire/shoot. Repeat. |
| **Going to a school dance** | | | |
| 1. Wheel the person onto the dance floor and spin around once or twice. | "What great music for dancing!! Let's go for it!" | Pause, observe | Verbally acknowledge and dance around with chair for 2–3 minutes. Repeat. |
| 2. Go to the refreshment table and get some punch. Brush the cup along the person's lower lip. | "Here's some punch. I bet you're thirsty from all that dancing." | Pause, observe | Verbally acknowledge and give a sip of punch. Repeat. |
| **Relay race** | | | |
| 1. As each team member runs and the line moves forward, the person's team partner shakes the wheelchair slightly before moving up in line. | "Okay, here we go, we need to move closer to the front to take our turn." | Pause, observe | Verbally acknowledge and move the chair forward. Repeat. |
| 2. Before taking a turn in the race, place the baton in the person's hands. | "Ready, on your mark, get set. . . ." | Pause, observe | Push wheelchair and run as required, then go to the back of the line when finished. |

a person with severe disabilities in the course of a day directly reflects the quality and quantity of integrated opportunities in his or her life. Thus, the focus of choice-making interventions often needs to be directed toward expanding opportunities rather than toward developing new and more sophisticated ways to teach people the essential skills.

*Age Appropriateness*    Options available in choice-making instruction for persons with severe disabilities should be appropriate for nondisabled people of the same age. With sufficient exposure and encouragement from friends and others, most people with severe disabilities will acquire sensitivity to age-appropriate cultural norms. Unfortunately, however, many individuals with severe disabilities have had limited exposure to age-appropriate experiences and when presented with such unfamiliar options, they may express no interest or may continue to choose options that are age-inappropriate. This presents communication facilitators with a dilemma: Do we offer *age-inappropriate* options when teaching choice making, since these are more motivating for the individual, or do we offer only *age-appropriate* options, although the person shows little interest in them?

The principle of today and tomorrow discussed in Chapter 7 offers a solution. This principle basically states that decisions for today should meet the user's immediate communication needs and match the current capabilities and constraints identified during assessment. Decisions for tomorrow are based on projections of future opportunities, needs, constraints, and capabilities as a result of instruction. In terms of this choice-making dilemma, the principle of today and tomorrow suggests that for today, choice-making options presented should be those that are valued by the individual, regardless of their age appropriateness. Nevertheless, the principle also *demands* that immediate steps be taken to expose the individual to varied age-appropriate options so that they can be incorporated into the choice-making repertoire for tomorrow. While the today decision may be necessary to provide motivation, it is certainly not an acceptable long-term decision.

**Augmented Language Learning**   "Augmented language learning" has been used successfully to teach a variety of communication skills, using voice output communication devices, to youngsters with moderate and severe retardation and severe spoken language impairments (Romski & Sevcik, 1992). In this project, words were represented on devices with abstract lexigrams accompanied by their printed English equivalents, and the devices were made available to the youngsters in integrated home and school settings. Facilitators were taught to operate the devices and to use them concurrently with speech in natural contexts throughout the day. For example, if a facilitator said to a youngster, "Let's get your coat and go outside," the facilitator might simultaneously activate the symbols for "coat" and "outside" on the communication display. Aside from this, "Communicative use of the device was not taught in the traditional sense. . . . Loosely structured naturalistic communicative experiences were provided to encourage, but not require, the children to use symbols when natural communicative opportunities arose [throughout the day]" (Romski & Sevcik, 1992, p. 119).

The results of this 3-year project are quite impressive. All of the youngsters learned to use the lexigraphic symbols, in combination with gestures and vocalizations, to request items, assistance, and information, to make comments, and to answer questions, among other functions (Romski & Sevcik, 1991, 1992). The children who began the project with spoken language comprehension of the words represented on their devices also learned to recognize at least 60% of the printed English words, independent of their related symbols, by the end of the first year. Seven of the thirteen children in the project began to produce intelligible speech by the end of the second year. This project clearly demonstrates the potential effectiveness of a loosely structured AAC intervention that utilizes naturally occurring communicative opportunities in multiple settings. Other clinicians have used iconic pictorial symbols, such as Picture Communication Symbols, and have reported similar positive results (e.g., Goossens', 1988; Goossens' & Crain, 1986b).

**Conversational Interventions**   The miniboard strategy for aided communication discussed in Chapter 10 for preschoolers is useful for ambulatory older individuals as well, as are aided formats such as communication books, wallets, and cards. Mirenda (1985) described a variety of strategies for designing and organizing aided devices by functional environment in order to facilitate their usefulness in integrated settings. For example, divider tabs can be used in communication books to separate activity sections and facilitate easy access, or core displays with supplemental border overlays may be provided for persons who use laptray aids (Goossens' & Crain, 1986b). Such strategies are important in order to provide a wide range of vocabulary items while allowing the AAC user to find a desired item quickly.

*Conversational Aids*   Unfortunately, communication aids provided to persons with severe disabilities usually contain vocabulary items that allow them to communicate primarily (or solely) about their wants and needs—symbols of preferred objects, activities, or people, for example. These vocabulary items, while necessary and important, do not readily facilitate conversational interactions between people with severe disabilities and their communication partners, and the result is that, often, these types of interactions do not take place.

If communication aids, whether electronic or not, are to be used in conversations, they must be constructed and designed with this goal in mind. Toward this end, the display should contain a number of photographs, magazine pictures, and line drawings of favorite people, pets, places, activities, and other items important in the person's life. Past and upcoming events should also be represented in some way. In addition, as discussed in Chapter 10, a variety of topic-setting strategies such as collections, topic-setter cards (Musselwhite, 1990) and remnants may be included. (Remember, a remnant is an item left over or otherwise related to an activity that the target individual has done or is planning to do.) One individual we know had a plastic bag containing grass clippings in his book, to remind him to tell his friends about learning how to mow the lawn over the weekend. Hunt, Alwell, and Goetz (1990) described a teenager who had a few pieces of dry cat food taped in her book to help her initiate conversations about taking care of her cat at home. The point is, through a combination of media, to provide AAC users with symbols that promote topics of conversation that are interesting and motivating both to them *and their communication partners.* These symbols should be changed and added so that current events in the person's life are reflected in the communication display.

In addition, it is often fun for people to have a few jokes in their displays that they can tell their friends. We particularly like "knock, knock" jokes because most people are familiar with the format and because they lend themselves readily to conversational turn taking. A series of pictures representing the parts of the joke will facilitate telling the joke. First, the AAC user touches a picture of someone knocking on a door accompanied by a written label such as "Wanna hear a cool joke? Knock, knock. . . ." After the partner has responded ("Who's there?"), the AAC user touches the next picture (e.g., a picture of plates and bowls labeled "dishes"). The partner responds ("Dishes who?") and the AAC user touches the final picture, which is a photo of him- or herself with the caption "Dishes me, who is you?", and everyone groans together! Of course, a similar format can be used for riddles and other types of humor.

Of course, the conversation aid should also *look* age appropriate, both in format and content. Polite though they may be, the co-workers of an adult with severe disabilities are not going to be interested for long in pictures of her dolls, or in his remnants from the movies "Bambi" and "Snow White." Similarly, the topic-setter collections appropriate for a 35-year-old (e.g., coupons, bottle caps, stamps, postcards, pop bottles, slogan buttons, magazines) are quite different from those appropriate for a preschooler. The covers of communication books should be attractive and, if they are decorated, done so in a manner appropriate to the individual's age. Finally, the device should be small enough to be carried around comfortably by ambulatory individuals, and small looseleaf binders (5 inches × 7 inches) or photo albums are particularly useful in this regard. A small carrying case with a Velcro or zippered closure (depending on the individual's abilities), such as a small purse, waistpack, camera bag, or travel pouch is recommended because regular-size backpacks or book bags are often too cumbersome for easy portability and manipulation (Hunt et al., 1990). Again, the point is to design an interesting, relevant device that can be used for conversations, in addition to interactions involving requests for desired items.

*Conversational Instruction*    A loosely structured strategy that holds real promise for teaching individuals with severe disabilities to use communication aids in conversation has recently been introduced (Hunt, Alwell, & Goetz, 1988, 1990, 1991a, 1991b). This strategy requires a facilitator to provide unobtrusive conversational "coaching" to the person with severe disabilities and to communication partners (friends, parents, or co-workers). The basic structure of this conversational strategy is displayed in Figure 13.1. (Hunt et al., 1991a).

The AAC user initiates conversation by taking the conversation aid from its carrying case and pointing to a picture, remnant, or other topic-setter device to ask a question or make a comment.

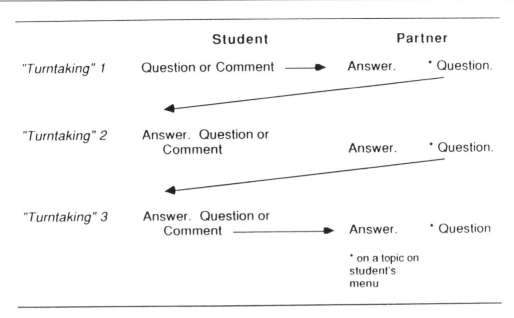

**Figure 13.1.** Basic conversational strategy. (From Hunt, P., Alwell, M., & Goetz, L. [1991b]. Interacting with peers through conversation turntaking with a communication book adaptation. *Augmentative and Alternative Communication*, 7, 120; reprinted by permission.)

The partner responds to the question or comment, makes additional comments about the topic, and ends his or her turn by asking the AAC user a question about something else represented in the communication aid. The AAC user answers the question, comments as desired, and asks another question, and the cycle repeats. Figure 13.2. is a summary of the conversational intervention strategy.

The results of several empirical studies regarding this strategy have indicated that AAC users with severe disabilities and little or no speech can learn to initiate and maintain augmented conversations independently after several weeks of instruction. The results also indicated that this occurs only when information is also provided to communication partners in the form of a 5-minute briefing that includes the following basic information:

> You always do three things in the conversation: (1) talk about what [Joe] just pointed to in the book and anything else you want to talk about; (2) then ask him a new question; and (3) then be sure to wait until [Joe] has a chance to talk about other things as well. (Hunt et al., 1990, appendix B)

This brief training also serves to emphasize the important role that facilitator training plays in AAC interventions, as is discussed throughout this book.

**Calendar/Schedule Box Strategies**    Calendar or schedule box strategies using real object symbols (see chap. 10, this volume) are applicable to communication interventions for elementary-age and older individuals with severe disabilities, including visual and dual sensory impairments. We have found the calendar/schedule box to be particularly effective in group homes for adults with disabilities as a way to provide individuals with information about upcoming events of the day. Of course, AAC users who are able to use photographs or line drawing symbols can use age-appropriate daily appointment books, wall displays, or other formats that contain their schedules in pictorial form (e.g., Baumgart, Johnson, & Helmstetter, 1990). Instruction in the use of these strategies is generally conducted in loosely structured naturalistic formats, using a hierarchy of prompts that are gradually faded.

**Loop Tape Strategies**    Single or multiple message loop tapes can also be used in a wide variety of situations with children, adolescents, and adults with visual, dual sensory or other mul-

A. Conversational Materials needed
   1. Conversation book, board, or wallet (see related section in chapter).
   2. Carrying case if the AAC user is ambulatory and requires portability (see chapter).

B. AAC User Instruction
   1. *Identify* naturally occurring conversational opportunities throughout the day in which interactions with non-disabled peers take place: during recess, break time at work, lunch at school, or transitions between classes. *Conduct* instruction in those settings.
   2. *Recruit* nondisabled peers as conversational partners.
   3. *Plan* for brief instructional sessions (preschoolers: 1–3 *turns* each, elementary students, 1–3 *minutes,* older students, 3–5 *minutes,* maximum).
   4. *Sit* by the AAC user and the partner and "coach" both through the steps involved. Use direct verbal and indirect verbal prompts (e.g., direct: "Point to the picture of your birthday party," indirect: "What could you say about that?"). Reinforce AAC user with subtle verbal praise or a pat on the back as necessary.
   5. *Fade* the coaching as quickly as possible by providing subtle gestural cues or whispered verbal cues.
   6. *Remember:* The point is to facilitate conversations that are as normal as possible: *Don't* be rigid about the conversational structure or intrusive in the conversations.
   7. *Facilitate* generalization: Teach across multiple settings and partners, ensure that AAC users have their books available at all times, provide sufficient information to potential partners regarding their roles, monitor and instruct to repair breakdowns.

C. Partner Information
   1. *Tell* the partner to make comments related to the pictures in the book.
   2. *Tell* the partner to end his or her turn by asking a question about something in the book.
   3, *Cue* the partner as needed during conversational training sessions.
   4. *Stay out of the partner's way as much as possible.*

**Figure 13.2.**   Summary of conversational intervention strategy. (Adapted from Hunt, Alwell, & Goetz, 1988, 1990, 1991a, 1991b.)

tiple disabilities (see chap. 10, this volume, for basic principles). For example, single message tapes can be used for greetings ("Hi, how are you today?"), farewells ("Goodbye, good to see you, let's get together soon"), single requests or active/passive choices (see Table 10.4.), conversational initiations ("So, how was your weekend?"), introductions ("Hi, my name is George, what's yours?"), and specific contextual messages (e.g., cheering "Go, team, go" at a pep rally, singing "For He's a Jolly Good Fellow" to a co-worker). Multiple message tapes or multiple tapes are used primarily for conventional requesting and choice making, although other uses are possible in environments where communicative exchanges are ritualized. For example, in many fast food restaurants, clerks are trained to take food orders in a standardized format (e.g., Clerk: "May I take your order, please?" Customer: Recites order. Clerk: Repeats order back to customer ending with, "Will there be anything else today?" Customer: Usually responds, "No, thanks." Clerk: "That will be [amount]." Customer: "Thank you.") This information can be identified by conducting an ecological inventory in a particular restaurant. If the format of the exchange remains the same, the essential phrases can be recorded on a multiple message loop tape, and the AAC user can learn to simply activate the tape during each of his or her turns in the interaction. Figure 13.3. displays suggestions and directions for implementing a simple tape recorder or loop tape system.

## Structured Interventions

Structured interventions either require the facilitator to arrange or set up communicative opportunities in some way and/or involve a need for structured teaching that may be conducted initially in isolated contexts. This is not to imply that these strategies are somehow not as good as those that are loosely structured. Indeed, some persons with severe handicaps may need systematic instruction in order to learn a beginning repertoire of communication skills.

   ***Strategies To Teach Basic Requesting***   The easiest communication function to teach is often to request a desired food, object, or action. This is because the contingent relationship be-

## Single Message Tapes

Directions:

There are probably numerous occasions when people need to communicate a single message to someone who doesn't know them very well, such as a store clerk or waitperson. These messages might include *greetings* ("Good morning, how are you today?" or "What do you think of the weather we've been having?"), *departure statements* ("Thank you very much. Goodbye." or "See you again soon."), or *simple requests* ("I'd like a large Coke with no ice, please " or "I would like to buy this birthday card ").

Below is a diagram of the equipment needed and how it all works together when the tape recorder is running on a battery (e.g., it is not plugged into the wall).

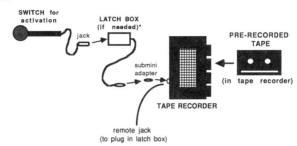

A latch box is needed if the individual is unable to depress the switch for a sufficient length of time. With the latch box, the AAC user hits the switch and the tape recorder stays activated until the switch is hit again. The latch box is available from Don Johnston Developmental Equipment, Inc., among other sources.

How To Operate:

1. Put the recorded message tape into the tape recorder.
2. Plug the individual's switch into the latch box (if needed) and then plug the latch box into the remote jack on the side of the recorder, or plug the switch directly into the tape recorder if no latch box is used.
3. Push the play button on the recorder and adjust the volume. Note: Nothing will happen at this point.
4. At the appropriate time, the individual hits the switch and activates the message. When the switch is hit again, the message is turned off.

## Suggestions and Ideas

1. A person of the same age and gender as the AAC user should record the messages. It is more important for the individual to have the opportunity to communicate than it is that the same person record all messages all of the time, although this is a good idea if it can be arranged.
2. Imagination and enthusiasm are the only limits to the ways this simple communication system can be used. It only takes 5–10 seconds to record a message, and new messages can be recorded over old ones so the same tape can be used over and over for different messages during a single outing into the community. For example, the AAC user could *order a drink* at a restaurant, then *say thank you* to the waitperson when the drink arrives, and then *say goodbye* to the cashier before leaving. These are three interactions that might not otherwise have been possible, for a total of maybe 30 seconds of recording time by the facilitator!
3. *What about talking on the telephone?* Help the AAC user compose a message to someone (a friend or family member) and then record it on tape. If you hold the receiver near the speaker on the tape recorder and the AAC user hits the switch, he or she can then "talk" to whoever is on the other end of the line. What a nice way to wish someone Happy Birthday, Merry Christmas, or to just chat about the past week! Remember: The message can be as long as the tape.

## Making Choices with Loop Tapes

Using the switch and tape recorder, the AAC user can also operate a *loop tape* with a series of recorded choices on it interspersed with 10-second pauses. The advantage of a *loop tape* is that it plays continuously and never needs to be rewound, so you only need to record each choice once, and the AAC user can play the tape as long as necessary before making his or her choice.

The set-up is the same as in the diagram, except that a loop tape is used instead of a regular cassette tape.

1. A person of the same age and gender as the AAC user should record (initially) a maximum of 2–3 options (choices) on the loop tape, with 10-second pauses (silences) between each choice. Example for a recreation/leisure choice: "I'd like to watch TV" (10-second pause), "I'd like to paint a picture" (10-second pause), "I'd like to do some sewing."
2. The user hits the switch to start the loop tape, listens until the desired option is spoken, and then stops the tape. The choice just before the tape was stopped is the one selected. If the tape is stopped accidentally in the middle of a choice, have the individual start over again (it was probably a mistake).
3. Confirm with the AAC user that the choice he or she made was accurate. If it wasn't, repeat step 2.
4. The individual can make choices about recreational/leisure activities to do at home, places to go, people to spend time with, clothes to wear, things to eat, for example. Ideally, there should be a number of tapes with choices of various types recorded on them, so that when it's time to make a choice, the facilitator can just pull out the tape, pop it in the tape recorder, and get on with it!

**Figure 13.3.** Using single message and loop tape techniques.

tween the request and its consequence is clear to the individual and can be arranged in advance by the facilitator. For example, if I am trying to teach a young woman to ask for her favorite item, a radio, I can place the radio within her line of visual regard but out of reach, to set up a communicative occasion. Once she has requested the radio with my instructional support, the relationship between her behavior (e.g., touching a photograph of a radio) and its effect (i.e., getting the radio) is straightforward. A number of structured interventions to teach basic requesting are summarized in this section.

*Milieu Teaching*    The term "milieu teaching" was introduced to describe a number of systematic natural context interventions (Hart & Rogers-Warren, 1978). Primary applications have been with language delayed and culturally disadvantaged children (Warren & Kaiser, 1986), although these interventions have also been used successfully to teach requesting to persons with severe disabilities (e.g., Halle, Baer, & Spradlin, 1981; Halle, Marshall, & Spradlin, 1979; Haring, Neetz, Lovinger, Peck, & Semmel, 1987; Oliver & Halle, 1982; Peck, 1985). Three strategies in particular, incidental teaching (Warren & Kaiser, 1986), the mand-model technique (Halle, 1982), and a time delay procedure (Halle et al., 1979, 1981) have been used singly or in combination.

There are similarities as well as distinct differences between the three strategies. All three are characterized by the use of dispersed (as opposed to massed) teaching trials in natural contexts, and by attempts to base teaching on the individual's interests in normal use. In addition, all three require that facilitators learn to identify potential communicative contexts throughout the day and use a variety of set-up strategies to create communication opportunities. Set-up strategies may include: 1) placing a needed or desired item out of the individual's reach, 2) passively blocking access to a desired item, 3) intentionally giving the individual materials that are inappropriate for the context (e.g., providing a cup when it is time to put on a coat), or 4) presenting two or more options so the individual can make a choice (Haring et al., 1987). All of these strategies are meant to elicit requesting behavior of some type.

Incidental teaching, the mand-model, and the time delay procedure are meant to be used in similar but distinctly different situations. The mand-model technique is used to teach basic requesting skills to individuals who have no such behaviors in their repertoire. Incidental teaching encourages initiation and builds more sophisticated communication skills in individuals who already communicate using at least simple gestures in response to verbal cues. The time delay procedure is used to encourage initiations when the individual already has the desired behavior in his or her repertoire but does not use it unless verbally prompted. The basic elements of the three milieu teaching strategies are summarized in Figure 13.4.

*Interrupted Behavior Chains*    The interrupted behavior chain is a technique used to teach requesting in natural settings. It is based on milieu teaching and uses natural routines, or "behavior chains," as contexts for communication (Alwell, Hunt, Goetz, & Sailor, 1989; Goetz, Gee, & Sailor, 1985; Hunt & Goetz, 1988b; Hunt, Goetz, Alwell, & Sailor, 1986). Behavior chains might include putting on a coat before going outside, or washing dishes after dinner, or any other multiple-step task that is done in the same way each time. The basic strategy is very similar to the scripted routine strategy discussed previously, except that it has been used primarily to teach the use of manual or pictorial symbols rather than natural gestures. Interrupted behavior chains are particularly useful for teaching requesting to individuals who are not motivated to initiate communication. First, pre-intervention assessment probes are conducted to identify intervention variables related to success. Using this information, instruction begins by having the individual complete the initial steps in the chain. Then, the chain is interrupted in some pre-arranged manner to elicit the targeted communicative behavior.

Basic assessment and intervention steps for using interrupted behavior chains are summarized in Figure 13.5. There is ample evidence to indicate that once an individual has learned to produce the target communication response in the context of several different behavior chains, generaliza-

**Mand-Model Technique** (Halle, 1982)

1. *Provide* communication opportunities in natural contexts. For example, have favorite foods or recreational/leisure items readily available.
2. When the target individual approaches the target item(s), the facilitator *initiates* communication by asking for a request signal, for example, "What do you want?"
3. If the individual does not respond, *expand* the request and *model* desired behavior. For example, "Show me (models gesture)" or "Show me the sign" (models) or "Show me the picture" (models).
4. *Pause* and observe for response.
5. If the individual still does not respond, *provide* a second model and a physical prompt if necessary to assist imitation. For example, "Show me what you want" + *model* + *pause* + physical *prompt* if no response during pause.
6. As soon as the individual makes the desired response, provide the target item along with verbal feedback.

**Incidental Teaching** (Haring, Neetz, Lovinger, Peck, & Semmel, 1987; Peck, 1985; Warren & Kaiser, 1986)

1. *Arrange* a variety of communication opportunities in natural contexts. For example, place desired or needed items out of reach, "forget" to put silverware on the dinner table, "lose" one of the individual's shoes prior to physical education class.
2. After the target individual has approached desired items and has attempted to get them through simple gestures (e.g., pointing, reaching, vocalizing), the facilitator *approaches* and *provides* instruction to elicit a more sophisticated response. Four levels of prompts may be used (from Hart & Risley, 1975):
   a. *Natural prompt,* such as a question ("What do you want?") or receptive *adult attention,* perhaps with a questioning look.
   b. *Minimum prompt,* a nonspecific verbal direction from the facilitator, such as "You need to tell me what you want."
   c. *Medium prompt,* a request for a partial imitation. For example, the facilitator might say "You need to tell me what you want. 'Want _____,' " while pointing to the individual's hands or communication board to signal that he or she should complete the sentence.
   d. *Maximum prompt,* the facilitator asks, "What do you want? You need to tell me. Say '(label),' " and simultaneously models the manual sign or points to the appropriate communication symbol.
3. When the individual responds correctly, *confirm* the response and *provide* the desired items.

**Time Delay Procedure** (Halle, Baer, & Spradlin, 1981; Halle, Marshall, & Spradlin, 1979; Oliver & Halle, 1982; Peck, 1985)

Required:
1. *Identify* and *arrange* communication opportunities.
2. When the individual stands by, looks at, or approaches a desired item, the facilitator *approaches* the individual within 3 feet but does not vocalize.
3. *Ensure* that the individual is aware of the facilitator's presence (e.g., via body language, clearing the throat).
4. *Pause* for at least 15 seconds for individual to initiate the desired response and provide desired item when this occurs.

Optional (if the target individual does not respond after the pause)
1. *Provide* a visual prompt (e.g., gesture broadly to the cassette on the shelf, hold up coffee cup).
2. *Exaggerate* facial expression/body language (e.g., pursed lips, raised eyebrows, shoulders shrugged as if to say "I don't know what you want ").
3. *Kneel* down to be on the individual's level.
4. *Last resort: Model* desired behavior or *use* incidental teaching prompts.
5. *Provide* desired item when desired communication behavior occurs.

**Figure 13.4.** Summary of milieu teaching strategies.

tion to noninstructional settings occurs with little difficulty (Alwell et al., 1989; Hunt & Goetz, 1988b). Use of the incidental teaching and time delay strategies discussed previously can help facilitate such spontaneous requesting.

*Generalized and Explicit Requesting and Use of an Attention-Getting Signal*   Generalized requesting is accomplished when the individual uses a single, uniform symbol (e.g., "want") in different situations to initiate requesting, which is then completed by offering real-object choices. Generalized requesting requires fewer symbol discrimination skills than does explicit requesting, which requires using more than one symbol to make requests. Requests that involve use of a single, specific symbol to obtain a specific item (e.g., a picture of ice cream to get ice cream) can also be taught using the strategy for generalized requesting, by simply substituting the specific symbol for the "want" symbol.

**Selecting Routines or Behavior Chains as Contexts for Instruction (Assessment)**

1. *Identify* several behavior chains (routines) throughout the day: 1) in which the target individual can at least initiate each step (may need some help completing some steps), and 2) that are not pivotal routines in the schedule (i.e., if they are not completed, an alternate activity can be substituted).
2. *Conduct* task analyses of the chains/routines.
3. *Choose* points in each chain where interruption and subsequent communication can occur (e.g., getting ready for recess routine: before zipping coat, dishwashing routine: before getting detergent from shelf).
4. *Allow* the individual to begin the routine, then interrupt the routine before the predetermined steps by:
   a. Passively blocking the individual from taking the next step
   b. Delaying presentation of the item needed for the next step
   c. Placing a needed item out of the individual's reach
   d. Removing an item needed for the activity from view
   e. Allowing a natural interruption to occur.
5. *Rate* the level of the target individual's: *frustration* at being interrupted (1 = low, 2 = moderate, 3 = high) and *motivation* to continue the chain (1 = low, 2 = moderate, 3 = high).
6. *Repeat* steps 4 and 5 on at least 3 occasions and average the ratings obtained.
7. *Select* chains for instruction for which individual has an average *frustration score* of 1–2 and *motivation score* of 2–3.

**Basic Instructional Procedure**

1. Have picture symbols available for the target requests or have manual signs selected.
2. *Begin* the routine.
3. *Interrupt* the routine at the pre-determined points using strategies in Assessment step 4. Do not use verbal cues.
4. Trial 1:
   a. *Wait* 5–15 seconds for the individual to initiate communication.
   b. If the individual initiates, *continue* the chain (go to step 6).
   c. If the individual does not initiate, *model or physically prompt* the desired communicative behavior (e.g., touching the picture or manually signing.).
   d. *Wait* 5–15 seconds.
5. Trial 2:
   a. If the individual initiates, *continue* the chain (go to step 6).
   b. If the individual does not initiate, *discontinue* the chain and initiate alternate activity.
6. *Record* correct (+), incorrect (−), and prompted (P) responses for Trials 1 and 2.
7. If step 5b is necessary for five consecutive sessions, *discontinue* instruction for that chain.

**Figure 13.5.** Assessment and instructional procedures of interrupted behavior chains. (Adapted from Alwell, Hunt, Goetz, & Sailor, 1989; Goetz, Gee, & Sailor, 1985; Hunt & Goetz, 1988a, 1988b; Hunt, Goetz, Alwell, & Sailor, 1986.)

In order to make generalized requests spontaneously, the individual must also be able to gain the attention of his or her communication partner. Attention getting is taught as part of the generalized requesting technique, although it can be taught separately. Keogh and Reichle (1985) noted that learners initially may use the attention-getting signal frequently until the novelty wears off. They emphasized the importance of being responsive to these initiations, even if they are not followed by completion of the request sequence. Burkhart (1988) and Fishman (1987) offered other suggestions for teaching the use of an attention-getting signal. A summary of the instructional steps for teaching generalized requesting and the use of an attention-getting signal are presented in Figure 13.6.

*Verbal Prompt-Free and Expectant Delay Procedures*   Requesting through the use of aided symbols (e.g., real objects, photographs) may be taught by a verbal prompt-free strategy (Locke & Mirenda, in press; Mirenda & Dattilo, 1987; Mirenda & Santogrossi, 1985; Mirenda & Schuler, 1988). A variation of this procedure, termed "expectant time delay," was introduced to teach choice making to students with severe physical disabilities (Kozleski, 1991). These strategies are particularly appropriate for individuals who tend to be so dependent on verbal prompts to communicate that they rarely initiate requests without cuing from their partners (e.g., "What do you want?" or "You need to tell me what you want"). Verbal prompt-free and expectant delay procedures require that the facilitator refrain from using any verbal prompts from the outset of instruction to avoid the need to fade them later. Both strategies can be used in natural contexts with both children and

**Teaching Self-Selection**
1. *Provide* an assortment of potentially reinforcing items (e.g., toys, food, drinks) on a cafeteria tray.
2. *Hold tray* within the target individual's reach for 10–20 seconds and encourage him or her to select an object.
3. *Accept* the individual's reach or point, as an indicator.
4. When an item has been selected, *remove* the tray, *provide* the item, and *record* the selected item as data.
5. If no response within 10–20 seconds, remove the tray, wait, and try again.
6. Repeat steps 1–6 until step 4 occurs three times in a row.
7. Repeat over 3–4 days to determine what the individual's preferences are, and how long each practice session should last.

**Teaching Use of a Generic "Want" Symbol to Arranged Cues**
1. *Place* a "want" symbol (e.g., a Picture Communication Symbol for "want") on a large cardboard in front of the individual within reach.
2. *Offer* the cafeteria tray with various items on it and ask, "What do you want?"
3. When the individual attempts to reach for a desired item:
   a. *Note* the item for which he or she was reaching,
   b. *Slide the tray* well out of reach,
   c. Physically (not verbally) *prompt* the individual to touch the "want" symbol.
4. After the "want" symbol has been touched, *provide* the desired item.
5. Over subsequent trials, gradually *fade* the physical prompt until the individual is consistently and independently touching the "want" symbol in response to "What do you want?"
6. Practice steps 1–5 in a variety of natural contexts with a variety of items (e.g., at breakfast with food items; at the library with books, or during a grooming session with self-care items). *Do not* practice in one context only, or the individual will fail to learn that "want" can be used anytime, anyplace.

**Teaching Use of an Attention-Getting Signal To Initiate Requests**
1. Be sure the "want" symbol is readily available to the individual.
2. Identify a manual or aided attention-getting signal that will be taught. Some possibilities include: tapping a listener's arm or shoulder (manual), raising a hand until attended to (manual), ringing a bell (aided), activating a call buzzer (aided).
3. If an aided call signal is selected, be sure it is accessible to the individual.
4. Use a physical prompt to teach the individual to use the signal to get a partner's attention.
5. When the partner's attention has been gained, the partner approaches the individual and repeats steps 2–6 of Teaching Use of a Generic "Want" Symbol.
6. Be sure to fade the prompt used to teach the attention-getting signal.
7. Make the attention-getting signal available to the individual during as much of the day as possible to encourage spontaneous requests.

---

**Figure 13.6.**   Teaching generalized requesting and use of an attention-getting signal. (Adapted from Keogh & Reichle, 1985; Reichle, York, & Sigafoos, 1991.)

---

adults with severe disabilities. The basic steps for use of the verbal prompt-free strategy in natural routines (e.g., meal, recreation, grooming contexts) are summarized in Figure 13.7. Readers are referred to Kozleski (1991) for a detailed description of the expectant time delay procedure.

   ***Strategies To Teach Basic Rejecting***   The ability to reject an undesired item and terminate a nonpreferred activity or event is as important as the ability to make requests. Teaching basic rejection can be accomplished through adaptation of many of the previously mentioned strategies or can be taught in a more structured manner (Reichle et al., 1991). For example, Reichle et al. (1991) described a basic strategy for teaching communicative "leavetaking" to individuals who usually cooperate in a particular activity for a brief period of time and then try to escape or otherwise terminate the activity (e.g., by having a tantrum). First, the consistent behavioral antecedents to escaping need to be identified. For example, perhaps the person begins to whine, or acts distracted, or stops working just before he or she tries to escape. Second, a "stop" symbol needs to be available during the activity (e.g., the manual sign for "stop," or a card with a small stop sign on it attached to a cord on the person's belt loop). Third, as soon as the individual begins to exhibit the antecedent behaviors, the facilitator physically prompts him or her to produce the "stop" symbol. This is followed by an immediate cessation of the activity for a few minutes. The physical prompt is faded gradually over subsequent trials until the person produces the "stop" symbol independently. When

**Basic Procedure:**
1. *Identify* natural contexts in which multiple requests for food or leisure items are appropriate (e.g., mealtime, break time at work, or a free-choice recreational/leisure activity).
2. *Identify* a number of items (at least 2–3) that may be requested and that are motivating to the target individual in the selected contexts, and *place* them within the individual's view.
3. *Choose* aided symbols (e.g., real objects, tangible symbols, photos, or line drawings) corresponding to the items identified in step 2.
4. *Position* self next to or across from the individual at a table and *place* one of the symbols on the table within the individual's reach.
5. *Wait* for 3–5 minutes. *Do not say anything.*
6. If the individual touches the symbol *accidentally or on purpose*, immediately *acknowledge* the touch verbally and *provide* the associated item (e.g., "Oh, you touched the picture of the juice—yes, you can have some juice! Here it is!").
7. If the individual does *not* touch the symbol within 3–5 minutes, *physically prompt* him or her to do so and *provide* the item associated with the symbol. Over subsequent trials, *fade* the prompt as quickly as possible.
8. *Repeat* steps 4–7 until the individual has independently touched the symbol (i.e., without any type of prompt) 5–6 times in succession.
9. If accidental touches are still occurring, begin to *ignore* them while *continuing to respond* to deliberate touches only until the individual is consistently touching the symbol deliberately.
10. *Add* a second symbol, and continue as in step 8 while alternating the positions of the symbols.
11. Continue to *add* one symbol whenever the step 8 criterion is met.
12. Once the requesting behavior is solidly in place across a number of symbols, begin to *deny* the request occasionally when appropriate (e.g., "No, sorry, it's not time for that now, you'll have to wait.").
13. *Place* symbols in a book or wallet that is portable and make it available in appropriate natural contexts.

**Figure 13.7.** Verbal prompt-free strategy. (Adapted from Locke & Mirenda, in press; Mirenda & Dattilo, 1987; Mirenda & Santogrossi, 1985.)

this basic rejecting behavior has been firmly established, the facilitator begins to delay stopping the activity for just a few seconds (e.g., "Oh, you want to stop. Okay, let's just finish wiping this one table") and gradually for longer periods. Reichle and colleagues (1991) also discussed variations of this procedure involving use of a "safety signal."

The individual may wish to reject an offered object or activity completely. Reichle, Rogers, and Barrett (1984) taught an adolescent girl this rejection behavior, using the manual sign for "no." She was offered a variety of nonpreferred items and asked, "Want one?" Initially, she was physically prompted to produce the sign for "no," and prompts were gradually faded. Whenever she produced the sign or an approximation, the nonpreferred item was removed. Once a rejecting behavior has been learned, it is important to honor it in situations that may not be as clear-cut, such as when the individual rejects a preferred item because he or she does not wish more (e.g., rejecting a third cup of coffee when the first two were accepted). Readers are referred to Reichle et al. (1991) for additional discussion.

***Strategies To Teach Conversational Commenting*** Buzolich, King, & Barody (1991) reported the successful use of a package of milieu teaching approaches to teach conversational commenting to three severely handicapped AAC users. The intervention consisted of a time delay procedure followed by graduated prompts, which were similar to those described by Hart and Risley (1975). Specifically, the intervention used an indirect verbal (i.e., "minimum") prompt, followed by a direct verbal (i.e., "maximum") prompt, followed by a model in which the facilitator demonstrated an appropriate comment with the AAC user's system. The comments consisted of phrases such as "This is fun," "Sounds good," "Yuck!" and "I didn't like it." Instruction was provided in the context of a regular communication group that occurred daily in the students' classroom. All three students learned to produce the comments appropriately using a range of electronic communication aids, and two students generalized this ability to novel contexts. This application of milieu teaching is an important first step in exploring the use of these approaches to teach conversational skills.

## COMMUNICATION AND BEHAVIOR

Numerous authors have suggested that all behaviors, including those that are socially inappropriate, can be interpreted as communicative and treated as such (e.g., Donnellan, Mirenda, Mesaros, & Fassbender, 1984; Reichle et al., 1991). Interventions based on this concept, which Carr and Durand (1985) referred to as "differential reinforcement of communication" (DRC), generally involve teaching the use of one or more communication modes that can be used in place of so-called inappropriate behaviors to achieve the same results. The success of this approach has been documented in relation to speech (Carr & Durand, 1985), manual signs (Horner & Budd, 1985), aided communication books (Hunt et al., 1988), and simple aided devices (Horner, Sprague, O'Brien, & Heathfield, 1990).

While an extensive discussion of this issue is not possible here, a number of strategies for differential reinforcement of communication should be noted. In fact, many of the techniques discussed previously in this chapter have been used successfully to teach substitute communication behaviors. *Conversational instruction* (Hunt et al., 1988) has been used with children and adolescents who displayed a variety of socially unacceptable attention-seeking behaviors directed at nondisabled peers, such as giggling, inappropriate touching, and acting out. When they had learned to get their friends' attention by initiating and maintaining conversations, the unacceptable behaviors virtually disappeared from the students' repertoires. Reichle et al. (1991) have used the *strategies for teaching rejecting* to teach acceptable substitutes for behaviors such as running away and having tantrums. Using a combination of *milieu teaching strategies*, Horner and Budd (1985) taught manual signs for desired items to replace request-motivated grabbing and yelling, and Horner et al. (1990) taught an adolescent to ask for help during difficult tasks instead of exhibiting physical aggression toward people or objects. Similarly, at least two studies have used a number of *milieu approaches* to teach children with autism to elicit attention or to avoid nonpreferred tasks by using functionally equivalent spoken language (Carr & Durand, 1985; Durand & Carr, 1991). Children who displayed tantrums, self-injury, and aggression have been taught to *make choices* among educational tasks, resulting in a marked decrease in their unacceptable behaviors (Dyer, Dunlap, & Winterling, 1990).

> People communicate in the most effective and efficient manner available to them at any given point in time.

Three important principles are common to all of these successful interventions. First is the *principle of functional equivalence* or *response effectiveness:* The substitute communication behavior must be as effective in achieving a particular outcome as the socially unacceptable behavior. This means that a holistic and often extensive analysis of the behavior of concern must be undertaken to identify its current functions so that an appropriate alternative can be designed (see Baumgart et al., 1990; Durand, 1990; O'Neill, Horner, Albin, Storey, & Sprague, 1990; Reichle et al., 1991 for procedures in this regard). For example, if the function of the behavior is to get attention, the new behavior must produce the same result, or if the current behavior allows the individual to avoid nonpreferred events, the new behavior must also accomplish this.

Second is the *principle of efficiency:* People communicate in the most time- and energy-efficient manner available to them at any given point in time. This means that the substitute behavior must be at least as easy for the individual to produce as is the problem behavior. Horner et al. (1990) demonstrated this principle empirically by comparing the results of teaching an adolescent to ask for help during difficult tasks in ways that were less efficient than his destructive behaviors and in ways that were more efficient. The young man used only the more efficient communication skill (pushing a single key on a Canon communicator to produce a "Help, please" message) as a behavioral substitute. Quite probably, if the less efficient alternative only had been available, he would have continued the unacceptable behavior rather than exert the additional effort. Failure to understand or incorporate this principle is one of the most frequent reasons that behavioral interventions are ineffective.

> Sometimes, the best response is to listen and then make changes in the environment.

Third is the *principle of appropriate listening:* When people communicate by way of an unusual behavior, sometimes the most appropriate response is to listen to what they are saying and respond accordingly rather than trying to teach a substitute behavior. Consider, for example, a person with a severe disability who is hanging out the window of a burning building, screaming and hitting herself. Most people would agree about the function of her behavior and her message: "Get me out of here! I'm really scared and it's getting hotter all the time!" probably comes pretty close. Everyone would also agree that the appropriate response would be to listen to her message and rescue her, not to try to teach her to produce a substitute behavior for screaming and hitting, such as a manual sign for "help" or a photograph of fire! Unfortunately for many people with severe disabilities, their "burning buildings" are not usually so obvious—they appear in the form of isolated, noninteractive settings; boring, nonpreferred tasks; and rigidly structured schedules over which the individual has no control or choice (see Brown, 1991, for examples). As noted by Carr, Robinson, and Palumbo (1990) in their eloquent discussion of this issue, the appropriate response in such situations is to focus on changing the environment or the sequence of events, not the person. As we learn more and more about the relationship between behavior and communication, it becomes increasingly important to remember that opportunities for control and choice making in the context of meaningful, interactive activities and environments is a critical factor for success.

# *Selected Resources for Changing Policies and Practices that Limit Communication Opportunity*

Biklen, D. (1985). *Achieving the complete school: Strategies for effective mainstreaming.* New York: Teacher's College Press.

Browder, D. (1991). *Assessment of individuals with severe disabilities: An applied behavior approach to life skills assessment* (2nd ed.). Baltimore: Paul H. Brookes Publishing Co.

Brown, F., & Lehr, D. (Eds.). (1989). *Persons with profound disabilities: Issues and practices.* Baltimore: Paul H. Brookes Publishing Co.

Brown, L., Long, E., Udavari-Solner, A., Davis, L., VanDeventer, P., Ahlgren, C., Johnson, F., Gruenewald, L., & Jorgensen, J. (1989). The home school: Why learners with severe intellectual disabilities must attend the schools of their brothers, sisters, friends, and neighbors. *Journal of The Association of Persons With Severe Handicaps, 14,* 1–7.

Brown, L., Long, E., Udavari-Solner, A., Schwarz, P., VanDeventer, P., Ahlgren, C., Johnson, F., Gruenewald, L., & Jorgensen, J. (1989). Should learners with severe intellectual disabilities be based in regular or in special education classrooms in home schools? *Journal of The Association of Persons With Severe Handicaps, 14,* 8–12.

Falvey, M. (1989). *Community-based curriculum: Instructional strategies for students with severe handicaps* (2nd ed.). Baltimore: Paul H. Brookes Publishing Co.

Ford, A., Schnorr, R., Meyer, L., Davern, L., Black, J., & Dempsey, P. (Eds.). (1989). *The Syracuse community-referenced curriculum guide for students with moderate and severe disabilities.* Baltimore: Paul H. Brookes Publishing Co.

Fullwood, D. (1990). *Chances and choices: Making integration work.* Baltimore: Paul H. Brookes Publishing Co.

Giangreco, M.F., & Putnam, J.W. (1991). Supporting the education of learners with severe disabilities in regular education environments. In L. Meyer, C. Peck, & L. Brown (Eds.), *Critical issues in the lives of people with severe disabilities* (pp. 245–270). Baltimore: Paul H. Brookes Publishing Co.

Mount, B., & Zwernik, K. (1988). *It's never too early, it's never too late.* St. Paul, MN: Metropolitan Council, Publication No. 421-88-109.

O'Brien, J., Forest, M., Snow, J., & Hasbury, D. (1989). *Action for inclusion: How to improve schools by welcoming children with special needs into regular classrooms.* Toronto: Frontier College Press.

O'Brien, J., & Lyle, C. (1987). *Framework for accomplishment.* Decatur, GA: Responsive Systems Associates.

Orelove, F.P., & Sobsey, D. (1991). *Educating children with multiple disabilities: A transdisciplinary approach* (2nd ed.). Baltimore: Paul A. Brookes Publishing Co.

Sailor, W., Anderson, J., Halvorsen, A., Doering, K., Filler, J., & Goetz, L. (1989). *The comprehensive local school: Regular education for all students with disabilities.* Baltimore: Paul H. Brookes Publishing Co.

Schnorr, R., Ford, A., Davern, L., Park-Lee, S., & Meyer, L. (1989). *The Syracuse curriculum revision manual: A group process for developing a community-referenced curriculum guide.* Baltimore: Paul H. Brookes Publishing Co.

Stainback, W., & Stainback, S. (1985). *Integration of learners with severe handicaps into regular schools.* Reston, VA: Council for Exceptional Children.

Stainback, W., & Stainback, S. (Eds.). (1990). *Support networks for inclusive schooling: Interdependent integrated education.* Baltimore: Paul H. Brookes Publishing Co.

Vandercook, T., York, J., & Forest, M. (1989). The McGill action planning system (MAPS): A strategy for building the vision. *Journal of The Association of Persons With Severe Handicaps, 14,* 205–215.

# Selected References on Communication for Multihandicapped Individuals with Visual or Dual Sensory Impairments

>>>>>>>>>>>>>>>>>>>>>>>>>>>>>>>>>>>>>>>>>>>>>>>>>>>>>>>>>>>

Bullis, M. (Ed). (1989). *Research on the communication development of young children with deaf-blindness.* Monmouth, OR: Teaching Research (345 N. Monmouth Ave., Monmouth, OR 97361).

Bullis, M., & Fielding, G. (Eds.). (1988). *Communication development in young children with deaf-blindness: Literature review.* Monmouth, OR: Teaching Research (345 N. Monmouth Ave., Monmouth, OR 97361).

Cress, P., Mathy-Laikko, P., & Angelo, J. (1988). *Augmentative communication for children with deaf-blindness: Guidelines for decision-making.* Monmouth, OR: Teaching Research (345 N. Monmouth Ave., Monmouth, OR 97361).

Downing, J., & Eichinger, J. (1990). Instructional strategies for learners with dual sensory impairments in integrated settings. *Journal of The Association for Persons With Severe Handicaps, 15,* 98–105.

Downing, J., & Siegel-Causey, E. (1988). Enhancing the nonsymbolic communicative behavior of children with multiple impairments. *Language, Speech, and Hearing Services in Schools, 19,* 338–348.

Durand, V. M., & Kishi, G. (1987). Reducing severe behavior problems among persons with dual sensory impairments: An evaluation of a technical assistance model. *Journal of The Association for Persons With Severe Handicaps, 12,* 2–10.

Goetz, L., Guess, D., & Stremel-Campbell, K. (Eds.). (1987). *Innovative program design for individuals with dual sensory impairments.* Baltimore: Paul H. Brookes Publishing Co.

Locke, P.A., & Mirenda, P. (1988). A computer-supported communication approach for a nonspeaking child with severe visual and cognitive impairments: A case study. *Augmentative and Alternative Communication, 4,* 15–22.

Mathy-Laikko, P., Iacono, T., Ratcliff, A., Villarruel, F., Yoder, D., & Vanderheiden, G. (1989). Teaching a child with multiple disabilities to use a tactile augmentative communication device. *Augmentative and Alternative Communication, 5,* 249–256.

Murray-Branch, J., Udavari-Solner, A., & Bailey, B. (1991). Textured communication systems for individuals with severe intellectual and dual sensory impairments. *Language, Speech, and Hearing Services in Schools, 22,* 260–268.

Reichle, J., Sigafoos, J., & Piche, L. (1989). Teaching an adolescent with blindness and severe disabilities: A correspondence between requesting and selecting preferred objects. *Journal of The Association for Persons With Severe Handicaps, 14,* 75–80.

Rich, J., & Rich, E. (1988). *Play activities for young children with sensory impairments.* Monmouth, OR: Teaching Research (345 North Monmouth Ave., Monmouth, OR 97361).

Rogow, S. (1982). Rhythms and rhymes: Developing communication in very young blind and multihandicapped children. *Child Care, Health and Development, 8,* 249–260.

Rogow, S. (1983, January). Social routines and language play: Developing communication responses in developmentally delayed blind children. *Journal of Visual Impairment and Blindness,* 1–4.

Rogow, S. (1988). *Helping the visually impaired child with developmental problems.* New York: Teachers College Press.

Rowland, C. (1990). Communication in the classroom for children with dual sensory impairments: Studies of teacher and child behavior. *Augmentative and Alternative Communication, 6,* 262–274.

Schweigert, P. (1989). Use of microswitch technology to facilitate social contingency awareness as a basis for early communication skills. *Augmentative and Alternative Communication, 5,* 192–198.

# Persons with Autism

> "For as she grew, the problem of her speech took precedence over all the others. It was through speech that she must join the human race," wrote Clara Claiborne Park about her autistic daughter (1982, p. 198).

Parents, professionals, and people with autism have consistently emphasized the important role of communication in the education and treatment of persons with this syndrome. A variety of approaches have been developed in response to this emphasis, ranging from structured behavioral interventions to those that emphasize intensive play, and from those that support a particular mode of communication such as manual signing or orthography to those that are multimodal. In addition, an innovative approach, "facilitated communication," which fundamentally challenges much of the existing research base concerning the nature of autism, has been implemented internationally with apparent success.

Given the broad array of (sometimes contradictory) AAC approaches used with people with autism, we experienced considerable difficulty when making decisions about the content of this chapter. Ultimately, we decided to present a range of both traditional and novel AAC strategies. Thus, in the final section of this chapter, we have included a summary of the newest AAC approach, facilitated communication, along with guidelines for its use. The more traditional approaches include all of those that have been discussed in Chapter 10 and Chapter 13. In fact, some of the more structured approaches discussed in Chapter 13 were originally developed for use with people with autism. In addition, the information in Chapter 11 regarding educational integration is certainly relevant, as students with autism have been placed successfully in regular classrooms in many instances (e.g., Biklen, 1988; Fenwick, 1987). Many of the adapted literacy techniques discussed in Chapter 12 may be applicable to those individuals with autism who can read and/or write. In this chapter, we endeavor to supplement, rather than reiterate, the information presented in Chapters 10–13.

## COMMUNICATIVE CHARACTERISTICS OF AUTISM

Professionals in the field of autism generally agree about the social/communicative strengths and deficits typically seen in individuals with autism, although their explanations for the source of the deficits may vary. People with autism appear to be limited in both the receptive and expressive language areas as well as in nonverbal communication (Ricks & Wing, 1976). Semantic and pragmatic aspects of their speech and language are more affected than are syntax, morphology, and phonology (Tager-Flusberg, 1981). In other words, aspects of language that most concern the specifics of speech coding are the least impaired. Nonetheless, from 25% (Paluszny, 1979) to 61% (Fish, Shapiro, & Campbell, 1966) of people with autism remain essentially mute and do not spontaneously develop imitative, gestural, or other nonverbal means to communicate. Given this profile, it is not surprising that the conventional wisdom of the field maintains that the mere provision of an AAC system does not automatically solve the pervasive communication problems encountered. Basic principles of communication need to be taught along with the specifics of the particular communication technique.

Another consideration pertains to the cognitive makeup of individuals with autism. Autistic individuals have been described as operating in a "gestalt" (Prizant, 1983), referring to an inflexible mode of information processing in which stimulus input is examined in its entirety rather than in terms of its component parts. This results in visual and auditory information being stored as unanalyzed wholes to be later reproduced. For example, entire spoken phrases may be memorized and reproduced in association with a particular context, person, or emotional overtone (i.e., echolalia), since the component parts were never recognized as such and understood (Prizant & Schuler, 1987). This holistic style of processing may account for the sometimes extreme rigidity exhibited by many people with autism who are unable to tolerate changes in their routines. This insistence on sameness clearly presents a number of challenges in the communication domain as well.

The combination of social/communicative and cognitive processing impairments appears to account for many of the unusual behaviors seen in these individuals. People with autism simply do not take in, interpret, or react to environmental input in the same ways that most people do. Temple Grandin, an adult with autism who has a Ph.D. in animal science from the University of Illinois, described some of the difficulties this presented for her when she was young:

> As a child, the "people world" was often too stimulating to my senses. Ordinary days with a change in schedule or unexpected events threw me into a frenzy, but Thanksgiving or Christmas was even worse. At those times our home bulged with relatives. The clamor of many voices, the different smells— perfume, cigars, damp wool caps or gloves—people moving around at different speeds, going in different directions, the constant noise and confusion, the constant touching, were overwhelming. . . . This is not unusual for autistic children because they are over-responsive to some stimuli and under-sensitive to other stimuli. . . . [They] have to make a choice of either self-stimulating like spinning, mutilating themselves, or escape into their inner world to screen out outside stimuli. Otherwise, they become overwhelmed with many simultaneous stimuli and react with temper tantrums, screaming, or other unacceptable behavior. (Grandin & Scariano, 1986, p. 24–25)

If, indeed, many of the behavioral difficulties experienced by these individuals are related to the quality and quantity of environmental stimulation, communication may serve not as the solution itself but as a way to mediate a solution. That is, if a person with autism can communicate, he or she can enlist the assistance of others to regulate the types of input that he or she receives. Thus, communication is critical because it allows the individual to exert a measure of control over the environment. In addition, communication is the bridge to social contact, an area that is especially problematic for these individuals.

## EARLY INTERVENTION

The optimum time for instituting communication and other interventions is when the autistic child is young. Prizant and Wetherby (1988) urged the development of more comprehensive and sensitive assessment practices so that children at risk for autism can be identified before the age of 2. These authors developed the Communication and Symbolic Behavior Scales in response to this concern, and these scales can be used to identify children who are at risk for developing problems in the social/communicative areas so that early intervention can be initiated (Wetherby & Prizant, 1990). Preventive interventions should be instituted as soon as problems are suspected, even if a diagnosis of autism has not been made.

---

Early is better than late. More is better than less. Positive is better than negative. Parental involvement in natural settings is better than isolated instruction by professionals only.

---

Simeonsson, Olley, and Rosenthal (1987) reviewed the outcomes of early intervention programs for 3-to-5-year-old children with autism, and they concluded that in programs with certain characteristics, a substantial number of these children were able to achieve near-normal levels of social and intellectual functioning by kindergarten. They identified the following common features among programs that provided the most comprehensive and positive data regarding outcomes: 1) training of parents to implement the program at home; 2) implementation before the age of 5; 3) an intense approach involving many hours a day, 5–7 days per week, year-round, at home and in a program setting; 4) emphasis on generalization by using natural settings and involving parents and peers; and 5) use of positive consequences. They also noted that most of the programs for which adequate data were available used a structured behavioral approach (e.g., Hoyson, Jamieson, & Strain, 1984; Lovaas, 1987). Nevertheless, there is considerable evidence from case reports to suggest that "child-directed" approaches that share the five characteristics mentioned above may also produce favorable outcomes, and these include such diverse interventions as the Option Method (Kaufman, 1976) and therapeutic play interventions based on a psychodynamic model (DesLauriers, 1978). Regardless of the theoretical rationale or the specific techniques employed, it appears that *early, intensive, positive* approaches that include *parents and nondisabled peers* as facilitators and that emphasize communication in *natural settings* hold the most promise for creating favorable communication outcomes.

## Building a Communication Foundation

A common mistake in teaching communication skills to children with autism is neglecting to build a strong communicative foundation for these skills. Initial interventions often involve introducing a formal symbolic communication system such as manual signing or pictures, although the individual does not enjoy communicating and does not understand many basic elements, such as turn taking, joint attending, and the role of other people as facilitators. In previous chapters we have discussed a number of these important communicative building blocks derived from a normal developmental model. According to this model, early forms of communication, such as gestures and vocalizations, are gradually augmented by new forms and eventually result in an integrated multimodal system. With a developmental model as the basis, interventions to promote the use of natural gestures and vocalizations in a variety of natural contexts are a good beginning point with children who may show little evidence of intentional communication. The goal of such interventions with young children should, of course, be the development of natural speech and language. If this does not occur, however, a strong foundation for later AAC interventions will have been built.

> "The most critical component of a model language intervention program for autistic children in the 1990s that differs dramatically from traditional behavioral programs is the emphasis on successful communicative interactions" (Wetherby, 1989, pp. 22–23).

What should such a model language intervention program be for young children with autism? A number of authors have emphasized the need to adopt a child-directed interaction style, in which the communication partner follows the child's lead when he or she initiates and controls enjoyable interactions using whatever communicative means are readily available (e.g., Mirenda & Donnellan, 1986; Rydell & Mirenda, 1991; Schuler & Prizant, 1987; Wetherby, 1989). This approach is in stark contrast to the "adult-directed" approach that involves training a series of essentially rote behaviors in response to specific cues. For instance, an adult-directed intervention might require that an individual be taught to give eye contact for a specified number of seconds when told to do so, or to produce manual signs for objects or pictures in response to the question "What is this?" (e.g., Lovaas et al., 1980). Unfortunately, such practices have little to do with real communication, and the person with autism who is being taught may only learn to do as he or she is told (Howlin, 1981). To develop real communication, it is critical to start by capitalizing on behaviors that are initiated by the autistic individual and directed toward responsive communication partners who appreciate the importance of reciprocal social interactions as precursors to communication (Wetherby, 1989).

"Children learn language in dyads involving people with whom they have meaningful relationships" (Wetherby, 1989, p. 5).

The contexts for communication are another important element of a child-directed communication approach. Everyday communication occurs for most of us because of our need for social cohesion, or "social relatedness." Very little of what we say in everyday contexts is motivated by a need to affect the physical world around us; rather, we are driven by a need to achieve or regulate social closeness. It is in this area of social closeness that individuals with autism are perhaps most deficient, because their motivation for social contact is very limited. Therefore, it is precisely in this domain that initial intervention is most appropriate, particularly with individuals who do not demonstrate communicative intentionality or turn-taking skills. The initial intervention must create enjoyable contexts in which a variety of motivating activities that the individual can control are available. Again, this contrasts with an adult-directed approach in which the communication targets are selected by the instructor in advance and are taught in highly structured settings in which the individual has little control over the instructional process.

The child-directed approach is exemplified by programs such as the Environmental Language Intervention (ELI) model (MacDonald, 1985), the transactional approach (Snyder-McLean, Solomonson, McLean, & Sack, 1984), and the Hanen Early Language Parent Program (Girolametto, 1988; Girolametto, Greenberg, & Manolson, 1986; Manolson, 1985; Weitzman & Mayerovitch, 1987). Each of these programs shares a similar operational philosophy, which can be summarized as follows:

1. Observe and interpret the child's gestures, vocalizations, and other behaviors as attempts to communicate.
2. Be playful, follow the child's lead, and focus on the child's interests.
3. Respond socially and contingently so the child will learn.
4. Keep the interaction going by taking turns.
5. Prompt the child as needed in order to teach new communication forms.

This operational philosophy is realized in contexts in which communication partners make music, share books, play games, and create art together to encourage interaction and language learning. The adaptive play strategies discussed in Chapter 10 are particularly appropriate in this regard, as are the scripted routine strategies described in Chapter 10 and Chapter 13.

The basic elements of a child-directed approach are also evident in more structured approaches, such as the the the "natural language teaching" paradigm (Koegel, O'Dell, & Koegel, 1987; Koegel et al., 1989; Laski, Charlop, & Schreibman, 1988) and the TEACCH communication curriculum (Watson, 1985; Watson, Lord, Schaeffer, & Schopler, 1989). Although these approaches employ a more behavioral perspective, they incorporate child-directed principles such as: 1) providing contingent, functionally related reinforcement for children's communicative attempts; 2) taking turns and allowing children to choose tasks; 3) varying tasks to prevent frustration or boredom; 4) sharing control of interactions; and 5) teaching during naturally occurring, functional activities using relevant contextual cues. Other important elements include active parental involvement in the teaching process, careful selection of instructional targets, and interspersing familiar tasks and activities with new ones.

As noted previously, the goal of communication interventions with young children with autism is the activation of natural speech and language development processes so that AAC interventions will not be needed. If, however, early interventions were not put in place, or if sufficient speech to meet the individual's ongoing, daily communication needs does not develop as a result of early intervention, a variety of AAC options are available. There are no specific "autistic AAC interventions"; indeed, all the strategies discussed in Chapter 10–Chapter 13 may apply to individuals with autism in particular circumstances. Thus, the discussion that follows does not review these options, but some special considerations and more innovative AAC techniques are presented with reference to the material covered in previous chapters.

## ACCESS INTERVENTIONS

The unique information processing problems experienced by people with autism becomes an important issue when decisions are being made about AAC techniques. The processing of *temporal information* that is sequentially coded appears to present significant difficulties for many of these individuals, since the information presented fades over time. This is unlike *spatial information*, which is concrete, permanent, and more predictable. Communication techniques can be arranged along a temporal–spatial continuum, with spoken language at the extreme temporal end, visual–spatial symbols such as pictures or traditional orthography at the spatial end, and manual signing in the middle (Fay & Schuler, 1980). Communication through spoken words involves the production of a series of individual speech sounds that are inherently temporal (i.e., transient) in nature. The articulation of the next speech sound entails the termination of the sound that preceded it (see Schuler & Baldwin, 1981). Sign language occupies an intermediary position between temporal and spatial techniques because it involves the presentation of information that, unlike speech, is spatially configured for at least a brief period of time. Nevertheless, like speech, it is ultimately transient (i.e., the sign does not remain in space indefinitely). The dual spatial and temporal organization of manual signing may explain the long-term positive results that have been obtained with some children using a total communication approach (e.g., Creedon, 1973; Konstantareas, 1987), although such success has certainly not been universal (Howlin, 1981; Kiernan, 1983).

Visual–spatial communication techniques such as line drawings, pictures, plastic chips, and written words allow for repeated examination over time and closely match the gestalt processing style common in persons with autism. Although reports on the use of visual–spatial techniques are few compared to those that pertain to sign language, what little information exists seems encouraging. Symbols such as plastic chips (Carrier & Peak, 1975), photographs and line drawing symbols (Mirenda & Santogrossi, 1985; Reichle & Brown, 1986), and traditional orthography (Biklen, 1990; Crossley, 1990) have all been used successfully with persons with autism. In addition, Panyan (1984) noted that computerized approaches that incorporate visual–spatial symbols are compatible with autistic cognitive styles and processing preferences. In short, it seems that a multimodal approach that incorporates whatever speech and natural gestures may be present, as well as the manual signs and visual–spatial symbols that best match the individual's participation needs and cognitive processing strengths, is most likely to provide an optimal solution.

### Unaided Communication

**Applicability to Persons with Autism**   Manual signs, as part of a program of total or simultaneous communication, are probably the form of augmentative communication used most often with persons with autism, at least in North America. This popularity is due to the perception that manual signs are easier to learn than are other types of symbols, a belief for which there is only equivocal evidence (Bryen & Joyce, 1986). As noted previously, the concrete and visual–spatial nature of signs relative to speech may be advantageous for some individuals with autism who are able to process at least some sequential information (Karlan, 1990). In addition, manual signs, like gestures, have practical advantages that include portability and accessibility, which are important considerations for autistic individuals, who are largely ambulatory. Manual sign languages permit the coding of an essentially infinite number of messages, and they allow nuances of meaning to be added through accompanying body language. However, manual signs are not usually taught to persons with autism as part of a system (as with persons who are deaf) but rather as individual symbols in conjunction with speech. Other considerations relevant to the effective use of manual signs include iconicity, motoric complexity, and intelligibility, and these are discussed briefly.

*Iconicity*  As discussed in Chapter 2, iconicity refers to the degree to which the meaning of sign is guessable by naive communication partners. Few studies have examined the impact of iconicity on the learning of manual signs by persons with autism. One such study (Konstantareas, Oxman, & Webster, 1978) found that transparent (i.e., highly iconic) verb and adjective signs were learned more easily by children with autism than were less iconic signs, but signs for nouns were not similarly affected by iconicity. Generally, this is in agreement with a number of studies that have indicated that the more iconic the sign, the easier it is to learn by persons with moderate and severe intellectual disabilities (Karlan, 1990). For this reason, facilitators may find it advantageous to select individual vocabulary items from several different manual sign systems (e.g., ASL, Signed English, Makaton signs) so that highly iconic signs can be used for initial instruction.

*Motoric Complexity and Other Considerations*  Reviews of the literature on manual sign learnability (Doherty, 1985; Karlan, 1990) have indicated that the easiest signs to learn are those that: 1) require contact between the hands, 2) are symmetrical (i.e., both hands make the same shape or movement), 3) are produced within the user's visual field, 4) require a single, simple handshape, and 5) require that the same hand movement be repeated. In addition, signs taught in the same environment or time frame should be dissimilar from other signs being taught; for example, teaching the signs for both "eat" and "drink" during lunch in the school cafeteria is probably not a good idea, since these signs are both motorically and conceptually similar. Finally, and most important, manual signs selected for instruction should be motivating and functional for the user. Selecting signs for initial instruction that meet all of these requirements is a formidable task, because it appears that functionality and learnability may be at least somewhat incompatible (Luftig, 1984). Nonetheless, Musselwhite and St. Louis (1988) provided a useful matrix to make decisions about signs to be included in an initial lexicon. We have modified this matrix and present it in Table 14.1.

*Intelligibility*  The majority of American Sign Language (ASL) and Signed English signs cannot be guessed by naive individuals such as those an individual with autism might encounter on buses, in stores, recreation facilities, and in other community environments (Lloyd & Karlan, 1984). This concern was illustrated in a study of two students with autism who were taught to use both manual signs and Picture Communication Symbols (Johnson, 1981, 1985) to order food in a restaurant (Rotholz, Berkowitz, & Burberry, 1989). On the average, between 0%–25% of the manual sign requests by one student and 0% of signed requests by the other student were successfully understood by the restaurant counterperson without assistance from the students' teacher. Average successful request rates of 80%–88% and 95%–100%, respectively, were reported when PCS symbols were used in the students' communication books. This study illustrates clearly the intelligibility limitations of manual signing when it is used with untrained community members, and this suggests that multimodal systems (e.g., manual signing + a pictorial communication book) may be necessary.

**Providing Instruction**  Instructional techniques that have been used successfully to teach manual signing to persons with autism include verbal prompts, modeling, and physical guidance combined with systematic fading procedures (Karlan, 1990). These instructional techniques are usually implemented in the context of milieu teaching approaches, including the time delay, inci-

**Table 14.1.**  Decision-making matrix for selecting manual signs for initial instruction

Directions:
Using input from family and other team members plus suggested core vocabulary lists, select a vocabulary pool of at least 15–20 items for initial instruction. Rate each sign relative to the relevant features, using the following code.

Code:
Numbers in parentheses in each category indicate weightings that reflect the relative importance of the factor. For example, "user preference" has a weight of 3, compared to "contact," which has a weight of 1. This indicates that user preference is considered to be 3 times more important than contact. A plus sign (+) = that the sign meets this requirement (1 point x weighting), a slash (/) = that the sign partially meets this requirement (.5 points x weighting), a minus sign (−) = that the sign does not meet this requirement (0 points).

Example:
Tim is a 10-year-old boy with autism who loves to eat and engage in self-stimulation by dangling strings in front of his eyes. He also enjoys music, although not as much as eating and strings. He does not particularly like physical contact. Note that the signs for "more," "eat," and "string" appear to be good initial instructional targets and that "toilet" (made here with the "t" sign) is least applicable, despite its high functionality. "Music" might be introduced at a later time after other more motivating signs, and "hug" should probably be eliminated from consideration because of its low "user preference" rating.

| | Learner and conceptual factors | | | | Motoric factors | | | | | |
| Sign | (3) User preference | (2) Used freq. | (1) Iconic | (1) Contact | (1) Symmetric | (1) Visible | (1) Simple handshape | (1) Simple movement | (1) Repetitive | Total score |
|---|---|---|---|---|---|---|---|---|---|---|
| More | +++ | ++ | / | + | + | + | + | + | + | 11.5 |
| Toilet | − | + | − | − | − | + | − | + | + | 4.0 |
| Eat | +++ | ++ | + | + | − | / | + | + | + | 10.5 |
| Music | ++ | + | − | − | − | + | + | + | + | 7.0 |
| Hug | − | − | + | + | + | + | + | + | − | 6.0 |
| String | +++ | ++ | + | / | + | + | − | + | − | 9.5 |

Based on Musselwhite and St. Louis (1988).

283

dental teaching, and mand-model procedures described in Chapter 13. Specific elements of these approaches are combined in natural language teaching (Koegel et al., 1987), which has been used successfully with children with autism to facilitate the development of natural speech. Because natural language teaching can be readily adapted to include instruction in manual signs concurrent with speech, it is discussed in some detail in the following section.

*Natural Language Teaching*　Koegel et al. (1987) compared their natural language teaching paradigm with a "traditional analogue" approach to instruction. In their study, the analogue intervention was conducted as follows: The clinician presented the instruction "Say + (desired child utterance)" while displaying a target object. The clinician paused and waited for the child to respond. If the child did not respond, the clinician prompted the child by a touch to the cheek, mouth, or lips. If the child imitated a correct approximation of the target word, he or she was reinforced with praise and an edible item (e.g., a raisin).

The analogue approach was compared to a natural language approach conducted as follows: Target items were selected by the child from a pool of available items. The clinician played with the child using the selected item and modeled a target response (e.g., "ball"). If the child did not imitate the model, play continued if the child was still interested, and a second model was provided. Any clear verbal attempt to respond, even if not related to the target word, was accepted, reinforced, and shaped over time. Praise and the continued opportunity to play with the target item were provided as reinforcers.

The results of this study were quite dramatic. Two young children with autism who had received traditional analogue instruction with very poor results for 2 and 19 months, respectively, began to imitate sounds with high frequency within 1 month of beginning the natural language instruction. The children showed evidence of spontaneous speech production, both in and out of the clinical setting, within a few months of beginning the new treatment. In a second study (Laski et al., 1988), parents and siblings were taught to use the natural language approach at home, and in clinical settings with eight children with autism, similar results were obtained.

Including simultaneous manual sign instruction as a component of natural language teaching requires a simple modification of the procedure. In addition to providing speech models, facilitators simply provide manual sign models as well. Of course, the efficacy of adding manual sign stimuli to the existing speech stimuli requires exploration. The issue of simultaneous sign + speech instruction versus sign-only or speech-only instruction is reviewed in the following section.

*Simultaneous versus Single-Mode Instruction*　The majority of studies support the use of a total communication rather than a sign-only approach to facilitate communication development in persons with autism (see Karlan, 1990; Kiernan, 1983). Simultaneous communication requires that manual signs be presented at the same time as words are spoken, usually in the context of a telegraphic or key word signing approach, as discussed in Chapter 2 (see Bonvillian & Nelson, 1978; Casey, 1978; Konstantareas, 1984; Schaeffer, 1980). For example, Barrera, Lobato-Barrera, and Sulzer-Azaroff (1980) found a combined manual sign + speech intervention to be more effective in establishing production skills than either mode taught singly. Brady and Smouse (1978) showed multiple-mode intervention to be superior to single-mode intervention in establishing an initial repertoire of comprehension skills. Other investigators, however, have reported that persons with autism may be more apt to attend to the manual sign component than the speech component when these two modes are combined (Carr, Binkoff, Kologinsky, & Eddy, 1978). Further, some research has suggested that the usefulness of simultaneous instruction may depend on whether the learner has mastered generalized imitation at the point of intervention (Carr & Dores, 1981; Carr, Pridal, & Dores, 1984).

There simply are no clearcut, empirically validated guidelines to use when making decisions about when and with whom to use manual signs and speech. Thus, facilitators must make such decisions based largely on experience and logic. The available evidence suggests that manual sign instruction does not appear to *reduce* an individual's motivation to use speech; thus, this need not be a concern for people with autism or other developmental disabilities (e.g., Creedon, 1973; Fulwiler & Fouts, 1976; Schaeffer, 1980; Silverman, 1989).

## Aided Communication

*Applicability to Persons with Autism*   Both low tech aids and electronic communication devices may also be used with persons with autism, since they can accommodate the many types of aided (i.e., visual–spatial) symbols discussed in Chapter 2. For example, low tech strategies such as calendar/schedule boxes, miniboards, and communication or conversation books and wallets have proved useful to many persons with autism. In addition, portable electronic devices with high quality diphonic or digitized voice output may be appropriate for many autistic individuals who are able to use pictorial or line drawing symbols. These include devices such as the Macaw and the Parrot (Zygo Industries, Inc.) and the IntroTalker (Prentke Romich Co.), among others. Individuals with "hyperlexic" reading or spelling skills, which are not uncommon in people with autism (Goldberg, 1987), may benefit from the use of keyboard-based devices ranging from the Canon Communicator to the RealVoice or other small computers (see Hedbring, 1985). An electronic device should be considered whenever the communication needs of the person with autism or the communication partners might benefit from voice or printed output. People with autism need all the help they can get in appropriately reaching out and participating with those around them, and voice output may be one way to provide assistance.

Portability, durability, intelligibility, and rate are other considerations related to the effective use of aided communication devices (Vanderheiden & Lloyd, 1986). In addition, systematic instruction in the use of such devices in natural settings should be provided. These issues are each discussed briefly in the following sections.

*Portability*   One common characteristic of people with autism is their mobility; most have gross motor skills that allow them to run, walk, and move adeptly. Thus, communication systems for these individuals must be lightweight and portable. In Chapter 13, we discussed a number of options in this regard, including small purses, waistpacks, camera bags, and travel pouches for carrying communication aids. Other options include sewing shoulder straps onto communication books, inserting symbols into wallets or credit card holders, or using one of the available carrying cases or straps for electronic aids. From the outset of intervention, the individual should learn to take his or her communication system from environment to environment. Alternatively, stationary communication miniboards can be placed in key areas of the home, school, or work so that the individual always has access to the symbols without having to transport them.

*Durability*   The issue of durability may require special attention for some individuals with autism who engage in self-stimulatory or other behaviors that result in property damage (e.g., tearing or crumpling paper). Symbols in communication books and wallets can be kept longer if they are laminated, placed in the clear plastic pages that are available in stationery stores, placed in clear, peel-back, self-adhesive photograph album pages, or placed in pockets of the clear vinyl pages used to protect baseball cards or slides. Alternatively, plastic cubes or small picture frames may be useful for some individuals. Stationary miniboards can be laminated or coated with clear acrylic before being hung in strategic locations. While most portable electronic devices are quite durable, it is advisable to consult various manufacturers about an individual's needs before deciding to purchase a device.

*Intelligibility*   Adaptations may be necessary to enhance the intelligibility of low tech devices, particularly for unfamiliar communication partners. For example, consider an adolescent girl with autism who is just beginning to use a communication book containing photographic symbols in her favorite recreational environment, the local bowling alley. She walks up to the counter, opens her communication book, and points to a photograph of bowling shoes that has the number "6" written underneath. The clerk, not understanding what she wants, asks questions, but the young woman becomes frustrated and the interaction breaks down quickly. This unfortunate situation could have been avoided with a notation placed on the partner's side of the symbol that read "I would like a pair of size 6 shoes, please." It is important to include listener-sensitive adaptations such as this when designing communication books and other aids, both to enhance functionality and to avoid communication breakdowns. This problem is more readily solved with many of the high tech devices, which can be programmed so that an entire phrase or sentence will be "spoken" when a single symbol is activated.

*Rate Enhancement*   A common strategy for rate enhancement is to use one symbol to represent an entire thought, rather than requiring the individual to communicate word by word. For example, a picture of fried chicken can be translated for the partner via orthography or synthetic speech to mean "One chicken leg, extra crispy batter, please." The ensuing communication exchange will certainly be more efficient than if the person is required to point to separate symbols for each word or phrase (e.g., the number "1," then a picture of a chicken leg, then a symbol for "extra crispy," and then a symbol for "please"). Another rate enhancement technique for individuals with extensive vocabularies is to categorize the symbols by environment rather than by grammatical usage (e.g., nouns, verbs) (see Goossens' & Crain, 1986b; Mirenda, 1985, for examples of categorization systems). On electronic devices, the use of levels or themes will also allow categorical organization along a number of dimensions.

**Providing Instruction**   The particular learning characteristics of individuals with autism have been well documented (e.g., Koegel, Rincover, & Egel, 1982). These learning characteristics include a propensity for stimulus overselectivity, prompt dependency, and perseveration in routines, all of which result in poor generalization across responses, persons, environments, and materials (Donnellan & Mirenda, 1983). Providing instruction in the actual settings where skills are required is critically important to offset these problems.

A number of instructional strategies described in Chapter 13 have been found to be useful with persons with autism (see Mirenda & Iacono, 1988). Several authors have reported the successful use of milieu teaching strategies to teach communication skills (e.g., McGee, Krantz, Mason, & McClannahan, 1983; Peck, 1985). The interrupted behavior chain strategy (Hunt & Goetz, 1988a) can be used unobtrusively in school and community settings, and is particularly well-suited to individuals with autism because of their reliance on routines. Another useful option is the verbal prompt-free strategy, which may be useful to teach beginning use of a communication device to individuals who tend toward dependence on verbal cues (Mirenda & Dattilo, 1987; Mirenda & Santogrossi, 1985). Although the verbal prompt-free strategy requires that initial instruction be presented in structured classroom rather than community settings, generalization of the spontaneous request behavior that the technique seeks to develop is usually good (Mirenda & Santogrossi, 1985). A more structured technique was used to teach an adult with autism to use a communication book to request and label objects (Reichle & Brown, 1986). This technique also requires that initial instruction be provided in structured contexts, but the spontaneous generalization of resulting communicative behaviors appears to be satisfactory. A well-planned instructional intervention is critical for persons with autism are to use their communication devices to initiate communication.

---

"I AMN NOT A UTISTIVC OH THJE TYP" ("I am not autistic on the typewriter"), wrote Evan, a 14-year-old with autism using facilitated communication (Biklen et al., 1991, p. 171).

## Facilitated Communication

In addition to unaided and aided AAC techniques, the approach referred to as "facilitated communication" is receiving considerable attention. Crossley (1988, 1990, 1991), the originator of this approach, first used it in 1977 with Anne McDonald, a young woman with cerebral palsy, who was diagnosed as profoundly disabled and was institutionalized in Australia. The story of Anne's progress with facilitated communication and her eventual release from the institution was described in detail in *Annie's Coming Out*, which she and Crossley wrote (Crossley & McDonald, 1984). Crossley used the approach subsequently with individuals at the DEAL (Dignity, Education, and Language) Communication Center in Melbourne, Australia, many of whom were diagnosed as having autism. The approach was introduced to a North American audience with the publication of a paper by Douglas Biklen, a professor of special education at Syracuse University, who spent several months in Australia observing Crossley's work and interacting with 27 facilitated communicators with autism (Biklen, 1990). Biklen has implemented the approach in his community with children and adults with autism and, with Crossley, has reported impressive results (Biklen & Crossley, 1990). These authors report that the majority of the people with autism with whom they have used facilitated communication have demonstrated reading, writing, and spelling abilities far beyond their measured intellectual abilities. Most of these individuals, even those with apparently severe language and communication impairments, have demonstrated receptive and expressive language and conversational skills that approach their age levels. The facilitated language approach has also been used successfully with individuals with Down syndrome and other developmental disabilities in several European countries (e.g., Denmark) as well as in Australia and the United States (Crossley, 1991).

"I THINKIT IS GOOD, I THIKNING IT HELPFS ME TALZKK. I LIKE THEEN TYPEWRITER AND THE COMPUTER AND THE BORD," typed a 6-year-old facilitated communicator with autism (Biklen & Schubert, 1991, p. 51).

Facilitated communication assumes communicative competence rather than impairment. Facilitators are encouraged to expect that their communication partners with autism will be able to produce meaningful, even complex, communicative messages with the proper supports. The technique involves the use of a keyboard communication device of some type (e.g., a Canon Communicator or small portable typewriter). The individual's forearm, wrist, and, if necessary, index finger are physically supported by the facilitator. The individual is introduced to the keyboard device gradually and is initially physically prompted to touch the correct letter keys in response to simple questions (e.g., "Where is the letter 'm'?" or "Show me which letter 'dog' starts with"). Errorless teaching, including positive verbal feedback for correct responses, is provided initially so that the person experiences successful interactions. The individual is gradually asked to type more complex responses, such as spelling his or her name, answering simple questions, or completing "fill in the blank" statements. The individual is eventually encouraged to initiate typing communicative messages and to carry on conversations, with facilitation. Gradually, prompts and other supports are faded, although the physical arm, wrist, and hand support is provided as long as the individual indicates a need for it. Figure 14.1. and Figure 14.2. provide details about the attitudinal and instructional techniques of facilitated communication.

Does facilitated communication work for all or most people with autism? If so, why? Crossley and Biklen, both of whom are well respected in their fields and deeply committed to the individuals with whom they work, have reported extensive verbatim transcription data produced by facilitated communicators that is impressive in this regard. In videotaped documentation, it certainly appears

Presentation/Intention

1. Don't patronize people with nervous jokes, excessive familiarity, or babying. Be candid.

2. Be reasonably vulnerable and self-effacing (e.g., make note of your own errors, personal limitations.).

3. Be apologetic about the assessment process. Invariably it involves asking questions that are too simple for the person being queried; apologize for speaking about the person in front of him or her (e.g., when asking a speaking person something about the person who is nonspeaking).

4. Being a dynamic support means being able to suborn your own ego or, at the very least, being able to carry on a two-sided conversation rather than imposing a one-sided, dominant relationship. You have to be comfortable touching, being close to people, and supporting without taking over.

5. Don't use labels; e.g., talk about "students like so-and-so," rather than referring to people as having a particular disability.

Assumptions/Beliefs

6. Assume the person's competence. "It's far better to overestimate than underestimate a person's ability."

7. Believe communication is important; conveying this belief will help convey to the person that you see him or her as important, as your peer, as someone worthy of being "heard." Respond to what is typed as if it were spoken.

Figure 14.1.    Attitudinal dimensions of facilitated communication. (From Biklen, D. [1990]. Communication unbound: Autism and praxis. *Harvard Educational Review, 60*[3], 219–314. Copyright © 1990 by the President and Fellows of Harvard College. All rights reserved; reprinted by permission.)

that people with autism are carrying out age-appropriate, sometimes sophisticated, communicative exchanges. They explain the success of the technique in terms of a motor dysfunction (i.e., apraxia) that heretofore has been undiscovered or unappreciated in people with autism and that can be overcome through physical facilitation (see Biklen, 1990).

"IM NOT RETARDED. . . . MY MOTHER FEELS IM STUPID BECAUSE IH CAN'T USE MY VOICE PROPERLY," wrote Louis, 24, typing for the first time with facilitated communication (Biklen, 1990, p. 296).

Information concerning the efficacy or dynamics of facilitated communication is so far unavailable, aside from extensive anecdotal and transcription data and a tentative theoretical explanation. A number of important research questions, aside from those related to efficacy, remain unanswered. These include, for example: What, exactly, are the motor, emotional, and other contributions made by successful facilitators? How can facilitators be trained so that greater generalization across people occurs? We have included facilitated communication as a possible AAC option because we believe that people with autism deserve to communicate successfully, even if we are unable to understand exactly how the technique helps them do so. We have also included it in the hopes that additional information concerning efficacy will be generated by people who utilize the technique.

Physical Support

1. Attend to the person's physical location: feet on ground, typing device slanted (e.g., at 30° angle), stabilized table, nonslip pad under device and person, relaxed atmosphere).

2. Initially, and only where necessary, provide physical supports under the forearm, or above the wrist, or by helping a person isolate the index finger to facilitate use of communication aid.

*(continued)*

Figure 14.2.    Facilitated communication practices. (From Biklen, D. [1990]. Communication unbound: Autism and praxis. *Harvard Educational Review, 60*[3], 219–314. Copyright © 1990 by the President and Fellows of Harvard College. All rights reserved; reprinted by permission.)

**Figure 14.2.** *(continued)*

3. Pull back the hand or arm after each choice so that the person takes enough time to make a next selection and to avoid repeating selections.

Being Positive

4. Progress through successful choices of pictures, words, sentences, letters, name spelling, first sentence, pulling back and reminding the person of the question or request whenever an incorrect or nonsensical choice is about to be made. Use semantic common sense (e.g., "n" does not come after "w"). In other words, help the person avoid errors.

5. Provide encouragement verbally and avoid telling the person that he or she has made an error or mistake during assessment (i.e., Don't say "No," "That was wrong," or "Incorrect"). Relate to the person naturally, conversationally.

6. Be direct and firm about the tasks: the need for practice, staying on task, focusing eyes, etc. Redirect the person to the tasks (e.g., "I'm going to count to 10—1, 2, 3. . . . 10" or, "You know the house rules, work before play.").

7. Keep your eyes on both the person's eyes and on the target (e.g., letter keys). This helps you identify and prevent errors caused by hand/eye coordination problems. It also helps you monitor whether the person is attending to the task.

8. Facilitated communication often requires the facilitator to do several tasks at once, for example, carrying on a verbal conversation with the person being assisted or with others in the room, watching the person's eyes, looking at the printed output thinking of the next question or activity and at the same time keeping your mind on the present activity, and so forth, in addition to providing physical support and encouragement.

Achieving Communication/Overcoming Problems

9. Communication is a process, including support, fading, training receivers, etc. It is important to see it as a process and to recognize that people generally get better (i.e., faster and more independent) at it over time. Ongoing support increases a person's speed; thus, independence is balanced by need for speed. Encourage lots of practice; practice builds accuracy and speed!

10. If a person is not communicating, is producing nonsensical communication, or is producing questionable or wrong communication (e.g., when you doubt the communication and believe that it might be you, the facilitator, who is initiating the choices of letters and words), revert to set, structured curricula (e.g., fill in blanks, math drills).

11. Look for small differences in communication style or behavior, such as 1) radial ulnar instability—when a person's index finger swings to one side when approaching a letter, thus consistently getting a typographical error; 2) habitual, meaningless repetitions of certain letters; or, 3) the tendency to revert to familiar, echolalic words or phrases.

12. Stop stereotyped utterances by ignoring them and focusing on the task of manual communication.

13. Ignore "behavior" such as screeches, hand slapping on desk, pushing desk away, and getting up by asking, for example, "What's the next letter you want?"

Curriculum

14. Don't use teaching or communication situations to "test" the person (e.g., "Is this a cup or a dollar bill?")

15. Give the student choices of work to do.

16. Use interesting materials: cartoons to be filled in, caption-less magazine pictures, crossword puzzles, and other activities that would not offend adults, teenagers, or other age groups with whom you are working.

17. Don't start communication by focusing on the expression of feelings; wait for feelings to come. Allow the person with whom you are working to initiate feelings at his or her own choosing.

18. Get nonspeaking people working together; group sessions can be encouraging and motivating as well as interesting to people who are developing familiarity with facilitated communication. It is often helpful for facilitators (also called receivers) to work with people other than their usual partners in group sessions.

# Persons with Visual and Dual Sensory Impairments

## with Kate Franklin and Kathleen Newman

≫≫≫≫≫≫≫≫≫≫≫≫≫≫≫≫≫≫≫≫≫≫≫≫≫≫≫≫≫≫≫≫

This chapter is distinctive in two ways. First, a speech-language pathologist, who has an extensive background in visual impairments, and a public school teacher, whose specialty is also vision, collaborated with us in writing this chapter. This joint authorship ensures that the information is as current and accurate as possible, since neither author of this book is an expert in the area of vision. Second, this chapter contains more technical information than others in the book, since much of the technology used in AAC applications for persons with visual and dual sensory impairments is quite specific and, therefore, is not described elsewhere.

The chapter highlights a number of issues to be considered in the assessment and development of AAC systems for individuals with visual impairments (VI). The first section of the chapter describes the nature of some of the most common visual impairments and provides an overview of the components of vision that may affect the selection of AAC systems in general. The second section describes techniques that can be used to augment the reading and writing skills of individuals with VI who are academically competitive. The third section reviews the communication techniques available to individuals with dual sensory impairments (i.e., hearing and visual impairments) who are academically competitive. Readers are referred to Chapter 2 and Chapter 13 for information concerning people with visual or dual sensory impairments and intellectual disabilities.

## VISUAL IMPAIRMENTS

### Demographics

There are approximately 44,300 children and young adults classified as legally blind in the United States (Tuttle, 1988). The number of visually impaired students receiving educational services in the United States has increased by 1,700 each year for the past 10 years, reflecting a rise of 62% since the passage of P.L. 94-142 in the mid-1970s (Tuttle, 1988). Estimates of school-age individuals with visual impairments of sufficient magnitude to interfere with the learning process range from 1:2,000 students (Scholl, 1986a) to 2:1,000 students (National Society to Prevent Blindness, 1980). It is important to note that the vast majority of these individuals are not totally blind. It is estimated that 80% of all individuals classified as legally blind have residual vision that is sufficient for use as a primary learning channel for reading, writing, and other school activities (Barraga, 1983).

The authors wish to acknowledge a number of individuals for their cooperation in providing materials for this chapter. Very special thanks to Dale Hayes, Technology Specialist, Nebraska Services for the Visually Impaired, Lincoln, Nebraska, for the many hours he devoted to sharing his experience, information, resources, and expertise. In addition, Susan Stokes, Resource Teacher for the Visually Handicapped, Lincoln Public Schools, Lincoln, Nebraska; and William Mann, Administrator, Nebraska School for the Visually Handicapped, Nebraska City, Nebraska, provided invaluable resources and input.

The rate of VI is much higher among persons with multiple disabilities than in the general population (Brett, 1983; Schorr, 1983). Approximately 50%–60% of school-age individuals with VI have additional impairments, with physical and or intellectual disabilities occurring most often (Gates, 1985; Sadowsky, 1985). Approximately 40% of persons with cerebral palsy have concurrent visual problems, including eye muscle imbalances (e.g., strabismus), visual field cuts, visual–perceptual problems, and loss of visual acuity (Mirenda & Mathy-Laikko, 1989). In addition, research has suggested that as many as 75%–90% of individuals with severe or profound intellectual disabilities are also visually impaired (Cress et al., 1981). Finally, a small but significant number of people experience both visual and hearing impairments, and these individuals are described in the final section of this chapter.

## COMPONENTS OF THE VISUAL SYSTEM

The term *visual impairment* is used generically to refer to a wide range of visual problems (Scholl, 1986b). These visual problems can be placed on a continuum that ranges from mild interferences in the visual system to total blindness, as depicted in Figure 15.1.

Assessment of an individual's visual status involves evaluation of a number of components, including *visual acuity, visual field magnitude, oculomotor functioning, light and color sensitivity,* and *visual stability.* Each component contributes to an individual's functional vision skills. The following sections define and discuss these components of vision and their implications for the design of AAC arrays in general.

### Visual Acuity

*Visual acuity,* or the clarity of vision, allows an individual to discriminate details. Visual acuity is expressed by notations that describe the size of a visual target and the distance at which the target is identified. Fractional notation is the most commonly used notation, with the numerator indicating the testing distance and the denominator the size of the test item that can be identified on an eye chart (see Figure 15.2.).

The arbitrary designation for *normal vision* is 20/20 (Cline, Hofstetter, & Griffin, 1980). Persons with acuities of 20/70–20/200 are considered to be *partially sighted,* and those with less than 20/200 vision are labeled *legally blind.* When vision decreases to the awareness of light only, the visual level is referred to as *light perception,* and a person is considered to be *totally blind* in the absence of light perception. Visual acuities are measured close up and at a distance, and "near" vision performance and "distance" vision performance may be different depending upon the task, the person's overall abilities, and the visual condition causing the impairment. For example, an individual who is visually efficient in her use of a communication board placed 18 inches in front of

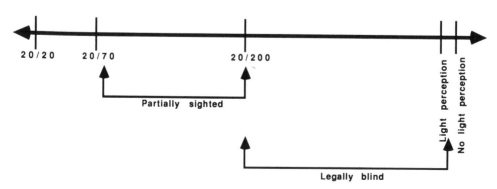

**Figure 15.1.**   Continuum depicting the range of visual impairments.

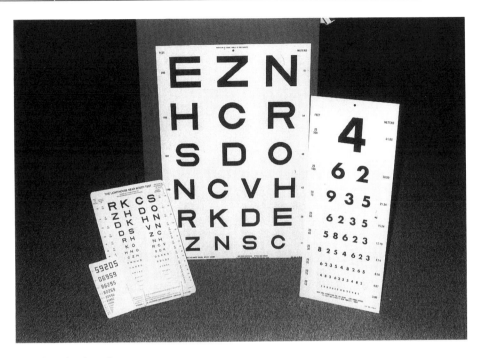

**Figure 15.2.**  Examples of eye charts.

her may be unable to see written material on a chalkboard in the front of the classroom. Visual acuity affects AAC intervention decisions concerning the type and size of symbols used in the display and the distance from the AAC user at which the display should be located.

## Visual Field

Visual field refers to the area in which objects are visible to the eye without a shift in gaze, normally extending in arcs of 150° from right to left and 120° up and down (Jose, 1983). The *central visual field* corresponds to the foveal and macular areas of the retina, which are the areas containing the cells most adapted to yield high visual acuity. Stimulation of these areas by visual impulses produces vision of the greatest clarity. Normal acuity decreases in proportion to the distance of the target from the fovea and macula. Thus, vision in the *peripheral visual field* is less clear than in the central field. The peripheral field is concerned with the detection of movement and with vision in conditions of decreased illumination (Cline et al., 1980).

There are many impairments associated with the visual field, including: 1) decreased vision in either the central or peripheral field; 2) depressed visual sensitivity in specific areas; 3) "blind spots" (also referred to as opacities or scotomas) of varying shapes and sizes; and 4) field losses that may occur subsequent to traumatic brain injury, stroke, or other causes, in which entire segments of the visual field are missing. These losses can occur in one or both eyes and are depicted in Figure 15.3.

An individual with a *central field loss* has difficulty seeing a visual target presented at the midline of the body. This person must shift his or her focus off center to bring a target into view, generally by moving the head or eye horizontally or vertically. Individuals with *peripheral field losses* tend to experience difficulties when moving, since they may be unable to detect movement or locate objects on the side or below. *Depressed sensitivity* results in areas of decreased acuity, which affect functional vision depending upon the location of the affected areas and their shape and size (Harrington, 1976). Similarly, *blind spots* or *hemispheric losses* in the visual field can create a

Central visual field loss

Peripheral visual field loss
with decreased central
sensitivity

Multiple "blind spots"
in the visual field

Loss of the left visual field

**Figure 15.3.** Examples of visual field impairments and their effects. (Picture Communication Symbols © 1981, 1985 by Mayer-Johnson Company; reprinted by permission.)

variety of problems that require adjustment of the point of visual fixation, the head position, and the placement of materials. Such adjustments are often difficult to achieve for individuals with visual impairments who use AAC, since they may experience additional physical impairments that interfere with their ability to move, maintain head control, or precisely direct their eye gaze. Careful assessment of visual field deficits is necessary in order to ensure proper placement and arrangement of communication symbols and devices for such individuals.

## Oculomotor Functioning

*Ocular motility* and coordination concern the functioning of the eye muscles that enable the eyes to move together smoothly in all directions. Specifically, these mechanisms allow the eyes to move into position and to place and maintain the image of an object on the optimum area of the retina. Oculomotor functioning includes movements that allow the eyes to establish and maintain visual fixation, locate and scan for objects, and follow moving objects.

Problems with oculomotor functioning impair an individual's ability to precisely direct his or her gaze. For example, a person with *strabismus* is unable to maintain the eyes in a position of binocular fixation because of weak eye muscles, and, thus, the eyes either converge (cross) or diverge. *Nystagmus*, another oculomotor disorder, is characterized by various involuntary movements of the eye and results in significantly reduced visual acuity. People with such oculomotor disorders often attempt to compensate for them by repositioning the eyes, head, and the materials being examined. Thus, the detection of oculomotor disorders is of particular importance when designing AAC systems for individuals with physical disabilities, since they may lack the ability to freely adjust their body positions in order to compensate for their oculomotor disorders. Decisions regarding the location of an AAC device, the configuration of a symbol array, and the spacing of items on the display are all affected by ocular motility and coordination.

## Light and Color Sensitivity

Light sensitivity must also be considered when evaluating an individual's visual status. Some disorders necessitate reduction or intensification of ambient light in order to achieve optimal visual functioning. For example, individuals with retinal problems may demonstrate abnormal sensitivity to light and require low light conditions for maximum performance. Individuals with conditions such as degenerative myopia (nearsightedness) require significantly increased levels of illumination in order to see.

In addition to various disorders affecting light sensitivity, glare is a consideration for all but the most severely visually impaired individuals. *Glare* is the dazzling sensation that is caused by bright light or the reflection of bright light that produces discomfort and interferes with optimal vision (Cline et al., 1980). Glare is a concern for all AAC users whose displays are laminated or otherwise covered by plastic, since such coverings heighten the reflection of light off the surface of the page. In addition, glare may be a problem for users of AAC devices with computer screen displays, especially those that are highly reflective. Attention to the ambient light sources used for illumination, as well as to the positioning of displays with reflective surfaces, are important in order to minimize glare. (Additional strategies for reducing computer screen glare were also discussed in Chapter 5.)

Color perception, which occurs when certain eye structures are stimulated by specific wavelengths of light, may be impaired in ways that affect accurate visual discrimination of contrast and detail. Generally, deficits occur in the ability of the eyes to interpret particular, but not all, wavelength frequencies, so that total color blindness is quite rare.

> The most common color impairment, which occurs in approximately 8% of males and 0.4% of females, involves confusion of red and green frequency wavelengths (Vaughan & Asbury, 1980).

People can be trained to accommodate color problems, but such problems may be difficult to identify in very young children or in those who have difficulty labeling or matching. Nonetheless, accurate identification of color deficits is important to ensure that functional implications are minimized. Colors used on AAC displays for organizational or coding purposes must be discriminable and helpful to the user. For example, color codes using the frequencies involved in an individual's particular color deficit may only serve to reduce communication accuracy and frustrate the AAC user.

## Visual Stability

Some individuals have eye conditions that are stable and relatively unchanging over time. Other individuals have conditions that fluctuate, sometimes daily, depending on their physical status or on environmental factors. Additionally, some conditions deteriorate over time, with variability in both the rate of deterioration and the final visual outcome. For example, individuals with *retinitis pigmentosa* (a progressive genetic visual impairment) experience a gradual reduction in the size of the visual field, along with night blindness, abnormal sensitivity to light, and color deficits. They may retain some vision throughout life, or they may eventually lose most or all vision. Since the condition is progressive and unpredictable, and since it cannot be treated at this time, these individuals must consider their current and potential visual status when making long-term decisions.

## Visual Impairment versus Visual Disability

Discussion thus far has centered on *visual impairments,* or identifiable defects in the basic functions of the eye or parts of the visual system (Sigelman, Vengroff, & Spanhel, 1984). The functional limitations that may result from these impairments are referred to as *visual disabilities*. Thus, a visual impairment is the physical aspect of vision loss, while the visual disability is the functional aspect or how the impairment actually affects an individual's life-style. Visual disabilities are quite variable and are determined by the type and extent of the impairment as well as by an individual's response to it. Thus, all visual impairments do not necessarily result in disability, and, in fact, the same impairment may result in different outcomes in different people, depending on how they compensate and on the visual demands of their life-styles. For example, consider two individuals with the same eye condition that results in identical visual acuities of 20/200 (legally blind). One person lives a normal life: She use adaptations to perform certain tasks, but continues to work, raise a family, and generally function adequately in society. Her counterpart functions much less independently, perceiving himself to be unable to perform even the most basic tasks, including those necessary for employment. The major difference between these two individuals is in their attitudes toward their impairments, not in the impairments themselves.

Such differences in performance are illustrative of the complexity of vision. Vision is a three-stage system that involves *sight*, which is the reception of sensory stimulation through the eye, the *transmission* of an image along the optic nerve, and the *interpretation* of the image in the visual cortex of the brain. It is during interpretation that images are transformed into meaningful information. The interpretation of the image is a result of all that an individual brings to the task, including motivation, experience, and self-image, which are the tools of functional vision.

---

People learn how to interpret information throughout life; thus, vision is a learned behavior that can be taught (Watson, Newman, & Neitzel, 1988).

---

How an individual actually uses and enhances his or her existing vision through various means is at least as important from a functional perspective as is the nature or severity of the visual impairment itself. This certainly applies to AAC system considerations, since it is not only important to consider the individual's impairment but also the AAC user's perceptions of his or her visual abilities and disabilities.

## AUGMENTED READING AND WRITING TECHNIQUES

Specialized reading techniques can be employed by individuals who are academically competitive and who experience various degrees of visual impairment. Specialized reading techniques include large-print text, braille text, low vision devices, computers, optical character recognition devices, speech systems, or some combination of these. The expressive communication and writing systems used by these individuals may include braille, typewriting, handwriting, audiorecordings, and computers. Individual preferences for particular techniques generally depend on a variety of factors, including the person's visual status and functional needs as well as the subject matter. The sections that follow review available systems for reading and writing used by literate persons with varying degrees and types of visual disabilities.

### Augmented Reading

***Regular Print***    Regular print may be a viable reading mode for individuals with less severe visual impairments. Regular print should be of high quality and good contrast in order to be maximally useful. Ability to read regular-print text may be limited if high quality materials are unavailable, or if visual fatigue (i.e., the effort required to perform the task) is a factor. Nonetheless, the ability to read regular print on even a limited basis may be advantageous so that an individual can read his or her mail, brief written messages, price tags, menus, and labels.

***Large Print*** Large print may be an option when individuals with VI cannot read regular print. Large print may be appropriate for individuals who need orthographic symbols enlarged in order to see them clearly, either when close or at a distance. Large-print texts are, however, cumbersome, expensive, and often not readily available. Some of the factors to consider about the usefulness of large print include "reading accuracy and rates, comprehension, reading comfort, and the fatigue factor for varying lengths and types of materials" (Heinze, 1986, p. 310).

***Braille*** Braille is the most widely used means of reading and writing for individuals with severe visual disabilities (Heinze, 1986). A general overview of braille as a symbol system was provided in Chapter 2, and readers are referred to that chapter for this information.

One of the primary advantages of braille is that it is the only medium in which individuals with severe visual disabilities can both write and read (Nolan, 1979). In addition, braille offers a method for learning spelling and punctuation, and it provides individuals with the ability to review their work and take notes independently. Disadvantages are that braille is expensive, bulky, time consuming to read and write, and requires good mechanical skills for mastery (Mack, 1984). Average reading rates with braille are much slower than with print.

---

"Braille . . . will most probably remain the major means of communication for individuals who are seriously visually impaired" (Olson, 1981, p. 7).

---

***Low Vision Devices*** Technology and optics are rapidly improving in the field of low vision. As a result, high quality and reasonably priced devices are now available to consumers. Low vision aids include nonoptical, optical, and electronic or projection aids that augment a person's ability to read various sizes of print. Some examples of these aids are shown in Figure 15.4.

Filters, reading stands, lamps, visors, guides, and special pens are among the available *nonoptical* low vision aids. *Optical devices* include magnifiers, telescopes, and telemicroscopes that aug-

**Figure 15.4.** Examples of optical and nonoptical low vision aids.

ment the user's vision at near, intermediate, or far distances. These can be hand-held, worn on the head, or placed on a stand. *Electronic* or *projection aids* use high magnification to enlarge print and enhance figure–ground contrast. Commonly referred to as closed circuit television systems (CCTV), these systems are large, heavy, and expensive. Nevertheless, CCTV can: 1) serve as reading or writing systems, 2) be adapted for use with typewriters and computers, 3) enhance many activities of daily living, and 4) "in some cases, [serve as] a viable alternative to braille as the primary mode of reading" (Miller-Wood, Efron, & Wood, 1990, p. 559). In addition, portable electronic magnifying systems that use hand-held cameras to detect print images and enlarge these images on a screen are also available. Most of the electronic systems can be readily interfaced with computers, and the MEVA (Miniaturized Electronic Visual Aid, TeleSensory Systems, Inc.) is an example of this technology.

Low vision devices are not a quick, easy remedy for visual impairments. Low vision devices, unlike regular prescription glasses, do not improve overall vision. Some are *limited-access devices* that enable individuals to read printed materials under specific conditions but do not improve their vision in all circumstances. The user of low vision aids is frequently in a "win some, lose some" situation in which trade-offs are inevitable. For example, a person who uses a telescope for enhanced distance vision loses his or her field of vision outside the telescope. An individual using a low power magnifier to read must move in closer to the printed text. If a high power magnifier is used, the focal distance is even closer and the area of visual clarity may be decreased. Certainly, low vision devices offer significant functional options for persons with VI. Nevertheless, they require realistic and functional goals related to their use, careful prescription, and follow-up in order to be maximally useful.

**Computers**   Computer technology allows individuals with VI to read computer screens via image enlarging systems consisting of specialized hardware, software, or both. Hardware can facilitate variable magnification and cursor tracking capabilities. One example is the IBM-compatible VISTA system, which can magnify computer screen information as much as 16 times its original size (TeleSensory Systems, Inc.). Software capabilities include text and graphic magnification and the ability to add windows, such as in the IBM-compatible LP-DOS program (Mark Christensen, Inc.). Large-text typing and editing capabilities are also available in word processing programs, such as Eye Relief for IBM-compatibles (Ski Soft Publishing Corporation) or inLarge (Berkeley Systems, Inc.), a Macintosh-based software program. Figure 15.5. illustrates a large-text typing display using Eye Relief software.

**Optical Character Recognition**   Optical character recognition (OCR) systems "translate printed material into an electronic format that can be stored and accessed via a computer monitor, a printer, or an adapted device like a speech synthesizer or braille display" (Converso & Hocek, 1990). Such systems incorporate: 1) a computer, which controls the system; 2) a scanner, which collects images from a printed page for transfer to the computer; 3) the OCR itself, which translates images into text characters; and 4) an output device, which permits the reader to read the information. The output may be in the form of print on a computer screen or on paper, in braille, or as synthetic speech (Converso & Hocek, 1990). Synthetic speech OCRs are discussed in a subsequent section, and other types of OCRs are reviewed briefly here.

One of the oldest and most widely known OCR systems is the Optacon (optical-to-tactual-converter), which was introduced in the 1970s (TeleSensory Systems Inc.). The Optacon provides output by converting the visual images on a printed page into tactile configurations via raised vibrating pins. While slow, inflexible, and limited in terms of the variety of printed information it can process, the Optacon provides accessibility to otherwise unavailable printed information. The Optacon can be used with typewriters, computers, and calculators, for example (Todd, 1986).

Another popular OCR system is OsCaR (TeleSensory Systems Inc.). OsCaR scans and converts print documents that can be read, modified, or saved on IBM-compatible computers. OsCaR

**Figure 15.5.** A large-text computer display using Eye Relief software.

is designed to be used with the manufacturer's large print, synthetic speech, electronic braille, or hard-copy braille output devices to display scanned information for reading (Focus on Technology, 1990–1991).

> TeleSensory Systems, Inc. is devoted exclusively to high technology equipment for persons with visual impairments.

### Speech Systems

*Aural Reading* Individuals who cannot efficiently read printed text may supplement reading with *aural reading* or "auding." This is "the process of hearing, listening, recognizing, and interpreting previously recorded language" (Swallow & Conner, 1982, p. 120). Successful auding depends on the individual's ability to process auditory and linguistic information efficiently and accurately. The individual must be able to grasp the main idea and details, remember and follow spoken sequences, and understand spoken word meanings (Swallow & Conner, 1982). These skills can and should be taught to individuals for whom auding may be a viable alternative to reading.

> Information about Talking Books and other resources can be obtained in the U.S. from the National Library Service for the Blind and Physically Handicapped.

In addition to the most common formats for auding, which are homemade tapes and Talking Books (National Library Service for the Blind and Physically Handicapped), compressed speech may be useful to some individuals with VI. Speech compressors (American Printing House for the Blind) enable control of the speed of audio output by deleting and shortening sounds. With compressed speech, "intelligibility is preserved, tonal quality is not adversely affected, and listening time for the same material is reduced" (Todd, 1986, p. 290).

There are also machines that allow listeners to hear recorded speech at increased speeds. However, as the output speed increases, the quality of the speech decreases, which makes accelerated speech less intelligible than regular or compressed speech.

*Synthetic Speech*    Aural readers have traditionally depended on human assistants or human-voice recordings for output. Computer technology has expanded the options to include digitized and synthesized speech output that can be used with adaptive software programs or with OCR devices.

Synthesized speech output usually requires a speech synthesizer card installed in the computer and a "screen reading" software program that allows the user to review displayed material and select desired information rather than listening to all of the text (Gage & Breda, 1986). One example of available software is Flipper (Omnichron), which can be used with a variety of speech synthesizers installed in IBM-compatible computers. Flipper allows selective voicing of portions of the screen, discovery of visual clues that communicate program features, and review of onscreen materials without affecting the operation of the software. (Raised Dot Computing, 1991).

Most speech synthesizers used with screen reading software are compatible with either Apple or IBM computers, and some are limited to use with a particular software program while others are more flexible. For example, the Accent PC synthesizer (Henter Joyce, Inc.) works with Job Access with Speech (JAWS) software (AICOM Corporation) in IBM-compatible computers.

---

"The 'Speaqualizer' is considered by many to be the 'Swiss army knife' of speech synthesizers" (D. Hayes, personal communication, February 22, 1991).

---

The Speaqualizer (American Printing House for the Blind) is IBM-compatible, as are the Symphonic 210 (Artic Technologies) and Vert Plus synthesizers (TeleSensory Systems, Inc.). Apple computer users often use the Slotbuster II synthesizer (RC Systems, Inc.), which operates with Appleworks software, or the Echo Commander (American Printing House for the Blind), a complete speech synthesis system for Apple IIe and Apple IIgs.

A "reading machine" is an optical character recognition device that provides synthetic speech output for persons with VI. The reading machine gives the user control of the speed and flow of the speech output and permits immediate repetition of a word or phrase, unlike a traditional OCR. The best known reading machines are the Xerox/Kurzweil Personal Reader (Xerox/Kurzweil Computer Products) and the Arkenstone Reader (Arkenstone, Inc.). The Xerox/Kurzweil is a portable optical scanner that reads typeset or typewritten text and outputs it as synthetic speech. This intelligent character recognition (ICR) system "is able to examine and analyze thousands of typefaces and styles and accurately convert the images into readable text" (Dixon & Mandelbaum, 1990, p. 495). It weighs less than 20 pounds and is available with hand and automatic scanner systems. The Xerox/Kurzweil can scan an 8½ inch by 11 inch page of printed text in 60–90 seconds and convert it to high-quality DECtalk speech (Digital Equipment Corporation). The Xerox/Kurzweil Personal Reader can automatically scan printed text and transmit it to other computer devices for storage and retrieval. This reading machine is compatible with a variety of word processing, communications, screen review, and braille conversion software programs.

---

The Xerox/Kurzweil Personal Reader is available through Xerox/Kurzweil Computer Products.

---

The Arkenstone Reader is a document scanner and an add-on character recognition board for IBM-compatible computers. The Arkenstone Reader must be combined with a personal computer and voice synthesizer to be used as a complete reading system. The Arkenstone Reader can translate almost any kind of book, magazine article, personal bill, or other printed document into synthetic speech output.

> It is important to keep in mind that reading machines represent a high tech option for aural reading. The availability of this technology *does not preclude* the importance of improving low tech (i.e., human voice) aural reading skills.

## Augmented Writing

Persons with VI have a variety of options for writing. These include machine- or hand-embossed braille, computerized braille, typesetting, and handwriting. These will be discussed in the sections that follow.

### Braille

*Noncomputerized Braille Production*    Braille serves as both a reading and a writing system for many individuals with VI who are literate. Written braille may be produced through a variety of methods. The most efficient method is to emboss braille characters using a "brailler," a device that resembles and serves the same function as a typewriter. The Perkins brailler was developed in 1950 at Howe Press on the campus of the Perkins School for the Blind, Watertown, Massachusetts. This machine produces embossed braille characters when combinations of keys, one for each braille dot, are pressed simultaneously. Also known as the Braillewriter (Roberts, 1986), this machine is more efficient than hand embossing with a slate and stylus (described below), requires fewer fine motor skills, and allows users to read their work as it is produced.

As mentioned, a slate and stylus may also be used to produce braille characters. This small (pocket-size) device is lighter, quieter, less expensive, and more portable than the Braillewriter, but it is also considerably more difficult to use. The technique requires the writer to have excellent fine motor skills, as well as the ability to write braille code backwards. With a slate and stylus, braille dots are pressed into place from the back of the paper, so, they must be embossed in reverse from right to left so that they are configured correctly when the paper is read. Figure 15.6. shows a brailler and a slate and stylus.

*High Tech Braille Production*    The computer is an extremely valuable option for writing. Appropriately referred to as a "forgiving typewriter" (Lauer, 1988), the computer allows information to be entered, corrected, and changed quickly and neatly. Computers also provide access to a wide variety of information sources as well as a way to produce multimedia output (i.e., print, synthetic speech, braille). For example, BEX (Raised Dot Computing) is an Apple-compatible word processing software program that translates print to braille and allows text preparation, editing, proofreading, and output in several modalities. Numerous other software programs that can be used by persons with VI for writing are also available (Berliss et al., 1989).

Computer technology provides an alternative to the brailler and slate/stylus techniques for braille production. For example, the VersaPoint-40 braille printer (TeleSensory Systems, Inc.) produces high quality braille documents with very sharp, high-contrast dots. The VersaPoint-40 braille printer can store up to 30,000 characters, offers bidirectional line print that produces a full line of braille at 40 characters per second, and can be used with both Apple and IBM-compatible computers.

> The VersaPoint-40 braille printer includes seven international computer braille translators that can produce English, French-Canadian, British, French, German, Swedish, and Spanish braille languages.

**Figure 15.6.**   A brailler and a slate and stylus for writing braille.

The Ohtsuki BT-5000 printer (American Thermoform), which is also Apple- and IBM-compatible, can output in braille, inkprint, or braille with an inkprint line below. Heavy-duty braille embossers that produce braille books and multiple-copy documents are faster than personal printers but are also much more expensive. Examples include the Thiel Printer (Blazie Engineering, Inc.) and the braille BookMaker Printer (Enabling Technologies Co.).

Additional writing innovations include numerous computerized paperless braille devices that store braille on audio cassettes or diskettes and that can be used with calculators, typewriters, and computers. Computerized paperless braille devices present output on the surface of the machine in a tactile array that changes as pins corresponding to braille dot configurations are raised and lowered at the touch of a button. This is referred to as a "refreshable" braille display. One example, the Braille N' Speak (Blazie Engineering, Inc.), is a pocket-size talking computer notetaker for persons with VI. It is easy to use to produce braille text, and the device incorporates a talking calculator, clock, and calendar and can be interfaced with Apple and IBM-compatible computers. The VersaBraille II (TeleSensory Systems, Inc.) is a portable, battery-operated system that allows the user to send and receive braille messages. The Versa Braille II features a refreshable braille display, a braille keyboard for sending messages, and complete word processing capabilities and can be connected to IBM-compatible computers as well as to printers, modems, and other peripherals. Braille-n-Print (Humanware, Inc.) produces both braille and print copies of documents created on a standard Perkins brailler. The Braille-n-Print snaps onto the bottom of the Perkins brailler and uses a buffer to send information to a serial or parallel port for conversion into print and braille output. BrailleMate (TeleSensory Systems, Inc.) is a hand-held, 1-pound device with a built-in speech synthesizer that organizes, stores, and retrieves information. BrailleMate allows the user to input either Grade 1 or 2 braille (see chap. 2, this volume), which is automatically converted to standard orthography and produced in either spoken or printed form.

*Typewriting*   The ability to produce typewritten materials expands an individual's expressive communication options, vocational options, and overall opportunities for independence. Touch typing on a standard keyboard is the most straightforward technique for written communication with the sighted world in school, at home, at work, and in other community settings. Not only does typing afford a means of expressive communication, it also encourages improved spelling and reading skills (Heinze, 1986).

Children with congenital or early onset vision losses that require the use of augmented writing should begin to learn touch typing skills as soon as they demonstrate the language and fine motor skills necessary to perform the task. These children will also need to learn to use one or more adapted methods for proofreading their products. The adapted methods for proofreading their typed products include the reading adaptations mentioned previously, such as low vision aids, electronic aids (i.e., CCTV), or some type of OCR device. Of course, live readers can also be used, but reliance on readers as the sole technique for proofreading is not advisable. (Simple software that can be used to teach keyboarding skills was reviewed in chap. 10 and chap. 12, this volume.)

*Handwriting*   Handwriting is an expressive communication skill that may be undervalued for persons with VI. Legible handwriting—especially the ability to sign one's name on legal documents, notes, and checks—is an important independent skill. Some individuals with good manual dexterity and partial sight may wish to learn more than basic handwriting so that they can take notes, write letters, or perform other brief personal or vocational writing activities.

A variety of aids are available to facilitate handwriting skills for persons with VI. These include special writing papers with raised or bold lines, varying contrast lines, and enlarged line spacing; specialized writing implements such as broad- and fine-tip markers and pens and pencils of various colors; and specialized materials to teach printed and cursive letter forms. Many of these handwriting aids provide tactile as well as visual feedback during the writing process.

---

[Here] is my list of lists: Long-term projects and obligations . . . daily tasks, projects, and obligations; spring cleaning tasks; items to be taken on overnight outings and trips . . . personal care schedule; phone numbers; books on loan from the National Library Service for the Blind and Physically Handicapped and from Recordings for the Blind, Inc.; two lists of physical therapy exercises; names and phone numbers of friends and former clients; names and addresses of out-of-town friends and family; calendar; medical and surgical supplies that must be stocked; and fears and questions I have concerning life with a progressive disease. Some of my lists are on large sheets of braille paper, other are in a loose-leaf binder. All are on cassette tapes. (Denise Karuth, a young woman who is blind as a result of multiple sclerosis, 1985, p. 27)

---

*Audio Recordings*   Recorded speech is another expressive communication option for persons with VI, although it not an augmented writing system per se. The student who records class notes or homework assignments on tape, the parent who maintains a recorded shopping list that is added to by other family members, and the employer who uses a Dictaphone to exchange brief messages with his or her secretary are all examples of individuals with VI who use recorded speech as a functional alternative to writing.

---

The Braille TeleCaption System uses the National Captioning Institute's broadcast signal to make television available in braille or large print (Biederman-Anderson, 1989).

---

## Summary

Persons with severe visual impairments have many options available to facilitate access to written communication. As with most AAC endeavors, the major challenge is to choose the options that are most appropriate to an individual's needs and abilities. Speed, accuracy, efficiency, opportunities for practice, fatigue, visual status, and prognosis are some factors that should be considered when choosing a reading and writing mode (McMillen & Kellis, 1982). When evaluating potential equipment, considerations such as ease of use, reliability, cost effectiveness, and individual preferences are paramount (D. Hayes, personal communication, March 1, 1991).

> Individuals with VI should not limited to a single reading or writing mode. Instead, they should be encouraged to become proficient in the use of a variety of media so that they have accurate and efficient access to literacy techniques across environments.

## DUAL SENSORY IMPAIRMENTS

### Demographics

Precise figures concerning people with dual sensory impairments (DSI) are difficult to obtain because of geographic variations in identification criteria, educational placements, and sampling procedures. Sims-Tucker and Jensema (1984) estimated that there are approximately 6,000 individuals with some degree of both hearing and visual impairments in the United States, approximately 75% of whom are also intellectually and/or physically disabled (Jensema, 1979). The number of public school students (birth–21) with dual sensory impairments in the United States is quite small and estimated at approximately 4,200 in 1986 (Fredericks & Baldwin, 1987). These authors also noted that approximately 94% of these 4,200 individuals have some residual hearing and/or vision, but their disabilities are such that the development of social/communicative interaction skills is seriously hindered.

> The vast majority of students with dual sensory impairments continue to be served educationally in residential schools, and in segregated classrooms for students with multihandicaps (Bullis & Otos, 1988).

The major causes of DSI among individuals below the age of 20 in North America include congenital rubella and Usher's syndrome. Rubella, also referred to as German measles, is a disease that causes severe damage to the eyes, ears, heart, and central nervous system of a developing fetus if contracted by the mother during the first trimester of pregnancy (Ward, 1986). A rubella epidemic in North America in the early 1960s resulted in the birth of many infants with DSI. This sudden increase in the number of children requiring specialized educational services was the impetus for the development in North America of many of the programs and services for this population.

Usher's syndrome is a genetic condition characterized by hearing loss and progressive visual loss from retinitis pigmentosa (Vernon, 1969). Usher's syndrome accounts for more than one half of the population of people with DSI in the United States (Davenport, O'Nuallain, Omen, & Wilken, 1978). Although most individuals with Usher's syndrome have profound hearing and visual losses, some individuals have less severe impairments in one or both areas (Boughman, Vernon, & Shaver, 1983; Brown, 1987). Hearing loss is typically present at birth and is often detected quite early, while night blindness, which is generally detected within the first 10 years of life, is typically the first symptom of retinitis pigmentosa. The visual symptoms usually increase during adolescence to include tunnel vision, decreased visual acuity, cataracts, photophobia, and problems with glare (Vernon, 1969).

In addition to rubella and Usher's syndrome, which are congenital disorders, vision and hearing losses may also occur through other disease processes or injuries. Helen Keller, who lost both her hearing and vision at a young age as a result of a brain infection, is perhaps the best known example of a person with acquired deafness and blindness. In addition, the secondary loss of hearing or vision by someone with a primary impairment in one of these areas may also occur. For example, a person with a hearing impairment may lose vision later in life as a result of an injury, infection, tumor, or cataract. Or, a child with retrolental fibroplasia, a severe visual impairment caused by prolonged use of highly concentrated oxygen with newborns, may experience decreased hearing due to frequent middle ear infections or a ruptured eardrum. When such *adventitious* (i.e., acquired) sensory losses occur, their impact greatly depends on the individual's age; his or her existing language, literacy, and motor abilities; and the rapidity of onset of the secondary impairment.

> The Association for Persons with Severe Handicaps (TASH) provides technical assistance to states, service providers, and parents of children with DSI from birth to 21. The Helen Keller National Center (HKNC) provides such assistance to people over age 22.

## Communication Options

Persons with DSI who are at the greatest risk of failure to develop adequate communication skills are individuals whose hearing and visual losses are congenital or were acquired at very young ages. Individuals who fit this profile generally have limited functional vision and hearing abilities that result in severely delayed cognitive development. (AAC techniques and strategies for persons with DSI and intellectual disabilities were discussed in chap. 10 and chap. 13, this volume, and are not repeated here.)

People whose visual and hearing losses develop after the age of 3 or 4—those with adventitious losses in one or both areas—are able to draw on a wealth of acquired visual and auditory experiences and information during the learning process. These experiences significantly enhance the cognitive, social, and communication development of these individuals with DSI and greatly increase the range of AAC options that may be useful to them. Many of the techniques described previously for persons with visual impairments can be used by individuals with noncongenital DSI, with modifications to meet their particular needs. For example, many speech output techniques (e.g., auding, synthetic speech) may be appropriate for persons with DSI who have adequate residual hearing or who use amplifiers or hearing aids to enhance sound. In addition, unaided and aided communication options have been developed specifically for individuals with various degrees of DSI. The following sections review some of these methods.

### Unaided Systems

*Oral Communication/Tadoma* Individuals who have minimal or no functional use of either visual or auditory modalities may use the Tadoma method to tactilely read the speech of others. With this technique, the person with DSI places his or her hand on the speaker's face. The thumb covers the speaker's mouth to feel movements of the lips, jaw, and tongue. The other four fingers are spread over the cheek, jaw, and throat to detect vibrations (Jensema, 1982; Mathy-Laikko, Ratcliff, Villarruel, & Yoder, 1987). Vanderheiden and Lloyd (1986) noted that this and other vibrotactile techniques are relatively easy to learn by persons who are not otherwise physically impaired.

*Gestures and Manual Signs* A variety of gestural and manual sign systems were discussed in detail in Chapter 2. People with acquired DSI generally have little difficulty producing symbolic gestures, since many of these are learned during the first years of life. Manual signs are most often used by persons with DSI who are congenitally hearing impaired and who lost their vision later in life (Jensema, 1982). Persons with DSI perceive the gestures or manual signs of their communication partners through residual vision or via direct hand-to-hand contact.

*Fingerspelling*     Fingerspelling is a mode of communication that uses handshapes to represent the letters of the alphabet. This one-handed manual alphabet is a form of tactile communication widely used by persons with DSI who are literate. Information is transmitted in fingerspelling by placing the hand of the information receiver over the hand of the individual formulating the letters (Jensema, 1982; Mathy-Laikko et al., 1987; Musselwhite & St. Louis, 1988). People with DSI who use fingerspelling can communicate directly only with partners who can read and transmit fingerspelled messages at a reasonably rapid rate.

*Morse Code*     Individuals with DSI can transmit messages using Morse code in a number of ways, including hand or finger taps to any part of a receiver's body or eye blinks. Similarly, they can receive Morse code messages via tactile input to any parts of their bodies and through the use of variable vibratory patterns (Jensema, 1982; Mathy-Laikko et al., 1987).

*Cross Code*     Cross code is a signal system that was developed by a man with DSI in order to communicate with his family. Cross code can be used to both transmit and receive messages. The message sender taps the back of the partner's hand or other designated body part in positions that represent specific letters of the alphabet (Jensema, 1982; Mathy-Laikko et al., 1987).

*Braille Hand Speech*     Braille hand speech enables an individual to send information to or receive information from a skilled communication partner. In this method, a sender positions the initial, middle, and ring fingers of both hands in a configuration that represents the six dots of the braille cell. Messages are transmitted tactilely by moving the fingertips against the receiver's hand or arm to send manual braille characters. Clearly, this method requires that the communication partner know braille (Jensema, 1982; Mathy-Laikko et al., 1987).

*Palm Writing*     In palm writing, the message sender spells out messages by using his or her index finger to draw the letters of the alphabet in the palm of the message receiver's hand. This method is most commonly used by persons who lost their vision after learning to read (Jensema, 1982; Mathy-Laikko et al., 1987).

*Glove Method*     In the glove method, the individual with DSI wears a thin white cotton glove that has the letters of the alphabet printed on the tips of the fingers, the joints, and the palm of the hand; and the numbers 1–10 printed on the fingernails and the knuckles. The communication partner touches the letters or numbers in order to spell out a message for the user (Jensema, 1982). This method is primarily used by people with DSI to receive, not to transmit, information.

*Cued Speech*     Cued speech is a system of eight handshapes that represent groups of consonant sounds and four positions around the face that represent groups of vowel sounds. Combinations of these hand configurations show the exact pronunciation of words in concurrent speech (Jensema, 1982; Musselwhite & St. Louis, 1988). The system was originally developed as a method for teaching spoken language and aiding in the development of English literacy skills with persons born deaf, although it is not used widely with this population at the present time (Woodward, 1990).

Information and materials are available from the Cued Speech Team at Gallaudet University and the Cued Speech Center.

*Braille Alphabet Card*     The pocket-size braille alphabet card, which contains both braille and printed letters, enables the person with DSI who reads braille to communicate with a sighted partner who has no special training. The person with DSI transmits messages letter by letter by touching braille characters, while the sighted partner views the corresponding printed letters. The sighted partner then places the user's fingertips on braille letters in order to send a message back (Silberman, 1986).

### Aided Systems

*Braille Transcription and Reception Systems*   Braille transcription and reception systems can be used to send printed messages between people who use braille or between a message sender who knows traditional orthography and a receiver who knows braille. An early example of a system is the Electro-Brailler (Jensema, 1982). This system consists of a braille transcriber that functions as a transmitter and a braille writer that functions to receive messages. The braille transcriber is an adapter that can be mounted on either a braillewriter, a braille keyboard, or an ordinary typewriter. When the keys of the transcriber are depressed, electrical impulses are produced and converted into braille dots, which, in turn, are interpreted and produced by the braille writer. Thus, the system is essentially a type of braille typewriter in which brailled material is formulated. The Braillemboss (Dalrymple, 1973), a similar device, is also capable of interfacing with a computer. Another option, the Teletouch (Silberman, 1986), resembles a miniature typewriter. When a key is pressed, the corresponding braille letter is mechanically raised on a braille cell on the back of the Teletouch, allowing the person with DSI access to brailled communication.

*Telephone Communication*   Several electronic devices have also been developed to facilitate telephone communication for individuals with DSI. The Tactile Speech Indicator (Lynch, 1990) enables people who are able to speak to obtain information by telephone. This device requires that telephone partners respond either "yes-yes," "no," or "I don't know" to questions initiated by the person with DSI in the phone conversation. The Tactile Speech Indicator then translates these responses into one ("no"), two ("yes-yes"), or three ("I don't know") vibrating pulses that are picked up by the individual with DSI via the fingertips.

The TeleBraille and TeleBraille II (TeleSensory Systems, Inc.) devices allow more flexible telephone communication. The original TeleBraille system requires that both individuals be proficient users of braille. The speaker sends a braille message using a keyboard similar to a brailler. This information is then converted to a signal that can be transmitted through the telephone system. On the other end, the message is converted back into braille characters that can be read by the receiver. The TeleBraille II system enables telephone communication between an individual with DSI and a partner who does not know braille. With this system, the speaker is able to send messages through the telephone system using a standard keyboard. As with the TeleBraille system, the information is converted into braille characters that can then be read by the message receiver with DSI.

## Summary

There are a number of communication options available to augment the receptive and expressive communication of individuals with DSI who are academically competitive. Given the heterogeneity of this population, the selection of appropriate AAC systems requires careful consideration. In addition to the options developed specifically for persons with DSI, many of techniques discussed in the first section of this chapter may also be appropriate with modifications made to meet individual needs. The individual's sensory loss, functional use of sensory modalities, current modes of communication, age, and cognitive and linguistic abilities (Jensema, 1982) are considerations in determining the appropriate communication options.

# *Adults with Acquired Physical Disabilities*

➢➢➢➢➢➢➢➢➢➢➢➢➢➢➢➢➢➢➢➢➢➢➢➢➢➢➢➢➢➢➢➢➢➢➢➢➢➢➢

"When I first realized that I would be unable to speak some day, I viewed it as losing my life. Communication was my life. Now I realize that was a little overly dramatic, but not much. Speechlessness is not a loss of life, but a loss of access to life. I find it difficult to access my friends. They used to stop by to chat, and I wished sometimes that they would leave me alone. Now if they stop at all, they stay for just a few minutes. They have difficulty tolerating my reduced ability to communicate. I have lost access to them. Because of that, I do not have the opportunities to discuss, joke, and most of all argue," wrote a lawyer with amyotrophic lateral sclerosis. (Beukelman & Garrett, 1986, p. 5)

The mechanics of spoken communication are so automatic for natural speakers that the content of interactions, not the speaking processes involved, is the primary focus of communicative exchanges. It is almost impossible for those who learned and continue to speak without difficulty to imagine what it would be like to be unable to speak due to an acquired disability. This chapter briefly summarizes assessment and intervention approaches to a number of such disabilities, including amyotrophic lateral sclerosis (ALS), multiple sclerosis (MS), Parkinson's disease, spinal cord injury, and brain stem stroke. Information related to the acquired disabilities of traumatic brain injury and aphasia secondary to stroke are discussed in subsequent chapters.

## A MODEL FOR INTERVENTION

A somewhat streamlined version of the Participation Model (Figure 7.1.) has been employed with adults who have severe acquired communication disorders. This model has been referred to as a "matching" (Coleman, Cook & Meyers, 1980) or "Communication Needs" model (Beukelman, Yorkston, & Dowden, 1985) and involves three simultaneous types of assessment, all of which are represented in Figure 7.1. The first assessment is an *identification of participation and communication needs,* the second is an *assessment of capabilities* in order to determine the available and appropriate communication options, and the third is an *assessment of external constraints.* In addition, strategies for *evaluating the effectiveness of* AAC interventions are important to this model. These components were discussed in detail in Chapter 7, so a brief review is sufficient at this point.

### Identify Participation Patterns and Communication Needs

*Participation Patterns*    Individuals who experience acquired physical disabilities that are so severe that their ability to communicate is affected usually experience other dramatic changes in their lives as well. Depending upon the progression of the condition or disease, these changes may come gradually, as with a degenerative disease, or more abruptly, as with trauma or stroke. Communication needs may be determined not only by individuals' physical disabilities, but also by their personal life-style preferences. For example, some people with severe degenerative disabilities such as ALS prefer to center their lives around their home environments. These individuals find that it is simply more efficient for them and less demanding on their families to establish their homes as their primary work and social setting, rather than to continue to participate in the larger community. Thus, they may work at home if they are active vocationally. Friends visit them at home, and they may travel only for health care services. Other individuals may adopt a different participation strategy and attempt to stay active in the community as long as they possibly can. These individuals may continue to work outside of the home and to attend recreational activities, church or synagogue functions, and social events with friends and family.

Such decisions about patterns of participation substantially affect an individual's communication needs and the AAC options to meet those needs. For example, an individual who communicates primarily at home may need an AAC system that can be moved to rooms in the house on a cart or computer stand with wheels, rather than an AAC device that is attached directly to a wheelchair. Individuals who participate actively in the community need communication systems that are self-contained, compact, and fully portable. It is important to consider the individual opinions and preferences of adults with acquired disabilities regarding participation and life-style patterns during assessment and intervention.

**Consensus Building**   It is important to develop a consensus among the people involved with the person of concern when developing a communication needs profile. One way to build consensus is to "organize" potential communication needs into specific and detailed components that can be designated as "mandatory," "desirable," "unimportant," or "may be mandatory in the future," as displayed in Figure 16.1.

A detailed needs assessment has advantages for both the person with the disability and his or her family or support networks. For example, it is not uncommon for adults with acquired communication disorders to insist that their AAC systems return (or maintain) all of the functions of natural communication to them. This is quite natural, since many people struggle to accept their disabilities and are often frustrated by their inability to communicate in the same way that was possible with natural speech. In the process of completing a communication needs inventory, such individuals are forced to go beyond the generic expectation of "being able to do everything that I could do before this happened" in order to identify *specific* communication needs and assign them priority.

In addition, it is not uncommon that family members and friends who surround a person with an acquired physical disability have differences of opinion regarding the person's communication needs. There is no way to predict what these differences will be, but it is important to try to achieve some degree of consensus among these individuals about the communication needs or, if that is impossible, to at least clarify what the differences of opinion are. If neither of these outcomes is accomplished early in the assessment process, it is nearly impossible to institute a successful intervention, since the communication needs perceived by one party will have been met, but the needs perceived by another will not have been met.

## Assess Specific Capabilities

As discussed in Chapter 7, assessments of cognitive, motor, language, and sensory capabilities are usually conducted with persons who have acquired physical disabilities. One particular aspect of the assessment process for these individuals involves predicting the natural course of various capabilities. For persons with degenerative diseases, it can be anticipated that some capabilities will deteriorate while others remain stable. For persons with stable conditions following brain stem stroke or spinal cord injury, it is often anticipated that some capabilities may improve naturally or with therapeutic intervention. These issues are discussed in more detail in subsequent sections of this chapter.

Name:
Date:
Interviewer:
Responders:

Please indicate whether the needs listed are:
M = Mandatory
D = Desirable
U = Unimportant
F = May be mandatory in the future

**Positioning**

In bed
   While supine                      _____
   While lying prone              _____
   While lying on side            _____
   While in a Clinitron bed      _____
   While in a Roto bed            _____
   While sitting in bed            _____
   While in arm restraints       _____
   In a variety of positions      _____
Related to mobility
   Carry the system while walking    _____
   Independently position the system  _____
   In a manually controlled wheelchair  _____
   In an electric wheelchair       _____
   With a lapboard               _____
   While the chair is reclined      _____
   Arm troughs                   _____

Other equipment
   With hand mitts               _____
   With arterial lines             _____
   Orally intubated              _____
   While trached                _____
   With oxygen mask            _____
   With electric wheelchair controls   _____
   Environmental control units     _____
   Other needs related to positioning  _____

**Communication Partners**

Someone who cannot read (e.g., child or nonreader)  _____
Someone with no familiarity with the system  _____
Someone who has poor vision  _____
Someone who has limited time or patience  _____
Someone who is across the room or in another room  _____
Someone who is not independently mobile  _____
Several people at a time  _____
Someone who is hearing impaired  _____
Other needs related to partners  _____

**Locations**

In one room only  _____
In multiple rooms in the same building  _____
In dimly lit rooms  _____
In bright rooms  _____
In noisy rooms  _____
Outdoors  _____
Traveling in a car or van  _____
Moving from place to place within a building  _____

*(continued)*

**Figure 16.1.** Communication needs assessment. (From Beukelman, D., Yorkston, K., & Dowden, P. [1985]. *Communication augmentation: A casebook of clinical management*, pp. 209–211. Austin, TX: PRO-ED; reprinted by permission.)

**Figure 16.1.**  *(continued)*

At a desk or computer terminal
In more than two locations in a day
Other needs related to locations

**Message Needs**

Call attention
Signal emergencies
Provide unique information
Make requests
Carry on a conversation
Express emotion
Give opinions
Convey basic medical needs
Greet people
Prepare messages in advance
Edit texts prepared by the user
Make changes in diagrams
Compile lists (e.g., phone numbers)
Perform calculations
Take notes
Other needs related to messages

**Modality of Communication**

Prepare printed messages
Prepare auditory messages
Talk on the phone
Communicate with other equipment (e.g., environment control units)
Communicate privately
Switch from one modality to another during communication
Via several modalities at a time (e.g., taking notes while talking on the phone)
Communicate via an intercom
Via formal letters or reports
On pre-prepared worksheets
Other needs related to modality of communication

## Assess Constraints

A variety of external constraints may affect the AAC decisions that are made for a specific individual, and some of these constraints commonly affect persons with acquired communication disorders. One constraint involves attitudes of family members and friends about the communication disorder in general and the recommended AAC intervention in particular. For example, families of some elderly persons appear to have difficulty accepting the use of electronic communication techniques for a spouse or parent. Families of teenagers or young adults may be resistant to low tech options, even if these are the most appropriate techniques, because they believe that their child "deserves the very best" and mistakenly equate sophisticated equipment with the best equipment.

A related constraint involves the availability of facilitators to learn about the operation and use of an electronic AAC system in order to assist the user to learn and maintain it. In some locations, adequate support may not be available for certain types of communication options. Another important external constraint involves the availability of funding for equipment and instruction. Funding patterns for AAC systems vary dramatically in different parts of the world. Some countries, provinces, or states fund AAC systems for children who are in educational programs but provide little financial support for adults. Other areas fund AAC systems for adults with acquired disabilities, while failing to support adults who are physically disabled because of congenital disorders. Still other areas severely restrict AAC funding for elderly individuals. It is impossible in this book to outline such funding constraints in detail. Suffice it to say that, as is the case for children, successful AAC interventions require that the AAC team assess constraints and focus on the remediation of these as vigorously as they focus on communication needs and capabilities.

## Evaluate Intervention Effectiveness

There are three primary reasons to measure the effectiveness of interventions with adults who have acquired physical disabilities. The first reason is to identify the communication needs that have and have not been met. When an intervention approach succeeds in meeting certain communication needs, it is important to document these, for the sake of the individual and his or her family. If an initial intervention does not meet certain communication needs, it is important to refine the approach and intervene in ways that will facilitate this over time.

The second reason to measure intervention effectiveness is to document the effectiveness of the AAC program. Agencies that provide funding for AAC interventions with adults usually demand this documentation for continued funding.

The third reason to measure intervention effectiveness is to document the overall AAC effort in a particular center or agency. If the effectiveness of AAC interventions for specific users is documented, administrative support for AAC efforts will probably be enhanced.

In the following sections of this chapter, AAC approaches that apply to specific diseases and syndromes are discussed. A complete clinical description of these conditions is not possible here, so only those aspects of the disease process that most directly influence AAC interventions are highlighted.

## AMYOTROPHIC LATERAL SCLEROSIS (ALS)

Amyotrophic lateral sclerosis (ALS) is a progressive degenerative disease of unknown etiology involving the motor neurons of the brain and spinal cord. Because 75% of persons with ALS are unable to speak by the time of their deaths (Saunders, Walsh, & Smith, 1981), the need for AAC services among individuals with ALS is extensive.

The mean age of onset for ALS is 56 years (Emery & Holloway, 1982). The most common early symptom is weakness, with approximately one third of those affected reporting initial upper extremity (arm and hand) weakness, one third reporting leg weakness, and one quarter presenting with bulbar (brain stem) weakness manifested by dysarthria and dysphagia. Extraocular muscle movements are usually spared, as is sphincter control. As the disease progresses, motor weakness may be pervasive, leaving the individual dependent upon others for personal care, mobility, and feeding. Fourteen to thirty-nine percent of individuals with ALS survive for 5 years, about ten percent live for up to 10 years, and a few may live 20 years after onset. Individuals with primarily bulbar (brain stem) symptoms tend to have a more rapid course, with a median survival of 2.2 years after the appearance of initial symptoms (Tandan & Bradley, 1985).

> The average worldwide incidence of ALS ranges between 0.4 to 1.8 per 100,000 of the population, and the prevalence rates range from 4 to 6 per 100,000 of the population (Tandan & Bradley, 1985). The male-to-female ratio is 2:1 (Emery & Holloway, 1982).

## Communication Symptoms

Persons with ALS usually do not experience language impairments as a result of their disease; however, dysarthria, a motor speech disorder, results from the weakness and spasticity inherent in the disease. Dysarthria of the mixed flaccid-spastic type is almost universally present at some point during the course of ALS (Darley, Aronson, & Brown, 1975; Dworkin, Aronson, & Mulder, 1980; Yorkston, Beukelman, & Bell, 1988). Persons with predominant bulbar (brain stem) involvement experience this speech disorder early in the disease process, and deterioration of their speech and swallowing functions may be rapid. Such individuals may be able to walk and even to drive, although they are unable to speak. Individuals with predominant spinal involvement, however, may retain normal or mildly dysarthric speech for a considerable period of time, even as they experience extensive motor impairments in their extremities.

Although the progression of speech symptoms may differ from individual to individual, most persons with ALS experience a severe communication disorder during the last months or years of their lives. In a retrospective study of 100 hospice patients with ALS, 28% were anarthric (unable to speak) and 47% were severely dysarthric at the time of their deaths. Only 25% were able to speak understandably during the terminal stage of the illness (Saunders et al., 1981). In a related study of the use of AAC devices by 40 individuals with ALS, it was reported that AAC systems were required, on the average, within 3 years after initial diagnosis, with a range from 6 months to 10 or more years (Sitver & Kraat, 1982).

### Identify Participation Patterns and Communication Needs

As noted previously, persons with ALS tend to adopt one of two life-style patterns. Some, such as Steven Hawking, the Nobel Prize-winning physicist, continue to participate outside the home in work and community affairs. These individuals require durable, portable AAC systems and, in some cases, powered mobility. Others tend to develop their homes as their social centers and work, socialize, and conduct their affairs within this stable and customized environment. For home-centered individuals, either movable (i.e., mounted on a table or cart) or portable AAC systems may meet their communication needs. These individuals may also use AAC systems that require extensive facilitator support (e.g., eye pointing or lip reading), since they rarely need to function as independently as do their counterparts who are active in the community.

"The [communication] system allowed Mark to communicate specific words and phrases when I could not understand him. This was especially good when he wanted to ask doctors a specific question or describe a specific symptom. The system was a good conversation piece. Mark enjoyed demonstrating the system to his friends. This often helped to ease their discomfort with his terminal disease. . . . Many friends were more willing to come by after they saw this system demonstrated. They felt it made Mark more comfortable, since he was able to communicate with them. In short, it helped remove the isolation factor when one has no speech. . . . [The communication system] gave Mark something to do. He was actively involved—no longer just a spectator. . . . He could write out notes and messages to the kids and to me at his leisure. . . . [However, the scanning approach was] not a comfortable mode of communication. Mark would get nervous after concentrating so hard," wrote Mark's wife, after he died from ALS. (Beukelman, Yorkston, & Dowden, 1985, p. 108)

### Assess Specific Capabilities

*Cognitive/Linguistic Skills*   Cognitive and linguistic functions are preserved as ALS progresses, although there are some reports of dementia in a small percentage (5%) of cases (Yorkston et al., 1988), but there is some doubt that this is directly related to ALS itself. The incidence of depression in ALS patients does not differ from that in other patients with chronic diseases, nor is the suicide rate unusually high. Thus, persons with ALS are able to understand and relate to the world around them and formulate messages much like other adults.

*Sensory/Perceptual Skills*   There is minimal evidence that ALS is associated with changes in sensory function. Impairment of motor control, however, is usually extensive.

***Motor Skills***   The pattern of motor control capability greatly affects the selection of an AAC system for an individual with ALS. These capabilities generally differ markedly from individual to individual, depending on whether the person first experiences bulbar or spinal symptoms.

*Bulbar ALS*   Persons with predominantly bulbar (brain stem) symptoms are usually able to control, for some time, AAC techniques that can be operated via direct selection using their hands or fingers. For example, Yorkston (1989) described an individual with ALS who pointed to letters on an alphabet board in order to communicate messages and supplement her distorted natural speech. During the initial stages of the disease, she was able to use handwriting for longer messages. Because she did not consider telephone communication as a pressing need, this individual decided to defer a decision regarding the use of a speech output device until her disease progressed. Another example is a man with ALS who used an alphabet board and a small portable typewriter. As his disease progressed, he continued to type using a single finger, and he moved his arm and hand with the assistance of a mobile arm support (Beukelman, Yorkston, & Dowden, 1985).

*Spinal ALS*   Persons with ALS who exhibit predominant spinal symptoms usually experience extensive motor impairments of their trunks and limbs at the same time as they are unable to meet their communication needs through speech. For these individuals, the need for an augmented writing system often precedes the need for a conversational system.

Individuals with severe impairments related to limb control usually require a scanning system of some type. For example, Beukelman, Yorkston, and Dowden (1985) described a man who communicated with an AAC system, the Living Center (Words +, Inc.), which is now known as the Equalizer system. The man was unable to move his upper or lower limbs, and using a direct selection optical pointer became too fatiguing after less than 1 minute. However, he demonstrated the ability to activate, release, and reactivate a switch that was mounted on a pillow beside his head when he was seated in a large easy chair. Since he had the head rotation capability needed for this, and it was accurate as well as nonfatiguing for him, he used this motor pattern to operate an automatic scanner until his death.

The motor control site for alternative access may need to be changed several times during the progression of the disease. For example, one AAC user we know was initially able to control her system using a single switch operated by either hand. In time, the switch was modified so that it could be controlled by minimal movement of a single finger. Finally, a different switch was mounted on her forehead, as depicted in Figure 16.2. She operated this switch by wrinkling her forehead slightly as she raised her eyebrow.

## Assess Constraints

Although not specifically mentioned in the Participation Model (Figure 7.1.), there are constraints that apply specifically to persons with ALS and their support systems, which are discussed in the following section.

***Operational Competence***   Persons with ALS, like most AAC users, require time and instruction in order to become competent with their AAC systems. Because ALS is predictably degenerative, these individuals are in the unique position of being able to select their AAC systems and learn to operate them while natural speech is still adequate to meet at least their most basic communication needs. In fact, if an AAC system is selected and implemented after an individual is no longer able to speak, the AAC experience often becomes extremely frustrating for all involved.

This raises the question of how to predict when a person with ALS will need to use an AAC system. Yorkston, Smith, Miller, and Hillel (1991) explored this issue in a retrospective survey of 77 persons with ALS. Their results indicated that, for the subject group as a whole, there was little or no relationship between the severity of the speech disorder and the length of time since diagnosis. For example, five subjects had functional speech 5 years post-diagnosis, while others spoke so poorly within 1 year of diagnosis that they required AAC systems. Although this work is ongoing, the following guidelines for clinical practice were suggested based on the initial data:

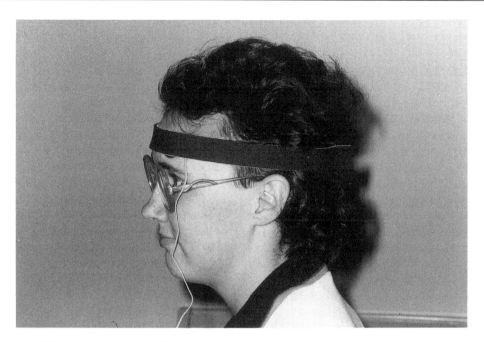

**Figure 16.2.** A P-switch worn on the forehead.

Although rapid decline of speech function [in ALS] is certainly not inevitable, it occurs frequently enough so that sound clinical management dictates early preparedness. In our clinic, exploration of augmentative options begins *when speech has slowed and intelligibility is inconsistent in adverse listening situations.* (Yorkston et al., 1991, p. 10, italics added)

**Facilitator Support**    Persons with ALS require ongoing support from facilitators to use their AAC systems. This support may include instruction in technical or other skills that enable the individual to operate the device efficiently and accurately. Facilitator support may also be needed to select and modify messages stored in the system. In addition, as the individual's capabilities change with progression of the disease, facilitators may need to change the motor control options and the positioning of the system. Instruction by facilitators in the social use of the AAC system may also be necessary.

Because persons with severe ALS often find travel to be difficult, locally available professional facilitator support is generally required. Several regional AAC centers have developed networks of professional service providers within their states or areas to meet the needs of persons with degenerative diseases. The regional center trains and supports network personnel concerning the needs of an individual AAC user. (Service delivery in AAC was discussed in detail in Chapter 6.)

**Equipment Availability**    Several features of ALS make the procurement of AAC equipment difficult. First, some people experience very rapid deterioration of natural speech abilities, and their need for AAC equipment becomes extremely urgent. Thus, delays in obtaining AAC services due to long waiting lists at regional centers, lack of funding for assessment services, and lack of funding for purchasing AAC devices can greatly impede the success of an intervention process. Second, because some persons with ALS will use their AAC systems for very brief periods of time prior to death, funding agencies may be reluctant to purchase systems for them. In order to counteract these and other equipment-related problems, an increasing number of regional programs for persons with neurologic diseases have established "lending libraries" of AAC equipment. As individuals' capabilities change, different AAC devices can be provided for as long as necessary, thus avoiding the need to purchase new devices for each limited-use period.

## MULTIPLE SCLEROSIS (MS)

Multiple sclerosis (MS) is a degenerative disease of the white matter of the central nervous system. The lesions of MS are multiple plaques that cause destruction of the myelin sheath, with preservation of the axon except in very chronic cases.

In the northern part of the United States, the prevalence of MS is about 1 in 1,000 of the population, and in the southern states, the prevalence is about one third to one half of this figure. Approximately 95% of all cases begin between the ages of 10–50 years, with a median onset age of 27 years. Although MS is considered to be a disease of young people, it is not uncommon for an initial diagnosis to occur between 50–60 years of age. The female-to-male ratio is 1.5:1 (Arnason, 1982).

The natural course of MS differs greatly from person to person. The clinical course of MS has been divided into five classes (Poser, 1984):

1. Relapsing and remitting: About 70% of young people with MS are in this category. They experience virtually full recovery from the neurologic signs and symptoms after each episode of relapse.
2. Chronic progressive: This is most commonly present in individuals who are older at the outset of the disease. The motor and neurologic symptoms gradually worsen over time, with no intermittent remissions.
3. Combined relapsing/remitting with chronic progression: This is the eventual outcome in the majority of individuals and results in a gradual deterioration of capabilities over time, although there are periods of relative remission.
4. Benign: About 20% of all individuals with MS have a normal life span with relatively normal functioning and little or no progression of the disease.
5. Malignant: A small percentage (5%–10%) of (predominantly) young people with MS show rapid and extensive involvement of cognitive, cerebellar, and pyramidal systems, which leads to death in a relatively short time.

The average life expectancy of young males with MS is about 35 years following the onset of the disease. The prognosis is worse: 1) in males than in females, 2) if the age at onset is greater than 35 years, 3) if a chronic progressive pattern is present at onset, or 4) if cerebellar symptoms occur at initial presentation (Poser, 1984).

### Communication Symptoms

Dysarthria is the most common communication problem associated with MS, but through the study of large groups of individuals with MS, it has become apparent that dysarthria is not a universal characteristic of this disease. A study of 144 individuals with MS reported that dysarthria was present in 19% of them (Ivers & Goldstein, 1963). Darley, Brown, and Goldstein (1972) reported that 41% of their MS sample demonstrated overall speech performance that was *not* "essentially normal" in terms of its impact on listeners. Nevertheless, when a self-report technique was utilized, only 23% of these individuals reported a "speech and/or communication disorder"; thus, it appears that a large percentage of this sample were unaware of the severity of their speech problems. Overall, a survey of studies related to the prevalence of dysarthria in MS reveals a range of occurrence of 19%–41%, depending on who makes the judgment and how the population was sampled.

Although a number of individuals with MS demonstrate impaired speech, most do not require AAC systems. Beukelman, Kraft, and Freal (1985) reported that 4% of 656 survey respondents with MS indicated that their communication was so severely impaired that strangers were unable to understand them.

> A man with MS recalls the following episode: "One evening . . . I had gone to the bathroom for a shower. . . . All was well as I entered the bathroom and showered. Then I began to wheel myself to the bedroom after I had finished. I tried to say something to my wife as I neared the door, but the words would not come and all I could manage was a babbling as I tried to express myself. My wife said to me, 'What did you do, flush your voice down the drain?' Now this is not a real funny line. However, under those circumstances, it sounded hilarious. We both burst into laughter. . . . My voice control did not return for a few days . . . [but it] did return." (Michael, 1981, p. 27)

## Identify Participation Patterns and Communication Needs

Because the onset of MS occurs relatively early in life, these individuals are usually in educational programs or employed when they first experience symptoms. The intermittent and gradual onset of symptoms usually does not require persons with MS to immediately modify their life-styles, although some persons with visual problems, quite common in MS, may require technological assistance to use computer screens or read detailed printed materials (see chap. 15, this volume). In time, however, disabilities that are unrelated to verbal communication often prevent these individuals from attending school or working. For example, Kraft (1981) reported that arm and leg spasticity is an important reason why many people with MS drop out of the employment market. Loss of balance, loss of normal bladder control, and fatigue also interfere with education or employment. In addition, a combination of weakness, spasticity, ataxia, and tremor may interfere with walking and necessitate the use of a wheelchair for mobility.

Because most persons with MS whose speech is so impaired that they require AAC systems are no longer able to attend school or work, they rarely experience communication needs related to these domains. Furthermore, some individuals with severe speech impairments require personal care assistance beyond what their families can offer, and they may live in residential or nursing centers, where their communication needs may be limited even further. Thus, the primary communication needs of many people with MS are conversational, although individuals may require assistance with writing as well.

## Assess Specific Capabilities

***Language Skills***   Although dysarthria is the most common communication problem associated with MS, aphasia has also been reported. Aphasia has been absent in several large reported studies of multiple sclerosis patients (Olmos-Lau, Ginsberg, & Geller, 1977). However, Beukelman, Yorkston, & Dowden (1985) noted that earlier authors reported the incidence of aphasia as ranging from 1% to 3% of persons with MS.

***Cognitive Skills***   The cognitive limitations of individuals with MS have been poorly documented, but definite evidence of cognitive impairment seems present in more than half of these individuals with MS. Neuropsychological testing reveals impaired abstract conceptualization and recent memory deficits most often (Poser, 1984). Although cognitive impairment in most individuals is unlikely to interfere with AAC intervention, the possibility should be considered and appropriate assessments undertaken. In particular, short-term memory impairments may make new learning difficult, and AAC approaches that build on old skills are more likely to be successful.

***Sensory/Perceptual Skills***   Vision limitations are common in MS. Optic neuritis, which is the acute or subacute loss of central vision in one eye with peripheral vision spared, is the first symptom in 16%–30% of persons with MS. Optic neuritis is often manifested initially by an inability to see text on a computer screen or to read small print in general. The visual limitations of MS are particularly problematic in the context of AAC interventions, since many AAC techniques require extensive visual capabilities. Complicated visual scanning arrays cannot be used by many of these individuals, and visual scanning arrays may need to be replaced by auditory scanning systems such as the one described in the section that follows. (See chap. 2, this volume, for examples of electronic auditory scanners.) Large-print text is a common requirement of persons with MS, as is synthetic speech feedback that echoes the letters and words selected in typing or from a communication display. For example, an AAC system designed for a 30-year-old woman with MS consisted of an expanded keyboard with 1-inch square keys and speech feedback (Honsinger, 1989). Readers are referred to Chapter 15 for additional information about AAC options for persons with visual impairments.

*Motor Skills*   Individuals' motor control capabilities in MS vary considerably, and, therefore, careful motor assessment is an important aspect of all AAC interventions. Intention tremor, which occurs in or is exaggerated by voluntary movement, is a prevalent motor control problem. The tremor is often disruptive when an individual attempts to access a keyboard or activate a switch. The body part involved in access sometimes can be stabilized sufficiently so that voluntary movement without tremor is possible. At other times, it may be necessary to attach a switch to a limb or hand so that the switch can move with the body part but still remain in position to be activated by a finger. Often, the motor control and visual impairments of MS combine to severely limit the AAC options. For example, Porter (1989) described an AAC intervention that occurred near the end of a person's life. The individual's visual and motor control limitations were quite extensive, but he learned to control a simple call buzzer and loop tape (auditory scanning) system using a pressure switch that was attached to a pillow beside his head. (Readers are referred to Chapter 10 and Chapter 13 for additional information about loop tape scanning.)

## Assess Constraints

Several characteristics of MS complicate AAC interventions. First, symptom patterns vary considerably across individuals. Although the clinical course of MS follows five general patterns of progression, individual manifestations can be complex and variable over time. Obviously, changes in an AAC system may be needed to accommodate this variability.

Second, as noted previously, visual impairments are quite common in MS and can make AAC interventions particularly challenging. Third, AAC interventions usually occur in conjunction with other efforts to compensate for the multiple impairments experienced by people with MS. Therefore, AAC interventions must be coordinated with other interventions in the context of changing symptom patterns.

## PARKINSON'S DISEASE

Parkinson's disease is a syndrome composed of a cluster of motor symptoms that include tremor at rest, rigidity, paucity (i.e., reduction in movement), and impaired postural reflexes. Parkinson's disease results from a loss of dopaminergic neurons in the basal ganglia (especially the substantia nigra) and the brain stem. The onset is typically insidious; in retrospect, many individuals recall stiffness and muscle aches, which they first attributed to normal aging. The symptom that often initiates the first visit to a physician is tremor in a resting position.

Medical treatment over the past few decades has greatly altered the natural course of Parkinson's disease. Prior to the availability of the pharmacologic agent levodopa (L-dopa), about one fourth of all individuals with Parkinson's disease died within the first 5 years following diagnosis, and 80% died after 10–14 years (Yorkston, Beukelman, & Bell, 1988). Although the changes in mortality rate due to L-dopa are not yet clear, the life-styles of persons with Parkinson's disease have been altered dramatically by this treatment. Individuals with Parkinson's disease are able to move much more freely and manage their lives much more independently with L-dopa than without it.

---

The average annual incidence of parkinsonism (excluding drug-induced cases) is 18.2 cases per 100,000 persons. The prevalence is estimated to be between 66–187 per 100,000. There is no significant difference between males and females. The incidence increases sharply above the age of 64, and peak incidence is between 75–84 years of age. There is a trend toward increased age at the time of diagnosis. In 1967, the mean age of onset was 55.3 years (Yorkston, Beukelman, & Bell, 1988).

---

Although pharmocologic treatment dramatically improves the performance of many persons with Parkinson's disease, some side effects of the medication can interfere with the use of AAC approaches. There may be individual fluctuations in response (also known as "on–off response"), probably due to differences in medication absorption and dopamine receptor responsiveness. With long-term therapy, some persons also experience the occurrence of involuntary movements that interfere with functional activities. These involuntary movements may be emotionally distressing as well.

## Communication Symptoms

The prevalence of speech disorders among persons with Parkinson's disease is quite high: of 65 individuals with Parkinson's disease studied by Buck and Cooper (1956), 37% had normal speech, 22% a moderate degree of speech involvement, and 29% had severely impaired speech. The percentage of individuals with impaired speech due to Parkinson's disease who might benefit from AAC techniques has not been determined.

Probably the most complete overview of parkinsonian speech characteristics comes from the work of Darley, Aronson, and Brown (1969a, 1969b, 1975), who studied 32 persons with dysarthria due to Parkinson's disease. They noted that the speech of this group was characterized by:

> reduced variability in pitch, loudness, reduced loudness level overall, and decreased use of all vocal parameters for achieving stress and emphasis. Markedly imprecise articulation is generated at variable rates in short bursts of speech punctuated by illogical pauses and often by inappropriate silences. Voice quality is sometimes harsh, sometimes breathy. (Darley, Aronson, & Brown, 1975, p. 175)

Nevertheless, speech disorders among persons with Parkinson's disease are not uniform. Some speakers are difficult to understand, primarily because they speak excessively fast. Their speaking rates may exceed those of normal speakers or exceed those that are optimum for persons with motor control disorders. Other speakers are difficult to understand because they speak with reduced intensity or loudness. Still others speak with such limited movements of the articulators that precise production of speech sounds is difficult. As Parkinson's disease progresses, many speakers demonstrate combinations of these speech disorders.

The natural course of symptoms in persons with Parkinson's disease who have communication disorders has not been documented. Clinical observations reveal the process to be gradual, with speech becoming increasingly difficult to understand. Most persons with Parkinson's disease communicate using natural speech to a greater or lesser extent. Therefore, when AAC techniques are used, they are part of a multimodal communication system that includes natural speech. Some strategies that utilize AAC approaches to support speech were summarized by Yorkston, Beukelman, and Bell (1988) and are highlighted in the following sections.

***Increased Speech Rate***    Individuals who speak too rapidly often benefit considerably from interventions designed to slow their speech rate. A slower speech rate may be accomplished by using several AAC techniques and is often accompanied by increased speech intelligibility. Alphabet board supplementation, introduced by Beukelman and Yorkston (1978), was among the first of such interventions documented in the literature. This procedure requires the speaker to point to the first letter of each word on an alphabet board or other type of AAC device as it is spoken. This not only forces speakers to slow their speaking rates but also provides their communication partners with extra information in the form of the first letters of words. For some speakers, the slowed speaking rate alone appears to be the major factor contributing to improved intelligibility. For others, the communication partner's knowledge of the first letter of the spoken word also contributes to more effective communication. In addition, when communication breakdowns do occur, speakers can use their alphabet boards to spell messages.

---

Mary's family complained that they were no longer able to understand her. She had difficulty initiating speech, as she seemed to freeze on the first word of some utterances. Once started, she spoke with bursts of excessive rate. Due to a lack of movement related to her Parkinson's disease, Mary showed no facial expression. Thus, during speech, her articulators barely moved.

Mary was taught to use a small alphabet board and point to the first letter of each word as she spoke. With this technique, her overall speaking rate was reduced to about 35–40 words per minute, and the rushes of excessive rate were eliminated. Her speech was quite understandable even when her listener did not observe the communication board to determine the first letter of each word. When she was difficult to understand, she simply spelled the message with her board.

Although this approach was quite successful for Mary, she was reluctant to use it. She felt that it looked strange. It also required more effort than simply speaking her messages. However, with encouragement from her family, she used the cued speech approach for several years. Toward the end of her life, Mary's motor control deteriorated to the point were she was unable to point efficiently. The alphabet board was abandoned and a dependent scanning approach was used instead until her death. (Beukelman, June, 1991, unpublished clinical anecdote)

---

**Articulatory Problems** The intelligibility of poorly articulated speech is usually improved considerably when the communication partner is aware of the topic of conversation. Thus, persons with Parkinson's disease may be encouraged to provide their listeners with the topic of a message or a conversation before beginning to speak. At times, the topic can be communicated successfully through natural speech, but it may be necessary to identify the topic using an AAC technique such as a topic board. Topic boards are often included on the same communication boards used for alphabetic supplementation of speech related to rate reduction. Figure 16.3 illustrates this combination.

It is important that persons with Parkinson's disease and their important communication partners act as informants and identify relevant topics to be included on the board. Some persons with Parkinson's disease may also find it useful to employ a remnant book, as described in Chapters 10 and 13. Remnants such as theater tickets, napkins from restaurants, traffic tickets, bank statements, programs from plays, church bulletins, and racing forms can be used to communicate topics as well as to clarify the details of an experience.

**Reduced Voice Loudness** Because many persons with Parkinson's disease speak with reduced voice loudness, portable speech amplification systems may be effective in improving communication interactions. Small, portable voice amplifiers such as the one illustrated in Figure 16.4. are most effective when speakers produce consistent phonation (voicing) during speech, although

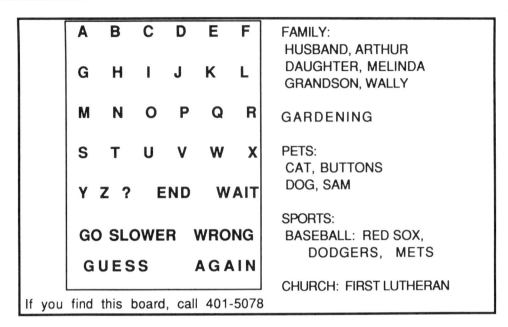

**Figure 16.3.** A combined alphabet and topic initiation communication board for a person with Parkinson's disease.

voice loudness may be severely reduced. In addition, many telephone adaptations are available to persons with Parkinson's disease and other disorders who have difficulty using the phone because of communication impairments (see Blackstone, 1991). If speech is whispered, however, amplification usually does not improve intelligibility.

> Two of the many voice amplifiers that may be used by persons with Parkinson's disease include the Rand Voice Amplifier (Luminaud, Inc.) and the Stanton ADDVox II Voice Amplifier (Stanton Magnetics).

***Voicing Disorders***   Some persons with Parkinson's disease who experience severe phonatory (voicing) disorders may be able to speak with an artificial larynx. This device, which is often used by persons with laryngectomies (i.e., surgical removal of the larynx), provides an alternative sound source for speech. The number of persons with Parkinson's disease who can use an artificial larynx profitably is limited, however, since motor problems such as tremor may prevent them from activating the device at the moment they wish to speak and turning it off promptly when they are finished speaking. Furthermore, the individual must be able to articulate sounds very precisely in order to be understood with an artificial larnyx, and this is often difficult because of dysarthria. We will discuss the use of electrolarynges further in Chapter 19.

## Identify Participation Patterns and Communication Needs

The communication needs of persons with Parkinson's disease depend on two primary factors. Many persons with Parkinson's disease are older, and most are retired. Therefore, their communication needs reflect, first of all, the social environments of their retirement. In addition, the range of physical impairments in Parkinson's disease varies greatly from person to person. Some people are so severely physically limited that they require extensive physical assistance from attendants or family members. The level of dependence greatly influences an individual's communication needs.

**Figure 16.4.** A portable speech amplifier.

## Assess Specific Capabilities

*Cognitive/Linguistic Skills*  Persons with Parkinson's disease acquire their disability late in life, and so they usually have developed normal language skills. Therefore, they are able to spell and read at levels necessary to support most AAC interventions.

Controversy exists as to whether dementia is a feature of Parkinson's disease (Morris, 1982). In some individuals, specific memory deficits are present on testing, and some complain of slowness in problem solving. The AAC team must consider whether such cognitive limitations are likely to interfere with AAC interventions. Additional instruction and practice may be provided in order to help the person compensate for learning or memory difficulties.

*Sensory/Perceptual Skills*  Disturbances in sensory function usually do not interfere with AAC interventions for persons with Parkinson's disease.

*Motor Skills*  There are clinical reports of persons who have successfully used direct selection AAC techniques such as alphabet boards, as discussed previously. Because few AAC interventions with parkinsonian speakers have been reported in the literature, however, the motor control problems that may influence such AAC interventions are not well documented. Clinical experience indicates that several motor control problems may need to be considered. Many individuals have reduced range and speed of movement due to the rigidity associated with Parkinson's disease. For these individuals, the size of the selection display (e.g., on an alphabet board) will need to be reduced. Other individuals experience extensive tremor that is usually worse when they are at rest. Many can dampen the tremor if their hands can be stabilized on the surface of a communication board or device. A keyguard is often helpful with devices using keyboards. Some persons experience hyperkinesia (excessive movement) as a side effect of the medication to control their parkinsonian symptoms. These excessive movements may interfere with the fine motor control required for some AAC options.

## Assess Constraints

Two types of constraints are usually associated with AAC interventions for persons with Parkinson's disease. First, because most persons with Parkinson's disease are able to speak to some extent, they may display some resistance toward the need for an AAC intervention. Some will blame their listeners for their communication failures, even if this is not the case. Communication partners need to actively encourage these individuals to use AAC techniques. Second, many persons with Parkinson's disease are elderly and have spouses and friends in the same age group. Therefore, the hearing limitations of their listeners may be a significant barrier to effective communication.

## SPINAL CORD INJURY

Persons with cervical spinal cord injuries (i.e., those that occur around the area of the neck) frequently experience writing impairments and may, on occasion, experience speaking impairments as well. Spinal cord lesions occur when the cord is bruised, crushed, or torn by a bone fracture, a dislocation (caused by disruption of the ligaments between individual vertebrae), or both.

A spinal cord injury progresses through several stages. During spinal shock, which occurs immediately following the injury, there may be paralysis, sensory loss, and loss of the reflexes below the level of the injury. Spinal shock lasts from several days to several weeks, after which time the reflexes return.

> If reflexes return before voluntary function is present, it [is] likely that voluntary function will never develop and the lesion is *complete*. In such an instance, the spinal cord injury interrupted all tracts to and from the brain. Frequently, however, a lesion will be referred to as being *incomplete*. (Donovan, 1981, p. 66)

Incomplete lesions may involve a localized portion of the spinal cord that is totally unable to transmit messages, while the remainder of the cord is near normal. Alternatively, an incomplete lesion may involve diffuse injury to the cord; in this case, certain nerve tracts still function, but they do so abnormally.

Recovery from a spinal cord injury varies from person to person. Individuals with complete lesions usually do not experience long-term recovery of neurologic function, while persons with incomplete lesions may recover neurologic function. In both cases, most people learn to compensate for their disabilities, at least to some extent, through active rehabilitation efforts.

---

The incidence of spinal cord injury is 25–30 injuries per 1,000,000 people per year. Automobile accidents account for 35% of all spinal cord injuries, falls add another 15%, gunshot wounds contribute 10%, and diving accidents cause 6%. The remaining 34% of spinal cord injuries are the result of a variety of other conditions. The mean age of a person with a spinal cord injury is about 30, and the median age (the age at which half of those injured are older and half are younger) is 25. The age group most represented is 18–21 year-olds (Donovan, 1981).

---

## Communication Symptoms

Spinal cord lesions in the cervical region usually interfere with handwriting. Keyboard control is also limited, because reduced finger control and strength occurs with low cervical and high thoracic injuries and arm and hand paralysis occurs with middle and high cervical injuries. Table 16.1. summarizes physiologic functions that are affected when various spinal motor root segments are injured.

If the spinal lesion occurs at or above the nuclei of the phrenic nerve (usually at the first or second cervical vertebra), the individual will be ventilator dependent due to loss of nerve innervation of the diaphragm. Most individuals who remain permanently ventilator dependent are able to learn to

**Table 16.1.** Muscles supplied and functions served by spinal nerve motor roots

| Root segment | Representative muscles | Function served |
| --- | --- | --- |
| C1 and C2 | High neck muscles | Aid in head control |
| C3 and C4 | Diaphragm | Inspiration (breathing in) |
| C5 and C6 | Deltoid<br>Biceps | Shoulder flexion, abduction (arm forward, out to side)<br>Elbow flexion (elbow bent) |
| C6 and C7 | Extensor carpi radialis<br>Pronator teres | Wrist dorsiflexion (back of hand up)<br>Wrist pronation (palm down) |
| C7 and C8 | Triceps<br>Extensor digitorum communis | Elbow extension (elbow straight)<br>Finger extension ("knuckles" straight) |
| C8 and T1 | Flexor digitorum superficialis<br>Opponens pollicis<br>Interossei (intrinsics) | Finger flexion (fist clenched)<br>Thumb opposition (thumb brought to little finger)<br>Spreading and closing the fingers |
| T2–T6 | Intercostals | Forced inspiration (breathing in)<br>Expiration (breathing out, coughing) |
| T6–T12 | Intercostals<br>Abdominals | Forced inspiration (breathing in)<br>Aid in expiration (coughing)<br>Aid in trunk flexion (sitting up) |
| L1, L2, and L3 | Iliopsoas<br>Adductors | Hip flexion (thigh to chest)<br>Hip adduction (thigh to midline, legs together) |
| L3 and L4 | Quadriceps | Knee extension (knee straight) |
| L4, L5, and S1 | Gluteus medius<br>Tibialis anterior | Hip abduction (thigh out to side, legs apart)<br>Foot dorsiflexion (foot up, walk on heels) |
| L5, S1, and S2 | Gluteus maximus<br><br>Gastrocnemius | Hip extension (thigh in line with trunk, hips straight,<br>    e.g., standing)<br>Foot plantar flexion (foot down, walk on toes) |
| S2, S3, and S4 | Anal sphincter<br>Urethral sphincter | Bowel function (fecal continence)<br>Bladder control (urinary continence) |

From Beukelman, D., and Garrett, K. (1988). Augmentative and alternative communication for adults with acquired communication disorders. *Augmentative and Alternative Communication, 4,* 111; reprinted by permission.

speak by venting air past their tracheostomy tube and through the larynx as the ventilator forces air into the lungs. For a more complete description of procedures in this area, readers are referred to Dowden, Honsinger, and Beukelman (1986) and Honsinger, Yorkston, and Dowden (1987).

> Keith was 25 years old when he sustained a neck injury at the level of the fourth cervical vertebra. His complete spinal cord injury left him unable to move his body, but he is able to speak. Prior to his injury, Keith was a civil engineer. Using a sip and puff switch, Keith learned to send Morse code that is translated by an emulator device, providing alternative access to an IBM desktop computer. This system was integrated into the mainframe computer of Keith's employer. With practice, he was able to write at a rate of 25–30 words per minute, error-free. For the past 8 years, Keith has worked full time, writing engineering reports by using the resources of both his desktop computer and the mainframe computer of the engineering firm (Beukelman, Yorkston, & Dowden, 1985).

## Identify Participation Patterns and Communication Needs

Since the 1970s, the opportunities available to persons with even the most severe spinal cord injuries have increased dramatically. Powered mobility, portable respiratory ventilation systems, modified public and private transportation, computer technology, and AAC interventions allow children with cervical spinal injuries to attend regular elementary schools, young adults to attend colleges, and adults to hold regular jobs. Increasingly, people who are ventilator dependent are able to be fully integrated into regular educational and vocational environments. These extensive opportunities greatly expand the communication needs for persons with spinal cord injuries. Analysis of these needs, especially in employment settings, is required to develop appropriate AAC interventions.

## Assess Specific Capabilities

*Cognitive/Linguistic Skills*    Persons with spinal cord injuries usually retain their pre-injury language and cognitive skills. Therefore, since most people are injured as adolescents or young adults, they are able to spell messages and learn to operate complicated AAC systems. Because a spinal cord injury may occur as the result of abnormal displacement of the head during an accident, traumatic brain injury may occur with a spinal cord injury. AAC interventions for individuals with both impairments must consider the learning and memory deficits associated with the traumatic brain injury.

*Sensory/Perceptual Skills*    Hearing and vision are not impaired as a result of a spinal cord injury. Nevertheless, tactile and impairments below the spinal cord lesion should be expected with complete lesions and may or may not be present with incomplete lesions.

*Motor Skills*    Since motor control is the primary problem resulting from spinal cord injuries, the goal of intervention is to provide alternative computer keyboard access that is efficient and minimizes fatigue. Beukelman and Garrett (1988) suggested that individuals with spinal cord injuries be divided into three groups, depending on their alternative access needs: 1) those individuals who have normal or near normal hand control, 2) those with limited hand function who can perform single finger typing with one or both hands, and 3) those who have little or no upper extremity control but who demonstrate normal or near normal control of the facial and neck muscles. Potential AAC interventions are discussed for each group of individuals.

*Normal Hand Function*    Individuals with normal hand function can usually operate a typewriter or computer keyboard, without modifications, provided that these devices are efficiently positioned in the individual's work space. An occupational therapist, vocational specialist, or rehabilitation engineer with knowledge about workplace modifications and work station development may need to be involved to facilitate such interventions.

*Limited Hand Function*    Individuals who can type with a single finger usually require several types of adaptive assistance in order to do so efficiently. Some individuals with limited hand function may benefit from the assistance of a universal cuff, such as the one illustrated in Figure 16.5., or will need to grasp a stick or pencil to activate the keyboard. Persons who are able to use only one hand will require keyboard assistance so that simultaneous double or triple key activations can be managed (i.e., shift key + letter for upper case). A number of standard computers contain a "sticky key" function that supports such multiple simultaneous keystroke commands. Alternatively, a number of adaptive software programs, such as EZKeys (Words +, Inc.), can be used in this regard.

Most single finger typists prefer to use some type of rate enhancement technique to increase their communication speed and to reduce fatigue. As discussed in Chapter 3, this can be accomplished through various encoding strategies that permit retrieval of entire words, messages, or even paragraphs. An alpha or alpha-numeric encoding strategy is generally selected by persons who were literate prior to their accidents.

---

Rate enhancement software packages that may be useful to persons with spinal cord injuries include Productivity Plus (Productivity Software International, Inc.), EZKeys (Words +, Inc.), and Handikey (Microsystems Software, Inc.).

---

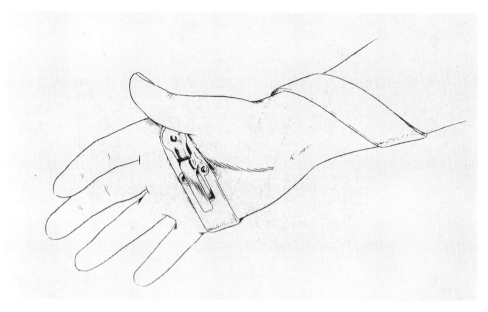

**Figure 16.5.** A universal cuff for typing. (From Kottke, F., & Lehman, J. [Eds.]. [1990]. *Krusen's handbook of physical medicine and rehabilitation* [4th ed.], p. 582. Philadelphia: W.B. Saunders; reprinted by permission.)

Individuals with limited hand function who have extensive writing needs may find that single finger typing is still too slow and laborious, even with rate enhancement. More rapid access approaches using Morse code or voice recognition, such as those described below, may be employed.

*No Functional Hand or Arm Movement*   Individuals who have no functional hand or arm control can operate computer and other AAC equipment through a variety of alternative access options. The best approach to use depends on the needs, capabilities, and preferences of the AAC user; the restrictions imposed by an educational agency, employer, and computer system; the abilities of facilitators; and the availability of funding. Generally, four options might be considered.

*Mouthsticks and headsticks* have been used for decades by individuals with spinal cord injuries to access typewriters, computers, tape recorders, and telephones. Mouthsticks and headsticks are appropriate for some applications, but this approach is often too slow and fatiguing for full-time employment or education. Fatigue occurs because of the precise positioning needed for backward and forward head, neck, and sometimes trunk, movements required for keyboard activation.

Efforts to reduce fatigue and muscle strain have led to the development of other access options that are controlled by the head. A variety of *head pointing options* that utilize light or sound have been developed and can be used with most standard desktop computer systems (see chap. 4, this volume). Usually, a light beam or sensor of some type is mounted on the user's head, and a receiving unit is positioned beside or on top of the computer monitor. The person then moves his or her head to direct the sensor at a screen-displayed keyboard in order to type. The receiving unit translates the head movements into cursor movements that can then be accepted either by a remote switch (usually a mouth control switch, as shown in Figure 16.6.) or by maintaining the sensor at the desired location for a specific time. The communication rates achieved with such head pointing systems may be enhanced with the use of rate enhancement software programs, as described previously.

*Morse code* AAC applications have also been reported for persons with spinal cord injury. Morse code emulators that translate the "dits" and "dahs" of Morse code into standard orthography or computer commands are available for most desktop computer systems. Readers are referred to Chapters 2 and 4 for more extensive discussions of this technique.

**Figure 16.6.**   Using a Headmaster with mouth control switch to operate a Macintosh computer.

---

Some of the Morse code emulators commonly used in AAC include: the Adaptive Firmware Card for Apple II computers, Ke:nx for Macintosh computers, and PC A.I.D. and PC Serial A.I.D. for IBM-compatible computers (distributed by Don Johnston Developmental Equipment, Inc.); WSKE Morse Code (Words +, Inc.); and Handicode (Microsystems Software, Inc.)

---

*Voice recognition* technology offers persons with spinal cord injuries an exciting alternative access option. Because most individuals with spinal cord injuries are able to speak, they can operate voice recognition systems as well as nondisabled individuals. Although this technology has been of interest in the AAC field, the number of messages that could be *accurately* recognized by early voice recognition systems was quite limited (e.g., Coleman & Meyers, 1991). In the 1990s, voice recognition systems with larger vocabulary capacities became commercially available at a cost that is reasonable for individual AAC users. Undoubtedly, such systems will be used increasingly by persons with spinal cord injuries, as well as by the nondisabled population. (Readers are referred to Chapter 4 for additional information.)

## BRAIN STEM STROKE

Strokes (i.e., cerebrovascular accidents) that disrupt circulation through the basilar artery that serves the lower brain stem often cause severe dysarthria or anarthria (i.e., an inability to produce speech). Because the nuclei of all the cranial nerves that activate the muscles of the face, mouth, and larynx are located in the brain stem, damage to this area of the brain may result in an inability, or reduced ability, to control these muscles voluntarily or reflexively. The nerve tracts that activate the trunk and limbs via the spinal nerves also pass through the brain stem. Therefore, severe damage to the brain stem may impair motor control of the limbs as well as the face and mouth.

## Communication Symptoms

Communication symptoms associated with brain stem stroke vary considerably with the level and extent of damage to the brain stem. Some people are dysarthric but able to communicate partial or complete messages through speech. The dysarthria experienced by these individuals is usually of the predominantly flaccid type due to damage to the nerve nuclei of the cranial nerves. A marked spastic component in addition to flaccidity may be present in other individuals. Many persons with brain stem stroke are unable to speak because of the severity of their impairments.

## Identify Participation Patterns and Communication Needs

Communication needs of persons who experience brain stem stroke are influenced by medical and life-style issues, as well as by the extent of their communication disorders. Extensive personal and medical care may be required for an individual, depending on the severity of the stroke and subsequent health condition. Persons who survive a brain stem stroke are usually unable to work, and some can be cared for at home, while others may live in settings that range from independent living to nursing care centers. Individuals who experience brain stem strokes are usually aware of the world around them and are able to exchange information and achieve social closeness through their message formulations. Thus, their communication needs may be extensive.

---

Ruby was 44 years of age when a severe brain stem stroke left her unable to speak or swallow. When we first met her on the rehabilitation unit, she was able to communicate by answering yes/no questions and by using a dependent scanning approach. She communicated "no" by closing her eyes and "yes" by leaving them open and raising her eyebrows slightly. The dependent scanning approach included a small chalkboard with the letters of the alphabet positioned vertically on the left and right sides. To communicate a message, Ruby's communication partner would point to each column of letters (A–L on the left side and M–Z on the right side). Ruby raised her eyebrows to signal the desired column of letters. Then her partner would scan down the column until Ruby signaled the preferred letter. In order to remember the letters that had already been chosen, the partner would write each letter on the chalkboard. Ruby's partners were encouraged to guess the remainder of a word or message when enough of a message had been communicated.

With proper positioning and head support, Ruby was able to move her head voluntarily to some degree, and she began to practice controlling a headlight pointer that was mounted on a head band and positioned over her right ear. In time, she was able to point to the letters on the chalkboard; with this technique, her communication rate was three times faster than with dependent scanning.

Finally, Ruby learned to access an electronic AAC device using an optical head pointing strategy. In time, the AAC device was mounted on her wheelchair and could also be transferred to her bed when needed. Ruby has used this system for about eight years (Beukelman, Yorkston, & Dowden, 1985).

---

## Assess Specific Capabilities

*Language Skills*   If the stroke does not affect the cortical or subcortical structures associated with language functioning, language skills should not be impaired as a result of brain stem stroke. Thus, the skills of persons with brain stem stroke reflect their pre-stroke linguistic performances.

*Cognitive Skills*   No accompanying cognitive limitations are expected if the stroke was limited to the brain stem. If the stroke extended higher into the brain or was associated with a more extensive medical episode that interfered with the supply of oxygen to the brain, a wide variety of cognitive deficits may be present. These need to be assessed on an individual basis.

***Sensory/Perceptual Skills***   A high brain stem stroke may affect the cranial nerve nuclei that control muscles for eye and eyelid movement, while a mid- or low brain stem stroke probably will not impair these muscles. Thus, visual functioning may or may not be impaired. In all cases, hearing is generally unimpaired, while tactile and position senses are often damaged.

***Motor Skills***   Persons with severe dysarthria or anarthria following a brain stem stroke usually experience motor control problems of their limbs as well as of their speech mechanisms. AAC interventions reported in the literature have employed eye or head pointing as the alternative access mode for these individuals who experience motor control problems. For example, Beukelman, Yorkston, and Dowden (1985) reported two case studies of persons with brain stem strokes who successfully used electronic AAC systems via optical pointers mounted on their eyeglasses. Both individuals were required to spend much time in bed for medical reasons, and so they learned to operate their AAC systems both while in their wheelchairs and lying supine. Special mounting systems were designed to support their systems in bed.

## SUMMARY

AAC interventions for persons with severe communication disabilities due to physical impairments are influenced by numerous factors. First, the diseases, conditions, and syndromes associated with the physical impairments usually require close medical monitoring. Therefore, frequent, detailed, and accurate communication with medical personnel is necessary.

Second, the medical and physical status of individuals with physical impairments can affect their capability levels. Since fatigue is common for persons with physical impairments, interventionists should take care to provide these individuals with AAC systems that they can control even when tired. In addition, these individuals' responses to medication can be variable. For example, persons with Parkinson's disease may experience a range of physical abilities, depending on their medication regimens. Finally, those with physical impairments may be susceptible to health problems such as infections and respiratory disorders, both of which limit physical endurance.

Third, persons with severe communication disabilities due to physical impairments often experience additional disabilities in areas such as mobility, object manipulation, eating, and swallowing. Their communication needs are usually influenced by the nature and severity of these associated disabilities. In order to obtain appropriate services, they must request assistance, instruct caregivers and attendants, and interact with professional personnel regarding the range of their disabilities. Thus, AAC interventions must be planned to accommodate other assistive technologies, such as powered wheelchairs, electronically controlled beds, and respiratory support equipment.

# Chapter 17

# Adults with Severe Aphasia

## with Kathryn Garrett

"I did comprehend somewhat vaguely what was said to me, but I could not answer except in gestures or by neologisms [made-up words]. I knew the language I used was not correct but I was quite unable to select the appropriate words. I recollect trying to read the headlines of the *Chicago Tribune* but they didn't make any sense to me at all. I didn't have any difficulty focusing; it was simply that the words, individually or in combination, didn't have meaning . . . " wrote Scott Moss, recalling the first days following his stroke. (1972, p. 4)

## PREVALENCE AND ETIOLOGY

Aphasia is an impairment of the ability to interpret and formulate language as a result of brain injury. Most individuals acquire aphasia as a result of a cerebral vascular accident, commonly known as a stroke, which occurs generally after the age of 60–70 years, after a lifetime of communicating normally. Usually without warning, individuals are left with impaired language and communication. Depending on the severity of the aphasia, some individuals are not able to meet their communication needs only for a short time, but many may never again communicate easily and effectively.

Each year there are 500,000 individuals who experience a stroke. The average age of these individuals is 70 years. Seventy to eighty percent of them survive their first stroke; the 10-year survival rate is about 50% (Beukelman & Yorkston, 1989).

Recovery patterns of persons with aphasia secondary to stroke vary considerably. Most motor recovery takes place within 3–6 weeks, although upper extremity functioning may continue to improve over 6 months. Language functioning may slowly return over a much longer period of time. Some individuals with aphasia experience a nearly complete recovery of their language capabilities. Others demonstrate mild or moderate language impairments that reduce the efficiency of their communication. This chapter focuses primarily on the significant number of persons with aphasia for whom very severe communication disorders are permanent. Individuals in this group can sometimes use an AAC intervention.

## COMMUNICATION DISORDER

Aphasia is not restricted to a single language process; rather, aphasic individuals usually have reduced abilities in all language and communication modalities, including speaking, auditory comprehension, reading, writing, and communicating through gestures or pantomime. The degree of the deficit in each modality may be different, which creates distinct patterns of impairment. For example, some people experience an auditory comprehension deficit that is relatively severe when compared to their other language deficits. Others have only mild comprehension problems but experience considerable difficulty expressing themselves, particularly in producing the correct names of people, objects, or places. Others comprehend well and are able to produce important words but have difficulty producing grammatically complete messages. These and other patterns of language disorders in aphasia have been widely described. A detailed discussion of the various types of aphasia is beyond the scope of this text, and the reader is referred to Johns (1985) and to Rosenbek, LaPointe, and Wertz (1989) for extensive descriptions of the classic aphasia taxonomy and neurologic aspects.

A standard classification system of the types of aphasia has been used to diagnose and plan interventions for persons with mild and moderate impairments. An alternative model for intervention seems more useful for persons with severe aphasia. This model approaches the communication difficulties these individuals experience from an integrative perspective that encourages the use of both residual speech and AAC techniques as appropriate. Thus, residual speech can be used to communicate a message if available. AAC options can be incorporated when residual speech is inadequate to meet a person's communication needs.

## THE PARTICIPATION MODEL

The Participation Model (Figure 7.1.) is an effective framework for organizing AAC interventions with persons who have severe aphasia. Since this model was discussed in considerable detail in Chapters 7 and 8, only a brief review of the application of the model to aphasia is provided.

### Participation Patterns and Communication Needs

The participation patterns and the communication needs of adults with acquired severe communication disorders depend on two factors: their life-styles and their communication capabilities. Life-style issues are discussed first, and capability issues are discussed in the section of this chapter concerning assessment. The life-styles of persons with aphasia are determined by factors such as their living environments, their friendships, and family networks, as well as by their lifelong interaction styles.

Persons with aphasia after a stroke live in a variety of different environments. Some continue to live in their homes, with a spouse, and have opportunities to interact with neighbors, friends, and relatives. Other individuals are no longer able to live in their homes and may live in retirement centers, nursing centers, or in the homes of children or relatives. Many people with severe aphasia who were employed prior to their strokes will have to retire because of residual impairments. Thus, the participation patterns of individuals with aphasia are often quite different after a stroke than before.

As mentioned in Chapter 1, Light (1988) suggested that communication interaction styles can be divided into four general categories: expression of basic wants and needs, information transfer, social closeness, and social etiquette. An assessment of an individual's communication needs must consider his or her life-style and living situation. In the sections that follow, examples of different environments are presented to illustrate the process of assessment.

*Pre-stroke*     The pre-stroke communication needs of many elderly individuals are depicted in Figure 17.1.

Before a severe stroke, many older persons are able to care for their own wants and needs. They can prepare their own food, manage their own clothing, and transport themselves from place to place. They may require occasional assistance with household chores, taking care of their property, or transportation, but, in general, they request minimal assistance with wants and needs.

In contrast to this, most elderly persons also strive for social closeness in their interactions. They spend much time interacting with their relatives, acquaintances, and friends. As they become older, their immediate families may play a more limited role in their lives, and they will often turn more to their social networks for interaction. With time and the disability and death of relatives and friends, older adults must add to their network of friends and acquaintances. Thus, for an elderly person, the ability to communicate for social closeness is a very important interaction function.

In addition to interaction to support social closeness, the ability to transfer information remains important for elderly persons. The purpose of information transfer, however, often changes as people get older. In raising a family and in their jobs, people generally need to transfer information primarily related to daily and upcoming activities and events. As people enter their seventh and eighth decades of life, however, information transfer increasingly reflects their cultural roles as "tellers" of the past. In such roles, they often reiterate the oral histories of their families, recount past events, and attempt to interpret present experiences in terms of their past (Stuart, 1991). Awareness of these information transfer issues is important in the design of AAC systems for elderly individuals. For example, AAC systems should be developed that will facilitate efficient communication of the narratives that an elderly person enjoys re-telling.

Most elderly individuals want to continue participating in the social etiquette routines of their cultures. For example, they often appreciate being able to thank other individuals for assisting them, and they may become unhappy or frustrated when they are unable to interact properly in terms of etiquette. The awareness of what is proper is usually retained unless there is significant cognitive deterioration.

---

Scott Moss's wife remembers the first verbal interaction she had with her husband after his stroke: "She [the nurse] apparently gave Scott the phone and he uttered a sound but that's all that it was; I could not make head or tail out of what he was trying to say to me. I remember feeling that I had just fallen down to China. My heart just dropped! And there he was just babbling something over the phone to me, but nothing that I could understand. At this juncture I knew that something was very wrong and I simply said to him, 'Well, let's hang up the phone and I'll be there in a few minutes.' I got over there as quickly as I could and when I saw him he could say absolutely nothing to me. He just looked at me. Apparently he understood me but he couldn't say anything back. . . . " (Moss, 1972, p. 21)

---

***Acute Medical Setting***  In an acute medical setting, it might appear that communication regarding wants and needs would take priority for elderly individuals with aphasia following a severe stroke. While communication about one's medical condition and personal needs is important, an analysis of acute medical settings reveals that many activities are proscribed by the daily routines and structures of the hospital. Meals arrive on schedule, doctors' visits occur at regular times, and medications are administered at prescribed intervals. Even visitors are allowed only during certain hours. In fact, many of the wants and needs of patients in acute medical settings are met automatically.

Information transfer needs in acute medical settings are also quite focused. First, the medical team is interested in the individual's past medical and social history, which is often provided by the family. Second, persons with aphasia are frequently asked for information as part of the evaluation process. Medical staff will often ask questions about age, marital status, occupation, and place of birth, for example, in order to evaluate an individual's memory and cognitive status. For persons

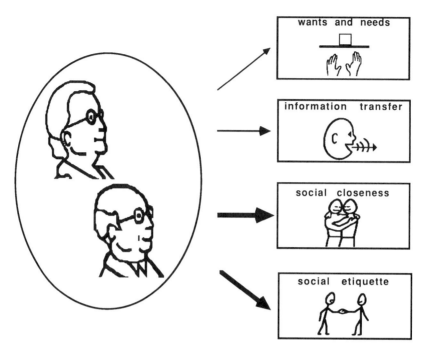

**Figure 17.1.** Pre-stroke communication needs of elderly individuals. (Picture Communication Symbols © 1981, 1985 by Mayer-Johnson Company; reprinted by permission. Some symbols have been adapted.)

with severe aphasia, these questions can be very frustrating, because their communication impairments can often mask their residual cognitive and memory skills. Thus, individuals may know the answers to these questions but be unable to provide them. Third, family members and business associates frequently need information from a person with severe aphasia. This information may relate to business, medical insurance, or financial investments. If the person or AAC team responsible for supporting the communication needs of an individual with aphasia can accommodate these information transfer needs, much of the frustration regarding this aspect of communication interaction is alleviated.

Communication needs related to social closeness often continue to predominate while the person is hospitalized and can often be met, at least in part, through alternative communication modes. Physical touch to express affection, affect displays (e.g., crying, smiling) to express emotion, and other nonverbal means may be used to achieve social closeness. In addition, residual drawing, writing, and other skills may also serve this function. Similarly, these alternative communication modes can be used for social etiquette routines such as thanking staff members for assistance. Social closeness interactions can be enhanced by providing patients with a means of recounting events related to the stroke and describing their current health status. These messages can be helpful when visiting with friends and family.

**Rehabilitation and Home Settings (Long-Term Care)**   An individual's communication needs change considerably when he or she is discharged from an acute medical to a rehabilitation setting. Another dramatic change in communication needs is experienced in the transition from an inpatient rehabilitation program to outpatient status. An individual's age, physical ability, and personality determine the interaction patterns that occur during these transitional phases. For example, some individuals may wish to participate only in family conversations and have little interest in social interactions outside of the home. Others may wish to communicate at home and in community activities, such as shopping, attending meetings, placing bets at the race track, or playing bingo, for example. Still others may wish to return to some level of employment. Obviously, it is difficult to develop an AAC plan without detailed knowledge of the individual's anticipated participation patterns.

The extent of communication related to wants and needs following discharge from a rehabilitation program depends a great deal on the individual's physical mobility. In most cases, people are able to move on their own following a stroke. If they are unable to use one hand, they can often use the other quite proficiently. Therefore, they can perform routine activities such as eating, pouring coffee, selecting their clothes, and performing simple chores around the house. A careful analysis should be made of activities that they cannot independently complete, since communication support to request assistance may be required for these activities.

The individual who returns home may also find that some interactions involve information transfer. For example, it may be extremely important to communicate the names of stores, medications, or grandchildren. Again, documenting such information transfer needs is an important part of an AAC assessment.

The social closeness interactions of elderly individuals following a stroke are a critical aspect of AAC interventions. Initially, spouses or family members may act as intermediaries or interpreters to assist the aphasic individual in communicating with family and friends, and vice versa. As time goes by, however, attempts should be made to initiate AAC techniques that allow independent communication of an increasing number of topics. Again, AAC specialists need to remember that the primary goal is social interaction, *not* information transfer. Thus, recounting past events, telling old stories, cracking timeworn jokes, and tying the present to the past (e.g., "That reminds me of the time . . . ") are very important *social interaction routines* for older persons. This may mean that once vocabulary items and other strategies have been instituted around particular topics (e.g., "When I was in the war" or "When I went to school"), they may not require much updating or revision, as the same events are likely to be recounted again and again. Obviously, this does not apply to topics that are more current, such as holidays, sports events, or politics.

The need for social etiquette interaction also increases when an individual leaves a medical or rehabilitation setting. In addition to simply thanking persons for assisting them, persons with aphasia may want to greet friends and acquaintances who come to visit, apologize for their difficulty in communicating or managing physical activities, tell people that they appreciate the assistance that is being provided, and communicate their pleasure that friends and family have taken the time to come and be with them. AAC strategies may be important if these routines cannot be communicated through natural speech or gestures.

## Assess Opportunity Barriers

It is important to be sensitive to the communication opportunities provided in specific contexts when assessing the ability of an individual with severe aphasia to participate in communication interactions. A common mistake is to provide an individual with an AAC system that has been set up for the wrong context. For example, it is not uncommon that people are discharged from rehabilitation programs with AAC supports that allow them to communicate quite effectively—as long as they are in rehabilitation settings! Such systems will probably be quite useless once the individual is at home or in an extended care facility where the communication opportunities and related needs are much different.

Families and friends of persons with severe aphasia play a vital role in determining communication opportunities. If families and friends do not attempt to include the individual, both physically and socially, in communicative interactions, successful participation will be difficult. It is also important, however, to remember that the communication patterns of the family before the stroke will eventually prevail. Thus, if the person with aphasia was not particularly social or talkative in the family prior to the stroke, it is unlikely that the family's interaction patterns will suddenly change to encourage much communication.

## Assess Specific Capabilities

Aphasia interventions traditionally emphasized the restoration of communication and linguistic processes. In keeping with this emphasis, assessment procedures were designed to identify the cognitive and linguistic deficiencies of an individual with aphasia, and interventions were designed to reduce these deficiencies.

This traditional approach has been inadequate for individuals whose communication disorders are so severe that they are unable to meet their daily communication needs. The traditional approach has meant that in many cases, people have lived without the ability to communicate adequately with their spouses, children, grandchildren, friends, and others. Thus, there has been a gradual shift to provide AAC supports of various types to persons with aphasia. These AAC approaches typically capitalize on an individual's residual capabilities. Garrett and Beukelman (1992) identified several such residual skills. Following the Participation Model, these are discussed in the following sections.

---

"We all use flowery adjectives to describe our opinion or rating of . . . experiences, but not Betty. She has adopted a short cut that is quite descriptive and effective, as well as being widely applicable. When asked how she likes the food in a restaurant, she may reply, 'B.' That is all, just 'B.' This means that it is almost tops, but not quite. A 'C' rating is pretty bad. The same system is used for movies, purchased items, perishable foods, television programs, art objects, etc.," wrote David Knox, referring to his wife, Betty, after her stroke. (1971, pp. 117–118)

---

**Linguistic Skills**    Although persons with aphasia may demonstrate extensive limitations in their linguistic systems, the words and structures with which they struggle are usually not lost or forgotten. Rather, they may not be immediately available for efficient communication. Some individuals with aphasia use telegraphic speech to communicate because they have difficulty accessing the grammatical aspects of language efficiently. Other individuals may retain a great deal of information about grammar, but have difficulty retrieving the content—that is, the specific words— that is important to their communication. In addition, the linguistic performance of a person with aphasia is often highly variable. Thus, an individual may be able to communicate a message at one point in time and have difficulty with the same message later on, or in a different context.

---

"Two months after the stroke I wanted to get a new head for my electric razor. I spent twenty minutes with the Yellow Pages and finally, in a sweat, asked [my wife] Jane to look up the store. I was within three pages but couldn't find it. After I had purchased the razor head, I couldn't install it because the directions were mildly complex. I was directed to: 'Remove the head, first pushing the blades to the down position and to the left, and insert new blades from the right, keeping them in the proper numerical order.' Clearly this was not written with an aphasic in mind," wrote Dr. Charles Clay Dahlberg, of his experiences after a stroke. (Dahlberg & Jaffe, 1977, p. 55)

---

To avoid underestimating the functional capabilities of individuals with aphasia, it is critical to be sensitive to the variability these individuals demonstrate when administering formal tests of language. Most tests are designed to be administered *acontextually*, so that linguistic processing capabilities can be measured without the influence of contextual supports, such as predictable conversational topics. Nevertheless, communication usually does not occur out of context, and many aphasic individuals find it very difficult to perform communicatively in such abstract, nonfunctional situations. Therefore, it may be necessary to supplement standard aphasia tests with assessments of the person's language performance in functional settings and with familiar people.

Many individuals with severe aphasia retain a considerable repertoire of nonverbal communication skills, such as gestures, facial expressions, pantomime , and vocalizations. Such skills allow some of them to communicate extensive information. Other individuals are impaired in their ability to produce nonverbal communication either consistently or efficiently. Instruction and practice are necessary in order for them to use this mode.

**Motor Skills**  Individuals with aphasia following a stroke usually retain the ability to control their limbs on at least one side of the body (usually the left). Therefore, they may be able to gesture, turn pages, or point to communication choices in a direct selection mode.

**Sensory Skills**  The visual system may be spared entirely following a stroke. Frequently, however, there may be a visual field cut, usually on the right side. This means that the person is unable to see images with the right side of both eyes. Thus, AAC or other materials that are positioned in the right visual field are visually inaccessible. A person's ability to scan the visual field or the extent of field cut should be determined. In addition, it is important to assess the individual's residual visual capabilities and identify any visual deterioration that has occurred naturally with age, as well as any new deficits.

**Perceptual Skills**  Persons with aphasia often understand many of the visual images that are used to represent the world. For example, they recognize various "icons of geography," such as maps, and "icons of events," such as logos and signs. They also usually retain the ability to identify photographs and drawings that relate to people and places. Many persons with aphasia retain knowledge about the relative relationships of size, shape, goodness, and importance among objects and experiences. For example, an aphasic individual may refer to another adult by gesturing to indicate his or her taller height as compared to a child.

Aphasic individuals may retain some ability to draw and can communicate messages through this modality (Lyon & Helm-Estabrooks, 1987). Although these individuals may never have considered themselves artists, they can often depict ideas clearly enough through drawing that knowledgable communication partners can understand their messages. Individuals with aphasia may often retain the chronology of events in their lives. For example, a person may indicate that a certain event, such as military service, occurred after high school but before marriage. Or, an individual may refer to important events in terms of their proximity to the birth dates of his or her children.

**Pragmatic Skills**  In addition to the generic skills that are identified in the Participation Model (Figure 7.1.), there are also specific skill areas that are particularly relevant to individuals with aphasia. One of these areas involves pragmatic skills, or the knowledge of how communication works. Because most individuals with aphasia have communicated using natural speech and writing for most of their lives, they are quite familiar with how communication works. That is, they are aware of the turn-taking skills, speaker–listener roles, and topic coordination that are required in communication. They can also recognize and attempt to clarify ambiguous communicative messages. Thus, when compared with individuals who have had few or no normal communication experiences, aphasic individuals are relatively aware of the structure and rules of conversational interaction.

**Experiential Skills**  Another skill area that is particularly relevant to persons with aphasia involves the experiential skill base underlying communication. Most individuals with aphasia have lived for a considerable period of time and have experienced relatively normal, routine life-styles, so their knowledge about the world is extensive. They have participated many times in the basic interactive routines of life. Therefore, although they may not have a strong linguistic base for communication, they are very aware of the settings in which communication normally occurs.

## Assess Constraints

*Partner Skills*    Because communication partners are so important in communication interactions with persons who have severe aphasia, it is useful to assess their capabilities as well. This
assessment usually cannot be formally conducted, so information about the communication skills
of partners is obtained from observing their interactions with the individual with aphasia. It is also
important to determine if the partner is able to learn or interested in learning new ways of communicating with the person with severe aphasia. The clinician should also formally evaluate potential
communication partners in basic skill areas that include handwriting legibility, reading skills,
hearing, and vision.

It is also important to assess how communication partners have adjusted to a spouse, parent,
or loved one following a stroke. Garrett and Beukelman (1991) provided a screening tool to assess
partner adjustment, as depicted in Figure 17.2.

## A NEW COMMUNICATION CLASSIFICATION SYSTEM

A new communication classification system of severely aphasic individuals to be used to plan and
initiate AAC interventions was introduced by Garrett and Buekelman (1991). They wrote: "As we
focus on enhancing the current communication performance of persons with aphasia and their
listeners, new descriptive classifications are necessary to guide clinical interventions" (p. 17). The
following categories are based on the severity of the communication deficits that affect individual
abilities to meet current needs and to participate in communication exchanges. The groups are
distinctive, and different AAC approaches are used for each group.

## Basic Choice Communicator

The basic choice communicator is so severely disordered that he or she requires maximal assistance
from a communication partner in order to express basic choices. For example, the individual might
make choices in order to clarify needs (i.e., bathroom or pain pill), participate in daily routines
(i.e., choosing clothing items during morning dressing), or communicate in the context of familiar
social activities (i.e., picking gift items from a simplified catalog). Although many types of aphasic

---

Patient: _____
Partner: _____
Date: _____

Circle the number that best describes your feelings

|  | | Disagree | | | | Agree |
|---|---|---|---|---|---|---|
| 1. | My family member/friend has changed since his or her stroke. | 1 | 2 | 3 | 4 | 5 |
| 2. | My family member/friend doesn't understand what's going on. | 1 | 2 | 3 | 4 | 5 |
| 3. | My family member/friend compensates well for his or her communication problems. | 1 | 2 | 3 | 4 | 5 |
| 4. | I think I have adjusted well to his or her disability. | 1 | 2 | 3 | 4 | 5 |
| 5. | We participate in as many activities as we used to. | 1 | 2 | 3 | 4 | 5 |
| 6. | We communicate as well as we did before the stroke. | 1 | 2 | 3 | 4 | 5 |
| 7. | I think my family member/friend should be more active than he or she is right now. | 1 | 2 | 3 | 4 | 5 |
| 8. | Our family has accepted the disability. | 1 | 2 | 3 | 4 | 5 |
| 9. | People don't understand what is wrong with my family member/friend. | 1 | 2 | 3 | 4 | 5 |
| 10. | I communicate with my family member/friend as often as I used to. | 1 | 2 | 3 | 4 | 5 |
| 11. | We have received enough information about stroke and aphasia. | 1 | 2 | 3 | 4 | 5 |
| 12. | I need to communicate better with my family member/friend. | 1 | 2 | 3 | 4 | 5 |
| 13. | My family member/friend respects himself or herself as much as before the stroke. | 1 | 2 | 3 | 4 | 5 |
| 14. | My family member/friend is frustrated. | 1 | 2 | 3 | 4 | 5 |

**Figure 17.2.**    Partner attitudinal survey. (From Garrett, K., & Beukelman, D. [1992]. Augmentative communication approaches for persons
with severe aphasia. In K. Yorkston [Ed.], *Augmentative communication in the medical setting*, p. 261. Copyright © by Communication Skill
Builders, Tucson, AZ; reprinted by permission.)

individuals function at the level of basic choice communicator shortly after their strokes, persons with persistent global aphasia and severe neurologic impairments may remain basic choice communicators for an extended period of time.

> "I have no memory of what I wanted to say—because it never got through. With utter confidence I pointed to each letter [on an alphabet board] and [my wife Jane] wrote them down and showed it to me. It was a combination of 'A,' 'I,' and 'U.' She tried to guess what I meant but couldn't. . . . If someone asked me to repeat a word I could not do it, but if someone showed me simple objects and asked me if I knew what they were, I could nod 'yes' or 'no' correctly. For instance, I could distinguish between a pencil and a coin. . . . Complicated directions . . . were impossible for me," wrote Dr. Charles Clay Dahlberg, describing his memories of the first days after his stroke. (1977, pp. 22–23)

The goal of AAC interventions with basic choice communicators is to provide them with a very simple system for communicating basic messages. Communication partners who are unfamiliar with these individuals will tend to use "20 questions, yes/no" for communicating basic messages. This strategy is often ineffective, however, because the individual becomes confused and is unable to manage this linguistic form. Instead, communication partners should be taught to provide simple choices from a limited number of options.

A second important partner skill involves learning to pause *without talking* for some time after offering a choice, to allow the individual to respond or to indicate that none of the choices are appropriate. This is quite important, as many basic choice communicators need considerable processing time in a quiet, nondistracting environment in order to formulate a message. Once the aphasic individual has made a choice, the partner then needs to learn to affirm it through a brief verbalization before proceeding (e.g., "Oh, you want the red shirt?"). Obviously, if the individual attempts to speak in response, this effort should be accepted and encouraged. The aphasic individual may, however, use other means for affirmation or negation at this point. Using the above example, for instance, some individuals may use prolonged eye gaze toward the red shirt to affirm their response. Others may simply reach for the shirt as a form of affirmation, or push it away if it is not the desired choice. Still others will nod their heads for affirmation and simply sit to indicate rejection. It is important for facilitators to become familiar with the simple accept/reject signals used by the individual so that they do not expect complex or sophisticated signals. Often, basic choice communicators will indicate a choice and then become confused when their communication partners engage in prolonged yes/no questioning or prodding to confirm the choice.

It is important to provide appropriate encouragement and instruction to those who facilitate communication for basic choice communicators. Facilitators must learn to analyze situations and predict the appropriate communication choices, which are skills that are initially unfamiliar and often frustrating. Elderly facilitators should not be rushed through training, and they should have ample time to observe someone else engaging their spouse or friend in basic choice communication. Younger listeners, such as children and grandchildren, often tend to present choices too rapidly. Younger facilitators often need to learn to be deliberate, to pause without talking so the person can respond, and to be patient and calm during communication interactions.

## Controlled Situation Communicator

Controlled situation communicators function more capably than basic choice communicators, because they can indicate needs by spontaneously pointing to objects and items. Controlled situation communicators are aware of daily routines and can participate in conversations structured by a skilled communication partner. Nevertheless, controlled situation communicators do not have the linguistic ability to initiate communication acts consistently. Thus, these individuals may be quite

isolated socially unless they are assisted to participate. With assistance, however, they can participate in controlled, predictable exchanges (e.g., introductions in a group), or in routine conversations when written or pictorial choices are provided by their communication partners. Some individuals with persistent global aphasia, Broca's aphasia, or Wernicke's aphasia may function as
controlled situation communicators.

---

"I . . . provided [Betty] with an identification paper on which was typed all the information
necessary to help her through any of the emergency situations that might occur. . . . I felt
that it was about as much protection as I could give her, as a driving aphasic. She was to carry
it in her purse always. [In addition to basic identification, the paper contained messages such
as 'My car will not start,' and 'I have a flat tire']. . . . Betty had driven to the dry cleaner's
with some clothes and when she came out the car would not start. She consulted her identification paper and decided to walk the two blocks to the nearest gas station. While walking
she repeated over and over the words from the instruction sheet, 'My car will not start,' so
she would not have to be embarrassed by pointing to the written sentence. The attendant
understood her and drove her back to . . . where her car was standing. . . . Next she tele-
phoned my office to ask me to pick her up, making use of the instruction sheet for the phone
number . . . " wrote David Knox, Betty's husband. (1971, pp. 65–66)

---

AAC interventions for controlled situation communicators attempt to provide the necessary
communication tools and techniques so that the person can engage in specific, restricted communication activities. Since these individuals often become confused if a variety of different communication activities are combined, simple and familiar contexts should be selected. These might include, for example, watching a baseball game, eating a meal, and celebrating a birthday party.

In order to facilitate choice making, partners must be trained to manage several communica-
tion-related tasks. First, when facilitating communication with an individual who is able to initiate
interactions, the facilitator needs to be able to identify the basic topic of interest. This can often be
determined intuitively, by examining the context of the interaction and taking cues from the daily
routine. For example, if the individual becomes agitated while watching a political debate on television, chances are fairly good that he or she wants to communicate something about politics or the
candidates. It may often be useful for the facilitator to provide symbols of some type that reflect
general topics that reoccur frequently, so that the individual can choose from the options.

A primary communication technique used with controlled situation communicators is "written choice communication" (Garrett & Beukelman, 1992). This technique requires the facilitator to
generate word choices pertinent to a conversational topic. The person with severe aphasia participates by pointing to the choices and making his or her opinions and preferences known. The clinician's role is to instruct the facilitators and to assist them to prepare notebooks containing choices to
support interactions.

During an AAC assessment, the appropriate types of symbols that can be used in conversations should be determined. Some controlled situation communicators are able to use only real
object symbols, while others are able to comprehend photographs or line drawings. For an individual who does not initiate communicative exchanges, the facilitator will need to offer such symbolized choices in order to start the conversation.

### Augmented Input Communicator

Augmented input communicators have auditory language processing difficulties that make it difficult for them to understand language. Thus, their communication partners need to augment or

support verbal input through gestures or visual symbols. As communication partners speak, they can provide individuals with aphasia with visual representations of their messages through writing, photographs, drawings, or other symbols representing key words and topics. Individuals with aphasia can then point to these same visual representations to identify aspects of the interaction that they have not understood or about which they want additional information. Visual representations may also help to clarify the range of choices that are being offered. For example, an individual with aphasia might be provided with pictures or written names of possible stores to visit during an afternoon shopping trip. This would be preferable to providing only verbal descriptions of the stores, if the individual experiences significant comprehension difficulties. The technique of augmented input is completely partner dependent, which means that communication partners must learn to resolve communication breakdowns by choosing the appropriate technique. The clinician can assist with this process by demonstrating the technique and by providing a notebook with instructions on the cover to partners.

Although a variety of individuals with severe aphasia may benefit from augmented input techniques at some point in their recovery, persons with Wernicke's aphasia often require augmented input permanently. Other individuals with aphasia who demonstrate intermittent auditory processing problems may also benefit from this technique.

> "On one occasion my wife read to me a story about a hedgehog, and I realized after a time that I had no idea what a hedgehog was. All her efforts to explain would not coax the concept back into my mind. She seemed to be describing something like a badger, but clearly it was not that. . . . When I tried to tell this anecdote, I was left feeling foolish because I could not remember the name for 'hedgehog,' and finally, by great effort, produced the word 'chair-horse'," wrote Guy Wint after his stroke. (1965, p. 26)

## Comprehensive Communicator

The comprehensive communicator has retained a variety of communication skills following the stroke, but these skills are often too fragmented or inconsistent for effective communication without support. Due to their typically independent life-styles, these individuals usually wish to participate in various types of conversational exchanges that occur in many environments. The comprehensive communicator often has a range of preserved skills that may include drawing, gestures, first-letter-of-word spelling, and pointing to words or symbols, in addition to limited speech. Many successful comprehensive communicators are individuals with Broca's aphasia. One individual with conduction aphasia was also an outstanding comprehensive communicator (Garrett & Beukelman, 1992). She was able to manage the social aspects of communication quite well but required extensive support when asked to communicate specific information to her friends, her lawyer, her doctor, and the bus driver.

AAC interventions for comprehensive communicators are quite complex. In addition to identifying anticipated participation patterns, clarifying communication needs, and identifying topics of interest, the AAC specialist must also teach the individual to manage a variety of AAC techniques. For example, Beukelman, Yorkston, and Dowden (1985) described a man with Broca's aphasia who used a series of AAC approaches as he progressed through various phases of recovery. Initially, he communicated with a simple communication book that contained photographs of familiar people, places, and activities, and his family provided picture albums identifying family members, interests, and experiences. In time, portfolios of this man's work as an interior designer were also used to augment his conversational efforts, by helping him to establish a topic and by providing pictorial support for specific words and ideas. Eventually, a multimodal AAC system was developed for him that included an electronic communication device with voice output, limited natural speech, gestures, a communication book, portfolios, books and blueprints on the walls of the design studio in his home, and a design assistant who also served as a facilitator.

An often overlooked but critical aspect of AAC interventions with comprehensive communicators is their need for substantial instruction and guided practice to teach them *when* to use the various AAC techniques provided. Garrett, Beukelman, and Low-Morrow (1989) described this process with a comprehensive communicator whose AAC system contained many different components, as outlined in Table 17.1.

Three to four months were required to teach this man ways to decide when to use a specific AAC technique and to become proficient in choosing the correct technique. He used the instructional sequence summarized in Figure 17.3. to guide his decision making in intervention sessions. He would first attempt to say a message using his natural speech. If he experienced a communication breakdown, he would then attempt to gesture, write, or repeat the spoken message. If he were still unsuccessful, he would use the word notebook, alphabet card, or new information pocket. Finally, he would direct his listener to the clues or control phrases.

Unfortunately, it is not uncommon in clinical practice to slight this training phase in a multimodal intervention. Other common reasons that comprehensive communicators often fail to use their AAC systems effectively include: 1) the vocabulary and content of the AAC materials provided are inappropriate, 2) important communication partners are not willing or encouraged to accept augmented modes of communication, and 3) teaching and training in naturalistic situations did not occur.

## Specific Need Communicator

The specific need communicator needs communication support in specific situations that require particular specificity, clarity, or efficiency. For example, an individual with aphasia might want to communicate on the phone, place bets at the race track, follow recipes, or write memos. Any individual with aphasia could have such well-defined, specific communication needs. Individuals who live in settings that demand some independence generally need this type of AAC technique.

**Table 17.1.**  Components of an AAC system for a comprehensive communicator with Broca's aphasia

| Communication component | Purpose | Comments |
|---|---|---|
| Word dictionary | To talk about frequently occurring topics of interest in conversations | Easier to use when words were organized topically rather than alphabetically |
| Alphabet card | To communicate unique information or to resolve communication breakdowns | Included first-letter-of-word cuing that allowed partner to deduce semi-intelligible spoken words |
| New information pocket | To communicate about current or recent events in conversations | Included newspaper clippings and remnants from the race track, for example |
| Breakdown resolution "clues" | To help resolve communication breakdowns | Included phrases to guide the partner through a structured form of 20 questions: "It's a place/person/event/thing/time" |
| Conversational control phrases | To enhance conversational control and to prevent or resolve breakdowns from rapid, unannounced topic shifts | Included phrases such as "I'm changing the topic now" and "Ask me questions" |
| Natural communication modalities | To enhance conversational efficiency | Included gestures, natural speech, drawing, and writing |

Adapted from Garrett, Beukelman, and Low-Morrow (1989).

Step 1: Natural Speech
    Try to say it

Step 2: Other Natural Modalities
    Use a gesture OR
    Write it OR
    Try to say it again

Step 3: Augmented Techniques
    Use the word dictionary OR
    Use the alphabet card OR
    Use the new information pocket

Step 4: Breakdown Strategies
    Use a clue phrase OR
    Use a control phrase

**Figure 17.3.** Instructional sequence for a comprehensive communicator with Broca's aphasia. (Adapted from Garrett, Beukelman, & Low-Morrow, 1989.)

AAC interventions for specific need communicators are usually limited in scope, since these individuals can often manage much of their communication through gestures and limited speech. When planning an intervention, it is first necessary to analyze the requirements of the specific communication task and to consider the person's current capabilities in light of the task. For example, an individual may need help setting up a system to allow verbal communication over the telephone. This can often be managed through a simple tape recorder system in which a pre-recorded message requests, "Please ask me questions that can be answered 'yes' or 'no.' " Another common need is to be able to communicate specific messages in a noisy place such as a cafeteria or bank. Often, a small communication card can be prepared with a restricted set of the messages that are needed in the situation. Careful analysis of specific, individual communication needs is required, because a variety of different communication events might need to be supported in this way.

## SUMMARY

Interest in applying AAC principles to persons with severe aphasia is increasing. With functional communication as the primary goal, people with aphasia are being provided with AAC options soon after their strokes. During rehabilitation, therapy to promote the recovery of natural speech is encouraged, and AAC systems are modified to support functional communication that cannot be managed through natural speech. As the recovery of natural speech stabilizes, the nature of the AAC system often stabilizes as well, so that the specific communication techniques no longer require modification. Nevertheless, it is essential that the *content* of an AAC system remain dynamic. As changes occur in the situations and contexts of an individual's life, the AAC system must reflect these changes, because, otherwise, motivation and interest in using the system will quickly diminish. Continual modification of the content of an AAC system requires that one or more facilitators, usually family members or caregivers, be trained to monitor and adjust the AAC system. Facilitators must also be able to train new people who enter the aphasic person's life (e.g., a son- or daughter-in-law or a new neighbor), so that they, too, can become effective communication partners. Failure to identify and adequately prepare facilitators is a common reason for AAC intervention failures among persons with severe aphasia.

# Chapter 18

# Persons with
# Traumatic Brain Injury

## THE CHANGING PHILOSOPHY OF AAC INTERVENTION

AAC interventions for persons who have experienced traumatic brain injury (TBI) have changed dramatically since the 1980s. Until recently, AAC interventions were initiated primarily with individuals who experienced severe, persistent anarthria or dysarthria following TBI. It was not uncommon to delay AAC interventions until the associated communication disorders "stabilized"; consequently, many persons with TBI were unable to speak functionally for months or even years after their accidents. The justification for this conservative approach had three bases. First, cognitive limitations during early phases of recovery make the operation of complex AAC techniques difficult for many persons with TBI. Second, because of the changing cognitive and motor performance of persons with TBI, an appropriate long-term AAC system is difficult to select. Third, clinical observations indicated that some individuals with TBI do recover functional speech and, therefore, do not require long-term AAC systems. With this view, the "safest" approach in recommending an AAC intervention was felt to be the most conservative approach.

The pattern of AAC services to persons with TBI has been changing. Increasingly, the goal of the AAC team is to provide communication assistance to individuals with TBI so that they are able to communicate to participate effectively in their rehabilitation programs, as well as meet their ongoing communication needs. Thus, the focus of intervention has shifted from providing a single, long-term AAC system to providing a series of AAC systems designed to meet short-term communication needs while continuing efforts to reestablish natural speech. For example, Table 18.1. illustrates the AAC intervention goals over a 3-year period for Ann, an adolescent with TBI (Light, Beesley, & Collier, 1988).

Because survivors of brain injury recover over an extended period of time, it is beyond the scope of this book to detail extensive AAC intervention concepts, techniques, and strategies developed for these individuals. Two detailed presentations of such information have been published and provide extensive information in this area (DeRuyter & Kennedy, 1991; Ladtkow & Culp, 1992). The purpose of this chapter is to outline the general approaches to AAC intervention for individuals with TBI.

## PREVALENCE AND ETIOLOGY

Injuries to the head that result in temporary or permanent brain damage are quite common. It is difficult to estimate the number of these injuries that occur each year, because many go unreported. Individuals who do not lose consciousness or do so only briefly are rarely admitted to the hospital, or even to an emergency room. The incidence of traumatic brain injury (TBI) as reported by emergency room records is approximately 200 per 100,000 people. Of the 500,000 individuals who sustain TBI in the United States each year, approximately 50,000–100,000 survive with impairments

**Table 18.1.**   Principal goals of intervention with Ann over a 3-year period

Phase One: 6–9 months post-trauma
1. To establish consistent and reliable yes/no responses.
2. To develop a preliminary communication display as a means to indicate basic needs and wants.

Phase Two: 13–16 months post-trauma
1. To provide a means to request attention.
2. To encourage more explicit "yes" response.
3. To develop a communication display as a means to share information and express needs and wants.

Phase Three: 22–23 months post-trauma
1. To provide access to a microcomputer for written communication.
2. To establish more explicit "no" responses for unfamiliar listeners.
3. To develop strategies to share information and generate novel vocabulary.

Phase Four: 36 months post-trauma
1. To develop breath control, articulation skills, and voicing.
2. To develop strategies to interact effectively with unfamiliar partners and in group activities.
3. To develop conversation skills around a range of topics.
4. To enhance the rate of written expression.

Phase Five: 40–44 months post-trauma
1. To continue to develop breath control, articulation skills, and voicing.
2. To recognize breakdowns in communication.
3. To use clarification strategies to repair communication.

From Light, L., Beesley, M., and Collier, B. (1988). Transition through multiple augmentative and alternative communication systems: A three-year case study of a head-injured adolescent. *Augmentative and Alternative Communication, 4,* 3; reprinted by permission.

that are so severe that they interfere with independent living. An additional 200,000 or more experience continuing sequelae that interfere with their ability to perform daily living skills (Gualtieri, 1988; Jennett, Snoek, Bond, & Brooks, 1981; Kalsbeek, McLauren, Harris, & Miller, 1981; Kraus, 1978; Olsen & Henig, 1983).

> Individuals with TBI do not represent a random sample of the total population. More than twice as many males as females are injured. The risk of TBI is also greater among children from four to five years of age, males from 15–24 years of age, the elderly (especially those over 75 years), and individuals who had previous TBI. (Beukelman & Yorkston, 1991, p. 4)

The causes of TBI are varied. Motor vehicle accidents are the most common cause, and falls of various types are second. Among students, recreational- and sports-related injuries such as those that occur from bicycling, skating, and horseback riding are common. Among adolescents and young adults, assaults are a common cause of TBI. The dramatic increase in the incidence of TBI among young adults occurs as a result of motor vehicle accidents.

Severe brain injuries dramatically affect the lives of survivors and their families. In 1988, most survivors of severe TBI:

> lived with their families, did not work or attend school, and were dependent upon others for skills, finances, and services outside the home. Due to the lack of available programs, families most frequently assumed the major responsibility for the survivor's long-term care despite no training in the area. (Jacobs, 1988, p. 425)

As they recover, persons with severe TBI usually progress through a continuum of care that begins in a trauma unit. Through hours, days, months, and years, these individuals recover abilities and functions at different rates. These complex but individual patterns of change affect nearly all aspects of their lives.

## CLASSIFICATION SYSTEMS

Several categorical scales have been developed in an effort to describe persons with severe traumatic brain injury. The Levels of Cognitive Functioning (LOCF) scale, which is used to describe cognitive and associated language behaviors that occur during recovery, is presented in Table 18.2.

## COMMUNICATION DISORDERS

Communication disorders associated with TBI are rooted in three areas of impairment. First, some of the language characteristics of persons with TBI are a consequence of *cognitive impairments*, as summarized in Table 18.2. The range of linguistic performance can be extensive depending on the cognitive level, as Table 18.2. shows. Second, language disorders may occur because of *damage to specific language processing areas* of the brain. A study of 125 individuals with TBI who were evaluated using the Battery of Language Test reported that 29% of subjects exhibited classic symp-

**Table 18.2.**  Levels of cognitive functioning and associated language behaviors

| General behaviors | Language behaviors |
|---|---|
| **I.  No Response**<br>     Patient appears to be in a deep sleep and is completely unresponsive to any stimuli. | Receptive and expressive: No evidence of processing or verbal or gestural expression. |
| **II.  Generalized Response**<br>     Patient reacts inconsistently and nonpurposefully to stimuli in a non-specific manner. Responses are limited and often the same, regardless of stimulus presented. Responses may be physiologic changes, gross body movements, or vocalization. | Receptive and expressive: No evidence of processing or verbal or gestural expression. |
| **III.  Localized Response**<br>     Patient reacts specifically, but inconsistently, to stimuli. Responses are directly related to the type of stimulus presented. May follow simple commands such as "Close your eyes" or "Squeeze my hand" in an inconsistent, delayed manner. | Language begins to emerge. Receptively: Patient progresses from localizing to processing and following simple commands that elicit automatic responses in a delayed and inconsistent manner. Limited reading emerges.<br>     Expressively: Automatic verbal and gestural responses emerge in response to direct elicitation. Negative head nods emerge before positive head nods. Utterances are single words serving as "holophrastic" responses. |
| **IV.  Confused-Agitated**<br>     Behavior is bizarre and nonpurposeful relative to immediate environment. Does not discriminate among persons or objects; is unable to cooperate directly with treatment efforts; verbalizations are frequently incoherent or inappropriate to the environment; confabulation may be present. Gross attention to environment is very short, and selective attention is often nonexistent. Patient lacks short-term recall. | Severe disruption of frontal–temporal lobes, with the resultant confusion apparent.<br>     Receptively: Marked disruption in auditory and visual processing, including inability to order phonemic events, monitor rate, and attend to, retain, categorize, and associate stimuli. Disinhibition interferes with comprehension and ability to inhibit responses to self-generated mental activity.<br>     Expressively: Marked disruption of phonologic, semantic, syntactic, and suprasegmental features. Output is bizarre, unrelated to environment, and incoherent. Literal, verbal, and neologistic paraphasias appear with disturbance of logico-sequential features and incompleteness of thought. Monitoring of pitch, rate, intensity, and suprasegmentals is severely impaired. |

*(continued)*

**Table 18.2.**  (*continued*)

| General behaviors | Language behaviors |
|---|---|
| **V. Confused, Inappropriate, Nonagitated**<br><br>Patient is able to respond to simple commands fairly consistently. However, with increased complexity of commands or lack of any external structure, responses are nonpurposeful, random, or fragmented. Has gross attention to the environment but is highly distractible and lacks ability to focus attention on a specific task; with structure, may be able to converse on a social-automatic level for short periods; verbalization is often inappropriate and confabulatory; memory is severely impaired; often shows inappropriate use of subjects; individual may perform previously learned tasks with structure but is unable to learn new information. | Linguistic fluctuations are in accordance with the degree of external structure and familiarity-predictability of linguistic events.<br><br>Receptively: Processing has improved, with increased ability to retain temporal order of phonemic events, but semantic and syntactic confusions persist. Only phrases or short sentences are retained. Rate, accuracy, and quality remain significantly reduced.<br><br>Expressively: Persistence of phonologic, semantic, syntactic and prosodic processes. Disturbances in logicosequential features result in irrelevances, incompleteness, tangent, circumlocutions, and confabulations. Literal paraphasias subside, while neologisms and verbal paraphasias continue. Utterances may be expansive or telegraphic, depending on inhibition–disinhibition factors. Responses are stimulus bound. Word retrieval deficits are characterized by delays, generalizations, descriptions, semantic associations, or circumlocutions. Disruptions in syntactic features are present beyond concrete levels of expression or with increased length of output. Written output is severely limited. Gestures are incomplete. |
| **VI. Confused-Appropriate**<br><br>Patient shows goal-directed behavior but depends on external input for direction; follows simple directions consistently and shows carryover for relearned tasks with little or no carryover for new tasks; responses may be incorrect due to memory problems but appropriate to the situation; past memories show more depth and detail than recent memory. | Receptively: Processing remains delayed, with difficulty in retaining, analyzing, and synthesizing. Auditory processing is present for compound sentences, while reading comprehension is present for simple sentences. Self-monitoring capacity emerges.<br><br>Expressively: Internal confusion-disorganization is reflected in expression, but appropriateness is maintained. Language is confused relative to impaired new learning and displaced temporal and situational contexts, but confabulation is no longer present. Social–automatic conversation is intact but remains stimulus bound. Tangential and irrelevant responses are present only in open-ended situations requiring referential language. Neologisms are extinguished, with literal paraphasias present only in conjunction with an apraxia. Word retrieval errors occur on conversation but seldom in confrontation naming. Length of utterance reflects inhibitory–initiation mechanisms. Written and gestural expression increases. Prosodic features reflect the "voice of confusion," characterized by monopitch, monostress, and monoloudness. |
| **VII. Automatic-Appropriate**<br><br>Patient appears appropriate and oriented within hospital and home settings, goes through daily routine automatically, but is frequently robotlike with minimal-to-absent confusion; has shallow recall of activities; shows carryover for new learning but at a decreased rate; with structure, is able to initiate social or recreational activities; judgment remains impaired. | Linguistic behaviors appear "normal" within familiar, predictable, structured settings, but deficits emerge in open-ended communication and less structured settings.<br><br>Receptively: Reductions persist in auditory processing and reading comprehension relative to length, complexity and presence of competing stimuli. Retention has improved to short paragraphs but without the abilities to identify salient features, organize, integrate input, order, and retain detail.<br><br>Expressively: Automatic level of language is apparent in referential communication. Reasoning is |

(continued)

**Table 18.2.**   *(continued)*

| General behaviors | Language behaviors |
|---|---|
|  | concrete and self-oriented. Expression becomes tangential and irrelevant when abstract linguistic concepts are attempted. Word retrieval errors are minimal. Length of utterance and gestures approximately normal. Writing is disorganized and simple at a paragraph level. Prosodic features may remain aberrant. Pragmatic features of ritualizing and referencing are present, while other components remain disrupted. |
| **VIII.   Purposeful and Appropriate**<br>      Patient is able to recall and integrate past and recent events and is aware of and responsive to the environment, shows carryover for new learning and needs no supervision once activities are learned; may continue to show a decreased ability relative to premorbid abilities in language, abstract reasoning, tolerance for stress, and judgment in emergencies or unusual circumstances. | Language capacities may fall within normal limits. Otherwise, problems persist in competitive situations and in response to fatigue, stress, and emotionality, characterized in reduced effectiveness, efficiency, and quality of performance.<br>      Receptively: Rate of processing remains reduced but unremarkable on testing. Retention span remains limited at paragraph level but improved with use of retrieval–organization strategies. Analysis, organization, and integration are reduced in rate and quality.<br>      Expressively: Syntactic and semantic features fall within normal limits, while verbal reasoning and abstraction remain reduced. Written expression may fall below premorbid level. Prosodic features are essentially normal. Pragmatic features of referencing, presuppositions, topic maintenance, turn taking, and use of paralinguistic features in context remain impaired. |

From Hagen, C. (1984). Language disorders in head trauma. In A. Holland (Ed.), *Language disorders in adults* (pp. 245–281). Austin, TX: PRO-ED; reprinted by permission.

toms associated with acquired aphasia. An additional 36% exhibited "subclinical aphasia," which was defined as "linguistic processing deficits on testing in the absence of clinical manifestations of linguistic impairment" (Sarno, Buonaguro, & Levita, 1986, p. 106).

Third, some communication disorders in TBI are caused by *damage to the motor control areas* of the brain that occurred at the time of injury. A detailed study of the incidence of dysarthria following TBI has not been completed. In a report of clinical work, approximately one third of a group of 96 persons with TBI demonstrated dysarthria during their "acute illness" (Rusk, Block, & Lowman, 1969). Several different types of dysarthria have been observed following TBI. The predominant type is ataxic dysarthria, which has been reported by Simmons (1983), Yorkston and Beukelman (1981), and Yorkston, Beukelman, Minifie, and Sapir (1984). In addition, flaccid dysarthria was described for a man with TBI (Netsell & Daniel, 1979). Mixed spastic-flaccid and mixed spastic-ataxic dysarthria have also been described (Yorkston & Beukelman, 1981).

## Recovery from Severe Communication Disorders

Communication disorders of individuals with TBI can change dramatically over the course of recovery. There is limited longitudinal research describing the patterns of these changes, but the results of two studies in this area can be summarized.

Ladtkow and Culp (1992) followed 138 persons with TBI over an 18-month period. They reported that 29 (21%) of these individuals were judged to be "nonspeaking" at some point in their recovery. Sixteen of these 29 individuals (55%) regained functional speech during the "middle phase" of recovery (i.e., Levels IV and V in Table 18.2). Thirteen individuals (45%) did not regain functional speech; unfortunately, the description of the cognitive recovery of those who did not regain functional speech is incomplete. The authors merely indicated that only three (10%) reached the late stage of recovery, corresponding to Levels VI, VII, and VIII.

In a related study, Dongilli, Hakel, and Beukelman (1991) investigated the recovery of 27 persons who were unable to speak on admission to inpatient rehabilitation following TBI. Sixteen (59%) individuals became functional natural speakers during inpatient rehabilitation, while the other eleven (41%) did not. All individuals who became functional speakers did so at Level V or VI. Of the 11 individuals who left inpatient rehabilitation unable to speak, 1 achieved functional natural speech almost 24 months post-injury, and another was making substantial progress toward becoming a functional speaker 48 months after the injury.

Adding to this limited information base regarding recovery from communication disorders are two case history reports of note. In one, Workinger and Netsell (1988) described a man who recovered intelligible speech 13 years post-injury, having used various AAC systems during the intervening years. In addition, Light et al. (1988) described the transitions of an adolescent with TBI through approximately 3 years of multiple AAC systems before she became a functional natural speaker (see Table 18.1.).

---

"[Judy] tried to talk several times during the day. Much of it sounded unintelligible, but occasionally we heard a 'Where am I?' or other words we could understand. We could not tell if she knew us, or understood anything we said. Then a few days later . . . Judy started trying to answer. . . . We spent the rest of the day hanging over her bed admiring her, as you might hang over the crib of a newborn baby. . . . The next day she responded less. This turned out to be a pattern. Nearly every day on which she showed definite improvement was followed by one of passivity or even apparent regression. It kept us on an emotional roller coaster," wrote Dorothy Thatch, recounting the first few days in the hospital after her daughter Judy's severe TBI. (Weiss, Thatch, & Thatch, 1987, p. 17)

---

## NATURAL ABILITY INTERVENTIONS: APPROACHES TO SUPPORT NATURAL SPEECH

As is apparent from the previous discussion, some individuals with TBI recover natural speech following the injury while others do not. At this point, the communication disorders field does not have enough information in order to predict the likelihood of natural speech recovery. Therefore, survivors of TBI, their families, and rehabilitation teams must address natural speech recovery on an individual basis. Some individuals may be able to produce a number of intelligible words, although they may not develop completely functional speech in all situations. Use of these words should be encouraged and improved if they allow the individuals to manage aspects of communication interaction.

Most individuals with TBI use multiple modes of communication at every stage of recovery. Thus, AAC systems must be integrated with reemerging natural speech. A person with TBI is likely to have communication needs that are unmet if he or she is receiving rehabilitation that emphasizes either reestablishing natural speech only or AAC only.

### Augmenting the Intelligibility of Natural Speech

Some persons with dysarthria following TBI are able to say many words, but the words may be unintelligible because of their impaired motor control. AAC techniques may be used to augment the intelligibility of natural speech.

*Topic Identification*  If a person's speech is marginally intelligible, his or her message can often be understood if the listener is aware of the semantic context or topic. Hammen, Yorkston, and Dowden (1991) reported that the improvement in speech intelligibility associated with contextual knowledge for a heterogeneous group of dysarthric speakers was: 1) 18.2% for the group with profound dysarthria (less than 35% intelligible without context), 2) 40.2% for the severe group (35%–50% intelligible without context), and 3) 29% for the moderate group (greater than

50% intelligible without context). Communication boards containing lists of frequently occurring topics can be used to establish context at the beginning of an interaction, to lessen the likelihood of a communication breakdown.

**Supplemented Speech** A "supplemented speech" strategy has been reported to substantially improve the speech intelligibility of dysarthric speakers (Beukelman & Yorkston, 1977). In supplemented speech, the speaker identifies the first letter of each word on an alphabet board or other type of AAC display as the word is spoken. This procedure provides listeners with information that allows them to restrict their word retrieval search to words that begin with the letter indicated. Beukelman and Yorkston (1977) described the impact of supplemented speech on the speech two dysarthric speakers, one of whom had sustained a TBI. When this young man spoke without AAC support, his sentence intelligibility was 33%, compared with 66% when he used supplemented speech.

**Portable Voice Amplification** Some persons with dysarthria following TBI speak so quietly that their speech is difficult to hear, especially in groups or noisy environments. A portable speech amplifier may be useful to increase the loudness of speech for these individuals. Readers are referred to Chapters 16 and 19 for more extensive discussion of this approach.

## ACCESS ASSESSMENT AND INTERVENTION

AAC approaches with persons who have traumatic brain injuries should be based on individual levels of cognitive recovery (DeRuyter & Kennedy, 1991; Ladtkow & Culp, 1992). AAC approaches have been described for three general phases of recovery: 1) the *early phase*, which involves Levels I, II, and III (Table 18.2.); 2) the *middle phase*, which includes Levels IV and V; and 3) the *late phase*, which includes Levels VI, VII, and VIII. Assessment and intervention goals and techniques differ considerably in these three phases (see Blackstone, 1989a for a summary).

### Early Phase (Levels I, II, and III)

**Assessment** It is almost impossible in the early phase of recovery to assess cognitive, language, or motor control capabilities, because the individual may be unable to stay awake or pay attention for any significant amount of time. Thus, very little formal assessment is attempted. Rather, systematic observations should be documented to identify changes in the individual's response patterns and to identify functional movements that may be used in a subsequent AAC program. Family members, friends, and other communication partners can also observe and chart such information if they spend a large amount of time with the individual. Because they know the person well, they are in a good position to document changes and responses.

As individuals with TBI become more alert, they are gradually able to differentiate between two or more people or objects. This is a positive sign, as it is often a precursor to the development of a yes/no response. The response mode for differentiation varies from person to person and may include eye pointing, moving a body part, or activating a beeper. The stimuli to which people are able to respond must be presented in a careful and controlled manner. Family members and communication partners can usually be trained in this approach. They can also provide information about the interests and pre-injury activities of the individual with TBI so that medical and rehabilitation personnel can provide the person with interesting and meaningful stimulation.

**AAC Intervention** During the early phase, persons with TBI are unable to speak functionally because of cognitive impairments. Some persons may have language or motor control deficits that further contribute to their communication disorder. Ladtkow and Culp (1992) suggested that "the primary treatment goal of early phase TBI recovery is for the person to emerge from coma and to begin to respond consistently to simple commands" (p. 154). Given this goal, the purpose of utilizing AAC techniques during this phase is to stimulate the individual and to facilitate consistent, purposeful responses.

AAC techniques utilized at this point vary considerably depending on the individual's overall neurologic involvement. For example, consider the individual who is functioning in the range of Levels I–III and who also has considerable motor control impairment. This individual might not be able to respond to stimuli consistently, not only because of cognitive problems, but also because of his or her motor weakness, spasticity, or incoordination. An AAC intervention for such a person might provide the individual with an alternative access mode, such as a single switch (Garrett, Schutz-Muehling, & Morrow, 1990). Then, as the individual begins to respond to various stimuli by making purposeful movements, contingency awareness (i.e., cause and effect) can be encouraged. For example, the individual might be encouraged to operate a tape recorder with a single switch to play favorite music or listen to recorded letters from family members or friends. In addition, the single switch with a control unit can be used to activate electrical appliances such as fans, radios, and lamps. As the individual becomes more purposeful, the single switch and tape recorder can be used to activate single-message tapes containing basic greetings and other social phrases (see chap. 10, this volume, for additional suggestions). Then, if motor control permits, two or more switches can be connected to different tape recorders so the individual can choose between different musical selections or letters.

## Middle Phase (Levels IV and V)

***Assessment***   In the middle phase of recovery, the individual may respond consistently to stimuli while still showing evidence of considerable performance and communication deficits due to attention and memory impairments. Individuals who do not have specific language deficiencies or severe motor control impairments usually begin to speak functionally during this phase, although the messages they produce may be somewhat confused (Dongilli et al., 1991; Ladtkow & Culp, 1992). In addition, people with TBI generally begin to indicate their basic needs at this point. These may include comfort messages such as hot/cold, hurt, hungry, or too loud. They may also be able to communicate messages related to their location, time of day, and other personal information. Family members and friends can assist with the selection of topics that are particularly important to persons in the middle phase of recovery.

The goal of assessment in the middle phase is to identify residual capabilities that can be utilized to achieve the specific communication needs mentioned previously. Most of the procedures for this assessment are nonstandardized and informal. The initial assessment often focuses on seating and postural issues, which should be coordinated with AAC concerns. Proper seating and positioning help to minimize reflex activity, excessive tone, and other movements that may interfere with verbal communication or AAC system usage (DeRuyter & Kennedy, 1991). Specifically, "the overall seating and positioning goals during the early rehabilitation phase should be to provide for a structurally appropriate and functional position in which minimal or no pain is encountered" (De Ruyter & Kennedy, 1991, p. 342).

Assessment of motor control capability is important to determine the individual's direct selection or scanning options. As discussed in Chapter 7, various access sites should be considered in terms of accuracy, efficiency, reliability, and endurance. This assessment may be difficult in some cases, since persons with TBI may require orthopedic surgical procedures that interfere, either temporarily or permanently, with their ability to use specific motor access sites (DeRuyter & Kennedy, 1991). Thus, it is important to coordinate medical procedures and AAC interventions closely by working with the medical team responsible for the individual's overall care.

Visual perceptual and visual acuity disturbances are common in TBI and should also be considered in the AAC assessment. At the lower cognitive levels, visual functioning is usually assessed by observing the individual's ocular response to threat, gross focus movements of the eyes, and the individual's ability to follow a bright object or familiar face (DeRuyter & Kennedy, 1991). At higher cognitive levels, many visual disturbances can be detected through standard ophthalmological examinations(see Table 7.12. for examples). A member of the AAC team should accompany the individual to such assessments to encourage the examiner to consider AAC-related issues, such as the optimum size for symbols and for the array and the optimum distance between the user and the display.

***AAC Intervention*** Depending on the nature of the brain injury, one or two major AAC goals are chosen for the middle phase. The goal may be to help the person compensate for attentional and memory deficiencies. This is particularly relevant for individuals with TBI who begin to speak during this phase, since they often need communication techniques to help them remember the names of people important to them and their schedule of activities, for example.

A second goal of intervention in the middle phase relates specifically to individuals who sustained damage to language or motor control areas of the brain. These individuals probably will not develop natural speech at this point in their recovery. Thus, AAC interventions should seek to provide them with techniques to support conversational interaction. In Levels IV and V, messages that relate to wants/needs and information sharing are more important to most individuals than are those that support social closeness and social etiquette (DeRuyter & Kennedy, 1991).

Most AAC interventions during the middle phase are nonelectronic and include alphabet boards, pictures, word boards, yes/no techniques, and dependent scanning, among others. In an effort to reduce the complexity of communication, context-specific miniboards are often used in this phase. For example, specific boards might be used to facilitate participation in cognitive rehabilitation activities, recreational events, or daily living routines. Depending upon the linguistic capabilities of the individual, the messages on these miniboards may be symbolized by photographs, line drawings, or printed words and phrases.

During the middle phase, single switches may continue to be used to activate call buzzers or appliances or to run tape recorders (see chaps. 10 and 13, this volume, for suggestions about these applications). Depending upon the physical capabilities of the individual, such switch control activities may serve as training for the operation of a long-term environmental control device.

---

DeRuyter and Donoghue (1989) described in detail the AAC interventions over a 28-week period for a young man who was unable to speak functionally due to TBI. During the first weeks of intervention (8 months after his injury), he established a reliable yes/no response by nodding his head, and he began to learn the visual–perceptual and upper extremity skills necessary for eventual use of a communication board. In addition, interventions designed to encourage the development of natural speech were initiated during this time. By the 10th week of intervention, he was able to use a simple alphabet board, 12 inches by 18 inches, with approximately 2-inch letters. Initially, he exhibited "extreme frustration" with the board because of his "motor planning deficits." By the 26th week of intervention, however, this young man exhibited "no hesitation in using his alphabet board when he was unable to communicate effectively verbally or gesturally" (p. 53). A SpeechPac, an electronic AAC device with voice output, was introduced at that time. With very little training on the SpeechPac, he was able to communicate at a rate of up to eight words per minute. At the time of his discharge from the inpatient rehabilitation facility, he communicated via limited speech, a sophisticated gesturing system, an alphabet board, and the SpeechPac with an expanded membrane keyboard.

---

Communication partners play an important role in structuring communication interactions during the middle phase. For example, partners may need to introduce topics for conversation, suggest the augmentative mode that can be used most productively at a particular time, assist with resolving communication breakdowns, and create motivating communication opportunities. Communication partners need to provide ample time for the formulation, clarification, and repair of messages for persons in the early and middle phases of recovery from TBI. Perhaps one of the most common partner errors is to rush or offer excessive encouragement during this phase by offering multiple suggestions of how to formulate or complete a message. This can be very distracting and frustrating to the individual with TBI who must concentrate very hard in order to think, plan, compose, and finally produce a communicative utterance. Thus, while communication partners should actively help to structure interactions, they should also be very patient and allow ample time for persons with TBI to prepare their messages.

### Late Phase (Levels VI, VII, and VIII)

**Assessment**   By this phase in recovery, most individuals have regained the cognitive capability to become natural speakers, and those who remain unable to speak usually experience severe specific language or motor control disorders. The Participation Model (Figure 7.1.) can be used effectively at this point for assessment and intervention planning.

Analysis of the *participation patterns* of individuals with TBI and their families is a particularly important part of this process. As people move from acute rehabilitation, to outpatient rehabilitation, to independent living, and eventually to employment, their patterns and expectations of participation change dramatically. These expectations greatly affect the nature and extent of their communication needs. It is also important to *assess opportunity barriers,* in much the same manner as was discussed in Chapter 7. *Identifying communication needs, assessing specific capabilities and constraints,* and matching these to *AAC system/device interventions* is an approach that is commonly used with persons in late-phase traumatic brain injury (DeRuyter & Kennedy, 1991; Ladtkow & Culp, 1992).

**AAC Intervention**   In the late phase of recovery, individuals with TBI are generally appropriate, oriented, and able to demonstrate goal-directed behavior. Learning new information may still be difficult, however, due to residual cognitive impairments. Some individuals may become natural speakers during Level VI, but by Levels VII and VIII, most individuals who are likely to become natural speakers without extensive intervention will have done so (Dongilli et al., 1991). Thus, by the late phase of recovery, many persons with TBI are able to interact and converse with their families and friends through natural speech. Nevertheless, even those individuals who regain speech may require augmented writing systems for an extended period. In addition, people with residual language and motor control impairments will continue to require long-term communication systems to meet their specific interaction needs. Many interaction needs are present at this point, including those related to communicating wants/needs, sharing information, achieving social closeness, and participating in social etiquette routines (DeRuyter & Kennedy, 1991).

During the late phase of cognitive recovery, traditional AAC techniques that resemble those used with other individuals who experience physical and cognitive impairments are often appropriate. Although persons with TBI who cannot speak usually experience a high incidence of physical problems, approximately 78% of those in one study were able to successfully utilize direct selection AAC techniques (DeRuyter & Lafontaine, 1987). Almost 75% of the direct selection users in this database operated their devices with their fingers or hands, while the remainder used eye pointing, headlight pointing, or chin pointing. Sixteen percent utilized dependent or independent scanning, and the remainder used other or no AAC techniques.

It might be assumed that due to the cognitive deficits associated with TBI, AAC systems that contain pictorial or other nonorthographic symbols will be required. This, however, is often not the case. It is important to remember that even late in the recovery process, cognitive impairments may mask considerable residual skills. One of the most important residual skills is the ability of many persons with TBI to read and spell. Thus, many of the individuals with TBI are able to utilize AAC systems that employ orthographic symbols, including letters, words, sentences, and alphabetic codes.

I met Joe many months after his accident. Because of residual motor control deficits, he was unable to speak but was able to communicate using a SpeechPac. He typed his messages using the index fingers of both hands. As I watched him begin to answer a question with his speech-language pathologist, I was initially impressed at the rate with which Joe prepared his answer. Then, he suddenly stopped typing, with his hands suspended above the keyboard. Seconds passed. No one prompted him. No one said anything while we waited patiently. Finally, after many seconds, Joe began to type again, rapidly, without missing a letter of his message. Why did this happen? Was he organizing himself and formulating his message? What would have transpired if we had interrupted him? This is not an uncommon pattern to observe in persons with TBI. (Beukelman, July, 1991, unpublished clinical anecdote)

Those who assist persons with TBI during the recovery process are well aware that new learning can be difficult and require considerable time and practice. This is an important consideration for those individuals who require long-term communication systems, since some AAC approaches require extensive training for operation. Examples are those approaches that are technically complex to operate or that require the user to learn a large number of messages using sequences of alphabetic or iconic codes. The AAC team should be cautious in deciding to introduce such techniques, and the AAC team should be careful not to make frequent changes in a system once it has been learned.

# AAC in Intensive and Acute Care Settings

> "When I was in the ICU [intensive care unit], I couldn't move my arms, and I had a halo [a brace to stabilize her neck] on my head, and I had a trach down my throat, and my eyes were swollen shut for 4 or 5 days. So, I couldn't communicate with anybody. I couldn't tell them when I hurt and where I hurt. So, I had mascara in my eyes for 9 days and my eyes watered and watered, for 9 days, until a nurse finally asked me enough pointed questions so that I could explain my eyes were hurting," wrote an ICU patient after her discharge from the unit. (Mitsuda, Baarslag-Benson, Hazel, & Therriault, 1992, p. 6)

Most hospitals contain intensive care units (ICUs) that serve a wide range of individuals who are unable to communicate, either temporarily or permanently. Such communication problems occur as a result of primary medical conditions, such as traumatic brain injury, stroke, and Guillain-Barré syndrome, or as a side effect of medical interventions such as intubation and tracheostomy. Providing AAC services in intensive and acute care medical settings is increasingly common, but it is still by no means universal.

Although the need for AAC services is extensive in medical settings, it is difficult for many AAC specialists to imagine initiating them, for several reasons. First, few AAC professionals have experience caring for patients in an ICU, and most have probably never been in one, except briefly, to visit a family member or friend. Therefore, most peoples' experiences are limited to visiting hours or to indirect experience of an ICU environment through television documentaries. As a result, there is a tendency to imagine that the patient in an ICU is very passive. It may seem as if patients are "having things done to them" constantly and that they are passive regarding their own care. This perception logically leads to the belief that because persons in intensive care are so ill and so passive, they do not need to communicate. This is not at all the case, with the exception of people who are unconscious. Most people in intensive care need to communicate regularly with hospital staff in order to participate in their own care, and they may feel an urgent need to communicate with family members at this uncertain and frightening time in their lives.

> You don't really know what's going on very much from the doctors because they don't try and talk to you directly. But the good things that were in the ICU was I had a lot of family support, so I had family there every day. . . . So I always knew I had somebody there that could help me, because you can't communicate with the nurses. It's like your family can understand you better for some reason. The nurses, they just give you the medicine and go about their business, but they don't really try and communicate at all in any way. So it's kind of a scary thing because you don't know exactly what's going on, and you don't know how bad you are. You just know that you are in a lot of pain and you are in bad shape. You don't know exactly what has happened even. (Mitsuda et al., 1992, p. 7)

In an ICU, communication also allows individuals to provide medical information to caregivers and serves as a critical link between the person and his or her support system, which includes family, friends, chaplains, and others. Depending on length of stay in an ICU, it may also be necessary to communicate about family finances, the operation of a business, the management of dependent children, and other personal matters.

## CAUSES OF COMMUNICATION DISORDERS IN ICU AND ACUTE CARE SETTINGS

### Primary Causes

A number of individuals in an ICU population are unable to speak because of their primary illness or condition. These include individuals with Parkinson's disease, stroke, traumatic brain injury, and amyotrophic lateral sclerosis (ALS). Some of these conditions, such as stroke, occur abruptly and without warning, and the people affected are usually completely unfamiliar with AAC approaches, as are their families and friends. Other primary conditions, such as ALS, are progressive, resulting in gradual physical deterioration. Many of these individuals will have used AAC systems prior to entering the hospital, and both they and their families may be familiar with a wide range of AAC approaches. Hospital staff, however, are unlikely to be as knowledgeable and will need to learn about the patient's system quickly. (Readers are referred to Chapters 16–18 for extensive discussion of these primary medical conditions and the AAC approaches typically used with them.)

Guillain-Barré syndrome . . . occurs in about 1.7 cases per 100,000 people (or about 3,500 cases per year in North America) and is among the most common neurologic causes of admission to the ICU. [It is] characterized by the acute onset of a symmetrical descending paralysis that extends from the legs to the trunk, arms, and cranial nerves. . . . Treatment includes ventilation in about one third of all cases . . . if respiratory failure occurs, the average period on a ventilator is 50 days, with a 108-day period of hospitalization. (Fried-Oken, Howard, & Stewart, 1991, pp. 45–46)

### Secondary Causes

A number of medical conditions may require respiratory support, either temporarily or permanently. These include, for example, Guillain-Barré syndrome, botulism, cardiopulmonary insufficiency, and extensive surgical interventions. Provision of such respiratory support often interferes with communication processes and a person's ability to speak. This is particularly true if endotracheal intubation or tracheostomy is required.

*Endotracheal Intubation*    Endotracheal tubes (Figure 19.1.) are designed to transport air from a ventilator to a patient's respiratory system. Endotracheal tubes are usually passed in emergency situations through the patient's mouth, pharynx, and larynx into the trachea (i.e., the airway below the larynx). This oral intubation interferes with communication in several ways. First, because the endotracheal tube passes through the oral cavity, it is impossible to articulate speech accurately. Second, because the endotracheal tube passes between the vocal folds, which are located in the larynx, it is impossible to produce sound (i.e., phonation). Thus, people who are orally intubated are unable to communicate using natural speech.

An endotracheal tube may also be passed through the nasal cavity into the trachea. Although in this case the tube does not interfere with articulation by passing through the mouth, the endotracheal tube does pass between the vocal folds. Therefore, an individual is unable to produce vocal sounds and efforts to communicate are limited to "mouthing" messages with the lips.

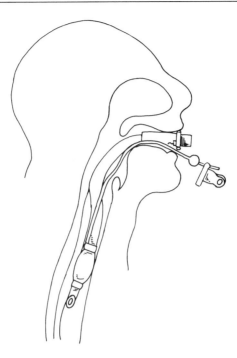

**Figure 19.1.**  An endotracheal tube in place.

Botulism [a form of food poisoning] clinically resembles Guillain-Barré syndrome. . . . [It] is an infection of the nervous system caused by the organism *Clostridium botulinum*, which when ingested produces widespread muscle weakness. The disease often occurs when someone eats uncooked canned food that has not been sterilized properly. (Fried-Oken et al., 1991, p. 46)

***Tracheostomy***   A tracheostomy is another way to transport air from a ventilator to an individual's respiratory system, and it is a surgical opening from the front wall of the lower neck into the trachea (i.e., the airway below the larynx). Tracheostomies are usually performed at the level of the second or third tracheal ring. Generally, the opening of the tracheostomy is maintained by inserting a tube or button through the neck wall into the trachea. As can be observed in Figure 19.2., the tracheostomy tube is curved to extend down into the trachea to keep it open for the movement of air. The ventilator is attached to the portion of the tube that extends anterior to the neck. A patient with a tracheostomy tube who is ventilator dependent has limited natural speech because air passes from the ventilator through the tube, rather than through the oral cavity and past the vocal folds.

Tracheostomy tubes may be left in place when ventilator support is no longer needed in order to maintain an open airway or permit suction of respiratory secretions. Nonetheless, air passes in and out of the trachea via the tracheostomy tube, bypassing the vocal folds. Thus, no phonation is possible and messages must be "mouthed." However, depending on the respiratory problem, some patients who are not ventilator assisted are able to inhale through the tracheostomy tube, then occlude the tube with their fingers or an external valve and exhale through the larynx and the oral cavity. In this way, air moves past the vocal folds on exhalation, and they are able to produce sound and speak naturally. In other cases, patients who can breathe on their own may be fitted with a

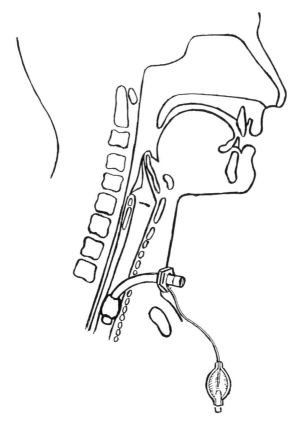

**Figure 19.2.**    Lateral view of a cuffed tracheostomy tube with the cuff inflated. (From Logemann, J. [1983]. *Evaluation and treatment of swallowing disorders,* p. 105. Austin, TX: PRO-ED; reprinted by permission.)

tracheal button that is used to maintain the tracheostomy through the neck wall (Figure 19.3.). These individuals can inhale through the button and then occlude the button with their finger or a valve to direct air past the vocal folds and produce speech.

## AAC SERVICE DELIVERY IN ICU AND ACUTE CARE SETTINGS

Effective, ongoing AAC services are usually provided by on-site professionals because ICUs are so organizationally complex. It is simply too difficult for a consultant to come intermittently to a hospital to provide AAC services, since the patient may be unavailable, too ill, or resting, or other medical treatments may take priority at the time of the consultant's visit. The core AAC team generally includes a speech-language pathologist, a physical therapist, and an occupational therapist who are employed by the hospital. In addition to their roles on the AAC team, these professionals may also be responsible for other therapy needs of patients in the ICU. They may consult with personnel from a regional center or with a local AAC specialist in the area.

The delivery of AAC services in ICU or acute care settings is structured differently than in typical rehabilitation or educational settings. A successful AAC program in an ICU or acute care setting must accommodate factors specific to these settings in order to be accepted and used by patients and medical personnel.

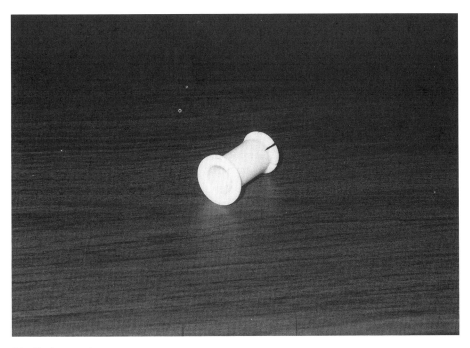

**Figure 19.3.** Tracheostomy button.

"When they put the tubes in, you get to the point of being helpless and you feel a need to communicate and talk to someone. You can't move. And you can't talk. And you want to say things. And you think, 'Now I'd like to ask some more questions. You explained to me what's going on. But no, I want to know more now. What's going to happen?' And all you can really do is just lay there. That's when you really, really get spooked the most," said Mike S., a 46-year-old man who had Guillain-Barré syndrome. (Fried-Oken et al., 1991, p. 43)

## Patient Issues

Patients in acute medical settings have serious medical needs that are critical to their survival. The delivery of AAC services simply cannot interfere with the delivery of medical care. Such services must be integrated into the overall care plan for the patient.

The intensity of medical care in an ICU affects the AAC program in a variety of ways. Medical staff are responsible for establishing and delivering an overall medical plan of which AAC may be a small part. Thus, AAC services cannot be provided without a request or referral from the medical team. The AAC team must clearly communicate the types of services they can deliver. They must consult with the medical team before and during AAC interventions to ensure that efforts coordinate well with the overall medical plan. Patients' AAC needs are likely to go unmet if these stipulations are not followed.

Because ICU patients receive such extensive medical support, it is not uncommon to find as many as 10–25 different professionals involved with each person during a 24-hour period, in addition to family members and friends present as visitors. Thus, AAC interventions must be readily understood by a variety of individuals. Instructions must be available, for example, via signs on the walls, written messages, or verbal instructions. AAC interventions in ICUs must be minimally complex and require minimal training and learning to be successful.

> "I think the staff should be trained separately from initial contact with the patient. I think they should already know how. At least the basic tools. . . . And they should have a separate kind of training so that whenever a patient comes in, any staff member can go up and say 'Here. Now let's use this here. A speech therapist will be down later. But right now, this is a basic method. And you can count on any nurse here knowing exactly how to use this and you can communicate with any of us.' We should have had at least that. Staff needs to be trained," said Alec K., a 35-year-old man who had Guillain-Barré syndrome. (Fried-Oken et al., 1991, p. 49–50)

## Medical Team Issues

Since *nursing personnel* are generally responsible for carrying out most day-to-day activities in the medical care plan, they have extensive contact with both patients and their family members. Thus, nurses are in an excellent position to assist the AAC team by monitoring the status of patients, coordinating AAC interventions with the medical care plan, documenting the individual's communication needs, and keeping family members informed of changes in the communication plan. The nursing coordinator in the ICU often assumes the role of patient advocate in the AAC area and actively encourages physicians to request AAC services.

*Respiratory therapists* are involved with a high proportion of the people in ICU and acute care units. Respiratory therapists are generally responsible for day-to-day management of patients' respiratory status, including patients with endotracheal or tracheostomy tubes. The AAC team must cooperate closely with respiratory therapists for successul AAC interventions. Ongoing *physician* education is also important, especially in training hospitals whose staffs consist of interns and residents as well as senior medical personnel. The AAC team may be invited to present their plan directly to the medical team in the ICU. Instruction about AAC services, however, usually occurs in the context of ongoing service delivery in the ICU.

> "[The scanning device] was a useless tool to me. There were two problems. First . . . it took too much effort to learn to hit the switch right. And once you did, you needed other words anyway. With so many things sitting around your bed, you need something that is always there, easily accessible, reasonably easy to understand and use. The machines don't fit that bill at all," said Alec K. (Fried-Oken et al., 1991, p. 47)

## ESTABLISHING AN AAC PROGRAM IN INTENSIVE CARE

It is beyond the scope of this chapter to provide an extensive discussion regarding how to develop an AAC program in an intensive or acute care medical setting. Readers are referred instead to a chapter by Mitsuda et al. (1992), which provides a detailed description of this process. These authors noted that AAC equipment needs for ICUs require careful attention, in addition to administrative, organizational, and personnel training issues. They suggested that the following equipment and materials can form the basis for many AAC interventions in ICU settings: 1) a lightweight neck-type electrolarynx; 2) an oral-type electrolarynx (i.e., one that delivers sound into the oral cavity through a tube); 3) materials to construct alphabet boards, word boards, and picture boards; 4) several Magic Slates (these are generally sold as toys, and consist of a sheet of plastic over a piece of coated board that can be written on; when the plastic is lifted, written messages are erased); and 5) a portable mounting system on wheels to hold cardboard message boards or eye pointing displays. These minimal equipment needs reflect the previously stated philosophy of simplifying AAC interventions in this area. This intention was supported by Dowden, Beukelman, and Lossing (1986):

> Clinicians with very few communication augmentation systems can nonetheless serve ICU patients quite well. . . . The majority of our patients were served with electrolarynges or . . . modified natural speech approaches. With additional access to the least expensive communication systems (plexiglass boards for eye-gaze . . . paper and pencil [and a few small typing systems]), we were able to serve all but a few of our patients. This means that even the smallest clinical program should consider serving patients in intensive care units. (p. 43)

More extensive electronic AAC devices may be necessary for persons who require a long-term communication intervention (e.g., people with high spinal cord injuries who need writing systems, or people with aphasia secondary to stroke). Because of the complexity of these systems and their learning requirements for both patients and staff, these AAC interventions are usually not initiated in the ICU. Rather, they are introduced either during inpatient rehabilitation or after discharge from the hospital.

## AAC INTERVENTION MODEL

The Participation Model (Figure 7.1.), described in detail in Chapters 7 and 8, has not been utilized for individuals in the ICU setting. Rather, a Communication Needs model, similar to that described in Chapter 16, has been used (Dowden, Honsinger & Beukelman, 1986; Mitsuda et al., 1992). Nevertheless, the Participation Model can be used quite effectively in intensive care settings to consider an overall AAC program.

## IDENTIFY PARTICIPATION PATTERNS AND COMMUNICATION NEEDS

The Participation Model supports the overall delivery of AAC services to persons in intensive care settings. Obviously, expected participation patterns are likely to be restricted, since patients are limited to essentially one communication environment (the ICU), have limited contact with persons in their social networks, and are not working. Thus, the communication needs of most ICU patients are quite limited in scope. A communication needs assessment checklist for intensive and acute care units is depicted in Figure 19.4. (Dowden, Honsinger, & Beukelman, 1986).

This checklist is similar to the assessment presented in Figure 16.1., but it contains a variety of options that are specific to ICU settings. Each of the needs listed is meant to be designated as "mandatory," "desirable," or "unimportant." The checklist should be completed by the AAC team with input from nursing personnel, family members (if available), and the patient (if he or she is able).

## ASSESS OPPORTUNITY BARRIERS

ICU patients deserve to have access to AAC services to meet even their restricted communication needs, and a lack of availability of AAC services can be considered to be an opportunity barrier. Few hospitals appear to have actual policies against AAC services, but there may be a number of practice or knowledge barriers that must be dealt with. These barriers may include: 1) medical teams that do not refer patients for AAC services, 2) nursing personnel who prefer not to be burdened with additional work in an already busy (and, perhaps, understaffed) ICU, and 3) professionals in speech-language pathology and other areas who are not familiar with conducting AAC interventions in ICU settings.

| | Indicate: Mandatory, Desirable, Unimportant |
|---|---|
| **Re: Environment:** | |
| Does individual need to: | |
| move from room to room | _____ |
| move within a room | _____ |
| communicate in w/c | _____ |
| manual chair | _____ |
| electric w/c | _____ |
| (controls: _____) | _____ |
| other w/c (specify: _____) | _____ |
| Does individual need to communicate: | |
| while lying supine | _____ |
| while lying prone | _____ |
| while side-lying | _____ |
| in several positions | |
| (specify: _____) | _____ |
| in a regular bed | _____ |
| in a roto-bed | _____ |
| in a Clinitron bed | _____ |
| while sitting in bed | _____ |
| while in a regular bed | _____ |
| at standing table | _____ |
| while on floor mat | _____ |
| while standing | _____ |
| with arterial lines in place | _____ |
| with hand mitts | _____ |
| while restrained | _____ |
| while orally intubated | _____ |
| while nasally intubated | _____ |
| while trached | _____ |
| with oxygen mask on | _____ |
| with NG tube in place | _____ |
| with a halo in place | _____ |
| while walking | _____ |
| in bathroom | _____ |
| in other locations | |
| (specify: _____) | _____ |
| outdoors | _____ |
| in van, car, bus-no w/c | _____ |
| in bright room | _____ |
| in dim room | _____ |
| in noisy room | _____ |
| in quiet room | _____ |
| **Re: Partners:** | |
| Does individual need to communicate: | |
| with anyone visually impaired | _____ |
| with anyone hearing impaired | _____ |
| with anyone who cannot read | _____ |
| with speakers of another language | |
| (specify: _____) | _____ |
| with anyone across the room | _____ |
| with more than one listener | _____ |
| with anyone with limited time | _____ |
| with anyone untrained on system | _____ |
| with anyone who cannot always look at display | _____ |
| with general public | |
| (specify where: _____) | _____ |
| **Re: Messages** | |
| In room, does individual need to: | |
| call attention | _____ |

*(continued)*

**Figure 19.4.**    Assessment of communication needs in an ICU setting. (From Dowden, P., Honsinger, M., & Beukelman, D. [1986]. Serving non-speaking patients in acute care settings: An intervention approach. *Augmentative and Alternative Communication, 2,* 31–32; reprinted by permission.)

**Figure 19.4.** (*continued*)
**Re: Messages**
In room, does individual need to:
   signal emergencies     _____
   answer yes/no questions     _____
   answer other questions     _____
   ask questions     _____
   provide unique information     _____
   make requests     _____
   carry on a conversation     _____
   express emotion     _____
   give his/her opinion     _____
   convey basic medical needs     _____
   greet people     _____
   leave messages/notes     _____
   prepare messages in advance

**Re: Modes**
Does individual need to:
   produce printed copy     _____
     take notes for self     _____
     leave notes for others     _____
   produce speech     _____
     produce quiet speech     _____
     produce loud speech     _____
   use telephone     _____
     talk on the telephone     _____
     take notes while on phone     _____
     access phone independently     _____
   switch from one mode to another     _____
     between print and speech     _____
     between print and telephone     _____
   switch tasks within one mode     _____
     during message preparation     _____
     during text preparation     _____

---

[While I was in the ICU], I wanted to communicate a friend's place where he works so they could tell him that I had been injured, and I had to blink the alphabet. But it took a while for them to figure out that I was blinking the alphabet because I was blinking so many times. Because first they wanted the phone number, and I kept telling them no there was no phone number because he didn't have a phone. He had just moved. So, then they finally realized, because I had blinked so many times because the first letter was an 'R,' they figured out that it was the alphabet so I could tell them the place that he worked through blinking the alphabet. (Mitsuda et al., 1992, p. 7)

## ASSESS ACCESS BARRIERS

As with other AAC assessments, those that occur in the ICU involve considerations of specific capabilities and constraints.

### Assess Specific Capabilities: Preliminary Screening

Many patients in the intensive care unit are unable to participate in extensive assessment procedures. A preliminary screening should be completed as the first step of an assessment to determine whether the individual is an appropriate candidate for a more complete AAC evaluation (Dowden, Honsinger, & Beukelman, 1986). Tasks in the initial screening are shown in Figure 19.5.

**Attending behaviors:**

| | | |
|---|---|---|
| Attends to spoken name? | yes | no |
| Attends to "Look at me"? | yes | no |

**Orientation questions:**

| | | |
|---|---|---|
| "Is your name (            )?" | yes | no |
| "Is the current year (       )?" | yes | no |
| "Is (            ) your home town?" | yes | no |
| "Are you married?" | yes | no |

**Single-step commands:**

| | | |
|---|---|---|
| "Close your eyes." | yes | no |
| "Open your mouth." | yes | no |

**Figure 19.5.** Initial Cognitive–Linguistic Screening Tasks for ICU Assessment. (From Dowden, P., Honsinger, M., & Beukelman, D. [1986]. Serving non-speaking patients in acute care settings: An intervention approach. *Augmentative and Alternative Communication, 2,* 31–32; reprinted by permission.)

In order to respond to these tasks, the individual must be able to follow simple directions and have some way of indicating "yes" and "no." Patients are rarely referred for evaluation unless this response is present, since this is often the first type of communicatiton that develops between patients and their staff or family members. Sometimes, however, the first step in assessment is to isolate or identify a yes/no response.

Dowden, Honsinger, and Beukelman (1986) described the use of the screening tasks in Figure 19.5. as follows:

> Patients are eliminated immediately if they are functional speakers or if they do not respond to either touch or their spoken name. Of those who are responsive, some may fail to pass the initial screening procedure, and are eliminated as too confused, agitated, or disoriented to cooperate with the communication augmentation intervention. (p. 25)

These authors reported that of the 42 patients who completed six or more of the screening tasks, 9% were provided with "limited switch approaches" (i.e., electronic scanning devices) that met communication needs, 53%–68% used oral or direct selection approaches that met their needs, and 70%–82% used several approaches simultaneously to meet their needs. Of eight patients in their study who completed fewer than six tasks accurately, three were not served because they died or were transferred to another hospital. The remaining five were seen for further assessment, but the AAC team was completely unsuccessful in providing them with AAC techniques to meet their communication needs. The authors drew two conclusions from these findings:

> First, it appears that the percentage of needs met may be related to the patient's cognitive status, as measured grossly by the cognitive screening tasks, because on the average, more communication needs were met for Group 2 patients [i.e., those who passed six or more items] than Group 1 patients [i.e., those who passed fewer than six items]. Second, within Group 2, the percentage of needs met appears to change with the type of intervention. For example, it appears that serving patients with multiple systems meets, on the average, more communication needs than serving the patient with a single system. (p. 43)

### Assess Specific Capabilities: Extended Assessment

Patients who successfully complete preliminary screening tasks undergo a more extensive assessment of their capabilities. Mitsuda et al. (1992) provided a flowchart to guide the decision-making process, which has been modified and is shown in Figure 19.6. Discussion of an extended capability assessment and related interventions follows.

#### Persons with Sufficient Oral Motor Control for Speech

*Oral Motor Control*   Many patients in an ICU have sufficient motor control for speech, provided that they have an adequate sound source for voicing. Thus, the first step in evaluating an ICU

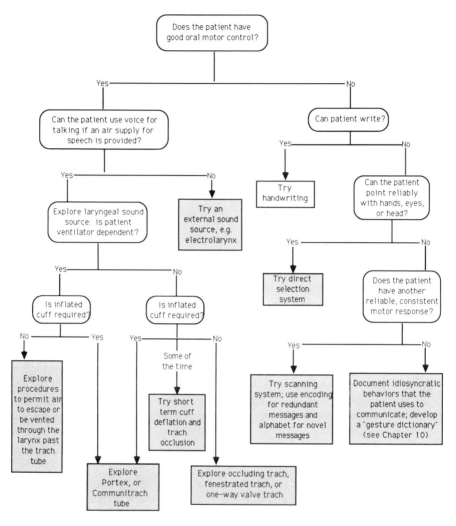

**Figure 19.6.**  AAC intervention planning flowchart for intensive care unit applications. (Adapted from Mitsuda, Baarslag-Benson, Hazel, & Therriault, 1992.)

patient should be assessment of oral motor capabilities. If these are adequate to support speech, the assessment should explore oral options. If oral motor control is inadequate, other options must be explored.

*Voicing Capabilities*    Many individuals who have adequate oral motor control for speech are unable to produce sound (i.e., voice) for one of several reasons. Some simply lack airflow past the vocal folds because of a tracheostomy, but are able to produce vocal sounds if this airflow can be reestablished temporarily. Other individuals may experience severe respiratory problems, or require ventilator supports that preclude any airflow past the vocal folds. Interventions related to these two options are discussed later in this chapter.

Still other people may not have the motor control necessary to produce voicing. For these individuals, an electrolarynx is often an effective intervention. These are usually of two types. A "neck-type" electrolarynx (Figure 19.7.) is positioned against the exterior neck wall and vibrates the air column within the vocal tract. "Mouthing words" then produces audible speech. The second is an "oral-type" electrolarynx (Figure 19.8.) that delivers sound into the oral cavity through a

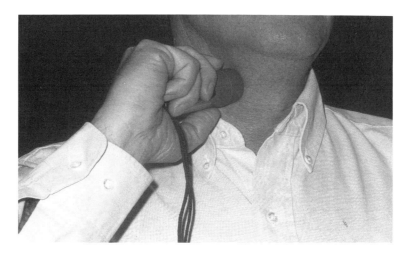

**Figure 19.7.**   A neck-type (Romet) electrolarynx.

tube or a catheter. The oral-type electrolarynx is useful for individuals who cannot use a neck-type electrolarynx due to extensive tissue damage, swelling, or surgical tenderness in the neck area or because they must wear cervical collars that obscure their necks.

   *Reestablishing the Airflow for Voicing*   The first step in initiating an intervention to re-establish the flow of air past the vocal folds is to determine if a cuffed tracheostomy tube is required and if the cuff must be inflated. (A cuffed tracheostomy tube was shown in Figure 19.2.) The air supply for respiration passes through the cuffed tube into the lungs. The cuff around the tube is inflated against the wall of the trachea to prevent air escaping from the ventilator and lungs

**Figure 19.8.**   Use of an oral-type (Cooper Rand) electrolarynx.

through the mouth, and to prevent food or liquid from moving through the mouth and pharynx into the respiratory system. Many individuals require the cuff to be inflated at all times. Devices are available, however, that allow the airflow to be directed through the vocal folds on exhalation although the cuffed tracheostomy tube is in place. These devices are usually operated by an external valve that directs the air stream. The Portex and Communitrach are examples of such "talking tracheostomy" products.

> The Portex tracheostomy tube is available from Portex, Inc., and the Communitrach is available through Implant Technologies, Inc.

Individuals who can tolerate the deflation of their tracheostomy cuffs for brief periods may achieve phonation by allowing air to escape from the respiratory system past the deflated cuff and vocal folds. They are able to produce natural speech in this way.

Another option is to use a tracheostomy tube that does not involve a cuff. This option may be appropriate for someone who requires a tracheostomy to maintain an open airway because of swelling or trauma to the neck area, but who is not ventilator dependent. In this case, air can be directed past the vocal folds by: 1) teaching the patient to occlude the tube with a finger during exhalation, 2) utilizing a fenestrated tracheostomy tube that has an opening on the top in the trachea, or 3) using a one-way valve that permits inhalation through the tube and exhalation through the vocal tract.

> "I think that board [a Magic Slate] was my preference over everything. You could communicate quickly and say what you wanted to say. You can write your letters and separate your words, like in normal writing. And it was much quicker and easier to understand by other people. I think they probably like it the best, too. So the Magic board was the best one, once I could start using my hands again. When I was unable to use my hands, of course the alphabet board [for dependent scanning] was the best, assuming that the other person understood how to use it, which many didn't," recalled Alec K. (Fried-Oken et al., 1991, p. 47)

### Patients with Insufficient Oral Motor Control for Speech

*Writing Options*   The flowchart assessment (Figure 19.6.) may reveal insufficient oral motor control for speech. In this case, the next assessment question is if the individual is able to write, since handwriting can be an effective communication mode in an ICU. Many people are comfortable and familiar with handwriting. Some individuals prefer to use a pencil and tablet so that as they write and save messages, they can begin to construct their own communication book. Then, rather than writing the same message again and again, they can simply refer to a question or a comment they have communicated previously. Others prefer to use a Magic Slate so that they can erase messages when they are finished and thus maintain privacy.

*Options for Persons Who Cannot Write*   Some individuals are unable to write by hand, but they can point accurately with their hands, eyes, or head. These individuals generally are encouraged to use a direct selection communication system. This direct selection system can be as simple as an alphabet board with some words or phrases on it. Other patients may prefer a small typing system. If hand or arm control is inadequate for use of these options, some individuals may use a headlight pointer to indicate words or letters on a wall or ceiling chart, or on a communication board placed on a mounting stand.

Some individuals may be limited to eye pointing in one of two forms. The first form is conventional eye pointing, in which the individual selects and gazes at a message on a display that is mounted on a transparent plastic board. The communication partner then interprets the direction of the patient's eye gaze and reads the related message. The second form, a technique known as "eye linking" may be used. In eye linking, the patient looks at the desired message, and the partner (who is positioned opposite the patient on the other side of the transparent communication board) moves the board until his or her eyes are "linked" directly across from the patient's. The message between the two at that point is the one that is read. Many individuals find this to be easier than eye pointing.

*Options for Persons Who Cannot Use Direct Selection*     Some individuals do not have the motor capability to engage in direct selection communication. If they have other reliable, consistent motor responses, individuals may be able to successfully use a scanning communication option. Many families can learn to use dependent scanning, in which an array of letters or messages is displayed on a communication board. The communication partner points to various message options, and the patient simply sends a "yes" signal when a desired message is reached via a gesture, eye blink, or by activating a beeper with a switch. Independent (i.e., electronic) scanning is more difficult to implement in an ICU setting and, as noted previously, the success of this option may be low as a result of this difficulty (Dowden, Beukelman, & Lossing, 1986). This type of communication is generally unfamiliar to most individuals, and the learning requirements for scanning may be too great for effective application of this option in an ICU environment.

## Assess Constraints

*Funding*     Constraints encountered in ICU settings are different than those experienced by individuals in other environments. For example, while AAC funding is often a problem for adults in general, this is not usually the case in the ICU. Funding for all medical-related services, including AAC services, are usually provided by the same funding sources responsible for the hospitalization.

*Instruction of Listeners*     The learning constraints in an ICU are quite extensive. First, the patients are very ill and under a considerable amount of stress. Many patients demonstrate little ability or tolerance for learning. Second, many professionals and others interact with these individuals over the course of their hospital stay. Thus, the most effective AAC interventions are those that require minimal listener training. As noted previously, complicated AAC systems are simply not used by patients or others in ICU settings.

# *Resources*

Adaptive Communication Systems, Inc., 354 Hookstown Grade Rd., Clinton, PA 15206
AICOM Corporation, 1590 Oakland Rd., Suite B112, San Jose, CA 95131
American Guidance Service, Circle Pines, MN 55014
American Printing House for the Blind, 1839 Frankfort Ave., P.O. Box 6085, Louisville, KY 40206-0085
American Thermoform, 2311 Travers Ave., City of Commerce, CA 90040
Apple Computer, 20525 Mariani Ave., Cupertino, CA 95014
Arkenstone, Inc., 540 Weddell Dr., Suite 1, Sunnyvale, CA 94098
Artic Technologies, 55 Park St., Suite 2, Troy, MI 48083
Artificial Language Laboratory, 405 Computer Center, Michigan State University, East Lansing, MI 48824-1042
Association de Paralysie Cérébrale du Québec, Inc., Centre de Ressources Bliss, 525 boul. Hamel est, Suite A-50, Québec QC G1M 2S8, CANADA
Attainment Company, 220 Mercer St., Windsor, Ontario N9A 7C2, CANADA
Auditec of St. Louis, 330 Selma Ave., St. Louis, MO 63119
*Augmentative and Alternative Communication*, Decker Publishing, Inc., One James St. South, P.O. Box 620, L.C.D.1., Hamilton, Ontario L8N 3K7, CANADA
Baggeboda Press, 1128 Rhode Island Ave., Lawrence, KS 66044
Berkeley Systems, Inc., 1708 Shattuck Ave., Berkeley, CA 94709
Blazie Engineering, Inc., 3660 Mill Green Rd., Street, MD 21154
Blissymbolics Communication International, 250 Ferrand Dr., Suite 200, Don Mills, Ontario M3C 3P2, CANADA
Boswell Industries, Inc., Suite 630–470 Granville St., Vancouver, British Columbia V6C 1V5, CANADA
Canon Corporation, One Canon Plaza, Lake Success, NY 11042
Closing the Gap, P.O. Box 68, Henderson, MN 56044
*Communicating Together*, P.O. Box 986, Thornhill, Ontario L3T 4A5, CANADA
*Communication Outlook*, 405 Computer Center, Michigan State University, East Lansing, MI 48824-1024
Communication Skill Builders, 3830 E. Bellevue, P.O. Box 42050-E91, Tucson, AZ 85733
COMPIC Development Association, P.O. Box 351, N. Baldwyn, Victoria 3104, AUSTRALIA
Crestwood Company, 6625 Sidney Pl., Milwaukee, WI 53209
Cued Speech Center, P.O. Box 31345, Raleigh, NC 27622
DEAL Communication Centre, 538 Dandenong Rd., Caulfield, Victoria 3162, AUSTRALIA
Digital Equipment Corp., 146 Main St., Maynard, MA 01754
Don Johnston Developmental Equipment, Inc., P.O. Box 639, Wauconda, IL 60084
Dragon Systems, Inc., 90 Bridge St., Newton, MA 02158
EARO, The Resource Centre, Black Hill, Ely, Cambridgeshire, ENGLAND
Easter Seal Communication Institute, 24 Ferrand Dr., Don Mills, Ontario M3C 3N2, CANADA
Enabling Technologies Co., 3102 S.E. Jay St., Stuart, FL 34997
First Byte, Inc., 3333 East Spring St. #302, Long Beach, CA 90806
Gallaudet University Press, Kendall Green, P.O. Box 300, Washington, DC 20002
Ginny Brady-Dobson, 89623 Demming Rd., Elmira, OR 97437
Hear Our Voices, c/o David Broehl, 105 Pine St., Wooster, OH 44691
Helen Keller National Center, 112 Middle Neck Road, Sands Point, NY 11050-1299 .
Henter Joyce, Inc., 7901 4th St. North, Suite 211, St. Petersburg, FL 33702
Humanware Inc., 6245 King Rd., Loomis, CA 95650
Imaginart Communication Products, 307 Arizona St., Bisbee, AZ 85603
Implant Technologies Inc., 7800 Metro Pkwy., Minneapolis, MN 55420
Institute of Applied Technology, Children's Hospital, Boston, MA 02115
Institute for Rehabilitation Research, Zandbergsweg 111, 6432 CC Hoensbroek, the NETHERLANDS
International Communication Learning Institute, 7108 Bristol Blvd., Edina, MN

*The ISAAC Bulletin,* P.O. Box 1762, Station R, Toronto, Ontario M4G 4AC, CANADA
Language Research Center, Georgia State University, Atlanta, GA 30303
Laureate Learning Systems, 10 East Spring St., Winooski, VT 05404
Luminaud, Inc., 8688 Tyler Blvd., Mentor, OH 44060
Makaton Vocabulary Development Project, 31 Firwood Dr., Camberley, Surrey GU15 3QD, ENGLAND
Mark Christensen, Inc., 927 11th Ave. North, St. Cloud, MN 56303
Mayer-Johnson Co., P.O. Box AD, Solana Beach, CA 92075-0838
Microcomputer Centre, University of Dundee, Dundee DD1 4HN, SCOTLAND
Microsystems Software, Inc., 600 Worcester Rd., Framingham, MA 01701
Mindscape Inc., 3444 Dundee Rd., Northbrook, IL 60062
Modern Signs Press, P.O. Box 1181, Los Alamitos, CA 90720
National Library Service for the Blind and Physically Handicapped, Library of Congress, 1291 Taylor St. NW,
    Washington, D.C. 20542
National Resource Center of Sweden, Educational Aids for Special Schools, Mariehemsv 2 902 36, Umeå,
    SWEDEN
National Support Center for Persons with Disabilities, P.O. Box 2150, Atlanta, GA 30005
Oakland Schools Communication Enhancement Center, Waterford, MI 48328
Omnichron, 1483 Oxford St., Berkeley, CA 94709
Peal Software, 5000 N. Parkway Calabasas #105, Calabasas, CA 91302
Phonic Ear, Inc., 3880 Cypress Dr., Petaluma, CA 94954-7600
Pictogram Centre, Saskatchewan Association of Rehabilitation Centres, Saskatoon, Saskatchewan, CANADA
Pointer Systems, Inc., One Mill St., Burlington, VT 054021
Portex, Inc., 42 Industrial Way, Wilmington, MA 01887
Prentke Romich Company, 1022 Heyl Rd., Wooster, OH 44691
Productivity Software International Inc., 1220 Broadway, New York, NY 10001
Raised Dot Computing, 408 S. Baldwin, Dept. 902, Madison, WI 53703
RC Systems, Inc., 121 W. Winesap Rd., Bothell, WA 98012
Royal Institute of Technology, Dept. of Speech Communication and Music Acoustics, Box 70014, Stockholm
    S-100 44, SWEDEN
Scholastic Software, 2931 E. McCarty St., Jefferson City, MO 65102
Scotlander Ltd., 74 Victoria Crescent Rd., Glasgow G12 9JN, SCOTLAND
Semantic Compaction Systems, 801 McNeilly Rd., Pittsburgh, PA 15226
Sentient Systems Technology, Inc., 5001 Baum Blvd., Pittsburgh, PA 15123
Ski Soft Publishing Corp., 1644 Massachusetts Ave., Suite 79, Lexington, MA 02173
Stanton Magnetics, 101 Sunnyside Blvd., Plainview, NY 11803
Sunburst Communications, 39 Washington St., Pleasantville, NY 10570
Street Electronics, 6420 Via Real, Carpinteria, CA 93013
Swedish Institute for the Handicapped, P.O. Box 303, Bromma S-151 26, SWEDEN
The Association for Persons with Severe Handicaps (TASH), 11201 Greenwood Ave. North, Seattle, WA
    98113
TeleSensory Systems, Inc., 455 N. Bernardo Ave., P.O. Box 7455, Mountain View, CA 94043
Trace Research and Development Center, S-151 Waisman Center, 1500 Highland Ave., Madison, WI 53705
*USSAAC Newsletter,* 1850 Sand Hill Rd., Apt. 10, Palo Alto, CA 94304
Votrax, Inc., 1394 Rankin Dr., Troy, MI 48083
Words+, Inc., P.O. Box 1229, Lancaster, CA 93535
Xerox/Kurzweil Computer Products, Personal Reader Department, 185 Albany St., Cambridge, MA 02139
Zygo Industries, Inc., P.O. Box 1008, Portland, OR 97207

# *References*

Abidin, P. (1983). *Parenting stress index*. Charlottesville, CA: Pediatric Psychology Press.

Adaptive Communication Systems, Inc. (1984). *ACS Speech PAC/Epson Instruction Manual*. Pittsburgh: Author.

Alwell, M., Hunt, P., Goetz, L., & Sailor, W. (1989). Teaching generalized communicative behaviors within interrupted behavior chain contexts. *Journal of The Association for Persons with Severe Handicaps, 14,* 91–100.

Amend, S. (1987). *Research report regarding Visual Phonics to the Sertoma Foundation*. Edina, MN: International Communication Learning Institute.

American Speech-Language-Hearing Association. (1981). Position statement on nonspeech communication. *Asha, 23,* 577–581.

American Speech-Language-Hearing Association. (1989). Competencies for speech-language pathologists providing services in augmentative communication. *Asha, 31,* 107–110.

American Speech-Language-Hearing Association. (1991). Report: Augmentative and alternative communication. *Asha, 33* (Suppl. 5), 9–12.

Anderson, R., Wilson, P., & Fielding, L. (1988). Growth in reading and how children spend their time outside of school. *Reading Research Quarterly, 23,* 285–303.

Angelo, J. (1987). *A comparison of three coding methods for abbreviation expansion in acceleration vocabularies*. Unpublished doctoral dissertation, University of Wisconsin-Madison.

Anthony, D. (1971). *Seeing Essential English* (Vols. 1 & 2). Anaheim, CA: Educational Services Division, Anaheim Union School District.

Apple Computer, Inc. (n.d.). *Apple Software Reference Guides*. Cupertino, CA: Author.

Aram, D., & Nation, J. (1982). *Child language*. St. Louis: C.V. Mosby.

Arnason, B.G.W. (1982). Multiple sclerosis: Current concepts and management. *Hospital Practice, 17,* 81–89.

Arthur, G. (1950). *The Arthur Adaptation of the Leiter International Performance Scale*. Chicago: C.H. Stoelting.

Arwood, E.L. (1983). *Pragmaticism: Theory and application*. Rockville, MD: Aspen Systems.

Bahadur, B. (1984). Liquid crystal displays. *Molecular Crystals and Liquid Crystals, 109*(1), 1–98.

Baker, B. (1982, September). Minspeak: A semantic compaction system that makes self-expression easier for communicatively disabled individuals. *Byte,* 186–202.

Baker, B. (1986). Using images to generate speech. *Byte,* 160–168.

Balick, S., Spiegel, D., & Greene, G. (1976). Mime in language therapy and clinician training. *Archives of Physical Medicine and Rehabilitation, 57,* 35–38.

Bambara, L., Spiegel-McGill, P., Shores, R., & Fox, J. (1984). A comparison of reactive and nonreactive toys on severely handicapped children's manipulative play. *Journal of The Association for Persons with Severe Handicaps, 9,* 142–149.

Barraga, N. (1983). *Visual handicaps and learning* (rev. ed.). Austin, TX: Exceptional Resources.

Barrera, R., Lobato-Barrera, D., & Sulzer-Azaroff, B. (1980). A simultaneous treatment comparison of three expressive language training programs with a mute autistic child. *Journal of Autism and Developmental Disorders, 10,* 21–38.

Barritt, L., & Kroll, B. (1978). Some implications of cognitive developmental psychology for research in composing. In C. Cooper & L. Odell (Eds.), *Research on composing: Points of departure* (pp. 49–57). Urbana, IL: National Council of Teachers of English.

Bashir, A., Grahamjones, F., & Bostwick, R. (1984). A touch-cue method of therapy for developmental verbal apraxia. *Seminars in Speech and Language, 5* (2), 127–128.

Batshaw, M., & Perret, Y. (1986). *Children with handicaps: A medical primer* (2nd ed.). Baltimore: Paul H. Brookes Publishing Co.

Baumgart, D., Johnson, J., & Helmstetter, E. (1990). *Augmentative and alternative communication systems for persons with moderate and severe disabilities*. Baltimore: Paul H. Brookes Publishing Co.

Beattie, W., Booth, L., Newell, A., & Arnott, J. (1990). The role of predictive computer programs in special education. *Augmentative and Alternative Communication, 6,* 89–90.

Beckman, P., & Kohl, F. (1984). The effects of social and isolate toys on the interactions and play of integrated and nonintegrated groups of preschoolers. *Education and Training of the Mentally Retarded, 19,* 169–174.

Berger, K. (1967). The most common words used in conversation. *Journal of Communication Disorders, 1,* 201–214.

Berliss, J., Borden, P., & Vanderheiden, G. (1989). *Trace resourcebook: Assistive technologies for communication, control, and computer access, 1989–1990 edition.* Madison, WI: Trace Research and Development Center.

Berlowitz, C. (1991, January 13). Ana begins to speak. *This World,* p. 16.

Berninger, V. (1989). Comparison of two microcomputer-assisted methods of teaching word decoding and encoding to non-vocal, non-writing and learning disabled students. *Learning and Educational Technology, 23,* 124–129.

Berninger, V., & Gans, B. (1986a). Assessing word processing capability of the nonvocal, nonwriting. *Augmentative and Alternative Communication, 2,* 56–63.

Berninger, V., & Gans, B. (1986b). Language profiles in nonspeaking individuals of normal intelligence with severe cerebral palsy. *Augmentative and Alternative Communication, 2,* 45–50.

Bernstein, L. (Ed.). (1988). *The vocally impaired: Clinical practice and research.* Needham Heights, MA: Allyn & Bacon.

Bernthal, J., & Bankson, N. (1988). *Articulation and phonological disorders* (2nd ed.). Englewood Cliffs, NJ: Prentice Hall.

Berry, J. (1987). Strategies for involving parents in programs for young children using augmentative and alternative communication. *Augmentative and Alternative Communication, 3,* 90–93.

Beukelman, D. (1986). Evaluation of the effectiveness of intervention programs. In S. Blackstone (Ed.), *Augmentative communication: An introduction* (pp. 423–445). Rockville, MD: American Speech-Language-Hearing Association.

Beukelman, D. (1989). There are some things you just can't say with your right hand. *Augmentative and Alternative Communication, 5,* 257–258.

Beukelman, D. (1990). AAC in the 1990s: A clinical perspective. In *Proceedings of the Visions Conference: Augmentative and Alternative Communication the Next Decade* (pp. 109–113). Wilmington, DE: Alfred I. duPont Institute.

Beukelman, D. (1991). Magic and cost of communicative competence. *Augmentative and Alternative Communication, 7,* 2–10.

Beukelman, D., & Garrett, K. (1986). Personnel preparation in augmentative communication. *Nebraska Speech, Language, and Hearing Journal, 24,* 5–8.

Beukelman, D., & Garrett, K. (1988). Augmentative and alternative communication for adults with acquired severe communication disorders. *Augmentative and Alternative Communication, 4,* 104–121.

Beukelman, D., Garrett, K., Lange, U., & Tice, R. (1988). *Cue-Write: Word processing with spelling assistance and practice manual.* Tucson, AZ: Communication Skill Builders.

Beukelman, D., Jones, R., & Rowan, M. (1989). Frequency of word usage by nondisabled peers in integrated preschool classrooms. *Augmentative and Alternative Communication, 5,* 243–248.

Beukelman, D., Kraft, G., & Freal, J. (1985). Expressive communication disorders in persons with multiple sclerosis: A survey. *Archives of Physical Medicine and Rehabilitation, 66,* 675–677.

Beukelman, D., & Mirenda, P. (1988). Communication options for persons who cannot speak: Assessment and evaluation. In C. A. Coston (Ed.), *Proceedings of the National Planners Conference on Assistive Device Service Delivery* (pp. 151–165). Washington, DC: RESNA, Association for the Advancement of Rehabilitation Technology.

Beukelman, D., & Yorkston, K. (1977). A communication system for the severely dysarthric speaker with an intact language system. *Journal of Speech and Hearing Disorders, 42,* 265–270.

Beukelman, D., & Yorkston, K. (1978). A series of communication options for individuals with brain stem lesions. *Archives of Physical Medicine and Rehabilitation, 59,* 337–342.

Beukelman, D., & Yorkston, K. (1979). The relationship between information transfer and speech intelligibility of dysarthric speakers. *Journal of Communication Disorders, 12,* 189–196.

Beukelman, D., & Yorkston, K. (1984). Computer enhancement of message formulation and presentation for communication augmentation system users. *Seminars in Speech and Language, 5,* 1–10.

Beukelman, D., & Yorkston, K. (1985). *Frequency of letter occurrence in the communication samples of augmented communicators.* Unpublished manuscript, University of Washington, Seattle.

Beukelman, D., & Yorkston, K. (1989). Augmentative and alternative communication application for persons with severe acquired communication disorders: An introduction. *Augmentative and Alternative Communication, 5,* 42–48.

Beukelman, D., & Yorkston, K. (1991). Traumatic brain injury changes the way we live. In D. Beukelman & K. Yorkston (Eds.), *Communication disorders following traumatic brain injury: Management of cognitive, language, and motor impairments* (pp. 1–14). Austin, TX: PRO-ED.

Beukelman, D., Yorkston, K., & Dowden, P. (1985). *Communication augmentation: A casebook of clinical management.* Austin, TX: PRO-ED.

Beukelman, D., Yorkston, K., Poblete, M., & Naranjo, C. (1984). Frequency of word occurrence in communication samples produced by adult communication aid users. *Journal of Speech and Hearing Disorders, 49,* 360–367.

Beukelman, D., Yorkston, K., & Smith, K. (1985). Third-party payer response to requests for purchase of communication augmentation systems: A study of Washington state. *Augmentative and Alternative Communication, 1,* 5–9.

Biederman-Anderson, L. (1989). Braille telecaptioning: Making real-time television accessible to deaf-blind consumers. *Journal of Visual Impairment and Blindness, 83,* 164–165.

Bigge, J. (1991). *Teaching individuals with physical and multiple disabilities* (3rd ed.). Westerville, OH: Merrill Publishing Co.

Biklen, D. (1985). *Achieving the complete school: Strategies for effective mainstreaming.* New York: Teacher's College Press.

Biklen, D. (Producer). (1988). *Regular lives* [Videotape]. Washington, DC: State of the Art.

Biklen, D. (1990). Communication unbound: Autism and praxis. *Harvard Educational Review, 60,* 291–314.

Biklen, D., & Crossley, R. (1990, December). *Facilitated communication: The Syracuse and Melbourne experiences.* Paper presented at the 17th annual conference of The Association for Persons with Severe Handicaps, Chicago.

Biklen, D., Morton, M., Saha, S., Duncan, J., Gold, D., Hardardottir, M., Karna, E., O'Connor, S., & Rao, S. (1991). "I AMN NOT A UTISTIVC OH THJE TYP" (I am not autistic on the typewriter). *Disability, Handicap, and Society, 6*(3), 161–180.

Biklen, D., & Schubert, A. (1991). New words: The communication of students with autism. *Remedial and Special Education, 12*(6), 46–57.

Blackstone, S. (1988a). Auditory scanning (AS) techniques. *Augmentative Communication News, 1*(5), 4–5, 8.

Blackstone, S. (1988b). Light pointing: Abandoned too soon? *Augmentative Communication News, 1*(2), 1–7.

Blackstone, S. (1989a). AAC after TBI: Silenced by the epidemic. *Augmentative Communication News, 2*(6), 1–5.

Blackstone, S. (1989b). For consumers: Societal rehabilitation. *Augmentative Communication News, 2*(3), 1–3.

Blackstone, S. (1989c). Individuals with developmental apraxia of speech (DAS). *Augmentative Communication News, 2*(2), 1–4, 6.

Blackstone, S. (1989d). M & Ms: Meaningful, manageable measurement. *Augmentative Communication News, 2*(3), 3–5.

Blackstone, S. (1989e). The 3 R's: Reading, writing, and reasoning. *Augmentative Communication News, 2*(1), 1–6, 8.

Blackstone, S. (1989f). Visual scanning: What's it all about? Visual scanning: Training approaches. *Augmentative Communication News, 2*(4), 1–5.

Blackstone, S. (1991). Telecommunication technologies. *Augmentative Communication News, 4*(4), 3–8.

Blackstone, S. W., Cassatt-James, E. L., & Bruskin, D. (Eds.). (1988). *Augmentative communication: Implementation strategies.* Rockville, MD: American Speech-Language-Hearing Association.

Blakeley, R. (1983). Treatment of developmental apraxia of speech: Method of Robert Blakeley. In W.H. Perkins (Ed.), *Current therapy of communication disorders: Dysarthria and apraxia* (pp. 25–33). New York: Thieme-Stratton.

Bliss, C. (1965). *Semantography.* Sydney, Australia: Semantography Publications.

Blissymbolics Communication International. (1984). *Picture your Blissymbols.* Toronto: Author.

Blockberger, S., Armstrong, R., O'Connor, A., & Freeman, R. (1990, August). *Children's attitudes toward a nonspeaking child using various augmentative and alternative communication techniques.* Paper presented at the fifth biennial conference of the International Society for Augmentative and Alternative Communication, Stockholm.

Blockberger, S., & Kamp, L. (1990). The use of voice output communication aids (VOCAs) by ambulatory children. *Augmentative and Alternative Communication, 6,* 127–128.

Bloom, L., & Lahey, M. (1978). *Language development and language disorders.* New York: John Wiley & Sons.

Bloomberg, K. (1990). Computer pictographs for communication. *Communication Outlook, 12*(1), 17–18.

Bloomberg, K., & Johnson, H. (1990). A statewide demographic survey of people with severe communication impairments. *Augmentative and Alternative Communication, 6*, 50–60.

Bloomberg, K., Karlan, G., & Lloyd, L. (1990). The comparative translucency of initial lexical items represented by five graphic symbol systems and sets. *Journal of Speech and Hearing Research, 33*, 717–725.

Boden, D., & Bielby, D. (1983). The way it was: Topical organization in elderly conversation. *Language and Communication, 6*(1/2), 73–79.

Boehm, A. (1986). *Boehm Test of Basic Concepts—Revised.* San Antonio, TX: The Psychological Corporation.

Bolton, S., & Dashiell, S. (1984). *INCH: Interaction Checklist for Augmentative Communication.* Wauconda, IL: Don Johnston Developmental Equipment, Inc.

Bonvillian, J., & Friedman, R. (1978). Language development in another mode: The acquisition of signs by a brain-damaged adult. *Sign Language Studies, 19*, 111–120.

Bonvillian, J., & Nelson, K. (1978). Development of sign language in autistic children and other language-handicapped individuals. In P. Siple (Ed.), *Understanding language through sign language research* (pp. 187–209). New York: Academic Press.

Bornstein, H. (1990). Signed English. In H. Bornstein (Ed.), *Manual communication: Implications for education* (pp. 128–138). Washington, DC: Gallaudet University Press.

Bornstein, H., Saulnier, L., & Hamilton, L. (1983). *The comprehensive Signed English dictionary.* Washington, DC: Gallaudet University Press.

Boubekker, M., Foulds, R., & Norman, C. (1986). Human quality synthetic speech based upon concatenated diphones. *Proceedings of the RESNA Ninth Annual Conference* (pp. 405–407). Washington, DC: RESNA, Association for The Advancement of Rehabilitation Technology.

Boughman, J.A., Vernon, M., & Shaver, K.A. (1983). Usher's syndrome: Definitions and estimates of prevalence from two high-risk populations. *Journal of Chronic Diseases, 36*, 595–603.

Bowles-Bridwell, L. (1987). Writing with computers: Implications from research for the language impaired. *Topics in Language Disorders, 7*(4), 78–85.

Bracken, B. (1984). *Bracken Basic Concept Scale (BBCS).* San Antonio, TX: The Psychological Corporation.

Brady, D., & Smouse, A. (1978). A simultaneous comparison of three methods for language training with an autistic child: An experimental single case analysis. *Journal of Autism and Childhood Schizophrenia, 8*, 271–279.

Brady-Dobson, G. (1982). *Brady-Dobson Alternative Communication (B-DAC).* Elmira, OR: Author.

Braun, U., & Stuckenschneider-Braun, M. (1990). Adapting "Word Strategy" to the German culture and language. *Augmentative and Alternative Communication, 6*, 115.

Brett, E.M. (1983). The blind retarded child. In K. Wybar & D. Taylor (Eds.), *Pediatric ophthalmology: Current aspects* (pp. 113–122). New York: Marcel Dekker.

Bridges Freeman, S. (1990). *Children's attitudes toward synthesized speech varying in quality.* Unpublished doctoral dissertation, Michigan State University, East Lansing.

Brigance, A. (1977). *Brigance Diagnostic Inventory of Basic Skills* (2nd ed.). Woburn, MA: Curriculum Associates.

Bristow, D., & Fristoe, M. (1984, November). *Systematic evaluation of the nonspeaking child.* Seminar presented at the annual conference of the American Speech-Language-Hearing Association, San Francisco.

Bristow, D., & Fristoe, M. (1987, November). *Effects of test adaptations on test performance.* Paper presented at the annual conference of the American Speech-Language-Hearing Association, New Orleans.

Bristow, D., & Fristoe, M. (1988). Effects of test adaptations on test performance. *Augmentative and Alternative Communication, 4*, 171.

Brodin, J. (1991). *To interpret children's signals: Play and communication in profoundly mentally retarded and multiply handicapped children.* Unpublished doctoral dissertation, University of Stockholm.

Broehl, D. (1990). Hear our voices—An empowerment initiative. *Communication Outlook, 12*(2), 12–13.

Brookner, S.P., & Murphy, N.O. (1975). The use of a total communication approach with a nondeaf child: A case study. *Language, Speech, and Hearing Services in Schools, 6*, 131–137.

Brothers, S. (1991). Let's talk! *Asha, 33*, 59–60.

Brown, C. (1954). *My left foot.* London: Secker and Warburg.

Brown, F. (1991). Creative daily scheduling: A nonintrusive approach to challenging behaviors in community residences. *Journal of The Association for Persons with Severe Handicaps, 16*, 75–84.

Brown, L., Long, E., Udavari-Solner, A., Davis, L., VanDeventer, P., Ahlgren, C., Johnson, F., Gruenewald, L., & Jorgensen, J. (1989). The home school: Why students with severe intellectual disabilities must attend the schools of their brothers, sisters, friends, and neighbors. *Journal of The Association of Persons with Severe Handicaps, 14*, 1–7.

Brown, L., Nietupski, J., & Hamre-Nietupski, S. (1976). The criterion of ultimate functioning and public: school services for severely handicapped students. In M. A. Thomas (Ed.), *Hey, don't forget about me!: Education's investment in the severely, profoundly, and multiply handicapped* (pp. 2–15). Reston, VA: Council for Exceptional Children.

Brown, S. (1987). Demographic characteristics and impairments of Louisiana students with Usher's syndrome. *Journal of Visual Impairment and Blindness, 81,* 106–109.

Bruno, J. (1986). Modeling procedures for increased use of communication functions in communication aide users. In S. Blackstone (Ed.), *Augmentative communication: An introduction* (pp. 301–306). Rockville, MD: American Speech-Language-Hearing Association.

Bruno, J. (1989). Customizing a Minspeak system for a preliterate child: A case example. *Augmentative and Alternative Communication, 5,* 89–100.

Bryen, D., Goldman, A., & Quinlisk-Gill, S. (1988). Sign language with students with severe/profound mental retardation: How effective is it? *Education and Training in Mental Retardation, 23,* 129–137.

Bryen, D., & Joyce, D. (1985). Language intervention with the severely handicapped: A decade of research. *Journal of Special Education, 19,* 7–39.

Bryen, D., & Joyce, D. (1986). Sign language and the severely handicapped. *Journal of Special Education, 20,* 183–194.

Buck, J., & Cooper, I. (1956). Speech problems in parkinsonian patients undergoing anterior choroidal artery occlusion or chemopallidectomy. *Journal of American Geriatric Society,* 1285–1290.

Bullis, M., & Otos, M. (1988). Characteristics of programs for children with deaf-blindness: Results of a national survey. *Journal of The Association for Persons with Severe Handicaps, 13,* 110–115.

Bureau of National Affairs. (1987). *VDTs in the workplace: New issues, new answers* (2nd ed.). Rockville, MD: Author.

Burgemeister, B., Blum, L., & Lorge, I. (1972). *Columbia Mental Maturity Scale* (3rd ed.). Cleveland: The Psychological Corporation.

Burkhart, L. (1980). *Homemade battery powered toys and educational devices for severely handicapped children.* (Available from author, 8503 Rhode Island Ave., College Park, MD 20740.)

Burkhart, L. (1982). *More homemade battery devices for severely handicapped children with suggested activities.* (Available from author, 8503 Rhode Island Ave., College Park, MD 20740.)

Burkhart, L.J. (1988). *Using computers and speech synthesis to facilitate communicative interaction with young and/or severely handicapped children.* Wauconda, IL: Don Johnston Developmental Equipment, Inc.

Burroughs, J., Albritton, E., Eaton, B., & Montague, J. (1990). A comparative study of language delayed preschool children's ability to recall symbols from two symbol systems. *Augmentative and Alternative Communication, 6,* 202–206.

Buzolich, M., King, J., & Baroody, S. (1991). Acquisition of the commenting function among system users. *Augmentative and Alternative Communication, 7,* 88–99.

Buzolich, M., & Weimann, J. (1988). Turn taking in atypical conversations: The case of the speaker/augmented communicator dyad. *Journal of Speech and Hearing Research, 31,* 3–18.

Calculator, S. (1988a). Evaluating the effectiveness of AAC programs for persons with severe handicaps. *Augmentative and Alternative Communication, 4,* 177–179.

Calculator, S. (1988b). Promoting the acquisition and generalization of conversational skills by individuals with severe handicaps. *Augmentative and Alternative Communication, 4,* 94–103.

California Research Institute. (1990a, August). Bridging the gap: Restructuring education in the 90's. *TASH Newsletter,* 7–10.

California Research Institute. (1990b). *The way to go* [Videotape]. Available from TASH, 11201 Greenwood Ave. North, Seattle, WA 98113.

Campbell, P. (1989). Dysfunction in posture and movement in individuals with profound disabilities. In F. Brown & D. Lehr (Eds.), *Persons with profound disabilities: Issues and practices* (pp. 163–189). Baltimore: Paul H. Brookes Publishing Co.

Carlson, F. (1981). A format for selecting vocabulary for the nonspeaking child. *Language, Speech, and Hearing Services in Schools, 12,* 140–145.

Carlson, F. (1985). *Picsyms categorical dictionary.* Lawrence, KS: Baggeboda Press.

Carlson, F., Hough, S., Lippert, E., & Young, C. (1988). Facilitating interaction during mealtime. In S. Blackstone, E. Cassatt-James, & D. Bruskin (Eds.), *Augmentative communication: Implementation strategies* (pp. 5.8-10–5.8-20). Rockville, MD: American Speech-Language-Hearing Association.

Carr, E. (1982). Sign language. In R. Koegel, A. Rincover, & A. Egel (Eds.), *Educating and understanding autistic children* (pp. 142–157). San Diego: College-Hill Press.

Carr, E., Binkoff, J., Kologinsky, E., & Eddy, M. (1978). Acquisition of sign language by autistic children: I. Expressive labeling. *Journal of Applied Behavior Analysis, 11,* 459–501.

Carr, E., & Dores, P. (1981). Patterns of language acquisition following simultaneous communication with autistic children. *Analysis and Intervention in Developmental Disabilities, 1,* 1–15.

Carr, E., & Durand, V. (1985). Reducing behavior problems through functional communication training. *Journal of Applied Behavior Analysis, 18,* 111–126.

Carr, E., & Kologinsky, E. (1983). Acquisition of sign language by autistic children: II. Spontaneity and generalization. *Journal of Applied Behavior Analysis, 16,* 297–314.

Carr, E., Pridal, C., & Dores, P. (1984). Speech versus sign comprehension in autistic children. Analysis and prediction. *Journal of Experimental Child Psychology, 37,* 587–597.

Carr, E., Robinson, S., & Palumbo, L. (1990). The wrong issue: Aversive vs. nonaversive treatment; The right issue: Functional vs. nonfunctional treatment. In A. Repp & N. Singh (Eds.), *Perspectives on the use of nonaversive and aversive interventions for persons with developmental disabilities* (pp. 361–380). Sycamore, IL: Sycamore Publishing.

Carrier, J., Jr., & Peak, T. (1975). *Non-SLIP (Non-speech language initiation program).* Lawrence, KS: H & H Enterprises.

Carrol, J., Davis, P., & Richman, H. (1971). *Word frequency book.* Boston: Houghton-Mifflin.

Carrow, E. (1973). *Test of Auditory Comprehension of Language.* Austin, TX: Learning Concepts.

Casey, L. (1978). Development of communicative behavior in autistic children: A parent program using manual signs. *Journal of Autism and Childhood Schizophrenia, 8,* 45–59.

Chadsey, C., & Wentworth, H. (1974). *The Grosset Webster Dictionary.* New York: Grosset & Dunlap.

Chaney, C. (1990). Evaluating the whole language approach to language arts: The pros and cons. *Language, Speech, and Hearing Services in Schools, 21,* 244–249.

Chumpelik, D. (1984). The prompt system of therapy: Theoretical framework and application for developmental apraxia of speech. *Seminars in Speech and Language, 5* (2), 139–156.

Clark, C. (1981). Learning words using traditional orthography and the symbols of rebus, Bliss, and Carrier. *Journal of Speech and Hearing Disorders, 46,* 191–196.

Clark, C., Davies, C., & Woodcock, R. (1974). *Standard rebus glossary.* Circle Pines, MN: American Guidance Service.

Cline, D., Hofstetter, H., & Griffin, J. (1980). *Dictionary of visual science* (3rd ed.). Radnor, PA: Chilton Book Co.

Cohen, C., & Palin, M. (1986). Speech syntheses and speech recognition devices. In M. Grossfeld & C. Grossfeld (Eds.), *Microcomputer applications in rehabilitation of communication disorders* (pp. 183–211). Rockville, MD: Aspen Systems.

Coleman, C., Cook, A., & Meyers, L. (1980). Assessing the non-oral client for assistive communication devices. *Journal of Speech and Hearing Disorders, 45,* 515–526.

Coleman, C., & Meyers, L. (1991). Computer recognition of the speech of adults with cerebral palsy and dysarthria. *Augmentative and Alternative Communication, 7,* 34–43.

Collier, B. (1991). Report on the ISAAC developing countries seminar. *Augmentative and Alternative Communication, 7,* 138–146.

Collins, T., & Price, L. (1987). Microcomputers and the learning disabled college writer. *Collegiate Microcomputer, 1,* 26–31.

Conn-Powers, M., Ross-Allen, J., & Holburn, S. (1990). Transition of young children into the elementary education mainstream. *Topics in Early Childhood Special Education, 9* (4), 91–105.

Converso, L., & Hocek, S. (1990). Optical character recognition. *Journal of Visual Impairment and Blindness, 84,* 507–509.

Cook, A., Coleman, C., Preszler, A., & Dahlquist, D. (1983). A hierarchy of augmentative communication system characteristics useful for matching devices to clients' needs and skills. *Proceedings from the Sixth Annual Conference on Rehabilitation Engineering* (pp. 185–186). Bethesda, MD: Rehabilitation Engineering Society of North America.

Cook, S. (1988). Using topic specific miniboards to allow individuals who use augmentative communication aids to initiate communication with school staff members. In S. Blackstone, E. Cassatt-James, & D. Bruskin (Eds.), *Augmentative communication: Implementation strategies* (pp. 5.3-24–5.3-30). Rockville, MD: American Speech-Language-Hearing Association.

Coston, C. (Ed.). (1988). *Proceedings of the National Planners Conference on Assistive Device Service Delivery.* Washington, DC: RESNA, Association for the Advancement of Rehabilitation Technology.

Crabtree, M., Mirenda, P., & Beukelman, D. (1990). Age and gender preferences for synthetic and natural speech. *Augmentative and Alternative Communication, 6,* 256–261.

Crary, M. (1987). *A neurolinguistic model of articulatory/phonological disorders.* Paper presented at the Boy's Town Institute Communication Series, Omaha, NE.

Creech, R. (1981). Attitude as a misfortune. *Asha, 23,* 550–551.

Creech, R. (1988). Paravocal communicators speak out. *Aug-Communique: North Carolina Augmentative Communication Newsletter, 6*(3), 12.

Creech, R., Kissick, L., Koski, M., & Musselwhite, C. (1988). Paravocal communicators speak out: Strategies for encouraging communication aid use. *Augmentative and Alternative Communication, 4,* 168.

Creedon, M. (1973). *Language development in nonverbal autistic children using a simultaneous communication system.* Paper presented at the annual meeting of the Society for Research in Child Development, Philadelphia.

Creedon, M.P. (Ed.). (1975). *Appropriate behavior through communications: A new program in simultaneous language.* (Available from Developmental Institute, Humana Hospital, 31st at Lake Shore Dr., Chicago, IL 60616).

Cregan, A. (1982). *Sigsymbol dictionary.* Hatfield, Herts, England: Author.

Cregan, A., & Lloyd, L. (1988). *Sigsymbols: American edition.* Wauconda, IL: Don Johnston Developmental Equipment, Inc.

Cress, P. (1987). Visual assessment. In M. Bullis (Ed.), *Communication development in young children with deaf-blindness: Literature review III* (pp. 33–44). Monmouth, OR: Teaching Research.

Cress, P., Spellman, C., DeBriere, T., Sizemore, A., Northam, J., & Johnson, J. (1981). Vision screening for persons with severe handicaps. *Journal of The Association for the Severely Handicapped, 6*(3), 41–50.

Crossley, R. (1988, October). *Unexpected communication attainment by persons diagnosed as autistic and intellectually impaired.* Paper presented at the fifth biennial conference of the International Society for Augmentative and Alternative Communication, Anaheim, CA.

Crossley, R. (1990, September). *Communication training involving facilitated communication.* Paper presented to the Australian Association of Special Education, Canberra, Australia.

Crossley, R. (1991). Communication training involving facilitated communication. *Communicating Together, 9*(2), 19–22.

Crossley, R., & McDonald, A. (1984). *Annie's coming out.* New York: Viking Penguin.

Crystal, D. (1987). Teaching vocabulary: The case for a semantic curriculum. *Child Language Teaching and Therapy, 3,* 40–56.

Culp, D. (1987). Outcome measurement: The impact of communication augmentation. *Seminars in Speech and Language, 8,* 169–181.

Culp, D. (1989). Developmental apraxia and augmentative or alternative communication—A case example. *Augmentative and Alternative Communication, 5,* 27–34.

Culp, D., & Carlisle, M. (1988). PACT: *Partners in augmentative communication training.* Tucson, AZ: Communication Skill Builders.

Cumley, G. (1991). *AAC facilitator roles and responsibilities.* Unpublished manuscript, University of Nebraska-Lincoln.

Dahlberg, C., & Jaffe, J. (1977). *Stroke: A doctor's personal story of his recovery.* New York: W.W. Norton & Co.

Dahle, A., & Goldman, R. (1990, November). *Perception of synthetic speech by normal and developmentally disabled children.* Paper presented at the annual conference of the American Speech-Language-Hearing Association, Seattle.

Dalrymple, G. (1973). Development and demonstrations of communication systems for the blind and deaf/blind. *Braille communication terminals and tactile paging systems: Final report.* Cambridge, MA: Massachusetts Institute of Technology, Sensory Aids Evaluation and Development Center.

Daniloff, J., Lloyd, L., & Fristoe, M. (1983). Amer-Ind transparency. *Journal of Speech and Hearing Disorders, 48,* 103–110.

Daniloff, J., Noll, J., Fristoe, M., & Lloyd, L. (1982). Gesture recognition in patients with aphasia. *Journal of Speech and Hearing Disorders, 47,* 43–56.

Daniloff, J., & Shafer, A. (1981). A gestural communication program for severely-profoundly handicapped children. *Language, Speech, and Hearing Services in Schools, 12,* 258–268.

Daniloff, J., & Vergara, D. (1984). Comparison between the motoric constraints for Amer-Ind and ASL sign formation. *Journal of Speech and Hearing Research, 27,* 76–88.

Darley, F., Aronson A., & Brown, J. (1969a). Cluster of deviant speech dimensions in the dysarthrias. *Journal of Speech and Hearing Research, 12,* 462–496.

Darley, F., Aronson, A., & Brown, J. (1969b). Differential diagnostic patterns of dysarthria. *Journal of Speech and Hearing Research, 12,* 246–269.

Darley, F., Aronson, A., & Brown, J. (1975). *Motor speech disorders.* Philadelphia: W. B. Saunders.

Darley, F., Brown, J., & Goldstein, N. (1972). Dysarthria in multiple sclerosis. *Journal of Speech and Hearing Research, 15,* 229–245.

Davenport, S., O'Nuallain, S., Omen, G., & Wilken, R. (1978). Usher's syndrome in four hard-of-hearing siblings. *Pediatrics, 62*(4), 578–583.

Deloria, E. (1943). *Speaking of Indians.* New York: Friendship Press.

Dennis, R., Reichle, J., Williams, W., & Vogelsberg, R. T. (1982). Motoric factors influencing the selection of vocabulary for sign production programs. *Journal of The Association for the Severely Handicapped, 7*(1), 20–32.

DeRuyter, F., & Donoghue, K. (1989). Communication and traumatic brain injury: A case study. *Augmentative and Alternative Communication, 5,* 49–54.

DeRuyter, F., & Kennedy, M. (1991). Augmentative communication following traumatic brain injury. In D. Beukelman & K. Yorkston (Eds.), *Communication disorders following traumatic brain injury: Management of cognitive, language, and motor impairments* (pp. 317–365). Austin, TX: PRO-ED.

DeRuyter, F., & Lafontaine, L. (1987). The nonspeaking brain injured: A clinical and demographic database report. *Augmentative and Alternative Communication, 3,* 18–25.

DesLauriers, A. (1978). Play, symbols, and the development of language. In M. Rutter & E. Schopler (Eds.), *Autism: A reappraisal of concepts and treatment* (pp. 313–326). New York: Plenum.

DiSimoni, F. (1978). *The Token Test for Children: Manual.* Allen, TX: DLM Teaching Resources.

Dixon, J., & Mandelbaum, J. (1990). Reading through technology: Evolving methods and opportunities for print-handicapped individuals. *Journal of Visual Impairment and Blindness, 84,* 493–496.

Dixon, L.S. (1981). A functional analysis of photo-object matching skills of severely retarded adolescents. *Journal of Applied Behavior Analysis, 14,* 465–478.

Doherty, J. (1985). The effects of sign characteristics on sign acquisition and retention: An integrative review of the literature. *Augmentative and Alternative Communication, 1,* 108–121.

Doherty, J, Daniloff, J., & Lloyd, L. (1985). The effect of categorical presentation on Amer-Ind transparency. *Augmentative and Alternative Communication, 1,* 10–16.

Doherty, J., Karlan, G., & Lloyd, L. (1982). Establishing the transparency of two gestural systems by mentally retarded adults. *Asha, 24,* 834.

Dongilli, P., Hakel, M., & Beukelman, D. (in press). Recovery of functional speech following traumatic brain injury. *Journal of Head Trauma Rehabilitation.*

Donnellan, A. (1984). The criterion of the least dangerous assumption. *Behavior Disorders, 9,* 141–150.

Donnellan, A., & Mirenda, P. (1983). A model for analyzing instructional components to facilitate generalization for severely handicapped students. *Journal of Special Education, 17,* 317–331.

Donnellan, A., Mirenda, P., Mesaros, R., & Fassbender, L. (1984). Analyzing the communicative functions of aberrant behavior. *Journal of The Association for Persons with Severe Handicaps, 9,* 201–212.

Donovan, W. (1981). Spinal cord injury. In W. Stolov & M. Clowers (Eds.), *Handbook of severe disability* (pp. 55–64). Washington, DC: U.S. Government Printing Office.

Dowden, P., Beukelman, D., & Lossing, C. (1986). Serving non-speaking patients in acute care settings: Intervention outcomes. *Augmentative and Alternative Communication, 2,* 38–44.

Dowden, P., Honsinger, M., & Beukelman, D. (1986). Serving non-speaking patients in acute care settings: An intervention approach. *Augmentative and Alternative Communication, 2,* 25–32.

Duffy, L. (1977). *An innovative approach to the development of communication skills for severely speech handicapped cerebral palsied children.* Unpublished master's thesis, University of Nevada, Las Vegas.

Duncan, J.L., & Silverman, F.H. (1977). Impacts of learning American Indian Sign Language on mentally retarded children: A preliminary report. *Perceptual and Motor Skills, 44,* 1138.

Dunn, L., & Dunn, L. (1981). *Peabody Picture Vocabulary Test—Revised.* Circle Pines, MN: American Guidance Service.

Dunn, L., & Marquardt, F. (1970). *Peabody Individual Achievement Test.* Circle Pines, MN: American Guidance Service.

Dunn, M. (1982). *Pre-sign language motor skills.* Tucson, AZ: Communication Skills Builders.

Durand, V. M. (1990). *Severe behavior problems: A functional communication training approach.* New York: Guilford Press.

Durand, V., & Carr, E. (1991). Functional communication training to reduce challenging behavior: Maintenance and application in new settings. *Journal of Applied Behavior Analysis, 24,* 251–264.

Dworkin, J., Aronson, A., & Mulder, D. (1980). Tongue force in normals and in dysarthric patients with amyotrophic lateral sclerosis. *Journal of Speech and Hearing Research, 23,* 828–837.

Dyer, K., Dunlap, G., & Winterling, V. (1990). Effects of choice making on the serious problem behaviors of students with severe handicaps. *Journal of Applied Behavior Analysis, 23,* 515–524.

Eagleson, H.M., Vaughn, G.R., & Knudson, A.B. (1970). Hand signals for dysphasia. *Archives of Physical Medicine and Rehabilitation, 51*, 111–113.

Easton, J. (1989). Oh the frustration! *Communication Outlook, 10*(3), 16–17.

Ecklund, S., & Reichle, J. (1987). A comparison of normal children's ability to recall symbols from two logographic systems. *Language, Speech, and Hearing Services in Schools, 18*, 34–40.

Edman, P. (1991). Relief Bliss, A low tech technique. *Communicating Together, 9*(1), 21–22.

Edmonds, R. (1979). Some schools work and more can. *Social Policy, 9*(5), 25–29.

Egof, D. (1988). *Coding communication devices: The effects of symbol set selection and code origin on the recall of utterances.* Paper presented at the third annual CEC/TAM conference, Baltimore.

Ehri, L., & Wilce, L. (1985). Movement into reading: Is the first stage of printed word reading visual or phonetic? *Reading Research Quarterly, 20*, 163–179.

Eisenson, J. (1968). Developmental aphasia: A speculative view with therapeutic implications. *Journal of Speech and Hearing Disorders, 33*, 3–13.

Eisenson, J., & Ingram, D. (1972). Childhood aphasia—An updated concept based on recent research. *Acta Symbolica, 3*, 108–116.

Ekman, P. (1976). Movements with precise meanings. *Journal of Communication, 26*, 14–26.

Ekman, P., & Friesen, W. (1969). The repertoire of nonverbal behavior: Categories, origin, usage, and coding. *Semiotica, 1*, 49–98.

Ellsworth, S., & Kotkin, R. (1975, November-December). If only Jimmy could speak. *Hearing and Speech Action, 43*, 6–10.

Emery, A., & Holloway, S. (1982). Familial motor neuron diseases. In L. Rowland (Ed.), *Human motor neuron diseases.* New York: Raven Press.

Engelmann, S., & Bruner, E. (1984). *Reading mastery program: DISTAR.* Chicago: Science Research Associates.

Erenberg, G. (1984). Cerebral palsy. *Postgraduate Medicine, 75*(7), 87–93.

Eulenberg, J. (1990). Dynamic displays and the future of augmentative communication. *Communication Outlook, 12*(2), 21–23.

Evans, I. (1991). Testing and diagnosis: A review and evaluation. In L. Meyer, C. Peck, & L. Brown (Eds.), *Critical issues in the lives of people with severe disabilities* (pp. 25–44). Baltimore: Paul H. Brookes Publishing Co.

Falvey, M. (1989). *Community-based curriculum: Instructional strategies for students with severe handicaps* (2nd ed.). Baltimore: Paul H. Brookes Publishing Co.

Fay, W., & Schuler, A. (1980). *Emerging language in autistic children.* Baltimore: University Park Press.

Fell, A., Lynn, E., & Morrison, K. (1984). *Non-oral communication assessment.* Ann Arbor, MI: Alternatives to Speech, Inc.

Fenwick, V. (1987). The Edward Smith school program: An integrated public school continuum for autistic children. In M. Berres & P. Knoblock (Eds.), *Program models for mainstreaming* (pp. 261–286). Rockville, MD: Aspen Systems.

Fiocca, G. (1981). *Generally understood gestures: An approach to communication for persons with severe language impairments.* Unpublished master's thesis, University of Illinois.

Fish, B., Shapiro, T., & Campbell, M. (1966). Long-term prognosis and the response of schizophrenic children to drug therapy: A controlled study of trifluoperazine. *American Journal of Psychiatry, 123*, 32–39.

Fishman, I. (1987). *Electronic communication aids.* Boston: College-Hill Press.

*Focus on Technology* (1990–1991a). OCR you can afford, 1–2.

*Focus on Technology* (1990–1991b). Tele Braille II debuts, 2.

Ford, A., & Mirenda, P. (1984). Community instruction: A natural cues and corrections decision model. *Journal of The Association for Persons with Severe Handicaps, 9*, 79–87.

Ford, A., Schnorr, R., Meyer, L., Davern, L., Black, J., & Dempsey, P. (Eds.). (1989). *The Syracuse community-referenced curriculum guide for students with moderate and severe disabilities.* Baltimore: Paul H. Brookes Publishing Co.

Forest, M. (1988). *With a little help from my friends* [Videotape]. (Available from Expectations Unlimited, P.O. Box 655, Niwot, CO 80544; Centre for Integrated Education, 24 Thome Crescent, Toronto, Ontario M6H 2S5, Canada.)

Foulds, R. (1980). Communication rates of nonspeech expression as a function in manual tasks and linguistic constraints. *Proceedings of the International Conference on Rehabilitation Engineering* (pp. 83–87). Washington, DC: RESNA, Association for the Advancement of Rehabilitation Technology.

Foulds, R. (1985). Observations on interfacing in nonvocal communication. In C. Barry & M. Byrne (Eds.), *Proceedings of the Fourth International Conference on Communication Through Technology for the Physically Disabled* (pp. 46–51). London: the International Cerebral Palsy Association.

Foulds, R. (1987). Guest editorial. *Augmentative and Alternative Communication, 3*, 169.

Foulds, R., Soede, M., & van Balkom, H. (1987). Statistical disambiguation of multi-character keys applied to reduce motor requirements for augmentative and alternative communication. *Augmentative and Alternative Communication, 3*, 192–195.

Francis, W., Nail, B., & Lloyd, L. (1990, November). *Mentally retarded adults' perception of emotions represented by pictographic symbols*. Paper presented at the annual conference of the American Speech-Language-Hearing Association, Seattle.

Franklin, K., Phillips, G., & Mirenda, P. (1991). *A comparison of five symbol assessment protocols*. Unpublished manuscript, University of Nebraska-Lincoln.

Frecks, K., Beukelman, D., & Mirenda, P. (1989). *The comprehension by aphasic individuals of three speech synthesizers and a natural speaker*. Unpublished manuscript, University of Nebraska-Lincoln.

Fredericks, H. D. B., & Baldwin, V. (1987). Individuals with sensory impairments: Who are they? How are they educated? In L. Goetz, D. Guess, & K. Stremel-Campbell (Eds.), *Innovative program design for individuals with dual sensory impairments* (pp. 3–12). Baltimore: Paul H. Brookes Publishing Co.

French, J. (1964). *Pictorial test of intelligence*. Chicago: Riverside Publishing.

Fried-Oken, M. (1989). *Sentence recognition for auditory and visual scanning techniques in electronic augmentative communication devices*. Paper presented at the RESNA/USSAAC annual conference, New Orleans.

Fried-Oken, M., Howard, J., & Prillwitz, D. (1988). Establishing initial communicative control with a loop-tape system. In S. Blackstone, E. Cassatt-James, & D. Bruskin (Eds.), *Augmentative communication: Implementation strategies* (pp. 5.1-45–5.1-51). Rockville, MD: American Speech-Language-Hearing Association.

Fried-Oken, M., Howard, J., & Stewart, S. (1991). Feedback on AAC intervention from adults who are temporarily unable to speak. *Augmentative and Alternative Communication, 7*, 43–50.

Fried-Oken, M., & More, L. (1992). Initial vocabulary for nonspeaking preschool children based on developmental and environmental language samples. *Augmentative and Alternative Communication 8*, 1–16.

Fry, E., Polk, J., & Fountoukidis, D. (1984). *The reading teacher's book of lists*. Englewood Cliffs, NJ: Prentice Hall.

Fullwood, D. (1990). *Chances and choices: Making integration work*. Baltimore: Paul H. Brookes Publishing Co.

Fulwiler, R., & Fouts, R. (1976). Acquisition of American Sign Language by a noncommunicating autistic child. *Journal of Autism and Childhood Schizophrenia, 6*, 43–51.

Gage, D., & Breda, D. (1986). Can we talk here? In D. Croft (Ed.), *The ultimate guide to peripherals for the blind computer user* (pp. 170–180). Boston: National Braille Press, Inc.

Galyas, K. (1990). The Multi-Talk concept for efficient communication. *Augmentative and Alternative Communication, 6*, 95.

Garrett, K., & Beukelman, D. (1992). Augmentative communication approaches for persons with severe aphasia. In K. Yorkston (Ed.), *Augmentative communication in the medical setting* (pp. 245–348). Tucson, AZ: Communication Skill Builders.

Garrett, K., Beukelman D., & Low-Morrow, D. (1989). A comprehensive augmentative communication system for an adult with Broca's aphasia. *Augmentative and Alternative Communication, 5*, 55–61.

Garrett, K., Schutz-Muehling, L., & Morrow, D. (1990). Low level head injury—A novel AAC approach. *Augmentative and Alternative Communication, 6*, 124.

Garrett, S. (1986). A case study in tactile Blissymbols. *Communicating Together, 4*(2), 16.

Gartner, A., & Lipsky, D. (1990). Students as instructional agents. In W. Stainback & S. Stainback (Eds.), *Support networks for inclusive schooling: Interdependent and integrated education* (pp. 81–93). Baltimore: Paul H. Brookes Publishing Co.

Gates, C. (1985). Survey of multiply handicapped visually impaired children in the Rocky Mountain/Great Plains region. *Journal of Visual Impairment and Blindness, 79*, 385–391.

Gillingham, A., & Stillman, B. (1970). *Remedial training for children with specific difficulty in reading, spelling, and penmanship*. Cambridge, MA: Educators Publishing Service.

Girolametto, L. (1988). Improving the social-conversational skills of developmentally delayed children: An intervention study. *Journal of Speech and Hearing Disorders, 53*, 156–167.

Girolametto, L., Greenberg, J., & Manolson, A. (1986). Developing dialogue skills: The Hanen Early Language Parent Program. *Seminars in Speech and Language, 7*, 367–382.

Gitlis, K.R. (1975, November). *Rationale and precedents for the use of simultaneous communication as an alternate system of communication for nonverbal children*. Paper presented at the 50th annual meeting of the American Speech and Hearing Association, Washington, DC.

Glass, A., Gazzaniga, M., & Premack, D. (1973). Artificial language training in global aphasia. *Neuropsychologia, 11*, 95–103.

Gleser, G., Gottschalk, L., & John, W. (1959). The relationship of sex and intelligence to choice words: A normative study of verbal behavior. *Journal of Clinical Psychology, 15*, 182–191.

Goetz, L., Gee, K., & Sailor, W. (1983). Crossmodal transfer of stimulus control: Preparing students with severe multiple disabilities for audiological assessment. *Journal of The Association for Persons with Severe Handicaps, 8*, 3–13.

Goetz, L., Gee, K., & Sailor, W. (1985). Using a behavior chain interruption strategy to teach communication skills to learners with severe disabilities. *Journal of The Association for Persons with Severe Handicaps, 10*, 21–30.

Goldberg, T. (1987). On hermetic reading abilities. *Journal of Autism and Developmental Disorders, 17*, 29–44.

Goldman-Eisler, F. (1986). *Cycle linguistics: Experiments in spontaneous speech.* New York: Academic Press.

Goodenough-Trepagnier, C., & Prather, P. (1981). Communication systems for the nonvocal based on frequent phoneme sequences. *Journal of Speech and Hearing Research, 24*, 322–329.

Goodenough-Trepagnier, C., Tarry, E., & Prather, P. (1982). Derivation of an efficient nonvocal communication system. *Human Factors, 24*, 163–172.

Goodglass, H. (1980). Naming disorders in aphasia and aging. In L. Obler & M. Albert (Eds.), *Language and communication.* Lexington, MA: Lexington Books.

Goossens', C. (1989). Aided communication intervention before assessment: A case study of a child with cerebral palsy. *Augmentative and Alternative Communication, 5*, 14–26.

Goossens', C., & Crain, S. (1986a). *Augmentative communication assessment resource.* Wauconda, IL: Don Johnston Developmental Equipment, Inc.

Goossens', C., & Crain, S. (1986b). *Augmentative communication intervention resource.* Wauconda, IL: Don Johnston Developmental Equipment, Inc.

Goossens', C., & Crain, S. (1986c). Establishing multiple communication displays. In S. Blackstone (Ed.), *Augmentative communication: An introduction* (pp. 337–344). Rockville, MD: American Speech-Language-Hearing Association.

Goossens', C., & Crain, S. (1987). Overview of nonelectronic eye-gaze communication devices. *Augmentative and Alternative Communication, 3*, 77–89.

Goossens', C., Heine, K., Crain, S., & Burke, C. (1987). *Modifying Piagetian tasks for use with physically-challenged individuals.* Birmingham, AL: Sparks Center for Developmental and Learning Disorders, University of Alabama.

Gorenflo, C., & Gorenflo, D. (1991). The effects of information and augmentative communication technique on attitudes toward nonspeaking individuals. *Journal of Speech and Hearing Research, 34*, 19–26.

Grandin, T., & Scariano, M. (1986). *Emergence: Labeled autistic.* Novato, CA: Arena Press.

Granlund, M., & Olsson, C. (1987). *Talspråksalternativ kommunikation och begåvningshandikapp* [Alternative communication and mental retardation]. Stockholm. Stiftelsen ALA.

Granlund, M., Ström, E., & Olsson, C. (1989). Iconicity and productive recall of a selected sample of signs from signed Swedish. *Augmentative and Alternative Communication, 5*, 173–182.

Grove, N., & Walker, M. (1990). The Makaton Vocabulary: Using manual signs and graphic symbols to develop interpersonal communication. *Augmentative and Alternative Communication, 6*, 15–28.

Gualtieri, C. (1988). Pharmacotherapy and the neurobehavioral sequelae of traumatic brain injury. *Brain Injury, 2*, 101–129.

Guess, D., Benson, H., & Siegel-Causey, E. (1985). Concepts and issues related to choice-making and autonomy among persons with severe disabilities. *Journal of The Association for Persons with Severe Handicaps, 10*, 79–86.

Guralnick, M. (1990). Social competence and early intervention. *Journal of Early Intervention, 14*, 3–14.

Gustason, G. (1990). Signing Exact English. In H. Bornstein (Ed.), *Manual communication: Implications for education* (pp. 108-127). Washington, DC: Gallaudet University Press.

Gustason, G., Pfetzing, D., & Zawolkow, E. (1980). *Signing Exact English* (3rd ed.). Los Alamitos, CA: Modern Signs Press.

Guyette, T., & Diedrich, W. (1981). A critical review of developmental apraxia of speech. In N. Lass (Ed.), *Speech and language advances in basic research and practice* (Vol. 5). New York: Academic Press.

Hagen, C. (1984). Language disorders in head trauma. In A. Holland (Ed.), *Language disorders in adults* (pp. 245–281). Austin, TX: PRO-ED.

Halle, J.W. (1982). Teaching functional language to the handicapped: An integrative model of natural environment teaching techniques. *Journal of The Association for Persons with Severe Handicaps, 7*, 29–37.

Halle, J., Baer, D., & Spradlin, J. (1981). Teachers' generalized use of delay as a stimulus control procedure to increase language use by handicapped children. *Journal of Applied Behavior Analysis, 14*, 389–409.

Halle, J., Marshall, A., & Spradlin, J. (1979). Time delay: A technique to increase language use and facilitate generalization in retarded children. *Journal of Applied Behavior Analysis, 12*, 431–439.

Hamblin-Wilson, C., & Thurman, S. (1990). The transition from early intervention to kindergarten: Parental satisfaction and involvement. *Journal of Early Intervention, 14,* 55–61.

Hammen, V., Yorkston, K., & Dowden, P. (1991). Index of contextual intelligibility: Impact of semantic context on dysarthria. In C. Moore, K. Yorkston, & D. Beukelman (Eds.), *Dysarthria and apraxia of speech: Perspectives on management* (pp. 43-53). Baltimore: Paul H. Brookes Publishing Co.

Hamre-Nietupski, S., Stoll, A., Holtz, K., Fullerton, P., Ryan-Flottum, M., & Brown, L. (1977). Curricular strategies for teaching selected nonverbal communication skills to nonverbal and verbal severely handicapped students. In L. Brown, J. Nietupski, S. Lyon, S. Hamre-Nietupski, T. Crowner, & L. Gruenewald (Eds.), *Curricular strategies for teaching functional object use, nonverbal communication, problem solving, and mealtime skills to severely handicapped students* (Vol. VII, Part I, pp. 94–250). Madison: University of Wisconsin-Madison and Madison Metropolitan School District.

Hanson, M., & Hanline, M. (1989). Integration options for the very young child. In R. Gaylord-Ross (Ed.), *Integration strategies for students with handicaps* (pp. 177–193). Baltimore: Paul H. Brookes Publishing Co.

Hardy, J. (1983). *Cerebral palsy.* Englewood Cliffs, NJ: Prentice Hall.

Haring, T., Neetz, J., Lovinger, L., Peck, C., & Semmel, M. (1987). Effects of four modified incidental teaching procedures to create opportunities for communication. *Journal of The Association for Persons with Severe Handicaps, 12,* 218–226.

Harrington, D. (1976). *The visual fields: A textbook and atlas of clinical perimetry* (4th ed.). St. Louis: C.V. Mosby.

Harrington, K. (1988). A letter from Annie. *Communicating Together, 6*(4), 5–7.

Harris, D. (1982). Communication interaction processes involving nonvocal physically handicapped children. *Topics in Language Disorders, 2*(2), 21–37.

Hart, B., & Risley, T. (1975). Incidental teaching of language in the preschool. *Journal of Applied Behavior Analysis, 8,* 411–420.

Hart, B., & Rogers-Warren, A. (1978). Milieu teaching approaches. In R. Scheifelbusch (Ed.), *Language intervention strategies.* Baltimore: University Park Press.

Hart, P., & Spellman, C. (1989). Tactual/tactile assessment. In M. Bullis (Ed.), *Communication development in young children with deaf-blindness: Literature review IV.* Monmouth, OR: Communication Skills Center for Young Children with Deaf-Blindness, Oregon State System of Higher Education.

Hart, V. (1977). The use of many disciplines with the severely and profoundly handicapped. In E. Sontag, J. Smith, & N. Certo (Eds.), *Educational programming for the severely and profoundly handicapped* (pp. 391-396). Reston, VA: Council for Exceptional Children.

Haynes, S. (1985). Developmental apraxia of speech: Symptoms and treatment. In D. F. Johns (Ed.), *Clinical management of neurogenic communicative disorders* (pp. 259–266). Boston: Little, Brown.

Hedbring, C. (1985). Computers and autistic learners: An evolving technology. *Australian Journal of Human Communication Disorders, 13,* 169–194.

Hedrick, D., Prather, E., & Tobin, A. (1984). *Sequenced Inventory of Communication Development* (rev. ed.). Seattle: University of Washington Press.

Hehner, B. (1980). *Blissymbols for use.* Toronto: Blissymbolics Communication International.

Heinze, T. (1986). Communication skills. In G. T. Scholl (Ed.), *Foundations of education for blind and visually handicapped children and youth: Theory and practice* (pp. 301–314). New York: American Foundation for the Blind.

Helfrich-Miller, K. (1984). Melodic intonation therapy with developmentally apraxic children. *Seminars in Speech and Language, 5*(2), 119–126.

Higginbotham, D. (1989). The interplay of communication device output mode and interaction style between nonspeaking persons and their speaking partners. *Journal of Speech and Hearing Disorders, 54,* 320–333.

Higginbotham, D. (1990, November). *An assessment of keystroke efficiency for five augmentative communication technologies.* Paper presented at the annual conference of the American Speech-Language-Hearing Association, Seattle.

Higginbotham, D., Mathy-Laikko, P., & Yoder, D. (1988). Studying conversations of augmentative communication system users. In L. E. Bernstein (Ed.), *The vocally impaired: Clinical practice and research* (pp. 265–294). Philadelphia: Grune & Stratton.

Hodges, P., & Schwethelm, B. (1984). A comparison of the effectiveness of graphic symbol and manual sign training with profoundly retarded children. *Applied Psycholinguistics, 5,* 223-253.

Hodson, B., & Paden, E. (1991). *A phonological approach to remediation: Targeting intelligible speech* (2nd ed.). Austin, TX: PRO-ED.

Hoffman, M. (1990). *The world almanac and book of facts.* New York: Pharos Books.

Hoffmeister, R. (1990). ASL and its implications for education. In H. Bornstein (Ed.), *Manual communication: Implications for education* (pp. 81–107). Washington, DC: Gallaudet University Press.

Hofman, A.C. (1988). *The many faces of funding.* (Available from A. C. Hofman, Editor, Phonic Ear, 3380 Cypress Dr., Petaluma, CA 94954.)

Honsinger, M. (1989). Midcourse intervention in multiple sclerosis: An inpatient model. *Augmentative and Alternative Communication, 5,* 71–73.

Honsinger, M., Yorkston, K., & Dowden, P. (1987, May–June). Communication options for intubated patients. *Respiratory Management,* 45-52.

Hooper, J., Connell, T., & Flett, P. (1987). Blissymbols and manual signs: A multimodal approach to intervention in a case of multiple disability. *Augmentative and Alternative Communication, 3,* 68–76.

Hoover, J., Reichle, J., Van Tassell, D., & Cole, D. (1987). The intelligibility of synthesized speech: Echo II versus Votrax. *Journal of Speech and Hearing Research, 30,* 425–431.

Horner, R., & Budd, C. (1985). Acquisition of manual sign use: Collateral reduction of maladaptive behavior and factors limiting generalization. *Education and Training of the Mentally Retarded, 20,* 39–47.

Horner, R., Sprague, J., O'Brien, M., & Heathfield, L. (1990). The role of response efficiency in the reduction of problem behaviors through functional equivalence training: A case study. *Journal of The Association for Persons with Severe Handicaps, 15,* 91–97.

Hoskins, B. (1990). Collaborative consultation: Designing the role of the speech-language pathologist in a new educational context. In W. Secord (Ed.), *Best practices in school speech-language pathology* (pp. 29–38). Houston, TX: The Psychological Corporation.

Houghton, J., Bronicki, B., & Guess, D. (1987). Opportunities to express preferences and make choices among students with severe disabilities in classroom settings. *Journal of The Association for Persons with Severe Handicaps, 11,* 255–265.

House, L., & Rogerson, B. (1984). *Comprehensive screening tool for determining optimal communication mode.* East Aurora, NY: United Educational Services.

Howes, D. (1966). A word count of spoken English. *Journal of Verbal Learning and Verbal Behavior, 5,* 572–604.

Howlin, P. (1981). The effectiveness of operant language training with autistic children. *Journal of Autism and Developmental Disorders, 11,* 89–105.

Hoyson, F., Jamieson, B., & Strain, P. (1984). Individualized group instruction of normally developing and autistic-like children: The LEAP curriculum model. *Journal of the Division for Early Childhood, 8,* 157–172.

Huebner, K. (1986). Curricula adaptations. In G. T. Scholl (Ed.), *Foundations of education for blind and visually handicapped children and youth: Theory and practice* (pp. 363–404). New York: American Foundation for the Blind.

Huer, M. (1983). *The Nonspeech Test.* Wauconda, IL: Don Johnston Developmental Equipment, Inc.

Huer, M. (1987). White's gestural system for the lower extremities. *Communicating Together, 5,* 3–4.

Huer, M., & Lloyd, L. (1988). Perspectives of AAC users. *Communication Outlook, 9*(2), 10-18.

Huer, M., & Lloyd, L. (1990). AAC users' perspectives on augmentative and alternative communication. *Augmentative and Alternative Communication, 6,* 242–250.

Hunnicutt, S., Rosengren, E., & Baker, B. (1990). Development of the Swedish language Minspeak Words Strategy. *Augmentative and Alternative Communication, 6,* 115–116.

Hunt, P., Alwell, M., & Goetz, L. (1988). Acquisition of conversation skills and the reduction of inappropriate social interaction behaviors. *Journal of The Association for Persons with Severe Handicaps, 13,* 20–27.

Hunt, P., Alwell, M., & Goetz, L. (1990). *Teaching conversation skills to individuals with severe disabilities with a communication book adaptation.* Unpublished handbook. (Available from P. Hunt, San Francisco State University, 14 Tapia St., San Francisco, CA 94132.)

Hunt, P., Alwell, M., & Goetz, L. (1991a). Establishing conversational exchanges with family and friends: Moving from training to meaningful communication. *Journal of Special Education, 25,* 305–319.

Hunt, P., Alwell, M., & Goetz, L. (1991b). Interacting with peers through conversation turntaking with a communication book adaptation. *Augmentative and Alternative Communication, 7,* 117–126.

Hunt, P., & Goetz, L. (1988a). Teaching spontaneous communication in natural settings through interrupted behavior chains. *Topics in Language Disorders, 9* (1), 58–71.

Hunt, P., & Goetz, L. (1988b). *Using the interrupted behavior chain strategy to teach initial communication skills to learners with severe disabilities.* Unpublished handbook. (Available from P. Hunt, San Francisco State University, 14 Tapia St., San Francisco, CA 94132.)

Hunt, P., Goetz, L., Alwell, M., & Sailor, W. (1986). Using an interrupted behavior chain strategy to teach generalized communication responses. *Journal of The Association for Persons with Severe Handicaps, 11,* 196–204.

Huntress, L., Lee, L., Creaghead, N., Wheeler, D., & Braverman, K. (1990). Aphasic subjects' comprehension of synthetic and natural speech. *Journal of Speech and Hearing Disorders, 55,* 21–27.

Hurlbut, B., Iwata, B., & Green, J. (1982). Nonvocal language acquisition in adolescents with severe physical disabilities: Blissymbol versus iconic stimulus formats. *Journal of Applied Behavior Analysis, 15,* 241–258.

Hussey, I. (1991). Beginning AAC in Zimbabwe. *Communicating Together, 9*(1), 19–20.

Hutchison, D. (1978). The transdisciplinary approach. In J. Curr & K. Peppe (Eds.), *Mental retardation: Nursing approaches to care* (pp. 65–74). St. Louis: C. V. Mosby.

Hymes, D. (1972). On communicative competence. In J. B. Pride & J. Holmes (Eds.), *Sociolinguistics* (pp. 269–293). Harmondsworth, United Kingdom: Penguin.

Iacono, T., & Parsons, C. (1986). A survey of the use of signing with the intellectually disabled. *Australian Communication Quarterly, 2,* 21–25.

Idol, L., Paolucci-Whitcomb, P., & Nevin, A. (1986). *Collaborative consultation.* Rockville, MD: Aspen Systems.

International Communication Learning Institute. (1986). *Introducing visual phonics* [Videotape]. Edina, MN: Author.

Ivers, R., & Goldstein, N. (1963). Multiple sclerosis: A current appraisal of symptoms and signs. *Proceedings of the Staff Meetings of the Mayo Clinic, 38,* 457–466.

Jacobs, H. (1988). The Los Angeles head injury survey: Procedures and initial findings. *Archives of Physical Medicine and Rehabilitation, 69,* 425–431.

Jastak, J., Bijou, S., & Jastak, S. (1978). *Wide Range Achievement Test.* Wilmington, DE: Jastak Assessment Systems.

Jennett, B., Snoek, J., Bond, M., & Brooks, N. (1981). Disability after severe head injury: Observations on use of the Glasgow Outcome Scale. *Journal of Neurology, Neurosurgery, and Psychiatry, 44,* 285–293.

Jensema, C. (1979). A review of communication systems used by deaf-blind people: Part 1. *American Annals of the Deaf, 124,* 720–725.

Jensema, C. (1982). Communication methods and devices for deaf-blind persons. *Directions, 3,* 60–69.

Johns, D. (1985). *Clinical management of neurogenic communication disorders.* Austin, TX: PRO-ED.

Johnson, J. (1986). *Self-Talk: Communication boards for children and adults.* Tucson, AZ: Communication Skill Builders.

Johnson, J. (1988). *Self-Talk stickers: Pictures and words for augmentative communication boards.* Tucson, AZ: Communication Skill Builders.

Johnson, R. (1981). *The Picture Communication Symbols, book I.* Solana Beach, CA: Mayer-Johnson Co.

Johnson, R. (1985). *The Picture Communication Symbols, book II.* Solana Beach, CA: Mayer-Johnson Co.

Johnson-Martin, N., Wolters, P., & Sowers, S. (1987). Psychological assessment of the nonvocal, physically handicapped child. *Physical and Occupational Therapy in Pediatrics, 7*(2), 23–38.

Johnston, J. (1991a) The continuing relevance of cause: A reply to Leonard's "Specific language impairment as a clinical category." *Language, Speech, and Hearing Services in Schools, 22,* 75–79.

Johnston, J. (1991b). Questions about cognition in children with specific language impairment. In. J. Miller (Ed.), *Research on child language disorders: A decade of progress* (pp. 299–308). Austin, TX: PRO-ED.

Jose, R. T. (Ed.). (1983). *Understanding low vision.* New York: American Foundation for the Blind.

Joseph, D. (1986). The morning. *Communication Outlook, 8*(2), 8.

Jung, J. (1989). *Genetic syndromes in communication disorders.* Austin, TX: PRO-ED.

Kalsbeek, W., McLauren, R., Harris, B., & Miller, J. (1981). The national head and spinal cord injury survey: Major findings. *Journal of Neurosurgery, 53,* 519–531.

Kamhi, A., & Catts, H. (1989). *Reading disabilities: A developmental language perspective.* Boston: Little, Brown.

Kamphuis, H. (1990). Enhancing communication rate: Two input systems for augmentative communication aids. *Augmentative and Alternative Communication, 6,* 95.

Kangas, K., & Lloyd, L. (1988). Early cognitive skills as prerequisites to augmentative and alternative communication use: What are we waiting for? *Augmentative and Alternative Communication, 4,* 211–221.

Karlan, G. (1990). Manual communication with those who can hear. In H. Bornstein (Ed.), *Manual communication: Implications for education* (pp. 151-185). Washington, DC: Gallaudet University Press.

Karuth, D. (1985). If I were a car, I'd be a lemon. In A. Brightman (Ed.), *Ordinary moments: The disabled experience* (pp. 9–31). Syracuse, NY: Human Policy Press.

Kates, B., & McNaughton, S. (1975). *The first application of Blissymbolics as a communication medium for nonspeaking children: History and development, 1971–1974.* Don Mills, Ontario: Easter Seals Communication Institute.

Kaufman, B. (1976). *Son rise.* New York: Warner Books.

Kaul, S. (1990). Sounds of silence. *Communication Outlook, 11*(3), 6–9.

Kearns, T. (1990). Training families as effective sign communication partners and teachers. *Augmentative and Alternative Communication, 6,* 103.

Kelford Smith, A., Thurston, S., Light, J., Parnes, P., & O'Keefe, B. (1989). The form and use of written communication produced by physically disabled individuals using microcomputers. *Augmentative and Alternative Communication, 5,* 115–124.

Kemper, S. (1988). Geriatric psycholinguistics: Syntactic limitations of oral and written language. In L. Light

& D. Burke (Eds.), *Language, memory, and aging* (pp. 58–76). Melbourne, Australia: Cambridge University Press.

Keogh, W., & Reichle, J. (1985). Communication intervention for the "difficult-to-teach" severely handicapped. In S. F. Warren & A. K. Rogers-Warren (Eds.), *Teaching functional language* (pp. 157–194). Austin, TX: PRO-ED.

Kiernan, C. (1983). The use of nonvocal communication techniques with autistic individuals. *Journal of Child Psychology and Psychiatry, 24,* 339–375.

Kiernan, C., Reid, B., & Jones, M. (1982). *Signs and symbols: Use of non-vocal communication systems.* London: Heinemann.

Kimble, S.L. (1975, November). *A language teaching technique with totally nonverbal, severely mentally retarded adolescents.* Paper presented at the 50th annual meeting of the American Speech and Hearing Association, Washington, DC.

Kipila, E., & Williams-Scott, B. (1990). Cued speech. In H. Bornstein (Ed.), *Manual communication: Implications for education* (pp. 139–150). Washington, DC: Gallaudet University Press.

Kirk, S., McCarthy, J., & Kirk, W. (1968). *Illinois Test of Psycholinguistic Abilities.* Champaign: University of Illinois Press.

Kirstein, I. (1981). *Oakland Schools Picture Dictionary.* Wauconda, IL: Don Johnston Developmental Equipment, Inc.

Kladde, A.G. (1974). Nonoral communication techniques: Project summary No. 1., 1967. In B. Vicker (Ed.), *Nonoral Communication System Project 1964/1973* (pp. 57–104). Iowa City: University of Iowa.

Klein, M. (1988). *Pre-sign language motor skills.* Tucson, AZ: Communication Skill Builders.

Klick, S. (1985). Adapted cuing technique for use in treatment of dyspraxia. *Language, Speech, and Hearing Services in Schools, 16,* 256–259.

Knapp, M. (1980). *Essentials of nonverbal communication.* New York: Holt, Rinehart & Winston.

Knox, D. (1971). *Portrait of aphasia.* Detroit: Wayne State University Press.

Koegel, R., O'Dell, M., & Koegel, L. (1987). A natural language teaching paradigm for nonverbal autistic children. *Journal of Autism and Developmental Disorders, 17,* 187–200.

Koegel, R., Rincover, A., & Egel, A. (1982). *Educating and understanding autistic children.* San Diego: College-Hill Press.

Koegel, R., Schreibman, L., Good, A., Cerniglia, L., Murphy, C., & Koegel, L. (1989). *How to teach pivotal behaviors to children with autism.* Santa Barbara: University of California-Santa Barbara.

Konstantareas, M. (1984). Sign language as a communication prosthesis with language-impaired children. *Journal of Autism and Developmental Disorders, 14,* 9–23.

Konstantareas, M. (1987). Autistic children exposed to simultaneous communication training: A follow-up. *Journal of Autism and Developmental Disorders, 17,* 115–132.

Konstantareas, M., Oxman, J., & Webster, C. (1978). Iconicity: Effects on the acquisition of sign language by autistic and other severely dysfunctional children. In P. Siple (Ed.), *Understanding language through sign language research* (pp. 213–237). New York: Academic Press.

Konstantareas, M., Oxman, J., Webster, C., Fischer, H., & Miller, K. (1975). *A five-week simultaneous communication programme for severely dysfunctional children: Outcome and implications for future research.* Toronto: Clarke Institute of Psychiatry.

Koppenhaver, D., Evans, D., & Yoder, D. (1991). Childhood reading and writing experiences of literate adults with severe speech and motor impairments. *Augmentative and Alternative Communication, 7,* 20–33.

Koppenhaver, D., & Yoder, D. (1990, July-August). *A descriptive analysis of classroom reading and writing instruction for adolescents with severe speech and physical impairments.* Paper presented at the International Special Education Conference, Cardiff, Wales.

Koppenhaver, D., & Yoder, D. (1992). Literacy issues in persons with severe physical and speech impairments. In R. Gaylord-Ross (Ed.), *Issues and research in special education* (Vol. 2, pp. 156–201). New York: Teacher's College Press.

Kottke, F., & Lehman, J. (Eds.). (1990). *Krusen's handbook of physical medicine and rehabilitation* (4th ed.). Philadelphia: W.B. Saunders.

Kozleski, E. (1991). Expectant delay procedure for teaching requests. *Augmentative and Alternative Communication, 7,* 11–19.

Kraat, A. (1985). *Communication interaction between aided and natural speakers: A state of the art report.* Toronto: Canadian Rehabilitation Council for the Disabled.

Kraat, A., & Sitver-Kogut, M. (1991). *Features of portable communication devices* [wallchart]. Wilmington, DE: Applied Science and Engineering Laboratories, University of Delaware/A. I. duPont Institute.

Kraft, G. (1981). Multiple sclerosis. In W. Stolov & M. Clowers (Eds.), *Handbook of severe disability* (pp. 111–118). Washington, DC: U.S. Department of Education.

Kraus, J. (1978). Epidemiologic features of head and spinal cord injury. *Advances in Neurology, 19,* 261–279.

Kravitz, E., & Littman, S. (1990). A communication system for a nonspeaking person with hearing and cognitive impairments. *Augmentative and Alternative Communication, 6,* 100.

Kynette, D., & Kemper, S. (1986). Aging and loss of grammatical forms: A cross-sectional study of language performance. *Language and Communication, 6*(1/2), 65–72.

Ladtkow, M., & Culp, D. (1992). Augmentative communication with traumatic brain injury. In K. Yorkston (Ed.), *Augmentative communication in the medical setting* (pp. 139–244). Tucson, AZ: Communication Skill Builders.

Lahey, M. (1990). Who shall be called language disordered? Some reflections and one perspective. *Journal of Speech and Hearing Research, 55,* 612–620.

Lahey, M., & Bloom, L. (1977). Planning a first lexicon: Which words to teach first. *Journal of Speech and Hearing Disorders, 42,* 340–349.

Landman, C., & Schaeffler, C. (1986). Object communication boards. *Communication Outlook, 8*(1), 7–8.

Langley, B. (1980). *Functional vision inventory for the multiply and severely handicapped.* Chicago: Stoetling.

Larson, V., & Steiner, S. (1985). Language intervention using microcomputers. *Topics in Language Disorders, 6*(1), 41–55.

Laski, K., Charlop, M., & Schreibman, L. (1988). Training parents to use the natural language paradigm to increase their autistic children's speech. *Journal of Applied Behavior Analysis, 21,* 391–400.

Lauer, H. (1988, September). Communication media for the visually impaired: Why one medium isn't enough. *RDC Newsletter,* 14–20.

Lebeis, S., & Lebeis, R.F. (1975). The use of signed communication with the normal-hearing, nonverbal mentally retarded. *Bureau Memorandum* (Wisconsin Department of Public Instruction), *17*(1), 28–30.

Lee, K., & Thomas, D. (1990). *Control of computer-based technology for people with physical disabilities: An assessment manual.* Toronto: University of Toronto Press.

Leonard, L. (1982). The nature of specific language impairment in children. In S. Rosenberg (Ed.), *Handbook of applied psycholinguistics: Major thrusts of research and theory* (pp. 295–328). Hillsdale, NJ: Lawrence Erlbaum Associates.

Leonard, L. (1991). Specific language impairment as a clinical category. *Language, Speech, and Hearing Services in Schools, 22,* 66–68.

Leonhart, W., & Maharaj, S. (1979). *A comparison of initial recognition and rate of acquisition of Pictogram Ideogram Communication (PIC) and Bliss symbols with institutionalized severely retarded adults.* Unpublished manuscript.

Lerner, J. (1988). *Learning disabilities: Theories, diagnosis, and teaching strategies.* Boston: Houghton Mifflin.

Leske, M. C. (1981). Speech prevalence estimates of communicative disorders in the U.S. *Asha, 23,* 229–237.

Levett, L.M. (1971). A method of communication for nonspeaking severely sub-normal children—trial results. *British Journal of Disorders of Communication, 6,* 125–128.

Levin, J., & Scherfenberg, L. (1988). *Selection and use of simple technology in home, school, work, and community settings.* Wauconda, IL: Don Johnston Developmental Equipment, Inc.

Light, J. (1988). Interaction involving individuals using augmentative and alternative communication systems: State of the art and future directions. *Augmentative and Alternative Communication, 4,* 66–82.

Light, J. (1989a). *Encoding techniques for augmentative communication systems: An investigation of the recall performance of nonspeaking physically disabled adults.* Unpublished doctoral dissertation, University of Toronto.

Light, J. (1989b). Toward a definition of communicative competence for individuals using augmentative and alternative communication systems. *Augmentative and Alternative Communication, 5,* 137–144.

Light, J., Beesly, M., & Collier, B. (1988). Transition through multiple augmentative and alternative communication systems: A three-year case study of a head-injured adolescent. *Augmentative and Alternative Communication, 4,* 2–14.

Light, J., Collier, B., & Parnes, P. (1985). Communication interaction between young nonspeaking physically disabled children and their primary caregivers: Part III. Modes of communication. *Augmentative and Alternative Communication, 1,* 125–133.

Light, J., & Kelford Smith, A. (in press). The home literacy experiences of preschoolers who use augmentative communication systems and their nondisabled peers. *Augmentative and Alternative Communication.*

Light, J., Lindsay, P., Siegel, L., & Parnes, P. (1990). The effects of message and coding techniques on recall by literate adults using AAC systems. *Augmentative and Alternative Communication, 6,* 184–201.

Light, J., McNaughton, D., & Parnes, P. (1986). *A protocol for the assessment of the communicative interaction skills of nonspeaking severely handicapped adults and their facilitators.* Toronto: Augmentative Communication Service, Hugh MacMillan Medical Centre.

Lindsay, P., Cambria, R., McNaughton, S., & Warrick, A. (1986, September). *The educational needs of non-speaking students and their teachers*. Paper presented at the fourth biennial conference of the International Society for Augmentative and Alternative Communication, Cardiff, Wales.

Linville, S.E. (1977). Signed English: A language teaching technique with totally nonverbal severely mentally retarded adolescents. *Language, Speech, and Hearing Services in Schools, 8*, 170–175.

Lippman, O. (1971). Vision screening of young children. *American Journal of Public Health, 61*(8), 1586–1601.

Lloyd, L., & Fuller, D. (1986). Toward an augmentative and alternative communication symbol taxonomy: A proposed superordinate classification. *Augmentative and Alternative Communication, 2*, 165–171.

Lloyd, L., & Karlan, G. (1984). Nonspeech communication symbols and systems: Where have we been and where are we going? *Journal of Mental Deficiency Research, 38*, 3–20.

Locke, P., & Mirenda, P. (1988). A computer-supported communication approach for a nonspeaking child with severe visual and cognitive impairments: A case study. *Augmentative and Alternative Communication, 4*, 15–22.

Locke, P., & Mirenda, P. (in press). An examination of the roles/responsibilities of special education teachers serving on teams that deliver augmentative and alternative communication services: *Augmentative and Alternative Communication*.

Loeding, B., Zangari, C., & Lloyd, L. (1990). A "working party" approach to planning inservice training in manual signs for an entire public school staff. *Augmentative and Alternative Communication, 6*, 38–49.

Loftus-Brigham, S. (1983). *Dyslexia need not be a disaster*. London: London Dyslexia Association.

Logan, J., Pisoni, D., & Greene, B. (1985). Measuring the segmental intelligibility of synthetic speech: Results from eight text-to-speech systems. *Research on Speech Perception (Progress Report No. 11)*. Bloomington: Indiana University.

Logemann, J. (1983). *Evaluation and treatment of swallowing disorders*. Austin, TX: PRO-ED.

Lord, J. (1984). Cerebral palsy: A clinical approach. *Archives of Physical Medicine and Rehabilitation, 65*, 542–548.

Lovaas, O. I. (1987). Behavioral treatment and normal educational and intellectual functioning in young autistic children. *Journal of Consulting and Clinical Psychology, 55*, 3–9.

Lovaas, O. I., Ackerman, A., Alexander, D., Firestone, P., Perkins, J., & Young, D. (1980). *Teaching developmentally disabled children: The me book*. Austin, TX: PRO-ED.

Luftig, R. (1984). An analysis of initial sign lexicons as a function of eight learnability variables. *Journal of The Association for Persons with Severe Handicaps, 9*, 193–200.

Lynch, M. (1990). Tactile Speech Indicator: Adaptive telephone device for deaf-blind clients. *Journal of Visual Impairment and Blindness, 84*, 21–22.

Lyon, J., & Helm-Estabrooks, N. (1987). Drawing: Its communicative significance for expressively restricted aphasic adults. *Topics in Language Disorders, 8*, 61–71.

MacDonald, J. (1985). Language through conversation: A model for intervention with language-delayed persons. In S. Warren & A.K. Rogers-Warren (Eds.), *Teaching functional language: Generalization and maintenance of language skills* (pp. 89–122). Baltimore: University Park Press.

MacDonald, J., & Gillette, Y. (1986a). Communicating with persons with severe handicaps: Role of parents and professionals. *Journal of The Association for Persons with Severe Handicaps, 11*, 255–265.

MacDonald, J., & Gillette, Y. (1986b). *Ecological communication system (ECO)*. Columbus, OH: Nisonger Center, Ohio State University.

MacGinitie, W. (1978). *Gates-MacGinitie Reading Tests*. Chicago: Riverside.

Mack, C. (1984). How useful is braille? Reports of blind adults. *Journal of Visual Impairment and Blindness, 78*, 313–331.

Magnússon, J. (1990). Experience with the ISBLISS symbolic processing system as a written communication aid. *Augmentative and Alternative Communication, 6*, 129.

Maharaj, S. (1980). *Pictogram ideogram communication*. Saskatoon, Saskatchewan: The Pictogram Centre, Saskatchewan Association of Rehabilitation Centres.

Manolson, A. (1985). *It takes two to talk: A Hanen early language parent book*. Toronto: Hanen Early Language Resource Center.

Marquardt, T., Dunn, C., & Davis, B. (1985). Apraxia of speech in children. In J. Darby (Ed.), *Speech and language evaluation in neurology: Childhood disorders* (pp. 113–132). New York: Grune & Stratton.

Marriner, N., Beukelman, D., Wilson, W., & Ross, A. (1988). *Implementing Morse code in an augmentative communication system for ten nonspeaking individuals*. Unpublished manuscript, University of Washington, Seattle.

Marvin, C., Beukelman, D., & Vanderhoof, D. (1991). *Vocabulary use patterns by preschool children in home and school contexts*. Manuscript submitted for publication.

Massey, H. (1988). Language-impaired children's comprehension of synthetic speech. *Language, Speech, and Hearing Services in Schools, 19*, 401–409.

Matas, J., & Beukelman, D. (1989). *Teaching Morse code as an augmentative communication technique: Learner and instructor performance.* Unpublished manuscript, University of Washington, Seattle.

Matas, J., Mathy-Laikko, P., Beukelman, D., & Legresley, K. (1985). Identifying the nonspeaking population: A demographic study. *Augmentative and Alternative Communication, 1,* 17–31.

Mathy-Laikko, P., & Coxson, L. (1984, November). *Listener reactions to augmentative communication system output mode.* Paper presented at the annual conference of the American Speech-Language-Hearing Association Convention, San Francisco.

Mathy-Laikko, P., Iacono, T., Ratcliff, A., Villarruel, F., Yoder, D., & Vanderheiden, G. (1989). Teaching a child with multiple disabilities to use a tactile augmentative communication device. *Augmentative and Alternative Communication, 5,* 249–256.

Mathy-Laikko, P., Ratcliff, A. E., Villarruel, F., & Yoder, D. E. (1987). Augmentative communication systems. In M. Bullis (Ed.), *Communication development in young children with deaf-blindness: Literature review III* (pp. 205–241). Monmouth, OR: Communication Skills Center for Young Children with Deaf-Blindness, Teaching Research Division, Oregon State System of Higher Education.

Mathy-Laikko, P., & Yoder, D. (1986). Future needs and directions in augmentative communication. In S. Blackstone & D. Bruskin (Eds.), *Augmentative communication: An introduction* (pp. 471–494). Rockville, MD: American Speech-Language-Hearing Association.

Mayer-Johnson Co. (1989). *Boardmaker.* Solana Beach, CA: Author.

Mayer-Johnson Co. (1990). *Talking symbols.* Solana Beach, CA: Author.

McCauley, R., & Demetras, M. (1990). The identification of language impairment in the selection of specifically language-impaired subjects. *Journal of Speech and Hearing Research, 55,* 468–475.

McDonald, E. T. (1987). Cerebral palsy: Its nature, pathogenesis, and management. In E. T. McDonald (Ed.), *Treating cerebral palsy: For clinicians by clinicians* (pp. 1–20). Austin, TX: PRO-ED.

McDonald, J., Schwejda, P., Marriner, N., Wilson, W., & Ross, A. (1982). Advantages of Morse code as a computer input for school-aged children with physical disability. *Computers and the handicapped* (pp. 95–106). Ottawa: National Research Council of Canada.

McGee, G., Krantz, P., Mason, D., & McClannahan, L. (1983). A modified incidental-teaching procedure for autistic youth: Acquisition and generalization of receptive object labels. *Journal of Applied Behavior Analysis, 16,* 329–338.

McGinnis, J. (1991). *Development of two source lists for vocabulary selection in augmentative communication: Documentation of the spoken and written vocabulary of third grade students.* Unpublished doctoral dissertation, University of Nebraska-Lincoln.

McKinney, J., & Feagans, L. (1984). Academic and behavioral characteristics: Longitudinal studies of learning disabled children and average achievers. *Learning Disability Quarterly, 7,* 251–265.

McLean, L., & McLean, J. (1974). A language training program for non-verbal autistic children. *Journal of Speech and Hearing Disorders, 39,* 186–194.

McLean, J., McLean, L., Brady, N., & Etter, R. (1991). Communication profiles of two types of gesture using nonverbal persons with severe to profound mental retardation. *Journal of Speech and Hearing Research, 34,* 294–308.

McMillen, R., & Kellis, T. (1982). Educating visually handicapped students at the secondary level. In S. S. Mangold (Ed.), *A teacher's guide to the special educational needs of blind and visually handicapped children.* New York: American Foundation for the Blind.

McNaughton, D., & Light, J. (1989). Teaching facilitators to support the communication skills of an adult with severe cognitive disabilities: A case study. *Augmentative and Alternative Communication, 5,* 35–41.

McNaughton, S. (1990a). Introducing Access Bliss. *Communicating Together, 8*(2), 12–13.

McNaughton, S. (1990b). StoryBliss. *Communicating Together, 8*(1), 12–13.

McNeil, M., & Prescott, T. (1978). *Revised Token Test.* Austin, TX: PRO-ED.

Mergler, N., & Goldstein, M. (1983). Why are there old people? *Human Development, 26,* 130–143.

Meyer, L., Peck, C., & Brown, L. (Eds.). (1991). *Critical issues in the lives of people with severe disabilities.* Baltimore: Paul H. Brookes Publishing Co.

Meyers, L. (1983). The use of microprocessors to promote acquisition of beginning language and literacy skills in young handicapped children. *Proceedings of the American Association for the Advancement of Science Conference on Computers and the Handicapped.* Washington, DC: American Association for the Advancement of Science.

Meyers, L. (1984). Use of microprocessors to initiate language use in young non-oral children. In W. Perkins (Ed.), *Current therapy of communication disorders.* New York: Thieme-Stratton.

Meyers, L. (1990). Technology: A powerful tool for children learning language. *OSERS News in Print, 3*(2), 2–7.

Meyers, L., Grows, N., Coleman, C., & Cook, M. (1980). *An assessment battery for assistive device systems recommendations: Part 1.* Sacramento, CA: Assistive Device Center, California State University.

Michael, P. (1981). *Multiple sclerosis: A dragon with a hundred heads.* Port Washington, NY: Ashley Books.

Miller, A., & Miller, E.E. (1973). Cognitive-developmental training with elevated boards and sign language. *Journal of Autism and Childhood Schizophrenia, 3,* 65–85.

Miller-Wood, D., Efron, M., & Wood, T. A. (1990). Use of closed-circuit television with a severely visually impaired young child. *Journal of Visual Impairment and Blindness, 84,* 559–565.

Mills, J., & Higgins, J. (1983). *Non-oral communication assessment and training guide.* Encinitas, CA: Author.

Minnesota Governor's Planning Council on Developmental Disabilities. (1987). *A new way of thinking* [Videotape]. Seattle: American Production Services.

Mirenda, P. (1985). Designing pictorial communication systems for physically able-bodied students with severe handicaps. *Augmentative and Alternative Communication, 1,* 58–64.

Mirenda, P., & Beukelman, D. (1987). A comparison of speech synthesis intelligibility with listeners from three age groups. *Augmentative and Alternative Communication, 3,* 120–128.

Mirenda, P., & Beukelman, D. (1990). A comparison of intelligibility among natural speech and seven speech synthesizers with listeners from three age groups. *Augmentative and Alternative Communication, 6,* 61–68.

Mirenda, P., & Dattilo, J. (1987). Instructional techniques in alternative communication for learners with severe intellectual disabilities. *Augmentative and Alternative Communication, 3,* 143–152.

Mirenda, P., & Donnellan, A. (1986). Effects of adult interaction style on conversational behavior in students with severe communication problems. *Language, Speech, and Hearing Services in Schools, 17,* 126–141.

Mirenda, P., Eicher, D., & Beukelman, D. (1989). Synthetic and natural speech preferences of male and female listeners in four age groups. *Journal of Speech and Hearing Research, 32,* 175–183, 703.

Mirenda, P., & Iacono, T. (1988). Strategies for promoting augmentative and alternative communication in natural contexts with students with autism. *Focus on Autistic Behavior, 3*(4), 1–16.

Mirenda, P., Iacono, T., & Williams, R. (1990). Communication options for persons with severe and profound disabilities: State of the art and future directions. *Journal of The Association for Persons with Severe Handicaps, 15,* 3–21.

Mirenda, P., & Locke, P. (1989). A comparison of symbol transparency in nonspeaking persons with intellectual disabilities. *Journal of Speech and Hearing Disorders, 54,* 131–140.

Mirenda, P., & Mathy-Laikko, P. (1989). Augmentative and alternative communication applications for persons with severe congenital communication disorders: An introduction. *Augmentative and Alternative Communication, 5,* 3–13.

Mirenda, P., & Santogrossi, J. (1985). A prompt-free strategy to teach pictorial communication system use. *Augmentative and Alternative Communication, 1,* 143–150.

Mirenda, P., & Schuler, A. (1988). Teaching individuals with autism and related disorders to use visual-spatial symbols to communicate. In S. Blackstone, E. Cassatt-James, & D. Bruskin (Eds.), *Augmentative communication: Intervention strategies* (pp. 5.1-17–5.1-25). Rockville, MD: American Speech-Language-Hearing Association.

Mirenda, P., & Schuler, A. (1989). Augmenting communication for persons with autism: Issues and strategies. *Topics in Language Disorders, 9,* 24–43.

Mitsuda, P., Baarslag-Benson, R., Hazel, K., & Therriault, T. (1992). Augmentative communication in intensive and acute care unit settings. In K. Yorkston (Ed.), *Augmentative communication in the medical setting* (pp. 5–58). Tucson, AZ: Communication Skill Builders.

Mizuko, M. (1987). Transparency and ease of learning of symbols represented by Blissymbols, PCS, and Picsyms. *Augmentative and Alternative Communication, 3,* 129–136.

Mizuko, M., & Esser, J. (1991). The effect of direct selection and circular scanning on visual sequential recall. *Journal of Speech and Hearing Research, 34,* 43–48.

Mizuko, M., & Reichle, J. (1989). Transparency and recall of symbols among intellectually handicapped adults. *Journal of Speech and Hearing Disorders, 54,* 627–633.

Moe, A., Hopkins, C., & Rush, R. (1982). *The vocabulary of first-grade children.* Springfield, IL: Charles C Thomas.

Montgomery, J. (1987). Augmentative communication: Selecting successful interventions. *Seminars in Speech and Hearing, 8,* 187–197.

Moran, M. (1988). Reading and writing disorders in the learning disabled student. In N. Lass, L. McReynolds, J. Northern, & D. Yoder (Eds.), *Handbook of speech-language pathology and audiology* (pp. 835–857) Toronto: B. C. Decker.

Morocco, C., & Neuman, S. (1986). Word processors and the acquisition of writing strategies. *Journal of Learning Disabilities, 19,* 243–247.

Morris, J. (1982). The manager of Parkinson's disease. *Australian and New Zealand Journal of Medicine, 12,* 195–205.

Morrow, D., Beukelman, D., Mirenda, P., & Yorkston, K. (in press). Vocabulary selection for augmentative communication systems: A comparison of three techniques. *American Journal of Speech-Language Pathology*.

Moss, C.S. (1972). *Recovery with aphasia: The aftermath of my stroke*. Urbana: University of Illinois Press.

Mount, B. (1987). *Personal futures planning: Finding directions for change*. Unpublished doctoral dissertation, University of Georgia, Athens.

Mount, B., & Zwernik, K. (1988). *It's never too early, it's never too late*. St. Paul, MN: Metropolitan Council, Publication No. 421-88-109.

Murray-Branch, J., Udavari-Solner, A., & Bailey, B. (1991). Textured communication systems for individuals with severe intellectual and dual sensory impairments. *Language, Speech, and Hearing Services in Schools, 22*, 260–268.

Musselwhite, C. (1985). *Songbook: Signs and symbols for children*. Wauconda, IL: Don Johnston Developmental Equipment, Inc.

Musselwhite, C. (1986a). *Adaptive play for special needs children: Strategies to enhance communication and learning*. San Diego: Singular.

X  Musselwhite, C. (1986b). Introducing augmentative communication: Interactive training strategies. *NSSLHA Journal, 14*, 68–82.

Musselwhite, C. (1990, August). *Topic setting: generic and specific strategies*. Paper presented at the sixth biennial conference of the International Society for Augmentative and Alternative Communication, Stockholm.

Musselwhite, C., & Ruscello, D. (1984). Transparency of three symbol communication systems. *Journal of Speech and Hearing Research, 27*, 436–443.

Musselwhite, C., & St. Louis, K. (1988). *Communication programming for persons with severe handicaps* (2nd ed.). Boston: College-Hill Press.

National Joint Committee on Learning Disabilities. (1991). Learning disabilities: Issues on definition. *Asha, 33* (Suppl. 5), 18-20.

National Society to Prevent Blindness. (1980). *Vision problems in the U.S.* New York: Author.

Netsell, R., & Daniel, B. (1979). Dysarthria in adults: Physiologic approach to rehabilitation. *Archives of Physical Medicine and Rehabilitation, 60*, 502–508.

Newell, A., Arnott, J., & Alm, N. (1990). An integrated development of computer-based alternative communication systems. *Augmentative and Alternative Communication, 6*, 97–98.

Nolan, C. (1979). Thoughts on the future of braille. *Journal of Visual Impairment and Blindness, 73*, 333–335.

Nolan, C. (1981). *Dam-burst of dreams*. New York: St. Martin's Press.

Nolan, C. (1987). *Under the eye of the clock*. New York: St. Martin's. Press.

Norris, L. (1991). ISAAC awards and scholarship program. *Augmentative and Alternative Communication, 7*, 62–64.

Norris, L., & Belair, B. (1988). The client's role on the AAC assessment team. *Augmentative and Alternative Communication, 4*, 168–169.

Nurss, J., & McGauvran, M. (1986). *Metropolitan reading test, Level II*. New York: Harcourt Brace Jovanovich.

O'Brien, J., Forest, M., Snow, J., & Hasbury, D. (1989). *Action for inclusion: How to improve schools by welcoming children with special needs into regular classrooms*. Toronto: Frontier College Press.

O'Brien, J., & Lyle, C. (1987). *Framework for accomplishment*. Decatur, GA: Responsive Systems Associates.

O'Connor, L., & Schery, S. (1986). A comparison of microcomputer-aided and traditional language therapy for developing communication skills in nonoral toddlers. *Journal of Speech and Hearing Disorders, 51*, 356–361.

Offir, C.W. (1976, June). Visual speech: Their fingers do the talking. *Psychology Today, 10*(1), 72–78

Ogden, C. (1968). *Basic English: International second language*. New York: Harcourt Brace Jovanovich.

Oliver, C., & Halle, J. (1982). Language training in the everyday environment: Teaching functional language use to a retarded child. *Journal of The Association for the Severely Handicapped, 8*, 50–63.

Olmos-Lau, N., Ginsberg, M., & Geller, J. (1977). Aphasia in multiple sclerosis. *Neurology, 27*, 623–626.

Olsen, D., & Henig, E. (1983). *A manual of behavioral management strategies for traumatically brain injured adults*. Chicago: Rehabilitation Institute of Chicago.

Olson, M. R. (1981). *Guidelines and games for teaching efficient braille reading*. New York: American Foundation for the Blind.

O'Neill, R., Horner, R., Albin, R., Storey, K., & Sprague, J. (1990). *Functional analysis of behavior: A practical assessment guide*. Sycamore, IL: Sycamore Publishing.

Ontario Crippled Children's Centre. (1974). *Ontario Crippled Children's Centre Symbol Communication Programme Year End Report*. Toronto: Author.

Oregon Research Institute. (1989a). *Bringing out the best: Encouraging expressive communication in children with multiple handicaps* [Videotape]. Champaign, IL: Research Press.

Oregon Research Institute. (1989b). *Getting in touch: Communicating with a child who is deaf-blind* [Videotape]. Champaign, IL: Research Press.

Osguthorpe, R., & Chang, L. (1988). The effects of computerized symbol processor instruction on the communication skills of nonspeaking students. *Augmentative and Alternative Communication, 4,* 23–34.

Otos, M. (1983). *Nonverbal prelinguistic communication: A guide to communication levels in prelinguistic handicapped children.* Salem: Oregon Department of Education.

Paget, R., Gorman, P., & Paget, G. (1976). *The Paget Gorman sign system* (6th ed.). London: Association for Experiment in Deaf Education.

Paluszny, M. J. (1979). *Autism: A practical guide for parents and professionals.* Syracuse, NY: Syracuse University Press.

Panel on Impact of Video Viewing on Vision of Workers. (1983). *Video displays, work, and vision.* Washington, DC: National Academy Press.

Panyan, M. (1984). Computer technology for autistic students. *Journal of Autism and Developmental Disorders, 14,* 375–382.

Park, C. C. (1982). *The siege.* Boston: Little, Brown.

Peck, C. A. (1985). Increasing opportunities for social control by children with autism and severe handicaps: Effects on learner behavior and perceived classroom climate. *Journal of The Association for Persons with Severe Handicaps, 10,* 183–193.

Peck, C., & Cooke, T. (1983). Benefits of mainstreaming at the early childhood level: How much can we expect? *Analysis and Intervention in Developmental Disabilities, 3,* 1–22.

Pecyna, P. (1988). Rebus symbol communication training with a severely handicapped preschool child: A case study. *Language, Speech, and Hearing Services in Schools, 19,* 128–143.

Perske, R., & Perske, M. (1988). *Circles of friends.* Nashville, TN: Abingdon.

Poole, M. (1979). Social class, sex, and linguistic coding. *Language and Speech, 22,* 49–67.

Porter, P. (1989). Intervention in end stage of multiple sclerosis. *Augmentative and Alternative Communication, 5,* 125–127.

Poser, C.M. (Ed.). (1984). *The diagnosis of multiple sclerosis.* New York: Thieme-Stratton.

Pratt, F. (1939). *Secret and urgent: The story of codes and ciphers.* New York: Blue Ribbon Books.

Premack, D. (1971). Language in a chimpanzee? *Science, 172,* 808–822.

Prinz, P.M., & Shaw, N. (1981, November). *Communication development by speech and sign in mentally retarded individuals.* Paper presented at the annual conference of the American Speech-Language-Hearing Association, Los Angeles.

Prizant, B. (1983). Language and communicative behavior in autism: Toward an understanding of the "whole" of it. *Journal of Speech and Hearing Disorders, 46,* 241–249.

Prizant, B., & Schuler, A. (1987). Facilitating communication: Theoretical foundations. In D.J. Cohen & A.M. Donnellan (Eds.), *Handbook of autism and pervasive developmental disorders* (pp. 289–300). New York: John Wiley & Sons.

Prizant, B., & Wetherby, A. (1988). Providing services to children with autism (ages 0 to 2 years) and their families. *Topics in Language Disorders, 9*(1), 1–23.

Pugach, M., & Johnson, L. (1990). Meeting diverse needs through professional peer collaboration. In W. Stainback & S. Stainback (Eds.), *Support networks for inclusive schooling: Interdependent integrated education* (pp. 123–137). Baltimore: Paul H. Brookes Publishing Co.

Pulli, T., & Jaroma, M. (1990). Exploring novel solutions for motivating simplified signing, pictorializing, and vocalizing. *Augmentative and Alternative Communication, 6,* 103.

Raghavendra, P., & Fristoe, M. (1990). "A spinach with a *V* on it": What 3-year-olds see in standard and enhanced Blissymbolics. *Journal of Speech and Hearing Disorders, 55,* 149–159.

*Raised Dot Computing, Inc.* (1991, March) Omnichron's Flipper: Screen access with Flipper 3.0, 7.

Ratcliff, A. (1987). *A comparison of two message selection techniques used in augmentative communication systems by normal children with differing cognitive styles.* Unpublished doctoral dissertation, University of Wisconsin-Madison.

Reichle, J., & Brown, L. (1986). Teaching the use of a multipage direct selection communication board to an adult with autism. *Journal of The Association for Persons with Severe Handicaps, 11,* 68–73.

Reichle, J., & Karlan, G. (1985). The selection of an augmentative system of communication intervention: A critique of decision rules. *Journal of The Association for Persons with Severe Handicaps, 10,* 146–156.

Reichle, J., Rogers, N., & Barrett, C. (1984). Establishing pragmatic discrimination among the communicative functions of requesting, rejecting, and commenting in an adolescent. *Journal of The Association for Persons with Severe Handicaps, 9,* 31–36.

Reichle, J., & Ward, M. (1985). Teaching the discriminative use of an encoding electronic communication device and Signing Exact English to a moderately handicapped child. *Language, Speech, and Hearing Services in Schools, 16*, 58–63.

Reichle, J., & Yoder, D. (1985). Communication board use in severely handicapped learners. *Language, Speech, and Hearing Services in Schools, 16*, 146–157.

Reichle, J., York, J., & Sigafoos, J. (1991). *Implementing augmentative and alternative communication: Strategies for learners with severe disabilities.* Baltimore: Paul H. Brookes Publishing Co.

Ricks, D., & Wing, L. (1976). Language, communication, and the use of symbols. In L. Wing (Ed.), *Early childhood autism* (2nd ed., pp. 93–134). New York: Pergamon.

Roach, E., & Kephart, N. (1966). *Purdue Perceptual Motor Survey.* New York: Charles E. Merrill.

Roberts, F. K. (1986). Education for the visually handicapped: A social and educational history. In G. T. Scholl (Ed.), *Foundations of education for blind and visually handicapped children and youth: Theory and practice* (pp. 1–18). New York: American Foundation for the Blind.

Robinson, C., Bataillon, K., Fieber, N., Jackson, B., & Rasmussen, J. (1985). *Sensorimotor assessment form.* Omaha, NE: Meyer Rehabilitation Center.

Rogers, B., Croker, K., Fishman, S., Bengston, D., Esser, S., Schauer, J., & Farrell C. (1985). *A journeyer's guide to the Trine System.* Madison, WI: Trace Research and Development Center.

Romski, M., & Sevcik, R. (1988a). Augmentative and alternative communication systems: Considerations for individuals with severe intellectual disabilities. *Augmentative and Alternative Communication, 4*, 83–93.

Romski, M., & Sevcik, R. (1988b). Augmentative communication system acquisition and use: A model for teaching and assessing progress. *NSSLHA Journal, 16*, 61–75.

Romski, M., & Sevcik, R. (1988c, November). *Speech output communication systems: Acquisition/use by youngsters with retardation.* Seminar presented at the annual conference of the American Speech-Language-Hearing Association, Boston.

Romski, M., & Sevcik, R. (1991). Patterns of language learning by instruction: Evidence from nonspeaking persons with mental retardation. In N. Krasnegor, D. Rumbaugh, R. Schiefelbusch, & M. Studdert-Kennedy (Eds.), *Biological and behavioral determinants of language development* (pp. 429–445). Hillsdale, NJ: Lawrence Erlbaum Associates.

Romski, M., & Sevcik, R. (1992). Augmented language development in children with severe mental retardation. In S. Warren & J. Reichle (Eds.), *Causes and effects in communication and language intervention* (pp. 113–130). Baltimore: Paul H. Brookes Publishing Co.

Romski, M., Sevcik, R., & Pate, J. (1988). Establishment of symbolic communication in persons with severe retardation. *Journal of Speech and Hearing Disorders, 53*, 94–107.

Romski, M., White, R., Millen, C., & Rumbaugh, D. (1984). Effects of computer keyboard teaching on symbolic communication of severely retarded persons: Five case studies. *Psychological Record, 34*, 39–54.

Rosegrant, T. (1985). Using the microcomputer as a tool for learning to read and write. *Journal of Learning Disabilities, 18*, 113–115.

Rosen, M., & Goodenough-Trepagnier, C. (1981). Factors affecting communication rate in non-vocal communication systems. *Proceedings of the Fourth Annual Conference on Rehabilitation Engineering* (pp. 194–195). Washington, DC: Rehabilitation Engineering Society of North America.

Rosenbek, J. (1985). Treating apraxia of speech. In D. F. Johns (Ed.), *Clinical management of neurogenic communicative disorders* (pp. 267–312). Boston: Little, Brown.

Rosenbek, J., Hansen, R., Baughman, C., & Lemme, M. (1974). Treatment of developmental apraxia of speech: A case study. *Language, Speech, and Hearing Services in Schools, 5*, 13–22.

Rosenbek, J., LaPointe, L., & Wertz, R. (1989). *Aphasia: A clinical approach.* Austin, TX: PRO-ED.

Rosenbek, J., & Wertz, R. (1972). A review of fifty cases of developmental apraxia of speech. *Language, Speech, and Hearing Services in Schools, 3*, 23–33.

Rosenberg, S., & Beukelman, D. (1988). The participation model. In C.A. Coston (Ed.), *Proceedings of the National Planners Conference on Assistive Device Service Delivery* (pp. 159, 161). Washington, DC: RESNA, Association for the Advancement of Rehabilitation Technology.

Rosenshine, B., & Stevens, R. (1984). Classroom instruction in reading. In P. Pearson (Ed.), *Handbook of reading research* (pp. 745–798). New York: Longman.

Rosenthal, R., & Rosenthal, K. (1989). *A model for mainstreaming handicapped kids: Handicapped kids are regular kids, too!* Lincoln, NE: Meadowlane Elementary School.

Rossi, P. (1986). Mathematics. In G. T. Scholl (Ed.), *Foundations of education for blind and visually handicapped children and youth: Theory and practice* (pp. 367–374). New York: American Foundation for the Blind.

Roth, F., & Cassatt-James, E. (1989). The language assessment process: Clinical implications for individuals with severe speech impairments. *Augmentative and Alternative Communication, 5*, 165–172.

Rotholz, D., Berkowitz, S., & Burberry, J. (1989). Functionality of two modes of communication in the community by students with developmental disabilities: A comparison of signing and communication books. *Journal of The Association for Persons with Severe Handicaps, 14,* 227–233.

Rowland, C. (1990). Communication in the classroom for children with dual sensory impairments: Studies of teacher and child behavior. *Augmentative and Alternative Communication, 6,* 262–274.

Rowland, C., & Schweigert, P. (1989). Tangible symbols: Symbolic communication for individuals with multisensory impairments. *Augmentative and Alternative Communication, 5,* 226–234.

Rowland, C., & Schweigert, P. (1990). *Tangible symbol systems: Symbolic communication for individuals with multisensory impairments.* Tucson, AZ: Communication Skill Builders.

Rule, S., Fiechtl, B., & Innocenti, M. (1990). Preschool environments: Development of a survival skills curriculum. *Topics in Early Childhood Special Education, 9*(4), 78–90.

Rumbaugh, D. (1977). *Language learning in the chimpanzee: The LANA Project.* New York: Academic Press.

Rush, W. (1986). *Journey out of silence.* Lincoln, NE: Media Publishing and Marketing, Inc.

Rusk, H., Block, J., & Lowman, E. (1969). Rehabilitation of the brain injured patient: A report of 157 cases with long term follow-up of 118. In E. Walker, W. Caveness, & M. Critchley (Eds.), *The late effects of head injury.* Springfield, IL: Charles C Thomas.

Rydell, P., & Mirenda, P. (1991). The effects of two levels of linguistic constraint on echolalia and generative language production in children with autism. *Journal of Autism and Developmental Disorders, 21,* 131–157.

Sadowsky, A. (1985). Visual impairment among developmentally disabled clients in California regional centers. *Journal of Visual Impairment and Blindness, 79,* 199–202.

Sailor, W., Anderson, J., Halvorsen, A., Doering, K., Filler, J., & Goetz, L. (1989). *The comprehensive local school: Regular education for all students with disabilities.* Baltimore: Paul H. Brookes Publishing Co.

Sailor, W., Utley, B., Goetz, L., Gee, K., & Baldwin, M. (1982). *Vision assessment and program manual for severely handicapped and/or deaf-blind students.* San Francisco: Bay Area Severely Handicapped Deaf Blind Project, U.S. Department of Education.

Salisbury, C., & Vincent, L. (1990). Criterion of the next environment and best practices: Mainstreaming and integration 10 years later. *Topics in Early Childhood Special Education, 10*(2), 78–89.

Sapon-Shevin, M. (1990). Student support through cooperative learning. In W. Stainback & S. Stainback (Eds.), *Support networks for inclusive schooling: Interdependent integrated education* (pp. 65–79). Baltimore: Paul H. Brookes Publishing Co.

Sarno, M., Buonaguro, A., & Levita, E. (1986). Characteristics of verbal impairment in closed head injury patients. *Archives of Physical Medicine and Rehabilitation, 67,* 400–405.

Saunders, C., Walsh, T., & Smith, M. (1981). Hospice care in the motor neuron diseases. In C. Saunders & J. Teller (Eds.), *Hospice: The living idea.* London: Edward Arnold Publishers.

Schaeffer, B. (1980). Spontaneous language through signed speech. In R. Schiefelbusch (Ed.), *Nonspeech language and communication* (pp. 421–446). Baltimore: University Park Press.

Schaeffer, B., McDowell, P., Musil, A., & Kollinzas, G. (1976). Spontaneous verbal language for autistic children through signed speech. *Research Relating to Children Bulletin 37* (ERIC Clearinghouse for Early Childhood Education). 98–99.

Schlanger, P.H. (1976, November). *Training the adult aphasic to pantomime.* Paper presented at the 51st annual conference of the American Speech and Hearing Association, Houston.

Schmidt, M.J., Carrier, Jr., J.K., & Parsons, S.D. (1971, November). *Use of a nonspeech mode in teaching language.* Paper presented at the 46th annual meeting of the American Speech and Hearing Association, Chicago.

Schnorr, R., Ford, A., Davern, L., Park-Lee, S., & Meyer, L. (1989). *The Syracuse curriculum revision manual: A group process for developing a community-referenced curriculum guide.* Baltimore: Paul H. Brookes Publishing Co.

Scholl, G. (1986a). Visual impairment and other exceptionalities. In G. Scholl (Ed.), *Foundations of education for blind and visually handicapped children and youth: Theory and practice* (pp. 137–144). New York: American Foundation for the Blind.

Scholl, G. (1986b). What does it mean to be blind? Definitions, terminology, and prevalence. In G. Scholl (Ed.), *Foundations of education for blind and visually handicapped children and youth: Theory and practice* (pp. 23–35). New York: American Foundation for the Blind.

Schorr, G. (1983). Visual impairment. In J. Blackman (Ed.), *Medical aspects of developmental disabilities in children birth to three* (pp. 227–231). Iowa City, IA: Department of Pediatrics, University Hospital School, University of Iowa.

Schuler, A., & Baldwin, M. (1981). Nonspeech communication and childhood autism. *Language, Speech, and Hearing Services in Schools, 12,* 246–257.

Schuler, A., & Prizant, B. (1987). Facilitating communication: Pre-language approaches. In D. Cohen & A. Donnellan (Eds.), *Handbook of autism and pervasive developmental disorders* (pp. 301–315). New York: John Wiley & Sons.

Schwab, E., Nusbaum, H., & Pisoni, D. (1985). Some effects of training on the perception of synthetic speech. *Human Factors, 27*, 395–408.

Secord, W. (Ed.). (1990). *Best practices in school speech-language pathology: Collaborative programs in the schools.* Houston, TX: The Psychological Corporation.

Seligman-Wine, J. (1988). A Blissymbol bar mitzvah. *Communicating Together, 6*(2), 16–17.

Sevcik, R., & Romski, M. (1986). Representational matching skills of persons with severe retardation. *Augmentative and Alternative Communication, 2*, 160–164.

Shakespeare, W. *Troilus and Cressida.* K. Muir (Ed.). (1982). New York: Oxford University Press.

Shalit, A., & Boonzaier, D. (1990). Macintosh-based semantographic technique with adaptive-predictive algorithm for Blissymbolics communication. *Augmentative and Alternative Communication, 6*, 129.

Shane, H., & Bashir, A. (1980). Election criteria for the adoption of an augmentative communication system: Preliminary considerations. *Journal of Speech and Hearing Disorders, 45*, 408–414.

Shane, H., & Cohen, C. (1981). A discussion of communicative strategies and patterns by nonspeaking persons. *Language, Speech, and Hearing Services in Schools, 12*, 205–210.

Shane, H., & Wilbur, R. (1989, November). *A conceptual framework for an AAC strategy based on sign language parameters.* Paper presented at the annual conference of the American Speech-Language-Hearing Association, St. Louis.

Shell, D., Horn, C., & Bruning, R. (1989, Oct.–Nov.). Technologies for the information age: Enhancing disabled persons' access and use of text based information. *Closing the Gap*, 24–27.

Shelton, I., & Garves, M. (1985). Use of visual techniques in therapy for developmental apraxia of speech. *Language, Speech, and Hearing Services in Schools, 16*, 129–131.

Shevin, M., & Klein, N. (1984). The importance of choice-making skills for students with severe disabilities. *Journal of The Association for Persons with Severe Handicaps, 9*, 159–166.

Shewan, C., & Blake, A. (1991). 1990 omnibus survey: Augmentative and alternative communication. *Asha, 31*, 46.

Siegel-Causey, E., & Downing, J. (1987). Nonsymbolic communication development: Theoretical concepts and educational strategies. In L. Goetz, D. Guess, & K. Stremel-Campbell (Eds.), *Innovative program design for individuals with dual sensory impairments* (pp. 15–48). Baltimore: Paul H. Brookes Publishing Co.

Siegel-Causey, E., & Guess, D. (1988). *Enhancing interactions between service providers and individuals who are severely multiply disabled: Strategies for developing nonsymbolic communication.* Monmouth, OR: Teaching Research.

Siegel-Causey, E., & Guess, D. (1989). *Enhancing nonsymbolic communication interactions among learners with severe disabilities.* Baltimore: Paul H. Brookes Publishing Co.

Sigelman, C., Vengroff, L., & Spanhel, C. (1984). Disability and the concept of life functions. In R. Marinelli & A. Dell Orto (Eds.), *The psychological and social impact of physical disability* (2nd ed.). New York: Springer.

Silberman, R. (1986). Severe multiple handicaps. In G. Scholl (Ed.), *Foundations of education for blind and visually handicapped children and youth: Theory and practice* (pp. 145–164). New York: American Foundation for the Blind.

Silverman, F. (1989). *Communication for the speechless* (2nd ed.). Englewood Cliffs, NJ: Prentice Hall.

Simeonsson, R., Olley, J., & Rosenthal, S. (1987). Early intervention for children with autism. In M. Guralnick & F. Bennett (Eds.), *The effectiveness of early intervention for at-risk and handicapped children.* New York: Academic Press.

Simmons, N. (1983). Acoustic analysis of ataxic dysarthria: An approach to monitoring treatment. In W. Berry (Ed.), *Clinical dysarthria* (pp. 283–294). Austin, TX: PRO-ED.

Simpson, S. (1988). If only I could tell them. . .!! *Communication Outlook, 9*(4), 9–11.

Sims-Tucker, B., & Jensema, C. (1984). Severely and profoundly auditorily/visually impaired students: The deaf-blind population. In P. Valletutti & B. Sims-Tucker (Eds.), *Severely and profoundly handicapped students: Their nature and needs* (pp. 269–317). Baltimore: Paul H. Brookes Publishing Co.

Sitver, M., & Kraat, A. (1982). Augmentative communication for the person with amyotrophic sclerosis (ALS). *Asha, 24*, 783.

Skelly, M. (1979). *Amer-Ind gestural code based on universal American Indian hand talk.* New York: Elsevier-North Holland.

Skelly, M., Schinsky, L., Smith, R., Donaldson, R., & Griffin, P. (1975). American Indian sign: A gestural communication for the speechless. *Archives of Physical and Rehabilitation Medicine, 56*, 156–160.

Skelly, M., Schinsky, L., Smith, R., & Fust, R. (1974). American Indian sign (Amerind) as a facilitator of verbalization in the oral apraxic. *Journal of Speech and Hearing Disorders, 39*, 445–456.

Smebye, H. (1990, August). *A theoretical basis for early communicatiion intervention.* Paper presented at the sixth biennial conference of the International Society for Augmentative and Alternative Communication, Stockholm.

Smith, A., Thurston, S., Light, J., Parnes, P., & O'Keefe, B. (1989). The form and use of written communication produced by physically disabled individuals using microcomputers. *Augmentative and Alternative Communication, 5*, 115–124.

Snyder, L. (1984). Developmental language disorders: Elementary school age. In A. Holland (Ed.), *Language disorders in children* (pp. 129–158). Boston: College-Hill Press.

Snyder-McLean, L., Solomonson, B., McLean, J., & Sack, S. (1984). Structuring joint action routines: A strategy for facilitating language and communication development in the classroom. *Seminars in Speech and Language, 5*, 213–228.

Spellman, C.R., DeBriere, T.J., & Cress, P.J. (1979). *Final report, Research and Development of Subjective Visual Acuity Assessment Procedures for Severely Handicapped Persons.*

Spragale, D., & Micucci, S. (1990). Signs of the week: A functional approach to manual sign training. *Augmentative and Alternative Communication, 6*, 29–37.

Stainback, W., & Stainback, S. (Eds.). (1990). *Support networks for inclusive schooling: Interdependent integrated education.* Baltimore: Paul H. Brookes Publishing Co.

Stainback, W., Stainback, S., Cortnage, L., & Jaben, T. (1985). Facilitating mainstreaming by modifying the mainstream. *Exceptional Children, 52*, 144–152.

Stark, R., & Tallal, P. (1981). Perceptual and motor deficits in language impaired children. In R. Keith (Ed.), *Central auditory and language disorders in children* (pp. 121–144). Boston: College-Hill Press.

Stauffer, R. (1980). *The language experience approach to the teaching of reading.* New York: Harper & Row.

Stedt, J., & Moores, D. (1990). Manual codes of English and American Sign Language: Historical perspectives and current realities. In H. Bornstein (Ed.), *Manual communication: Implications for education* (pp. 1–20). Washington, DC: Gallaudet University Press.

Steiner, S., & Larson, V. (1991). Integrating microcomputers into language intervention with children. *Topics in Language Disorders, 11*(2), 18–30.

Stemach, G., & Williams. W. (1988). *Word Express: The first 2,500 words of spoken English.* Novato, CA: Academic Therapy Publications.

Stephens, R. (1987, September). *Write/read/write some more.* Paper presented at the fourth annual Conference on Adult Reading Problems, Chicago.

Sternberg, L. (1982). Communication instruction. In L. Sternberg & G. Adams (Eds.), *Educating severely and profoundly handicapped students* (pp. 209–241). Rockville, MD: Aspen Systems.

Stevenson, J., & Richman, M. (1976). The prevalence of language delay in a population of three-year-old children and its association with general retardation. *Developmental Medicine and Child Neurology, 18*, 431–441.

Stillman, R., & Battle, C. (1984). Developing prelanguage communication in the severely handicapped: An interpretation of the Van Dijk method. *Seminars in Speech and Language, 5*, 159–170.

Stillman, R.D., & Battle, C. (1985). *The Callier-Azusa Scales for the Assessment of Communicative Abilities.* Dallas: University of Texas, Callier Center.

Stuart, S. (1988). Expanding sequencing, turn-taking and timing skills through play acting. In S. Blackstone, E. Cassatt-James, & D. Bruskin (Eds.), *Augmentative communication: Implementation strategies* (pp. 5.8-21–5.8-26). Rockville, MD: American Speech-Language-Hearing Association.

Stuart, S. (1991). *Topic and vocabulary use patterns of elderly men and women in two age cohorts.* Unpublished doctoral dissertation, University of Nebraska-Lincoln.

Stuart, S., Vanderhoof, D., & Beukelman, D. (in press). Topic and vocabulary use patterns of elderly women. *Augmentative and Alternative Communication.*

Sutton, A. (1989). The social-verbal competence of AAC users. *Augmentative and Alternative Communication, 5*, 150–164.

Swallow, R., & Conner, A. (1982). Aural reading. In S. Mangold (Ed.), *A teacher's guide to the special educational needs of blind and visually handicapped children.* New York: American Foundation for the Blind.

Swartz, S. (1984). Blissymbols go to India. *Communicating Together, 2*(1), 4–6.

Sweeney, L., & Finkley, E. (1989). Early manual communication skills assessment. In D. Blackstone, E. Cassatt-James, & D. Bruskin (Eds.), *Augmentative communication: Intervention resource* (pp. 3-159–3-168). Rockville, MD: American Speech-Language-Hearing Association.

Swiffin, A., Arnott, J., Pickering, J., & Newell, A. (1987). Adaptive and predictive techniques in a communication prosthesis. *Augmentative and Alternative Communication, 3*, 181–191.

Swisher, L. (1985). Language disorders in children. In J. Darby (Ed.), *Speech and language evaluation in neurology: Childhood disorders* (pp. 33–96). New York: Grune & Stratton.

Tager-Flusberg, H. (1981). On the nature of linguistic functioning in early infantile autism. *Journal of Autism and Developmental Disorders, 11,* 45–56.

Tandan, R., & Bradley, W. (1985). Amyotrophic lateral sclerosis: Part 1. Clinical features, pathology, and ethical issues in management. *Annuals of Neurology, 18,* 271–280.

Teller, D. Y., McDonald, M.A., Preston, K., Sebris, S.L., & Dobson, V. (1986). Assessment of visual acuity in infants and children: The acuity card procedure. *Developmental Medicine and Child Neurology, 28,* 779-789.

Thompson, C. (1988). Articulation disorders in the child with neurogenic pathology. In N. Lass, L. McReynolds, J. Northern, & D. Yoder (Eds.), *Handbook of speech-language pathology and audiology* (pp. 548–591). Toronto: B.C. Decker.

Tijerina, L. (1984). *Video display terminal workstation ergonomics.* Dublin, OH: Online Computer Library Center, Inc.

Todd, J. (1986). Resources, media, and technology. In G. T. Scholl (Ed.), *Foundations of education for blind and visually handicapped children and youth: Theory and practice* (pp. 285–296). New York: American Foundation for the Blind.

Tomblin, J. B. (1991). Examining the cause of specific language impairment. *Language, Speech, and Hearing Services in Schools, 22,* 69–74.

Toulotte, J., Baudel-Cantgrit, B., & Trehou, G. (1990). Acceleration method using a dictionary access in a Blissymbolics communicator. *Augmentative and Alternative Communication, 6,* 122.

Trace Research and Development Center. (1991). HyperABLEDATA (4th ed.). [compact disc]. Madison, WI: Author.

Trevor, K., & Nelson, N. (1989). *Vocabulary use by children in first, third, and fifth grade classrooms.* Unpublished research project, Western Michigan University, Kalamazoo.

Tronconi, A. (1990). Blissymbolics-based telecommunications. *Communication Outlook, 11*(2), 8–11.

Tuttle, D. (1988). Visually impaired. In E. Meyen & T. Skrtic (Eds.), *Exceptional children and youth* (3rd ed., pp. 352–385). Denver: Love Publishing Company.

Ulatowska, H., Cannito, M., Hayashi, M., & Fleming, S. (1985). *The aging brain: Communication in the elderly.* San Diego, CA: College-Hill Press.

U. S. Department of Education. (1988). To assure the free and appropriate public education of all handicapped children. *Tenth Annual Report to Congress on the Implementation of the Education of the Handicapped Act.* Washington, DC: Government Printing Office.

Valentic, V. (1991). Successful integration from a student's perspective. *Communicating Together, 9*(2), 9.

Van Coile, B., & Martens, P. (1990). Development and evaluation of two speech aids which are based on Dutch text-to-speech synthesis. *Augmentative and Alternative Communication, 6,* 123.

Vandercook, T., York, J., & Forest, M. (1989). The McGill Action Planning System (MAPS): A strategy for building the vision. *Journal of The Association of Persons with Severe Handicaps, 14,* 205–215.

Vanderheiden, G., & Kelso, D. (1987). Comparative analysis of fixed-vocabulary communication acceleration techniques. *Augmentative and Alternative Communication, 3,* 196–206.

Vanderheiden, G.C., & Lloyd, L. (1986). Communication systems and their components. In S. Blackstone (Ed.), *Augmentative communication: An introduction* (pp. 49–162). Rockville, MD: American Speech-Language-Hearing Association.

Vanderheiden, G., & Smith, R. (1989). Application of communication technologies to an adult with a high spinal cord injury. *Augmentative and Alternative Communication, 5,* 62–66.

Vanderheiden, G., & Yoder, D. (1986). Overview. In S. Blackstone (Ed.), *Augmentative communication: An introduction* (pp. 1–28). Rockville, MD: American Speech-Language-Hearing Association.

Van Dijk, J. (1966). The first steps of the deaf-blind child towards language. *International Journal for the Education of the Blind, 15*(4), 112–114.

Van Dijk, J. (1967). The non-verbal deaf-blind child and his world: His outgrowth toward the world of symbols. *Jaarverslag Instituut voor Doven, 1965–1967* [Annual Report of the Institute for the Deaf] (pp. 73–110). Sint Michielsgestel, the Netherlands: Instituut voor Doveno.

Van Oosterum, J., & Devereux, K. (1985). *Learning with rebuses.* Cambridgeshire, England: EARO, The Resource Centre.

Van Tatenhove, G. (1989). *Power in play.* Wooster, OH: Prentke Romich Co.

Vaughan, D., & Asbury, T. (1980). *General ophthalmology* (9th ed.). Los Altos, CA: Lange Medical Publications.

Vernon, M. (1969). Usher's syndrome—deafness and progressive blindness: Clinical cases, prevention, theory, and literature survey. *Journal of Chronic Diseases, 22,* 133–151.

Viggiano, J. (1981) Ignorance as handicap. *Asha, 23,* 551–552.

Vincent, L., Salisbury, C., Walter, G., Brown, P., Gruenewald, L., & Powers, M. (1980). Program evaluation and curriculum development in early childhood/special education: Criteria of the next environment. In W. Sailor, B. Wilcox, & L. Brown (Eds.), *Methods of instruction for severely handicapped students* (pp. 303–328). Baltimore: Paul H. Brookes Publishing Co.

Wacker, D., Wiggins, B., Fowler, M., & Berg, W. (1988). Training students with profound or multiple handicaps to make requests via microswitches. *Journal of Applied Behavior Analysis, 18,* 331–343.

Walker, M. (1987, March). *The Makaton Vocabulary: Uses and effectiveness.* Paper presented at the first international AFASIC symposium, University of Reading, England.

Walker, M., Parsons, F., Cousins, S., Henderson, R., & Carpenter, B. (1985). *Symbols for Makaton.* Camberley, England: Makaton Vocabulary Development Project.

Wallach, G., & Liebergott, J. (1984). Who shall be called "learning disabled?": Some new directions. In G. Wallach & K. Butler (Eds.), *Language learning disabilities in school-age children* (pp. 1–14). Baltimore: Williams & Wilkins.

Ward, M. (1986). The visual system. In G. Scholl (Ed.), *Foundations of education for blind and visually handicapped children and youth: Theory and practice* (pp. 35–64). New York: American Foundation for the Blind.

Warren, S., & Kaiser, A. (1986). Incidental language teaching: A critical review. *Journal of Speech and Hearing Disorders, 51,* 291–298.

Wasson, P., Tynan, T., & Gardiner, P. (1982). *Test adaptations for the handicapped.* San Antonio, TX: Educational Service Center.

Watson, L. (1985). The TEACCH communication curriculum. In E. Schopler & G. Mesibov (Eds.), *Communication problems in autism* (pp. 187–206). New York: Plenum.

Watson, L., Lord, C., Schaeffer, B., & Schopler, E. (1989). *Teaching spontaneous communication to autistic and developmentally handicapped children.* New York: Irvington.

Watson, L., Newman, K., & Neitzel, G. (1988). Enhancing vision and motor skills in the learning environment. In W. Padula (Ed.), *A behavioral vision approach for persons with physical disabilities.* Santa Ana, CA: Optometric Extension Program Foundation, Inc.

Webb, A. (1984). Dustin—3: Augmented communication for a preschool child. *Communication Outlook, 6*(2), 4–5.

Weiss, L., Thatch, D., & Thatch, J. (1987). *I wasn't finished with life.* Dallas, TX: E-Heart Press.

Weitzman, E., & Mayerovitch, J. (1987). *A pilot program for the parents of young children with autism: A modified Hanen program.* Unpublished manuscript, Hanen Early Language Resource Centre, Toronto.

Westby, C. (1985). Learning to talk—talking to learn: Oral-literate language differences. In C. Simons (Ed.), *Communication skills and classroom success: Therapy methodologies for language-learning disabled students* (pp. 181–213). San Diego: College-Hill Press.

Wetherby, A. (1989). Language intervention for autistic children: A look at where we have come in the past 25 years. *Journal of Speech-Language Pathology and Audiology/Revue d'orthophonie et d'audiologie, 13*(4), 15–28.

Wetherby, A., & Prizant, B. (1990). *Communication and Symbolic Behavior Scales (CSBS).* Tucson, AZ: Communication Skill Builders.

White, S. H. (1980). Cognitive competence and performance in everyday environments. *Bulletin of The Orton Society, 30,* 29–45.

Williams, R. (1989). *In a struggling voice.* Seattle, WA: TASH, The Association for Persons with Severe Handicaps.

Williams, B., Briggs, N., & Williams, R. (1979). Selecting, adapting, and understanding toys and recreation materials. In P. Wehman (Ed.), *Recreation programming for developmentally disabled persons* (pp. 15–36). Austin, TX: PRO-ED.

Wills, K. (1981). Manual communication training for nonspeaking hearing children. *Journal of Pediatric Psychology, 6*(1), 15–27.

Wilson, P.S. (1974, April). *Sign language as a means of communication for the mentally retarded.* Paper presented at the Eastern Psychological Association Conference.

Wilson-Favors, V. (1987). Using the visual phonics system to improve speech skills: A preliminary report. *Perspectives for Teachers of the Hearing Impaired, 6*(2), 2–4.

Windsor, J., & Fristoe, M. (1989). Key word signing: Listeners' classification of signed and spoken narratives. *Journal of Speech and Hearing Disorders, 54,* 374–382.

Windsor, J., & Fristoe, M. (1991). Key word signing: Perceived and acoustic differences between signed and spoken narratives. *Journal of Speech and Hearing Research, 34,* 260–268.

Wint, G. (1965). *The third killer: Meditations on a stroke.* New York: Abelard-Schuman.

Wolfensberger, W. (1975). *The origin and nature of our institutional models.* Syracuse, NY: Human Policy Press.

Wolverton, R., Beukelman, D., Haynes, R., & Sesow, D. (1992). Strategies in augmented literacy using microcomputer-based approaches. *Seminars in Speech and Language, 13*(2).

Wood, C. (1990). Blissymbol talk: New Blissymbols for teaching human sexuality. *Communicating Together, 8*(3), 12–13.

Wood, P. (1980). Appreciating the consequences of disease: The WHO classification of impairments, disabilities, and handicaps. *The WHO Chronicle, 34,* 376–380.

Woodcock, R. (1987). *Woodcock Reading Mastery Tests—Revised.* Circle Pines, MN: American Guidance Service.

Woodcock, R., Clark, C., & Davies, C. (1968). *Peabody rebus reading program.* Circle Pines, MN: American Guidance Service.

Woodward, J. (1990). Sign English in the education of deaf students. In H. Bornstein (Ed.), *Manual communication: Implications for education* (pp. 67–80). Washington, DC: Gallaudet University Press.

Workinger, M., & Netsell, R. (1988). *Restoration of intelligible speech 13 years post-head injury.* Unpublished manuscript, Boys Town National Communication Institute, Omaha, NE.

Wright, C., & Nomura, M. (1987). *From toys to computers: Access for the physically disabled child.* Wauconda, IL: Don Johnston Developmental Equipment, Inc.

Writer, J. (1987). A movement-based approach to the education of students who are sensory impaired/multihandicapped. In L. Goetz, D. Guess, & K. Stremel-Campbell (Eds.), *Innovative program design for individuals with dual sensory impairments* (pp. 191–223). Baltimore: Paul H. Brookes Publishing Co.

Yoder, D., & Kraat, A. (1983). Intervention issues in nonspeech communication. In J. Miller, D. Yoder, & R. L. Schiefelbusch (Eds.), *Contemporary issues in language intervention. ASHA Reports 12,* 27–51. Rockville, MD: American Speech-Language-Hearing Association.

York, J., Nietupski, J., & Hamre-Nietupski, S. (1985). A decision-making process for using microswitches. *Journal of The Association for Persons with Severe Handicaps, 10,* 214–223.

York, J., & Vandercook, T. (1989). Strategies for achieving an integrated education for middle school aged learners with severe disabilities. In. J. York, T. Vandercook, C. MacDonald, & S. Wolff (Eds.), *Strategies for full inclusion* (pp. 1–20). Minneapolis: University of Minnesota, Institute on Community Integration.

Yorkston, K. (1989). Early intervention in amyotrophic lateral sclerosis: A case presentation. *Augmentative and Alternative Communication, 5,* 67–70.

Yorkston, K., & Beukelman, D. (1981). Ataxic dysarthria: Treatment sequences based on intelligibility and prosodic considerations. *Journal of Speech and Hearing Disorders, 46,* 398–404.

Yorkston, K., Beukelman, D., & Bell, K. (1988). *Clinical management of dysarthric speakers.* San Diego: College-Hill Press.

Yorkston, K., Beukelman, D., Minifie, F., & Sapir, S. (1984). Assessment of stress patterning in dysarthric speakers. In M. McNeil, A. Aronson, & J. Rosenbek (Eds.), *The dysarthrias: Physiology, acoustics, perception, management* (pp. 131–162). San Diego: College-Hill Press.

Yorkston, K., Beukelman, D., Smith, K., & Tice, R. (1990). Extended communication samples of augmented communicators II: Analysis of multiword utterances. *Journal of Speech and Hearing Disorders, 55,* 225–230.

Yorskton, K., Dowden, P., Honsinger, M., Marriner, N., & Smith, K. (1988). A comparison of standard and user vocabulary lists. *Augmentative and Alternative Communication, 4,* 189–210.

Yorkston, K., Fried-Oken, M., & Beukelman, D., (1988). Single word vocabulary needs: Studies from various nonspeaking populations. *Augmentative and Alternative Communication, 4*(3), 149.

Yorkston, K., & Karlan, G. (1986). Assessment procedures. In S. Blackstone (Ed.), *Augmentative communication: An introduction* (pp. 163–196). Rockville, MD: American Speech-Language-Hearing Association.

Yorkston, K., Smith, K., & Beukelman, D. (1990). Extended communication samples of augmented communicators I: A comparison of individualized versus standard vocabularies. *Journal of Speech and Hearing Disorders, 55,* 217–224.

Yorkston, K., Smith, K., Miller, R., & Hillel, A. (1991). *Augmentative and alternative communication in amyotrophic lateral sclerosis.* Unpublished manuscript, University of Washington, Seattle.

Yoss, K., & Darley, F. (1974a). Developmental apraxia of speech in children with defective articulation. *Journal of Speech and Hearing Research, 17,* 399–416.

Yoss, K., & Darley, F. (1974b). Therapy in developmental apraxia of speech. *Language, Speech, and Hearing Services in Schools, 5,* 23–31.

# Index